The English Revolution and the Wars in the Three Kingdoms, 1638–1652

MODERN WARS IN PERSPECTIVE

General Editors: *H. M. Scott and B. W. Collins*

This ambitious series offers wide-ranging studies of specific wars, and distinct phases of warfare, from the close of the Middle Ages to the present day. It aims to advance the current integration of military history into the academic mainstream. To that end, the books are not merely traditional campaign narratives, but examine the causes, course and consequences of major conflicts, in their full international political, social and ideological contexts.

ALSO IN THIS SERIES

The English Revolution and the Wars in the Three Kingdoms, 1638–1652

Ian Gentles

PEARSON
Longman

Harlow, England • London • New York • Boston • San Francisco • Toronto
Sydney • Tokyo • Singapore • Hong Kong • Seoul • Taipei • New Delhi
Cape Town • Madrid • Mexico City • Amsterdam • Munich • Paris • Milan

PEARSON EDUCATION LIMITED

Edinburgh Gate
Harlow CM20 2JE
United Kingdom
Tel: +44 (0)1279 623623
Fax: +44 (0)1279 431059
Website: www.pearsoned.co.uk

First edition published in Great Britain in 2007

© Pearson Education Limited 2007

The right of Ian Gentles to be identified as author of this work has been
asserted by him in accordance with the Copyright, Designs and Patents Act 1988.

ISBN: 978-0-582-06551-2

British Library Cataloguing in Publication Data
A CIP catalogue record for this book can be obtained from the British Library

Library of Congress Cataloging-in-Publication Data
Gentles, I. J.
    The English Revolution and the wars in the three kingdoms, 1638–1652 / Ian Gentles. —
1st ed.
        p. cm. — (Modern wars in perspective)
    Includes bibliographical references and index.
    ISBN-13: 978–0–582–06551–2 (pbk.)
    ISBN-10: 0–582–06551–8 (pbk.)
    1. Great Britain—History, Military—1603–1714.   2. Great Britain—History—Charles I,
1625–1649.   3. Great Britain—History—Puritan Revolution, 1642–1600.   4. Great
Britain—History—Civil War, 1642–1649.   5. Scotland—History—Charles I, 1625–1649.   6.
Ireland—History—1625–1649.   I. Title.

DA405.G45 2007
941.06′2—dc22

                                                                        2006049201

10   9   8   7   6   5   4   3   2   1
10   09   08   07

Set by 35 in 10/13.5pt Sabon
Printed in Malaysia

The Publisher's policy is to use paper manufactured from sustainable forests.

To Gerald Aylmer,
Conrad Russell
and Austin Woolrych
in memoriam

Contents

List of Maps

Acknowledgements

We are grateful to the following for permission to reproduce copyright material:

Map 2 courtesy of Cambridge University Press; map 3 courtesy of McGill-Queen's University Press.

All attempts at tracing the copyright-holder of *Edgehill, 1642* (maps 4 and 8) by Peter Young were unsuccessful, as were attempts to locate the copyright-holder for cartography, P. Vaughan Williams.

In some other instances we have been unable to trace the owners of copyright material, and we would appreciate any information that would enable us to do so.

Preface

Over the years that it has taken to write this book I have incurred many debts of gratitude. Tim Wales was an invaluable research assistant, who not only broke the codes of a number of important letters, but provided intelligent commentary on the various manuscripts that he transcribed. David Scott read every word of the book, subjected it to searching scrutiny, challenged my arguments, and saved me from many errors. With John Morrill I have had many stimulating conversations about the period that we both love. He and his wife Frances extended hospitality to me on many occasions. I have also benefited tremendously from conversations with other leading scholars in the field: Barbara Donagan, Blair Worden, Kevin Sharpe, Ronald Hutton, Jane Ohlmeyer, Micheál Ó Siochrú, Tadhg Ó hAnnracháin, Toby Barnard, Allan Macinnes, John Adamson, James Scott Wheeler, Edward Furgol, Jonathan Scott, Stephen Porter, Colin Davis, Barbara Taft, Sarah Barber, Paul Griffiths, Jason Peacey, Patrick Little, Sean Kelsey, Robert Armstrong, Frances Henderson and Andrew Barclay. Maija Jansson kindly gave me access to the Yale Center for Parliamentary History's transcript of Sir Simmonds D'Ewes's diary, and Anne Steele Young completed the work of transcription to 1645. I owe an immense debt to Ian and Helen Roy, who have entertained me frequently. Ian, my old tutor, has shared unstintingly his unrivalled knowledge of the royalist army, as well as furnishing many insights into the sources. Tony Wrigley was extremely helpful on the demographic implications of England's 'troubles'. Many archivists and librarians have given invaluable assistance, but I would like to pay special tribute to Mary Robertson at the Huntington, Godfrey Waller at the Cambridge University Library, and Jean-Pierre at the Bodleian for their exceptional graciousness and good humour. Hamish Scott, the publisher's editor has been a source of considerable encouragement. I am thankful too to Hetty Reid, Jenny Oates, Melanie Carter and Christina Wipf Perry for their patience and their helpfulness in seeing the book through the press.

On many occasions Lesley and Alan Leclaire, Ursula Aylmer, Andrew and Sarah Ingersoll, Ann and Bruce Saunders, Harold and Pauline Norman, Maija Jansson and Paul Bushkovitch, Richard and Carol Downer, and Kay Senior have welcomed me into their homes and added greatly to the sum of (my) human happiness. The members of my family – my mother, Caroline, Emma, Stephen, Peter, Ginny and Erin – have been wonderfully supportive throughout.

The research for the book was made possible by grants from the Social Sciences and Humanities Research Council of Canada, the Huntington, Folger and Beinecke Libraries, and Glendon College, as well as visiting fellowships at Clare Hall and Wolfson College, Cambridge. I am also grateful for the encouragement of my colleagues at Tyndale College, and indebted to the staffs of the British Library, the Bodleian Library, the National Archives (formerly the PRO), the House of Lords Record Office, the Cambridge University Library, the Corporation of London Records Office, the Guildhall Library, Dr Williams's Library, New College and Christ Church Oxford, The Huntington Library, The Folger Shakespeare Library, the Beinecke Library, the National Archives of Scotland (formerly the SRO), the National Library of Ireland and Marsh's Library, Dublin for the high standard of service they have given.

This book is dedicated to the memory of three giants in the field, who have died recently: Gerald Aylmer, Conrad Russell and Austin Woolrych. Each of them gave to me generously of his time, knowledge and wisdom, and answered many questions. Austin Woolrych in particular took me under his wing, imparting much insight into the military and political history of the period, often during long walks in the Pennines.

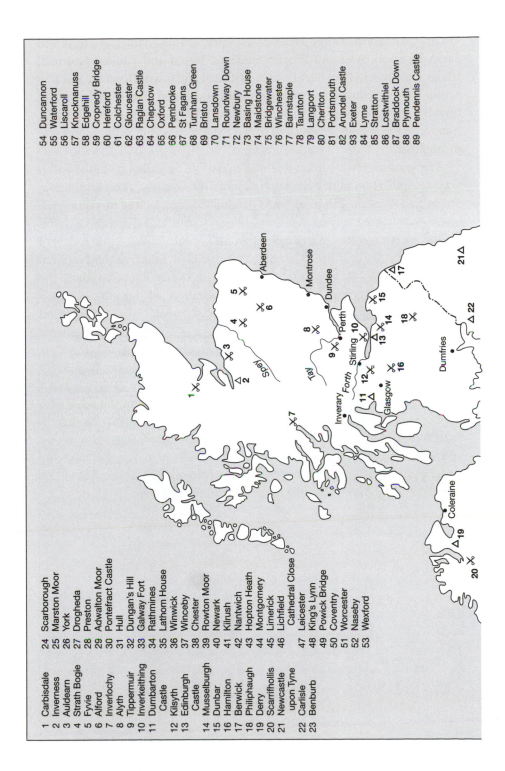

1 Carbisdale
2 Inverness
3 Auldearn
4 Strath Bogie
5 Fyvie
6 Alford
7 Inverlochy
8 Alyth
9 Tippermuir
10 Inverkeithing
11 Dumbarton Castle
12 Kilsyth
13 Edinburgh Castle
14 Musselburgh
15 Dunbar
16 Hamilton
17 Berwick
18 Philiphaugh
19 Derry
20 Scarrifhollis
21 Newcastle upon Tyne
22 Carlisle
23 Benburb

24 Scarborough
25 Marston Moor
26 York
27 Drogheda
28 Preston
29 Adwalton Moor
30 Pontefract Castle
31 Hull
32 Dungan's Hill
33 Galway Fort
34 Rathmines
35 Lathom House
36 Winwick
37 Winceby
38 Chester
39 Rowton Moor
40 Newark
41 Kilrush
42 Nantwich
43 Hopton Heath
44 Montgomery
45 Limerick
46 Lichfield Cathedral Close
47 Leicester
48 King's Lynn
49 Powick Bridge
50 Coventry
51 Worcester
52 Naseby
53 Wexford

54 Duncannon
55 Waterford
56 Liscaroll
57 Knocknanuss
58 Edgehill
59 Cropredy Bridge
60 Hereford
61 Colchester
62 Gloucester
63 Raglan Castle
64 Chepstow
65 Oxford
66 Pembroke
67 St Fagans
68 Turnham Green
69 Bristol
70 Lansdown
71 Roundway Down
72 Newbury
73 Basing House
74 Maidstone
75 Bridgewater
76 Winchester
77 Barnstaple
78 Taunton
79 Langport
80 Cheriton
81 Portsmouth
82 Arundel Castle
93 Exeter
84 Lyme
85 Stratton
86 Lostwithiel
87 Braddock Down
88 Plymouth
89 Pendennis Castle

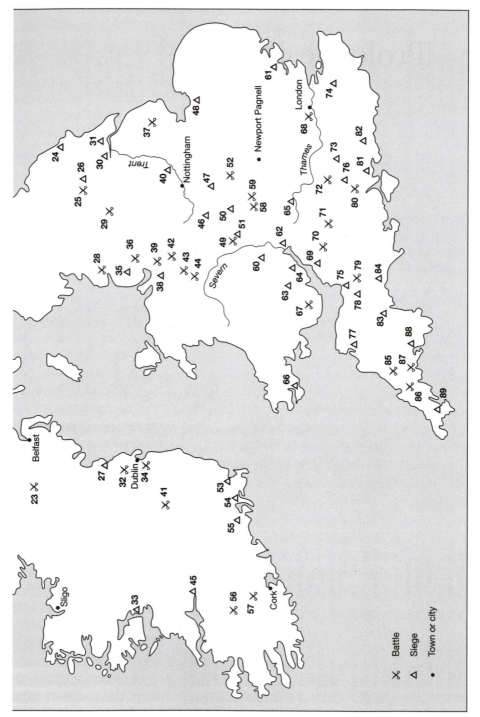

MAP 1 *The three kingdoms: battles and sieges*

Prologue

Could a nation which God had chosen reject him? ...
We call the resultant disaster the English Civil War.[1]

It has been said that without Charles I there could have been no civil war in England, and consequently no political and cultural transformation such as took place in the 1640s and 1650s.[2] Those who are drawn to speculate about the contingent nature of human events enjoy the thought of how differently the history of seventeenth-century England, Scotland and Ireland might have unfolded had Henry, son of James I and heir to the thrones of the three kingdoms, not suddenly died of typhoid fever in 1612. Until the time of his much-lamented death he had shown every promise of becoming the longed-for Protestant paladin who, had he lived, would have rescued Frederick the Elector Palatine from the clutches of the Habsburg monarchy, and who without hesitation would have thrown himself into the battle against Antichrist (meaning the forces of international popery), alongside the House of Orange, Gustavus Adolphus, king of Sweden, and the German Lutheran princes.

Instead, hopes had to be pinned henceforth on his shy, diminutive, stammering younger brother, to whom little attention had been paid before Henry's death. Charles Stuart turned out to be a big disappointment to everyone who harboured dreams of a European Protestant empire under English leadership. It is often assumed that a monarch not burdened by

[1] Patrick Collinson, *The Birthpangs of Protestant England: religious and cultural change in the sixteenth and seventeenth centuries*, 20.
[2] Conrad Russell, *The Causes of the English Civil War*, 208–11.

Charles's rigidity, duplicity, political incompetence and fatal attraction for Roman Catholicism could have skirted the Puritan challenge to kingly power, while cutting an impressive figure on the European stage during the Thirty Years' War. Those who view Charles I as the most pathetic individual ever to have sat on the thrones of the three kingdoms overlook the reality that if there had not been some minimum of competence and kingly charisma, had Charles not commanded the loyalty of a sizeable proportion of both nobility and commoners in his leading kingdom, there would have been no civil war. An utterly disastrous monarch would have been deposed in a palace coup similar to the ones that unseated his ancestors Edward II and Richard II. By the same token a king of the calibre of Henry VII or his son would never have allowed their realm to become embroiled in political and religious conflict to the point that a significant percentage of the people were prepared to take the route of treasonous resistance to their monarch.

As Charles I's most recent biographers have reminded us, this king was far from being a thoroughgoing incompetent. It was his strengths, every bit as much as his weaknesses, that made civil war possible in all three of his kingdoms. Willing to consult and compromise, he was normally committed to reconciliation with his adversaries. He was a subtle and responsive tactician with an ability to think ahead and plan a political campaign. He was also conscientious, dignified, eloquent and inspiring, both in speech and on paper.[3] As the 1640s would show, he was a fairly able military commander, capable of chalking up at least two significant victories and a number of 'drawn' matches on the battlefield.

When in 1642 Essex clothworkers wrote to the Long Parliament to explain their attacks on certain members of the gentry class in their county, they did not invoke social or economic causes, even though they were suffering acutely from a depression in the cloth trade. Quite the contrary: they indicted parliament for its timorousness in confronting the religious crisis. The root cause of the present troubles, in their eyes, was parliament's failure to stand up to popery, rampant both at home and in Ireland, where a popish rising had led to the massacre of countless innocent Protestants. Set beside the need for religious reform, which was foundational, the social and economic problems of the realm were mere superstructure. Take care of religion and the economy would look after itself. That was the message

---

[3] Richard Cust, *Charles I*, 115, 155, 174, 300, 356; Mark Kishlansky, 'Charles I: A case of mistaken identity', *Past & Present* (hereafter *P&P*), 189 (2005). See also the article co-authored by Mark Kishlansky and John Morrill in the Oxford Dictionary of National Biography (hereafter *ODNB*).

of these clothiers.[4] Were they right? One of the aims of this book is to listen to the voices of those who lived through the 15 years from 1638 to 1652, to attend to what they had to say, and to refrain from subjecting them to the enormous condescension of posterity.

Scotland and Ireland are the bookends of the present work, and they are also at its heart. Their insurgencies against the Stuart monarchy in 1638–40 (Scotland) and 1641–42 (Ireland) mark the opening of our story, while their subjugation by the English republic in 1649–52 (Ireland) and 1650–51 (Scotland) signal its close. Scotland by its rebellion gave the example to Ireland, as the leaders of its insurgency freely acknowledged. By stripping the king of his rights over his Scottish kingdom, reducing him in effect to a figurehead, and establishing the parliament of Scotland as the sovereign power there, the Scots blazed the trail that the Westminster parliament would follow a year or two later. Another achievement of the Scottish rebels was to raise their nation from a condition of military helplessness and place it in the forefront of Europe's military revolution. By sheer force of will they created a popular revolutionary army under centralized direction and with seasoned professional commanders. They achieved this in 1639, fully six years before the organization of a similar force by the English parliament.

As John Morrill has recently reminded us, there is no stable, agreed title for the events explored in this book. They have been variously labelled the Great Rebellion, the Puritan Revolution, the English Civil War, the English Revolution, and most recently, the Wars of the Three Kingdoms. Because of this failure to agree over nomenclature they constitute 'the historical moment that dare not speak its name'.[5] Yet because they turned hundreds of thousands of people into actors in the public sphere, they deserve the tag, 'the People's Revolution'. For the first time farmers, yeomen, craftsmen and traders – the 'middling sort' – seized the moment to voice their religious and political opinions. They did this in taverns, in churches, at grand jury and common council meetings, and on the streets. Their vehicles were pamphlets, newsbooks, petitions, street demonstrations, lay sermons, prophesyings and extemporaneous prayer. Not all of the actors were radicals, still less revolutionary republicans. For every Leveller, commonwealthman, fifth monarchist, Quaker or anabaptist, there were at least as many underground Anglicans, papists and vociferous royalists. But while

---

[4] *Three Petitions*, E134/13, 2, 6; John Walter, *Understanding Popular Violence in the English Revolution: The Colchester Plunderers*, 311–13.

[5] I am grateful to John Morrill for sending me the text of his Ford Lectures in advance of publication.

these events attracted massive popular participation, they were decidedly not the major socio-economic upheaval that turned the three kingdoms into a modern nation. Still less were they a critical turning point on the road leading from the Reformation to the Enlightenment and the modern secular state. True, these events carried with them more than a whiff of anti-clericalism, anti-authoritarianism, and the democratization of public utterance. The democratizing spirit arguably went further in Scotland (as we have seen) and in Ireland where a broad franchise was established by the Catholic Confederation, and where in 1651 the Earl of Clanricard campaigned for universal male suffrage, than it did in England. The celebrated debates at Putney, on the outskirts of London, in 1647 were much more about what to do with the king and how to discern the will of God than they were about expanding the franchise or writing a new constitution for England.

The research of the past 40 years has made it no longer tenable to view the crisis in the three kingdoms as the product of social, still less of class, conflict. The king attracted just as many lower-class followers – butchers, porters, watermen, labourers and the like – as did parliament. The gentry were split down the middle, while a significant minority of noblemen opposed the king. None of the other measures of social status – office holding, rising or declining wealth for example – can be correlated with support for king or parliament. The recent suggestion that the divide between the supporters and enemies of the king ran along ethnic and cultural lines is much more plausible than the socio-economic interpretation. The New English Protestant planter class of Ireland, the Scottish Covenanters led by the Earl of Argyll, as well as the English puritans and their sympathizers, were opposed by a royalist coalition that consisted of a largely celtic, often Catholic 'fringe' drawn heavily from the west country, Wales, Highland Scotland and Gaelic Ireland.[6]

Under a variety of titles, there have been several excellent accounts of the three kingdoms' troubles written in the past two decades. The main justification for the present study is that it attempts to weave together the twin narratives of politics and war, which are so often treated separately. It also takes seriously the thoughts of those who were the chief actors in the drama, in the conviction that thought can be an engine for action at least as often as action can be a generator of new thought. Finally, it attempts an assessment of the human and economic costs of these 15 years of warfare.

[6] Mark Stoyle, *Soldiers and Strangers: An Ethnic History of the English Civil War.*

CHAPTER 1

Rebellion in the north

Who knows but this great work which is begun in Scotland now when it is going into England, and it has taken some footing there, but the Lord He will make it to go over the sea? Who knows but the Lord will make Scotland, who is a worm indeed in comparison of other nations, to be a sharp threshing instrument, to thresh the mountains and to beat the hills to pieces? Who knows but He will make them a sharp threshing instrument to beat Rome and the Pope and Antichrist to pieces . . . ?[1]

Scotland was where Charles I's troubles began. His father James VI had occupied the throne of that kingdom until 1603, when he inherited the English crown, thereby uniting the kingdoms of Britain. Scots had initially welcomed this union, believing it would enable them to share in the greater wealth of England, not least by plucking some ripe plums of patronage for themselves. And indeed, Scots were very much in evidence at the English court during the early years of James I. Disillusionment soon set in, however. In the first place parliament threw cold water on the king's cherished scheme to join the two kingdoms into one. Secondly, after a decade in England James began showing more and more favour to his English courtiers. Basking in the greater opulence, flattery and formality of the southern court, the first Stuart king gradually lost interest in Scotland, revisiting his bleak northern capital only once (in 1617) during his twenty-two-year reign.

[1] 'Fear not, thou worm Jacob' (22 August 1640), in Samuel Rutherford, *Quaint Sermons of Samuel Rutherford*, 36. The text of Rutherford's sermon was from Isaiah 41:14–16.

It did not take long for religion to emerge as a further cause of strain between the king and his Scottish subjects. In the middle of the sixteenth century Scotland had undergone a Calvinist revolution. Led by John Knox, the nobility had risen up against the French-dominated Mary Stuart and overturned her Catholic regime, substituting a Protestant regency until the infant James grew to manhood. Calvinism's three distinctive tenets were: original sin, or the universal depravity of the human race consequent upon the fall of the first man, Adam; the irresistibility of God's grace to those whom He had selected for salvation; and, the predestination of every human being to salvation or everlasting damnation. There was little room for free will.

The Scottish version of Calvinism, called Presbyterianism, entailed a new form of Church government. Lay elders, selected by their congregations, combined with ministers as delegates to presbyteries, which were groupings of parishes. (There were just over 1,000 parishes divided among 66 presbyteries in early seventeenth-century Scotland). The presbyteries in turn elected delegates to the general assembly, which governed the Kirk, as the Scottish Church was known.

James insisted on grafting bishops onto this structure, mainly to act as agents of royal power. He enhanced their authority by giving them courts of High Commission through which to enforce their judgements. The king's insistence on a state-dominated Church rather than a Church-dominated state as the Presbyterians would have desired, prompted the latter to band together locally in covenants. From the 1590s they developed the concept of people uniting themselves under a sacred oath as a way of concretizing the spiritual bond between God and his elect people. The political potential of covenants remained latent until after Charles had come to the throne.

The potency of the Scottish Kirk was grounded not only in its militant Calvinist theology, but in the self-confidence of its educated clergy who were also well paid in comparison with their English counterparts. The religious assurance of these men and their congregations was distilled in the words of the Confession of Faith: 'the church of Scotland through the abundant grace of our god is one of the most pure churches under heaven this day, both in respect of truth and doctrine and purities of worship'.[2] The adherents of this perfect Church did battle with James over the bishops, and they resisted his attempts to move in the direction of Arminianism – a Dutch brand of Protestantism that asserted free will against Calvinist predestination.

[2] Quoted in Allan I. Macinnes, *Charles I and the Making of the Covenanting Movement 1625–1641*, 27.

Royal promotion of a Crown- and bishop-dominated Church espousing a diluted version of Calvinism could never have been stopped by the clergy alone. The country's dominant socio-economic classes had to be enlisted in the struggle as well. Fortunately for the Presbyterian clergy, the nobility, the lairds (as the untitled landowners were called), and the merchants of the burghs all had their reasons for being unhappy with Scotland's absentee monarchy. At the end of the sixteenth century the nobility had undergone a severe cultural and economic crisis, though a few had profited from new patronage opportunities when James VI ascended the English throne. Prolonged inflation, whose effects were accentuated by the practice of granting perpetual leases at fixed rents, was made still worse by disastrous weather and crop failures in the 1590s. When partial recovery occurred after 1610, the nobles found themselves beset by ever-increasing taxes and predatory lawyers. The doubling of the size of the nobility from 50 to about 100 within half a century, and the intellectual attacks on the honour culture added to their anxiety. As if all this were not enough, in 1625 they were confronted by Charles I's Revocation. The young king announced his determination to recover all royal land alienated since an unspecified date in the past. While his aim was the disinterested one of strengthening church revenues, the landed classes saw the very basis of their property under threat. More than a decade later the king finally thought better of his attempted land-grab, but after their hair-raising experience nobles and lairds would never trust him again.

What supplied the combustible element to convert smouldering resentment into flaming rebellion was religion. The nobility long bore a grudge against the bishops, whose power James I had persistently tried to increase. The bishops were partly blamed for the religious 'Perth' Articles of 1621, which required Scots to bend their stubborn knees while receiving communion. To many, kneeling was a sign of creeping Anglicisation, if not outright popery. By the time Charles I visited Edinburgh in 1633 for his coronation, word had got around about his plans for a more centralized, authoritarian and Arminian Church. His heavy-handed manipulation of the Scottish parliament, and his efforts to intimidate opponents by personally taking notes of their speeches, were deeply worrying. When a group of lords led by the Earl of Loudoun, Lord Balmerino, implored the king not to force religious changes on the Scottish people, he brushed them aside, and went ahead with his plans for a new prayerbook and canons. No representative body was consulted: the new canons were simply published in 1636, while the reform of the prayerbook was announced in a royal proclamation issued by the Scottish privy council at the end of that year.

The canons, which were the laws governing the clergy, banned extemporaneous prayer, because it offended Charles's desire for order and decency in worship. The new prayerbook was devised by Scottish bishops according to Charles's specifications. It stipulated that ministers were to be strictly subordinated to bishops and bishops to the king. The communion table was to be removed out of the body of the church into the chancel. Key words were excised from the formula spoken by the minister as he distributed the bread and wine at communion, so that it no longer implied that the service was simply a memorial of Christ's Last Supper. One minister said of the new book, which had been submitted to no representative ecclesiastical body whatsoever, that it was more popish than the English prayerbook. Even though its use was not to become compulsory until the summer of 1637, discontented people, among them Balmerino, and a knot of militant Presbyterian ministers, began organizing meetings around the country months ahead of time. Women, from the rank of maidservant to matron in the mercantile community, were in the forefront of the public protest in Edinburgh. They were there of their own volition, as 'holy and religious women', not because they had been put up to it by men, as sometimes happened in other riots.[3]

On a fateful Sunday in July 1637 several members of the Scottish privy council, nine or ten bishops, and the lords of the session (Church leaders) assembled in St Giles Cathedral, Edinburgh with a large congregation. As soon as the dean began to read from the new prayerbook there were cries of 'the mass is entered among us' and women began to shout insults, 'calling them traitors, belly-gods, and deceivers'.[4] Rising to their feet, they hurled their folding stools, one of them just missing the bishop for whom it was intended, and striking the dean on the head. The women then stormed out of the cathedral to continue their rioting in the street. When the Bishop of Edinburgh emerged after the service they chased him with stones and insults.

Now that the breadth of the opposition to the new liturgy had been shown the nobility moved to take charge of the movement. Under their inspiration a Supplication was framed attacking not only the prayerbook and canons, but also the bishops. What amounted to a counter-government was set up. Going under the name of the Tables, it consisted of four committees, the first comprising the nobility, the other three the representatives

---

[3] Macinnes, *Covenanting Movement*, 159–60, 165.
[4] Quoted in Kevin Sharpe, *The Personal Rule of Charles I*, 788; David Stevenson, *The Scottish Revolution, 1637–1644*, 61.

of the clergy, the gentry and the boroughs. The Fifth Table was an executive committee made up of the nobles' Table, and four representatives from each of the other three. Their mandate was to concert resistance to the new order of service. Charles for his part made negotiations awkward by insisting that he and not the bishops was responsible for the new prayerbook.

The National Covenant

This fresh evidence of Charles's recalcitrance and political ineptness impelled the Tables to commission 'a band of mutual association' for the Scottish people. They appointed a respected Presbyterian minister, Alexander Henderson, and a young firebrand lawyer, Archibald Johnston of Wariston, to draw it up. Published as the National Covenant in February 1638, it was, in Allan Macinnes's words, 'a nationalist manifesto asserting the independence of a sovereign people under God'.[5] Signatories swore to defend 'the true reformed religion' and abstain from all innovations not approved by the Kirk assemblies or parliament. Only a 'covenanted king' who agreed to defend 'the true reformed religion' (meaning Presbyterianism), and to rule according to the laws of the realm as defined by parliament would be obeyed by his subjects. If the king failed to uphold Presbyterianism or to govern according to the law, the people were morally required to resist him. This was nothing less than a revolutionary attack on the powers of kingship. Yet the Covenant's promoters recruited many thousands of signatories within the space of a few months. Many adherents, we are told, 'subscribed with tears on their cheeks, and . . . some did draw their own blood, and used it in place of ink to underscribe their names'.[6] In Edinburgh thousands wept as they assembled in Greyfriars churchyard to sign the document inscribed on parchment. Expressing the general mood of exaltation, Wariston proclaimed 'the glorious marriage day of the kingdom with God', while Samuel Rutherford identified 'little Scotland' as the bride of Christ.[7] Anyone who held back was ostracized as a papist.

Why did the covenant evoke such powerful emotion among the Scottish people? It was because of the heightened sense of national destiny

[5] Macinnes, *Covenanting Movement*, 173.
[6] James Gordon, *History of Scots Affairs from MDCXXXVII to MDCXLI*, Vol. 1, 45.
[7] Roger Mason, 'Aristocracy, episcopacy and the revolution of 1638', in T. Brotherstone (ed.), *Covenant, Charter and Party*, 14.

that it imparted to those who swore their allegiance to it. It was not just a contract between individuals and their God. It was a collective act in which all the signatories were bound to one another as well as to God. Not only did many Scots sincerely believe that their brand of Protestantism was purer than any other; with the covenant they became only the second people in the world – after the ancient Israelites – to make a pact with God. They accordingly regarded themselves, like the Jews, as a chosen people. Their special role in carrying out God's providential design was to assist in the overthrow of popery and the establishment of Christ's reign on earth. Some Scots went further, extending this apocalyptic vision to all three British kingdoms, and even to all of Christendom.[8]

The political significance of the covenant was that it embraced the whole people, whereas before only the leaders of society had been involved in the political process. Equally momentous, the insistence on contractual obligation, derived directly from Calvinist federal theology, made resistance to monarchical authority possible.[9] There were dissenters of course. Less than half the Scottish nobility were actively pro-Covenant, and most of the population of the Highlands were opposed to it. Aberdeen was a particularly strong centre of loyalty to the king, although the fact that the region's most powerful nobleman, the Marquess of Huntly, was a Catholic weakened the royalist cause.

Seeing that his northern kingdom was out of control, Charles decided to backtrack. Again he was too late. His offer to surrender the prayerbook if Scotland would surrender the covenant got him nowhere. He told Hamilton that if he had to live under the covenant he would have no more power than a doge of Venice. All of Hamilton's suggestions for compromise he rejected. 'I will rather die than yield to these impertinent and damnable demands', he wrote.[10] But when his own advocate, Sir Thomas Hope, refused to declare that there was anything in the covenant contrary to the laws of Scotland, he made it impossible to proclaim its signatories traitors. The ground had been cut from under Hamilton's feet. At length the king consented to the summoning of a Kirk assembly, with the proviso that the bishops must be allowed to take their proper place in it. Because

---

[8] Macinnes, *Covenanting Movement*, 174–5, 183–4, 206; David Scott, *Politics and War in Three Stuart Kingdoms, 1637–1649*, 26.

[9] Margaret Steele, 'The "politick Christian": the theological background to the National Covenant', in John Morrill (ed.), *The Scottish National Covenant in its British Context*, 45, 54.

[10] Gilbert Burnet, *The Memoires of the Lives and Actions of James and William, Dukes of Hamilton*, 55–6, 59.

Edinburgh had proved itself a rebellious city, the assembly was convoked in Glasgow, thought to be more amenable to royal influence since it was adjacent to the Marquess of Hamilton's ancestral estates.

The king sent Hamilton to Edinburgh at the beginning of June 1638 to try and reassert royal control there. Hamilton's reception demonstrated more the power of the covenanters than any respect for the king's emissary. At Leith, the port of Edinburgh, he was met by thirty noblemen, backed up by a line of gentry strung out along the seaside in a line a mile-and-a-half long. He next had to pass by 600 ministers in close ranks, while between Leith and Edinburgh 20,000 people waited. During the next several months leading up to the assembly, the commissioners of the Tables encouraged thousands of people to flock to Edinburgh in order to support their deliberations and nullify any effort by Hamilton to mobilize royalist support.

Charles knew that if the Covenanters were successful, kingly authority would be no more than a cipher in Scotland. Equally, he knew that if he gave way in Scotland he would soon be called upon to give way in England as well. He would have dearly loved to put down the revolters by a decisive show of force, but with only £200 in the Exchequer that summer, he knew that that option was closed to him.

Meanwhile, throughout the lowlands of Scotland people not only thronged to the capital, but met also in countless societies for prayer and fasting prior to the elections to the General Assembly of the Kirk in Glasgow. For moving political mountains these are formidable engines. The elections to the Glasgow Assembly were subject to rigid, oligarchic, centralized supervision. Almost all of the 66 presbyteries were under Covenanter control. In a portentous break with the past the Fifth Table dictated that laymen should be elected to the assembly as well as ministers. Thus 100 of the 250 commissioners who assembled in Glasgow on 21 November were non-clergy. The lay presence was further bolstered by Fifth Table instructions that ruling elders plus four gentlemen from all presbyteries, all commissioners from the royal burghs, and any other associates willing to volunteer their services should converge on Glasgow. Scotland's revolution, religious though it was, was emphatically not to be clerically led. Thanks to covenanting manipulation the Kirk Assembly was turned into a meeting of the revolutionary Tables. The mobilization of large crowds before and during the assembly had the desired effect of intimidating the opposition – bishops in particular – into absenting themselves. Straitjacketed on every side by these ruthlessly coordinated measures, Hamilton wrote a long gloomy letter to Charles just prior to the inauguration of the assembly, bitterly lamenting his failure and saying of Scotland 'next Hell I hate this place'.[11]

From the opening day of the Glasgow Assembly the covenanting leadership demonstrated how carefully they had prepared the ground for political victory. Denied support from assembly members, Hamilton, the king's commissioner, was outwitted at every turn. Criminal charges were entered against the bishops, who on this pretext, were excluded from the meeting until they should be tried. Hamilton's attempt to challenge the assembly's legality on the grounds of its admitting lay representatives, was sidetracked until a moderator and clerk were elected. It had been arranged prior to the assembly's opening that they should be Alexander Henderson, a leading Presbyterian minister, and Archibald Wariston, a leading lawyer. Now firmly under covenanting control, the assembly easily turned back Hamilton's challenge to the legality of its elections, and his demand to have the bishops' protest against their exclusion read out. Eloquent but impotent in his anger, Hamilton then pronounced their meeting unconstitutional, and ordered them to disperse or be regarded as traitors. At this critical moment Archibald Campbell, the eighth Earl of Argyll, rose to speak. A short man of ungainly appearance, he had just recently come into his inheritance as the greatest magnate in Scotland and leader of the Campbell clan. He was not a member of the gathering – he had not even signed the covenant; but his words carried all the more weight for that. 'I have not striven to blow the bellows', he assured his hearers, 'but studied to keep matters in as soft a temper as I could, and now I desire to make it known to you that I take you all for members of a lawful Assembly and my honest countrymen.'[12] Having crossed his political rubicon, Argyll at once became, along with Rothes and Montrose, a leader of the covenanting movement. 'He is so far from favouring episcopal government, that with all his soul he wishes it totally abolished', wrote Hamilton to the king. Astutely Hamilton predicted that Argyll would 'prove the dangerousest man in this state'.[13]

The assembly continued to sit in defiance of Hamilton's orders. It quickly proceeded to abolish episcopacy and to remove the clerical estate

[11] Philip York, 2nd Earl of Hardwicke (hereafter Hardwicke, *State Papers*), *Miscellaneous State Papers from 1501 to 1726*, Vol. 2, 119.

[12] Quoted in C.V. Wedgwood, *The King's Peace 1637–1641*, 220.

[13] Hardwicke, *State Papers*, Vol. II, 115. According to Clarendon, Argyll's own father labelled him 'a man of craft, subtlety and falsehood' (Clarendon, Edward Earl of, *History of the Rebellion and Civil Wars in England*, ed. W. Dunn Macray, 6 vols (hereafter Clarendon, *Hist.*), Bk 2, para. 58).

from parliament. Boldly it asserted the inherent right of the Kirk to hold general assemblies at least once a year rather than at the king's whim. As the Covenanters were well aware, this stripping away of the royal prerogative could never be acceptable to Charles. Armed confrontation was now inevitable.

The army of the Covenant

Under Argyll's leadership Scotland was placed on a war footing. Committees were set up in the shires and presbyteries to levy, equip and train troops, and to assess a compulsory contribution from the whole country. The main administrative burden was carried by Presbyterian committees, nominated by the Tables, composed entirely of laymen and led by the gentry. For military purposes the country was divided into twenty districts spread over seven military regions. Recruits were selected by their own communities. In the burghs the councils functioned as the recruiting agencies. In rural parishes it was the clergy and church elders, assisted by local landowners, who were charged with enlisting eligible men. Clergy played a special role in both town and countryside by publicizing the levies and encouraging men to join up. The major problem with which the Covenanters had to grapple was that in 1638 few of these men had any military training or experience. Thanks to the union of the thrones Scotland had grown rusty in the exercise of war.

There was a military reserve, however. It consisted of the Scots mercenaries who had fought on the continent. Like other poor countries, Scotland earned foreign currency by exporting its young men. An estimated 40,000 had already served in the Thirty Years' War, fighting in Germany for Holland and Sweden. When the word went out at the end of 1638 that they were needed at home, thousands returned. In recognition of their expertise, one of their number, Alexander Leslie was named field marshal and lord-general. It was a wise choice, not only because he was the best Scottish soldier of his day, but also because the appointment of one of the nobles as general would have provoked jealousies among the others. In spite of his small stature and unprepossessing appearance, 'such was the wisdom and authority of that old crooked soldier, that all, with an incredible submission, from the beginning to the end, gave over themselves to be guided by him'.[14] Alexander Hamilton, another continental veteran,

[14] Robert Baillie, *The Letters and Journals*, ed. David Laing (3 vols) (hereafter Baillie, *Letters*), Vol. 1, 213–14.

was named general of the artillery. The Tables shrewdly decided to allot thirty-two officers' positions in every regiment to veterans: the colonel, lieutenant-colonel, lieutenants and sergeants were to be 'sent for out of Germany and Holland'. The captains and ensigns could be nominated by the Tables from the nobility and gentry of the shire.[15] By the former provision the Covenanters assured the military competence of their army; by the latter they won its support from the landed classes throughout the country.

While we cannot be precise about the number of men raised, we do know that up to 11,000 were occupied in the north-east in the spring of 1639, taking control of Aberdeen and keeping the Marquess of Huntly's forces at bay. Leslie commanded between 12,000 and 20,000 men on the eastern border, facing Charles's army near Berwick. An unknown number defended the Forth coastline against the Duke of Hamilton's seaborne royal troops. In sum, both in 1639 and 1640 the Covenanters put into the field roughly 2.5 per cent of their country's population. This was a feat exceeded only by the kingdom of Sweden.[16]

Leslie and the other continental mercenary officers brought back with them an up-to-date knowledge of the methodology and technology of warfare pioneered by the Dutch and carried on by the Swedes: weapons drill to achieve maximum firepower, thinner lines with infantry in the middle and cavalry on the wings, the protection of bodies of pikemen by bodies of musketeers on each flank, and an increased proportion of musketeers to pikemen in each foot regiment. Under Leslie the ratio was three to two. The ideal deployment was to divide the army into two lines, each the depth of a regiment (three ranks deep according to the Dutch plan). The second line would be so arranged as to cover the gaps between the regiments in the first line. In addition, a reserve might also act as a smaller third line. A 'forlorn hope' of 200 men or more could be posted several hundred feet ahead of the front line with the mission of conducting sallies against the enemy line to 'soften it up'.

What of weapons? In 1638 Scotland was almost bare of them; neither could it boast a native munitions industry. The Covenanters therefore looked overseas, chiefly to the Netherlands. During the six years ending in

---

[15] Calendar of State Papers, Domestic Series, 1637–53 (hereafter CSPD), 1638–39, 409.

[16] Edward M. Furgol, 'Scotland turned Sweden: the Scottish Covenanters and the military revolution, 1638–1651', in Morrill (ed.), The Scottish National Covenant, 140.

1644 they imported from Zeeland alone 31,673 muskets, 29,000 swords, 8,000 pikes, 500 pairs of pistols and 12 pieces of field artillery. The principal field gun was a small portable cannon, the saker, which fired 6-pound shot. Mobile artillery was new in Britain, which gave Leslie a tactical advantage. By 1640 his train of artillery comprised over sixty pieces.[17]

To summarize, in two short years the Covenanters pulled Scotland from military incoherence into the military revolution of the seventeenth century. They created a standing army for national service under centralized control – an achievement that would not be matched in England until the emergence of the New Model Army six years later. Indeed, the force that Leslie presented for royalist inspection at Duns Law near Berwick drew widespread admiration. John Aston was one of a party of royalists who were entertained by Leslie in his camp. After noting Leslie's skill in his choice of ground, and the good discipline of his men, Aston went on:

It was a very graceful sight to behold all the army so united together in such a ground, and all the soldiers standing to their arms, their drum beating and colours flying . . . They were all or most part of them well timbered men, tall and active, apparelled in blue woollen waistcoats and blue bonnets.

While the bulk of them were lowlanders, there was a contingent of about 1,000 highlanders. 'Some carry only a sword and targe [small shield]; others muskets, and the greater part bows and arrows, with a quiver to hold about six shafts.'

Aston also observed the high morale of the covenanting army: 'The confidence of the Scots in their cause, and experience of their general was of much more value to them than their [armed] strength, for of their 12,000 soldiers there was not one of them that had any defensive arms, not so much as a head piece, and as for their offensive weapons, their muskets were many of them birding pieces, and their pikes but half ones, and many young boys amongst them to manage them.'[18] Not to be overlooked among the contributors to high morale was the 'extraordinary crop' that had been harvested in southern Scotland the previous autumn.[19] Without this plentiful supply of food the Covenanters might not have been able to contemplate war in 1639.

---

[17] Ibid., 137, 145.
[18] John Aston, *Diary*, 28–9.
[19] Baillie, *Letters*, Vol. 1, 213.

The army of Charles I

Charles I's army was relatively well supplied, but it suffered from disastrously bad morale. Pieced together from reluctant militiamen, conscripts and the levies of noblemen no longer skilled in war, it was supported by no national consensus about the justice of the king's cause. Involving almost no one in his strategic preparation, Charles conceived the grandiose scheme of conquering the Covenanters by a three-pronged invasion. Thomas Wentworth, Lord Deputy of Ireland, and the Earl of Antrim, would lead an Irish force against the west coast of Scotland. The Marquess of Hamilton would bring an amphibious force from Yarmouth into the Firth of Forth to take Edinburgh. The king himself would lead the main royal army in a march to the Scottish border in the north-east. Wentworth was sceptical of the plan, and scornful of the Earl of Antrim's military competence. In London almost no one except Hamilton knew of the king's plans.

To raise his army Charles toyed with several expedients, each one worse than the last. First he thought of summoning the county militia or trained bands, through the medieval instrument of the Commission of Array. The problem with this idea was that the trained bands could not be expected to leave their native counties unless the country was in immediate peril of foreign invasion. Continuing the medieval train of thought, Charles next thought he could command the nobility to recruit and arm cavalry at their own expense. Those who wished to avoid the summons would pay the medieval fine called scutage. Embarrassingly, it was the Catholic nobility and gentry who most readily accepted the king's call to arms. Conscious of the tepid enthusiasm of most of his magnates, Charles next thought of hiring mercenaries. The Roman Catholic colonel, Henry Gage, who was serving in the Spanish army undertook to recruit 6,000 veteran Spanish infantry and 400 cavalry, and ship them from Dunkirk to seize Edinburgh Castle. This scheme of pitting soldiers from the most hated Catholic power in Europe against his Protestant subjects would have been a public relations disaster of the first order. Luckily for Charles the scheme failed to materialize. At this point the king turned his attention to the army in Ireland. Lord Deputy Wentworth's loyal force in the Pale seemed well suited to his needs. There was only one drawback: he had no money to pay it, which is why Wentworth vetoed the idea: the most he would consent to was the sending of 500 men to garrison Carlisle. Finally there was the scheme of the rootless court Catholic, Randal MacDonnell, Earl of Antrim, the man who had left his native Ireland in the 1630s to marry the Duke of Buckingham's widow. Antrim, a charming, voluble man for whom Wentworth had bottomless contempt, almost persuaded Charles to let him recruit men from his own estates in north-west Ireland, combine them with Catholics under Colonel Eoin O'Neill, and invade western Scotland to do battle with the clan Campbell under the Earl of Argyll, and incidentally recover land that Antrim believed they had taken from him and his ancestors. This scheme, which again would have pitted Catholics against the king's Protestant subjects, would have unleashed a conflagration similar to the Thirty Years' War throughout his kingdoms. Thanks to the resolute opposition of Wentworth Antrim's offer to throw Catholic troops into the scales came to nothing in 1639, though it would resurface later to do irreparable damage to the king's cause.[20]

In the event Charles's armies in 1639 and 1640 were composed partly of feudal levies furnished by the nobility, partly of the county trained bands and partly of pressed men. Together, the infantry and cavalry of the trained bands, or militia, totalled almost 100,000 men, mostly men of the 'middling sort' – yeomen, smallholders and artisans. So great was their reluctance to depart from their native counties that the privy council made the fateful decision to allow members of the trained bands to buy out their obligation and send substitutes.[21] In place of the experienced men of the local militia the king had to be content with many labourers lacking military skills. Another several thousand men were recruited by conscription through the Commission of Array. Constables and justices of the peace were responsible for recruitment, and they often exempted skilled workers and labourers who were needed to bring in the harvest. Much recruiting was done in taverns, inns and alehouses where officials scooped up an unpromising collection of sturdy rogues, vagabonds and petty criminals. Small wonder that most of them either deserted or performed poorly on the battlefield.

The royal Ordnance Office did a reasonable job of supplying artillery, hand weapons and munitions to the army in 1639 and 1640. Much existing equipment was broken or unusable, while there were no big arms suppliers in London. The Gunmakers' Company had not kept abreast of the latest technology, being slow to adopt the wheel-lock or snaphance musket in which a spark from a flint ingnited the powder, rather than a flaming piece of fuse or match, as with the more primitive matchlock version. The Ordnance Office was better served by sword merchants, chiefly because

---

[20] The two preceding paragraphs are based on Mark Fissel, *The Bishops' Wars: Charles I's Campaign Against Scotland, 1638–1640*, 152–70.

[21] Ibid., 195, 203, 210.

the Cutlers' Company had to cope with the competition of Benjamin Stone, a maverick sword merchant in Hounslow. Stone supplied at least half the edged weapons used by the royal forces in the two wars. For the rest of the matériel needed by the king the Ordnance Office resorted to foreign suppliers. The Dutch, who had filled large orders for the Scots, cheerfully did the same for the English, but the Ordnance Office sent back a high proportion of their shipments. It may be that the Dutch expressed their sympathies in these wars by trying to fob off their poorer quality arms on the English.[22]

The king ordered his nobility, trained bands and impressed levies to attend the royal standard at York at the beginning of April. His commanding general was the Catholic Earl of Arundel, a man of indifferent abilities. Most of his other officers were inexpert and uninspiring, with the notable exception of Sir Jacob Astley, sergeant-major-general of the infantry who had gained valuable experience in the service of the king of Denmark and the Dutch states.

Leadership was not the only factor that made the prospect of war an inauspicious one for Charles in the spring of 1639. The two garrisons which it was essential for him to hold, Carlisle and Berwick, had been virtually unmanned. Wentworth had filled the gap at Carlisle by sending 500 men from his army to reinforce it.[23] The garrison at Berwick numbered barely two dozen until Astley installed a 2,000-man force at the last minute. The experienced Earl of Essex, who had been denied the generalship of the cavalry, in favour of the queen's much inferior favourite Holland, was sent to command the garrison.[24] While most of the peers had obeyed the royal summons to York, their hearts, like most of their countrymen's, were not in it. Knowing this, Argyll, Lothian and several other covenanting nobles wrote to the Earl of Essex in that month trying to build a bridge between them and their English counterparts. At York, Viscount Saye and Sele and Lord Brooke flatly refused to swear the military oath pledging their fortunes and their lives in the king's quarrel with Scotland. 'I find you averse to all my proceedings', said Charles as he sent them

---

[22] I owe this point to Edward Furgol.

[23] Bodl. MS Ashmole, vol. 800, fo. 50v.

[24] Charles knew that Essex was incomparably the better choice, but his wife had just lost their seventh child, and nearly perished into the bargain. How could he deny her impassioned request for her favourite, the incompetent Holland, to be made commander of the cavalry?

home. The king's Scottish councillor Sir Thomas Hope said that they were 'intelligencers to the Scots nobles', which was almost certainly true.[25]

Few of the king's military backers had much affection for the present bench of bishops. One officer thought they were the cause of all the trouble. Nor did it escape the notice of several others that the overthrow of the Scottish Covenanters would ineluctably draw England closer to Charles's goal of becoming an absolute monarch in all his kingdoms. The poor morale of the nobility manifested itself in quarrels over precedence, an example that was echoed in petty disputes between the privy chamber men and the gentlemen pensioners over who should guard the king at Alnwick. So preoccupied were the leaders by their mutual jealousies that during all their time at York in the month of April they never once mustered, much less trained or disciplined, their regiments.

The rank and file had more serious things to worry about: shortages of bread and fresh water led to mutinies. Sleeping in the open air did not improve their tempers or their resistance to disease. Many fell sick and died from the wet. By 1 May there was a graver worry: smallpox had broken out in the English camp. When they finally left York on 1 May the gloomy Sir Edmund Verney remarked 'there was never so raw, so unskilful, and so unwilling an army brought to fight'.[26] Part of their demoralization stemmed from their knowledge of how little support there was for the war in England. In London, Secretary Windebanke had remarked despairingly on the 'coldness of the citizens' towards Charles's demands.[27] Wentworth took an equally dismal view of the English army's capacity for battle. His advice was to postpone any engagement with the enemy until next year. In the meantime a parliament would have to be called so that the king could explain to the nation why war was necessary, and enlist its financial support.

The First Bishops' War, 1639

Notwithstanding these negative prognostications the royal army of 21,000 trudged with measured step through Durham and Newcastle, reaching Berwick and the Scottish border by the end of May. Neither the king nor

---

[25] Quoted in Peter Donald, *An Uncounselled King: Charles I and the Scottish Troubles, 1637–1641*, 145.

[26] Camden Society, *Letters and Papers of the Verney Family Down to the End of the Year 1639* (hereafter *Verney Papers*), ed. John Bruce, 228.

[27] Clarendon, Edward Earl of, *State Papers Collected by Edward, Earl of Clarendon*, eds R. Scrope and T. Monkhouse, 3 vols (hereafter *CSP*), Vol. 2, 45.

his chief adviser Hamilton had any notion of the value of time. The Covenanters took advantage of their leisurely pace to secure Aberdeen, seize Edinburgh and Dumbarton castles, and arrest the Marquess of Huntly, the chief royalist noble in the north-east. When they tried to coerce him into signing the covenant he spurned them with a choice piece of royalist bravado: 'You may take my head from my shoulders but not my heart from my Sovereign.'[28] These ringing words did not alter the fact that in every theatre the king's efforts to overcome the Scots had been checkmated. From the west nothing had been heard of Antrim's vaunted attack on Argyll's territories. In the east Hamilton's mission to blockade, then capture Edinburgh was stalled by the vigilance of the inhabitants who watched his eight warships from the hilltops and lit beacons against him every step of the way. His own mother, the dowager marchioness, who still controlled his inheritance, embraced the covenant, loudly announcing that she would shoot her son if he tried to land his army.

Meanwhile the king's main army at Berwick also suffered humiliation. On 3 June the Earl of Holland set out at the head of 1,000 cavalry and 3,000 foot to probe the Scottish line at Kelso. Their departure was marred by an angry altercation between Holland and the Earl of Newcastle, governor of the Prince of Wales, whose troop carried the prince's arms on their colours. Without success Newcastle attempted to argue that his troop should march in the van. Holland failed to compel the cavalry to stay close to the lumbering infantry whose pace slowed to a crawl under the weight of their packs and the sun's oppressive heat. Suddenly the cavalry found themselves on the verge of being surrounded by what appeared to be a well ordered body of perhaps 6–8,000 Scots infantry advancing on them in crescent formation. Rather than hurl himself into the jaws of this trap Holland prudently withdrew. In fact Leslie had employed a ruse: by drawing up his infantry in shallow formation and equipping them with extra sets of colours he had made them look more numerous than they actually were. Derisive shouts from the Scottish foot echoed in the ears of Holland's men as they turned tail and retreated. No lives were lost in this humiliating episode, but it led Verney to the rueful reflection that whereas the Scots seemed to know exactly where the English troops were at any moment, the movements of Leslie's army were shrouded in mystery. 'We are betrayed in all our intelligence', he moaned.[29]

---

[28] S.R. Gardiner, *History of England, 1603–1642*, 10 vols (1883–84) (hereafter Gardiner, *Hist.*), 5–6.

[29] *Verney Papers*, 244.

With food running out, and acutely aware of the superior condition of the Scots forces, the whole of the English camp was now plagued by doubt and irritation. The turning point arrived when the Earl of Bristol entered Charles's tent for a two-hour heart-to-heart talk. The gist of his advice was the same as Wentworth's: he must call parliament before proceeding any further in the religious policy that had driven the Scots to revolt. Crestfallen, Charles saw that his dream of a short, sharp victory against the Covenanters could not be realized in the current fighting season.

Is it possible that Charles, had he kept his nerve, might have beaten the Scots in 1639? Was his decision to open negotiations 'arguably the greatest single mistake' of his life? It has been observed that his troops outnumbered Leslie's army by several thousand, and that the latter was if anything more poorly supplied and disease ridden. According to one English intelligence report the Scots believed 'that if we had come to blows we should have beaten them'.[30] In fact the cessation of hostilities came not a moment too soon for the Scots. By a superhuman effort they had fielded a sizeable army, but their money and food alike were nearly exhausted. Had Charles been able to hold out for another week or two, their army might well have disintegrated.

The pacification of Berwick

Thanks to the good relations between many of nobility on both sides, negotiations were courteous. The only sour note was struck by the unaristocratic Wariston who embarrassed his colleagues by openly expressing distrust towards Charles. The king, he declared, was playing for time. The Kirk assembly and the parliament that he promised them meant nothing, since he intended ultimately to overrule them by force. Charles's hurt anger – 'the devil himself could not make a more uncharitable construction' – in fact reflected the penetrating accuracy of Wariston's jibe.[31]

Yet it is arguable that delay benefited the Covenanters even more than the king. With every passing day they were gaining more friends in England; they were consolidating support for their position in the Netherlands and France; the holding of an assembly and a parliament in Scotland could only enhance their constitutional position.

[30] BL. Add. MS 11045, fo. 32 [Rossingham to Viscount Scudamore, 25 June 1639], cited by John Adamson, 'England without Cromwell: What if Charles I had avoided the civil war', in Niall Ferguson (ed.), *Virtual History, Alternatives and Counterfactuals*, 100.

[31] Scottish Historical Society (hereafter SHS), *Diary of Sir Archibald Johnston Lord Wariston 1639* (hereafter Wariston, *Diary*), Vol. 26 (1896), 85.

These were the concessions that Charles was compelled to yield in consequence of his failure to put down the Covenanters' revolt. He undertook to withdraw his forces, to summon a general assembly of the Kirk as well as a parliament, and to accept the legislation they passed. Both institutions would meet in Edinburgh within two months. Apparently then Charles was agreeing in advance to the abolition of the bishops that he had disputed so bitterly with the Covenanters. However, his commissioner, the Earl of Traquair, with misguided subtlety, had advised the king that if the bishops were prevented from sitting in parliament he could declare the proceedings null and void. He could therefore allow the parliament to meet without the bishops, secure in the knowledge that he could reintroduce episcopacy whenever he felt strong enough to do so. Once again Charles allowed himself to be seduced by bad advice.

For their part, the Covenanters agreed to disband their army without having obtained the king's formal ratification of the acts of the Glasgow Assembly or the removal of the bishops. As the basic demand had been that 'we shall be governed by general assembles in matters ecclesiastical, and by parliament in matters civil',[32] there was a widespread conviction in Scotland that the covenant had been betrayed. Few appreciated the fragility of the spectacle that had just been staged for the king's benefit.

Kirk, Tables and estates: the Scottish parliament of 1639

The Kirk Assembly met first, again with lay representatives, and without the bishops. It adopted the revolutionary programme of the Glasgow Assembly and confirmed the abolition of episcopacy dubbing it 'antichristian'.[33] The Kirk, as Alexander Hamilton wrote in an internal memo, had abjured episcopacy several times, 'and spewed it out; we must not return to our vomit'.[34] Henceforth no churchman would be eligible to hold any civil office. Charles knew that parliament had even worse things in store for him. Before it met Hamilton had already counselled him to prepare for a renewal of war.

Scotland's parliamentary system was different in several important respects from England's. Unicameral in structure, meaning that it lacked an upper chamber, it had originally consisted of four estates: the nobility,

---

[32] Wariston, *Diary 1639*, 40.
[33] Quoted in Donald, *Uncounselled King*, 132.
[34] Quoted in ibid., 129.

bishops, barons or gentry and burgesses, with a total membership somewhat under 150. A small body drawn from parliament and known as the Lords of the Articles, acted as an executive or senate which continued to meet during the long periods when parliament was not in session. The Articles comprised up to a dozen representatives from each estate. Before 1639 the bishops and nobility had elected the representatives from the other two estates. The reason for this provision was to preserve royal and upper-class control of the Articles. While parliament was in session the function of the Lords of the Articles was to frame legislation for parliamentary assent. Parliament could not amend such legislation, only pass or reject it. The Lords of the Session, or judiciary, were appointed by the Crown, as was the privy council. Under Charles I the latter body had come to be increasingly dominated by bishops.

Elections to the 1639 parliament were carefully controlled by the Tables, which were the political committees of the Covenanters. More than one-third of the members – 50 nobles, 47 gentry and 52 burgesses – had sat in the Glasgow Assembly. The agenda of the 1639 parliament had already been set by the Covenanters before it met; it was nothing less than constitutional revolution. First on the agenda was ratification of the religious settlement hammered out in Glasgow. Next was modification of the Lords of the Articles. Each estate would from now on elect its own representatives. This new executive arm of parliament would be called the Committee of Estates, the Scottish version of a revolutionary committee of public safety. This was a momentous change, as it eliminated kingly power over parliament. Next was parliamentary control over the appointment of officers of state, privy councillors and Lords of the Session. The effect of this measure was to reduce Charles to the status of a 'Doge of Venice'. The next provision was a guarantee that the future existence of parliament would not be subject to the whim of the king. A triennial act would be passed to ensure the summoning of parliament every three years. Finally was the abolition of the clerical estate in parliament. The bishops had already been warned not to attend. A statute would make their exclusion permanent. The aim here was not so much the secularization of the state as the extinction of prelacy.

With the aim of bolstering both the autonomy of parliament and enshrining its superiority to the Crown in the Scottish constitution, several further provisions were agreed on. First, there was to be no proxy voting. Powerful men would no longer be able to come to parliament, their pockets stuffed with other men's votes. Secondly, 'strangers' (meaning Englishmen) who had been awarded Scottish peerages, but who owned no land in Scotland, would be denied a vote in the nobles' estate. The king would thus be unable to pack that estate with his own nominees from outside the country. Thirdly, instead of the gentry casting one vote per shire, each of the two commissioners from every shire would vote. Gentry voting strength in parliament was thereby doubled. Fourthly, privy councillors were liable to censure and removal by parliament. Fifthly, no Lords of the Session were to be appointed without the prior advice of the nobles and gentry in parliament. The judiciary, in other words, was placed firmly under parliamentary control.

From London the king had made up his mind to ratify none of this legislation, but to overthrow it by force. Traquair, who had presided over the revolutionary deliberations of the Edinburgh parliament, did everything in his power to sidetrack them, including adjourning parliament for over two months (7 September to 14 November). When the legislation was passed nevertheless, the king withheld his assent to any of it on the ground that it lacked Traquair's signature. He then ordered parliament prorogued until 2 June 1640.

The parliamentarians did not take this threat to their existence lying down. Protesting that they were indeed a sitting parliament, they empowered the new revolutionary executive, the Committee of Estates, to remain in Edinburgh, exercising full parliamentary authority, and awaiting a more favourable reply from the king. The Committee of Estates was effectively the Tables under a new name. As such it took upon itself to organize the second round of the armed struggle with the king. While military preparations went on apace the committee continued to hector Charles with demands for three further concessions: First, his agreement that parliament could not be prorogued without its own consent; secondly, the abolition of the Lords of the Articles and their replacement by the Committee of Estates, directly accountable to parliament; and third, that no governor be appointed to any garrison without parliamentary consent. Taken together these demands signified the transfer of sovereignty from the king to parliament, and his conversion into a figurehead ruler. Almost every one of the Scottish parliament's demands foreshadowed those of the Long Parliament. Not for the last time Scotland had led the way.

The Second Bishops' War

To no one's surprise, the king would hear of none of this. The storm clouds of war continued to darken. By November 1639 Charles had formed a committee of eight of his most trusted privy councillors, including

Wentworth, Laud and Hamilton, to advise him on Scottish affairs. The most powerful member of the committee was Wentworth, who counselled the king to rule Scotland directly. He further persuaded Charles to summon the English parliament in order to generate money and public support for an invasion of the northern kingdom.

The council of war meanwhile drew up plans for an army of 23,000. With Wentworth's (he was now Earl of Strafford) blessing the Earl of Northumberland was given the supreme command. Secretary Windebanke lobbied hard for the king to detach the Earl of Essex from the disaffected peers by appointing him general of the horse: 'he is a popular man, and it will give extraordinary satisfaction to all sorts of people to see him in employment again'.[35] The plea fell on deaf ears and the commission went to Lord Conway. Strafford then left for Ireland, where in March 1640 he convened the Irish parliament. Led by its Catholic members, this body denounced the Covenanters and authorized the lord-lieutenant to levy an army of 9,000 men to fight them. The English parliament, which met the following month, proved much less cooperative. Preferring to debate the accumulated grievances of eleven years, the MPs gave the king's councillors a dusty answer when they urged subsidies of £840,000 for the projected war. The 'Short' Parliament was dissolved after three weeks.

In the face of mounting evidence of popular hostility to his quarrel with Scotland, Charles nevertheless broke off negotiations with the commissioners from that kingdom. The man who more than anyone incited him to take a hard line was Strafford, back in England once again. 'Go on with a vigorous war', he is reported to have said, 'loose and absolved from all rules of government; being reduced to extreme necessity.' What did it matter that Charles had little support in England? 'You have an army in Ireland [that] you may employ here to reduce this kingdom . . . Scotland shall not hold out five months.'[36]

More fundamental than the shortage of money was popular disenchantment with the king's cause. The Yorkshire gentry refused to mobilize the county's trained bands unless Charles would foot the bill.[37] Elsewhere

---

[35] *CSP*, Vol. 2, 95.

[36] Royal Commission on Historical Manuscripts (hereafter HMC) HMC 3, *Fourth Report* (House of Lords MSS), 3. Henry Vane's notes. These were the words that would send Strafford to the scaffold barely a year later. It is quite clear, however, that he intended the Irish army to be used not against England, but Scotland.

[37] David Scott, '"Hannibal at our gates": loyalists and fifth columnists during the Bishops' Wars – the case of Yorkshire', *Historical Research* (hereafter HR), 70 (1997), 282–3.

recruitment became increasingly difficult. In Lincolnshire for example, the most able-bodied men fled into the forest in order to avoid being taken. Only the 'lame, sick and unserviceable' remained.[38] In response to the wholesale refusal of the militia to serve, the disastrous policy of substitution was re-invoked, even though the Marquess of Hamilton had called it 'the greatest cause of these misfortunes' in 1639. Thus the ablest soldiers were able to shield themselves from military service. It is no surprise that Sir Jacob Astley condemned the 4,000 troops who reached him at Selby in July as 'all the arch knaves of the kingdom'.[39] Many of them had neither shoes nor stockings, and their officers were not drilling them.

Leading Yorkshire gentry, in concert with a faction of twelve disaffected English noblemen, worked systematically to subvert their own country's cause. Three times in the summer of 1640 the Yorkshire gentry petitioned the king against the ruinous effect that his Scottish policy was having on the county. Their refusal to bring out the Yorkshire militia was of critical importance in early August when the king's army was still not ready for service. The non-appearance of the Yorkshire militia can only have encouraged the Scots in their invasion plans. There is evidence too of collusion between the Yorkshire gentry and the disaffected nobility, whose communication with the Scots was coordinated by Lord Savile. In June, during his sojourn in London, Lord Loudoun had been in touch with Savile, who had assured him that many English peers sympathized with the Scots. Later Wariston wrote to Savile, asking for money for the invading army. Savile at once drafted a letter to which he and six other peers – Essex, Warwick, Mandeville, Bedford, Saye and Brooke – attached their signatures, promising the Scots everything they wanted. This was a significant factor in giving the Covenanters confidence to launch their invasion.[40]

Dénouement at Newburn

On 20 August the Scots army – 20,000 foot and 2–3,000 horse – crossed the River Tweed at Coldstream. The royal strategy had dictated the strengthening of Berwick and its garrison in preparation for a strike against Edinburgh. But Leslie and the Covenanters simply bypassed Berwick and

[38] Quoted in Fissel, *Bishops' Wars*, 211.
[39] *CSP*, Vol. 2, 101.
[40] Peter Donald, 'New light on the Anglo-Scottish contacts of 1640', *HR*, 62 (1989), 221–9; Scott, ' "Hannibal at our gates" ', 276–8, 292 and n. 44.

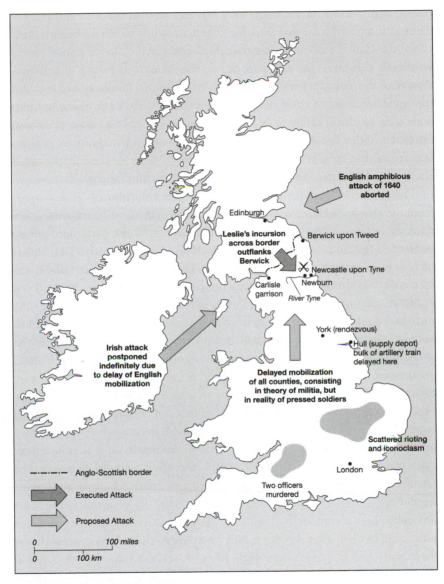

MAP 2 *The Second Bishops' War*

Adapted from Fissel, Mark, *The Bishops' Wars: Charles I's Campaigns Against Scotland*
(Cambridge University Press, 1994)

plunged straight into England. With them came herds of sheep and cattle
to feed them, and money to pay for whatever they took. Besides being well
provisioned the covenanting army's discipline and cohesion was maintained
by religious exercises. Every night on their march southwards 'there was
nothing to be heard almost through the whole army but singing of psalms,

prayer and reading of the scripture by the soldiers in their several huts'.[41] Charles's departure for the north had left his councillors in London at their wits' end when the news arrived that the Scots had invaded. Charles's presence had a galvanizing effect in the north, however. By 27 August the armies of the two sides were about equal in number if not in quality. But the royal army was split in two, half with the king at York, the other half with Conway and Astley at Newcastle. Leslie's force had now advanced more than 50 miles down the eastern side of England without encountering opposition. It was evident that their target was Newcastle, the third city of the kingdom, and the shipping point for the vital trade between London and the Durham coalfields. It did not help matters that – apart from the elite – the citizens of Newcastle were unwilling to do anything for the king.[42] The city's governor was Lord Conway. Weak man that he was, he tried to realize two incompatible objectives simultaneously. Two-thirds of his troops he left to garrison the city. Then, with his remaining 3,000 foot and 1,500 horse he set out to hold the ford across the River Tyne at Newburn, six miles upstream. Bolstered by only a few cannon (for the ordnance had not been brought north from the arsenal at Hull), he commanded his men to take up and defend an untenable position on the southern bank. Two sconces or breastworks were each occupied by 400 musketeers and four sakers (small cannon firing 6-pound shot). The horse, divided into squadrons, were drawn up in a meadow behind them. On the other side of the river, only a few hundred feet to the north, was a height of land. Here Leslie set up his cannon, somewhere between forty and eighty in number, mostly demi-culverins firing $10^3/_4$-pound ball. It was now low tide, and the river easily fordable. Leslie therefore sent down a party of horse, but Wilmot, commissary-general of the horse, charged and drove them back across the river. From this commanding position Leslie then unleashed his cannon on the English breastworks. After a number of direct hits, which killed several officers and many men, the soldiers threw down their arms and fled from their little forts. A second time Wilmot's horse entered the fray. Some of them held back, however, and seeing this, Leslie threw all his horse into the scales, supported by 10,000 musketeers, according to Conway's account.[43] As Vane, who was also there, put it, 'our horse did not behave well. Many ran away and did not second those that were first charged.'[44] The routed horse fled all the way to Durham, while

---

[41] John Livingstone, *A Brief Historical Relation of the Life of Mr. John Livingston*, 25.
[42] *CSP*, Vol. 2, 100.
[43] Ibid., 109.
[44] Hardwicke, *State Papers*, Vol. 2, 162.

the Scottish infantry crossed the ford without hindrance. Leslie restrained his men from slaughtering the panic-stricken English foot, who took refuge in Newcastle. Since the town lacked adequate fortification, they had no choice but to evacuate it next day. Leslie's army occupied the town on 30 August.

The consequences of Newburn were momentous. The Scots' victory meant that Scotland would not be Anglicized in religion; that Scotland would keep its distinctive identity within a British union; and, that the Scots would become a force in English politics.[45]

It is worth reviewing the causes of this devastating blow to Charles's power and prestige. First of all, his army was composed of poor material – raw, untrained, mutinuous men. Secondly, with the exception of General Astley, the English leaders inspired little confidence. Strafford was a novice; Northumberland was ill; Conway was indecisive and showed poor judgement in his choice of ground. When his request for money to fortify Newcastle was turned down, he did little to remedy his situation. Thirdly, the English army was poorly supplied with artillery. Conway's handful of heavy guns was no match for Leslie's 40 to 80. Charles actually had the ordnance he needed; the trouble was that most of it was in Hull, miles away from the scene of action. Fourthly, the refusal of the Yorkshire militia to turn out obliged Charles to keep half his forces in York. This inexorably dictated that Conway at Newcastle would face an army twice the size of his own. Fifthly, wherever he turned in the winter and spring of 1640 Charles found himself straitjacketed by lack of money. The poor and middling sort balked at paying their taxes, while the wealthy declined to lend. The drying up of revenue reflected a sixth and deeper problem for the king: the popular perception that the struggle truly was a 'bishops' war'. Few people saw any reason to risk their lives or their purses on behalf of the Scottish episcopate. Many had a more than sneaking sympathy for the supposed enemy: a stridently Calvinist people who were appealing for English support in their quest for liberty from an Arminian, episcopally-dominated system of Church government and worship. The Yorkshire gentry were so disaffected to the king's cause that, as Conway put it, 'if Hannibal were at our gates, some had rather open them than keep him out'.[46] Indeed, as recent scholarship has shown, the king's war effort against the Scots in 1640 was deliberately sabotaged by elements within the English nobility and gentry.[47] Charles and his councillors were quite

[45] Conrad Russell, *The Fall of the British Monarchies*, 145.
[46] *CSP*, Vol. 2, 105.
[47] See above, n. 40.

aware of this treasonous activity, and their knowledge set up a chain of threats and coercion in British politics that carried all three nations into war and ultimately destroyed the king himself.

Another astonishing fact, as we shall see, is that most of the bill for the Scots' defeat of the English was footed by the English. Not until January 1639 did the Covenanters begin preparing to raise money on the scale required to support an army. The Tables sent a letter to the shires ordering the levying of forces and the assessment of the rents of each parish so that the burden of supporting these forces could be distributed equally. In the meantime 200,000 merks (about £11,000 sterling) was borrowed from the richest merchant in Edinburgh. Smaller sums were also borrowed, and all available silver was assembled and sent to Edinburgh for coining. Loans, the coining of silver, the raising of men at the expense of their parishes and the supplying of arms and provisions on credit thus financed the first Bishops' War.

In January of 1640 a convention of estates met and ordered a valuation of the nation's wealth. Everyone was ordered to pay a tenth of his yearly rent. The tenth penny, as it became known, was the first national tax imposed by the Covenanters. Its originality consisted in attempting to tax all kinds of income; in employing an entirely new valuation of property in both shires and burghs; and in using the presbytery as a unit of collection. In 1643 further taxes were added: the excise or value-added tax, and the monthly maintenance, both of which were based on the principles of spreading the burden as fairly and widely as possible.

The money was raised through a combination of coercion and inspiration. There was also heavy reliance on anticipated revenue from England. At the beginning of August, with their pre-emptive invasion less than three weeks away, the covenanting army faced a crisis of finance and supply. An appeal was made to Edinburgh for immediate support. After a solemn fast followed by prayer and exhortation the citizens offered £100,000 Scots (£8,333 sterling) plus 3,000 sheets which the women of the city fashioned into tents for the soldiers. Similar scenes were doubtless repeated in other centres, but as Robert Baillie admitted, a large part of the army's maintenance was based on 'hopes from England'.[48] Between 1638 and 1641 the covenanting movement spent almost half a million pounds (£5,746,351 Scots). Only 9 per cent of this sum was collected in Scotland. Just under 85 per cent was received from England in the form of the 'brotherly assistance' (only half the promised £300,000 was actually received) and the

---

[48] Baillie, *Letters*, Vol. 1, 255.

daily payment of £850, which totalled £266,050 for the 313 days of occupation. The remaining six–seven per cent was unpaid debt. The belief that Puritan Englishmen would pay a covenanting Scottish army to invade their country was based to a large extent on the letter of the seven peers promising just that. The Covenanters took the leap of faith, and in the short term at least, were vindicated. Had it not been for the promise of English money their invasion would have quickly collapsed.[49]

On the king's side, before and during the bishops' wars, there was neither prayer nor fasting nor exhortation. Nor was there any attempt to revamp the national system of taxation in order to spread fairly the burden of fighting the Scots. In 1639 and 1640 the receipts from Ship Money virtually dried up. The medieval tax called Coat and Conduct Money was equally unpopular. When in May 1640 the king told the Lord Mayor and Aldermen of London that he needed to borrow from them, he was met with blank refusal. Nor could the magistrates be brought to raise the 4,000 men they were expected to contribute to the war. The Short Parliament of April 1640 voted nothing, while the parliament in Ireland did only a little better. Attempts to borrow in Genoa and France also failed, as did the attempts to squeeze money from English Catholic recusants. By July the royal exchequer had nothing in the cupboard beyond a loan of £60,000 secured on the future customs revenue. Charles seriously contemplated seizing Spanish bullion from the Tower of London, and debasing the coinage, but backed off when financiers protested that he would destroy London's position as a leading financial centre. To no one's surprise the army that marched north in the summer of 1640 was ill equipped, dispirited and poorly paid.

The English-Scottish conflict of 1638–40 was full of portent. The Scots had thrown out their bishops and their Anglican order of service, putting back Calvinist worship and Presbyterian church government in their place. The upper-class laity had taken control of the church. The Scottish nation had twice faced down a threatened invasion by the king, and the second time had turned the tables on him by invading and occupying England's two north-eastern counties, and defeating an English army in pitched battle. Prior to this stunning military achievement rebellious Covenanters had seized control of the government of Scotland, creating a new executive arm

---

[49] The above analysis is based on Stevenson, 'Financing the cause of the covenants, 1638–51', *Scottish History Review* (hereafter SHR), 51 (1972), 89–95; Macinnes, *Covenanting Movement*, 205–6; Wariston, *Diary*, 97–8; Baillie, *Letters*, Vol. 1, 255–6.

called the Committee of Estates. Through the parliament of Scotland they asserted control over the appointment of leading officers of state: privy councillors and judges (lords of the session). They also saw to it that parliament's existence would no longer be subject to the whim of the king by passing an act guaranteeing that it would be summoned at least once every three years. Most important of all, they wrested the sword, the fundamental attribute of sovereignty, from the king's hands. Since 1637 there had been a torrential unleashing of spiritual and political energy in Scotland, testimony to the remarkable power of the National Covenant in winning hearts and minds at all levels of Scottish society.

These events had been watched with the greatest interest in Ireland and England. It would not be long before the pioneering revolutionary example of the Covenanters was imitated in these other two kingdoms.

CHAPTER 2

The Irish insurgency, 1641–42

The example of Scotland was catching. Before spreading to England, however, the contagion of rebellion jumped across the Irish Sea to Ireland. On 1 November 1641 the news reached London that Ireland's northern province of Ulster was aflame with revolt. Led by Sir Phelim O'Neill, the financially troubled landowner who was descended from the Earl of Tyrone and cousin to Owen Roe O'Neill, 10,000 armed Gaelic Irish had gone to war to recover the lands that had been confiscated from them by English and Scots settlers, and win the freedom to practise their Catholic religion. In a matter of days they had overrun a string of castles and other strongholds, and were practically in control of most of the province. Soon the common people and younger sons of the gentry were flocking to the rebel standard. English settlers were pillaged, and warned that their throats would be cut if they tried to take refuge in Dublin. Although most of the clergy tried to restrain the insurgents, a few priests and friars egged them on. One was reported to have preached that 'it was no sin to kill all the Protestants for they were all damned already'; another that 'it was as lawful to kill Englishmen as a dog'.[1] Terrified, many settlers disobeyed the rebels' command to stay in their homes, and headed for British-held territory. On the way they were attacked by crowds who took everything they had, including the clothes off their backs. In the bitter cold many died from exposure.

Sir Phelim and other leaders of the revolt tried to halt the plundering and cruelty of the civilian population, but so deep and abiding was the hatred towards the English, that the leaders were often helpless to curb

---

[1] Quoted in Michael Perceval-Maxwell, *The Outbreak of the Irish Rebellion of 1641*, 231.

the activities of their supporters. Not only did many die – often at the hands of women – but buildings and crops were destroyed and livestock slaughtered, sometimes after the animals had been convicted at mock trials.[2]

News of the rising was brought to England by Owen O'Connolly, a Protestant, and servant to the MP and landowner in Ireland, Sir John Clotworthy. O'Connolly's foster brother, Colonel Hugh MacMahon was one of the conspirators who informed him of the plans while he was in his cups one night, four days before the rebellion was due to erupt. The Irish, as he reported, 'had prepared men in all parts of the kingdom . . . to destroy all the English inhabitants there' and 'all Protestants should be killed this night'.[3] After passing on this information to the government in Ireland, he crossed over to England where he brought it to the attention of the Earl of Leicester, the recently appointed Lord Deputy of Ireland. Leicester in turn informed the English House of Commons. The story was soon embellished in the telling. The Earl of Northumberland's secretary wrote a few days later that 'those popish hellhounds' were 'murdering, ravishing, burning and taking what they could'.[4] Before long London was flooded with pamphlets purporting to describe, in the most lurid detail, the genocidal acts of the Catholic Irish against the Protestant English settlers. Both the number and the nature of these atrocities were wildly exaggerated, but apparent verisimilitude was lent to the published reports by the stream of refugees who soon began disembarking at the western ports of England. Some were maimed; many had lost their families; most were destitute. Their appeals for relief from parish vestries in London, where many of them ended up, wrenched the hearts of those who heard them. Their stories, and the images they conjured up, stayed in people's minds, and drove a deeper wedge between Charles I and his English parliament. Many concluded that events in Ireland were only the prologue to a Catholic rising in England with foreign support, and accompanied by parallel atrocities. More than a year after this panic first seized Londoners the MP Sir Simonds D'Ewes wrote of the terrible fear of the 'bloody murtherers like to descend upon us like a swarm of caterpillars'.[5] It was the considered opinion of the Puritan divine, Richard Baxter, that

[2] Ibid., 232–3.
[3] Ibid., 210–11.
[4] Ibid., 270.
[5] Bodl., MS Tanner 64, fo. 97.

above all, the two hundred thousand killed in Ireland, affrighted the
Parliament and all the land. . . . There was nothing that with the people
wrought so much as the Irish massacre and rebellion.[6]

It did not matter that the entire Protestant population of Ireland numbered
only half the total Baxter believed to have been killed there: most politically aware English people became unshakeable in their conviction of a
bloody popish plot to wipe out all Protestants in all three kingdoms. The
royalist historian Clarendon later reflected that but for the Irish rebellion
'all the miseries which afterwards befell the king and his dominions had
been prevented'.[7] This was of course an oversimplified and Anglocentric
reading, since in reality the rebellions in all three kingdoms sprang from
one interlocking crisis, with many common causes.

Conquest, religion, land and ethnicity: the background of the 1641 rebellion

The destinies of England and Ireland had been wedded ever since the
Norman conquest of both countries in the eleventh century. By an act
of Henry VIII (1541) Ireland had been made a kingdom 'united and knit
to the Imperial crown of the realm of England'. In other words it was
a dependency, not of the English parliament, but the English Crown.
Ireland's chief executive, or viceroy, who bore the title of lord deputy or
lord lieutenant, was appointed by the king, and reported only to him.
From the late twelfth century Norman settlers had taken up residence in a
small area within forty miles of Dublin known as the Pale. Never a large
presence, they eventually numbered 2,000 families, and came to be known
as the Old English. By 1641 they controlled a third of the profitable land
in Ireland, about $2^1/_4$ million acres.

Because of its physical proximity to England, Ireland had loomed large
in English strategic thinking since the Middle Ages. English rulers could
not shake off the fear that one of the larger European powers, whether
Spain, France or the papacy might use Ireland as the staging point for an
invasion of England. In the pithy words of a 1641 pamphleteer, it was dangerous 'to have the pope keeper of the keys to your back door'.[8] Politically,

---

[6] Richard Baxter, *Reliquiae Baxterianae*, 37, 28.
[7] Clarendon, *Hist.*, Bk 15, para. 2.
[8] Quoted in T.W. Moody F.X. Martin and F.J. Byrne, *The New History of Ireland.*
Vol. 3: *Early Modern Ireland 1534–1691* (hereafter *NHI*, Vol. 3), 233.

therefore, Ireland was kept on a tight leash. By Poynings' Law (1494) no bill could be introduced into the Irish parliament unless it had first been approved by the lords justices (the Irish executive, equivalent to the English privy council), and the privy council in London.

At the Reformation neither the native Gaelic Irish nor the Old English chose to convert to Protestantism. As Nicholas Canny has pointed out, from the Reformation onwards it was at all times the policy of the English government to eradicate Catholicism and dispossess Catholics of their property in favour of Protestants.[9] A policy of colonization or plantation as it was called was implemented by Elizabeth I, and then at a quickening pace, by James I. The religious question, together with the fear of Spanish infiltration into Ireland was what spurred Elizabeth's policy. The reality of Spanish meddling was made manifest in the Earl of Tyrone's rebellion of the 1590s, the most formidable challenge to English rule since the Norman conquest.

The flight of Tyrone and his fellow earls in 1607 under suspicious circumstances, combined with a minor rebellion the following year, were enough to impel James I to resort to outright confiscation of six counties in the northern province of Ulster. In a revolutionary transfer of land from Catholic to Protestant, English and Scottish undertakers were invited to come and take up permanent settlement. The consequence of this and other confiscations was that the percentage of land owned by Catholics steadily declined, to 59 per cent by 1641, and 14 per cent by the end of the century.[10] In 1609 James I presented the citizens of London with 40,000 acres in County Derry. Londonderry, as it was known, stood as a stark symbol of Ireland's colonial status.

The English and Scottish planters who arrived in Ireland came up against an economy that was by their standards primitive, pastoral and semi-nomadic. Many Irish peasants still migrated each summer with their livestock to the hills and wastelands in search of fresh pasture. Cattle, highly prized, were still occasionally treated as a form of currency. Sheep and horses were also reared. With manufacturing nearly non-existent, the chief articles of export were hides, fish and wool. The impact of the planters was to quicken the pace of economic growth by the introduction

[9] Nicholas Canny 'The attempted Anglicisation of Ireland in the seventeenth century: an exemplar of "British History"', in J.F. Merritt (ed.), *The Political World of Thomas Wentworth, Earl of Strafford, 1621–1641*, 157–86. Canny enlarges on this theme in *Making Ireland British 1580–1650*.

[10] *NHI*, Vol. 3, 1.

of progressive agricultural techniques, but as English land tenure replaced the looser form of ownership traditional to the country, the price of land rose, and the wandering way of life became untenable. Rising national prosperity went hand-in-hand with a declining standard of living for the mass of the population. By 1641, as Aidan Clarke observes, 'the depression of small freeholders was almost complete'.[11] By this time the profitable land was held by no more than 6,000 proprietors – about 40 per cent by New English and Scots, and 30 per cent each by Gaelic Irish and Old English.

Alarmed at the prospect of being dispossessed of all their land, the Catholic Old English approached Charles I soon after he ascended the throne with a series of requests. Their timing was auspicious, because Charles had already gone to war against Spain, and as he prepared to attack Cadiz Ireland's strategic importance loomed large once again. So in return for an Irish commitment to raise money and men to defend the country against an apprehended invasion from Spain, the king offered 26 'matters of grace and bounty'. These included the suspension of recusancy fines (for refusal to attend the established Protestant church), the abolition of religious tests for inheritance, appointment to public office, and the right to practise the law. Most important was his promise to apply to Ireland the English statute of 1624 which guaranteed security of title to anyone who had possessed his estates for 60 years or more. This promise of nearly equal rights for the Catholic population provoked a backlash from the New English planter class. In 1627 the Protestant bishops castigated Charles for putting religion up for sale. In the face of this division within the country Charles invited representatives from both groups – Old and New English – to come to England. The following year a delegation dominated by Old English representatives arrived in London with a list of 51 demands under their arm. Charles said yes to them, provided he could be guaranteed £40,000 a year for three years and more thereafter. To this demand the Irish agreed with alacrity. These 'royal instructions and graces' represent the apex of Old English political achievement. It seemed, assuming the king could be trusted, that Catholics could take their place in the public life of their country, that Ireland would, for the first time since the Reformation, become safe for Catholicism. The English privy council gave the green light for them to be introduced into the Irish parliament, but with significant exceptions. The offer to suspend recusancy fines was dropped, and the promise to secure the right of Catholics to hold public office was

[11] Ibid., 170.

rebuffed. The centrality of Protestantism as a determinant of social and political status was reaffirmed.

With the ending of the threat from Spain came an end to the need to cater to Irish Catholic opinion. Responding to New English planter pressure, Charles ordered Lord Deputy Falkland to suppress religious houses in Dublin and other major towns. His failure to execute this policy led to his recall. For the next three years no lord deputy was appointed, and Ireland was ruled by two lords justices, Richard Boyle, Earl of Cork and Lord Chancellor Adam Loftus. Under their rule the interests of the New English planters were vigorously promoted. Thanks mainly to his accumulation of confiscated Irish estates, the Earl of Cork became the greatest landowner in all three kingdoms. Like his friend and supporter on the English privy council, Viscount Dorchester, he was a man of Puritan conviction. For both men, as John Reeve emphasises, 'Ireland was an arena in which they could express the religious intensity of their souls'.[12] Thus in 1630 Cork undertook the confiscation of the religious houses. Recusancy fines were reimposed in order to strengthen the Dublin garrison and the standing army that was thought necessary to defend the planter community. Once again the religious life of the people retreated underground.

The rise and fall of Thomas Wentworth, Earl of Strafford, 1633–41

In 1633 there arrived in Dublin the man who was to dominate Ireland for the next seven years. The overwhelming force of his personality, together with his dramatic end on the scaffold at Tower Hill in 1641 have made Thomas Wentworth an object of fascination from that day to this. One of the king's harshest critics in the 1628 parliament, he switched sides that same year, was elevated to the peerage, and joined the king's privy council. Though a believer in parliamentary government he also held that parliament must ultimately submit to the king's will. At root he was an authoritarian with absolutist yearnings.[13] Endowed with formidable intelligence and vigour, he was well equipped to realize the policy goals he set for himself. He thought clearly, connectedly and constructively, and made decisions without hesitation. While he was a skilled political infighter, he

[12] John Reeve, 'Secret alliance and Protestant agitation in two kingdoms: the early Caroline background to the Irish rebellion of 1641', in Ian Gentles, John Morrill and A. Blair Worden (eds), *Soldiers, Writers and Statesmen of the English Revolution*, 25.

[13] Anthony Milton, 'Thomas Wentworth and the political thought of the Personal Rule', in Merritt (ed.), *Political World of Thomas Wentworth*, 156.

did not mix well with people, and lacked the gift of empathy that would have enabled him to appreciate the legitimacy of an opposing point of view. Nor – with a few exceptions – did he have the knack of bringing out the best in the people he worked with.[14]

Judgements about his career are at least as extreme as his policies were, and almost all are negative. In Clarendon's eyes he was 'a man of great parts and extraordinary endowments of nature . . .', yet 'of all his passions his pride was most predominant'.[15] To Macaulay he was 'the lost Archangel, the Satan of the Apostasy'.[16] Among modern historians, C.V. Wedgwood found his policy in Ireland 'fundamentally incoherent'.[17] 'An overwhelming failure' is the verdict of Terence Ranger; 'above all a man who brought disaster' the view of H.F. Kearney, who also indicts him for causing the Irish uprising of 1641.[18]

There is no doubt about his talent for making enemies. The list of the powerful whom he alienated and who thirsted for revenge included men from all three groups: among the Gaelic Irish the Earl of Antrim and the O'Byrnes; among the Old English the Earl of Clanricarde – the leading Catholic peer in Ireland – and the Earl of Westmeath; and, among the Protestant New English, the Earl of Cork, the greatest landowner in Ireland, Lord Chancellor Adam Loftus, Vice-Treasurer Lord Mountnorris, and Sir John Clotworthy, a Presbyterian well connected in England. For good measure, he also despised the Marquess of Hamilton, Charles's chief counsellor for Scotland, and hated all puritans for 'their narrow and shrivelled up hearts'.[19] He upset the whole Irish parliament with his 'scornful language' and his blunt statement that Ireland was 'a conquered nation and must expect laws as from a conqueror'.[20] So impartial was he in his hatreds that by 1640–41 he had, as Conrad Russell notes, 'achieved the distinction of being perhaps the only Englishman to have obliterated the religious divide in Irish politics'.[21]

---

[14] Aidan Clarke, 'The government of Wentworth, 1632–40', in *NHI*, Vol. 3, 243; C.V. Wedgwood, *Thomas Wentworth, First Earl of Strafford, 1593–1641*, 397.

[15] Clarendon, *Hist.*, Bk 3, paras. 204–5.

[16] Quoted in Wedgwood, *Thomas Wentworth*, 70.

[17] Ibid., 174.

[18] Terence Ranger, 'Strafford in Ireland', *Past & Present* (hereafter *P & P*), 19 (1961), 30, 44.

[19] Wedgwood, *Thomas Wentworth*, 251.

[20] *Calendar of the State Papers, Ireland* (hereafter *CSPI*) 1633–47, 262 (19 February 1641).

[21] Russell, *Fall of the British Monarchies*, 382–3.

The pole star of Wentworth's life was the principle of unswerving loyalty to the king. His objective in Ireland was to turn the kingdom into a prosperous state, humming with economic activity, and generating steadily increasing revenues for the Crown. A risk taker, he invested in new industries – linen, glass and horse breeding – but they did not pay off. Yet he did sweep the Irish Sea clear of pirates, and within five years had almost tripled the customs revenues, a quarter of which went into his own pocket.[22]

Wentworth had little regard for the common law and Magna Carta. Lawyers and judges who stood in the way of the Crown were a nuisance, while parliament's main job was to vote taxes. If it failed in this duty, the king was entitled to raise the money in whatever way he saw fit. Wentworth's strategy for making Ireland a revenue producer for the Crown was to play one social group off against the other. Thus, he did not hesitate to lock horns with Protestant landowners, most notably the Earl of Cork, for their alleged swindling of crown and Church. Cork, the richest and most powerful man in Ireland next to the lord deputy, was hauled up in front of the prerogative court of Castle Chamber, fined heavily and obliged to disgorge much of the land he had gobbled up. By contrast, in parliament Wentworth appeared to smile benignly upon the Old English, leading them to believe (wrongly) they could expect statutory confirmation of the Graces once they had voted generous subsidies for the king. He also initially won favour in Irish eyes by his imperious attitude towards the City of London over its plantation in Londonderry.

In return for the king's grant of 40,000 acres in the province of Ulster the citizens of London had been expected to send settlers ('planters') who would spread both Protestantism and modern agricultural techniques, and generate tax revenue. In the event Londonderry was a disappointment. Few settlers arrived, and little revenue materialized; so in 1635 Charles took the estate back from the Londoners, and turned it into his personal fiefdom. Londoners were greatly aggrieved at the loss of their Irish property, and blamed Wentworth.[23]

Meanwhile, with the Irish parliamentary subsidies mostly paid into the exchequer, Wentworth announced that he did not think it advisable for the

---

[22] *CSPI 1633–47*, 273. Customs revenue rose from £22,553 in 1632–33 to £57,387 in 1637–38, but fell back to £51,874 in 1639–40.

[23] For an excellent account of the multiple kingdoms dimension of the struggle over Londonderry, see Jane H. Ohlmeyer, 'Strafford, the "Londonderry Business" and the "New British History"' in Merritt (ed.), *Political World of Thomas Wentworth*, 209–29.

king to confirm the Graces. This was the first public indication that he had no intention of making Ireland safe for Catholics. On the contrary, his close friendships with William Laud, and John Bramhall, Bishop of Derry, were a sign of his determination to Protestantize and Anglicize Ireland. A set of Laudian, Arminian canons was imposed on a hitherto Calvinist church, while Protestant landowners were bullied into surrendering the lands they had taken from the church, so that its endowment might be restored.[24]

In his private correspondence Wentworth made plain his hostility to Catholicism: ultimately he wanted to expel all priests from the country.[25] In the short term he resorted to legal manoeuvres to strip Roman Catholic boroughs of their charters. Between 1634 and 1640 he succeeded in reducing Catholic representation in the Irish parliament by a third. The effect of his campaign was to give the Protestants a clear majority of 89 seats[26] – this in a country whose population was over 90 per cent Catholic.

An even clearer sign of his hostility to Catholicism was his aggressive policy of confiscation and plantation in the provinces of Connacht and Leinster. Since the time of James I six Ulster counties had already been turned into a bastion of English and Scottish Protestantism. Through his Commission for Defective Titles Wentworth challenged Catholic property rights in Galway, Mayo, Tipperary and Kilkenny. No Catholic landowner any longer felt that his property was safe. With 'stern looks and insolent and impious and insupportable pride'[27] he bullied juries into returning verdicts favourable to the Crown. Those whose titles were found to be defective were allowed to have three-quarters of their land back as tenants-in-chief of the king. The remaining quarter was reserved for Protestant settlers. Even when the Catholics had recovered three-quarters of their estates, they would owe knight service and regular payments to the Crown. Attached to the tenure of knight service was the requirement that the grantees and their heirs take the Oath of Supremacy. Catholics were unable to take this oath; thus if it were rigidly applied, all the native proprietors whose estates had been scrutinized would be forced to become Protestants or surrender their land. Clearly what Wentworth referred to as 'the great work of Plantations' amounted to the confiscation of most of the

[24] See John McCafferty, ' "God bless your free Church of Ireland": Wentworth, Laud, Bramhall and the Irish Convocation of 1634', in Merritt (ed.), Political World of Thomas Wentworth, 187–208.

[25] Canny, 'Attempted anglicisation of Ireland', 181.

[26] Aidan Clarke, The Old English in Ireland, 1625–42, 126.

[27] BL. Egerton MS 917, quoted in Clarke, Old English, 93.

land in Ireland remaining in Catholic possession. A glimpse of his agenda was provided by his attack on the lands of the Earl of Clanricarde. In 1635 Wentworth personally conducted an inquisition into the earl's property in County Galway. A cowed jury found Clanricarde's title defective, and all his lands subject to confiscation by the Crown. Clanricarde died shortly thereafter, and it took his young heir until 1639 to persuade Charles I to reverse the finding of Wentworth's Galway jury.

What was lost by Wentworth's policy of confiscation and plantation was not merely a few hundred thousand acres of land, but the privileged status upon which every member of the Old English group had relied to protect his property. Yet new Protestant settlers were slow to arrive. Not a single one had taken up residence in Connacht by 1640.[28] Had Charles allowed Wentworth a completely free hand in Ireland he could well have run into armed opposition from Catholic landowners, perhaps with the support of Irish soldiers who had returned from service in continental Europe. There might have been an Irish rebellion in the mid-1630s rather than in 1641. However, in the earlier period Wentworth and the king would have been able to count on the united support of Protestants in England, Scotland and Ireland. A war whose ultimate objective was to Protestantize and Anglicize Ireland would have been winnable. It would also have contributed to the formation of a coherent British monarchy. Charles I, however, was not the man to contemplate a war on behalf of militant Protestantism. Like his predecessors, he was inclined to support those who professed loyalty to him. Catholics like the Earl of Clanricarde, who had good connections at the English court, lobbied successfully to get Wentworth's policies diluted. Thus, as Nicholas Canny has argued, 'the collapse of the British monarchy occurred not because of the policies that were pursued by Charles, but because he failed to endorse a scheme of government for Ireland that was considered just and reasonable by the vast majority of the more influential subjects in the three kingdoms'.[29]

Another object of Wentworth's hostility was the kingdom of Scotland, 'the veriest devil that is out of hell' as he saw it.[30] When in the autumn of 1638 the Scots Presbyterians of Ulster showed signs of linking up with their compatriots, even to the point of arming themselves, Wentworth retaliated by ordering arms from the Netherlands. Those who dared to

---

[28] Clarke, *Old English*, 107, 110.

[29] Canny, 'Attempted anglicisation of Ireland', 184–5. See also Canny's powerful elaboration of this argument in *Making Ireland British 1580–1650*, ch. 7.

[30] Quoted in Perceval-Maxwell, *Outbreak of the Irish Rebellion*, 55.

take the National Covenant were hailed before the Court of Castle Chamber in Dublin, and forced to swear an oath renouncing 'their abominable Covenant' as 'seditious and traitorous'.[31] Soldiers were stationed in Ulster in the spring of 1639 to enforce the oath throughout the province.

On 23 July 1639, having been humiliated by the Scots at Berwick, the king wrote to Wentworth asking him to come to England. The lord lieutenant responded with alacrity to this invitation to realize his ambitions on a larger stage. Over the next year he was Charles's chief adviser and strategist for the war against the Scots. At the same time he kept a close watch on Ireland, losing no opportunity to put down his enemies there. In November for example, in the privy council he violently attacked Adam Viscount Loftus, the Irish Lord Chancellor, for his assorted misdeeds.[32]

An essential ingredient in Wentworth's plan for subduing the Scots was the raising of an army of 8,000 foot and 1,000 horse in Ireland. To this end a parliament was summoned, and Wentworth, having at last been elevated to the coveted earldom of Strafford and promoted to lord lieutenant of Ireland, returned to Dublin in March 1640 to oversee its proceedings. The opening of the parliament could not have been more auspicious. The MPs expressed warm support for the government, and the king's resistance to the Scots, backing up their words with a vote of four subsidies totalling £180,000 to finance the army that was intended to fight the Scots that year. Basking in the seemingly unanimous approval of his regime, Strafford now felt confident enough to return to England. And indeed, from an Irish perspective, the few storm clouds that were on the horizon seemed trivially small. The panegyrics that had been uttered about Ireland as a kingdom of peace and plenty were supported by objective evidence. The population had grown almost uninterruptedly since the turn of the century, until it was now around 2 million, including about 100,000 Protestants. The flourishing state of the economy was attested by the impressive rise in customs revenue after Wentworth's arrival in 1633, and a £100,000 surplus in the treasury.[33] Even the violently pro-catholic author of the *Aphorismical Discovery* was constrained to admit that in 1641 Ireland, 'one of the best islands in Europe stood in fairer terms of happiness and prosperity than ever it had done these 500 years past . . .

---

[31] *NHI*, 3, 268. The latter phrase was used by the Scots commissioners in their indictment of Strafford in December 1640. Huntington Lib., Ellesmere Collection (Bridgewater MSS), EL 7060.

[32] Huntington Lib., Ellesmere Collection (Bridgewater MSS), EL 7811, John Castle to the Earl of Bridgewater, 12 November 1639.

[33] Perceval-Maxwell, *Outbreak of the Irish Rebellion*, 30–2.

she had enjoyed the sweet fruits of a long peace, full of people and riches . . .'.[34] It is true that there had been a sharp economic downturn since 1638, but this could be blamed on three years of bad weather and bad harvests, and on the Scottish crisis, which were beyond Strafford's control.[35]

Defying his sea captain's advice to wait for calmer seas, Strafford set off for England again at the beginning of April 1640. Laid low by dysentery before and during the voyage, he arrived in a weakened state, and was of little use to the king during the Short Parliament of that month. In the latter half of the 1630s he had suffered declining health on account of a variety of afflictions: gout, the stone, 'strangurie' (a urinary disease) and dysentery. These painful conditions may have contributed to his frequent outbursts of temper, and his refusal to suffer corruption or folly gladly. Bad health would continue to haunt him throughout the year leading up to his death.[36]

The sterility of the Short Parliament, abruptly dissolved after its refusal to vote money to fight the Scots, left the government desperate. Support from Ireland became more crucial than ever before. At a critical meeting of the privy council on 5 May 1640 Strafford raged like a wounded lion against those who thwarted the royal strategy. Sir Henry Vane senior, who nursed a venomous hatred towards him, recorded his fateful words on that day: 'You have an army in Ireland [that] you may employ here to reduce this kingdom [meaning Scotland] . . . Scotland shall not hold out five months. One summer well employed will do it. Venture all I had, I would carry it or lose it.'[37] In the hands of his accusers these words would be twisted to suggest, not that he wished to conquer Scotland, but that he had treasonously urged reducing the English parliament to the king's will. It did not matter that the army in question would not be ready for another two months, or that the parliament it was supposed to overawe would not even be convened for another six.

The signs of Strafford's growing physical and political debility in England supplied his enemies in Ireland the courage to attack him there. At the second session of the Irish parliament, which met in June 1640, all the elements aggrieved by his regime submerged their differences to present a united front against him. The Commons voted to restore the

[34] Printed in John T. Gilbert (ed.), *A Contemporary History of Affairs in Ireland from 1641–1652* (hereafter Gilbert, *Contemp. Hist.*), Vol. 1, 1.

[35] Perceval-Maxwell, *Outbreak of the Irish Rebellion*, 38, 41–2.

[36] Huntington Lib., Ellesmere Collection (Bridgewater MSS), EL 7835–7.

[37] HMC 3, *Fourth Report* (House of Lords MSS), 3.

disenfranchised Catholic boroughs, to cut back sharply the previously voted subsidies, and to halt the plantation of Connacht. News of this about-face, when it reached England, further undermined Strafford's position at court. Charles, in his frantic search for money to continue his war against Scotland, appointed Strafford's arch-enemy, the Earl of Cork, to the privy council. He hoped that this would win over the New English and encourage them to loosen their purses. The military success of the Scots at the end of the summer completed the undermining of what remained of Strafford's power base. Though too sick to be present at the débâcle, he had nevertheless been the commander-in-chief of the forces humiliated at Newburn.

At the third session of the Irish parliament in October, Strafford's enemies came out into the open. Working in concert with his enemies in England, the Irish Protestant–Catholic alliance drafted a crushing indictment of his government in the shape of a Remonstrance which was adopted on 7 November 1640. In order to preserve the coalition of unlikely political bedfellows, the 16 clauses made no mention either of religious toleration, or the lenient enforcement of the laws against Catholics. Instead, it focused on the high-handed and predatory activities of the courts of Castle Chamber and High Commission, and of the various commissioners for defective titles, plantations, and Londonderry, who, the MPs alleged, had brought the nation 'very near to ruin and destruction'.[38] John Bramhall, Bishop of Derry was the man who had implemented the religious policy that had united Protestants and Catholics against the lord lieutenant and his royal master. The political hurricane that promised to blow him and his reforms away was beyond his comprehension. 'I dare not to propose the causes of these distempers', he wrote, in bewilderment to Archbishop Laud.[39]

More remarkably, Strafford appeared momentarily to have united all three kingdoms against him. The Irish indictment had been foreshadowed in September by the petition of the disaffected peers in favour of the punishment of the counsellors who had proposed the Scottish war, and

[38] Though formally addressed to the Lord Lieutenant of Ireland, the Remonstrance was really intended for the eyes and ears of the recently convened English parliament. With an accompanying petition to the king, it was engrossed on heavy parchment with over 80 signatures. Identical original copies were sent, not to Charles I, but to the Commons and the Lords: BL. Egerton MS 1048, fos. 13–14.

[39] Huntington Lib., Hastings Collection, MS HA 14061 (Bramhall to Laud, 4 November 1640).

the bringing in of an Irish army.[40] A month after the Irish Remonstrance the Scots commissioners chimed in with their own indictment of the lord lieutenant's ruthless treatment of the Scottish covenanters in Ulster. Even though he had been brought low by the God-given success of the covenanting army, 'yet this firebrand still smoketh . . . and taketh upon himself to breathe out threatenings against us as traitors and enemies to monarchical government'. There could be only one answer: the unrepentant 'incendiary' must be 'put to a trial and . . . have his deserved punishment'.[41] The stage was set for Strafford's impeachment for treason.

The chief intermediary between the English, Scots and Irish malcontents was Sir John Clotworthy. A New English planter, who sat in both the Irish and English parliaments, he, like the Earl of Cork, harboured a consuming malice towards Strafford, not only because he had been stripped of his interest in the Londonderry plantation, but also because he was a zealous Presbyterian. Clotworthy seconded John Pym's motion for a committee of the whole house to consider Irish affairs, orchestrated the legal case against Strafford, and testified against him on several occasions. Laud aptly termed him 'a firebrand brought from Ireland to inflame this kingdom'.[42]

As a substantial landowner in County Antrim, in the province of Ulster, Clotworthy enjoyed close connections with several important Ulster political families. Through his mother he was related to Lord Chancellor Loftus. By marriage he was related to John Pym, and in the Long Parliament became a client of the Earl of Warwick, as well as developing a close relationship with the Earl of Holland, another of Strafford's great enemies at Court. In his Commons speech of 7 November Clotworthy dwelt at length on the arbitrary nature of Strafford's government, and his raising of a Catholic army to put down the Scots. A member of the committee of five that recommended that Strafford be tried for treason, he, along with the lord lieutenant's other Irish enemies – the Earl of Cork, Viscount Ranelagh (Lord President of Connacht), Lord Mountnorris and Sir Piers Crosby – furnished the bulk of the information at Strafford's trial.[43]

For all the energy and determination of those who prosecuted Strafford's impeachment, it faced a nearly insuperable obstacle. How

---

[40] HMC 3, *Fourth Report* (House of Lords MSS), 2.

[41] Huntington Lib., Ellesmere Collection (Bridgewater MSS), EL 7060 (16 December 1640).

[42] Ohlmeyer, 'Strafford, the "Londonderry business"', 226.

[43] *NHI*, Vol. 3, 279; Ohlmeyer, 'Strafford, the "Londonderry business"', 216–17.

could they prove that he had 'endeavoured to subvert the fundamental laws and government of the realms of England'[44] when he had spent most of the preceding eight years in Ireland? It was questionable whether the English parliament could convict him of treason as Lord Deputy of Ireland, when it was the king alone, with his privy council, who had jurisdiction over that kingdom. Whatever his offences during his brief period as general in the Second Bishops' War, he could easily demonstrate that he had only been carrying out the king's commands. When it became apparent that the House of Lords would not find Strafford guilty as charged, the Commons leaders dropped the impeachment in favour of a simpler expedient: a bill of attainder. By means of an attainder the accused could be found guilty by simple resolution of both houses. The bill passed easily through the Commons, and the pressure of angry crowds milling outside the Lords' chamber soon brought the peers to heel. The only catch was that it still required the king's signature, and Charles had earlier pledged to protect Strafford's life. However, when Strafford himself wrote absolving the king from his pledge and urging him to sign the bill for the sake of the kingdom's peace and his own family's safety, Charles gave his consent. It was a betrayal for which he would never forgive himself.

While Strafford was embroiled in his own legal defence, his enemies in Ireland continued their attacks on his policies. The Queries passed in February 1641 demanded for Ireland the same political and civil rights as England. As Conrad Russell has commented, they 'represent the fullest flowering of . . . Anglo-Irish constitutionalism, and again show how deeply Irish thinking had been influenced by the Parliament of 1628'.[45] The Catholic MPs who voted for the Queries were slow to appreciate that in claiming the benefit of the laws of England, they might inadvertently make themselves subject to the authors of those laws – the parliament of England. At the same time, the Old English delegates in London, led by Clanricarde, returned to the longstanding issue of the Graces, and lobbied the king to confirm the 24th Grace that guaranteed security of title for lands occupied for over 60 years. Acting too late, as he would so often in his ill-starred career, Charles yielded this highly prized concession. Why did he now at last grant what for 13 years he had withheld? Certainly not to save Strafford's life. His hope was that this concession would help him

---

[44] John Nalson, *An Impartial Collection of the Great Affairs of State, From the Beginning of the Scotch Rebellion in the Year Mdcxxxix to the Murther of King Charles I*, Vol. 2, 8.

[45] Russell, *Fall of the British Monarchies*, 386.

to keep his Irish army on foot.[46] But in the event, no money was forthcoming in either country to pay this army, so the grand gesture gained him nothing.

Confirmation of the Graces meant that the nearly century-old policy of plantation would be stopped in its tracks. This deeply offended the lords justices and the whole Irish Protestant establishment, who fought a rearguard action against Charles's decision all that summer. To Secretary Vane they wrote,

. . . the plantations . . . have been the very original and preservation of the peace and happiness which of late years this kingdom has enjoyed . . . By them several English towns, castles, houses of strength, and churches have been built in many remote and desolate parts of the kingdom . . . religion, civility, schools, manufacture, and trades in a good measure for the time introduced . . . and the lands by habitation generally raised to values far above former times . . . There was no way to reduce this kingdom to the English laws and obedience of the Crown, and to free England of the perpetual charge thereof, but only a full conquest or a politic reformation by plantations. . . . Plantations have certainly kept the peace and encouraged the Protestant religion.[47]

It was a classic apology for colonialism, cogently put.

The Irish council then lobbied their friends in the English House of Lords to support them. In the end this two-pronged attack on the king worked, and he was prevailed upon to do what he already wished to do: renege a second time on the confirmation of the Graces. Here we have one of the few examples of skilful political footwork by the second Stuart king. While bitterly disappointing the Old English he made it seem the fault of Protestant interests on both sides of the Irish Sea. This enabled the Old English to preserve their cherished illusion that Charles was basically sympathetic to their aspirations.[48]

The rising in Ulster and its spread to the other provinces

To contemporaries, as well as some modern historians, the rebellion of October 1641 came like a thunderbolt out of a cloudless blue sky, 'a

---

[46] Ibid., 389.

[47] *CSPI 1633–47*, 277–8.

[48] Russell, *Fall of the British Monarchies*, 390.

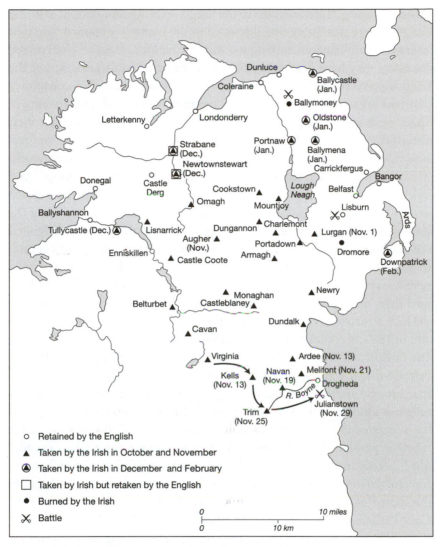

MAP 3 *The Ulster Rising, October 1641–February 1642*

Adapted from Perceval – Maxwell, M., *The Outbreak of the Irish Rebellion of 1641* (McGill-Queen's University Press, 1994)

startling interruption of a mood of peaceful cooperation'.[49] Just before it broke out, Sir John Temple remembered, 'all men sat pleasantly enjoying the comfortable fruits of their own labour'.[50] Indeed, a mere three weeks

[49] Aidan Clarke, 'Ireland and the general crisis', *P & P*, 48 (1970), 86.

[50] Sir John Temple, *The Irish Rebellion: Or, an History of the Beginnings and First Progresse of the Generall Rebellion Raised within the Kingdom of Ireland, upon the Three and Twentieth Day of October, in the Year, 1641. Together with the Barbarous Cruelties and Bloody Massacres which Ensued Thereupon*, 16.

before the rising, Temple wrote to the king's secretary in London, assuring him that there was little being discussed in the Irish privy council, and that 'there is in this kingdom nothing worthy of your knowledge'.[51] Unexpected the rising may have been to Temple and the other lords justices, but the English privy council had been kept regularly informed of a conspiracy that had been brewing as early as September 1639. Irish malcontents in Spain were said to be plotting a return to their homeland to claim their ancestral estates and liberate the Catholic Church from foreign oppression.[52] The government's informant expressed the fear that if Wentworth were absent for long from Ireland there would be 'evil consequences'. And indeed, hearing of Wentworth's second departure for England in the spring of 1640, the Irish exiles stepped up their preparations. Before tracing the lead-up to the rebellion, it is worth recalling that the fuel which ignited the conflagration had existed for generations. First was England's refusal to allow the Gaelic Old Irish the liberty to practise the Roman Catholic religion; second was the steady eating away of what remained of the Irish birthright through the policy of Protestant colonization. All attempts by the Irish to arrest the confiscation of their lands had failed. Twice, in 1628 and in 1641, the king had promised in the Graces security of tenure to the Old English and the Old Irish. Twice he had reneged on that promise. Ranger believes that it was the oppressive, corrupt regime of Thomas Wentworth that brought on the Catholic uprising. Kearney argues that Wentworth's religious absolutism was its chief cause.[53] More perceptively, Wedgwood has suggested that it was not his policies, but his overthrow, that made the rebellion possible. Had he continued in power a rebellion probably would not have occurred, but even if it had, given his administrative ability and forceful personality, Wentworth could almost certainly have crushed it. In the short run, however, it was not his overthrow, but other actions of the Long Parliament that furnished the tinder to ignite the Irish rising.

At the same time that they were engaged in bringing down Strafford, the pro-Scottish faction in the Westminster parliament were pursuing the disbandment of Strafford's, now the Earl of Ormond's 'Catholic army' in Ireland. A joint address from both houses put this demand on the table

[51] BL. Add. MS 78268 (Evelyn Papers), unfol. (Temple to Edward Nicholas, 2 October 1641).

[52] See the letters from Sir Arthur Hopton in Madrid to Secretary Windebanke in *CSP*, Vol. 2, 69, 70, 80.

[53] Hugh F. Kearney, *Strafford in Ireland 1633–41: A Study in Absolutism*, 220; Ranger, 'Strafford in Ireland', 30.

on 15 March 1641.[54] On 28 April the king answered the houses in his
Banqueting Hall, with an assurance that no one desired to dismantle the
Irish army more than he.[55] He then ordered Ormond to commence the process, and on 21 May the earl informed Secretary Vane, 'I have disbanded
the new Army.'[56] A thousand of these soldiers were prepared for immediate despatch to Spain, with the eventual intention of shipping 7,000,
practically the whole force, to that country. Conscious of the geopolitical
implications of aiding Europe's leading militant Catholic power, the
English House of Commons blocked this scheme in August. This move had
an ironic consequence: the unemployed troops who had been denied leave
to emigrate were available to the organizers of the rebellion two months
later.[57] Meanwhile in London the pro-Scottish faction had stepped up
its attack on popery. A week before Strafford's death, because 'they find
popery to grow' they prevailed upon all members of both houses to adopt
a Protestation swearing among other things to 'maintain and defend . . .
the true reformed Protestant religion . . . against all popery and popish
innovation within this realm'.[58] Parliament then sent the oath out for

[54] Nalson, *Impartial Collection*, Vol. 1, 789.

[55] Ibid., 808.

[56] *CSPI 1633–47*, 289–90.

[57] Whether the king engaged the Earl of Antrim to mobilize these troops into an army
for use against the Scots or the Long Parliament is still a matter of debate. Jane
Ohlmeyer has argued for the reality of Antrim's 'plot', while Conrad Russell and
Michael Perceval-Maxwell have rejected it. See Jane H. Ohlmeyer (ed.) *Ireland from
Independence to Occupation, 1641–1660*, 306; Jane H. Ohlmeyer 'The "Antrim Plot"
of 1641 – a myth?', *Historical Journal* (hereafter *HJ*), 35 (1992), 905–19; see also her
'The "Antrim Plot" of 1641 – a rejoinder', *HJ*, 37 (1994), 431–7; Conrad Russell, 'The
British background to the Irish rebellion of 1641', *HR*, 61 (1988), 177–9; Russell, *Fall
of the British Monarchies*, 393–5; Perceval-Maxwell, *Outbreak of the Irish Rebellion*,
194–211; and his 'The "Antrim Plot" of 1641 – a myth? A response', *HJ*, 37 (1994),
421–30. William Pius Kelly supports Jane Ohlmeyer's argument: 'The early career of
James Butler, twelfth earl and first Duke of Ormond (1610–1688), 1610–1643' (PhD
thesis, Cambridge University), 188–90. My own view is that the Long Parliament, by its
veto of the export of Irish troops to the continent, made it possible for some of these
troops to be used by the leaders of the rising of 1641. This was quite separate from a
supposed scheme of Antrim to place a 'catholic army' at the disposal of the king. To me
Antrim's alleged testimony in 1650, when he was trying to curry favour with the English
republic, and had everything to gain by blackening the reputation of the deceased
Charles I, is highly suspect.

[58] S.R. Gardiner, *The Constitutional Documents of the Puritan Revolution*, 3rd edn
(hereafter Gardiner, *Const. Docs.*), 84.

national subscription. The Protestation was generally understood as an anti-Catholic covenant, and most of those who refused to swear it were regarded as recusant Catholics. Throughout the early weeks of May rumours of Catholic plots swirled about the capital. The queen's supposedly malevolent role was more openly criticized. Mobs attacked the Spanish and Portuguese embassies where armed Catholics were thought to be hiding out. A general search and arrest of priests and Jesuits was ordered.[59] In Ulster Protestant petitions for the reform of the Church, both 'root and branch', were circulating. Other ominous developments were Pym's objection in principle to Irish religious toleration, and the news that Strafford's successor as lord lieutenant was to be the strongly Protestant Earl of Leicester.

Some time in February 1641 Rory O'More, a Gaelic gentleman who had lost his hereditary lands, invited another Old Irish landowner, the young, debt-laden Conor, Lord Maguire, to his house in Dublin. At their meeting O'More proposed that the time was ripe for a rising to regain what they had lost to the British. Claiming that many in Leinster and Connacht would support a rising if they could count on the Catholic gentry of Ulster, he reminded Maguire of how precarious his finances were, and how great the estate of his ancestors had been prior to the British plantations. He also underlined how the English parliament 'intends the utter subversion of our religion.' With these arguments he obtained Maguire's backing.[60] Other Ulster leaders were contacted, notably Sir Phelim O'Neill, regarded in the province as 'chief of his name'. Since May 1640 he had been in direct contact with his cousin Owen Roe O'Neill, who was then in the king of Spain's service in Flanders. The most talented military leader among the Old Irish, Owen Roe had promised to come back to Ireland should a rising take place there. Noting that the English and Scots were preoccupied with their own troubles, and that the well-equipped army raised by Strafford was available, they were, O'More argued, presented with an unparalleled opportunity. Over the next several months expatriate Gaelic Irish flooded back to the country from Spain, France and the low countries. In June, according to the lords justices, Dublin was swarming with hundreds of Jesuits, friars and priests. They were seen talking to disbanded soldiers, urging them not to take up service in the Spanish army,

---

[59] Caroline Hibbard, *Charles I and the Popish Plot*, 194–5.

[60] For Maguire's account of this meeting see Nalson, *Impartial Collection*, Vol. 2, 543–4; see also Patrick J. Corish, 'The rising of 1641 and the Catholic confederacy, 1641–5', in *NHI*, Vol. 3, 290ff.

since 'there might be use for them soon'.[61] Later in the summer the Irish parliament swung behind the Westminster parliament in opposing the sending of Irish soldiers abroad, officially because they might be used on the Catholic side in the war for the Palatinate. Catholics in the Irish parliament, such as Sir Phelim O'Neill, may have supported the resolution because they saw the advantage of keeping the men at home for their projected rebellion.[62] By the end of the summer the signs were accumulating that Ireland had begun the descent into anarchy.[63]

Charles I also shared responsibility for the rising. His failure to promulgate the Graces at the beginning of August prompted the conspirators to move into top gear with their planning. Their only hesitancy arose from the reluctance of the Old English of the Pale to commit themselves to the scheme.

In the absence of Old English support it became evident that the uprising would have to be based in Ulster. On 11 October it was reported that disaffected men, some 'broken . . . in their estates and fortunes' had been seen congregating at Sir Phelim O'Neill's house in Tyrone on the pretext of raising men for the king of Spain.[64] The date they fixed for the rising in Ulster was 23 October. Dublin Castle would be seized on the same day by a contingent of the troops pretended for Spain. Control of the castle would both paralyse the administration and secure a great quantity of arms for the rebels. Up to this point the objectives of the rising were still limited: the occupation of some key military posts in order to establish a negotiating position. However, the attempt on Dublin Castle was a fiasco. A few days before the strike one of the conspirators, while in his cups, blurted out the details to a servant of Sir John Clotworthy. Forewarned, the government then ordered all strangers to leave the city and arrested two leading conspirators, Hugh MacMahon and Lord Maguire.[65]

Thanks to the successful defence of Dublin, there was little alarm in official circles when the news of the rising first broke. Sir Henry Vane senior, who more than half a year earlier had anxiously flagged the anticipated rebellion, now wrote complacently to the Earl of Ormond that 'this storm will blow over'. Sir William St Leger, president of Munster, dismissed the rebels as 'a company of ragged naked rogues that with a few

---

[61] The lords justices to Sir Henry Vane, 30 June 1641: *CSPI 1633–47*, 307–8.

[62] Russell, *Fall of the British Monarchies*, 394–5.

[63] See William Wandesforde's letter of 20 August 1641 about the sharp rise in forcible entries in Bodl. MS Carte 80, fo. 652.

[64] Thomas Carte, *The Life of James Duke of Ormond* (hereafter Carte, *Life*), Vol. 3, 35.

[65] Bodl. MS Carte 2, fo. 9.

troops of horse would be presently routed'.[66] A few days later he changed his tune, as news reached the capital that the Ulster rebellion was spreading like wildfire. Within a week the insurgents had turned south, captured Dundalk and Ardee, and advanced to besiege Drogheda a few miles north of Dublin. Sir Phelim O'Neill chose this moment to explode a political bombshell that would do incalculable damage to Charles's cause in England. He published a proclamation, purportedly from the king himself, dated 1 October, and bearing the Great Seal of Scotland, authorizing the Gaelic Irish to take up arms in his defence 'and also to arrest and seize the goods and estates and persons of all English Protestants within the kingdom [of Ireland]'.[67] The implausibility of a Protestant king authorizing a group of Catholic conspirators to arrest his Protestant subjects was plain to many people at the time, and there is no modern historian who doubts that the commission was a forgery.[68] Although Charles did not officially denounce the rebellion until the end of December,[69] he did issue three commissions in mid-November to Protestant commanders to raise 3,000 foot and 700 horse 'for service in Ireland'.[70] Nevertheless, O'Neill's forged commission helped to win many wavering Irishmen to the rebels' side, while it threw Irish Protestant royalists into disarray. Towards the end of November some officers wrote to their commander Ormond asking what they should do if the commission turned out to be genuine. Would it then be lawful, they asked, to use their arms against the king's authority?[71] For many in England O'Neill's 'commission' was the final proof that the king was the chief agent in the popish plot against the English people and their religion. For the next seven years Charles would be dogged by the suspicion that he had in fact stamped the Irish revolt with his approval, and therefore bore personal responsibility for the unspeakable atrocities perpetrated in that kingdom against the English Protestant population.

No longer confined to Ulster, the insurgency had spread by the second week of November to Connacht, where County Leitrim quickly fell to the rebels, and counties Sligo and Roscommon became fiercely contested

[66] Carte, *Life*, Vol. 3, 30, 37, 38.

[67] Bodl, MS Carte 68, fo. 349v.

[68] One of the rebel military leaders boasted to the English Protestant Edward Leech that 'all the kings in Christendom (except the king of England and king of Denmark)' had given the rebels support (Bodl. MS Carte 68, fo. 384v). This statement implicitly contradicted the claim of Sir Phelim O'Neill that Charles I backed the Irish uprising.

[69] *CSP*, Vol. 1, 222 (Charles I to the House of Lords).

[70] Bodl. MS Carte 2, fos. 51, 53, 55.

[71] Bodl. MS Carte 2, fo. 108.

territory. Counties Mayo and Galway, the latter under the dominance of the still loyal Earl of Clanricarde, remained quiet for the moment.[72] Immediately south of Dublin the rebels were besieging Wicklow Castle, and making forays into Carlow and Kilkenny, and almost up to the gates of Dublin itself. County Wexford too was engulfed by rebellion, and Arklow, Fort Chichester and Limerick quickly fell, and then Counties Louth and Meath, adjacent to the capital. By 21 November the rebels were laying siege to Drogheda with 2,300 troops.[73] At first the government had been too stunned by the sudden and sweeping nature of the uprising to do any more than defend its own narrow enclave. Six weeks elapsed before it was able to offer a serious check to the rebel advance. By then the insurgents had celebrated their first dramatic military success: the defeat at Julianstown of a government force sent from Dublin to relieve Drogheda. More decisive than the large haul of captured arms, was the psychological impact upon the Old English gentry of the Pale of this victory. Already their allegiance to the Dublin government had become unglued by its failure to supply them with arms from the great store in Dublin Castle to defend themselves against marauding rebels. Disillusion had been deepened by the savagery of Protestant hardliners such as Sir Charles Coote.

Even more critical for the Old English were the activities of the English parliament: its steady encroachment upon the king's prerogatives, and its threat to the independence of the Irish parliament. A weak king would offer little protection against an aggressively intolerant Puritan parliament. In November the tenuous loyalty of the Old English hung on the result of a mission by one of their number, the Protestant Lord Dillon of Costello, to the king. On their behalf he journeyed to London with a promise to put down the revolt in return for a guarantee of toleration for Catholicism. Unfortunately John Pym got a copy of Dillon's paper, ordered him arrested, and with Scots help rammed through a motion in the Westminster parliament declaring that popery would not be tolerated in Ireland. This performance convinced the Old English that the rising power of the 'Puritan' parliament was in itself a fundamental obstacle to peace in Ireland.[74] In a petition to Charles on 19 December they called upon him to summon a parliament in Dublin, adding that for the time being they had no alternative but to take up arms on their own behalf and join with the

---

[72] Ulick, Marquis of Clanricarde, *The Memoirs and Letters of Ulick, Marquis of Clanricarde and Earl of Saint Albans*, 11.
[73] Bodl. MS Carte 2, fos. 45, 72, 84; 68, fo. 373v.
[74] Russell, *Fall of the British Monarchies*, 396–8; Clanricarde, *Memoirs*, 67.

Gaelic forces of Ulster. Their justification was the refusal of the Dublin government to issue them with arms for their own defence. This, combined with Sir Charles Coote's campaign of terror against Roman Catholics, had convinced them that they must look out for themselves.[75] Charles's condemnation of the rebellion, made first in a statement to the House of Lords, and then published as a proclamation on 1 January 1642 caused considerable discomfiture among the Old English when it reached them at the end of February. His offer to raise 10,000 English volunteers to suppress the rebellion, on the face of it proved the falsity of Sir Phelim O'Neill's pretended commission. The Old English had always thought of themselves not as rebels, but conservatives. Their fixed aim was to preserve the king's prerogative as a firewall between themselves and the vengeful, expansionary Protestantism of the Westminster parliament. Circumstances had now transformed them into reluctant revolutionaries.[76]

The atrocity stories and their impact

Before long the accusations of each side about the terrible inhumanity of the other were matched in emotional intensity. Beliefs about what was happening were of more consequence than the events themselves. It is nevertheless worth trying to clear away as much of the thicket of propaganda as we can, and seek an approximation of historical truth with reference to these events.

For the first several weeks after the rebellion's outbreak the private correspondence of those who were in Ireland contained few references to anything beyond 'spoils', 'robberies' and the slaughter of livestock, chiefly cattle and sheep. What transformed the insurgency into a full-blown peasant uprising of uncontrolled, incandescent anger were the insurgents' military setbacks following their failure to capture Dublin Castle. Protestant vengeance was rapid, merciless and devastating, as befitted the fortress mentality of a colonialist, occupying people. The first Protestant victory was at Lisnegarvy on 28 November, when 700 Irish were put to the sword. Then, the implacable Sir Charles Coote marched out a day or two later with 500 foot and 80 horse to relieve Wicklow Castle, under siege by the rebels. After raising the siege he executed a number of men and women

---

[75] See the 'Humble apology of the lords, knights, gentlemen and other inhabitants of the English Pale of Ireland for taking arms' (19 December 1641), in Carte, *Life*, Vol. 3, 47–9.

[76] *CSP*, Vol. 1, 222 (no. 1545); Carte, *Life*, Vol. 3, 53; Clarke, *Old English*, 232–4; Canny, *Making Ireland British*, 523.

'with indiscriminate and sadistic violence'.[77] Later he took another expedition to Clontarf near Dublin, and burned the village to the ground.[78] It was widely believed by the Old English Lords of the Pale that he had advised the lords justices 'to execute a general massacre upon all of our religion' and offered to perform it himself.[79] At the beginning of December Sir William St Leger, President of Munster, wreaked vengeance on the rebels at Mohill who had robbed an English farmer of several hundred sheep and cattle. Riding all night through craggy, snow-covered terrain, he pursued them beyond Waterford, slew 140 and took another 50 prisoner. His intent was to execute all his prisoners by martial law. 'How this may stand with Magna Carta I know not', he confessed to the lords justices, but expressed confidence that they would approve. More expansively he boasted that his ruthless action had for the moment cleared the rebels from the province of Munster, but recognized that those who had got away before he could kill them 'may endeavour some revenge for the loss of their fellows, and that other incursions or insurrections may happen'. Unconsciously he was admitting that the vicious circle of violence, once initiated, would not cease.[80]

According to one interpretation it was these acts of unrestrained killing, sanctioned by the Protestant rulers of Ireland, that ignited the pent-up anger of the agricultural lower classes against their British overlords. And indeed it is true that most Catholic atrocities occurred after the savage killings by Protestants in late November and early December. Most, but not all. The first massacre conducted by Catholic Irish occurred at Portadown in mid-November. A large number of English Protestant settlers had already been imprisoned in Loughgall church for nine days, during which time 'many of them' according to a Protestant eye witness, 'were sore tortured by strangling and half hanging'. Then as many as 100 were 'driven like hogs about six miles to a river called the Bann' where they were forced onto the bridge and driven to jump into the river at sword-point.[81] Those who tried to swim ashore were shot. The next most horrific

---

[77] Clarke, *Old English*, 177–8.

[78] *NHI*, Vol. 3, 294.

[79] Carte, *Life*, Vol. 3, 52.

[80] Bodl. MS Carte 2, fo. 144v. So great was St Leger's reputation for cruelty that he was seriously accused by the Lord of Upper Ossory of having ordered a pregnant woman executed by disembowelling, and her unborn babies impaled on spears. Carte, *Life*, Vol. 3, 51.

[81] Hilary Simms, 'Armagh', in Brian Mac Cuarta (ed.), *Ulster 1641: Aspects of the Rising*, 124.

episode after Portadown was the massacre at Shewie in the parish of Kilmore, County Armagh, in early December, or perhaps February 1642. About twenty people were herded into a house which was then locked and set on fire, burning them all alive. The instigator of the atrocity was a former Protestant, Jane Hampson. She and others may have been helped by Sir Phelim O'Neill's men who were returning after their repeated defeats at Lisnegarvey (Lisburn) in November.[82] In December or January at least 32 of the Protestant tenants on Sir Phelim O'Neill's estate at Kinnard near Tynan were murdered by Catholics. Among the victims were Sir Phelim's nurse and her child. The murders were evidently committed without O'Neill's knowledge, for he hanged eight of the nine perpetrators.[83] A second mass drowning of between 12 and 45 people took place under the direction of the wife of Brian Kelly, a rebel captain, in or near Loughgall. Another 16 people were also drowned in a nearby bog. It was County Armagh where some of the worst atrocities occurred. Hilary Simms, who has made a thorough study of them, concludes that between 600 and 1,300 died there between November 1641 and May 1642. Much barbarity was also alleged in County Monaghan.[84] Even assuming that the highest estimate for Armagh prevailed in the other eight Ulster counties, the total for the province cannot have exceeded 12,000, and was probably much lower.[85] By contrast, one of the witnesses at the time estimated that Ulster's population was reduced by 154,000, a figure frequently quoted, despite the fact that the entire Protestant population of Ulster was less than half that total.[86]

---

[82] Sir Phelim O'Neill attacked Lisburn, where 1,000 British soldiers had been stationed, on 8, 22 and 28 November. He was thrown back each time, suffering severe losses in the last attempt. Portadown was only a few miles from Lisburn, but if, as Hilary Simms states, the drownings there occurred about the middle of November, they can hardly have been the consequence of O'Neill's humiliation at Lisburn: Perceval-Maxwell, *Outbreak of the Irish Rebellion*, 214–15; Simms, 'Armagh', 127–8.

[83] Mac Cuarta (ed.), *Ulster 1641*, 130–1.

[84] Huntington Lib., Hastings Collection (Irish Papers), HA 15009.

[85] Interestingly, it is also Patrick Corish's view that we shall probably never better Lecky's surmise in the nineteenth century, that in all perhaps 4,000 Protestants were murdered in the rising and that a further 8,000 refugees died from their privations: Corish, 'The rising of 1641', in *NHI*, Vol. 3, 291–2.

[86] Temple, *Irish Rebellion*, 126; Mac Cuarta (ed.), *Ulster 1641*, 134. The archdeacon of Down, who gave the estimate cited by Temple, presumably included those who had fled the province in his total.

After picking his way through more than 3,000 sworn depositions about the acts of cruelty perpetrated in Ulster against the English settler population, Nicholas Canny has concluded that one factor which made the settlers more vulnerable to the wrath of their Catholic tenants was the lack of unity between Scots and English. For the most part Scottish settlers in Ulster tried to save their own skins by abandoning the English to their fate.[87] Ethnicity, as distinct from economic or religious grievances, seems to have been a significant factor. There is plenty of evidence that anything identified as English – people, Bibles, churches, buildings or cattle – was specially targeted, while the Scots, initially at least, attracted much less hostility.[88] Canny has analysed the escalation in the attack on English settlers into three categories: first the seizure or destruction of property, whether land, money, records of indebtedness, goods or livestock; secondly, stripping settlers of their clothing and casting them out of doors into a bitterly cold winter; thirdly, killing them, sometimes with sadistic cruelty, and then sometimes subjecting their corpses to ritual humiliation. Another aspect of the revolt, which marks it as a peasant uprising rather than merely an attempted seizure of power on the part of an elite, is the active involvement of women and children in the most violent acts.[89]

Outside Ulster, it was not until 25 November that we have the first report of English settlers being 'stripped naked and banished . . .' from counties Wicklow and Wexford in Leinster 'by the fury of the rebels, whose great multitudes do so terrify'.[90] Writing to the new, absent lord lieutenant, the Earl of Leicester, on 14 December, the lords justices of Ireland noted that the rebels' policy, after destroying all English cattle and laying waste the habitations of the Protestant settlers, was to deny them any relief. Their explicit aim was to eradicate the English presence in Ireland. The intention to uproot a people is not far different from genocide, even if it did not necessarily involve putting them all to the sword. It was at Longford Castle in mid-December that the first real massacre outside Ulster was reported. After the Protestant defenders of the castle had surrendered on promise of quarter, a Catholic priest 'with sheen [dagger] in hand' led the besiegers in killing them all 'most perfidiously'. It was further

---

[87] Canny, *Making Ireland British*, 480–1.
[88] Kathleen M. Noonan, ' "The cruel pressure of an enraged, barbarous people": Irish and English identity in seventeenth-century policy and propaganda', *HJ*, 41 (1998), 163–4; Canny, *Making Ireland British*, 522–3. I do not think the evidence supports Noonan's contention that ethnicity was at least as important a factor as religion.
[89] Canny, *Making Ireland British*, 542–4.
[90] Bodl. MS Carte 68, fo. 373.

reported that the rebels in the Pale had forced people to convert to Roman Catholicism, 'openly professing that no Protestant shall be suffered to live in Ireland'.[91] Yet, according to Nicholas Canny, priests as a rule did their best to curb the violence of the peasants, and may perhaps be credited with the low incidence of reported rape during the uprising.[92] In March 1642 there was a slaughter of English near the bridge at Jellyancton, County Meath.[93] Many English had already taken the hint, and fled by sea at the first word of these atrocities. In Connacht there was much seizure and destruction of property and livestock, particularly in County Leitrim where Sir Charles Coote's estate was located, but almost no deliberate killings. This was due partly to the moderating influence of the Earl of Clanricarde, and partly to the small planter population in that province. In Munster Lord Mountgarret 'and his rabblement of young devils' 10,000 strong, were reported to have carried out much property destruction and wanton killing in early March 1642 at the Earl of Cork's plantation at Tallowe. After pillaging and firing, and slaughtering 50,000 sheep, they then 'killed man, woman and child'.[94]

By the standards of the modern world the extent of killing in 1641–42 was modest. The death toll a decade later was to be much higher. The benefit of a larger historical perspective should not, however, inoculate us against the emotional experience of the people who lived through the events. It is a worthwhile exercise to re-imagine the sheer physical terror induced by the first reports of slaughter. The drowning of English Protestants at the bridge at Portadown – even if only a few dozen – would have given nightmares to all Protestant inhabitants of Ireland, acutely aware of how vastly outnumbered they were by their Catholic neighbours.

Soon reports of the Portadown drownings and other shocking episodes reached England, sending a thrill of horror through all who heard about them. When, a few weeks later, refugees began docking at the west coast ports, and finding their way to London, where they threw themselves on the mercy and charity of parish churches, the citizens of the capital knew that a major upheaval was underway. The presence of refugees with their stories of cruelty and privation electrified the London population, quite

---

[91] Bodl. MS Carte 68, fos. 382v, 384v5.

[92] Canny, *Making Ireland British*, 502.

[93] House of Lords Record Office (hereafter HLRO), Main Papers, 17 March 1642, fo. 44/1.

[94] NLI, MS 2541 (Cadogan Papers), 23.

apart from the inflammatory impact of the pamphlets with their grossly exaggerated accounts and gruesome drawings of alleged atrocities.[95]

The Gaelic Irish and Old English populations were of course already afflicted by their own nightmares, in which they were stalked by Sir Charles Coote, Sir William St Leger, Murrough O'Brien Lord Inchiquin, and others of that ilk. The nightmares had only just begun, however. Soon expeditions arrived from England and Scotland to assist the beleaguered New English. The government in Dublin recovered its nerve, and the scale of Protestant terror escalated. Before the end of 1641 Sir Simon Harcourt arrived at the head of Lord Lisle's English expedition, consisting of 1,500 troops, followed shortly by another 1,900. These soldiers slaughtered 'man, woman, child' and hanged the inhabitants without mercy. It was the habitual practice of an otherwise civilized man like Edmund Verney to grant no quarter to Irish rebels.[96] This became official policy when in February 1642 the lords justices authorized the Earl of Ormond, Charles's commander in Ireland, to 'kill and destroy all the men [near Dublin] able to bear arms'.[97] The ruthlessness of the Scots was even more drastic. Many of them were veterans of the continental wars, and were militarily far superior to their untrained opponents. The west was terrorized by their Laggan corps, and in the east they defeated the Irish at Lisburn. On 15 April 1642 General Robert Monro arrived at Carrickfergus with an advance party of 2,500 men from Scotland. These were the first fruits of the recent alliance between the Westminster and Edinburgh parliaments (see Chapter 3). At once he went on the offensive, capturing Newry and putting all within to the sword on 1 May.[98] Between July and September the English forces waged a systematic campaign of terror in the south-west and then in Galway. The predictable consequence was that bitterness of catholics increased and their political unity solidified.[99]

In sum, while it was the Gaelic Irish who committed the first notorious massacre (Portadown), the New English and Scots settlers, and their compatriots from England and Scotland soon equalled, if not exceeded, the Irish in vindictive ruthlessness and in the sheer efficiency of their killing.

[95] Keith Lindley, 'Irish adventurers and godly militants in the 1640s', *Irish Historical Studies* (hereafter *IHS*), 29 (1994), 3.

[96] Gardiner, *Hist.*, Vol. 10, 75.

[97] Carte, *Life*, Vol. 3, 61.

[98] Gardiner, *Hist.*, Vol. 10, 174; Corish, 'The rising of 1641', in *NHI*, Vol. 3, 293; Mac Cuarta (ed.), *Ulster 1641*, 130.

[99] *NHI*, Vol. 3, 303.

Ireland had begun its descent into the maelstrom of untrammelled violence from which it would not emerge for a decade and more.

It is now time to return to England and the year 1640, in order to understand how the parliament that had been summoned to deal with the Scottish war was plunged into crisis and civil war by the rising in Ireland.

CHAPTER 3

The outbreak of civil war in England, 1640–42

Did the English Revolution have long-term causes? To attempt an answer to this question is to enter a minefield of controversy. For almost a generation revisionist historians have called into doubt the notion that there was any highroad to civil war in the sixteenth or early seventeenth centuries. Yet the argument that fundamental long-term economic, social and intellectual changes prepared the ground for a civil war and revolution in the mid-seventeenth century continues to have an irreducible validity.

First there are the economic preconditions. In the context of early-modern Europe England stood out as a mature capitalist economy. The country's population had almost doubled between 1541 and 1641.[1] To feed this population agricultural production had almost kept pace, thanks to technical improvements, better fertilizers and the consolidation of farms through enclosure and engrossment. Crop yields rose, and more and more food was produced for the market rather than subsistence. England was a country in which landlord–tenant relations were governed by the marketplace, even if the moral economy of customary relations of service continued to tug at landlords' sleeves. For centuries a unified, centralized state had recognized and protected the rights of individual private property. By the early seventeenth century there were many industries in the countryside; there was an impressively large coal industry based in Newcastle; internal and overseas trade were growing by leaps and bounds; London

---

[1] E.A. Wrigley and R.S. Schofield, *The Population History of England 1541–1871: A Reconstruction*, 528. The methods and assumptions underlying this book have recently been seriously questioned, but its statistical findings are still the best we have: John Hatcher, 'Understanding the population history of England, 1450–1750', *P & P*, 180 (2003), 83–130.

had been growing fast for over a century, and was poised to overtake Paris as the largest city in western Europe.

Secondly, England was a country undergoing significant social change. The non-titled landed class known as the gentry grew much faster than the population, more than trebling in numbers during the century 1540 to 1640.[2] It is difficult to exaggerate the prosperity and economic independence of the English landed class. Better educated than ever before, they were becoming a political force to be reckoned with. The same was true of the urban middle classes, lawyers and overseas merchants in particular. In the century before 1640 there was a massive shift of wealth away from the Crown and the Church towards the gentry and professional classes. During this century there arose a comparatively large, well informed, experienced 'public', with a keen appetite for news, and capable of political action and influence.[3] At the same time the traditional ruling class, comprising Crown, Church and nobility, were undergoing a relative decline in wealth and hence social prestige. Under Henry VIII and Elizabeth I the Crown dissipated much of its patrimony in expensive wars against France and Spain. Its financial poverty meant that it was unable to maintain a standing army or more than a very tiny paid bureaucracy. Since local administration was carried out by unsalaried sheriffs, deputy lieutenants and justices of the peace, it was difficult for the central government to make these officials obedient to its will. Nor was it easy to discipline wealthy tax evaders. There had been no reform of the subsidy since its introduction in 1522; consequently the yield from the subsidy shrank steadily, all the while that the country was swelling in population and wealth.

The venality and outright corruption of many Crown officials was a source of alienation between monarchy and subject. In the terminology of the day, the king was the fountain of bounty and justice, and also head of the body politic. If that fountain became polluted, then the whole of society would become diseased. Thanks to flattering sycophants and evil counsellors, the playwright Webster declaimed, 'death and diseases through the whole land spread'. The political remedy was similar to the preferred medical ones of the age: purging and bloodletting.[4]

The nobility had different problems from those of the Crown. While few any longer believed that they were undergoing a profound economic

---

[2] Lawrence Stone, *The Causes of the English Revolution*, 72.

[3] Richard Cust, 'News and politics in early seventeenth century England', *P & P*, 112 (1986), 60–90.

[4] Linda Levy Peck, *Court Patronage and Corruption in Early Stuart England*, 208–10.

and moral crisis, or losing political influence, they were still experiencing a military crisis. The causes of this crisis were partly ideological: Renaissance humanism and Reformation Protestantism were encouraging warriors to become politicians. Or, as Mervyn James has observed, a polity structured in terms of unconditional obedience was undermining the aristocratic concept of honour as a code of political dissidence.[5] With the Tudor crack-down on private armies of feudal retainers, more and more noblemen sought to exercise power not as great territorial magnates, but as courtiers and counsellors to the monarch. Noblemen still found an outlet for their military ambitions in foreign conflicts, especially the Thirty Years' War (1618–48). By the eve of the civil war over two-thirds of them could boast military experience.[6] At the same time both the nobility and the monarchy had been left behind by the military revolution, which had multiplied both the scale and the cost of warfare.[7] Although they may have been tamed by the Tudors, individual noblemen such as the earls of Northumberland, Warwick, Essex, Worcester and Hertford continued to occupy estates that dwarfed those of any gentleman. Their political influence correspondingly overshadowed that of individual gentry.

The Church, traditionally a pillar of the Crown's authority, was also becoming enfeebled. The Reformation had resulted in the confiscation of half its land, with the rest being subject to unscrupulous raiding by the Crown – particularly under Elizabeth. The changes in doctrine entailed by the alternation between Protestant and Catholic monarchs had sapped public confidence in the Church's moral and intellectual authority. Already the invention of the printing press in the late fifteenth century had made it increasingly difficult for the Church to control the circulation of reli-gious and political ideas. The translation of the Bible into English and the gradual expansion of literacy aroused expectations of religious and polit-ical participation, and exposed large numbers of humble people to the radically subversive message of the New Testament. Thomas Hobbes later testified to the empowering effect of Bible-reading upon the lower classes when he complained that 'after the Bible was translated into English, every

[5] Mervyn James, *Society, Politics and Culture: Studies in Early Modern England*, 358.
[6] Roger Manning goes so far as to write of a 'remilitarization' and 'rechivalrization of English aristocratic and gentry culture' during these decades: Roger B. Manning, *Swordsmen: The Martial Ethos in the Three Kingdoms*, 17–19. This corrects Lawrence Stone's estimate that only one peer in five had experienced battle: Lawrence Stone, *The Crisis of the Aristocracy, 1558–1641*, 266. It is not true that '. . . Charles lost the Civil Wars [because] the English aristocracy no longer knew how to fight'.
[7] Geoffrey Parker, *The Military Revolution*, 6–44.

man, nay, every boy and wench, that could read English, thought they spoke with God Almighty, and understood what he said . . .'[8]

There were other sources for the growing intellectual challenge to the idea of untramelled royal authority. The ideology of the common law, fostered by a burgeoning legal profession,[9] was used to re-erect barriers for the protection of private property, private interests and private persons against the encroachments of a would-be centralizing state.[10] The diligently cultivated myth of Magna Carta as the foundation stone of individual liberties would in the end be a powerful tool in the common lawyers' attack on the royal prerogative courts.

What was once thought to be a third major intellectual current to challenge royal authority turns out to have been a myth: the supposed dichotomy between Court and country: the widespread conviction that the country was the repository of personal and political virtue, and (under James I at least) the Court the sink of all iniquity, hypocrisy, double-dealing ambition and extravagance. Modern research has uncovered a much fuzzier picture. There were plenty of ardent royalists in the countryside, whereas the climbing courtier could be popularly viewed as a seditious malcontent. In fact most courtiers hailed from gentry backgrounds, and retained strong ties with their counties. Greater than the gulf between the Court and the country was the contrast between the Jacobean and Caroline courts. James I had set the tone at his Court by engaging in reckless financial extravagance, the selling – and thereby cheapening – of honours and titles, drunkenness and sexual excess. His highly moral son was an exemplar of happy, fruitful, married love. Drunkenness and profane talk were banished from his Court; the sale of honours and titles halted; the principal form of financial extravagance – which only slightly dented royal finances – was the purchase of European paintings and the staging of masques. Charles was impatient of court parasites. Far more energetically than his father, he drove the landed class back to their estates, issuing proclamations threatening to imprison any gentleman caught in London without excuse. He followed up these threats with prosecutions in Star Chamber. Charles I's Court became a place of exalted, classical ideals. Poets and artists cultivated an equilibrium of passion and reason, freedom and restraint. In politics the Court took an aloof and authoritarian attitude

---

[8] Thomas Hobbes, *Behemoth, or the Long Parliament*, 21.

[9] Geoffrey Holmes, *Augustan England: Professions, State and Society, 1680–1730*, 137.

[10] Christopher Hill, *Intellectual Origins of the English Revolution*, 233–46, 253, 256–8.

which it combined with an ethic of service to the state derived from stoicism. Most courtiers shared a deeply ingrained fear of mankind's violent
and anarchic tendencies, which they had learned from the Roman historian
Tacitus, Sir Francis Bacon and Ben Jonson.[11] In short, there was not a great
deal to complain about in the Court of Charles I.

David Underdown substituted for the Court–country polarity a clash
of two fundamentally opposed cultures. The first stressed tradition, custom and the cooperative, harmonious 'vertical' community. The second
exalted moral reformation, individualism, the ethic of work and personal
responsibility. Taking his cue from an intriguing observation by the
seventeenth-century antiquarian John Aubrey, about the contrast between
the people who lived in arable, open field country ('the chalk') of his native
Wiltshire, and those who dwelt in the upland wood–pasture country ('the
cheese'), Underdown linked this cultural clash to geography. The people
of the arable or mixed farming regions were usually under the thumb of
a local parson or squire, and hence tended to be deferential; they also set
much store by neighbourliness and group loyalty. Those of the pasture–
woodland regions, as well as the clothing and industrial towns by contrast,
tended to be more individualistic, less deferential and inclined towards
Puritanism.[12]

The problem with Underdown's thesis is that it is not proven by his
data. There is too much blurring around the edges, and besides, there
were just not enough people living in pasture–woodland areas to launch
a successful challenge to royal power. Indeed, it was mainly townsmen,
according to Underdown's own evidence, who manned both royalist and
parliamentarian armies. Overwhelmingly, the parliamentary armies were
recruited from London and the clothing and industrial towns such as
Norwich, Bradford, Birmingham, Northampton, Leeds and Marlborough.

We are on firmer ground if we seek the origins of the civil war in the
clash between the theories of divine right monarchy and the so-called
'ancient constitution'. The early Stuart monarchs believed that they
derived their authority from God, not the people; therefore they were
accountable to Him, not them. They also held that kings were the fountain
of the law; indeed, the king *was* the law, 'a living, a speaking, an acting

[11] R. Malcolm Smuts, *Court Culture and the Origins of a Royalist Tradition in Early
Stuart England*, 67, 74–5, 78, 106–7, 193, 263; Kevin Sharpe, *Criticism and
Compliment: The Politics of Literature in the England of Charles I*, ch. 1; Sharpe,
Personal Rule, 209–35.

[12] David Underdown, *Revel, Riot, and Rebellion: Popular Politics and Culture in
England, 1603–1660*, 72–8 and passim.

law' as Justice Berkeley put it in the Ship Money judgment of 1638.[13] This is not to say they believed in the unfettered right to exercise the powers of a tyrant. Kings were obligated to govern according to the law, and to consult their Great Council (the peerage) and the Commons assembled in parliament. They could only make sovereign law through parliament, and they could not take their subjects' property except by the law of the land. But the final authority was theirs. They were absolute in the sense that they possessed discretionary powers which they wielded without oversight from any other body. Against divine right theory common-law jurists like Sir Edward Coke stressed not only that kings were obliged to govern according to the laws of the realm, but that they were subordinate to the laws, and could not alter them without the agreement of parliament. Parliament also had the power to call the king's counsellors to account, and even impeach them, when the occasion required, of high crimes and misdemeanours. The main purpose of parliament's checking function was to protect property, and in so doing to preserve human liberty.[14]

Support for the ancient constitution in the late sixteenth and early seventeenth centuries was also grounded in concrete grievances. Towards the end of Elizabeth's reign there was mounting impatience with non-parliamentary vehicles of revenue collection such as purveyance, wardship and monopolies. Under James the grievances were monopolies, increased customs duties known as impositions and the corruption of royal minis-ters. In the early part of Charles I's reign the issues were freedom of speech, unparliamentary taxation, the application of martial law to the civilian population and arbitrary arrest and imprisonment. This bundle of finan-cial and constitutional grievances was made more combustible by the dawning apprehension that the government of Charles not only harboured authoritarian ambitions, but was seriously out of step with the Protestant consensus in most of the country. Charles's embrace of Arminianism, and his resolute efforts to reorient both the theology and the liturgy of the Church away from Calvinistic Protestantism and towards an exalted sacerdotal doctrine of kingship, combined with a more Catholic form of worship, roused the spectre of a Crown-led drift towards popery. The Dutch theologian Arminius had rejected predestination in favour of free

---

[13] Gardiner, *Const. Docs.*, 122.

[14] There is an enormous literature on the theories of divine right, absolutism and the ancient constitution. Two excellent, recent presentations of opposing views are Glenn Burgess, *Absolute Monarchy and the Stuart Constitution*, and Johann P. Sommerville, *Royalists and Patriots: Politics and Ideology in England 1603–1640*.

will. English Arminians, most notably the king, with the support of his Archbishop of Canterbury, William Laud, made their hostility to Calvinistic theology visible and concrete by their insistence that the priesthood wear traditional vestments, by their reintroduction of the practice of bowing at the name of Jesus, the sign of the cross in baptism, kneeling for communion, and by replacing wooden communion tables with raised stone altars encircled by railings and positioned at the east end of the church. Attempts were also made to bring back candles, incense, stained glass windows, sculptures and paintings. All these liturgical changes were summed up in William Laud's phrase 'the beauty of holiness'. To puritans, or the 'hotter sort of Protestants' as they were also known, it all smacked of popery. Their fervent desire was to cleanse public worship of all Catholic vestiges, and to present a strong front against the incursions of internal popery. The landed class also became alarmed by Laud's systematic attempt to increase Church revenue by reclaiming impropriated tithes and land that had been raided from it by unscrupulous laymen.

Paradoxically, the rise of a religious and political opposition was made easier by the fact that the Stuart dynasty, boasting a plentiful male progeny and no visible rivals for the throne, was more secure than any other in the last three centuries. With the passage of the Elizabethan Poor Law in 1598 (revised in 1601) England had became Europe's first welfare state. The relative generosity of the Law's provision for the poor did much to render the lower classes quiescent, and so the spectre of an insurrection of the poor steadily receded in the early decades of the seventeenth century. Finally, England's continental neighbours were preoccupied with a destructive and debilitating war from 1618 until 1648. Under these circumstances the middle and upper classes felt that they could indulge the luxury of challenging the authority of monarchical government without thereby imperilling the survival of the nation itself.

So much for the long- and medium-term causes of the outbreak of civil war. According to revisionist historians none of these causes made a civil war inevitable. The revisionist school was launched in 1965 when Sir Geoffrey Elton published a seminal essay, 'A high road to civil war?'.[15] His argument for the contingency of the events that led to civil war was quickly taken up and advanced by Alan Everitt, Conrad Russell, John Morrill, Anthony Fletcher, Kevin Sharpe, Mark Kishlansky, Paul Christianson, Glenn Burgess and John Adamson, among others. According to the revisionists

[15] Geoffrey Elton, 'A high road to civil war?', repr. in his *Studies in Tudor and Stuart Politics and Government*, Vol. 2, 164–82.

none of the long-term changes in the English polity made a revolution inevitable. In spite of many people's worries about 'disorder' England enjoyed a high degree of social stability, and an almost complete absence of violence in the decades before 1640.[16] Furthermore, it was the king who was on the cutting edge of change, while his critics were stuck in the past. Looking at Europe as a whole what do we witness but the decay of representative institutions, the strengthening of links between Church and state, the triumphal progress of a resurgent Catholicism, and the well-nigh universal growth of absolutist government? The concept of the royalists as men of the future receives unexpected demographic confirmation in the remarkable finding that the parliamentarian MPs in the Long Parliament were on average eleven years older than the royalists.[17] John Adamson has uncovered a similar disparity in the ages of royalist and parliamentarian peers. Had Charles I been a more mainstream Protestant; had he been a more skilful ruler less addicted to cloak and dagger conspiracies; had he chosen more cautious and far-sighted advisers, he might have navigated his way through the storms of upper-class discontent. None of the problems bequeathed to him by his two predecessors was insoluble. Nor was there any reason why a robustly capitalistic society should not have thriven under an absolutist regime enlightened enough to pay attention to the religious susceptibilities and economic requirements of improving landowners and thrusting entrepreneurs.

Instead, Charles engaged in the high-risk policy of locking horns with the leading power groups in the country. The revenues of landowners were threatened by arbitrary taxation in the form of a forced loan in 1626, a new assessment called Ship Money in the 1630s, and a revival of fiscal feudalism in the form of the forest laws, distraint of knighthood, and the energetic prosecution of the royal rights to wardship. The merchants and monied men of London were exploited and bullied. In 1628–29 for example, the Levant Company saw some of its leading members thrown into jail for refusing to pay an arbitrary increase in the imposition on currants. The City of London was harried ruthlessly over its failure to turn the Londonderry plantation into a profitable venture. Common lawyers saw their livelihoods threatened by the steady expansion of the jurisdiction of prerogative courts. The mainstream Protestant sensibilities of the political

---

[16] John Morrill, 'Politics in an age of revolution, 1630–1690', in John Morrill (ed.), *The Oxford Illustrated History of Tudor and Stuart Britain*, 362; Anthony Fletcher and John Stevenson (eds), *Order and Disorder in Early Modern England*, 31, 38, 40.

[17] Douglas Brunton and D.H. Pennington, *Members of the Long Parliament*, 16.

nation were offended by a pro-Catholic, pro-Spanish, foreign policy in the decade before 1640, and an aggressively pursued attempt to wean the Church of England from its Calvinist tutelage in preference to a sacramental, Arminian worship redolent of popery.

Yet there was little public protest against these policies after 1629, and even less resistance. Ship Money, a new tax imposed to pay for the navy, was collected successfully right up to the end of the decade. When a Buckinghamshire gentleman, John Hampden, challenged the constitutionality of this non-parliamentary tax, the common law judges rejected his arguments, though by a margin of only seven to five. There were no other protests to speak of until the tax strikes of 1640. Charles had no desire to lay the foundations of an absolutist tyranny. Admittedly, those who criticized the religious policies of his bishops were hailed before the Court of Star Chamber, which subjected them to savage corporal punishments – whippings, the pillory and mutilation. The lawyer William Prynne had his ears cropped twice for the same offence. Yet by the standards of the day, Charles provided his people with mild government. During the time he was in power there was not a single execution for treason or crimes of state.[18] The bishops encountered little resistance as they promoted the beauty of holiness and sought to reclaim the church's patrimony from lay predators. The privileged Levant, East India and Merchant Adventurers companies continued to return royal favours by lending to the Crown on a large scale, right up until 1640. In the end it was the difficulty of governing multiple kingdoms, intersecting with the explosive issue of religion, that precipitated the disintegration of the regime at the end of the 1630s. Yet even as late as the beginning of 1642 civil war was not inevitable. Had things gone a little bit differently Charles might well have defeated the Scots in the first Bishops' War, thereby obviating the need to summon parliament in the autumn of 1640.[19] When parliament met, the king made huge political, financial and religious concessions to his critics. Most people who backed either the king or parliament, as well as the great majority of the population, who were interested mainly in local issues, had no desire for armed conflict.[20]

Almost from the beginning the revisionist account of the reasons for England's civil war came in for searching and sustained criticism.

[18] Sharpe, *Personal Rule*, 930.
[19] Adamson, 'England without Cromwell', 100–1.
[20] Russell, *Causes of the English Civil War*, 213; John Morrill, *Revolt in the Provinces: The People of England and the Tragedies of War, 1630–1648*, 62–3.

Revisionists were accused of doing a better job of explaining why a civil war did not happen rather than why it did. They were charged with exaggerating the extent of intellectual consensus in early Stuart England, while overlooking the substantive ideological differences between the king and his political opponents. Far from caring only about local, county matters, many people outside London had a lively interest in national issues, and were avid readers of political news from the capital, as well as the continent. The provinces were just as deeply divided over politics and religion – popery in particular – as was the metropolis. Not only was most of the country gripped by a terrible fear of international Catholicism, there was great resentment against the absolutist pretensions of the Stuart monarchy. Arbitrary arrest and imprisonment, unparliamentary taxation, and the king's claim to be above the law were all deeply divisive issues in the decades leading up to the outbreak of civil war. Ann Hughes, Norah Carlin and others have argued that the civil war was also the product of broad social and cultural conflict. It is therefore unsatisfactory to explain the outbreak of civil war merely through a detailed narrative of high politics. The attitudes and actions of 'ordinary people' had a direct impact on events, and perceptions of their power helped structure elite behaviour.[21]

There are profitable insights to be derived from the work of both revisionist and post-revisionist scholars. The contribution of revisionists has been to force everyone to study the evidence more closely, dig more deeply, and go back to archival sources. They have insisted on the contingency of events: things might easily have turned out differently. They have reminded us that explaining historical phenomena can be a tricky business: because 'a' is followed by 'b' does not prove that 'a' has caused 'b' (the *post hoc ergo propter hoc* fallacy). They have insisted that the extent of political conflict before 1641 should not be exaggerated: at many other times in British history conflict was more bitter, yet civil war did not result. They have underlined the vital role of personality: with a different set of *dramatis personae* the play would have turned out differently. They have stressed the intractable difficulty of governing three very different kingdoms.

---

[21] The anti-revisionist critique has been mounted by several historians, among the most distinguished of whom are Clive Holmes, Derek Hirst, David Underdown, Johann Sommerville, Peter Lake, Richard Cust, Ann Hughes, John Walter, Thomas Cogswell, Andy Wood and David Cressy. Their work is ably summarized in two short books bearing the same title: Ann Hughes, *The Causes of the English Civil War*, and Norah Carlin, *The Causes of the English Civil War*.

Finally, far from downplaying the role of ideas in the lead-up to the civil war, they have insisted on the crucial role of religion in stirring people up to passionate commitment and a readiness to risk their lives on behalf of their convictions.

The anti-revisionists are right to point out that a surface of apparently unruffled calm does not prove that all was well in the English polity before 1640, any more than it was in the USSR before communism collapsed in 1989. Many people were profoundly dissatisfied with the policies and conduct of their government, its military incompetence and its willingness to appease the Catholic powers of Europe. Their anxiety about national and international politics is seen in their continual hunger for news about doings at Court and in parliament, as well as in Europe. People well down the social scale manifested this keen interest in political and religious affairs.

To round out this survey of the causes of the civil war in England there are three remaining questions to be considered: the three kingdoms problem, the overlapping question of religion, and the personality of the key player, Charles I.

A ruler far more gifted than Charles I would have found it a challenge to master three distinct kingdoms, each with its own council, parliament, legal system and brand of religion. At the Reformation the Irish people had declined the invitation to convert to Protestantism; they remained 80 to 90 per cent Catholic a century later. The small established Irish Protestant Church was more firmly Calvinist than its English counterpart, but attracted few adherents, even though Catholics were liable to fines and in theory suffered a wide range of civil and legal disabilities. By Poynings' Law no statute could be passed in the Irish parliament unless it had first been ratified by the English privy council. The English parliament, however, had no jurisdiction over Irish affairs. Scotland suffered no demeaning equivalent to Poynings' Law. In the 1560s the nation had fervently embraced Calvinist Presbyterianism, a form of Protestantism that was both anti-hierarchical and insistent upon its independence from the state. James VI had imposed bishops on this Presbyterian structure, but was not able to endow them with much of the governing power of the English bishops.

The basic dilemma, common to most multiple kingdoms, was whether to permit in one kingdom practices and beliefs which were prohibited in another. A ruler could not govern any one of his kingdoms simply in its own interests. Constantly he had to be looking over his shoulder at the effects of what he did there on his other kingdoms. To Charles I's orderly mind it was scandalous that most of his Scottish subjects worshipped in a Calvinistic Presbyterian way, most of his Irish subjects in a Roman Catholic way, while in his chief kingdom of England most of his subjects worshipped in a Protestant episcopal way. Charles, a religious revolutionary who was repelled by lay and popular Protestantism, sought to link the sacramental worship of God with the rituals of divine kingship. His Caesaro-sacerdotalism fractured the religious consensus that his father had patiently constructed.[22] A king less zealous and less insistent on religious uniformity throughout his realms might have saved both his throne and his head.

Religion was the most intractable of all the problems that Charles had to face. By 1640 in England the century-long tradition of anti-Catholicism had become an almost fixed element in the national identity. The tradition started with John Foxe's chronicling of the suffering of Protestant martyrs in the 1550s under Mary Tudor. First published in 1563, Foxe's *Acts and Monuments* was reprinted many times down to the nineteenth century. Anti-Catholicism was reinforced by the papal bull solemnly excommunicating and deposing Queen Elizabeth in 1570, by the plotting of Mary Stuart and her adherents against the life of Elizabeth, and by the launching by Philip II of Spain's armada in 1588 to implement the Pope's deposition of the queen. In the early seventeenth century the flames of anti-Catholicism were kept bright by the 'Gunpowder Treason' of 1605 – a plot to blow up the royal family, nobility, bishops and commons in parliament, and install a Catholic regime in England – by the presence of a proselytizing Catholic Court around Charles's wife Henrietta Maria, and by the growth of anti-Calvinism, or Arminianism, under the direct sponsorship of the king. The Catholic phenomenon was made to seem more menacing by the reality that it was an upper-class religion. Strong among the gentry, it also commanded the allegiance of a fifth of the nobility.

As Caroline Hibbard, Peter Lake and others have shown, there was substance to popular fears. Charles did in fact wink at Court conversions; he welcomed the first papal agent to enter England since the Reformation, and he all but ended persecution of Catholic priests. In early 1640, on the eve of the Short Parliament, the papal agent Rossetti urged him to rely on extra-parliamentary sources of money, including a loan from the Pope. Charles would have been glad of the loan, but negotiations foundered

---

[22] Julian Davies, *The Caroline Captivity of the Church: Charles I and the Remoulding of Anglicanism, 1625–1651*, 17–18, 21.

on his refusal to convert to Catholicism. A similar attempt to borrow from the Catholic king of Spain also fell through, but not before details of the negotiations had leaked out. At the same time, and throughout the 1640s, he relied heavily on the Somerset family, the Catholic earls of Worcester, who not only lent generously but rallied troops for the king from Wales and the marches. Throughout the summer of 1640 the Earl of Strafford was authorized to waive the bar against Catholics in his recruitment of 9,000 troops to assist the king in fighting the Scots. Montreuil, the French ambassador, reported that the king was considering using these troops 'as much to obtain satisfaction from his English subjects as for the Scottish war'.[23]

Once parliament resumed people were quick to make known their unhappiness with the king's religious policies. The House of Lords manuscripts are full of complaints, largely against the Arminian clergy; indeed no fewer than 800 petitions critical of the Laudian church poured in during the early months of the Long Parliament.[24] Many landowners were offended by Laud's attempts to restore the finances of the Church at their expense. Others were offended by his injunction to refuse communion to anyone who would not kneel at the altar rail. It was not only Puritanism that was divisive.[25] In that period religion was the main issue that divided the House of Commons. The MPs were only reflecting a broader division throughout the country. The Puritan divine Richard Baxter noted that most of the people called puritans, 'that used to talk of God and heaven and scripture, and holiness', adhered to parliament. Those who did not do these things, or were tolerant of dancing and recreation on Sundays, backed the king.[26] As the royalist Earl of Clarendon conceded, the imputation that the king intended to bring in or was 'conniving at or tolerating popery' made 'a deep impression on people'.[27]

On the other hand, it cannot be denied that the religion of Charles and Laud enjoyed a certain attraction. It was after all a form of worship that appealed – through the 'beauty of holiness' – to all five senses. 'It was a faith that welcomed all the people to kneel to receive their risen Lord at the altar rail, and which did not condemn many of them to sit around, as a godly clique commemorated what God had achieved for *them*, the elect in his death and resurrection.' Yet at the same time it was hugely unpopular,

[23] Quoted in Hibbard, *Popish Plot*, 156.

[24] HMC 3, *Fourth Report* (House of Lords MSS), 47, 49, 63–4, and passim; John Morrill, *The Nature of the English Revolution*, 76.

[25] Carlin, *Causes*, 64–5.

[26] Baxter, *Reliquiae Baxterianae*, 31.

[27] Clarendon, *Hist.*, Bk 5, para. 441 n. 3.

mainly because it reeked of popery.[28] But when parliament unleashed popular iconoclasm by its official sanctioning of the destruction of idolatrous
images and altar rails, and the replacement of altars with communion
tables, there were many who were appalled by the destruction of objects
that were both beautiful and costly. Such people were the nucleus of the
royalist party. The crowd that rallied to defend Norwich Cathedral and its
organ at Shrovetide 1642 is 'somewhere near the epitome of royalism'.[29]
Those who would deny that a radical disagreement about religion was
the fundamental cause of the civil war can only do so by ignoring what
the people alive at the time had to say. Take for example, the petition of the
peers in September 1640 exhorting Charles to summon parliament. The
chief grievance agitating the nation was 'the great increase of popery'.[30] Or
again, look at the statement of parliament itself, in the autumn of 1642 to
the Scots commissioners that 'the cause of these troubles [is] the malignant
design, now in hand by force of arms to hinder reformation of religion
and church government and to introduce popery and superstition'.[31] John
Morrill is right: it was the religious split in the Long Parliament that made
civil war necessary.[32] And Richard Tuck is also right that at the beginning
of the English Civil War the work of ideological opposition to the king was
done largely by radical Calvinism and its derivatives.[33] And Alan Orr is
right that because of the Erastian nature of the English church, 'power over
souls was more important than power over lives, goods and estates'.[34]
Conrad Russell is also right that religion was a primordial cause of the civil
war because Charles decided that it should be. The king was willing, reluctantly, to conciliate men over legal, constitutional issues, but he chose not
to conciliate men who put religious issues first – men such as the Earl
of Warwick, Viscount Saye and Sele, John Pym, Oliver St John and Sir
Robert Harley. 'It was religion which divided the parties because Charles
decided it should be so.'[35] Which brings us to the question of how much

[28] Morrill, *Oxford Illustrated History of Tudor and Stuart Britain*, 362.
[29] R.W. Ketton Cremer, *Norfolk in the Civil War*, 142–3, cited in Russell, *Causes of the English Civil War*, 22.
[30] Gardiner, *Const. Docs.*, 135.
[31] Bodl. MS Tanner 64, fo. 73 (23 October 1642). The fact that this statement was framed for Scottish consumption should not lead us to dismiss it as mere propaganda.
[32] Morrill, *Nature of the English Revolution*, 85.
[33] Richard Tuck, *Natural Rights Theories: Their Origin and Development*, 144.
[34] D. Alan Orr, 'Sovereignty, supremacy and the orgins of the English Civil War', *History*, 87 (2002), 490.
[35] Russell, *Fall of the British Monarchies*, 527.

responsibility for the outbreak of civil war should be laid at the feet of the king. The question can be explored under two headings: his inadequacies and his strengths.

The second Stuart king seems to have endured an unhappy childhood, being overshadowed until the age of 12 by his dazzling and much lamented elder brother Prince Henry. His intense personal insecurity was not helped by his diminutive height, and it was eloquently symbolized by a lifelong stammer. Perhaps to compensate for these shortcomings he was drawn to propagate a high conception of kingship. In Charles's universe resistance to the royal will was illegitimate, and if persisted in, treasonous. His belief in divine right kingship made him scornful of everyday political skills. The opposite of a supple, sinewy politician, he had no comprehension of the truth which every successful political leader carries in his bones, that power is a rapidly wasting asset which must be won afresh every day. Nor would he have agreed that politics is the art of the possible. When driven by necessity to make concessions he did so with ill grace, almost invariably he made them too late, and he tried to reverse them as soon as possible.

His sense of personal inadequacy made him obsessively concerned about his subjects' loyalty, from the first years of his reign. People were quick to pick up on the new king's self doubt. One of the earliest pieces of evidence was his complaint to the Earl of Manchester on the opposition of the Scottish privy council to his plan to raise soldiers there: 'You durst not have done so to my father.' Fifteen years later in 1641 when Sir Patrick Wemys saw him in Edinburgh he reported that 'there was never any king so much insulted . . . It would pity any man's heart to see how he looks . . . Glad he is when he sees any man that he thinks loves him.'[36]

Charles's high but rigid principles gave him tunnel vision. He could never appreciate that those who disagreed with him did so from principles just as sincere as his own.

What of his strengths? The second Stuart king was a man of considerable artistic taste and intelligence; moreover, he eschewed the buffoonery and sensual self-indulgence of his father. Happily married to the French princess, Henrietta Maria, to whom he was completely devoted, he sired a large family whose Protestant education he conscientiously oversaw. His governing ideals were honour, order and defence of the established Church. At least until the meeting of the Long Parliament Charles showed himself to be a flexible ruler, willing to compromise, priding himself on being a man of his word, and basing his decisions on the advice of his

[36] Quoted in Russell, *Causes of the English Civil War*, 204; Bodl. MS Carte 1, fo. 460v.

councillors.[37] His high-mindedness is exemplified in his refusal to let his servants take the blame for policies that went awry. His readiness to stick to his principles even at the cost of his own life has commanded respect if not admiration since his lifetime.

It is important not to lose sight of the fact that there could have been no civil war had Charles not commanded the fervent loyalty of a significant proportion of the English people. Had he been as universally despised as Edward II or Richard II he would have been as easily and quickly overthrown as they. Consider Charles's speech to his troops at Selby in August 1640, just before the battle at Newburn. It was reported to be 'so princely and so pathetic [emotional] that it moved tears in many gentlemen that heard it, who before were of another kind of temper, and indeed of the more stubborn'.[38] The next month, when he addressed the English nobility assembled at York, an anonymous witness wrote,

had you seen and heard the king as I did, with what vivacity of spirit, with what noble courage, with what reason, and upon what grounds of truth he alleged his own arguments, disproved the Scots' causeless complaints, implored our Lords' counsel and assistance, explained some difficulties, etc. you would think with me he were (as certainly he is) the most incomparable and accomplished prince in the world, of admirable wisdom and of indefatigable industry and patience, and one that, in regard of his great abilities, wants nothing but more kingdoms to govern, but better people.[39]

It is ironic that these effusive words were penned just after Charles, having dismissed the Short Parliament, and gone to war on an empty treasury, had suffered ignominious defeat at the hands of Scotland, much the economic inferior of his two British kingdoms. Yet the testimonies just quoted are a reminder that not all of Charles's contemporaries considered him a pitifully incompetent ruler. It was his strengths as well as his weaknesses that helped precipitate the civil war.

Another precipitant was the trouble with Scotland. As the lawyer MP Bulstrode Whitelocke later observed, the Scottish rising 'was the trouble from whence our ensuing troubles did spring'.[40] This crisis prompted the

---

[37] Kishlansky, 'Charles I: a case of mistaken identity', 51, 56, 58–60.

[38] Huntington Lib., Ellesmere Collection (Bridgewater MSS), EL 7856, 28 August 1640.

[39] Huntington Lib., Ellesmere Collection (Bridgewater MSS), EL 7740, 25 September 1640. (Anonymous letter describing the first proceedings of the Great Council of Peers at York.)

[40] Quoted in Sharpe, *Personal Rule*, 952.

City financiers to call in their loans, to invest their capital abroad, and thereby to create a climate of economic instability. After military failure in the first war of 1639 Charles's government lost the active cooperation of the country magistracy in executing its orders and commands. The Earl of Strafford was his first councillor to point out to him that he could not fight the Scots a second time unless he summoned parliament.[41] The failure of the Short Parliament of April 1640 to vote any money meant that Charles went to war that summer on an empty treasury. His hopes were pinned on Strafford and the Irish army of 9,000, as well as a promised Spanish loan of £300,000. But the loan fell through, the army was not recruited in time to fight the Scots, and Strafford was so ill from dysentery and gout that he was unable to play an effective role as lord general of the king's forces. The 'froward people' of the City of London declined to advance any money; in fact the common people were said to be on the edge of insurrection. The capital, in one writer's memorable phrase, was like 'a ball of wildfire' which if not checked, would soon engulf the whole kingdom.[42] Both the king and his adversaries were conspiring dangerously against each other. Charles was said to be planning to use Strafford's army in England after he had subdued the Scots.[43] Meanwhile, several disaffected peers and gentlemen, notably the Earl of Warwick, Viscount Saye and Sele, Viscount Mandeville, Lord Brooke and John Pym, had been plotting with the Covenanters to effect an invasion of England. Saye's son, Nathaniel Fiennes, had been in Edinburgh during the months leading up to the invasion. All these men were part of a Puritan network going back to the 1620s that extended into each of the three kingdoms. In England their involvement in two colonial ventures – the Providence Island Company and the Saybrook Project – furnished the opportunity for private meetings where they concerted their plans. The involvement of these men in what was nothing less than treason, and their awareness that Charles knew of their activities, made them utterly dependent on a Scottish victory and the continuing occupation of England by the Scots until they had gained the upper hand over Charles.[44]

---

[41] Huntington Lib., Ellesmere Collection (Bridgewater MSS), EL 7814, 6 December 1639.

[42] Huntington Lib., Ellesmere Collection (Bridgewater MSS), EL 7835, 7838.

[43] Hibbard, *Popish Plot*, 156.

[44] Russell, *Causes of the English Civil War*, 24; Russell, *Fall of British Monarchies*, 151–3; Donald, 'New light on the Anglo-Scottish contacts', 221–9; Donald, *Uncounselled King*, 246–8; Scott, *Politics and War*, 24.

The English army meanwhile was in an appalling state of demoralization. Some units had murdered two Catholic officers on their way north. One of the commanders, Sir Jacob Astley, wrote that many of his troops had already deserted, and the rest he was afraid to arm for fear they would turn on their officers.[45] This unpaid, leaderless army, acutely conscious that the nation did not support its struggle, succumbed before the Scottish onslaught at Newburn on 27 August. Newcastle then surrendered without a shot the next day. The second humiliating defeat in two years at the hands of England's ancestral enemy produced a rapid unravelling of Charles's regime. The radical nobility moved to exercise control, twelve of their number petitioning the king to meet a council of the entire peerage at York at the end of September. At this council the peerage attempted to take charge of the country, as they had done in similar crises in earlier centuries.[46] Their chief demands were that parliament be summoned to deal with the financial mess, and that some of them be appointed commissioners to conclude a treaty with the Scots. They got their way, but Charles tried to pre-empt them by announcing at the start that he had decided to call a parliament on 3 November.

In the north, meanwhile, people were beginning to feel the iron heel of a foreign oppressor. Whatever disenchantment they may have felt about the king's exactions and his billeting of soldiers, was as nothing compared to the dismay caused by the pillaging that followed in the wake of the Scottish occupation.[47] By contrast, for the radical peers and their allies in the House of Commons the value of the Scottish presence in the north could not be overestimated. It gave them the leverage necessary to extract concessions from the king that he would not otherwise have granted. The Scots for their part insisted on negotiating, not with Charles, but with the commissioners he appointed with parliament's approval. The great majority of these commissioners were directly implicated in the treasonous invitation to the Scots to invade. They would continue to depend on the Scots to protect them against the king for another four years.[48]

---

[45] Huntington Lib., Ellesmere Collection (Bridgewater MSS), EL 7844.

[46] I am grateful to John Adamson for letting me read some early chapters from his book *The Noble Revolt* in advance of publication. Published July 2006, Weidenfeld and Nicolson.

[47] For an impassioned denunciation of the Scots army that was scattered in the streets of Newcastle, see Bodl. MS Tanner 65, fos. 37–8.

[48] Conrad Russell, 'The Scottish party in the English parliament, 1640–2 OR the myth of the English Revolution', *HR*, 66 (1993), 46–52.

Constitutional revolution: the Long Parliament and the people, 1640–42

Almost immediately upon its assembling in November 1640, the Long Parliament set about purging Charles's government of evil counsellors, at the same time ignoring the king's pleas to be thrown a financial lifeline. The first grant that it did vote was a 'brotherly assistance' of £300,000 to the Scots. Within six months half the privy councillors who had been present for the opening of the Long Parliament had fled, been disgraced, or were in prison. The Commons' first target was the Earl of Strafford, President of the Council of the North and Lord Deputy of Ireland, whom they impeached of treason. Unlike Secretary Francis Windebanke, who took off for France out of fear that his negotiations for papal troops and papal gold would be revealed, Strafford strode south to Westminster to face the music. The charges against him were British in scope: 'endeavouring to subvert the ancient and fundamental laws and government of England and Ireland', erecting an 'arbitrary and tyrannical government' in Ireland, and provoking war against the Scots. His enemies in the other two kingdoms were if anything more determined to have his blood than those in England. There was only one trouble with this case: by any fair interpretation of the law Strafford could not be convicted of treason. Everything he had done was in obedience to the instructions of the king, who had complete confidence in him. Strafford, with his incisive intellect and impassioned eloquence, cut the impeachers' case to ribbons. His prosecutors then resorted to an attainder. The advantage of this instrument was that unlike an impeachment it did not require judicial proof; it was merely a parliamentary resolution declaring the accused person guilty. The attainder passed by a large margin in the Commons and by a lesser margin in a thinly attended upper house.[49] Many lords had been kept away by fear of the crowd. There remained a last hurdle: attainders, unlike impeachments, still required the king's assent. Charles had promised Strafford that he would never abandon him, but in a heroic gesture the earl told the king he should sign the attainder in order to preserve the peace of the kingdom. Stunned by the readiness of his chief minister to sacrifice his life, Charles dithered and gave in, hoping that by throwing Strafford to the lions he

[49] A recent study of the trial of Strafford argues that while he 'got a raw deal', his attainder was not an illegal act, because Strafford, by unlawfully appropriating the powers of the king, had effectively destroyed the law: D. Alan Orr, *Treason and the State: Law, Politics and Ideology in the English Civil War*, 100.

would preserve his family from the rage of the mob. It was a decision he instantly regretted. As he later told the Duke of Hamilton, he viewed the civil war as God's punishment for having betrayed Strafford.

'Black Tom Tyrant' might yet have been spared had it not been for the discovery at the beginning of May of a plot by a group of army officers to seize the Tower of London, release him, and threaten parliament with dissolution, possibly with the assistance of French or Dutch troops. What was not known at the time, but which has been established by Conrad Russell, was the complicity of Charles in this 'First Army Plot'. Panicked, both houses passed a bill against the dissolution of the parliament without its own consent. Charles gave his assent on 10 May, two days before Strafford's execution. Next, the Commons drew up an oath of association along the lines of Scotland's National League and Covenant. It was tendered to all MPs after which 11,000 copies were printed and circulated throughout the country. Known as the Protestation, it pledged its adherents to uphold four things: 'the true reformed Protestant religion . . . against all popery and popish innovation'; 'His Majesty's royal person and estate'; 'the power and privileges of Parliament'; and 'the lawful rights and liberties of the subjects'. As David Cressy and John Walter point out, it drew more people into the political process than ever before, and was of foundational importance in fashioning 'a pro-Parliamentary, popular political culture'.[50]

Parliament was united behind the oath of Protestation, as it was behind the attack on 'evil counsellors'. The next day, with imperturbable courage, Strafford met his death on Tower Hill before a hostile crowd of 100,000. Archbishop Laud, who had also been impeached of treason, was left to moulder in the Tower until 1645 when he too was despatched. Lord Keeper Finch and six other judges who had upheld Ship Money were also impeached but not executed; Finch, like Windebanke, fled to the continent.

Parliament's unity against the king and his counsellors began to fall apart as soon as it turned seriously to tackle the question of religion. Almost from the start parliament was inundated with petitions calling for the abolition of bishops. Most celebrated was the so-called Root and Branch Petition of December 1640, whose London promoters claimed 15,000 signatures. It indicted the institution of episcopacy as 'a main cause and occasion of many foul evils, pressures and grievances' and demanded

---

[50] Walter, *Understanding Popular Violence*, 292; David Cressy, 'Revolutionary England 1640–1642', *P & P*, 181 (2003), 70.

its abolition along with 'all its dependencies, roots and branches'.[51] During the course of 1641 similar anti-episcopal petitions were generated from nearly twenty counties in England. But the Commons debate on Root and Branch in February 1641 opened up bitter divisions. Its advocates, men such as Lord Saye's son Nathaniel Fiennes, argued that only the abolition of bishops could protect the Church from men like William Laud, and prepare the way for a godly commonwealth. Others urged reform. Let us not, pleaded Lord Digby, 'root up a good tree because there is a canker in the branches'.[52] Virtually all those who spoke for root and branch – men such as Denzell Holles and Oliver Cromwell – would end up fighting against the king. Of those who wanted to keep the bishops and restore the primitive purity of the institution virtually all went over to the king's side when war became imminent in 1642. Nothing was as predictive of civil war allegiance as the attitude people took towards the Church.

The root-and-branchers were not allowed to monopolize the public sphere. Until Judith Maltby brought it forcefully to our attention, most historians were unaware of the strength and depth of popular loyalty to the established Church on the eve of the civil war. In the year 1641–42 no fewer than 26 petitions from over 20 counties were submitted to parliament in defence of the Church. Notably, they were all different, in sharp contrast to the root-and-branch petitions, many of which were formulaic and followed the lead of Westminster. Most of the pro-Church petitions were lay- rather than clergy-inspired. Typically they were drafted by the gentry (very few originating in urban centres), and were circulated at assizes and quarter sessions. While they evinced little affection for either bishops or king, they spoke feelingly of the Book of Common Prayer as England's strongest bulwark against popery. Threading its way through many petitions was a vein of panic at the threat to the social order posed by iconoclastic disruptions and irreverent behaviour in church. Signatories numbered from a few hundred to many thousands. The six counties of North Wales claimed 30,000 hands to their petition, calling themselves undivided churchmen 'who cannot without some trembling entertain a thought of change'.[53] It was not only local leaders who spoke up for the established Church; support came from a cross-section of society. Indeed,

---

[51] Gardiner (ed.), *Const. Docs.*, 137–8.

[52] John Rushworth, *Historical Collections* (hereafter Rushworth, *Hist. Coll.*), Vol, 3 (1692 edn), 172.

[53] Judith Maltby, *Prayerbook and People in Elizabethan and Early Stuart England*, 86–7, 109, 242, 244.

one critic of the Devon petitioners derided them as mainly 'hedgers at the hedge, plowmen at the plow, threshers in the barns'.[54]

The message of these petitions was not one that the leaders of parliament wanted to hear. Sometimes they attempted to frighten the petitioners in order to deter others from imitating their example. Thus the four MPs who promoted the Kent petition of March 1642 were arrested and had impeachment proceedings slapped on them.[55]

Besides bringing down a large number of the king's counsellors, and waging war against the bishops and liturgy of the established Church, the leaders in parliament effected a peaceful constitutional revolution. First, they swept away ship money, forced loans and any other forms of non-parliamentary taxation. Next they introduced legislation for the summoning of parliament at least once every three years, and forbidding the dissolution of the present parliament without its consent. Then at different times they abolished the prerogative courts: High Commission, Star Chamber and Wards. The judicial powers of the privy council, the council in the north and the council in the marches were suppressed. Feudal finance in the form of knighthood fines, forest fines, wardships and purveyance, was abolished. By these fiscal measures England became the first European country to complete the abolition of feudalism and enshrine the unfettered right to private property. All these elements of the constitutional revolution received the king's assent.

Members of the 'Junto' (as the ruling group at Westminster soon came to be known) now moved to consolidate their gains by getting their hands on the levers of power. With the aim of placating them Charles agreed to several 'bridge-appointments' – the Earl of Bedford as Lord Treasurer, John Pym as Chancellor of the Exchequer, and Oliver St John as Solicitor-General. He hoped that in return they would rescue the Crown from bankruptcy. But after Bedford's sudden death from smallpox in May 1641 the Junto failed to agree on measures to overhaul royal finances. As Conrad Russell astutely observes, if it had been Charles I rather than Bedford who died in May 1641 civil war would have been almost impossible to imagine.[56]

Distrust between the king and the Junto continued to mount during the spring and summer of 1641. The Junto goaded the king by their continued

[54] Quoted in Ibid., 96.

[55] Judith Maltby, 'Approaches to the study of religious conformity in late Elizabethan and early Stuart England: with special reference to Cheshire and the diocese of Lincoln' (PhD thesis, Cambridge University), 166–7. The impeachments were later dropped.

[56] Russell, *Causes of the English Civil War*, 211.

support of the Covenanters, their withholding of royal revenues, and their aggressive stance towards the queen. When Charles announced his intention of visiting Scotland mistrust was screwed a notch higher. Some MPs feared that he was going to rally both the English and Scottish armies for an attack on parliament. In June he had already attempted to sound out his officers about the feasibility of bringing the army down to London to control the turbulent populace.[57] In the event it came to nothing since the officers in the north rebuffed the royal advances. At the same time Charles was negotiating through his wife for papal financial support.

In this atmosphere of rising tension and mistrust John Pym put a series of resolutions known as the Ten Propositions, before both houses. Among the most provocative were those asking for the disbandment of the armies, for the king's journey to Scotland to be delayed, and for ministerial responsibility to parliament. Other propositions demanded the removal of Catholics, both from Court and from attendance on the queen. The two houses adopted them virtually without dissent.

After giving way on some minor points Charles rejected the Ten Propositions, and in mid-August departed for Scotland. Once there he was able to reach an agreement with the representatives of his northern kingdom. The Scottish army was paid off, withdrawn from England and disbanded. In return Charles guaranteed that English or Irish troops would not be deployed against Scotland without the consent of the English parliament. But he threw away whatever goodwill he might have gained from these concessions by furtively working to build up a royalist party in Scotland. In October he was disastrously implicated in the so-called 'Incident', which was nothing less than an attempt by royalist agents to arrest and possibly murder Argyll and Hamilton.[58] Why Hamilton, hitherto his chief agent in Scotland? The subtlety of Hamilton's political manoeuvring had induced Charles to believe that his previously loyal servant was guilty of treason. The exposure of the plot completely discredited him in Covenanter eyes. On the day (27 October) when news arrived of the insurrection in Ireland Charles headed out for an afternoon of golf.[59] This

---

[57] The conspiracy would not come to light until November: *The Journal of Sir Simonds D'Ewes*, ed. Willson Havelock Coates, 155–8.

[58] Beinecke Lib., Osborn MSS 76.12.3 (Howard of Escrick Papers), Captain William Stewart's deposition (10 October 1641); Scott, *Politics and War*, 29.

[59] Scottish National Archives (hereafter SNA), GD 406/1 (Hamilton Papers), 1447 (Vane to Hamilton), cited in John Joseph Scally, 'The political career of James, third Marquis and first Duke of Hamilton (1606–1649) to 1643' (PhD thesis, Cambridge University), 313.

nonchalance in the face of a major political crisis confirmed many Scots in their suspicion that Charles's hand was somehow in the uprising. When he then asked for Scottish help in suppressing the uprising the Scots answered that they must have the consent of the English parliament before they could intervene.

In this seriously compromised position Charles proceeded to give away the store. He agreed that the acts of parliament of June 1640 could be published without having been touched by his sceptre. In other words, bills no longer required royal assent in order to become law. He also agreed to the removal of most royalists from his Scottish privy council. Finally, he accepted the creation of four commissions, and heaped rewards on recent enemies in the hope of purchasing their neutrality. The Earl of Argyll was elevated to a marquess; Alexander Leslie became Earl of Leven; the lawyer Archibald Johnston of Wariston was knighted. But royalists who had risked their lives and squandered their fortunes for the king got neither reward nor thanks. Still the Covenanters did not feel secure in the concessions they had extorted from him. They were sure that if Charles ever got the upper hand against his English parliament he would then try to overthrow the Covenanters in Scotland. It was this appreciation of the interdependence of events in the two kingdoms that drew the Covenanters to the conclusion that their political safety lay ultimately in a confederal union with England. This became the chief item on their agenda for the next three years.[60]

Meanwhile in England Sir Henry Vane the younger was kept informed by the parliamentary commissioners in Edinburgh about the constitutional advances being made there. On 20 October the Westminster parliament resumed sitting after a six-week recess. Supporters of the king seemed to be gaining ground until the political terrain was transformed by the news of rebellion in Ireland, followed by Sir Phelim O'Neill's shocking claim that the insurgents had a commission from the king for their rising. Even though the 'commission' was almost certainly a forgery, the Junto at Westminster claimed it as the irrefutable argument for excluding the king from the command of the army that was to put down the rebellion.

Pym chose this moment of almost unbearable tension to introduce into the Commons a 'Grand Remonstrance' cataloguing the abuses of Charles's government ever since his accession to the throne in 1625. Chief villains in this sorry tale of misgovernment were 'Jesuited Papists' and 'Jesuited counsels'. The Remonstrance called for an end to the 'exorbitant power' of

---

[60] Stevenson, *Scottish Revolution*, 234, 239–42.

'prelates' and a thorough reformation of religion. In future royal appoint-ments should go only to those in whom 'the parliament may have cause to confide'.[61] This of course was a concession which Charles had already yielded in Scotland, but which he had no intention of yielding in England. After a furious debate the Remonstrance was finally passed by eleven votes (159:148) at 2 a.m. on 23 November. So frayed were MPs' tempers that some took their sheathed swords out of their belts and made ready to draw them. The near-resort to violence reflected the radical, divisive nature of the Remonstrance. It trashed the Book of Common Prayer; it pretended to be an address to the king, when in fact it was an inflammatory appeal to the public; its sponsors made no attempt to seek the peers' concurrence. The king's friends were appalled by the subsequent decision to print and distribute the Remonstrance. Kentish MP Edward Dering, previously a critic of the bishops, spoke for many when he said that he 'did not dream that we should remonstrate downwards, tell stories to the people, and talk of the king as of a third person'.

The king still had influential friends in the City of London. To celebrate his return from Scotland the lord mayor and aldermen threw a lavish ban-quet at Guildhall on 25 November. On that day the streets of the City rang with shouts of 'God bless and long live King Charles and Queen Mary'. The power of the men responsible for the banquet would soon be ended, however, by the municipal elections a month later which saw radicals replace conservatives in almost every ward. The king's popularity in the City was even more evanescent, being quickly blown away by swelling popular horror at the stories emanating from Ireland about the massacres in Ulster and the spread of the insurgency to Leinster and Munster. Pym and the Junto took advantage of the Irish crisis to widen their assault on Charles's authority. At the end of the month an armed crowd filled up Palace Yard shouting 'no bishops!' By December the capital was almost out of control. On the eleventh a delegation of London merchants and tradesmen delivered a petition to the Commons supporting Pym's policies. It purported to bear 20,000 signatures.[62] There were many other petitions along similar lines in late 1641 and 1642.

A small knot of radical magistrates – Aldermen Isaac Penington, John Ven and John Fowke, and Captain Randall Mainwaring – were prominent in organizing these petitions, which were also promoted by radical Puritan clergy. Also prominent were Star Chamber victims Sir Richard Wiseman

---

[61] Gardiner, *Const. Docs.*, 205.
[62] *The Citizens of London's Humble Petition* (11 December 1641), E 180/16.

and John Lilburne. Signatures were probably collected by ward committees that sat in taverns and 'in divers private houses in London'. Puritans appear to have sought minor offices of authority in the wards and parishes. When the time came they were able to exploit these offices to promote a radical agenda. In the panic-stricken weeks after the news of the Irish rebellion hit the capital canvassing would have been easy, for refusal to sign a petition could mark a man as a secret papist or papist sympathizer.[63]

By late December large crowds of apprentices and 'poor artificers' were demonstrating menacingly on a daily basis outside parliament, their main demand being the exclusion of bishops from the House of Lords. As the French agent observed 'If this were any other nation, I believe the city would be in flames and blood flowing within 24 hours.'[64] At the end of the month bishops were forcibly prevented from taking their seats and several demonstrators were injured. At the same time growing numbers of armed gentlemen were gathering near Whitehall Palace to express their support for the king. It was during these 'December Days' that the terms roundhead and cavalier came into common parlance to designate the two groups who frequently clashed near the gates of Whitehall: on one side royalist gentlemen; on the other, parliamentarian apprentices and other young men from the City, who typically wore their hair cut short. The use of these labels was an implicit recognition that there was a class dimension to the more fundamental conflict over religion and the constitution.

The steady crescendo of street violence convinced the king that the capital was sliding into anarchy. His determination to halt the slide led him into a major political blunder. On 3 January 1642, obsessed by mounting rumours that the Junto was about to impeach Henrietta Maria for her role in the 'popish plot', he issued articles of high treason against six members: Pym, Holles, Sir Arthur Hesilrige, John Hampden, William Strode and Viscount Mandeville (the future Earl of Manchester) accusing them, among other things, of encouraging the Scots to invade England. Few in London or in parliament seemed to care that this last charge was quite true. On 4 January Charles burnt his bridges by personally leading a party of armed men to the House of Commons to arrest the five members of the lower house. It was an unheard-of assault on parliamentary privilege, and it ended in fiasco. Alerted ahead of time, the five fled the Commons by boat – only minutes ahead of the king – and took refuge in the City. When he arrived in the chamber Charles demanded that the five members be turned

---

[63] Brian Manning, *The English People and the English Revolution*, 121–2.
[64] National Archives (hereafter NA), PRO31/3 (Baschet transcripts), Vol. 73, fo. 5v.

over to him. He was met with blank silence. Scrutinizing the hostile assemblage for several minutes he failed to identify the culprits. He asked the Speaker where they were. The normally timorous William Lenthall fell on his knee and cried, 'May it please your Majesty, I have neither eyes to see, nor tongue to speak in this place, but as this House is pleased to direct me, whose servant I am here.'[65] The Speaker, hitherto the servant of the king, in this moment and henceforth, became the servant of the House of Commons. Charles concluded disconsolately that 'all the birds are flown', and retreated amid shouts of 'Privilege! Privilege!'. The next day the Commons adjourned to Guildhall in order to avoid further royal intrusion. In effect they had thrown themselves on the mercy of the people of London. At this decisive juncture the people chose to back parliament rather than the king. When he turned up the next day to explain himself to a meeting of Common Council, one group cried 'God bless the king', while another shouted 'Privileges of parliament!' But when he walked through the outer hall, filled with lower-class people, the unanimous cry was 'privileges of parliament!'.[66] The next night (6–7 January) no one slept a wink in the City out of fear of a cavalier counterattack. The trained bands stood to attention in their full arms, while thousands more turned out with halberds, swords, clubs and whatever other weapons they could lay their hands on. The gates of the City were bolted shut, portcullises lowered and chains put across the streets to stop the cavaliers. Women built barricades out of furniture, and boiled water 'to throw on the cavaliers'. But none materialized, so towards morning the citizens retired to bed. Three days later (10 January), judging his family to be in jeopardy from the mob, the king packed up and took them all to Hampton Court, a few miles upstream on the Thames.

Even the royalist historian Clarendon acknowledged that the whole episode could not have been a greater disaster. Public indignation was 'great and general', and the king's conduct severely undermined his 'dignity . . . majesty and safety.'[67] Lord Digby was blamed for having counselled the escapade in the first place. The members of the Junto were confirmed in their conviction that the king would stop at nothing to destroy them, while Charles, by vacating the capital, handed it over to his enemies. For the next seven years parliament would benefit immensely from its control of the vast arsenal, treasurehouse and store of manpower

[65] Gardiner, *Hist.*, Vol. 10, 140.
[66] Manning, *The English People and the English Revolution*, 161.
[67] Clarendon, *Hist.*, Bk 4, para. 193.

that was London. While disaffection with the parliamentary cause would steadily increase over those years, Charles was never able to reverse the precipitate and unthinking surrender of the capital to his enemies.

The ill-fated attempt to arrest the five Commons ringleaders marks the final, total breakdown of trust between Charles and the parliamentary Junto. It is also the effective beginning of the war between king and parliament, although the official declaration lay another eight months in the future.[68] On 11 January the MPs returned to Westminster, with the five Commons members in their midst, to the huzzahs of the crowd. On that same day 4,000 men from Buckinghamshire, perhaps the most radical county in England, marched on Westminster. They tendered a petition protesting against the slur cast on their MP John Hampden, and offered to place themselves at the defence of parliament.

While both sides silently jockeyed for military advantage in the run-up to the war, there was a very noisy paper war for the allegiance of the great numbers of undecided people. This war for public opinion was waged through the medium of petitions, pamphlets, proclamations, declarations and ordinances. Both sides were anxious not to forfeit the constitutional high ground. Between December 1641 and the formal outbreak of war in August 1642 all but two of the English counties, as well as Wales, sent in petitions supporting parliament. Many petitions had similar wording, were submitted around the same time, and may well have been orchestrated from the centre. There is little doubt, however, that the petitioners subscribed to the positions advanced.[69] Typically a petition would originate in more or less formal meetings of the gentry, with close cooperation between the organizers and the shire knights in preparing the ground, while clergy were often active in collecting signatures. Fear of popery, which acquired an urgent immediacy from the Irish rebellion and the arrival of boatloads of refugees in London and the western ports, was the dominant theme running through the petitions. They were also a response to the Protestation of May 1641 and the Grand Remonstrance of November. They echoed these manifestoes in demanding the suppression of popery, the removal of evil counsellors and the completion of the unfinished business of Reformation.

In Anthony Fletcher's words, 'the petitions present incontrovertible evidence of the hold parliament had obtained on the nation's mind. In this sense it was in 1642 that the representative body of the nation finally came

---

[68] Clarendon, *Hist.*, Bk 4, para. 203.
[69] Walter, *Understanding Popular Violence*, 291, 320.

into its own.'[70] There was only one difference between the petitioners and the Junto at Westminster: the petitioners were not zealous for war. Indeed, the hope they expressed was that it could be staved off. Far from expressing enmity towards the king, 'they were suffused with loyalty to Charles as well as parliament'.[71] Similarly, many peers cooperated with the Junto, not in order to promote a war, but to disable the king from starting a war against the Commons. Many who would soon accept office under the Militia Ordinance apparently did so in the hope that they could ensure no belligerent use was made of the militia where they held sway. Several leading peers were in these months pursuing 'a sort of conciliarism which would enable the peers and great officers to continue government in the king's name unless or until he came to his senses and tried to reach an agreement with his opponents'.[72]

Regardless of the peaceful intentions of most petitioners, the Junto used their expressions of support to push their own much more radical programme. At the end of January, when Pym presented massive petitions from London and three neighbouring counties, he exploited the occasion to launch a hard-line attack on the king. Charles, he insinuated, was to blame for the war with Scotland, the rebellion in Ireland, the corruption of religion, the suppression of liberty in England and the subversion of parliament. Many of the rebel Irish leaders had been allowed back into Ireland 'by His Majesty's immediate warrant'.[73]

The king did not take these attacks lying down. In response to the Junto's campaign to portray him as a traitor to his own country, he used the pens of backers such as Edward Hyde, Sir John Culpeper and Viscount Falkland to paint himself as a reasonable, flexible man, dedicated to upholding Protestantism, English liberties and the ancient constitution. It was the skilfull propaganda of these royalists that helped to win for the king a party with which to fight the civil war. To begin with, the declarations issued in his name took all possible credit for the many concessions he had already granted, especially in the legislation of 1641. They went on to express his total condemnation of the Irish rebellion, and his devotion to the laws of the land, which they claimed were now being violated by parliament. They represented him as the defender of order against lawless tumults and seditious petitions. Above all they repeatedly affirmed his

---

[70] See Anthony Fletcher, *The Outbreak of the English Civil War*, 222.

[71] Ibid., 226.

[72] Russell, *Fall of the British Monarchies*, 472.

[73] Ibid., 469.

commitment to the true Protestant religion, as embodied in the Church of England.[74]

This propaganda resonated with what many people were thinking by the spring of 1642. Witness the Kentish petition, crafted by the former parliamentarian Edward Dering in March. The most passionate passage in the petition is its defence of the clergy and liturgy of this ancient church, celebrated

by the piety of holy bishops and martyrs who composed it, established by the supreme law of this land, attested and approved by the best of all foreign divines, confirmed with subscription of all the ministers of this land, a clergy as learned and able as any in the Christian world, enjoyed and with holy love embraced, by the most and best of all the laity, that this holy exercise of our religion may, by your authority, be enjoyed, quiet and free from interruptions, scorns, prophanations, threats and force of such men, who daily do deprave it, and neglect the use of it in divers churches, in despite of the laws established.[75]

In its combination of devotion to a 'traditional' Church and to the rule of law, the Petition was, as Russell puts it, 'the essence of what was to become the Royalist cause'.[76]

The king was much less successful on the legislative than on the propaganda front. At the end of January he committed his second major strategic blunder within a month by summoning fourteen of the lords to attend him at Windsor. The departure of these and other peers lost the king his majority in the upper house. In short order the depleted chamber passed the Bishops Exclusion Bill (5 February), which had been previously bottled up there for several weeks, and the Impressment Bill to raise troops for Ireland. Charles ratified both of them, but he rejected the Militia bill that followed hard on their heels (15 February). The Militia bill empowered parliament to appoint the commanders of the army without reference to the king. It was a straightforward attempt to wrest from his hands the most fundamental attribute of sovereignty, the power of the sword. When Charles balked, the houses re-passed the bill as an ordinance, stipulating that even without the king's assent it had the force of law.

People did not remain passive as the nation descended into the vortex of civil war. Protesting against the higher taxation already being levied, the

---

[74] Austin Woolrych, *Britain in Revolution, 1625–1660,* 220–1.
[75] *House of Lords Journal* (hereafter *LJ*), Vol. 4, 677.
[76] Russell, *Fall of the British Monarchies,* 499.

gentry of Somerset urged the king to bring an end to 'the misunderstandings between him and parliament'.[77] Movingly the gentry of Yorkshire spoke of the 'piercing anguish of our souls' and implored the king and parliament to be reconciled with each other. Their greatest worry was the menace of popery represented by the Irish rising.[78] Such anxieties were expressed all around the country.

On 2 June the houses once again threw down the gauntlet in the shape of the Nineteen Propositions. Far from being a negotiating position, the document was an ultimatum. All privy councillers were henceforth to be approved by the two houses; those not approved were to be immediately removed. Sixteen of the most senior officers of state were to be chosen with the approval of both houses. The king was to accept the Triennial Act and the Militia Ordinance. He was also to enforce more rigorously the existing laws against 'Jesuits, priests & popish recusants', and to grant a full pardon to the six members. Most insultingly of all, he was to turn over the education of his children to Protestant tutors nominated by parliament.

A fortnight later Charles issued his answer to the Nineteen Propositions. Drafted by Viscount Falkland and Sir John Culpeper, it was a propaganda masterpiece. What the houses were demanding, the king declared, amounted to 'a total subversion of the fundamental laws and [the] excellent constitution of this kingdom'. He then solemnly pledged to defend the present system of 'regulated monarchy', to uphold the rule of law, and thereby to prevent the 'eternal factions and dissensions . . . [the] dark, equal chaos of confusion' into which parliament's demands threatened to plunge the nation.[79]

While singing this melody of peace and sweet reasonableness, Charles, like parliament, was strengthening the sinews of war for the conflict both knew was inevitable. It is to these military preparations that we now turn.

[77] Beinecke Library, Osborn shelves, fb 157/1.

[78] Beinecke Library, Osborn shelves, fb 156/9v (John Browne Papers); see also Bodl., MS Tanner 64, fo. 113.

[79] His Maiesties Answer to the XIX Propositions of Both Houses of Parliament (Oxford, 1642 [Wing C2121]), 23, 26, 28. See also David Smith, A History of the Modern British Isles 1603–1707, 126; David Smith, Constitutional Royalism and the Search for Settlement, c. 1640–1649, 90–1.

CHAPTER 4

Building and fuelling the machinery of war: recruitment, finance, logistics

War in England: preliminary manoeuvres, January–August 1642

Both sides now accelerated their preparations for the armed conflict that all knew was inevitable. We have seen that trust had broken down irrevocably with the king's attempt on the six members and his subsequent flight from London. Shortly afterwards he had secretly appointed the Earl of Newcastle Governor of Hull and sent Captain Legge, his agent in the Army Plot, to secure its magazine and ensure the citizens' obedience. Hull was the depot for most of the weapons and artillery that had been amassed for the war with Scotland – enough to arm 16,000 men. But the Commons got wind of the design and ordered Sir John Hotham to take possession of Hull with the Yorkshire trained bands. It was a striking example of the Commons's readiness to give direct orders that plainly infringed on the royal prerogative. At the same time the politically reliable Philip Skippon was ordered to place a guard on the Tower of London, and the great naval base at Portsmouth was secured. On 14 January the MP for Cambridge, Oliver Cromwell, asked for a committee 'to put the kingdom in a posture of defence'.[1] In late January another radical MP, John Hampden, moved that the Tower and other forts, as well as the trained bands of every county, should be put in the charge of men whom

[1] W.C. Abbott (ed.), *The Writings and Speeches of Oliver Cromwell*, Vol, 1, 149.

parliament could trust. London, Hull and Portsmouth: within a month the kingdom's most strategic strongholds had been secured for parliament.

Next came the struggle over the Militia Ordinance, with the king declaring that he would never give up the power of the sword, and the two houses voting that the country was in imminent danger and that the ordinance 'ought to be obeyed by the fundamental laws of the kingdom'. On the same day (15 March) they claimed the right of directing the armed forces by sea as well as by land. On 8 April Charles announced that he intended to go to Ireland in person with a force armed from Hull. The Commons at once ordered the contents of the Hull magazine shipped to the Tower of London to keep them out of the king's hands, but this time they were blocked by the Lords. The struggle for Hull paved the way for the first open military clash between king and parliament. On 23 April Charles attempted in person to claim possession of the arsenal, having been stung into action by the scornful words of his wife. When he approached the town at the head of 300 horse, Hotham, in a state of fretful trepidation, closed the gates of the city, raised the drawbridges, and came out on the wall to tell the king that he could not enter. There was a brief argument, with Charles denouncing Hotham as a traitor and his followers calling out to the garrison within to kill Hotham and throw him over the wall. No one took up the invitation, so, angry and crestfallen, the king backed off. He had better luck at Newcastle-on-Tyne, where at the end of June the Earl of Newcastle made himself master of the town. With Newcastle came control of the Durham coalfield, and the option of either strangling London by denying it fuel, or profiting from the revenues of the trade. Now too he had a port on the east coast where he might receive supplies from Holland. Public opinion in Yorkshire seemed to be moving in his direction. Early in the summer upwards of 40,000 freeholders and farmers of the county gathered on Heworth Moor, close to York. Charles rode among them, and copies of his appeal for loyalty were read out. Disappointingly, no definite pledge of support emerged from the county, and the day ended in confusion.

The navy

Of far greater significance than control of the north was the navy. During the previous decade Charles had overseen a major ship-building programme which had added several powerful vessels to the fleet. What he had failed to notice was that few of those who manned the fleet sympathized with his policy of benevolent neutrality towards Spain. In the spring of 1642 the Earl of Northumberland, who had been a less than impressive lord high admiral, begged to be relieved of his commission, pleading ill health. Without consulting the king the House of Lords persuaded Northumberland to nominate the Earl of Warwick in his place. Charles was outraged, for Warwick's Puritan and parliamentarian sympathies were well known. Charles tried to replace him with Sir John Pennington, but parliament outmanoeuvred him by ordering a phoney investigation into Pennington's conduct. The king backed down, fondly believing that he could get rid of Warwick whenever he liked. Tough, quick-witted, and popular with the seamen, Warwick acted with energy and decision to take control of the navy for parliament. He then intercepted a vessel bearing arms from the queen in Holland. When in late June the king attempted to relieve Warwick of his commission and replace him with the 70-year-old Pennington, parliament rushed through an ordinance confirming Warwick as admiral, and the higher officers of the navy recognized his authority. The five ships that held out for the king were soon brought to heel. As Clarendon later observed, 'this loss of the whole navy was of unspeakable ill consequence to the king's affairs', and made a greater impression on Charles than any of his later misfortunes.[2] Clarendon was right. Winning control of the navy in 1642 was not only a military, but a financial coup for Parliament. It guaranteed that the bulk of the customs revenues would flow into parliamentary, not royal coffers. If Charles had hung onto the navy he could have freely brought in supplies from the continent. He could also have blockaded the Thames, cutting off deliveries of food and fuel to the capital, and choking its economy. In such circumstances parliament would have had little choice but to sue for peace.[3] As it was, a king without a fleet cut a poor figure in the chancelleries of Europe.

Recruitment

England

In a country where most of the population deplored the coming war, and wished to fight for neither side, how did king and parliament recruit the armies they needed to wage their struggle – not only recruit about 140,000 men between them, but arm, pay and supply them as well? The summer

---

[2] Clarendon *Hist.*, Bk 5, paras. 377, 382.
[3] Bernard Capp, 'The war at sea', in John Kenyon and Jane Ohlmeyer (eds), *The Civil Wars: A Military History of England, Scotland, and Ireland 1638–1660*, 157.

and early autumn of 1642 witnessed intensive efforts to raise the forces to wage war. Each side deployed quasi-legal instruments, and each tried to thwart the recruitment campaign of the other. The king resorted to a medieval instrument, the feudal Commission of Array. Inscribed in Latin on a parchment roll, and stamped with the Great Seal, it empowered the leading men of each county or city to take charge and arm their locality for the king. Mistrusting many of his subjects, Charles committed the tactical blunder of bypassing the system of lord and deputy lieutenants that had been established in the reign of Elizabeth. In several counties he disarmed the trained bands, and attempted to confiscate their weapons and ammunition for his national armies. By doing so he belied his protestations of constitutionalism and earned the enmity of many. Only 11 counties responded positively to the Commission of Array. They ran in a long strip on the western side of England, from Cornwall in the south, through Monmouthshire and the Welsh marches to Cheshire, Lancashire and Yorkshire.[4] A vivid glimpse of how the commission worked when it was successful comes from Myddle in Shropshire. The commissioner called all local people to a meeting on Myddle Hill, where a recruiting agent 'with a paper in his hand and three or four soldiers' pikes stuck upright in the ground by him' offered volunteers four shillings and four pence a week. To agricultural workers this was an attractive sum, and 20 men from three villages signed on the spot.[5]

In 12 counties the commissions were scotched or abandoned.[6] Other counties, such as Worcestershire, Gloucestershire, Devon, Warwickshire, Cheshire, Leicestershire, Norfolk, Derbyshire, Hampshire and Rutland, were sharply divided. The Worcestershire quarter-sessions and assizes for example, see-sawed back and forth during the summer, the sessions first going royalist in response to pressure from the local gentry, and the assizes later swinging back to the parliamentary camp after intense lobbying by the county MPs.[7] The defects of the Commission of Array often furnished the pretext for disobeying the royal command. In Cornwall, Robert Bennett, a man of Puritan piety, and a future parliamentarian colonel, justified his initial disobedience with the argument that the commission was 'set on foot without the advice and consent of parliament . . .' What made his disobedience easier was the parliamentary order of 20 June

---

[4] Fletcher, *Outbreak of the English Civil War*, 356–7.
[5] Richard Gough, *The History of Myddle*, ed. David Hey, 71.
[6] Fletcher, *Outbreak of the English Civil War*, 361.
[7] Ian Roy, 'The royalist army in the first civil war' (D.Phil. thesis, University of Oxford), 18ff.

to sheriffs and justices of the peace to arrest all who tried to put the Commission into effect.[8] Indeed, strenuous exertions were made to undo the royalists' work, by intercepting letters and suppressing the publication or reading of the Commission of Array or the proclamation summoning loyal subjects to arms. Thus the inhabitants of Buckinghamshire and adjacent counties were active in frustrating the attempts by the Earl of Northampton to remove the county ordnance from them for the king's use. Money collected for the king at York was seized and diverted to Guildhall. A large crowd in Nottinghamshire stopped Lord Newark, the sheriff and John Lord Byron and Sir Nicholas Byron from making off with the county magazine. A royalist justice of the assize confided to Secretary Nicholas that Devon and Dorset were 'much possessed with the illegality of the Commissions of Array', mainly, it seemed, because of 'the unlimited power' it entrusted to the commissioners.[9]

The king did not just rely on Commissions of Array; he issued proclamations 'requiring the aid and assistance of all his subjects'; and he handed out commissions to individual colonels. Lord Paget was typical. Like most aristocrats he reached into his own pocket for the money to finance his regiment, and found some of his recruits among his own tenants. He then went further afield, to Lichfield and other places in the south and west of his native county of Staffordshire, to raise men. For his captains he chose a mixture of younger sons of Staffordshire gentry, and gentry from other counties. By this ramshackle process he put together a regiment within a month.[10] Thus, if few men turned out at Nottingham on 22 August when Charles raised the royal standard there, the situation was very much better by mid-October. When he mustered his forces at Bridgnorth in the west of England 6,000 foot appeared, along with 2,000 horse and 1,500 dragoons (mounted infantry). At the battle of Edgehill, less than two weeks later, the royalist army numbered probably around 15,000 men – 2,800 horse, 11,000 foot, 1,000 dragoons, and perhaps 100 in the train of artillery. The parliamentary army under the Earl of Essex was much the same size – 2,150 horse, 12,000 foot, 720 dragoons.

In addition to dozens of country gentlemen and minor nobility, great magnates such as the marquesses of Worcester and Hertford, and the earls of Newcastle, Derby and Carnarvon, played their part. Nor should we overlook the loyal clergy. In 1641 and early 1642 they had served their

---

[8] Folger Lib., MS X.d.483 (Bennett Papers), fos. 4, 5.
[9] *CSPD, 1641–43*, 367–8, 375–6.
[10] Ronald Hutton, *Royalist War Effort 1642–1646*, 22–3.

political apprenticeship by promoting petitions for episcopacy and resisting the Protestation of parliament. They then transferred their energies to
mobilizing the royalist armies. In some localities they were such effective
recruiting agents that it would be only a slight exaggeration to label them
the storm troopers of royalism. Public relations blunders by parliament,
aided by the perceived moderation of the king, also helped recruitment.
When in September 1642 parliament declared that the king's active supporters would pay for their delinquency by having their estates confiscated
it gave a fillip to the royalist recruitment drive.[11]

On the other hand, the presence of high numbers of Catholics in the
northern royalist armies furnished a banquet for parliamentary propagan-
dists. It would have been hard for the king to snub a group of subjects
who for the most part were passionately loyal to him, which is why he
responded favourably to a petition from Lancashire Catholics to be allowed
to arm themselves. According to parliamentary accusations the Earl of
Newcastle's army was half Catholic in December 1642. Exaggerated as
this accusation doubtless was, Peter Newman suggests that of the officers
at least one-third were Catholic, a much higher percentage than the
Catholic share of the population in the north.[12] Elsewhere the Catholicism
of certain commanders acted as a brake to royalist recruiting. The Welsh
of Monmouthshire for example, refused to rise for Lord Herbert, because
'they had rather perish than be under the power of a papist'.[13]

The armies of both sides were like mushrooms: shooting up almost
overnight, and then shrivelling away almost as quickly. Citing numbers
can give a misleading sense of precision, since the size of all armies fluctuated week by week. With this caveat in mind, the following figures are
offered as no more than a rough guide to the size of the different royalist
armies. Charles's main army, based at Oxford for most of the war, peaked
at 15,000 at Edgehill; most of the time it was under 10,000. In the north
the Earl of Newcastle mobilized an impressively large army, drawn chiefly
from Northumberland, Durham and Yorkshire. It grew steadily to reach
19,000 (3,000 of whom were cavalry) by the summer of 1643. At the
opposite end of the country Sir Ralph (later Lord) Hopton raised a small
force of about 3,000 in Cornwall, Devon, Dorset and Somerset. In addition Colonel George Goring put together his own force of 5,000 foot and

[11] S.R. Gardiner, *History of the Great Civil War*, 4 vols (hereafter Gardiner *GCW*),
Vol. 1, 17–18.
[12] Roy, 'Royalist army', Vol. 1, 25; Peter Newman, 'The royalist armies in northern
England, 1642–1645' (PhD thesis, University of York), 10, 85.
[13] BL. Add. MS 18980 (Rupert Papers), fo. 42.

5,000 horse at Taunton, while in Wales Charles Gerard is reported to have recruited a field force of 2,000 foot and 700 horse. In addition the Earl of Derby sent significant numbers from Lancashire to the main army in Oxford.

During the winter of 1642–43 the Earl of Essex's army shrank from its Edgehill peak of 15,000 to a third that size. Yet by April 1643, when he advanced on Reading, it had swollen to 16,000 foot and 3,000 horse. With that garrison's capitulation one-third of Essex's men promptly departed. By July two-thirds of his army were reported sick, dead or missing. While the horse had remained fairly steady at 2,500, the foot had collapsed to only 3,000 able-bodied men.[14]

In East Anglia the Earl of Manchester was authorized to raise at first 14,000 and later 21,000 men. In reality his infantry, nearly all conscripted, never rose above 6,600, his dragoons 263, and his cavalry 4,000.[15] In Yorkshire Ferdinando Lord Fairfax managed to mobilize an army that – thanks to impressment – grew slowly from 900 in 1642 to 8,000 by early 1645.[16] Headquartered in Gloucester, Colonel Edward Massie's Western Brigade numbered some 6,000 when it was finally disbanded in the autumn of 1646. Finally the many provincial garrisons were manned by units ranging from a few dozen to – in the cases of Hull, Bristol, York, Newark, Reading, Gloucester, Newcastle and Newport Pagnell – a few thousand men.

Both sides received significant reinforcements from outside the kingdom. The king suffered a grave propaganda setback from his employment of French mercenaries, perhaps four regiments in all between 1643 and 1645.[17] The cease-fire or 'cessation of arms' in Ireland (September 1643) enabled the Marquess of Ormond to ship about 9,000 men from the king's Irish army.[18] The bulk of these troops were Protestants, while the Catholics who served tended to be of Old English stock; none of the officers was a Confederate catholic. Moreover, many of the Irish troops were stationed in Welsh garrisons, and took little part in active fighting.[19] By the spring of

[14] *LJ*, Vol. 6, 160.

[15] Clive Holmes, *The Eastern Association in the English Civil War*, 236.

[16] *LJ*, Vol. 6, 442; Jennifer Jones, 'The war in the north: the northern parliamentarian army in the English Civil War 1642–1645' (PhD thesis, York University [Toronto]), 415.

[17] Roy, 'Royalist army', 146.

[18] Stoyle, *Soldiers and Strangers*, 61, 210. Stoyle's figures are authoritative, and replace all previous estimates.

[19] Roy, 'Royalist army', 125, 160; Hutton, *Royalist War Effort*, 123–4, 148; Peter M. Darman, 'Prince Rupert of the Rhine: a study in generalship, 1642–1646 (M.Phil. thesis, University of York), 165; Peter Newman, *The Old Service: Royalist Regimental Colonels and the Civil War, 1642–1646*, 229.

1645 at any rate, there were only 1,200 Irish veterans left in England to bolster the royalist army. The opprobrium the king suffered from his importation of Irish troops cost him more than any benefit gained from their presence.

By contrast on the parliamentary side the Scots played a crucial role in the key battle of the civil war, Marston Moor. Early in 1644, 21,500 experienced Scots troops entered England under the Earl of Leven following a treaty negotiated the previous autumn. Because the Scots were Protestant, and had never been hated to the same degree as the Irish, parliament paid no discernible propaganda price for its importation of foreign troops. Parliament also profited from the technical expertise of a number of Dutch, Walloon and German officers and men whom it imported throughout the 1640s.

Scotland

In 1638, facing imminent war against England, the covenanting regime in Scotland recalled its mercenary veterans from the continent. Under the direction of Alexander Leslie, Earl of Leven, they imitated the Swedish model of recruitment by dividing the country into about 20 military districts, nominating colonels, authorizing the levying of troops, and establishing quotas by shire. Shire committees were appointed and ordered to report to the central government. The committees set the quotas for each burgh or parish, and supervised the collection of the 'cess' or taxation. Throughout the country clergy played a key role in listing men for military service. With a population only a fifth of England's to draw on, the Covenanters mobilized a remarkable number of soldiers over the following 12 years. In 1640 they fielded 24,000 men, rising to over 30,000 by 1644 – 10,000 under Major-General Robert Monro in Ireland and 21,500 under Leven in England. In the mid-1640s the Marquesses of Huntly and Montrose raised close to 6,000, mainly highland troops, to fight for the king. In 1648 the Engagers under the Duke of Hamilton raised a force of about 14,000 men, over the strenuous opposition of the covenanting clergy, to invade England on behalf of the king. By 1650 the Covenanters had thrown in their lot with Charles II, and mustered 16,000 foot and 7,000 horse to face the Cromwellian invasion of that year.[20]

[20] Edward Furgol, 'The civil wars in Scotland', in Kenyon and Ohlmeyer (eds), *The Civil Wars*, 42–4, 50, 51–3, 64–5.

Ireland

In Ireland the time-honoured fashion of recruitment was for grandees to summon their followers, tenants and kinsmen to arms. The Irish standing army, a Protestant force, numbered about 3,200 horse and foot at the time of the Catholic rising in October 1641. Led by the Earl (later Marquess) of Ormond until 1647, and aided by commanders of implacable ruthlessness such as Sir Charles Coote and Sir Henry Tichbourne, this army's numbers ranged up to 7,000, and received a fillip from the arrival of 2,600 foot from England in the winter of 1641–42. When in 1647 this 'Dublin' or Leinster army was taken over by Colonel Michael Jones on behalf of the Long Parliament, it grew even larger. After the 1641 rising the Protestant community outside Leinster had immediately rallied and begun raising troops to supplement the Dublin-based army. In Munster Richard Boyle, Earl of Cork, spent vast sums revamping local defences and buying guns and powder. He also lent money to local commanders, and raised and maintained two companies at his own expense. During the 1640s Protestant troop strength in Connacht and Munster combined fluctuated between 2,000 and 6,000, normally hovering around 4–5,000. They were commanded by Murrough O'Brien, Baron Inchiquin. In western Ulster Protestant landlords under the leadership of Sir William and Sir Robert Stewart raised the so-called 'Laggan army' which peaked at close to 11,000 troops in 1643, and never sank below 5,000 during the decade. They were strengthened by the 10,000 Scots brought over by Robert Monro in the spring and summer of 1642. Monro's force suffered steady attrition, falling to 3,500 by 1647. Overall, Protestant troop strength in Ireland ranged between 14,000 and 38,000 prior to the arrival of Cromwell in 1649.[21]

By December 1641 the Ulster insurgents had forged an alliance with the leading Old English lords of the Pale. By May the following year the Catholic Confederation had been formed, with a national assembly and a hierarchy of provincial and county councils. Each province was assigned its own army, in theory consisting of 6,000 foot and 400 horse, as well as a 'running army' of 2,000 foot and 200 horse. Each county was expected to recruit a quota of men between the ages of 18 and 60 for service. Local power-brokers were charged with drilling and maintaining 'trained bands' to be drawn upon in times of emergency. Men were recruited by a mixture

---

[21] Jane Ohlmeyer, 'The civil wars in Ireland', in Kenyon and Ohlmeyer (eds), *Civil Wars*, 75, 79–82; Scott Wheeler, 'Four armies in Ireland', in Ohlmeyer (ed.), *Ireland from Independence to Occupation*, 50.

of impressment and voluntary enlistment. The Leinster army under Colonel Thomas Preston mustered at just over 5,000 men in May 1646, but had dropped to under 4,000 by 1649. The Munster army under Theobald Lord Taaffe began at 2,000 in 1642, and grew as large as 8,000 by 1644. When Owen Roe O'Neill returned from Spain in the summer of 1642 he quickly recruited 8,000 troops in Ulster, and kept his army at close to this strength until a few months before his death in November 1649. In Connacht Ulick Burke, Earl of Clanricard, initially backed Ormond's Protestant royalist force, but later threw in his lot with the Confederation. His small force, which fluctuated between 2,000 and 6,000, did not play a major military role. Overall, Catholic troop strength in the four provinces ranged between 11,000 and 24,000 during the 1640s, reaching peak strength in 1646–47. Protestant troop levels at least matched and often exceeded those of the Confederacy for much of the decade. It is clear that at least 45,000 men served in arms in Ireland during the 1640s.[22]

Desertion plagued all armies, those of the royalists in particular. Early in the war many of the troops garrisoned in Dublin fled to Wales and England, while others deserted to the Confederates, sometimes on a large scale. In the parliamentary armies it became an increasingly familiar pattern for large numbers to depart after a major victory. This happened to Essex's after Reading, to Ferdinando Lord Fairfax's after Marston Moor, and to the New Model after Naseby. The New Model Army had been given a targeted strength of 22,000, besides officers in the spring of 1645. The goal was quickly reached, but after Naseby, where 17,000 were engaged, about 4,000 of the foot went home to dispose of their booty. Few returned. Large-scale victories were scarcer on the royalist side, but Prince Rupert did undergo the chastening experience of sizeable desertions after his capture of Bristol in 1643.[23]

Desertion, far more than death on the battlefield, was the reason for haemorrhaging of numbers on each side. Men frequently 'straggled' before they even saw their first military action. Once in the army, lack of pay, clothing or arms could cause them to steal away or refuse to march. Defeat in battle could trigger large-scale desertions, with many infantry immediately taking up service with the victorious enemy. At Lostwithiel in September 1644, for example, several thousand of Essex's infantry enlisted with the king after the articles of surrender were signed. Likewise, many of the king's infantry changed sides after Naseby. Not surprisingly, impressed

[22] Ohlmeyer, 'The civil wars in Ireland', 79–80, 82; Wheeler, 'Four armies in Ireland', 51.
[23] Darman, 'Prince Rupert', 117.

men were likelier to desert than volunteers. Another headache for the commanders of both sides was the reluctance of men to march outside their county or region. The king failed to persuade any of the Yorkshire gentry to follow him to Nottingham in the summer of 1642. Both Essex and Sir William Waller were unnerved by the cry 'home, home!' from the London trained bands who became increasingly anxious the further they found themselves from the capital – at Gloucester (September 1643) under Essex, for example, or Basing (November 1644), and Cropredy Bridge (29 June 1644) under Waller.

If the king was initially hampered by his decision to resort to an obsolete feudal instrument to raise troops, parliament was embarrassed by the illegality of its preparations to wage war against its sovereign. Early in the year it had drafted a bill setting up committees in each county to train the inhabitants for war, name deputy lieutenants and appoint officers. But the king refused his assent (although he did agree to a bill for conscripting soldiers for Ireland), so instead of a statute it was called an ordinance. Illegal though it was, the Militia Ordinance's strength was that it worked through the existing system of county trained bands, and did not attempt to confiscate local supplies of weapons and ammunition. The records of the county committee in Norfolk show that it met weekly to plan and organize the war effort in the county. The gentry were mobilized, and voluntary pledges of money, plate and horses for parliament were collected. Catholics and others who refused to contribute to the cause were disarmed and their horses confiscated.[24] In summoning the trained bands the gentry of many counties felt secure that they were performing a traditional, precautionary act, a minimum gesture in defence of their locality.[25] Transferring these men to a national army was another matter. When after several weeks few volunteers materialized, the militia committees, with the parliamentary Committee of Safety breathing down their necks, resorted to conscription. Even in Essex a 'great backwardness' was reported, and royalism and neutralism were troubling in their persistence. Fathers tried to protect their sons, and masters their servants from impressment. Marginalized and outcast individuals – the unemployed, strangers, the too-young and the too-old – were often shovelled into the army to make up county quotas.[26] By August, alarmed at the shortfall in recruits, parliament

[24] Bodl. MS Tanner 64, fos. 95–147, esp. fos. 95, 122.

[25] Fletcher, Outbreak of the English Civil War, 355–6.

[26] BL. Egerton MS 2646, fos. 261, 163, cited in William Cliftlands, 'The "well-affected" and the "country": politics and religion in English provincial society, c. 1640–1654' (PhD thesis, University of Essex), 20–1, 25–7.

diverted troops ostensibly raised for the universally approved expedition to Ireland, into the army being raised against the king. Money and clothing being collected for that expedition were similarly diverted.[27] Charles did not fail to exploit the propaganda opportunity handed to him by this parliamentary sharp practice.

In summary, all sides began the wars fondly believing that they could rely on volunteers to man their armies. The personal prestige of great men, the promise of steady pay, and the merits of the cause, whether defending king and Church, upholding the covenant, struggling for religious freedom, or combating popery, were thought to be inducement enough. When voluntarism failed every army resorted to coercion. The size of armies would shoot up after energetic recruitment drives, only to collapse just as quickly from desertion. Battle deaths and disease were a lesser cause of attrition. Armies were most vulnerable to desertion, not just after defeat, when many infantry crossed over to the enemy side, but also after victory, when soldiers crept away to find safe lodging for their plunder.

Finance

The first call upon the treasury of the Long Parliament after it had voted £300,000 for the 'brotherly assistance' to the Scots, was for money to fight the Irish insurgency. The London merchant community was approached for a loan. In November the City pledged £50,000; in December the Merchant Adventurers put up £100,000. In June 1641 the Livery Companies were induced to subscribe £100,000. In February 1642 a group of London merchants, later to be known as the Irish Adventurers, floated a scheme to raise £1 million in return for 2.5 million acres of Irish land. Less than a third of the hoped-for sum was raised in 1642 (£306,718), with more trickling in later. In the event much of the money, as well as the soldiers and arms, was diverted to parliament's war against the king.

Apart from misappropriating the funds raised to fight the Irish insurgency, parliament tried to finance its war against the king initially through loans and contributions. Between 1640 and 1645 the Drapers' Company lent £150,000. Sympathizers living in the United Provinces sent £31,215 during the years 1643–48. Parliament also sought to obtain money and materials by asking for contributions from the public at large. The Propositions, issued on 9 June 1642 called for money and plate, as well as horses

---

[27] *CSPD 1641–43*, 366, 374.

and arms. The response was impressive. In the years 1642–45 over £1 million was raised in this way. Parliament was nevertheless disappointed at the failure of some people to contribute. In May 1643 it imposed a tax of one-fifth on the personal estate and one-twentieth on the real estate of non-contributors.

It was not long before loans and voluntary contributions had run their course. Parliament then turned to taxation. From the beginning most taxes were assessed and collected locally through centrally appointed county committees. On 24 February 1643 the houses made their first order for a weekly assessment, initially for a three-month period. It replaced the so-called 'weekly pay', a voluntary subscription that had mostly dried up by the end of 1642. The new tax was assessed in the same way as Ship Money and the £400,000 tax for Ireland. Individuals were assessed by notables in their county, and the sums due were collected by the constables. John Morrill has likened the weekly assessment to the raising of a parliamentary subsidy of £70,000 every second week.[28] London and Westminster were assessed far more heavily than any other part of the kingdom – £11,000 per week. But taxpayers dragged their feet, with the consequence that it proved quite inadequate to pay the main field armies. It was renewed for a further three months in May and again for two months in July 1643. Owing to the explosive political situation in the capital London was wholly exempted from the tax for these final two months.

In the summer of 1643, desperate for new expedients to increase parliament's income, the Saye–Pym Junto introduced an excise tax, the first in English history, which became law on 22 July. Initially it was applied to non-essentials such as tobacco, alcohol, imported groceries and luxury goods. By January 1644 many other items had been added to the list including meat and salt. Between 1643 and 1645 the excise provided the main income for the field armies. Parliament frequently borrowed money against the future receipts of the excise. Between September 1644 and September 1646 well over £400,000 of future revenue was mortgaged in this fashion. Despite the fierce resentment it provoked, the excise continued throughout the interregnum, and has lasted to the present day under the name of a value-added tax (VAT).

In March 1643 the two houses approved the Sequestration Ordinance, providing for the seizure of enemy property. The task of administering confiscated land was carried out locally by agents appointed by county committees. Royalist 'delinquents' whose land was seized were allowed to retain up to a fifth of their estate so that their families would not be

---

[28] John Morrill, *Revolt of the Provinces: Conservatives and Radicals in the English Civil War 1630–1650*, 85.

destitute. In time more and more 'delinquents' were allowed to 'compound', meaning recover their estates in return for paying a fine equivalent to a certain number of years' rent, depending on the perceived seriousness of their 'malignity'.

The heavy shower of money from sequestration rents and composition fines was never enough to sate the ravenous maw of the military juggernaut parliament had set in motion. The next expedient was to sell off confiscated lands. In the autumn of 1646 the bishops' lands were put on the auction block, essentially to raise money to rid the Scottish army from English soil. Whatever was left over was devoted to reducing parliament's public faith debt. Next it was the turn of the cathedral estates, known as the dean and chapter lands, which were put up for sale in 1649 in order to finance the invasion of Ireland. In July of the same year the Crown lands were dumped onto the market in order to reduce the arrears of all the parliamentary armies, which stood at £2.8 million in January 1648. Finally, in 1651, it was the turn of the remaining 'delinquent' or royalist lands. They were offered for sale in order to fund the coming war with the United Provinces.

In 1645 the excise was overtaken as the leading instrument of military finance by the monthly assessment. Initially set at £53,000 a month in order to finance the New Model Army, the monthly assessment was later raised to £60,000, then £90,000, and ultimately £120,000 a month as it became the chief source of income for all the parliamentary armies. For much of this time £20,000 a month was also being levied to support the parliamentary war effort in Ireland, in addition to £21,000 a month in 1644 and 1645 for the Scottish army in England, and a further £10,000 a month levied on Yorkshire from December 1644 for Ferdinando Lord Fairfax's northern army. In June 1645 the northern associated counties were assessed £15,000 a month for the northern army.[29]

The assessment's strong point was that it was locally calculated and collected on the basis of up-to-date estimates of people's income. Its weakness lay in the tendency of officials to spend it locally, usually on garrison forces. The centrifugal pull of localism remained strong despite the best centralizing efforts of parliament. As a consequence field armies, even the New Model Army, often went underpaid. Again and again we read of officers on both sides reaching deep into their pockets to pay their men and prevent them from running away.[30] For every officer who grew rich from

[29] Jones, 'War in the north', 132–5. The counties of the Northern Association were Yorkshire, Lancashire, Westmorland, Cumberland, Durham, Northumberland and Nottinghamshire.

[30] An article is waiting to be written about the many officers on all sides who not only risked their lives but made great financial sacrifices on behalf of the cause they believed

the civil war there were at least ten who emerged poorer. This is the most eloquent testimony of all to the strength of commitment of the several thousand officers who fought on both sides.

TABLE 4.1 *The main sources of parliamentary revenue, 1643–59*

A: Taxation[31]

	£
Customs	5,251,195
Assessment	12,165,390
Excise	5,050,542
Total	22,467,127

B: Land sequestration and confiscation[32]

	£
Sequestration rents; delinquents' fines and compositions	1,830,364
Bishops' lands	676,387
Dean and chapter lands	1,170,000
Crown lands	1,434,249
Crown fee-farm rents	816,834
Royalist ('delinquent') lands	1,224,916
Total	7,152,750

in. Here are a few references: BL. Add. MS 18980, fo. 116 (Ralph Hopton); Bodl. MS Clarendon 22, fo. 37 (Alexander Popham); 22, fo. 36v (Hercules Langrish); Bodl. MSS Tanner 60, fo. 449 (John Birch); 61, fos. 289–90 (Scots officers in Ulster); 62, fo. 587 (Lionel Copley); 62, fo. 580 (John Barkstead + 8); 62, fo. 426 (Tho. Windham); 62, fo. 453 (Earl of Denbigh) 64, fo. 119v (Sir John Hotham); NLI MS 2310 (Ormonde Papers), 135 (Chas. Townley); Folger Lib. X.d.483 (Bennett Papers) (nos. 12,15) (Robt Bennett); Bulstrode Whitelocke, *Diary*, ed. Ruth Spalding, 149 (Rowland Wilson *et al.*); *House of Commons Journal* (hereafter *CJ*), Vol. 4, 675–6; *LJ*, Vol. 8, 512 (Edward Massie); Jones, 'War in the north', 137, 154–5, 159 (Capt. Hugh Bethell and numerous other officers in the northern army); Martyn Bennett, *The Civil Wars Experienced*, 106 (Sir Francis Bassett, Sir Richard Vyvyan). Another nail in the coffin of the materialist interpretation!

[31] James Scott Wheeler, 'English army finance and logistics 1642–1660' (PhD thesis, University of California, Berkley), 74. This splendid dissertation provides more information about parliamentary finance during the English Revolution than anything else written.

[32] The figures for rents, fines and compositions are drawn from NA, AO 1/361/15, 16 (Audit Office, Goldsmiths Hall, Treasurers' Accounts, Revenue from Sequestrated

Royalist finances[33]

Right from the start the king was hampered by several disadvantages in comparison with his foes. He could not tax in a parliamentary way. Because he had surrendered London he had forfeited the great bulk of the customs revenue, which was collected there. To set against these disadvantages he enjoyed the support of many of the richest landowners in the country, both nobles and gentry. During the early months of the war it was the hundreds of thousands of pounds furnished by men such as the marquesses of Worcester and Newcastle and the Earl of Derby, as well as the great merchant Sir Nicholas Crispe, that enabled him to put an army into the field. The universities also contributed £25,000. At the Restoration Worcester and Newcastle each asserted that he had been set back by almost a million pounds. Crispe had been ruined, ending his life in debtors' prison.

The king was able to tap other resources unavailable to parliament. The queen took the Crown jewels and her own jewellery to the Netherlands, where she raised £180,000 for the war effort. She also got the Stadtholder Frederick Henry to borrow 300,000 guilders for her. In addition, Charles marketed titles and honours as unashamedly as his father had. Dozens of baronetcies were sold; men paid dearly to enter the peerage; the Earl of Worcester, for example, put £100,000 on the table for his marquessate in 1643.

Before long the king imitated parliament's financial expedients. The Contribution was his answer to the monthly assessment. Also known in Yorkshire as 'the great sesse' it was levied quarterly; in some counties people found themselves paying £3 a year. It was a more decentralized tax than the parliamentary assessment, since the king insisted that it be approved by grand juries or groups of freeholders in each county. An excise was also imposed, and collected on a wider range of goods than the parliamentary excise. Royalist financial records are fragmentary, but we do know that in Yorkshire the Earl of Newcastle levied £30,000 a month during much of 1643. For a time the 15 counties under royalist control contributed £6,700 a week, almost all of which was spent on the army.

Delinquents' Estates, 1643–1655). The figure for crown land sales is from NA, E351/603/87 (Exchequer, Accounts of Sir John Dethick, Treasurer for the Sale of Crown Lands [1662]). The remaining land sale figures are taken from H.J. Habakkuk, 'Public finance and the sale of confiscated property during the interregnum', *Economic History Review* (hereafter *EcHR*), 2nd ser. 15 (1962–63), 87.

[33] The following paragraphs are based on Roy, 'Royalist army', 224–42 and Jens Engberg, 'Royalist finances in the English Civil War', *Scandinavian Economic History Review*, 14 (1966), 73–96.

Much of the tax was paid in the form of livestock and agricultural produce. The king also drew a steady income from customs receipts, mainly in Newcastle and Bristol, but also south-western ports such as Dartmouth, Exeter and Falmouth. Despite Charles's misgivings about attacking property rights, enemy estates were also sequestered, without any humanitarian provision for landowners' families. Sequestration turned out to be much less lucrative for the king than parliament because he controlled less and less territory as the war went on, and perhaps too because parliamentarians owned smaller estates on average than royalists. In the 12 months beginning November 1642 John Ashburnham, the Treasurer at War received over £180,000, of which £117,000 was dedicated to the army. These figures do not include the money that was raised and spent locally, but even so, royalist income was a trickle compared to the flood of money that streamed into parliament's coffers. The royalists' inability to meet their obligations to suppliers meant also that they were chronically short of crucial commodities such as gunpowder and musket shot. This materially affected their military fortunes at the Second Battle of Newbury and other engagements after 1644.

Scotland: Covenanter finances

Like both Charles I and the Westminster parliament the Covenanters began by asking their supporters for a loan. In the shires the sum was set at one dollar for every 1,000 merks of income, or £1 6s. 8d. for every £666 Scots (there were £12 Scots to every pound sterling). They also asked for voluntary contributions. The richest merchant in Edinburgh put up £11,000 in 1639, was never repaid, and ended his life a bankrupt. As late as the spring of 1643 an appeal for money had netted £168,000 Scots within three months. Great sums were borrowed from Edinburgh merchants in anticipation of revenue, such as the 'brotherly assistance' from England.

By the spring of 1639 taxes were being raised at the local level. Everyone was called upon to surrender a tenth of their yearly rent. The 'tenth penny', as it was called, was soon extended to all forms of wealth, not just land. The tax was administered through the presbytery, with local assessors allocating individual sums. By late 1645 over £395,000 Scots had been raised, but the kingdom's known public debt totalled £1,635,000. Nevertheless, by the end of 1643 nearly 84 per cent of the tenth penny had been paid and accounted for.[34] In addition, forced loans were imposed as the country's financial plight deteriorated. To pay for the 10,000 Scots

[34] Stevenson, 'Financing', 98–9.

troops in Ireland a forced loan of £800,000 Scots was raised, because the English parliament was so slow in honouring its promise to foot the bill for that army. When England also fell behind on its promise to pay for the 21,500-strong Scots army in England, the Convention of Estates imposed an excise modelled on the English one. The estates of bishops and other enemies of the covenant were seized for public use. The outbreak of civil war in Scotland in 1644 led also to the sequestration of the estates of malignants and the fining of those who submitted. In January 1645 parliament voted to allow the sale of enemy property in order to obtain sufficient funds to meet the threat from Montrose. By 1646 income from malignants' fines constituted the largest source of revenue.

As in England much of the equipping of troops was done by individuals rather than at public expense. Yet the Committee of Estates did spend substantial sums on military supplies. In August 1643, for example, it borrowed £40,000 Scots to pay for outfitting the army. By the time of the Cromwellian conquest of Scotland in 1651 the country had been utterly exhausted by fighting in all three kingdoms. The Covenanters' biggest mistake had been to depend on the promises of English financial support. Only half of the £300,000 sterling pledged for the Ulster army was ever paid. By the Westminster parliament's own admission the Scots received less than half what they had been promised between October 1643 and November 1645 for sending 21,500 troops to England. Scotland's support of the king in the second civil war gave Westminster the excuse to cancel its outstanding debts, which were probably not far short of £1 million sterling.

In February 1645 the Covenanters introduced the 'Maintenance', a tax modelled on the monthly assessment of the Westminster parliament. Its initial purpose was to raise £108,000 Scots a month, the sum reckoned to be needed to pay for the forces mustered to combat Montrose. In November of the same year the quota was raised to £135,000, and the Maintenance remained the principal Scottish tax until the Cromwellian conquest, by which time collections were hopelessly in arrears.

Ireland: royalists and confederates[35]

In 1642 the Protestant forces under the Earl of Ormond resisting the Catholic insurgency cost £607,452 to maintain, which was seven times the

---

[35] These paragraphs are based on Raymond Gillespie, 'The Irish economy at war, 1641–1652', in Ohlmeyer (ed.), *Ireland from Independence to Occupation*, 160–80; and Wheeler, 'Four armies in Ireland', 43–65; Perceval-Maxwell, *Outbreak of the Irish Rebellion 1641*, 274–84.

country's income in 1640. The Westminster parliament had earmarked £400,000 to put down the rebellion, but most of that money was diverted to fighting the king in England. When Ormond signed a cessation of hostilities with the Confederates in September 1643 he eased his financial situation by demobilizing some of his troops and receiving money from the Confederates. However, their finances were almost as precarious as Ormond's. Ireland, like Scotland, was a much poorer kingdom than England, and to make matters worse, much of the money that was raised for defence was wasted on the wages of government bureaucrats. The Confederates looked abroad to the Catholic powers to support their struggle. They were rewarded with sympathy but little else. Spain and France, each embroiled in its own wars, contributed £5,000 and £7,300 respectively. In the event the most generous supporter was the Pope who sent £56,000.

Failing to attract foreign support, both royalists and Confederates were thrown back on their own resources. Royalist commanders often used their own money to buy arms for their troops, while civilians also gave or lent money. In Munster the Earl of Cork bankrolled the royalist war effort, while in Connacht the Earl of Clanricard complained that his entire fortune had been consumed in the king's service. The Confederates found financial backing among the merchant elite. Cash was so scarce throughout Ireland that Ormond called in plate and turned it into currency. The Confederacy established a mint at Waterford, while in Munster the Protestant Lord Inchiquin minted his own coins in 1643. The Church also made sacrifices. Two-thirds of tithes and church revenues were allocated to maintain the Confederate armies. The population was taxed on one-third of their freeholds and one-tenth of their movable goods. As if that was not enough, individuals were required to contribute one-quarter of their estates to the war effort. When these sources ran dry the applotment was introduced. Similar to the English assessment and the Scottish tenth penny, it effectively tapped local wealth, by assigning quotas to each county. Most of the revenue was raised in Leinster and Munster. Royalists too levied an assessment, or cess, on both urban and agricultural property, but as Dublin and other cities became depopulated revenues shrank.

Sequestration of enemy property was also practised, and the rents often had a significant impact on war finance. Customs were another steady source of income, though the dislocations of war caused them to dwindle alarmingly. In Dublin for example, the customs fell from £5,000 a year in the early 1630s to £600 by 1647. At Derry the customs simply stopped being collected; at Waterford, Wexford and Ross they were negligible.

Then there was the excise, coming hard on the heels of the English tax of the same name. Though it was levied on liquor, tobacco and cattle, such was the state of anarchy that receipts were derisory for royalists and Confederates alike. Ormond and the Confederates both used the anticipated receipts of the excise as collateral to raise loans. Before the end of the 1640s the two sides had come to the end of the line with their creditors. Interest rates spiralled upwards, and lenders became increasingly risk shy. Ormond's adviser told him to exploit the customs and excise as he prepared for the arrival of Cromwell in 1649. However, the amounts he was able to raise were small change in comparison with Cromwell's fat war chest.

In summary, the 14 years of war and civil war from 1639 to 1652 strained the financial resources of the three kingdoms as never before. In England the monthly assessments extracted revenue at a rate anywhere from seven to seventeen times greater than Ship Money in the 1630s. On top of that was the unprecedented excise tax, introduced everywhere in 1643. The capital resources of all three kingdoms were run down by the confiscation, plunder and sale of land belonging to the enemy. Small wonder that some people were reduced to despair by the incessant demands for ever greater contributions; and that in most regions it was soldiers who collected the taxes, their authority backed up with swords and muskets.[36]

Logistics

Food

Given that an army is a great beast which marches upon its belly, the importance of regular feeding of the beast can scarcely be exaggerated. The dietary requirements of seventeenth-century soldiers were rudimentary; nevertheless, great financial and administrative ingenuity was called for to ensure that they did not go hungry. Hunger would cause morale to plummet, as well as bringing on its concomitants: desertion and disease.

In both royalist and parliamentary armies the daily minimum ration was the same: a pound of bread or biscuit and half a pound of cheese. Biscuit was simply bread in hardened form, which may have been less appetizing than the normal loaf, but had the twin merits of being more compact and less quick to go mouldy. English soldiers adamantly insisted on wheaten bread; they refused to eat rye-, barley- or oat-bread. What they

---

[36] For people reduced to tears by taxes in Hertfordshire see Samuel Luke, *Letter Books of Sir Samuel Luke, 1644–45*, ed. H.G. Tibbutt, 599; for military collection of taxes: M.J. Braddick, *Parliamentary Taxation in Seventeenth-Century England*, 155, 158.

got was some version of household or servants' bread, baked with a coarse, mixed flour in which the leading component was wheat, but which sold for half the price of pure wheaten bread. With justification it was later said that 'Scotland and Ireland were conquered by timely provision of Cheshire cheese and biscuit'.[37]

But the soldiers did not live by bread and cheese alone. In the royalist Oxford army the private soldier who had a penny to spare could quaff a quart of beer with his dry rations.[38] Many officers also saw to it that their men were provided with beef, mutton, pork or bacon. In the garrison of Trim the men were issued four lbs of beef per week instead of cheese.[39] In general the army fed better than the navy, and soldiers in garrison enjoyed a more varied diet than those on the march. Beans and peas, rich in protein, were also staple fare. Johnston of Wariston tells us that soldiers of the covenanting army in 1639 were provided with 2 lbs of oat bread and 28 oz ($1^3/_4$ lbs) of wheat bread plus a pint of ale per day.[40] Royalists – officers in particular – seem to have drunk a lot more wine than their parliamentary or covenanting counterparts.[41]

Diet would be adjusted to local specialties. At Plymouth in January 1646 the New Model Army arrived just in time to benefit from a nearly miraculous haul of mullet by resident fishermen.[42] When wages were interrupted and soldiers quartered on the population they could become very demanding. Some civilians grumbled that the soldiers expected to be treated to chicken boiled in butter and wine. Around the time of Naseby, according to the inhabitants of Northamptonshire and Warwickshire, the newly recruited army descended like a cloud of locusts, consuming mammoth quantities of sheep, lambs, pigs, calves, butter, cheese, bacon, beer, wheat, barley, peas, oats, meal and malt. Their horses, which numbered 7–8,000, ate their way through whole meadows and pastures of fresh

---

[37] Quoted in C.W. Firth, *Cromwell's Army*, 223.

[38] Roy, 'Royalist army', 260.

[39] NLI. MS 2541 (Cadogan Papers), 317–19 (a quarter of beef per week for every seven men).

[40] Wariston, *Diary*, 40.

[41] For the abundance of wine consumed in the king's armies see Sharpe, *Personal Rule*, 894; *Calendar of the State Papers, Venetian Series* (hereafter *CSPV*) 1643–47, 57; Bodl. MS Tanner 60, fo. 77; NLI MS 2313 (Ormond Papers), 391; Aston, *Diary*, 6; BL, Add. MS 18981, fo. 114; Thomas Carte (ed.), *A Collection of Original Letters and Papers, Concerning the Affairs of England, From the Year 1641 to 1660*, 2 vols (hereafter Cacte, *Orig. Letters*), Vol. 1, 88.

[42] Joshua Sprigge, *Anglia Rediviva, England's Recovery*, 165.

grass.[43] When the New Model embarked for Ireland in July 1649, besides vast quantities of biscuit, wheat and beer, it carried with it rye, oats, peas, barley and cheese. Surprisingly, there were also 274 barrels of raisins and 230 bags of rice.[44] Rice pudding was evidently on the menu for this expedition.

There were four ways to organize the feeding of an army. The army's commissariat could purchase staple items and transport them to the troops either overland in carts and wagons, or where possible by coastal and inland shipping. In return for being fed by the commissariat the private soldier would have fourpence a day deducted from his pay; higher ranks would see much greater sums taken off. This was the method typically used when an army was being launched – such as the New Model in 1645 – or a hazardous expedition undertaken – for example the invasions of Ireland and Scotland in 1649 and 1650. Normally, however, armies lived off the territory through which they passed. Soldiers were expected to use a large proportion of their pay to buy food in local markets or hostelries. When pay ran out they fell back on free quarter. Householders and innkeepers would be issued with vouchers for accommodating and feeding so many men and their horses for so many nights. The chances of getting these vouchers redeemed were slender at the best of times, especially when they were issued by the royalists. The records of the 1640s are full of bitter complaints against the 'intolerable burden' of free quarter. Free quarter was in fact an impossible burden if it lasted more than a few days. Hence, armies that relied on it had to keep moving so as not to exhaust utterly the resources of the districts through which they passed. The third way of feeding any army was for the army itself to organize a network of magazines or storage depots stocked with staple foods for the troops that were in the region. George Monck, capable and far-sighted military administrator that he was, established such a system for his campaign in the Scottish Highlands in the summer of 1654. Throughout the period when he commanded the occupying force in Scotland Monck also saw to it that his garrisons were stocked with a ten-month supply of stores.[45]

Fourthly, there was a private enterprise commissariat, 'the market which is appointed to follow the army with provisions from our rear'.[46] Cornchandlers, mealmen and sutlers took it upon themselves to follow the

[43] NA. State Papers (hereafter SP) 28, Vols. 171–3, passim (Northants); Vol. 136, fo. 51, Vols 182–6, passim (Warwicks).

[44] SP25/118/55–65 (Council of State, charges for the war in Ireland).

[45] Firth, *Cromwell's Army*, 224–5.

[46] HMC 29, *Thirteenth Report, Portland MSS*, Vol. 1, 293.

army and supply it with food for a profit. This system had certain administrative and financial advantages. Enterprising merchants assumed the risks and costs of buying and transporting food, of employing drivers, drovers, butchers and bakers. Whatever inventory or capital equipment was lost or destroyed was their responsibility, not the army's. The great strategic advantage of this system was that the army could remain concentrated; it did not have to dilute its combat power by spreading itself thinly across the countryside in order to absorb local farm surpluses. Such a system appears to have worked briefly for the New Model Army in 1645–46. It depended on the conjunction of several factors. To make it worth the merchants' while the army had to be well financed with ready cash. There had to be a plentiful supply of cheap grain. As Joan Thirsk has demonstrated, the prices of grains and field crops remained low in England and Wales during the early 1640s, and did not begin climbing until 1646. Livestock prices were at or below average levels until 1650.[47] The size and wealth of London gave it the purchasing power to pull foodstuffs from elsewhere in the country. Even though the capital produced no food of its own it commanded a market large enough to enable it to supply the army. Finally, the Chamber of London, which was the corporation's own financial office, operated as a central bank, enabling parliament to borrow freely against anticipated tax revenues. Thus the armies of Essex, Waller and Fairfax were launched or renewed in 1643 and 1645 thanks to loans against various assessments. A steady stream of cash flowed to the parliamentary armies, making it possible for the private commissariat to operate with confidence. When in October 1646 the assessment was suspended for several months and excise revenue dried up the system ground to a halt.[48]

Supplies

Parliament

London, Southwark, Westminster and the adjacent suburbs constituted a great industrial powerhouse at the service of parliament from the beginning

[47] Joan Thirsk (ed.), *The Agrarian History of England and Wales, Vol. 5(2), 1640–1750, Agrarian Change*, 828, 840.

[48] Aryeh J.S. Nusbacher, 'The triple thread: supply of victuals to the army under Sir Thomas Fairfax 1645–1646' (D.Phil. thesis, University of Oxford), 24, 32, 42, 72, 83, 123–5, 143–5; Aryeh J.S. Nusbacher, 'Civil supply in the civil war: supply of victuals to the New Model Army in the Naseby campaign, 1–14 June 1645', *EHR*, 115 (2000), 145–60.

of the civil war. Other urban centres made a significant contribution: Bristol, Birmingham and Manchester most notably, but all together their industrial power amounted to only a fraction of the metropolis's. Surviving supply warrants show that London arms makers produced over 30,000 pikes, 102,000 swords and 111,000 firearms between 1642 and 1651.[49] It would be reasonable to expect that this heavy demand for weapons would produce some instances of monstrous war profiteering, but the only people who seem to have enriched themselves were parliamentary officials. The Committee of the Army drove hard bargains with its contractors, judging by the fact that muskets and pistols halved in price between 1642 and 1645, while pikes and swords declined by a third.[50] Prices continued to fall after 1645. Not only did parliamentary officials keep a downward pressure on prices; they saw to it that orders were executed with dispatch.

All parties were constantly threatened with shortages of munitions, because gunpowder was forever being used up, and when it was not it decayed and became useless. Gunpowder was mixed from three ingredients: saltpetre (potassium nitrate) – 75 per cent; charcoal – 15 per cent; and brimstone (sulphur) – 10 per cent. Until 1641 its manufacture had been a royal monopoly, and until 1643 parliament merely used up existing supplies. By the mid-1640s, however, powder mills had been built in more than half a dozen centres, including Leicester, Northampton, Stafford and Coventry. The royalists had their powder mills at Oxford, Bristol, Chester, Shrewsbury and Worcester. Saltpetre and brimstone were in chronic short supply, and had to be imported. The Scots could boast no native gunpowder industry; the 45,000 pounds of powder they brought with them to England in 1644 must have come from the United Provinces and Sweden. The Irish were also big importers of powder, although after a time the Confederates – but not the royalists – were able to develop a small gunpowder industry using imported materials.

To ignite their cannon- and musket-charges armies also required large supplies of match – the hempen cord that was soaked in saltpetre and lime water and dipped in melted sulphur. Every musketeer had to carry half a pound of match coiled around his arm, ready to be lit at any moment. Large consignments of match were imported through Amsterdam into all three kingdoms.

---

[49] Peter Edwards, *Dealing in Death: the Arms Trade and the British Civil Wars*, 71.
[50] Ben Coates, *The Impact of the English Civil War on the Economy of London, 1642–50*, 96; Edwards, *Dealing in Death*, 72.

Artillery, or ordnance, was manufactured in the Weald of south-east England, South Wales and the Forest of Dean. Most cannon were cast from iron, but brass ordnance was also cast in London. Gun founding was a royal monopoly, which until 1641 had been held by John Browne in Surrey. His decision to throw in his lot with parliament was not as great a blow to the king as might appear. There were more ironworking sites in royalist territory – South Wales, the Welsh border, the West Midlands and the north-east – than in parliament's territory. Gun foundries were soon built at Oxford, York and Sheffield. The Covenanters had a much harder time of it because iron ore was not available locally. They did manage to cast a certain number of cannon by melting down domestic utensils. Cannon played an important role in the Irish wars where sieges were common and towns such as Dublin, Limerick and Galway were heavily fortified. Some small foundries had been built in the 1630s; their numbers were augmented in the next decade.

Of all military supplies ammunition was the easiest to produce. Cannonballs could be made of iron, stone or lead; musketballs were lead. They were manufactured on a large scale in London and many other centres, but could also be made in the field with simple equipment that was routinely issued to armies. Lead was produced in the Peak District of Derbyshire, as well as the Mendips, Durham, Northumberland and the Yorkshire Dales. In a pinch lead could also be mined from the roofs and gutterings of large buildings – Worcester Cathedral for example.

Royalists, Scots, Irish

It might be assumed that military production on the royalist side was pathetic by comparison with parliament, but Ian Roy has concluded that the royalists were not held back by a lack of matériel, at least in the war's first two years. Royalist war production was based in several centres: Oxford, Bristol, Reading, Shrewsbury, Chester, Newcastle and York principally. Oxford quickly became a leading arms manufacturing centre, its mills, forges, workshops and furnaces producing all kinds of ordnance and munitions. The English royalists did not match parliament's production levels but they were far higher than what the Scottish Covenanters were able to achieve. Edinburgh was the main centre for weapons manufacture in Scotland; its craftsmen produced modest quantities of muskets, pistols, swords and pikes. Ireland was worse off, with no local arms industry to speak of. Both kingdoms relied heavily on imports. In Ireland the imports failed to arrive fast enough. Had the Catholic insurgents not lacked arms, artillery and explosives in October 1641 they might have overrun Dublin in a matter of days.

Clothing and equipment

Wool and cloth remained by far the largest industries in the three kingdoms until well into the early-modern period. In England the making of broadcloth, the basic material from which coats were fashioned, was concentrated in the West Country, parts of Suffolk and Essex. Kersey, a lighter material, was used to make breeches. Parliament was supplied from East Anglia; the royalists from Gloucestershire. London merchants employed hundreds of workers to fashion tens of thousands of coats, stockings, shirts, breeches, knapsacks and shoes. At its founding in 1645 the New Model Army adopted the red coat that became the standard uniform of the British army until the nineteenth century. Then as now, Northampton was also a major shoemaking centre, supplying the king as well as parliament. As they did with weapons, parliamentary officials bargained hard over clothing prices, leaving merchants little opportunity for profiteering. Harder to control were sharp practices such as using cheap, poor quality cloth and skimping on materials. This type of corruption was brought to an end when the New Model Army instituted rigorous quality control by inspectors before deliveries would be accepted. The prices of many articles of clothing, as well as saddles, were driven down during the 1640s, thanks to the negotiating power of parliament. The Army Committee had no difficulty enforcing a maximum price of 25 shillings to outfit a recruit with a suit (coat and breeches), shirt, stockings, shoes and knapsack.[51] Nevertheless, these prices were no lower, and sometimes significantly higher than the median prices that prevailed between 1660 and 1700.

The royalists did not suffer excessively from their lack of access to the London clothing market, for there were many towns in royalist territory that specialized in textile manufacturing. Within a few months of the outbreak of the civil war the king's troops were adequately supplied with uniforms. Scotland had its own clothing and shoe industries based in Glasgow, Dundee and Aberdeen, but much cloth had to be imported from England – broadcloth and kersey in particular. In Ireland the clothing of soldiers in the initial stages of the insurrection was desperately difficult. Many royalist soldiers were dispossessed settlers who had fled with little

---

[51] Ian Gentles, *The New Model Army in England, Ireland and Scotland, 1645–1653* (hereafter Gentles *NMA*), 44.

TABLE 4.2 *Prices paid for clothing by the English parliament, compared with the later seventeenth century*[52]

	1644–8	1660–1700
Shirts	2s. 6d.–2s. 10d.	2s. 6d.
Coats	9s. 6d.	6s. 8d.
Breeches	7s. 6d.	4s. 11d.
Shoes	2s. 3d.–3s.	2s. 4d.
Cotton stockings	1s.–1s.1 1/2d.	
Woollen, silk or leather stockings	2s. 6d.	1s. 3d.

more than the shirts on their back. There were plentiful local supplies of wool, flax and leather, but they were mostly exported to England, to be re-imported as finished breeches, shirts, stockings and shoes. When civil war broke out in England the supply of clothing and footwear virtually dried up, causing much suffering to the royalist armies. The Confederates, with greater access to essential raw materials, appear to have suffered less.

Armour and equipment

People who made military equipment were skilled craftsmen – turners, metalworkers and girdlers. Unlike textile workers their numbers were limited; consequently it was difficult to step up production quickly in wartime. During the Scottish campaigns of 1639–40, and the early years of the civil war in England, much armour – pots (helmets), backs, breasts and corslets in particular – had to be imported from Amsterdam. Bandoliers (shoulder belts with loops for cartridges) were domestically made. Production started to improve in 1644, and by the time it came to equip the New Model Army native industry was able to supply a large proportion of the armour required. London manufacturers were also able to fill thousands of orders for belts and knapsacks.

---

[52] For the mid-1640s: Edwards, *Dealing in Death*, 136–9; for the later seventeenth century: Margaret Spufford, 'The cost of apparel in seventeenth-century England, and the accuracy of Gregory King', *EcHR*, 53 (2000), 694; for prices paid by the New Model Army in 1645: State Papers (hereafter SP) 28/29/200, 30/340 (lockeram shirts); SP28/30/355, 32/366–7, 37/407 (suits of coats or cassocks and breeches); SP28/29/195, 30/652 (shoes); SP28/29/194, 32/28, 36/188–9 (cotton stockings).

The Royalist Ordnance Papers indicate that much armour was manufactured in or near Oxford – backs, breasts, gorgets (throat armour), pots. But Royalists continued to be dependent upon imports, especially from the Low Countries and Denmark. Scotland too appears to have possessed limited armour- and equipment-making capacity, while for Ireland there is no information at all.

Horses

Horses were an indispensable component of any seventeenth-century army – not only as mounts for officers, and cavalry and dragoon troopers, but also as draught animals. Unlike manufactured goods, horses could not be produced overnight. Riding mounts took four years to mature, draught animals longer. The great majority of horses were bred and reared in Britain, reflecting the great improvements that had occurred in English horse breeding over the previous century. Because the supply was inflexible, steady demand exerted an upward pressure on prices: before the conflict had come to an end the price of horses had risen 50 per cent over 1638 levels.[53] There was as much variation in the price of horses as there is with modern motor cars. For dragoon horses the New Model Army paid £4, for draught horses £7, and for troop horses £7 10s. Major Thomas Harrison, who always took pride in his personal accoutrements, managed to wangle £50 'to furnish himself with two horses'.[54]

In 1642 horses were being collected several months before the formal declaration of war, especially by parliament under the terms of the Propositions. London and the Home Counties were the most enthusiastic for the cause. In the 12 months after June 1642 the inhabitants of London and the nearby counties donated 6,704 horses for the defence of the capital. Royalists, through the Engagement, instigated a similar scheme. By 1643 the voluntary sources were evaporating, and so parliament introduced enforceable quotas for every county. The royalists followed suit in 1644. A number of officers spent their own money to buy horses for their troops. Parliament also obtained many horses from dealers in the Smithfield Market in London, notably when the New Model Army was being fitted out in early 1645. Horses were always in short supply, a situation exacerbated by their high attrition rate. Not only were many killed in

---

[53] Edwards, *Dealing in Death*, 173.
[54] NA. SP28/29/204, 32/349 (dragoon horses); 32/338 (draught horses); 31/439, 32/347 (troop horses); 31/547 (Maj. Harrison).

battle, or captured by the enemy, soldiers and deserters would sometimes sell them illegally to civilians, especially when pay was in arrears.

Scotland and Ireland

Most of the saddle horses in Scotland and Ireland were too small to serve as cavalry mounts. This accounts for cavalry being relatively less important in these kingdoms than in England. In Scotland the Covenanters only established separate horse regiments after David Leslie returned from Sweden in 1643. Previously, horse units were brigaded with the foot or served as independent troops.[55] Montrose relied almost entirely on his Highland and Irish infantry. Even when the covenanting army entered England in 1644 many of its cavalry were poorly horsed on 'the veriest nags'.[56] In Ireland the Confederates focused on sieges and skirmishes rather than formal battles because of the scarcity of troop horses. For Protestants the situation was worse, given that most of the country was in Catholic hands. Ormond's royalists could find no horses to pull their ordnance, while the parliamentarians under Colonel Michael Jones in Dublin in 1647 lacked carts and carriages, implying a corresponding lack of horses. When Cromwell arrived two years later he brought with him 900 draught and carriage horses for the artillery train alone.[57] The Confederates relied on oxen, still the main draught animals in Ireland, but slower and weaker than horses.

Provisions for horses were a huge budget item in all pre-mechanized armies. To feed a warhorse cost upwards of 12d. a day. Not only did it consume 14 lbs of hay; this basic diet had to be supplemented with more nutritious feed: oats, peas and barley. A common soldier could be fed for a third the price.

Imports

All sides in all three kingdoms needed to import arms on a large scale in order to fight effectively. The Irish were most dependent on foreign suppliers, the Scots somewhat less, followed by the English royalists and parliamentarians in that order. By the late 1640s the Westminster parliament had become nearly self-sufficient in war matériel. Earlier in the decade, however, imports had streamed in from every part of Europe between

---

[55] Furgol, 'Scotland turned Sweden' 143.
[56] Quoted in John Kenyon, The Civil Wars of England, 91.
[57] NA. SP 25/118, 88–91.

Spain and Germany, with the lion's share originating in the Low Countries. Dutch sources reveal that from Amsterdam alone tens of thousands of muskets, pistols, swords, sword blades, pikes and bandoliers were shipped to England between 1639 and 1645. While the Dutch appeared to trade impartially with anyone who could furnish ready cash, there is some evidence that they supplied Covenanters and parliamentarians with better quality products, palming off their shoddy merchandise on the royalists.[58]

Had it not been for their massive imports of matériel from Dutch, German and Swedish ports the Covenanters could not have faced Charles I in 1639 and 1640. Similarly, the Catholic Confederates imported arms on a large scale from French, Flemish and Spanish ports. The worsening situation in England in 1642–43 made it easier to move such supplies by sea. To give but one example: four ships reportedly laden with 120,000 arms sailed from Nantes on the French coast to Waterford in early 1642.[59]

Despite their desperate need for supplies and matériel to fight the Confederate Irish, both the royalists under Ormond and the Scots Ulster army under Monro received little help from the Westminster parliament. The royalists tried to force parliament's hand by ordering arms from Amsterdam to fight the Irish and sending the bill to London. On the two occasions when they did this parliament refused to pay up. The royalists then fell back on importing arms from abroad and footing the bill themselves. When Ormond came back to Ireland in September 1648 to head an allied force of royalists, Confederates and Inchiquin's men he brought with him arms for 4,000 foot and 1,000 horse, paid for by the French. Over the previous six years, however, the Confederates had generally experienced greater success in obtaining arms from abroad than the royalists.

The English Civil War

In March 1642 Queen Henrietta Maria arrived in The Hague looking to buy material help for her husband's cause. With the cooperation of Stadtholder Frederick Henry she was able to organize a shipment from Amsterdam at the end of July: four siege cannon, ten pieces of field artillery, mortars, petards, ammunition, 100 barrels of gunpowder, 200 firelock- and 3,000 matchlock-muskets, 1,000 carbines, 2,000 pairs of pistols, 1,000 pikes and 3,000 saddles.[60] When she herself finally left for

---

[58] Edwards, *Dealing in Death*, 179–80.
[59] Ibid., 191.
[60] *August. 5. Two Letters* (1642), E109/12, 8.

home in February 1643 she took with her, besides brass and iron cannon, arms for 10,000 men. Royalist imports from the Low Countries did not stop with the queen's return. In March 1644 the king's representative there obtained a licence to export 10,000 muskets with bandoliers and rests, 3,000 pistols and 3,000 carbines, as well as 1,000 suits of cuirassier armour, 1,000 corslets and 1,000 saddles. Yet the United Provinces were officially neutral in the dispute between king and parliament, and for public consumption at least, forbade the export of arms to either side. But among the mercantile elite there was warm sympathy for the parliament-arian cause. In the summer of 1642 a number of arms ships sailed from Amsterdam, Flushing and Middleburg to London bearing gunpowder, muskets, pistols, carbines and pikes. Indeed, in the first year of the war parliament imported far greater quantities of firearms, match, shot, ban-doliers, pikes, halberds, partizans and armour than it produced at home. The officially neutral United Provinces were the major supplier.[61] Even after home production improved imports remained vital to parliament.

Because of family connections the royalists also expected help from France and Denmark, but they were disappointed. In spite of her presence in France from 1644 onward, Henrietta Maria was able to pry nothing out of her brother Louis XIV. Charles I's uncle, Christian IV of Denmark sporadically sent supplies, but exacted payment and concessions in return. The Orkney and Shetland Islands had to be offered as security, which turned into another public relations setback for the king's party.

In summary, imports were important to all parties in the wars of the three kingdoms. That is why the royalists' loss of Weymouth, Dartmouth, Falmouth, Newcastle and Bristol in 1644 and 1645 crippled their ability to wage war. Of all the parties, the Westminster parliament was least dependent on imports, but at the start it too had little gunpowder and match and was heavily dependent on the Amsterdam connection. The shortage of matériel did not begin to be overcome by home production until the end of 1643. By the time of the founding of the New Model Army in early 1645 domestic manufacturers were providing over half the arms and armaments needed. Imports were still required for gunpowder, match and self-igniting firearms. But by the time of the Irish and Scottish campaigns of 1649–52 parliament was able to purchase the bulk of its supplies at home.[62]

[61] Edwards, *Dealing in Death*, 200.
[62] Ibid., 211.

Transport

Once the powder, ammunition, weapons, clothing, food and other supplies had been accumulated they had to be delivered to their destination. Wherever possible, goods were moved by water either along the coast or through navigable rivers. There were hazards: tides and winds, privateers and enemy ships.

As we have seen, parliament won a tremendous advantage with the defection of the navy in 1642. However, the royalists' capture of almost all of the south-western ports in the first eight months of 1643 enabled Charles to create a substitute navy. By early 1644 the Earl of Warwick calculated that the royalists could draw on 260 ships of 50 to 300 tons.[63] Given that many of them were foreign and operated virtually as privateers, the royalist navy was a much more decentralized institution than parliament's. The Irish Confederates also developed a fleet of sorts by issuing letters of marque to privateers. By the mid-1640s their fleet may have numbered 50–60 warships, almost all of them 'Dunkirk frigates'. Twenty-one were based at Wexford, the remainder at Waterford. Small, but heavily armed and extremely swift, these frigates were among the most sophisticated warships in early-modern Europe. They intercepted merchant shipping all around the British Isles, and also ventured as far as the Baltic and the Atlantic coast of Spain.[64]

Each side tried to blockade, capture or destroy the ships of the other. In 1642–43 however, parliament, preoccupied with its conflict with the king, failed to stop many arms shipments from reaching the Irish Confederates. It similarly failed to prevent many shipments reaching the royalists in England. But after 1644 it was quite effective in blockading the royalist ports in Ireland: Dublin, Cork, Kinsale and Youghal. The parliamentarian blockade also hampered the Earl of Antrim's expedition to the Western Isles, led by Alistair MacColla in 1644. On the other hand the Confederates, operating out of ports like Wexford and Waterford, attacked parliamentary shipping daily and took many 'Puritan prizes'. By 1648, emboldened by the mutiny of the parliamentary fleet, the privateers shifted their theatre of operations to the Channel where they continued to wreak much havoc on parliamentary shipping.

---

[63] J.R. Powell, *The Navy in the English Civil War*, 91–2.

[64] Jane Ohlmeyer, ' "The Dunkirk of Ireland": Wexford privateers during the 1640s', *Journal of the Wexford Historical Society*, 12 (1988–89), 24–7; Jane Ohlmeyer 'Irish privateers during the civil war, 1642–50', *Mariner's Mirror*, 76 (1990), 122–3.

On land thousands of people and draught animals were employed in transporting war supplies. For haulage, horses were preferred to oxen because they were stronger and faster, though more expensive to feed. The containers consisted of four-wheeled wagons or two-wheeled carts, wains or tumbrels. Packhorses were also used for transport over rough terrain. In Scotland most of the carriage work was performed by such animals, but sleds were sometimes used to move bulky items short distances.

Parliament was in a better position to move arms and equipment from the point of manufacture or collection to the place where they were needed. From the capital, goods made locally or imported could be sent out via the river system or round the coast. The Eastern Association established its supply base at King's Lynn, while in 1645 Reading became the storage depot for the New Model Army, and numerous barges, laden with munitions and weapons, plied the Thames. The royalists also used the Thames, sending cargoes from Oxford to various garrisons on the river. The Severn was used to transport goods between Shropshire and Worcester, and from there overland to Oxford.

Moving goods by road could be just as dangerous as sending them by sea, and so armed escorts and convoys had to be provided. In October 1645, even though the royalists were in full retreat it was still thought necessary to provide an armed guard of 1,000 dragoons and 500 horse to accompany the chests of silver containing the New Model Army's pay to the west.[65] Nothing was more cumbersome to move around the country than artillery. It could take eight horses to draw a culverin or as many as 70 to draw the largest piece, the three-and-a-half-ton cannon royal.[66]

Ultimately, parliament's superiority in sea- and land-transport, which in turn flowed from its financial superiority, was what made the conquests of Ireland and Scotland possible between 1649 and 1652. It took 130 ships to move Cromwell's army of 12,000 and all their supplies across the Irish Sea in July and August 1649.[67] Over the following three years 20 merchantmen were employed on a regular basis to keep the troops supplied. For the conquest of Scotland, while the army marched to its destination, at least 140 ships were hired to transport supplies and money. Cromwell's artillery train alone needed 1,300 horses to haul its 50 gun carriages and additional wagons. Enormous quantities of hay, oats, wheat, biscuit,

---

[65] *A Diary or an Exact Iournall*, 2–9 Oct. 1645, E304/13.

[66] *The Royalist Ordnance Papers, 1642–1646*, ed. Ian Roy, 2 pts (1963–4, 1971–3), Pt 1, 61; Firth, *Cromwell's Army*, 149–50; Kenyon, *Civil Wars of England*, 86.

[67] Gentles, *NMA*, 354.

cheese and butter were also sent by wagon to Scotland in 1650 and 1651 for the simple reason that the Scots' scorched earth policy made it impossible for an invader to live off the land. A major reason why Cromwell was able to beat the Scots instead of being beaten by them – as Charles I was 1640 – was his mastery of transport and logistics.[68]

Conclusion

Financially and logistically the royalists were less well organized than parliament; after 1649 the Irish royalist Confederates and the Scots Covenanters were less well organized than the English republic. For all the king's aristocratic backing, in the long run parliament had the deeper pockets. From its financial superiority flowed logistical dominance, which in turn was assisted by its command of the navy and its possession of London with its huge financial, commercial and manufacturing base. These structural advantages did not begin to tell until the second year of the war, when the rise to dominance of the Independents made their full exploitation possible. Before that moment the king might well have pulled off a quick victory over his adversaries. By heroic exertion the Scots Covenanters, the Irish Royalists and the Catholic Confederates were able to maintain sustained war efforts on several fronts for a decade and more. In the end, though, their financial and logistical weakness contributed fatally to their undoing.

[68] James Scott Wheeler, 'The logistics of the Cromwellian conquest of Scotland 1650–1651', *War and Society*, 10 (1992), 10, 12, 14.

CHAPTER 5

Popular allegiance in the English Civil War

Popular allegiance

How did people choose sides in the onrushing conflict? Much as they might have preferred to avoid making any choice, both parliament, by its passage of the Militia Ordinance, and the king, by his promulgation of the Commissions of Array, required at least the able-bodied male segment of the population to declare itself. The mainsprings of popular allegiance has been a question no less contested than the causes of the war.

For the Earl of Clarendon, writing in the 1650s and 1660s, the explanation was straightforward: the nobility, the gentry and the Church backed the king, while the common people – both the 'middling sort' and those without property – backed parliament. What drove on the common people was envy of the rich and hatred of authority, especially in the towns. The Marquess of Hertford and a few other royalists at the time supported this interpretation.[1] Such a view of popular allegiance as essentially class-based has found many modern adherents.[2]

---

[1] Clarendon, *Hist.*, Bk 2, paras. 226, 318; David Underdown, 'The problem of popular allegiance in the English Civil War', *Royal Historical Society, Transactions* (hereafter *TRHS*), 5th ser. 31 (1981), 71.

[2] Christopher Hill, *The English Revolution 1640*; Manning, *The English People and the English Revolution*; Stone, *Causes of the English Revolution*; Underdown, *Revel, Riot and Rebellion*; Robert Brenner, *Merchants and Revolution: Commercial Change, Political Conflict, and London's Overseas Traders*. Although Underdown would maintain that he advances a culturally or ecologically based interpretation of popular allegiance, I agree with Buchanan Sharp that what it boils down to is 'a largely neo-Whig or neo-Marxist view' – in other words a class analysis: Buchanan Sharp, 'Rural discontents and the English revolution', in R.C. Richardson (ed.), *Town and Countryside in the English Revolution*, 263.

Another influential contemporary explanation held that the civil war was a battle between elites, and that the great bulk of the population had no allegiance in any active sense. The common people resented having to pay taxes, Baxter reminds us, while according to Hobbes, they were willing to fight for whichever side offered better prospects of pay and plunder.[3] Some modern historians have sought to dignify perceived lower-class indifference to the conflict by redefining it as neutralism or localism – a desire to avoid bloodshed by keeping the civil war out of their region.[4] Others have suggested that deference is the key: the common people followed the lead of their 'betters'. Thus, according to Alan Everitt, rural society was organized around a series of rival landed-family connections, leaving little room for autonomous lower-class political activity.[5]

Another interpretation that has fascinated many derives from geography. Beginning with the widely remarked fact that the prosperous and heavily populated south and east of England more or less supported parliament, while the poorer, less populated north and west (including Wales) mostly supported the king, David Underdown, Christopher Hill and (with qualifications) Ann Huhes have concluded that industrial and urban areas – cloth towns and ports in particular – as well as pasture–woodland areas – the 'cheese' – tended to be 'progressive', Puritan and parliamentarian in allegiance. The downland, arable- and mixed-farming, fielden areas – the 'chalk' – were culturally more traditional and therefore tended to be royalist. This interpretation was chiefly inspired by the publication of Joan Thirsk's seminal essay on 'The farming regions of England', after which it was remarked that the geographical breakdown of allegiance in the civil war roughly corresponded to the boundaries of the two principal farming regions that Thirsk had identified. In Underdown's succinct summation, '. . . the arable, fielden areas were more likely to be royalist, and the forests and pasturelands parliamentarian'.[6]

---

[3] Baxter, *Reliquiae Baxterianae*, 17; Hobbes, *Behemoth or the Long Parliament*, 2.

[4] Morrill, *Revolt of the Provinces*. More recently Morrill has offered a different interpretation, in which religion becomes the mainspring of popular allegiance.

[5] Alan Everitt, *The Community of Kent and the Great Rebellion, 1640–60*, 83. See also Peter Laslett, *The World We Have Lost*, 170–8; Holmes, *Eastern Association*, 19–22, 26, 34–48.

[6] Thirsk (ed.), *Agrarian History*, Vol. 4; David Underdown, 'The chalk and the cheese: contrasts among the English clubmen', *P & P*, 85 (1979), 26, 48; Underdown, *Revel, Riot, and Rebellion*, 204–7; Christopher Hill, *The World Turned Upside Down*, 37–8, 46; Ann Hughes, *Politics, Society and Civil War in Warwickshire, 1620–1660*, 151. Hughes modified her position after being charged with 'ecological determinism':

In a moment we shall look at what I consider to be the crucial determinant of popular allegiance. First, however, what are the merits of the interpretations outlined thus far? The geographical or ecological basis of allegiance is ingeniously argued, but its chief exponent, David Underdown, rests his case mainly on three southern counties. It may be true, as Joan Thirsk tentatively suggests, that pastoral regions were 'the most fertile seedbeds for Puritanism and dissent', but they were not the heavily populated areas of the country. If the arable, fielden regions tended towards royalism, how is it that the heartland of parliament's support lay in the populous, arable farming areas of the Midlands and East Anglia?[7] The class interpretation also runs up against a stone wall of conflicting evidence. In its favour it can be said that a majority of the nobility and the higher gentry – the great landowners – with varying degrees of enthusiasm, supported the king. The gentry as a whole were split, however, with rather more supporting the king than parliament, but a sizeable majority avoiding a clear commitment. This was a source of considerable anxiety to parliamentary recruiters. In August 1642, according to Norfolk MP Sir John Potts' correspondent, the Earl of Essex's army was 'attended with but a very small number of the gentry'.[8] On the other hand a high proportion of the 'middling sort' – craftsmen, tradesmen, yeomen, prosperous husbandmen – backed parliament. But beyond these broad brushstrokes the class interpretation breaks down. Clarendon, however masterful an analyst of high politics, was a poor sociologist. Underdown, in his examination of Somerset, Dorset and Wiltshire, has uncovered among the major-generals' lists of royalist suspects butchers, bakers, chandlers, blacksmiths, carpenters, weavers and a 'hundred and one other trades', proving that 'the royalists, no less than the parliamentarians, had their following among the middling and industrious sorts of people'.[9] Nor is it true that the poor were universally indifferent, deferential or parochial in outlook. In London, by the late 1640s if not before, porters, watermen and butchers were expressing defiantly royalist opinions. Some of them flocked to join the besieged

---

Andy Wood, 'Beyond post-revisionism? The civil war allegiances of the miners of the Derbyshire "Peak Country"', *HJ*, 40 (1997), 27; Hughes, *Causes of the English Civil War*, 139.

[7] Joan Thirsk, 'The farming regions of England', in Thirsk (ed.), *Agrarian History*, Vol. 4, 112. Underdown concedes this problem with the ecological hypothesis in 'The chalk and the cheese', 48.

[8] Bodl. MS Tanner 63, fo. 125.

[9] Underdown, *Revel, Riot and Rebellion*, 200–1.

royalists in Colchester during the summer of 1648. In Bristol at the outbreak of the civil war, John Corbet related that while 'the middle rank, the
true and best citizens' were on parliament's side, both 'the wealthy and
powerful men' and the 'basest and lowest sort' supported the 'king's cause
and party'. In early 1643 a considerable number of sailors and portside
labourers joined leading merchants in a plot to betray the city to Prince
Rupert.[10] In December 1642 a gentry-led mob of 'the meaner sort of people'
seized Chichester for the king.[11]

I would go further and suggest that anyone having a passing familiarity
with the primary sources for the 1640s will have encountered numerous
examples of popular, lower-class royalism. The phenomenon was irrepressible; it bursts through the surviving sources in the most unexpected
places. Thus, worried correspondents reported serious manifestations
of it in supposedly parliamentarian strongholds such as Hertfordshire,
Rutland, Norfolk and Northamptonshire.[12] Jacqueline Eales has found
that the royalist rebels in Kent in the summer of 1643 were not gentry-led,
but were independent-minded yeomen, husbandmen and craftsmen.[13]
Indeed, one outraged landowner dismissed them as 'men of very mean
and base condition [who] chiefly aimed at enriching of themselves by
the robbing and spoiling of such as were wealthy, intending to destroy the
gentry'.[14] At a victualer's house in Gracious Street, London, a fiddler and
his boy were asked for 'a song of mirth', and responded with 'a scurrilous
rude song in disgrace and disparagement of the parliament'.[15] While parliamentarian language of the street include jeering references to 'popish'
or 'anti-Christian' 'whores', there are many more instances of royalist
mockery of 'roundhead rogues', 'parliament dogs' and 'parliament
whores'.[16] Admittedly, cursing is often the recourse of the weak, the powerless and the defeated, and so one would expect to hear more of it from
lower-class royalists than lower-class roundheads, but the frequency of the
maledictions uttered against parliament is striking nonetheless.

---

[10] Quoted by David Harris Sacks, 'Bristol's "wars of religion"', in Richardson, *Town
and Countryside*, 109–10.

[11] Anthony Fletcher, *A County Community in Peace and War: Sussex 1600–1660*, 261.

[12] Bodl. MS Tanner 63, fos. 147, 142v, 151, 163.

[13] Jacqueline Eales, *Community and Disunity: Kent and the English Civil Wars,
1640–1649*, 18.

[14] BL. Harley MS 165 (D'Ewes diary), fo. 131.

[15] Bodl. MS Tanner 63, fo. 40.

[16] The papers of the Indemnity Commissioners (NA, SP 24) contain many such phrases
from most parts of England.

Popular royalism was rampant in rural and urban areas alike. David Scott informs us that it was strong in York, so much so that the 'malignant' element came near to overwhelming the ruling roundhead minority in the second civil war.[17] In Norwich at Shrovetide 1642 a crowd of 500 wielding muskets, swords and pistols rallied to defend the cathedral's organ against Puritan iconoclasts who would have destroyed it.[18] 'Overtaken with drink', an apprentice in Salisbury declared to anyone who would listen that 'he did not care a pin for the parliament, saying they were a company of rebels'.[19] In Canterbury the cathedral was also a centre of royalist resistance to parliament.[20] The city of Cambridge was reported to be dangerously malignant by the county committee in the summer of 1643, as were King's Lynn, Great Yarmouth and Wisbech.[21] Writing to the Earl of Essex in August 1643 Francis Lord Willoughby of Parham wrung his hands over 'the baseness and cowardliness' he encountered in Lincolnshire. The people of Boston were 'so out of hand' he feared, that 'they will all give themselves up to the enemy'.[22] On the other side of the country Worcester and Chester were strongly royalist throughout the 1640s.[23] Ann Hughes has noted signs of royalism among the common people in Warwick in 1642, despite the political dominance of the Puritan Lord Brooke. In the same year Nehemiah Wharton found Southam to be 'a very malignant town'.[24] Nottingham Castle was under firm parliamentary control from the beginning, but the county committee reported the great majority of the townsfolk were 'so malignant that they were ready to deliver up the town to the enemy'.[25] In London in the early autumn of 1642 a royalist mob wearing red ribbons in their hats drove out an iconoclast mob that had

[17] David Scott, 'Politics and government in York, 1640–1662', in Richardson, *Town and Countryside*, 57.

[18] Russell, *Causes of the English Civil War*, 22.

[19] Bodl. MS Tanner 63, fo. 66.

[20] Jacqueline Eales, 'Kent and the English civil wars, 1640–1660', in F. Lansberry (ed.), *Politics and Government in Kent, 1640–1914*, 8–9, 13.

[21] Bodl. MS Tanner 62, fos. 299, 192, 222.

[22] Bodl. MS Tanner 62, fo. 232.

[23] Philip Styles, 'The city of Worcester during the civil wars 1640–60', in R.C. Richardson (ed.), *The English Civil War: Local Aspects*, 210; Huntington Lib., Ellesmere Collection (Bridgewater MSS), EL 7764.

[24] Hughes, *Causes of the English Civil War*, 141; Hughes, *Warwickshire*, 140; Charles E. Carlton, *Going to the Wars: The Experience of the British Civil Wars, 1638–1651*, 110.

[25] Bodl. MS Tanner 62, fo. 295 (26 August 1643).

broken into St Paul's to pull down the organ.[26] Three months later those who petitioned and demonstrated noisily in favour of peace with the king and against the levying of taxes by parliament included not only great merchants, but apprentices, a clown, the master of the Southwark bear garden, ship's chandlers, tapsters, brewers and other tradesmen. Hostile pamphlet- and newsbook-writers grudgingly admitted that they represented 'a considerable part of London'.[27]

Broadly speaking the poorer, more sparsely populated north and west of England did support the king, while the richer, more densely populated south and the east aligned itself with parliament. But allegiance was almost never undivided. Wales is usually thought of as unreservedly royalist, yet the Welsh were violently allergic to popery, and their revulsion against the Irish revolt put them firmly in parliament's camp in 1641. With the outbreak of civil war in 1642, however, there was a general stampede to the royal standard.[28] Most of the gentry and their tenants, as well as the bards, ballad-mongers and clergy, who were the chief agents for disseminating news and propaganda, backed the king, and Wales became renowned as the nursery of the royalist infantry.[29] On the other hand the south-western county of Pembrokeshire, an outpost of Puritanism, was strongly parliamentarian, while Montgomeryshire and Monmouthshire were sharply divided. Mark Stoyle has demonstrated that Devon, far from being a bastion of royalism, was deeply divided, and largely parliamentarian.[30] David Underdown has shown that west Dorset, north Wiltshire and north Somerset were predominantly parliamentarian. Indeed Somerset was overwhelmingly anti-royalist at the beginning of the war, raising thousands of men to drive the royalists out of the county.[31] As for the north, the king raised few troops in Cumberland and Westmorland, while the West Riding of Yorkshire largely supplied the 8,000-strong army of volunteers that Ferdinando Lord Fairfax raised for parliament. Lancashire turned out to

---

[26] Gardiner, *GCW*, Vol. 1, 38.

[27] *An Answer to the London Petition* ([14 December] 1642), E130/18, p. 2. See also *A Continuation of Certaine Speciall and Remarkable Passages* (8–15 December 1642), E244/10, p. 5; *A Continvation of Certaine Speciall and Remarkable Passages* [a different publication] (19–22 December 1642), E244/22, p. 3.

[28] A.H. Dodd, *Studies in Stuart Wales*, 86–7.

[29] W.S.K. Thomas, *Stuart Wales 1603–1714*, 19–20.

[30] Mark Stoyle, *Loyalty and Locality: Popular Allegiance in Devon during the English Civil War*, 30–2.

[31] David Underdown, *Somerset in the Civil War and Interregnum*, 37–48.

be a disappointing recruiting ground for the king, while Manchester, Salford and Bolton held out stubbornly for parliament.

Conversely, East Anglia, the south-east and the East Midlands, bastions of parliamentarianism, were riddled with royalism and neutralism. Nottinghamshire was a mainly royalist county.[32] Derbyshire, Hampshire and Sussex were split. The situation in East Anglia was summed up succinctly by Thomas May, who observed that while the common people backed parliament, 'a great and considerable number of the gentry . . . were disaffected to the parliament, and were not sparing in their utmost endeavours to promote the king's cause'.[33] The truth of this statement is borne out in Suffolk by the petition of the Great Inquests at the Assizes in July 1642. After thanking the king for his care for the safety of the kingdom and of religion, they urged him to stop the growth of 'Anabaptism and other schisms', pledging themselves to the 'preservation of your sacred person, and of your crown and dignity'.[34] In Lincolnshire vast crowds turned out to greet the king in July 1642, and the gentry, who were 'most of them ill affected to the parliament', promised to raise 400 cavalry for him.[35] As early as September 1641 Sir Thomas Barrington, one of the leading puritans in Essex, was perplexed by 'the strange tepidity' he observed in that county in executing the parliamentary ordinance for the disarming of papists.[36] In July 1642 the Grand Jury of Essex delivered a loyal address pledging 'to assist your majesty with our persons, lives, and fortunes whensoever you shall command us'.[37] In April 1643 the parliamentarian Walter Long wrote from Essex to Speaker William Lenthall, 'I am among strangers here.' Only because he was backed up by military force was he able to collect the weekly assessment from the county.[38] In August 1642 Lord Mandeville's correspondent in Huntingdonshire warned him of strong popular disaffection there, '. . . the country nothing persuaded to accommodate the parliament either with horse, arms, plate, or monies'.[39]

[32] Stoyle, *Loyalty and Locality*, 253.
[33] Thomas May, *The History of the Parliament of England: which Began November the Third, M.DC.XL. with a Short and Necessary View of Some Precedent Years*, Bk 3, Ch. 4, 78.
[34] Bodl. MS Tanner 63, fo. 110.
[35] Clive Holmes, *Seventeenth-Century Lincolnshire*, 145, 147.
[36] Beinecke Library, Osborn MSS 76.12.3 (Howard of Escrick Papers).
[37] *CSPD 1641–3*, 357.
[38] Bodl. MS Tanner 62, fo. 35.
[39] HMC 1, *Manchester MSS*, Pt 2, 59.

Similarly, there was strong royalist and anti-war sentiment among the gentry of Cambridgeshire and Hertfordshire. Both counties were only secured for parliament by the dispatch of troops from London.[40]

Industrial districts, cloth towns and ports were largely parliamentarian, but there were important exceptions. The tin miners of Cornwall and Devon, having long benefited from royal favour, fiercely backed the king. The Devonshire tinners' regiment was fully comparable in dedication and bravery to Newcastle's famous Whitecoats. The Derbyshire lead miners, locked in a struggle with local landowners, appealed to the king for support, and when they got it returned the favour by sending several hundred volunteers to his army.[41] The workers in the coal and iron industries in the same county also rallied in large numbers to the royalist side. The metal workers of Dudley (near Birmingham) were also royalist.[42] The inhabitants of Westbury and Warminster – cloth towns in south-west Wiltshire – similarly threw in their lot with the king.[43] City merchants in general tended to be wary of civil conflict, acutely aware that it almost invariably disrupted their normal economic activities. Their bias was towards accommodation and a cessation of hostilities once they had begun.[44]

To sum up, the geographical basis of allegiance was roughly as the traditional interpretation informs us: Wales and the north and west of England were mainly royalist; the east and south were mainly parliamentarian. There were, however, many dissenting voices within all regions, in addition to the large segment, almost certainly constituting the majority, who deplored the war and sought peace at every opportunity.

But geography, or ecology, was clearly not the primary basis of allegiance. What was? Most people at the time were in little doubt about the answer: it was religion. Religion was about more than doctrine, Church governance and the fear of Catholics, though it was about those things as well. At root it had to do with conceptions of morality, how God ought to be worshipped, and what kind of society people wanted England to be. Richard Baxter, who unlike Clarendon did have a nose for sociology, defined the difference as well as anyone.

---

[40] Holmes, *Eastern Association*, 53, 55.

[41] Andy Wood, *The Politics of Social Conflict: The Peak Country, 1520–1770*, 271.

[42] Hughes, *Causes of the English Civil War*, 1st edn (1991), 144; 2nd edn (1998), 139.

[43] Sharp, 'Rural discontents', 256.

[44] Roger Howell, Jr., 'The structure of urban politics in the English Civil War', *Albion*, 11 (1979), 117.

the generality of the people . . . who were then called puritans, precisians,
religious persons, that used to talk of God, and heaven, and Scripture,
and holiness, and to follow sermons and read books of devotion, and
pray in their families and spend the Lord's Day in religious exercises, and
plead for mortification, and serious devotion, and strict obedience to
God, and speak against swearing, cursing, drunkenness, prophaneness,
&c., I say, the main body of this sort of men, both preachers and people,
adhered to the parliament. And on the other side, the gentry that were not
so precise and strict against an oath, or gaming, or plays, or drinking, nor
troubled themselves so much about the matters of God and the world to
come, and the ministers and people that were for the king's Book [of
Sports], for dancing and recreation on the Lord's days; and those that
made not so great a matter of every sin, but went to church and heard
Common Prayer, and were glad to hear a sermon which lashed the
puritans, and which ordinarily spoke against this strictness and
preciseness in religion, and this strict observation of the Lord's Day,
and following sermons and prayers extempore, *and talking so much of*
scripture and matters of salvation, and those that hated and derided them
that take these courses, the main body of these were against the
parliament . . .[45]

There is a paradox here that Baxter does not explore. We can safely
assume that those who did not make a great fuss over every sin, who were
content with the Book of Common Prayer, and who were happy to hear
sermons that mocked the puritans, greatly outnumbered the strict precisians who pursued holiness and spoke out against sin. Yet it was the
latter who supported parliament, which in turn raised more money than
the king, fielded more troops and ultimately beat him. How was this
minority able to overcome the majority? The answer has to do with passion and intensity of their commitment. In a memorable comment Lord
Falkland wryly stated that 'they who hated bishops hated them worse
than the devil, and that they who loved them did not love them so well as
their dinner'.[46] As John Morrill points out, men such as Robert Harley, Sir
William Brereton and Alexander Rigby – and dozens of others – 'were fired
by the vision not simply of ecclesiastical reconstruction, but of building a
godly commonwealth'. By contrast, many of those whose chief interest
was legal and constitutional reform got cold feet when war stared them in

---

[45]   Baxter, *Reliquiae Baxterianae*, 31.
[46]   Clarendon, *Hist.*, Bk 3, para. 242.

the face in 1642.[47] Lucy Hutchinson wrote that many who fought saw themselves defending 'just English liberties' against royal tyranny, but as John Pym aptly observed, 'the greatest liberty of our kingdom is religion'.[48] When Sir John Potts wrote to his countrymen in November 1642 he appealed to them to support parliament 'for maintenance of the true Protestant religion'.[49] Nor was it just educated landowners and merchants who were fired by this religious vision. The trained bands and volunteers of Essex declared that they were resolved to shed their 'dearest blood' for liberty and peace, but also for 'religion, more precious than both'.[50]

John Walter has brought to light a major episode of popular protest that on the face of it appears to be a class conflict, but on closer inspection turns out to be about religion. In Essex's Stour Valley, as the country lurched towards civil war, crowds in their thousands invaded and plundered the houses of the landed classes. With the exception of one prominent royalist family (the Lucases) all those attacked were, or were suspected of being, Roman Catholics. Plebeian as well as gentry Catholic families were attacked. If we are to avoid what E.P. Thompson called 'the enormous condescension of posterity' we need to pay attention to what the crowds themselves said motivated them. It was anti-popery.[51] Those from Colchester put it this way:

We find the trade of clothing, and new drapery, upon which the livelihoods of many thousands, men, women, and children in this town do depend, to be almost wholly decayed, and poverty abundantly to grow upon us. Which is occasioned . . . by the high breaches of the privileges of parliament, and the want of a thorough reformation in matters of religion, which we conceive have been hindred by the opposition made thereunto by the bishops and popish Lords, and by the insolencies of papists in this land, and the outrageous cruelties of the rebels in Ireland.

[47] Morrill, *Nature of English Revolution*, 66.
[48] Lucy Hutchinson, *Memoirs of the Life of Colonel Hutchinson*, ed. J. Sutherland, 53; Jacqueline Eales, *Puritans and Roundheads: The Harleys of Brampton Bryan and the Outbreak of the English Civil War*, 200.
[49] Bodl. MS Tanner 64, fo. 94.
[50] *Repromission and Resolution of the Trained Bands of Essex* (1642), Thomason 669.f.6/33, quoted in Cliftlands, 'The "Well-Affected" and the "Country" ', 18. For a similar statement see the petition of the Essex militia and volunteers to the Earl of Warwick: *LJ*, Vol. 5, 118 (7 June 1642).
[51] Walter, *Popular Violence*, 234, 284.

In order to put the cloth trade back on its feet they proposed that 'a discipline and government may be established according to the word of God'.[52]

Other petitioners from London, Essex, Suffolk, Middlesex and Hertfordshire expressed the same concerns and pronounced the same solutions: disarming of papists, crushing of Irish rebels and reforming the Church.[53] Much of this religious–political activity can be traced back to the Protestation of 1641, and its circulation throughout England. With its denunciation of 'all popery and popish innovation', it played a key role in shaping a pro-parliamentary popular political culture.[54] That phrase furnished the justification for many acts of popular iconoclasm in the lead-up to the civil war. Attacks on the houses of Catholics were similarly a response to the cues that parliament and preachers had given. Such attacks were conducted not only by clothworkers in Essex and Suffolk. Sailors on the east coast were keenly anti-popish, and also drew on the Protestation to justify their disorderly acts. In other parts of England too anti-popery provided the basic language of political analysis in a popular culture that reminded itself continually of the black acts of papists in the time of Mary Tudor, the Spanish Armada and the Gunpowder Treason of 1605. Anti-popery was more than merely an irrational prejudice: there was an objective basis to the popular fear that international Catholicism posed a mortal threat to the survival of Protestant England.[55] Parliament's denunciations of popery seem to have provided the inspiration and legitimation for crowds comprising poor, middling sort and gentry in Gloucestershire, Wiltshire, Devon and Somerset to rise up and stop the raising of the Commission of Array.[56] In the crowds' mental universe religion was foundational: if parliament would only deal with the problem of popery, secondary economic and political issues would take care of themselves.

In 1644 captured parliamentary soldiers were quoted as explaining their allegiance in these terms:

---

[52] *Three Petitions . . . brought by many thousands of the County of Essex* ([20 January] 1642), E134/13, 2.

[53] *LJ*, Vol. 4, 537–40; *A Continuation of Certaine Speciall and Remarkable Passages* (24 November–1 December 1642), E242/31, 1, 6.

[54] Walter, *Popular Violence*, 292–3.

[55] Robin Clifton, 'The popular fear of Catholics during the English Revolution', *P & P*, 52 (1971), 38, 41; Robert Clifton, 'Fear of popery', in Conrad Russell (ed.), *The Origins of the English Civil War*, 149, 154–6; Peter Lake, 'Antipopery: the structure of a prejudice', in Richard Cust and Ann Hughes (eds), *Conflict in Early Stuart England*, 80, 97.

[56] Walter, *Popular Violence*, 339–40.

'Tis prophesied in the Revelation, that the Whore of Babylon shall be destroyed with fire and sword, and what do you know, but this is the time of her ruin, and that we are the men that must help to pull her down?[57]

It was no accident that common soldiers were thinking these thoughts. Wherever militant Protestantism was strong, preachers on the eve of the civil war were stirring up any who would listen with denunciations of popery, malignancy and vice, and painting inspiring word pictures of the New Jerusalem that was waiting to be fashioned in England. A concomitant of Puritan preaching was the construction of a godly people, which reinforced the idea of an active citizenship. Stephen Marshall for example, repeated his parliamentary fast sermon of February 1642, *Meroz Cursed*, no fewer than 60 times. The burden of his message was that those who were lukewarm in God's cause would be cursed. The MPs were instructed to do three things: pray unceasingly for the Church; give unstintingly of their money to the cause; and be prepared to sacrifice their lives. Memorably he declared that 'praying spirits [are] in truth . . . the very chariots and horsemen of Israel' and that 'some of you may be called, as soldiers, to spend your blood in the Church's cause'.[58] Marshall's was only the first of a long series of incendiary sermons in which people were exhorted to storm heaven with their prayers and fasting. Clarendon and other royalists were in no doubt about the power of godly preaching. 'This strange wildfire among the people', he wrote, 'was not so much and so furiously kindled by the breath of the parliament as of the clergy, who both administered fuel and blowed the coals in the Houses too.'[59]

Soldiers from as far away as Herefordshire quoted Marshall's sermon, and the royalist chaplain Edward Symmons tried, ineffectually, to subject it to a line-by-line refutation.[60] We know that in Coventry as well, similar preaching under the patronage of the Puritan Lord Brooke produced 'a high state of godly excitement', resulting in hundreds of volunteers for Brooke's army.[61] There was also much 'combustible material' in the sermons of godly preachers in the West Riding of Yorkshire on the eve of the

[57] Edward Symmons, *Scripture Vindicated* (Oxford, 1644), E27/12, sig. A3r.

[58] Stephen Marshall, *Meroz Cursed* (1642), E133/19, 47, 51, 53.

[59] Clarendon, *Hist.*, Bk 6, 39. H.R. Trevor-Roper, *Religion, The Reformation and Social Change*, 307–8.

[60] Marshall, *Meroz Cursed*; Clarendon, *Hist.*, Bk 6. 39; Tom Webster, *Stephen Marshall and Finchingfield*, 4, 5, 17, 18; Symmons, *Scripture Vindicated*, sig. A3v, 1ff.

[61] Anne Hughes, 'Coventry and the English Revolution', in Richardson, *Town and Countryside*, 79–80.

civil war. While the preachers did not advocate armed resistance to the king, they gave their hearers a clear view of where the right lay in the coming conflict. They may justly be regarded as examples of what Clarendon called 'conductors' who carried the people into rebellion.[62] Conrad Russell has shown too that a long tradition of godly preaching was the common factor in those communities that raised volunteers for parliament.[63]

As with preaching, so it was with written communication. Fear of popery was the thread running through the petitions sent up from the counties to parliament in early 1642.[64] The great bulk of pamphlets and books published in 1641–42 were not about constitutional issues but about religion. There were no constitutional militants in 1642, for 'it was the force of religion that drove minorities to fight, and forced majorities to make reluctant choices'.[65]

Fluctuating allegiance

The last aspect of popular allegiance to be noted is that it was not static but almost everywhere in constant flux. This phenomenon is witnessed most dramatically in London. To say that the capital was parliamentarian in the civil war is to ignore the profound shift in public opinion that occurred there during the 1640s. Between 1639 and 1642 London was vehemently antagonistic to the king. Pro-Scots in the bishops' wars, its moneyed men refused to lend to the Crown, while its citizens declined to enlist in his armies.[66] When the Long Parliament was summoned Londoners showed themselves militantly pro-parliament and anti-royalist. Through the media of pamphlets, petitions and popular demonstrations they opposed king and prelates at every turn.[67] When war became imminent they freely donated large quantities of money, horses and weapons to the parliamentary cause, and flocked to fight under its standard. When taxation became necessary, London assented to a burden far higher than that of any other jurisdiction: £10,000 a week from February to April 1643. Londoners'

---

[62] William Sheils, 'Provincial preaching on the eve of the Civil War: some West Riding fast sermons', in Anthony Fletcher and Peter Roberts (eds), *Religion, Culture and Society in Early Modern Britain: Essays in Honour of Patrick Collinson*, 292; Clarendon, *Hist.*, Bk 5, 444.

[63] Russell, *Causes of the English Civil War*, 21–2.

[64] Fletcher, *Outbreak*, 200.

[65] Morrill, *Nature of English Revolution*, 47.

[66] *CSP*, Vol. 2, 53, 54–5, 64.

[67] Cressy, 'Revolutionary England 1640–1642', 35–71.

intoxicating enjoyment of their conflict with the king soon drained away, however. After the sobering experience of large-scale casualties at Edgehill those who hated the war found their voice and demonstrated repeatedly, in December 1642 and January 1643, for peace and against war taxation. Such was popular disillusionment with the war that when a second weekly assessment was introduced in July 1643, London was completely exempted from it. Parliament's alertness to London sensitivities was not sufficient to head off large-scale peace demonstrations the following month, however. At the same time voluntary enlistment in parliament's armies virtually dried up, and for the rest of the civil war recruitment in the capital had to be carried out by force.

Sir Edmund Waller attempted to tap this popular disenchantment with parliament's war. His attempted royalist coup in May 1643 turned into a fiasco, but his analysis of where royalist support lay may have been near the truth. Royalists were still outnumbered three to one within the city walls, he thought, but he was sure that in the 'outparts' they exceeded the supporters of parliament by a ratio of five to one.[68] We now know that at that time only 38 per cent of the metropolitan population resided within the walls; the other 62 per cent dwelt in Westminster, Southwark and the various suburbs.[69] Thus, to judge by this admittedly biased source, metropolitan London by 1643 had already become strongly royalist. Beleaguered parliamentarians lashed out against people who sported such tokens of their royalist allegiance as medallions bearing the king's image. Even women who wore them were liable to be 'despoiled' by angry round-heads.[70] As we shall see in later chapters, London's allegiance continued to shift until, by the spring of 1648 royalists were lighting bonfires through-out the city and suburbs in celebration of Charles's coronation day, and brazenly stopping coaches in the street, and forcing their occupants to drink the king's health. In the months before and after the king's trial royalist publications triumphed in the court of public opinion with their biting satire and penetrating political commentary on the king's tormentors. From Marchamont Nedham's *Mercurius Pragmaticus*, with its frequently accurate revelations about the deliberations of the radical parliamentarians,

---

[68] BL. Harley MS 164 (D'Ewes diary, YCPH transcript), fo. 397.

[69] Roger Finlay and Beatrice Shearer, 'Population growth and suburban expansion', in A.L. Beier and Roger Finlay (eds), *London 1500–1700, The Making of the Metropolis*, 45.

[70] Christchurch, Oxford, Browne Letters, Box A–C. Christopher to Richard Browne, 17 August 1643 [now transferred to BL: Add. MS 78268].

to John Crouch's *Man in the Moon* with its hilariously scatalogical attacks on the leaders of the future republic, they provided Londoners with a diet of compulsively readable news and gossip.[71] Combined with the evidence of pamphlets and pulpit oratory, this suggests that very few Londoners supported the regicide.

Allegiance was equally unstable in other parts of the country. In the petitions he has tracked from 38 counties in 1641–42 Anthony Fletcher has found 'incontrovertible evidence of the hold parliament had obtained on the nation's mind'.[72] Yet he also acknowledges that within months of the outbreak of war there were many petitions to king and parliament urging peace and accommodation.[73] John Morrill has documented a powerful impulse towards non-involvement in the form of neutrality pacts in 22 counties, where people sought to keep the two sides out of the shire completely, or to reach a demilitarization agreement between them.[74] Equally, Judith Maltby has found petitions defending the Book of Common Prayer and episcopacy from 22 English and six Welsh counties, as well as London, Westminster, Southwark and the universities of Oxford and Cambridge over almost the same period (1640–42).[75] Support for bishops and prayerbook was a sure pointer towards royalist allegiance. Sometimes a change in the fortune of battle would trigger a change in allegiance. The parliamentarian stronghold at Gloucester became very shaky after Bristol fell to the royalists in July 1643. The governor, Colonel Edward Massie, wrote that the citizens, who depended heavily on trade with Bristol, had become much less supportive of parliament: '. . . we have cause to distrust many of their fidelities'. Worse, his soldiers were running away 'hourly from us', and there was much complaining by civilians against the burden of billeting and feeding the soldiers.[76] Similarly, in Essex parliament's failure to protect the county against the depredations of its soldiers alienated opinion and reduced both the breadth and intensity of 'well-affected' support. In the second civil war, however, many turned against the royalist insurgents when their promises of protection against plunder proved to be

[71] David Underdown, *A Freeborn People: Politics and the Nation in Seventeenth-Century England*, 99–111.

[72] Fletcher, *Outbreak*, 222.

[73] Anthony Fletcher, 'The coming of war', in John Morrill (ed.), *Reactions to the English Civil War 1642–1649*, 40–1.

[74] Morrill, *Revolt in the Provinces*, 54.

[75] Maltby, *Prayerbook and People*, appendix 1.

[76] Bodl. MS Tanner 62, fos. 199, 197v.

false.[77] Parliament had a similar experience after its capture of Newbury. By March 1646 its garrison there, 'half starved . . . and for want of pay . . . very desperate', had earned the cordial hatred of people in Berkshire by 'ranging about the country and breaking and robbing houses and passengers and driving away sheep and other cattle before the owners' faces'.[78] In Somerset and Devon many fell away from parliament in the summer of 1644 as the king advanced towards his victory against the Earl of Essex at Lostwithiel. In a melancholy letter Essex recorded that the people in these counties could not be relied upon, and that the king, 'if he is not hindered', would likely recruit many soldiers from among them. In both counties the movement of clubmen profited even more than the king from popular disillusionment with parliament.[79]

A year or so later the shoe was on the other foot. In Staffordshire, the country people, 'much exasperated against the pressures of the soldiers' were ready to rise against the royalist garrisons.[80] In Devon and north Cornwall it was the royalist cavalry commander George Goring who was regarded as the oppressor. The Prince of Wales admonished him that his financial exactions would 'very much hinder' the prince's efforts to mobilize the countryfolk for the king. But even if Goring's behaviour had been above reproach he could not have prevented the previously loyal Cornish from throwing in their lot with Fairfax, whose army was carrying everything before it in its sweep through the south and south-west. Everywhere in the west people switched their allegiance to Fairfax in 1645–46, when they saw that his army held out the best hope for bringing an end to the ravages of war. This even extended to the Welsh, whose royalist ardour cooled rapidly after the battle of Naseby. 'From the Welsh, good Lord deliver me', wrote a royalist recruitment officer at the time. Most Welsh counties either retreated into neutralism or threw in their lot with parliament.[81]

Briefly then, parliament commanded its maximum popular allegiance during the two years between its summoning in November 1640 and the outbreak of civil war two years later. From then on, with the increasingly radical attacks on the Church, the steadily more burdensome conscription of men and money, the ever rising cost of the war in human lives and broken bodies, and the perception that roundhead tyranny was at least as

[77] Cliftlands, 'The "Well-Affected" and the "Country"', 20, 80.
[78] Bodl. MS Tanner 60, fo. 491.
[79] Bodl. MS Tanner. 60, fo. 547; 61, fos. 32, 63.
[80] *The Pythouse Papers*, ed. W. Ansell Day, 20.
[81] Thomas, *Stuart Wales*, 44–5.

oppressive as the cavalier variety, more and more people transferred their allegiance either to the Club and peace movements, or to the king. The Clubmen of Sussex spoke for many when in September 1645 they complained of

The insufferable, insolent, arbitrary power that hath been used amongst us, contrary to all our ancient known laws, or ordinances of Parliament . . . by imprisoning our persons, imposing of sums of money, light horses, and dragoons, and exacting of loans by some particular persons stepped into authority who have delegated their power to men of sordid condition whose wills have been laws and commands over our persons and estates by which they have overthrown all our English liberties and have endeavoured thereby to make us desperate.[82]

Combat motivation

We have seen the complexity that underlay popular allegiance both at the outset and during the civil war. Before telling the story of the war itself we must address the somewhat different question of what brought men to fight. Each side had many hundreds of thousands of adherents, but in the end only 140,000 took up arms, and many of those were coerced. What motivated the ones who fought freely and with zeal?

For many royalists the primordial argument may have been fear. High-profile supporters of the king such as the marquesses of Worcester and Hertford, and the earls of Newcastle, Antrim, Ormond and Derby knew that if the king was defeated they could say goodbye to their property, and probably their lives as well. The fate of Strafford was never far from their minds. Others acted out of religious fear. It was not only Laudian clergy who dreaded that the puritans in parliament would abolish the Book of Common Prayer, extirpate the established Church root and branch, and replace it with a Presbyterian worship and doctrine. Nor was it only in Cornwall that people were spurred on to fight by a 'spontaneous political conservatism and deep attachment to traditional ways in the church'.[83] More justified in their fears than the defendants of the established liturgy were Roman Catholics. Out of all proportion to their numbers they flocked to the king's standard in the hope of finding refuge from intolerant Puritanism.

[82] Bodl. MS Tanner 60, fo. 254, quoted by Robert Ashton, 'From cavalier to roundhead tyranny, 1642–9', in Morrill, *Reactions*, 201.
[83] Fletcher, *Outbreak*, 311.

A sense of honour drove many royalists on, particularly among the officers. The ideals of medieval chivalry – courtesy, reckless courage, the conviction that a man's word is sacred, loyalty to one's lord, and a hunger for fame – all these still entranced the imaginations of fighting men in the seventeenth century. The king may have been an inept politician and an indifferent soldier, but as their anointed sovereign, he commanded the unwavering loyalty of men as diverse as the Marquess of Worcester, Sir Jacob Astley and Sir Ralph and Edmund Verney. As Edmund wrote to his brother, 'I beseech you, consider that majesty is sacred. God saith touch not mine anointed.'[84] Simple loyalty, the belief that in serving the king they were honouring the father of their country and thus obeying the Fifth Commandment stiffened many to fight. Lord Capel made this point specifically in his dying speech in 1649. Lord Paget explained in 1642 why he chose to obey the king rather than parliament: 'I . . . am now on my way to his majesty, where I will throw myself down at his feet and die a loyal subject.'[85]

Many moderates, less bewitched by the medieval cult of honour, threw in their lot with the royalist cause out of an abhorrence of puritan narrowness and dogmatism. Men such as Edward Hyde, Lord Falkland and the earls of Southampton and Carnarvon favoured a balanced constitution, a hierarchical social order, and a moderate Church. Others of less reputable lives, such as Colonel George Goring and Sir Edmund Waller instinctively knew that royalism was more forgiving of the sins of the flesh. It was men such as these who would give the cavalier cause its notoriety for plunder, drinking, whoring and swearing. Finally, there were a few who gambled that victory in war would lead to riches from plunder and confiscation of their enemies' property. Those of a predatory disposition were, however, vastly outnumbered by those who freely staked large sums of their own money with little hope of return.

Many parliamentarians too were driven by fear. Men who had openly defied the king, invited the Scots to invade, or sent the favourite royal counsellor to the scaffold, feared that if they did not go on to defeat Charles in war they too would face execution. John Pym, Sir Philip Stapleton, Denzil Holles, William Strode, the earls of Essex and Manchester, Viscount Saye and Sele, the Fairfaxes, Oliver Cromwell and others were at all times conscious of the fate that awaited them should the king wrest a military triumph from their hands. At the very least they knew

---

[84] Quoted in Gardiner, GCW, Vol. 1, 5.
[85] J.G. Marston, 'Gentry honor and royalism in early Stuart England', *Journal of British Studies* (hereafter *JBS*), 13 (1973), 38. *LJ*, Vol. 5, 152.

they would be ruined in their estates. More powerful and more widespread was religious fear, engendered by the conviction that there was a Jesuitical plot to impose the popish religion on England and exterminate all godly Protestants who refused to convert. The ongoing nightmare of the Irish uprising fuelled this fear for the remainder of the 1640s. Fear that the Catholic rebels, if once triumphant, would invade England was pervasive. The conviction that the king was actually encouraging the Irish in their murderous designs was an article of faith to many. They were helped to conquer this religious fear by the assurance that a providential God would not permit his godly people to suffer such a fate. Such an assurance released tremendous energy and confidence, exemplified in John Hampden's statement that the county of Essex was a powerhouse of the parliamentary cause: 'The power of Essex is great, a place of most life of religion in the land.'[86] The certainty that they were waging God's battles gave many men the courage to stand and fight rather than turn tail and flee. Oliver Cromwell understood this when, at the beginning of the wars 'he had', as Richard Baxter wrote, 'a special care to get religious men into his troop'. Baxter explained Cromwell's reasoning in these terms:

he that maketh the felicity of Church and State his end, esteemeth it above his life, and therefore will the sooner lay down his life for it. And men of parts and understanding know how to manage their business, and know that flying [fleeing] is the surest way to death, and that standing to it is the likeliest way to escape . . . By this means he indeed sped better than he expected.[87]

The Earl of Essex also sought religious men for his regiments, though with less success than Cromwell. The Earl of Denbigh strove to stir up his men with the proclamation that 'now they are employed in a service that tends to God's glory; now they are carrying on a work of reformation'.[88] There was a wide streak of millenarianism among the parliamentary and military preachers who stoked the fires of war. Stephen Marshall returned to this theme often in his fast sermons to parliament. He interpreted Revelation 15: 3–4, to mean that the peoples of England, Scotland, and other European countries would 'shake off the yoke of Antichrist'. 'In the end, all the kingdoms of the world shall be the kingdoms of our Lord and his

---

[86] Quoted by Gardiner, *GCW*, Vol. 1, 153n.
[87] Baxter, *Reliquiae Baxterianae*, 98.
[88] Gardiner, *GCW*, Vol. 1, 154; Bodl. MS Tanner 62, fo. 381v.

saints, and they shall reign over them.' Hugh Peters in 1648 told parliament that the army must root up monarchy not only in England but in France and other kingdoms round about.[89] Robert Ram in his *Souldier's Catechisme* told the soldiers that their task was nothing less than 'the pulling down of Babylon, and . . . the advancement of Christ's kingdom'.[90] We see this same certainty at work in the army of the Scottish Covenanters, who without embarrassment regarded themselves as God's chosen people. 'Zeal for religion transports men beyond themselves', wrote one witness from Edinburgh in 1640. 'We are busy preaching, praying and drilling', added another.[91]

More significant than these random pronouncements are the visual statements made by the thousands of officers on both sides who put their lives and their fortunes on the line when they volunteered for the armies of king or parliament. Drawings of nearly 500 of the banners designed by field and regimental officers for their units have survived. These battle standards, or 'colours' to use the proper military term, not only served the practical function of rallying troops on the battlefield, they also publicized the cause each commanding officer believed that he was advancing. Normal practice was for every officer to design his own colour; thus the several hundred drawings that survive constitute exceptionally revealing evidence for combat motivation. Among the parliamentary banners 72 per cent contained a religious reference, in contrast to only 50 per cent of the royalist colours. More important than this discrepancy is the contrasting flavour of roundhead and royalist piety. Both sides thought that God was backing their cause, but for the roundheads this assurance led to aggressive confidence in military victory, and many expressions of Protestant zeal. 'Let God arise and his enemies be scattered' (Psalm 68: 1), was the choice of several officers. 'If God is with us, who can be against us', was another Biblical favourite. Philip Skippon, the future major-general of the New Model infantry, designed a flag showing a sword of heaven and a Bible, with the slogan 'Pray and fight: Jehovah helps, and he will continue to help'. One of Oliver Cromwell's cavalry captains pictured a walled city above a clutch of flaming hearts and the motto 'aflame with love for Sion'. Only a handful of parliamentary religious standards were negative:

---

[89] Quoted in Christopher Hill, *The English Bible and the Seventeenth-Century Revolution*, 303.

[90] Thomas Swadlin, *The Souldier's Catechisme Composed for the King's Armie* (Oxford 1634), E 1185/5, 9.

[91] Quoted in Carlton, *Going to the Wars*, 34.

anti-bishop or anti-Catholic. One of the most striking portrayed the pope being pushed off his throne beneath the text 'Antichrist must down'. Other banners referred to the alleged horrors of the Irish rebellion. Others pictured Magna Carta, symbol of liberty and England's protection against royal tyranny. Still others suggested that the king had been led astray by evil counsellors. Scottish covenanting banners are less interesting because they all bear the virtually identical mottoes: 'Covenant for religion, king and kingdoms'. Those designed by the officers of the Irish Catholic Confederation boasted more variety, but were overwhelmingly focused on the twin themes of defending Catholicism while remaining loyal to the king. Thus, 'It is just to die for Christ/Long live King Charles', and 'You have overcome all heresies/Long live King Charles', the latter beside a picture of the Virgin Mary holding the infant Jesus, her heel crushing a serpent's head.[92]

Royalist banners, right from the beginning, were less triumphalist than those of parliament. There was much stress on the theological obligation of loyalty to the king. Some flags almost prefigured his defeat. Thus a royalist colour captured at Marston Moor displayed the three crowns of England, Ireland and Scotland, with the motto, 'the fourth [meaning the heavenly crown after death] will be eternal'. This embracing of martyrdom echoed what Thomas Swadlin had to say in his *Soldiers Catechisme Composed for the King's Armie*.[93] Political colours portrayed the parliamentarians as traitors – in particular the six members whom Charles had tried to arrest in January 1642 – and proclaimed the royalist virtue of fidelity. 'Love loyalty', exhorted the Marquess of Winchester's colour. A number of colours expressed class consciousness verging on social panic. Sir John Berkeley's displayed an opulent, peaceful landscape of houses and cornfields being invaded by a crowd of beggars and posed the question, 'Will a barbarian reap these crops?' Finally, a minority of colours on both sides invoked the classical virtues of stoicism, moderation, honour, contempt for death, and martial valour.[94]

---

[92] Alan R. Young, *Emblematic Flag Devices of the English Civil War 1642–1660*, 27–31, 7, 34.

[93] Swadlin, *The Soldiers Catechisme*, p. 9. Robert Ram, in his *Catechisme* for the parliamentary soldiers, had next to nothing to say about martyrdom. See also Margaret Griffin, *Regulating Religion and Morality in the King's Armies 1639–1646*, 207.

[94] I. Gentles, 'The iconography of revolution: England, 1642–1649', in Gentles, Morrill and Worden (eds), *Soldiers, Writers and Statesmen*, 98–113; Ian Gentles 'Why men fought in the British civil wars, 1639–1652', *History Teacher*, 26 (1993), 409–14.

In summary, the several tens of thousands of men who voluntarily put their lives on the line during the civil wars did so partly out of fear of what their enemies would do to them if they did not fight, partly out of desire for material gain, partly from social panic (royalists), partly on account of political and constitutional grievances (mostly parliamentarians), partly out of loyalty and a sense of honour, and, more than anything else, out of zeal for religion – whether the defence of the established church and its liturgy, or the desire to build a godly commonwealth. It was religion more than political principle that separated the two armies at the start of the civil war.

CHAPTER 6

War in England: the first year, 1642–43

The king's declaration of war cleared the air. Both sides now knew what they had to do. The king's task was to retake London and drive the rebels out of parliament. Once this was accomplished it would be relatively easy to bring the navy to heel again and resume the unhindered exercise of sovereignty. For parliament the challenge was to expand its power base beyond London, the home counties and East Anglia to the rest of the country. Only when they had secured the surrender of royalist forces in all parts of England and taken the king into custody would they have any chance of imposing their political will.

The road to Edgehill

The first stages of the conflict were not auspicious for the king. As far as the rest of Europe was concerned Charles, having lost his navy and been stripped of so much power, was hardly any longer a sovereign authority. During the summer and autumn of 1642 parliament erected the administrative framework to conduct a war. A Committee of Safety, with representatives from both Lords and Commons, was appointed. It planned military strategy, developed an intelligence system, and acted as a liaison between field commanders and the houses of parliament. Besides allocating men, money and supplies, it also oversaw the buying and delivery of war materials. At the same time it oversaw parliament's relations with the king, with Scotland and Ireland and the counties, and as well supervised state security and foreign policy.[1] Until it was replaced by the Committee of Both Kingdoms it was parliament's nearest equivalent to the privy

[1] Lotte Glow, 'The Committee of Safety', *EHR*, 80 (1965), 291–2, 295.

council. In the Commons 'the director of the whole machine',[2] almost until his death in December 1643, was John Pym. In the Lords it was Viscount Saye and Sele. Together they headed what came to be known as the Junto that directed the war effort. They used the Committee of Safety to frame policy, and to screen and manipulate the news that parliament was allowed to hear. In addition to setting up a central executive, and fielding an army under the Earl of Essex, they created several regional groupings, of which the Eastern Association under the Earl of Manchester's command was the most successful.

Outside the capital Bristol and Plymouth declared for parliament, while parliamentary forces moved swiftly to increase the number of coastal fortresses under their control. Dover Castle was taken, thanks to the bravery of a handful of soldiers who scaled the forbidding walls in the dead of night, discovering to their delight that it was garrisoned by no more than 20 men.[3] At the beginning of September Sir William Waller forced George Goring to hand over Portsmouth, the greatest naval port on the south coast. The next month a small parliamentary force took the royal bastion of Hereford by deception. They tricked the defenders into believing that the 900 foot and two troops of horse they saw before the walls were just the vanguard of the full parliamentary army.[4]

The king's only significant strategic success was the occupation of Newcastle-Upon-Tyne by the Earl of Newcastle. Newcastle would be the only significant royalist port on the east coast. Not only did it control the vital coal trade, it was the crucial entry point for the enormous quantities of matériel that would soon arrive from United Provinces.

Before leaving Yorkshire Charles made a second attempt to take Hull. Hotham had begun to waver in his adherence to parliament and let it be known that he would turn over the garrison if the king would make a respectable show of besieging it. Charles accordingly approached with 8,000 troops and fired a few cannon shots at the walls. Parliament, however, had anticipated this eventuality, and installed 1,500 additional soldiers under Colonel John Meldrum, a tough veteran with continental experience. On 27 July he sallied out of Hull with his troops and pounced on the unsuspecting royalist foot, spreading panic among their ranks. Their ignominious conduct obliged Charles to abandon the siege.

[2] *CSPV 1643–1647*, 53.
[3] Rushworth, *Hist. Coll.*, Vol. 4, 783.
[4] *CSPD 1641–1643*, 398.

The king then decided to embark on his grand strategy, the capture of London and the expulsion of the rebels from parliament. To do this he had to leave Yorkshire for a more central location from which he could launch his campaign for the capital. He first chose Nottingham, a town which lay athwart the main north–south communication routes of England. However, the reluctance of the Yorkshire gentry to follow him south with their troops meant that the royal muster at Nottingham was a drab, disappointing affair. On a wet windy 22 August the standard was raised, and the proclamation read summoning loyal subjects, but the king had written in so many changes that the herald stumbled over the words. Despite this inauspicious start, the king's army reportedly numbered 3,200 by 10 September. The parliamentary army assembling about 50 miles to the south at Northampton was already much larger, so it was decided to shift the royal headquarters to friendlier territory at Shrewsbury.

Confident in his superior numbers, the Earl of Essex decided to shadow the king, leaving Northampton on 19 September, then advancing quickly to Coventry, Warwick and Worcester. The letters of Sergeant-Major Nehemiah Wharton who was a Londoner with the army have left an unforgettable picture of the confident, jolly, carnivalesque atmosphere that pervaded this untried force. Along the way the soldiers amused themselves by plundering papists, defacing churches, burning altar rails, tearing apart copies of the prayerbook, dressing up in clerical vestments and ducking a hapless whore in the river. These satisfying exploits were punctuated with feasts of venison poached from the estates of 'malignant' royalists. Often the day would be rounded out with an inspirational sermon by Obadiah Sedgwick (Wharton's favourite chaplain), Stephen Marshall or Simeon Ashe, firing the men up for the coming conflict, and at the same time preparing them to die.[5]

Although the king was clearly preparing to move on London, the Earl of Essex decided to continue journeying west to Worcester, thereby allowing the enemy forces to interpose themselves between him and his base. Essex thought that he could score an easy victory against Sir John Byron who was stationed in Worcester with only one regiment of horse. But as his advance guard crossed Powick Bridge on the River Teme south of the city, they were attacked and badly cut up by Rupert's cavalry. Their casualties were between 100 and 150, while Rupert suffered hardly any. The date was 23 September 1642. Essex's troops nonetheless occupied Worcester soon after, avenging their recent humiliation by arresting the

[5] *CSPD 1641–1643*, 372, 379, 382, 387.

mayor, sacking the cathedral, and tearing down the sweet-toned organ that had been the joy and pride of the region. Because this was the first action of the civil war its moral impact was out of all proportion to its military importance. Led by an austere, energetic man of 23, the cavaliers had drawn the first blood. In Clarendon's words this 'gave his troops great courage, and rendered the name of Prince Rupert very terrible indeed . . . In all places [the roundheads] talked loud of the incredible and irresistible courage of Prince Rupert and the king's horse.'[6]

The king began his march from Shrewsbury towards London on 12 October. Essex had positioned himself poorly. Not only had he allowed the enemy to get between him and his base, he had dispersed much of his army in garrisons – Hereford, Worcester, Coventry, Northampton, Banbury and Warwick Castle. This prevented him from acting with any decisiveness against the royalist army. But the king has his problems too. Atrocious weather, and all the extra baggage represented by the artillery train, senior officers' coaches, pack animals and soldiers' families, slowed the army's pace to a crawl. Essex's army lumbered out of Worcester a week after the king had left Shrewsbury. Poor intelligence and inadequate reconnaissance on both sides meant that neither army knew where the other was. Essex had not yet even appointed a scoutmaster-general.

The battle

When detachments from the royalist and parliamentarian armies bumped into each other by accident at Wormleighton, near Edgehill on the night of 22 October, their units were widely dispersed in villages between Cropredy and Edgecote. By the following morning they had concentrated their forces, the king's at the bottom of the steep, 300-foot incline called Edge Hill, and Essex's in the field halfway between Edge Hill and the village of Kineton. On the parliamentary side the main body of infantry occupied the centre, two lines deep, and hemmed in by cavalry on both wings. There was also a small cavalry reserve of two regiments stationed behind the infantry. Beyond the cavalry on either wing were detachments of dragoons. On the left Sir James Ramsey had stationed about 300 of them in an advanced position at right angles to the line. This was so that they could subject any attacker to enfilading fire, meaning shoot into its flank. In line with recent advances the guns of the parliamentary ordnance were placed in pairs between the bodies of infantry in the front line. Both the Swedes

---

[6] Clarendon, *Hist.*, Bk 3, 236–7.

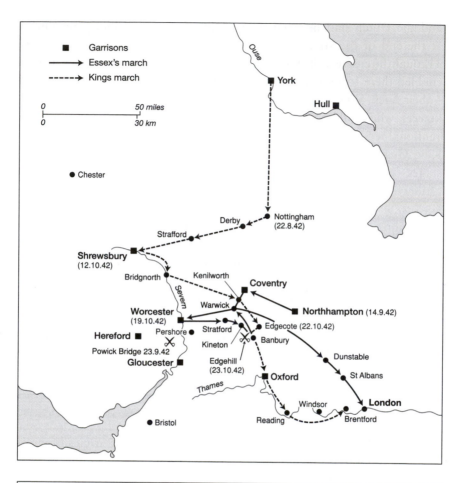

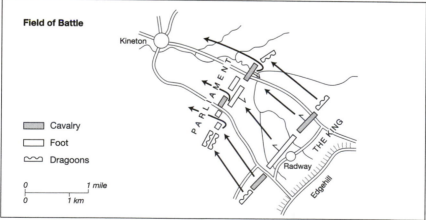

MAP 4 *The Battle of Edgehill, 23 October 1642*
Adapted from Young, Peter, *Edgehill, 1642 (Great Battles)* (Cassell Military, 1995)

and the Dutch had been pioneers of the European military revolution at the end of the sixteenth and beginning of the seventeenth centuries. Through intensive drill they achieved superior discipline, which in turn enabled them to reduce the size of their units and thin out – and widen – their lines. Superior discipline meant shorter re-loading times for musketeers, who could now be stationed eight ranks deep instead of the conventional ten. Twenty-five per cent more men could now give fire at once. King Gustav II Adolph of Sweden took the Dutch innovations several stages further by reducing his lines to six ranks, adding copious field artillery, and interlacing his squadrons of horse with detachments of musketeers. Sir James Ramsey on the left wing adopted the advanced Swedish formations, while Charles Essex's brigade of foot, also on the left wing, followed the simpler Dutch practice by arranging his regiments into a single line, eight ranks deep. Although he had superior numbers and was comforted by the knowledge that Warwick Castle lay behind him as a refuge, the earl did not feel confident enough to take the offensive. For one thing he was still expecting three more regiments of foot, eleven troops of horse and more guns to arrive in the next day or so. Secondly, he was worried about killing the king during the unpredictable action of a battle. So he waited.

The royalists meanwhile were arguing about how to draw up their army in battle formation. The Earl of Lindsey, as commander-in-chief, favoured the Dutch plan. Rupert, whose commission required him to take orders only from the king, argued for the more complex Swedish formation. Charles eventually backed his nephew. Lindsey resigned his generalship in a huff and went off to lead his own regiment of foot.

After a brief artillery duel Rupert ordered his cavalry to advance. As they rode forward with increasing speed, finally reaching a gallop, Ramsey's horse stood still, hoping to absorb the impact. However, they committed the grave error of firing their carbines before the royalists were in range, then lost their nerve and fled. Rupert's men pursued them into Kineton, cutting many down. Sir John Byron's two regiments, which comprised the second line of Rupert's wing, now joined the charge. This was a blunder: they ought to have stayed back and attacked the exposed flank of the parliamentary foot. It was the same story on the royalist left. Wilmot swept away Lord Feilding's regiment, and Lord Digby, commanding the second line, joined in the pursuit. Only a few hundred royalist cavalry remained to participate in the main battle.

A bitter struggle now raged as the two infantries came to push of pike. In the words of a parliamentary eye witness it was 'as bloody a battle as [could] possibly be imagined'.[7] Except for the flight of Charles Essex's parliamentary brigade, both sides stood their ground, and kept up the fight until nightfall. The parliamentary observer boasted that 'our foot . . . plied their business so well, that it seemed to be for the space of four hours only one continued peal of thunder'.[8] Essex had wisely kept two horse regiments (Balfour's and Stapleton's) in reserve. These he now threw into the fray. In conjunction with four foot regiments they attacked Sir Nicholas Byron's brigade, broke into it, and drove it back. The Earl of Lindsey and Sir Edmund Verney fell in the fighting, while Sir Nicholas himself was wounded.

By the end of the afternoon the main body of royalist horse was drifting back to the battlefield, but both riders and their mounts were worn out. For this reason the royalist foot made an orderly withdrawal to the bottom of the Edge Hill escarpment where they spent the night. The battle had ended in a stalemate of mutual exhaustion. It used to be thought that the king might have savoured the fruits of victory had Rupert not allowed the cavalry on both wings to leave the battlefield in reckless pursuit of their fleeing adversaries. But the greater blunder was Sir John Byron's, and also Lord Digby's, both of whom should have prevented the second line of cavalry under their respective commands from joining the pursuit. Had Byron and Digby led their four regiments in attacking the flanks of Essex's infantry, they would likely have carried the day.

Despite the arrival of reinforcements during the night, Essex, contemplating the destruction of the four regiments of Colonel Charles Essex's brigade, had lost his appetite for battle. The king was no better off: many of his horse and about a third of his foot were missing. So the two sides disengaged, the king heading back to his previous quarters, and the earl to Warwick Castle.

Edgehill was a draw. Losses on each side were about equal, totalling 1,500. Charles lost more of his officers, but he had cleared the road to London and captured seven guns to reinforce his feeble artillery train. While both sides had demonstrated sophistication in their deployment of troops along the Swedish pattern, they had thrown away whatever advantages that might have brought them in the first few minutes of battle.[9]

---

[7] *A Trve Relation of the Disastrous and Most Bloody Battell* (1642), Beinecke Lib., Brit. Tracts 1642, T783, 2.

[8] Ibid., 3.

[9] There are good accounts of Edgehill in Gardiner, *GCW*, Vol. 2 and C.V. Wedgwood, *The King's War, 1641–1647*, 134–8. The most authoritative modern account is Peter Young's *Edgehill, 1642*. See also Peter Young and Richard Holmes, *The English Civil War: A Military History of the Three Civil Wars 1642–1651*, 73–81.

The march on London

In the wake of the battle Prince Rupert was all for attacking London at once. That this was not just the reflection of a young man's impetuosity is suggested by the intelligence the king received that 'my Lord of Essex was so shattered and dispersed at the battle . . . that the City of London would declare for him if he approached.[10] But in the Council of War, George Lord Digby prevailed upon the king to defer a strike against the capital.[11] He stopped instead in Oxford to regroup his army and convert the university city into his chief fortress and capital for the next four years. In early November he resumed his advance on the capital, reaching Colnbrook on 11 November. There he received word, through the nascent peace party led by the earls of Northumberland and Pembroke, that parliament desired a truce. This did not deter him from authorizing Rupert to attack the parliamentarian outpost at Brentford the following day. The town was held by two of the best regiments of Essex's infantry, those of Lord Brooke and Denzil Holles. When Prince Rupert's forces swept into Brentford at dawn, both regiments were pushed right back into the Thames. Many drowned, and the two units were effectively destroyed leaving Rupert's men to pillage at their leisure. On their way they had already ruthlessly plundered the country houses of two leading parliamentarians: Viscount Saye and Sele and Bulstrode Whitelocke.

The trauma of the sack of Brentford and the loss of two London-raised regiments stiffened the determination of the citizens of the capital not to allow the metropolis to suffer the same fate. Essex had already hurried back with the remnants of his army and entered London from the east. After Edgehill the Commons had authorized the enlistment of apprentices to beef up the trained bands. They mustered, 6,000 strong in Chelsea Fields. On the night of 12 November Essex received word that the king's forces were on the move. Hastily leaving his seat in the House of Lords, he went into the City, where he spent the next few hours exhorting the citizens to rise in arms to defend the capital. By the next morning he had put together an impressive force of 24,000, which was nearly twice the size of the king's army. It drew up on Turnham Green, a few miles west of the City. Major-General Philip Skippon, the commander of the trained bands, rode from company to company encouraging the soldiers with the words,

[10] Folger Lib., MS V.a.216 ('A briefe relation of the life and memoires of John Lord Belasyse'), unfol.
[11] BL. Add. MS 62084B (Pythouse Papers), fo. 11.

'Come my brave boys, let us pray heartily and fight heartily.' Essex did the same with his regiments. They responded by throwing their caps in the air, shouting 'Hey for old Robin!' For the whole day the two armies eyed each other, as a large crowd of Londoners who had packed picnic lunches and come to watch the spectacle, looked on. The cartloads of food and wine brought out by the City women lent a festive air that belied the real tension of the day. From time to time a party from one army would advance towards the other, prompting many spectators to scatter in the direction of London, while a number of the less courageous soldiers slunk away.[12] At the end of the day, it was the king who withdrew his forces, but in the view of the militants in parliament Turnham Green was a defeat for the over-cautious Essex. To them it became a symbol of lost opportunities.

Peace or mass mobilization (i)?

The political struggle of late 1642 and early 1643

The close shave at Turnham Green sharpened the argument between the pro-war Junto led by Viscount Saye and Sele, John Pym and William Strode, and the budding peace group under the earls of Northumberland and Holland, Denzil Holles and Bulstrode Whitelocke. For the former the narrow escape from royalist clutches, together with the news that the Prince of Orange, the French king and other friends of the queen had recently added £1.2 million to royalist coffers stirred up fear and bitterness. Their answer was to redouble efforts to defeat the foe. Petitions were drummed up demanding that parliament should go on vigorously with the war, turning a deaf ear to any call for pacification. Other voices were heard demanding that the Scots should be invited to help with their army. Nerves frayed as the news from various battlefronts worsened. In the south-west Hopton had occupied most of Devon and placed Plymouth under siege. Lord Wilmot stormed Marlborough, while at almost the same time Worcester was abandoned by the regiment Essex had left behind to hold it for parliament.

In Yorkshire, Newcastle, with an army that had by now grown to 8,000 men, had relieved York from its parliamentarian besiegers. He went on to occupy Pontefract, thereby cutting the parliamentary defence of Yorkshire in two. In mid-December the Earl of Stamford had to abandon Hereford and fall back to Gloucester. The only good news was that Sir

---

[12] Whitelocke, *Diary*, 139–40.

William Waller recovered Winchester and Chichester in quick succession for parliament.

The almost unrelieved gloom induced by these despatches from the north, south and south-west prompted the hard-line war party member Henry Marten, 'whose custom it was to bark at everybody', to voice the first public dissatisfaction with the Earl of Essex's leadership. Referring to his stationary presence at Windsor Marten declared rhetorically 'that all these miseries proceeded from his slowness . . . It was summer in Devonshire, summer in Yorkshire and only winter at Windsor; and therefore desired that we might speedily send to the Lord General to move forward.'[13] A week later, John Pym chose the occasion of the announcement that the queen was on her way from the United Dutch Provinces with troops and money for the king, to launch into a 'violent and vehement speech'. It was all the more notable for the rarity with which the Commons Junto leader paraded his emotions in public. He exhorted his fellow members to declare that

this war was for religion and that his Majesty's army consisted for the most part of papists and was raised for the extirpation of the true religion; that the Earl of Ormond was joined with the rebels against us in Ireland . . . and that therefore we should advise all true-hearted Protestants to take up arms for the defence of their profession.[14]

Pym's outburst was prompted not only by a sense of desperation at parliament's dismal military situation, but also by a wish to exploit the steadily accumulating evidence of the heavy involvement of papists in the royal cause. It was no secret that several weeks earlier, in reply to a petition from Lancashire Catholics, Charles had granted a general permission for any Catholics to join his army.[15] Pym was also worried about the growing peace movement. As awareness of the carnage at Edgehill sank in increasing numbers took fright at what had been unleashed. For Holles the reality of the war struck home when he lost his regiment at Brentford; for Bulstrode Whitelocke the moment of truth was the sack of his house in Buckinghamshire; for William Pierrepont it was the realization that his elder brother, the royalist Lord Newark, now classified as a delinquent by parliament, faced complete financial ruin. They were joined by other men such as Robert Glynne and Edmund Waller in favour of an accommodation

---

[13] BL. Harley MS 164 (D'Ewes diary), fo. 243.
[14] Ibid., fo. 264.
[15] Rushworth, *Hist. Coll.*, Vol. 5, 49–50.

with the king. Many Londoners, despite their heroic defence of their city, were also coming around to the accommodationist view. Peace pressure strengthened with the realization that the financial demands of war had only just begun.

In late November a resolution calling for the disbandment of both armies attracted wide support. In early December there were four days of disturbance, climaxing in a tumultuous peace demonstration at Haberdashers' Hall, where the joint Lords and Commons Committee for Advance of Money were meeting. Claiming that the earls of Bedford and Essex were now for peace, the overwrought crowd, angry at the prospect of more and heavier taxes, shouted for propositions to be sent to the king. They then turned their attention to the Common Council, whom they besieged at Guildhall. In the end they had to be dispersed by the Trained Bands. A fortnight later the mayor, aldermen and sheriffs themselves endorsed a peace petition. The main demand, which was to be repeated many times over the next six years, was that the king should be brought to London. The hope was that his mere presence would prompt such an outpouring of support that parliament would have no recourse but to end the war. Popular pressure for peace became even heavier in January: 3,000 apprentices brought a petition to Westminster and similar petitions sprang up in the pro-war heartland of Bedfordshire, Essex and Hertfordshire.

The public agitation forced parliament's hand. The peace propositions that had been framed in the Lords and for so long blocked in the Commons were finally adopted and sent to the king, over the angry objections of Sir Henry Vane and other partisans of the war. But the fiery spirits were strong enough to force the adoption of 'killer amendments' such as a long list of 'delinquents' who would not be pardoned. In this way the forthcoming negotiations at Oxford were doomed before they started.

January to July 1643: the royalist high point

Meanwhile behind the scenes the partisans of war on both sides were preparing for a resumption of conflict as soon as the weather improved. The king continued to fortify Oxford, as Prince Rupert readied his troops for a decisive strike against the Earl of Essex. For his part the parliamentary lord-general, operating from his outpost at Windsor, tried to tighten the noose around the royalist capital. The Junto had not given up the project for a national association with Scotland in spite of the coldness with which it was received in the Commons. Pym was encouraged to hear from his correspondent in Edinburgh that the 'coals now only want blowing from England and this kingdom will soon be on fire.'[16] Once the peace movement had temporarily quietened, and the treaty at Oxford broken down, parliamentary finances were at last established on a firm footing with the passage of the weekly assessment.

The south

Early in the new year the royalists made a number of small gains which did not materially alter the strategic picture, but which heightened apprehension on the parliamentary side. The previous autumn the cavaliers had been driven out of Somerset and split up: the Marquess of Hertford joining the king at Edgehill, and Sir Ralph Hopton becoming the general of the Cornish cavaliers and twice invading Devon. Under its leaders, the MPs Alexander Popham, William Strode and John Pyne, Somerset was a parliamentary stronghold, which had mobilized up to 12,000 foot in the late summer of 1642. Dorset held out for the royalists, with Sherborne Castle being the focus of their strength. Devon, however was contested territory. Attempts by Hopton and Sir Bevil Grenville to take Plymouth and Exeter were nimbly foiled by Lord Ruthin. Gaining confidence, the roundheads now advanced into Cornwall. In mid-January Hopton and Grenville fell upon Ruthin, whose forces had become separated from Stamford's army, and routed him at Braddock Down, taking 1,250 prisoners, as well as valuable heavy guns and ammunition. It was the infantry that won the day. The moral results of the victory were even more important than the material. Lord Ruthin had gone against the orders of the Earl of Stamford, and found his cavalry wanting. Hopton, a Somerset man, had won the trust of the Cornish, and emerged as a general of real merit. The Cornish royalists followed up this victory by taking Saltash and Okehampton, and again besieging Plymouth. Stamford, however, drove them back, and by the end of February they were content to sign a 40-day truce.

In the south Sir William Waller rolled up an impressive string of victories that gave him the popular title 'William the Conqueror' and cast his superior, the Earl of Essex, in a poor light. Waller's swing through the south had been prompted first by the ill-advised attempt of a small group of royalist Sussex gentry to seize the city of Chichester for the king. Led by the county sheriff, and sure of the support of the cathedral clergy, they took the city by trickery, and set about repairing its decayed wall and fortifications. The merchants and citizens, with their Puritan and political traditions, however, did not rally to the cause. When the Earl of Essex sent

[16] HMC 21, *Hamilton MSS*, Vol. 2, 65–6.

Sir William Waller to retake it, the number of royalist defenders was so small that they soon had to give up. Waller added Arundel and Farnham Castles to his list of conquests, and then turned west to continue his triumphant march. He took Gloucester from Lord Herbert before robbing the cavaliers of Tewkesbury and Hereford. The last two victories proved ephemeral, but Gloucester stayed roundhead till the end of the war, acting as a major obstruction to communications between Oxford headquarters, Wales and the west midlands.

At the beginning of February Prince Rupert left Oxford at the head of five regiments of foot and dragoons, his own troop of lifeguards, and a small train of artillery. His objective was Cirencester, which controlled communications between the royalist capital, Bristol and the south-west. He threw the garrison off guard by making a feint against Sudeley Castle. As he intended, many of the 2,000 soldiers in Cirencester sallied out to help their comrades in Sudeley. Rupert then fell on the relievers, and drove them back past their hedges towards the town. Defenders and attackers entered the town pell mell, the infantry demolishing the chains across the streets, so that the horse could ride through unobstructed. Rupert enhanced his already considerable charisma by riding up and down through 'the hottest volleys' giving commands and encouragements, first to the gunners, then to the infantry. After an hour-and-a-half the battle was over, the royalists having lost only 20 men, and taken 1,200 prisoners as well as large quantities of supplies. It then transpired that the defenders had coerced their men into fighting. Within the town the gentry and clothiers threatened urban workers with the loss of their jobs if they did not join up. Other men asserted that they had been dragged from their ploughs and threatened with being shot if they did not agree to defend the town.[17] Cirencester was a relatively small victory, but its knock-on effect was the capitulation of Sudeley, Berkeley, Tewkesbury, the Vies and Malmesbury. Gloucester, however, the most important prize of all, did not capitulate. Secure behind strongly fortified walls and gates, its governor, Edward Massie, could not be intimidated into surrender. Rupert declined to endanger his troops with either a storm or a siege. His prudence on this and other occasions belies his reputation for recklessness.

Elsewhere in the Midlands the king's forces continued to gain ground, taking the vitally important town of Newark which controlled communications with the north-east, as well as Ashby-de-la-Zouch, Tamworth,

---

[17] *A Particular Relation of the Action before Cyrencester* ([Oxford], 1642), Wing P597, 2, 9, 14–15.

Lichfield, Stafford and Stratford-on-Avon. But they were still stymied by parliament's control of Bristol and Gloucester in the west, Brereton's check-mating of the Earl of Derby in Cheshire and Lancashire, the Hothams' control of Hull, and the Fairfaxes' dominance of the West Riding of Yorkshire in defiance of Newcastle's much larger force.

The north

When the king quit York in the summer of 1642 he left behind the Earl of Cumberland to raise men and money for him. This was an unfortunate choice, for he was, as Clarendon observed, 'in his nature inactive and utterly inexperienced in affairs . . . of that nature'.[18] Before long the Earl of Newcastle, who was also governor of Newcastle-upon-Tyne, eclipsed Cumberland, and was made commander of all the king's forces in the north. The 50-year-old earl completely lacked military experience. Next to the Marquess of Worcester, he was the wealthiest of the king's supporters and no dilettante. Skilful at horsemanship and fencing, he also boasted administrative experience. Whether thanks to training or personal loyalty, his infantry would distinguish themselves by their extraordinary courage at the battle of Marston Moor. His lieutenant-general and chief of staff was the Scot James King, later Lord Eythin, a man of extensive Swedish service, who had fought along side Prince Rupert in 1638. He and the prince unfortunately did not trust each other. Newcastle's commander of horse was Colonel George Goring who had served under the Dutch, and in the Bishops' Wars. In 1642 he had failed to hold Portsmouth for the king and received a harsh notice from the Earl of Clarendon, but in spite of his affection for the bottle, and carelessness about the conduct of his men, he was a brave and skilful battlefield commander of horse.

Parliament had given charge of its forces in the north to Ferdinando Lord Fairfax, but then undermined his authority and abandoned him to his own devices. At the age of 59 Fairfax was no longer an able battlefield commander, but this deficiency was more than made up by the fiery energy of his son. Barely 30, Sir Thomas had already served under Sir Horace Vere in the Netherlands. He equalled Rupert in his ability to inspire his troops. Off the battlefield he was a mild, sickly, religious man, who read widely, and was a zealous 'gadder' to sermons, where he took copious notes. The Fairfaxes were hampered in their efforts to secure the north for parliament by lack of money, and by the hostility of the Hothams, father and son, who had barricaded themselves behind the double walls of Hull,

[18] Clarendon, *Hist.*, Bk 6, 260.

and obtained from parliament an independent authority. Armed with this authority they cut off supplies to the West Riding and recalled all of their troops from Fairfax's army to Hull. The power base of the tiny northern army was the rich clothing towns of the West Riding: Bradford, Leeds, Halifax, Wakefield, Doncaster and Cawood. In the North Riding the main parliamentarian outpost was the port of Scarborough, held by Sir Hugh Cholmley, whose shaky allegiance would soon become apparent.

Once he had secured Leeds Fairfax projected his power southward, taking in Sheffield and Rotherham. By February 1643 his army of less than 3,000 was overextended. The Earl of Newcastle, who had already recruited 10,000 men by the previous November, continued to receive fresh accessions of strength. While parliament controlled the fortress at Hull, the earl had secured Newcastle-upon-Tyne and choked off shipments from the Durham coalfields to London. Throughout the winter of 1642–43 parliamentarians watched the price of coal skyrocket in the capital, and fretted lest the populace mutiny against the war.[19] The queen's arrival in Newcastle bringing cash, sixteen cannon, arms, ammunition and 1,000 experienced soldiers provided a great emotional and material boost for the Earl of Newcastle's army. From Newcastle she processed to York. Soon after her arrival there Sir Hugh Cholmley paid her a visit, and fell under her spell. Once back in Scarborough he announced that he had a commission from Henrietta Maria to hold the garrison for the king.

With the East Riding now in enemy hands, and in the absence of cooperation from Hull, Fairfax had no recourse but to reduce his perimeter. He evacuated Selby, recalled the garrisons from Tadcaster and Doncaster, and dismissed the soldiers at Cawood. In order to cover his retreat to Leeds, he ordered his son Sir Thomas to stage a diversionary manoeuvre. Taking three troops of horse, 300 foot and some clubmen, he made a feint towards York, hoping to distract Colonel Goring. But Goring, with a force nearly twice as large, advanced quickly and trapped him at Seacroft Moor near Tadcaster. As Sir Thomas scrambled to back away, he found that his untrained foot had dispersed into houses in search of refreshment. Goring seized this moment to pounce on the disordered party, killing 200 and taking 800 prisoner. Despite this disaster Sir Thomas had facilitated the larger strategic objective of ensuring that his father's forces reached Leeds unmolested. Nevertheless, from that point until the end of June Newcastle's army, apart from one setback, went from strength to strength. In April, if not earlier, Sir John Hotham and his son Captain John had

---

[19] BL. Harley MS 164 (D'Ewes diary), fo. 209v (30 May 1643).

deserted parliament and pledged their service to the earl.[20] At the end of April Newcastle took Rotherham by storm, sparing the common soldiers, many of whom showed their gratitude by joining the royalist army. Rotherham gave access to Nottinghamshire. Four days later he took Sheffield, most of whose garrison fled to Leeds. This conquest opened the way through Derbyshire. Sheffield also became a major source of munitions for the northern royalist army. Fuelled by these conquests, Newcastle's army grew apace. Every day fresh recruits of horse and foot flowed into his ranks, swelling them, according to Fairfax, from 12,000 to 24,000 within a few months. Given the reluctance of southern forces to come to his aid, the only hope of salvation, said Fairfax, was the Scots.[21]

Just when his military fortunes seemed to have reached their nadir, Fairfax launched a successful counterstrike. Taking 1,500 men – 60 per cent of his army – from the garrisons of Leeds, Bradford, Halifax and Howley, he put them under the command of his son, who moved against Wakefield on 20 May. When Sir Thomas reached the town he found the royalists on the alert, and 500 musketeers lining the hedges outside it. Thinking that the garrison was only 800 or 900 strong, he decided to storm the works in three places. Once his men had opened a breach Sir Thomas charged through it himself at the head of his own troop. Thanks to this daring assault, resistance collapsed and some 1,500 royalists were captured, including 80 officers, among whom was Colonel Goring himself. The roundheads were astonished to discover that with minimal losses they had just taken a garrison of no less than 3,000 infantry and seven troops of horse. With their overstretched army, they could not hold Wakefield, but the conquest gave a badly needed fillip to the morale of Fairfax's army.[22]

The euphoria of success did not last long for Lord Fairfax and his northern roundheads. This was mainly due to the lack of success in organizing help from the south. Never was there more than a trickle of money for his army; meanwhile the crucial royalist stronghold at Newark had fended off an attack by Major-General Ballard and a scratch force of 6,000 from Lincolnshire, Nottinghamshire and Derbyshire. Controlling the passage over the Trent, and access to Lincolnshire and the north, Newark would remain in royalist hands until the end of the first civil war.

[20] The captured letters from the Hothams to Newcastle are in Bodl. MS Tanner 62, fos. 71, 83, 88, 90.

[21] BL. Harley MS 164 (D'Ewes diary), fo. 385. Letter from Ferdinando Lord Fairfax, Leeds, 1 May 1643. Fairfax probably exaggerated Newcastle's numbers by a good 20 per cent.

[22] *A fuller relation . . . Wakefield* (29 May 1643), Wing F2491A, 4–6.

A month later, at the end of March, a force sent by the Earl of Newcastle had overrun Grantham in Lincolnshire. In May Oliver Cromwell's effort to mass several thousand men for a fresh attack on Newark broke down because of quarrels among local roundhead commanders: notably Sir John Gell in Derbyshire and Lord Grey at Leicester. There was also the reluctance of men from East Anglia and Leicestershire to move north. In exasperation Lord Fairfax wrote to all these commanders at the beginning of June peremptorily ordering them to advance and help him 'to suppress this popish army here'.[23]

After the queen left York with 7,000 troops at the beginning of June to join her husband at Oxford, the Earl of Newcastle was at last free to turn his full attention to Ferdinando Lord Fairfax and his vexatious little roundhead army. The distraction of having to protect the queen, as well as his own excessive caution, had prevented Newcastle from eradicating an opponent whose numbers rarely reached even a fifth of his own. On the contrary, Fairfax had been able to hang on, while chalking up occasional morale-boosting victories at Leeds and Wakefield. This helped the northern roundhead army to develop into a confident fighting force. But not before it encountered a disaster that would set it back for a whole year.

Adwalton Moor

In mid-June Newcastle's army, now 18,000 strong, poured out of York in search of the foe. Fairfax was in an impossible position. Denied refuge in Hull, short of food, his treasury bare, he had no alternative but to stay at Bradford and fight. He knew that if he let himself be bottled up by a siege it would mean certain surrender within two weeks. He therefore marched out of Bradford on 30 June with his own 2,500 troops, plus 1,500 from Lancashire, and an unspecified number of ill-armed, untrained country folk. They faced an enemy roughly four times their number. Fairfax's hope had been to surprise the royalists by launching his attack very early in the morning. The plan failed because his army was not ready to move until 8 a.m. By that time royalist scouts had signalled to Newcastle their approach, and he had put his own troops into battle formation on Adwalton Moor. The battle itself was a confused affair of cavalry charges and counter-charges, but at the end of the day the Fairfaxes had to abandon Bradford with heavy losses: 500 men killed and another 1,400 taken prisoner. The royalists suffered few casualties.

[23] *Fairfax Correspondence*, ed. Robert Bell, Vol. 3, 47.

The knock-on effect of Adwalton Moor was immediate and far reaching. In Leeds the 700 royalist captives broke out of the prison and seized the town, waiting for Newcastle to relieve them. Parliament's sympathizers in the north were now 'so disheartened and afraid' that 'none dare appear'. The deputy-lieutenants of East Anglia reported that the counties of Norfolk, Suffolk, Cambridge and East Anglia, parliament's 'present magazines both for money and provisions', were in peril. Small wonder that the Junto tried to prevent the report on Adwalton from being read to the Commons.[24] But now, just as the future looked blackest for the northern roundheads, a ray of light shone out. The citizens of Hull rose up, arrested Hotham, and reclaimed the town for parliament. They then invited the Fairfaxes to take refuge there. And so, at the beginning of July, father and son, by separate routes, crept into Hull along with a few hundred miserable, bedraggled soldiers. In a handsome gesture Newcastle sent Lady Fairfax, who had been captured near Bradford, in his own coach to rejoin her husband. Safe now within the mighty fortress on the north-east coast, Ferdinando and Sir Thomas began the arduous process of rebuilding their near-extinct army. Newcastle's men were exuberant: their victory at Adwalton Moor 'gave new strength, courage and health to every soldier'.[25] Now that he was in control of all the north-east with the exception of Hull, it remained to be seen how Newcastle would exploit his first major victory.[26]

The west Midlands

In the western half of the country the picture was far more blurred for most of 1643. Rupert's seizure of Cirencester was offset by Waller's capture of Malmesbury, and his surprise attack on Lord Herbert's 2,000-strong Welsh army at Highnam, just across the river from Gloucester on 24 March. With professional skill and speed Waller crossed the river so stealthily that Herbert's troops were unaware of his presence. He then encircled them from behind, while troops from Gloucester garrison made a sharp sally. The Welsh cavalry fled, while the infantry surrendered without a fight. In addition to 1,400 men, the king had lost, and Waller gained in one fell swoop, a valuable supply of arms, powder and artillery.

[24] BL. Harley MS 165 (D'Ewes diary), fos. 118v, 107v.

[25] Sir Henry Slingsby, *The Diary*, ed. Daniel Parsons, 97.

[26] This account of Adwalton Moor is drawn chiefly from two PhD theses: Jones, 'The war in the north', 100–21; and Newman, 'The royalist armies in northern England', 183–98; as well as Young and Holmes, *English Civil War*, 111–13.

Meanwhile, Lord Brooke, the roundhead commander of Warwickshire and Staffordshire, took Lichfield from the royalists. This little victory, however, cost him his life. Brooke died instantly when a sniper in the cathedral tower shot him through the eye, and parliament had lost one of its finest commanders. Further north Sir William Brereton, parliament's chief commander in Cheshire, and Sir John Gell, his counterpart in Derbyshire, were planning to unite their forces in order to wrest the town of Stafford from the cavaliers. To counter them the Earl of Northampton, a continental veteran, and Colonel Henry Hastings of Ashby-de-la-Zouch, agreed to concert their efforts. Combined, they were able to put 1,200 men in the field against Brereton and Gell's 1,500 at Hopton Heath, three miles north-east of Stafford. A telling factor in the cavaliers' favour was their demi-cannon, a 29-pounder that they had christened 'Roaring Meg'. Its first shot killed or wounded ten of the enemy, while the second 'made such a lane through them that they had little mind to close again'.[27] Having thus demoralized Gell's stand of pikes, they made a general onslaught against the roundhead centre. Northampton in person led the charge, clearing both Gell's and Brereton's horse from the field in less than a quarter of an hour. But the infantry stood rooted to the ground, and, helped by hedges and a field pocked with coal pits and rabbit holes, held the royalist cavalry at bay. Northampton himself was unhorsed and cut off from his men. Surrounded by enemies and told to surrender, he answered that he 'scorned to take quarter from such base rogues and rebels as they were'.[28] His reward for this haughtiness was to be despatched by a blow to the head from a halberd. Not until darkness fell did the roundhead foot slip silently away, leaving 'great fires and lighted matches on sticks' to cover their retreat.[29]

The centre: Reading

Northampton's death was as great a blow to the king as Brooke's was to parliament. In the hope of remedying this disaster Prince Rupert was ordered to fill the vacuum. He marched north and took the Puritan town of Birmingham on 3 April. The artisans who had crafted thousands of swords for the parliamentary forces were punished by seeing their houses set on fire. Although the firing of the town had been against the express orders of

[27] Sutherland Papers, Vol. 2, fo. 69, quoted in Young and Holmes, *English Civil War*, 118.
[28] Clarendon, *Hist.*, Bk 6, 280.
[29] Bodl. MS Clarendon 23, fo. 121.

Rupert, the memory of it lingered as a blot on his reputation for the remainder of the war.[30] On 21 April Rupert took Lichfield. He had thereby restored an essential link in the communication between Oxford and Yorkshire, and also opened the way for the queen's safe journey from York to rejoin her husband. The same purpose had been served by the recent royalist successes at Newark, Ashby-de-la-Zouch, Tamworth and Stratford-on-Avon.

All these little gains were overshadowed by the mortal threat now being posed to the royalist garrison at Reading. Strategically the town was of the utmost importance: situated half way between the headquarters of king and parliament, it stood astride the main road from London to the west. It also commanded the passage of the River Thames. Whoever possessed it was in a position to strike at the heart of the other. Charles I had placed Sir Arthur Aston, a papist, in charge of the garrison, with 2,000 foot, a regiment of horse and four cannon. He spent the winter of 1642–43 strengthening its fortifications, erecting palisades, adding bastions and redans and digging a ditch.[31] The time of testing came on 15 April when the Earl of Essex, stung by criticism of his inactivity, marched from Windsor with 1,600 foot and 3,000 horse. By then the royalist garrison had swelled to 3,300 horse and foot. The king, who was only too aware of the significance of the roundhead threat, wrote urgently to Rupert recalling him from Lichfield. Secretary Nicholas outlined the ominous implications of a rebel victory: 'they will grow very insolent at London . . . you will have no place of security in these parts, and the rebels will with ease pour down men very fast upon you by water from London'.[32]

Belying his reputation for lethargy, Essex's troops swept round the southern outskirts of the town and seized Caversham Bridge, in order to block a relieving force from Oxford. An attack on Reading itself seemed imminent. With the arrival of Lord Grey of Wark and 5,000 reinforcements from Hertfordshire, Essex now enjoyed overwhelming superiority. But Aston contemptuously rejected the summons to surrender, prompting Essex to begin battering the town's defences with his two heavy guns. Under Major-General Philip Skippon the town was completely encircled, while each day the lines crept closer and closer. Just as negotiations were getting underway for Reading's surrender, the king and Prince Rupert arrived at the head of most of the Oxford army – some 10,000 men. They

[30] Rupert, *Memoirs of Prince Rupert and the Cavaliers*, Vol. 2, 154–5.
[31] Bodl. MS Tanner 62, fo. 76v.
[32] Rupert, *Memoirs*, Vol. 2, 171; BL. Add. MS 18980, fos. 50v, 52v.

found themselves powerless to act because Colonel Richard Feilding, who had taken over from the wounded Aston, had promised not to resort to arms during the period of the truce. Such was his code of ethics 'that if the king himself should . . . command him to do it, he could not forfeit his honour and the faith he had pledged during the truce'. According to Clarendon the king met Feilding during the night and authorised him to surrender the town on condition that the men could march away with all their arms and baggage.[33] These terms were agreed upon, and on 28 April the garrison marched out 'with colours flying, arms and four pieces of ordnance, ammunition, bag and baggage, lighted match, bullets in their mouths, drums beating and trumpets sounding'. The articles of surrender were violated when the soldiers were not only reviled, but disarmed, and their wagons plundered. Essex and his officers witnessed these violations but were powerless to prevent them. The shame of Reading would be often cited in the future as an excuse for similar royalist violations of surrender articles.

Essex had been victorious partly through good luck, but more because he had been well supplied from London with food, money and ammunition. The besieged garrison, though well provisioned, suffered from low morale, as the foot accused the horse of conspiring to desert them. At the beginning of the siege Aston had complained to Rupert about the poor quality of his men.[34] The townsfolk also had no appetite for a long siege.[35]

Many at the Oxford court now accused Feilding of treachery in giving up Reading. Charles himself felt that his honour had been undermined by the article, which he had neither seen nor approved, stipulating that parliamentary soldiers who had deserted to the cavaliers must be handed over to Essex. 'I have not known the king more afflicted than he was with that clause', wrote Clarendon. He felt personally responsible for 'giving up those poor men, who, out of their conscience of their rebellion, had betaken themselves to his protection, to be massacred and murdered by the rebels whom they had deserted.' The unfortunate Feilding was condemned to die, but the king vacillated in imposing the sentence. Twice Feilding mounted the scaffold, and twice he was reprieved, thanks to the pleading of Rupert and the young Prince of Wales.

The quarrel over Feilding's fate epitomized the plummeting morale at the Oxford headquarters caused by the loss of Reading. No longer

---

[33] Clarendon, *Hist.*, Bk 6, 35.
[34] BL. Add. MS 18980, fo. 43.
[35] Bodl. MS Tanner 62, fo. 75.

could courtiers harbour the comfortable illusion that they were well insulated from immediate danger. Lethal feuding erupted among the officers.
Duels led to one officer's death and the wounding of another. But no one
was punished, 'and therefore nothing but disorder can be expected', was
Secretary Nicholas's melancholy reflection to Rupert. Some officers poached
from each other's regiments and paranoia was rife. Rupert sulked.[36]

If at this moment Essex had marched on Oxford the king would have
fled to Newcastle. Fortunately for Charles Essex had his own insurmountable problems. Because his soldiers had been required to sleep on the ground
in frost and rain for two weeks during the siege, many had succumbed to
lethal illnesses. The region between Reading and Oxford continued to be
inundated by rain and flooding, making another prolonged siege a frightful
prospect. Those who were not cut down by disease deserted. By 13 May
the queen's convoy of arms and munitions had arrived at Woodstock.
Henrietta Maria herself arrived two months later with 3,000 well-armed
men and a plentiful supply of cash. When the king greeted her rapturously
on the battlefield of Edgehill, Essex's window of opportunity to attack the
royal headquarters slammed shut. In spite of the manpower and the treasure that she brought, the queen's arrival had an ominous significance that
soon became apparent. With her came a list of demands for her personal
favourites – she even refused a private interview with her husband until he
promised to grant them. And so 'from that hour discontent, heart-burnings,
and jealousies were rife in the king's court and camp'.[37]

By the end of May there were just as many heart-burnings in parliament
over the Earl of Essex's failure to follow up his victory at Reading. Finally,
on 10 June, under the prodding of his critics, he advanced his headquarters
to Thame, barely ten miles from Oxford. While doing so he continued to
complain about his terrible shortage of men, money and horses. The king's
forces by contrast were growing daily stronger. Far from being intimidated
by the approach of the sluggish earl, Prince Rupert saw in it an opportunity to win honour once again. With the king's permission he took a
small party out on a reconnaissance mission.[38] Crossing the River Thame
he destroyed a roundhead troop of horse, then pushed on to Chinnor where
he surprised and overran Sir Samuel Luke's newly raised Bedfordshire
dragoons. After these successes, he turned back towards headquarters. But

---

[36] See Secretary Nicholas's remarkably revealing letter in BL. Add. MS. 18980, fos. 59–
60, repr. (with slight errors) in Rupert, *Memoirs*, Vol. 2, 188–90.
[37] Rupert, *Memoirs*, Vol. 2, 229–30.
[38] BL. Add. MS 62084B (Pythouse Papers), fo. 12.

a larger parliamentary force pursued him and forced him to fight before he could get back across the Thame. After a short struggle Rupert's forces routed the roundheads by attacking them in the flank. Their most grievous loss was John Hampden, who received two bullets in the shoulder, and died a week later. Hampden, a leading member of the war party, was also an icon of principled resistance to unconstitutional taxation. Respected for his intelligence and statesmanship, he had played a valuable role in preventing a breakdown of relations between Essex and parliament. His tact and boundless energy would be badly missed.

The disaster of Chalgrove, the gathering strength of the Oxford army, and the accumulation of royalist victories brought the parliamentary leadership to the edge of breakdown in the month of July. Criticism of Essex as the general who had an army 'which lay still and did nothing' continued to mount. Even the death of John Hampden was blamed on Essex's 'improvidence'.[39] When John Pym wrote him 'that the people began now to think it more safe to be under command of the king's army than under his', the earl was so stung that he offered to surrender his commission. Since they did not yet want to get rid of Essex altogether, Pym and the 'hot spirits' were forced to back-pedal.[40]

The south-west

While this political drama in Westminster was being played out the military struggle for the west of England was approaching its climax. A few months earlier all the south-western counties except for Cornwall had seemed securely under parliament's control. From his base in Plymouth the Earl of Stamford watched over Devon. The populous county of Somerset was a great reservoir of manpower for the parliamentary armies, ably recruited by Sir John Horner, Colonel Alexander Popham and John Pyne. The royalist general in the West, William Seymour, Marquess of Hertford was such an uninspired leader that few paid him much attention. His lieutenant-general of cavalry, the king's nephew and Rupert's younger brother, Prince Maurice, was little better. One commander on the royalist side was, however, quickly emerging as a man of real talent. He was Sir Ralph Hopton, a native of Somerset. In concert with Sir John Berkeley and some of the leading Cornish he had raised a Cornish army that eventually numbered 3,000 foot, 500 horse and 300 dragoons. His first victory had been against the parliamentary magnate John Lord Robartes at Braddock

[39] BL. Harley MS 164 (D'Ewes diary, YCPH transcript), fo. 233v.
[40] BL. Harley MS 165 (D'Ewes diary, YCPH transcript), fo. 100v.

Down. This had been followed by setbacks at Okehampton, Medbury and Sourton Down. At every engagement, however, the Cornish army gained in experience, and its reputation for sobriety, clean living, and respect for civilians spread. Hopton and the other commanders were strict disciplinarians, who also believed in the power of religion to transform raw recruits into a courageous and formidable army. Hopton's chief instrument was 'solemn and frequent actions of devotion'.[41] Gradually he turned the tide. At Stratton in Cornwall, he tried the novel tactic of sending three converging columns up a hill against a force twice his number under the Earl of Stamford. The result was a remarkable victory. By the end of May he had overrun all of Devon except for Plymouth. He then marched into his native Somerset to a rendezvous with the Marquess of Hertford at Chard. Their combined numbers were 8,000 foot, 4,000 horse, 600 dragoons and 31 or 32 guns.[42] Together they took Taunton – 'the fairest, largest and richest town'[43] – Bridgwater and Dunster Castle in quick succession. They went on to drive the roundheads from Glastonbury and reoccupy Wells.

It was now the looming threat to Bristol and Gloucester that brought Sir William Waller scurrying from his siege at Worcester to bolster the beleaguered forces of Stamford in the south-west. He had earlier disobeyed Essex's order to march south.[44] In fact he was the only available parliamentary commander thought to be a match for Hopton in agility and tactical resourcefulness. Hopton and Waller were fitting antagonists, having fought together 20 years earlier in the German wars. Hopton, hoping that he might be able to win over the conqueror by friendly argument, invited him to a private meeting. But in a memorable letter Waller refused the meeting:

Certainly my affections to you are so unchangeable, that hostility itself cannot violate my friendship to your person, but I must be true to the cause wherein I serve . . . The great God, which is the searcher of my heart, knows with what a sad sense I go upon this service, and with what a perfect hatred I detest this war without an enemy . . . We are both upon the stage and must act these parts that are assigned us in this tragedy; let us do it in a way of honour, and without personal animosities, whatsoever the issue be . . .[45]

[41] Clarendon, *Hist.*, Bk 7, 98.
[42] Ralph Hopton, *Bellum Civile*, ed. C.F.H.C. Healey, Vol. 18, p. xxvii.
[43] Ibid., 78.
[44] M.D.G. Wanklyn and Frank Jones, *A Military History of the English Civil War, 1642–1646*, 103.
[45] Quoted in Mary Coate, *Cornwall in the Great Civil War and Interregnum, 1642–60*, 77.

Once he had set up his base in Bath, about ten miles south-east of Bristol, Waller could discern the contours of royalist strategy. Hopton, Prince Maurice and Lord Hertford would march out of Somerset to join forces with the king's main army at Oxford. In conjunction with a further 5,000 troops that the queen was expected to bring from Newark they would then be in a position to roll back Essex's army and overrun London.[46] He used this nightmarish prospect to panic officials in the capital into sending him more men and money. In June he was strengthened by a regiment of cuirassiers or armoured cavalry under the command of Sir Arthur Hesilrige. The cavaliers nicknamed this regiment 'the lobsters' because of the bright iron shells that covered three-quarters of their bodies. The exact size of Waller's force is not known. In addition to Hesilrige's 'lobsters' he had his own cavalry from London, and 1,200 horse and dragoons sent by Stamford. While he probably outnumbered his opponents in cavalry, his infantry bore no comparison with Hopton's experienced Cornish foot.

Lansdown

At the beginning of July Hopton led his forces towards Bath. Waller in turn stationed his troops on nearby Lansdown Hill. With its broad flat top and its steep ridge, it was an exceptionally strong position. On 5 July, after some preliminary skirmishing, Hopton decided to fall back to Marshfield in order to conserve ammunition. Waller sent about 1,000 horse and dragoons to attack them in the flank and rear. This led the cavaliers to turn around and mass their entire army at the base of Lansdown Hill. With superior discipline they dislodged the parliamentarian horse and dragoons, who struggled to find their way back up the hill. In response to his Cornishmen's cry to press on, Hopton ordered a three-pronged advance, the same tactic he had used at Stratton. The middle prong, consisting of Sir Bevil Grenville's pikemen took the road that went straight up the hill, and drove forward in the teeth of withering musket and cannon fire, in addition to three cavalry charges, in the last of which Sir Bevil was struck down. The obstinacy of the Cornish pikemen saved the day for the

---

[46] BL. Harley MS 164 (D'Ewes diary), fo. 234. See also Bodl. MS Tanner 62, fo. 128. This was much closer to the king's actual strategy in 1643 than the imagined 'three-prong strategy' for an attack on London from the north, the west and the south posited by Gardiner and repeated in many textbooks since his time. Wanklyn and Jones in their *Military History*, 92–3, have authoritatively refuted Gardiner.

royalists. In Richard Atkyns's account we have an unforgettable image of them standing at the crest of the hill against the third charge, 'as upon the eaves of a house for steepness, but as unmovable as a rock . . . The air was so darkened by the smoke of the powder, that for a quarter of an hour together . . . there was no light seen, but what the fire of the volleys of shot gave . . .'.[47] At length Waller's troops fell back, as the musketeers who had climbed the hill on the right subjected them to galling fire from the woods. On both sides the cannon roared ceaselessly until it was dark, 'legs and arms flying apace' as Colonel Slingsby recounts.

Technically Lansdown was a royalist victory, but they could ill afford to win many more of this sort. The horse were dispirited by the devastation they had suffered – of the original 2,000 only 600 were still able to fight. Nor had they displayed anything like the valour of the foot. The Cornishmen for their part felt no exhilaration, but 'drooped for their lord [Sir Bevil] whom they loved'. To top it off, as the royalists were trundling back to Marshfield, an ammunition wagon caught fire and blew up eight barrels of powder, killing all the prisoners in it, and two officers. Hopton himself, who was on horseback near the wagon was severely burned, temporarily blinded and paralysed.[48] He would never recover his former vitality or ingenuity. Other leading officers had also been wounded: Lord Arundel of Wardour, Colonel Sir George Vaughan and the Earl of Caernarvon.

Roundway Down

When Waller heard of Hopton's mishap, he called for reinforcements from Bristol and set out in pursuit, hoping to recoup his loss. Learning that Waller wanted a return match, the Marquess of Hertford sent him a message urging 'that we might fight no more in holes'[49] but in open country. Waller agreed, and took up a position on Roundway Hill, just outside Devizes where the royalists were encamped. Outnumbered, short of food, their ammunition depleted, and chilled by the hostility of the surrounding population, the royalists convened a council of war to debate their next move. Hopton, half blind, muffled in bandages, and confined to a chair,

---

[47] Richard Atkyns, *Vindication*, printed in Peter Young ed. ' "The praying captain" – cavalier's memoirs', *Journal of the Society for Army Historical Research* (hereafter *JSAHR*), 35 (1957), 54.

[48] Bodl. MS Clarendon 23, fo. 37. He had already been shot through the arm at the beginning of the battle (ibid., fo. 49v).

[49] Firth, *Cromwell's Army*, 133.

was still able to perceive what had to be done. With the infantry he would stay holed up in Devizes, keeping Waller at bay, while Hertford, Maurice, the Earl of Caernarvon and all the horse rode to Oxford for help.

All that Oxford could spare were Lord Wilmot's and Sir John Byron's brigades, 900 men in all, besides 300 of Prince Maurice's who were still fit to fight. The Earl of Crawford added another 600 horse and a convoy of ammunition. Waller for his part took few precautions, confident that Essex would block any relief force that left Oxford.

In the early afternoon of 13 July two cannon shot were heard. It was Wilmot, three miles off, signalling his approach. Waller at once marched his army of 2,500 foot, 500 dragoons, 2,000 horse and eight field guns onto Roundway Down. There he drew them up into a conventional battle formation with their backs to the steeply descending slope on the west side. His own horse he stationed on the left, Hesilrige's lobsters on the right, the foot in the middle, in conventional fashion. The artillery was distributed between the horse and the foot. Hopton's and Wilmot's combined forces were still outnumbered by Waller's. Hopton's council of war feared that the infantry would be entrapped if they left the safety of Devizes. In vain the ailing Hopton tried to persuade them to move. When at length they came around to his view it was too late; the battle was already underway.

Not waiting for the Cornish foot, Wilmot advanced alone with his 1,800 cavalry diagonally against the right wing of Waller's army commanded by Hesilrige. This diagonal approach converted Hesilrige's regiment from the right wing of Waller's army into its advanced guard. By the same token, Waller's brigade was no longer the left wing, but a rather superfluous rearguard. Wilmot was able to execute this manoeuvre because he had no infantry to slow him down. His complete mobility allowed him to pick off the two wings of Waller's horse consecutively rather than having to tackle them at once. In the first skirmish the royalist forlorn hope drove their roundhead opponents back into their main body, somewhat disordering it. Wilmot then led his own brigade against Hesilrige's cuirassiers, who stayed rooted to the spot, firing their carbines and pistols too early. The ground was then hotly disputed, but after rallying once Hesilrige's 'impenetrable regiment' at length gave way when Byron seconded Wilmot's charge. Crawford's small brigade stayed back as a reserve. Two royalist captains and a cornet all discharged their pistols at point-blank range against Sir Arthur Hesilrige, while one of the captains slashed at him repeatedly with his sword. Hesilrige's armour was so thick that he was impervious to these assaults and was eventually rescued by his men.[50] Byron now turned his

---

[50] The story is told by Richard Atkyns in his *Vindication*, 58–60.

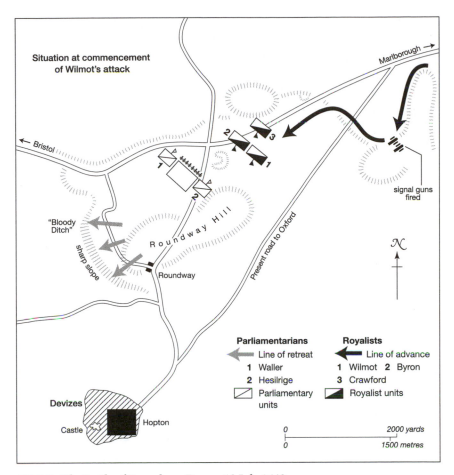

MAP 5 *The Battle of Roundway Down, 13 July 1643*
Adapted from Young, Peter and Holmes, Richard, *The English Civil War: A Military History of Three Civil Wars, 1642–51* (Wordsworth Editions Ltd, 1999)

attention to Waller's brigade. His men obeyed his order not to discharge their pistols until the enemy had spent all their shot. With nothing but empty carbines and pistols facing them, they then fired at point-blank range. Waller's horse did not quit their ground immediately; in fact it took a long tussle before they fell back on their own reserves. Confused panic spread through the troops. In their haste to flee many of them tumbled over the edge of the escarpment, and ended up in a twisted mass of horse- and man-flesh in the 'bloody ditch' at the bottom.

The roundhead infantry were now in grave peril. Waller personally formed them into two bodies, where they grimly defended themselves against cavalry attacks and artillery fire. By this time the royalist commanders in Devizes had been persuaded to despatch the Cornish foot to the battle-field. Waller's officers, seeing the game was up, now mounted their horses and flew off as fast as they could. For parliament it was a dismal defeat. With 600 killed and 800 taken prisoner, Waller's army had for practical purposes ceased to exist. Lord Wilmot had led the Oxford cavalry to a tremendous victory. It was eloquent testimony to the high quality of both his and Byron's brigades. Lightly armed and outnumbered, they had faced down the cream of the parliamentarian cavalry, otherwise known as Hesilrige's 'lobsters' or armoured cuirassiers. The training of Prince Rupert had paid off. As at Edgehill they had not discharged their firearms till the enemy had spent all his shot. This tactic was 'punctually observed', so that the cavaliers were able to fire with impunity upon their foe at close range. Rupert had also trained them to advance as close together as possible, keeping their unsheathed swords in their hands.[51] Wisely Wilmot had avoided tangling with the enemy foot until he had taken out their horse. The infantry were in any event incapable of inter-vening in the cavalry duel, and could only stand on the sidelines and gape. When confronted with a truly professional force Waller had been embar-rassed to find that he possessed few cavalry officers who really knew their business. With all these factors accounted for, Wilmot's victory was still, in Peter Young's words, 'well-nigh incredible'.[52]

The way now lay open for the king's forces to complete the conquest of the west. Waller took refuge in London, leaving the royalists to possess Bristol. Prince Maurice then led a small force to reduce Dorchester and Weymouth, and besiege Exeter.

The political fall-out at Westminster

In London, while there were bitter recriminations behind the scenes, the public were shielded from the full knowledge of the disaster until August. The ambiguous result of Lansdown was trumpeted as a parliamentary victory. The news was manipulated in such a way that Waller's army and Sir Arthur Hesilrige's role in it were given maximum coverage.[53] Hesilrige's

---

[51] Firth, *Cromwell's Army*, 133.

[52] Peter Young, 'The royalist army at the battle of Roundway Down, 13th July, 1643', *JSAHR*, 31 (1953), 129.

[53] See for example, *A True Relation of the Great and Glorious Victory . . . Obtained by Sir William Waller, Sir Arthur Haslerig, and Others . . .* (1643), E60/12, and *A Copie of a Letter Sent from the Maior of Bristoll unto a Gentleman . . . in London* (Bristol, 8 July 1643), E59/25.

courage, and the fact that he was wounded in the thigh, redounded greatly to his credit. Much was made of the fact that his lobsters were 'the first that made any impression upon the king's horse, who . . . were not able to bear a shock with them'.[54] Much was also made of the fact that Waller had led four charges in person. Hesilrige's and Waller's confidential letter to the Speaker told a different story. While they minimized their casualties and bragged about their own roles, they paid tribute to the Cornish infantry, and conceded that 'we lost that day'. They went on to request that Essex protect them from any intervention by the king's Oxford army. But since this request was penned on the eve of the battle of Roundway Down, it was too late for Essex to do anything about it.[55] Not even the MPs at Westminster were allowed to know the full story of what had happened in the west. As the news gradually trickled out the war party's spin doctors turned it into yet another of the Earl of Essex's failures, and used it as a pretext to press for a new general for the army.[56] Bulstrode Whitelocke, an astute moderate, recorded that Roundway Down did cause a diminution of Waller's fame. But the damage was controlled when Waller posted quickly back to London and by his presence 'silenced invectives against him'.[57]

The hapless Earl of Essex can only have felt a terrible sense of injustice. His signal victory at Reading in April had scarcely been noticed; instead he had been blamed for Hampden's death in June. Now he found himself being charged with responsibility for Waller's defeat at the hands of a divided, numerically inferior and under-equipped enemy in the west. The best military advice he could offer to his political masters was to seek peace with the king. Essex's new-found role as a peace advocate stemmed in part from his own deeply felt frustration, and in part from the skilful lobbying of a coalition of peace peers led by the Earl of Northumberland. His proposal drew from Pym the answer that peace was not possible with 'an enemy that delights in cruelty, that spoils not only for necessity or gain, but of purpose to consume and to destroy'.[58] Defeat on the battlefield and

---

[54] Quoted in D.A. Costa, 'The political career of Sir Arthur Hesilrige' (D.Phil. thesis, University of Oxford), 172–3.

[55] Bodl. MS Tanner 62, fo. 164. It is likely that Waller also wrote directly to Essex asking him to block royalist reinforcements from leaving Oxford, but the letter has not survived.

[56] BL. Harley MS 165 (D'Ewes diary), fos. 127, 128.

[57] Bulstrode Whitelocke, *Memorials of the English Affairs* (hereafter Whitelocke, *Memorials*), Vol. 1, 205.

[58] Bodl., MS Tanner 62, fo. 168. This was the letter that Pym drafted for Speaker Lenthall's signature.

the political squabbling to which it gave rise, were bad for recruitment. Essex complained that his once-proud army had shrunk to 5,500 because of sickness, desertion, lack of pay, clothes and other necessaries, and the widespread belief that a different army was soon going to be raised. He bluntly demanded that his own force should be rebuilt before any other was set on foot, that he should be the only one to grant commissions for the raising of troops, and that there should be an inquiry into the reasons for the losses in the west. The Commons grudgingly agreed that he should have 4,000 infantry recruits.[59]

Bristol and the undermining of Viscount Saye and Sele

The political conflict in London was only intensified by the loss of Bristol at the end of July. As the second city in the kingdom and the leading port on the west coast, Bristol was a rich prize. Its governor was Nathaniel Fiennes, son of Viscount Saye and Sele. He was not a gifted soldier, and seems to have owed his appointment to political influence. Conscious at all times of the enmity of Bristol's merchant class, he had nevertheless spent the winter of 1642–43 building up the town's defences, and raising men and money for parliament's war in the west. The original city was endowed with a natural moat in the form of the Rivers Avon and Frome, which almost surrounded it. The unmoated gap on the east side had long ago been plugged by a massive castle covering 18 acres, equal in size to the White Tower in London. Its high walls were 12 feet thick at the base. After the civil war broke out Fiennes had supervised the extension of the fortifications, throwing up an earthen wall five feet high and three feet thick. Running north of the River Avon beyond the town's western side, it was punctuated by five forts, each surrounded by a dry ditch and palisades. The trouble was that the perimeter had now grown to five miles, and by the summer of 1643 the fortifications were not yet complete. A great number of men and guns were required to defend Bristol adequately. While he had nearly 100 guns, Fiennes was down to a mere 1,800 men in the garrison, because he had previously given 1,200 to Waller, as well as sending half of Colonel Alexander Popham's regiment into Somerset.

After Roundway Down Fiennes offered shelter to Waller's shattered army. But Waller judged the town indefensible and retired to London. Both cities became royalist targets. On 18 July Prince Rupert left Oxford at the head of 14,000 troops and a formidable train of artillery.

[59] BL. Harley MS 165 (D'Ewes diary, YCPH transcript), fo. 132v.

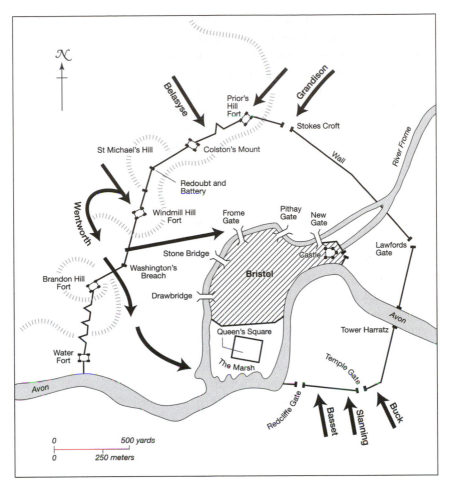

MAP 6 *Royalist capture of Bristol, 26 July 1643*
Adapted from Young, Peter, and Holmes, Richard, *The English Civil War: A Military History of Three Civil Wars, 1642–51* (Wordsworth Editions Ltd, 1999)

On the 23 July Rupert rendezvoused with the western army, which took up a position south of the town, facing Redcliffe and Temple Gates. Our sources do not specify the size of their cavalry, but the foot numbered only 1,000. Always impatient with sieges, the prince carried the Council of War in favour of a storm. After Fiennes rejected the summons to surrender the storm was unleashed on the morning of 26 July. The Cornish infantry tried several times to scale the wall but were beaten back by showers of bullets and stones. Counted among their heavy losses were several leaders: Sir Nicholas Slanning, Colonel Buck and Colonel Trevanion. Major-General Bassett and Colonel Sir Bernard Astley were both wounded. Meanwhile on the opposite side Lord Grandison's tertia was repulsed three times from Prior's Hill Fort, and retreated, the younger Grandison mortally wounded. The only group to penetrate the outer defences was Colonel Wentworth's tertia which hurled grenades as the men stormed the line and tore a breach in the earthworks with their halberds, partisans and bare hands. Once inside the breach the cavalry met stubborn resistance from pikemen, musketeers and dragoons. Then infantrymen with flaming pikes arrived and turned the tide. According to de Gomme 'these firepikes did the feat'.[60] Many of the defenders fled crying 'wildfire'. It was now 4 p.m., but the fight was far from over. There ensued a desperate struggle to break the town's inner defences through Frome Gate. Colonel Lunsford was shot through the heart, Rupert lost his horse, and the attackers were 'much tired'. But the timely arrival of reinforcements, and Rupert's repeated interventions saved the day.

Having recovered another horse, he rode up and down from place to place where most need was of his presence: here directing and encouraging some; and there leading up others. Generally it is confessed by the commanders that had not the Prince been there, the assault, through mere despair, had been in danger to be given over in many places.[61]

Rupert had been advised to make things easier for himself by setting fire to the city, but he was determined to preserve it in good condition for the king. Fiennes, with his 1800 defenders, had put up a remarkable resistance to an attacking force that outnumbered them by almost ten to one, and had made them pay dearly for their conquest. Not only had the king lost several fine officers, 500 of the choice Cornish infantry had been slain and many wounded. Clarendon thought that the royalists could not afford many more such victories.[62]

Rupert readily granted Fiennes's request for a truce, and agreed to generous terms. The garrison was allowed to march out and guaranteed a safe convoy to Warminster. The guarantee was not honoured by the common soldiers who, citing their mistreatment by Essex's men at the surrender of Reading three months earlier, plundered the defeated roundheads as they emerged from the town. Rupert and Maurice were furious at this breach of

---

[60] Sir Bernard de Gomme's 'Journal', printed in C.H. Firth (ed.), 'The siege and capture of Bristol by the royalist forces in 1643', *JSAHR*, 4 (1925), 192.
[61] Ibid., 194.
[62] Clarendon, *Hist.*, Bk 7, 131.

honour, and rode among the plunderers hacking and slashing them with their swords. Richard Atkyns was sure that the dishonouring of the articles of surrender at Bristol caused the parliamentary garrisons at Plymouth and Gloucester to hold out when they had been on the verge of yielding.[63] Rupert later sent a formal apology to Fiennes for his troops' behaviour.[64]

As the son of Viscount Saye and Sele, one of the radical leaders in parliament, Nathaniel Fiennes found himself the object of a vicious attack by Saye's enemies at Westminster. The attack was led by the Presbyterians Clement Walker and the redoubtable William Prynne. Ignoring the weakness of the garrison in manpower, as well as the intrinsic difficulty of defending a city with so large a perimeter, they impugned Fiennes's honesty, courage and judgement. There was no let-up in their campaign of vilification for the remainder of the year. They sneeringly compared his speedy surrender to Major-General Massie's tenacious and successful resistance at Gloucester. But a close reading of their indictments reveals that their animus had less to do with Fiennes's supposed military incompetence than with politics and religion. They accused him of underhandedly ousting a political foe, Colonel Charles Essex, as governor of Bristol. They referred to his 'powerful solicitor' in parliament, namely his father Lord Saye, and hinted darkly at the latter's corrupt dealings. They blamed the alienation of Bristol's population from the parliamentary cause on Fiennes's favouring of religious radicals, and the abuses they had committed in various churches. In the end all these slurs produced the desired effect: Fiennes was court-martialled for premature surrender and sentenced to death. The Earl of Essex reprieved him, but his career was finished. For Lord Saye the consequences were if anything more serious. Politically he was hobbled, and his influence did not revive for many months.[65]

Peace or mass mobilization (ii)?

The struggle for London in late 1643

The attack on Nathaniel Fiennes was merely one aspect of the larger political crisis that gripped the capital in the wake of parliament's multiple

---

[63] Young (ed.), ' "The praying captain" ', 63.

[64] *A relation Made in the House of Commons, by Col: Nathaniel Fiennes, concerning the Surrender of the City and Castle of Bristoll* (5 August 1643), E64/12, 10.

[65] See for example BL. Add. MS 18778 (Yonge's diary), fo. 36 (9 September 1643), where Sir Edward Bainton was reported to have accused Saye, along with Pym, of having 'betrayed the west'.

military defeats in the spring and summer of 1643. The royalist plot to overthrow London from within, followed by Newcastle's victory at Adwalton Moor, Hopton's at Lansdown, Wilmot's at Roundway Down, a royalist rising in Kent in defence of the Book of Common Prayer, and a host of smaller victories had, by the end of July, shaken the parliamentary leadership to its core. Why had the royalists done so well, given that parliament controlled London, the navy and the more prosperous part of the nation? In the long run parliament's greater economic depth would be a telling factor, but in the beginning the royalists were quicker off the mark. The king was able to tap the resources of his wealthy supporters, who not only placed large sums of money at his disposal, but also mobilized large numbers of troops. It is often overlooked that while in most parts of the country the two sides raised roughly equal numbers of troops, in the northeast the royalists out-recruited the parliamentarians by a ratio of at least five to one. The royalists could also boast more and better cavalry, and, in Rupert, Wilmot and Goring, better commanders. Not until 1644 did the roundhead armies develop commanders of equivalent or better calibre.

Meanwhile, in the face of failure, the Lords and the Commons became more faction-ridden than ever. Three contradictory solutions were proposed to the crisis. The 'violent spirits' wanted to replace the Earl of Essex as lord-general with Sir William Waller. The shrinkage in the army's size would be overcome by a 'general rising' of the people. Throughout most of July and early August the radicals threw their energies into mobilizing a volunteer army for Waller, but in the end hardly anyone signed up. The experience was instructive. After a brief initial burst of enthusiasm most people, as revolutionaries are always disappointed to learn, quickly tire of the struggle. They then have to be coerced into fighting for the cause in order to stave off collapse.

The second solution was advanced by the Northumberland–Holles peace group, who almost won the Earl of Essex to their side. On 10 July the lord-general wrote parliament urging serious peace talks with the king. If the talks failed then the armies of both sides ought to meet at an agreed-upon battlefield, the king being absent, and settle the conflict by a single battle. This idea, a throwback to the medieval trial by battle, drew mockery from the radicals. While Essex's letter was being read out D'Ewes saw several of them 'pluck their hats over their eyes'.[66] Both Lords and Commons voted it down.

---

[66] BL. Harley MS 165 (D'Ewes diary), fo. 122v.

The peace party peers did not give up. For the rest of the month they continued their efforts to detach Essex from the Saye–Pym Junto. They also devised a new negotiating package that went a long way towards meeting the king's requirements.[67] They laid the scheme before the House of Commons on Saturday 5 August. In the Commons the Junto denounced it as a complete capitulation, a surrender of the power of the sword into the king's hands. But after a long tussle their attempt to kill the scheme was turned aside: the majority agreed to continue the debate after the weekend. It looked as though the Northumberland–Holles peace party was poised to carry the day, in which case Essex might very well have thrown in his lot – and his army – with them. This prospect stirred the Junto to organize an intimidating demonstration of 5,000 militants to overawe moderate and pro-peace MPs when they came to parliament on the Monday morning. The manoeuvre worked. Even though the peers were enraged by the mob's violence, and threatened to adjourn the upper house and bring parliament to a halt, the Junto was not deflected from its objective. Enough MPs were frightened off for the peace package to be rejected by a narrow margin in the Commons. A women's peace demonstration orchestrated by the Northumberland–Holles group two days later was ruthlessly crushed. It was an instructive lesson about who still controlled London.[68]

The collapse of the movement for a general rising of the people, and the failure of the peace peers' initiative cleared the way for the Saye–Pym Junto to put a third solution on the table. Since the end of June the Junto, after criticizing Essex for his dilatory conduct of the war, had turned to cultivating the prickly earl. In late July they redoubled their efforts to increase parliament's revenue in order to feed, clothe and equip his pathetically shrunken army. The Excise ordinance was passed. A fresh weekly assessment was levied on every county (but not London). A new committee – the Council of War – was voted. Dominated by Pym and other war-party moderates, it effectively supplanted the increasingly discredited Committee of Safety on which Henry Marten had been an all-too-loud voice.[69] On 10 August an ordinance was passed authorizing the deputy lieutenants in the counties, and the London militia committee to impress men for the war effort.[70] The Junto also deployed all its negotiating skills to extract from the sullen lord-general an undertaking to make Waller major-general of

[67] HMC 4, *Fifth Report* (House of Lords MSS), 99.
[68] Scott, *Politics and War*, 64.
[69] Glow, 'The committee of safety', 309–10.
[70] *LJ*, Vol. 6, 175.

the London forces, even if, as Essex pointedly noted, 'he did therein wrong to Serjeant-Major-General Skippon who was a gallant man' and who, after all, had been in charge of the London militia since the start of the war.[71] The Council of War now addressed itself to mustering infantry recruits from London to fight under Essex.

The tide begins to turn

The sense of impending disaster in London can only have been heightened by the news from East Anglia. On 28 July Oliver Cromwell and Sir John Meldrum had relieved Gainsborough, Lincolnshire from a royalist blockade. But their success was short-lived: within hours the Earl of Newcastle's entire army appeared before the town, forcing their precipitate retreat, and Gainsborough fell into royalist hands. By mid-August Newcastle controlled almost all Lincolnshire, with his forces raiding up to the walls of Boston. The parliamentary heartland, crucial for food, manpower and cash, was now in jeopardy. Responding to recommendations from a committee of East Anglian MPs, parliament agreed on 16 August that the Earl of Manchester should mobilize an army of 20,000 men to defend the six associated counties of Norfolk, Suffolk, Essex, Cambridgeshire, Huntingdonshire and Hertfordshire. Newcastle, by his inaction, allowed the Association to get off the ground. Cromwell was then able to score a major success by linking up with the Yorkshire cavalry under Sir Thomas Fairfax. On 11 October they routed a substantial force of royalist cavalry at Winceby. On the same day Lord Fairfax dealt another body blow to the northern royalists when he sallied out from Hull and overran Newcastle's siegeworks. In the face of these two setbacks Newcastle abandoned his march on London and retired to York. Manchester capitalized on the situation by taking Lincoln on 20 October. The victory at Winceby had been organized by Manchester and largely executed by Sir Thomas Fairfax. Much was also due to Oliver Cromwell's training of the Eastern Association horse. The result was the first big victory of parliamentary over royalist cavalry, and a big shot in the arm to the morale of the parliamentary armies.[72]

Parliament's impressment ordinance had not come in time to supply Essex with enough troops for his next expedition – the relief of Gloucester. Four trained bands regiments of the London militia, however, were thrown into the breach. From the poorer parishes fronting on the Thames, and

[71] BL. Harley MS 165 (D'Ewes diary), fo. 146v.
[72] Holmes, *Eastern Association*, 94–6; Alfred H. Burne and Peter Young, *The Great Civil War*, 114–18.

'being honest men and well affected', they did not share the pro-peace sentiments of their more prosperous fellow-citizens.[73] In spite of the revitalization of his army, Essex found it difficult to forgive Waller for blaming him for his defeat at Roundway Down. He still refused to grant Waller a commission unless it was limited in duration, and hedged in with restrictions – he denied him the independent power to commission colonels, for example.[74] Finally, just in time for the trek to Gloucester, the quarrel was patched up. Since London had come up with the money and the men, Essex reciprocated by issuing an unrestricted commission for a sergeant-major-general of ten regiments of horse and ten of foot. But he saved face by requiring parliament, not himself, to fill in the name of the person who was to receive the commission. Waller for his part made conciliatory noises, exclaiming that he was now ready to die at Essex's feet.[75]

The siege of Gloucester

Immediately after the storming of Bristol there was a big debate in the royalist Council of War over whether to attack London or Gloucester. As the news flowed in of the collapse of resistance in one town after another, and the demoralization of the parliamentary leadership in London, a bold strike against the capital seemed to recommend itself. The king had plenty of friends there, and royalist uprisings had occurred in Kent and Norfolk. But there were also reasons for delay. The Earl of Newcastle, for all his victories in Lincolnshire, refused all entreaties to bring his army further south. His excuse was that Hull was still controlled by the enemy, and his best regiments were loath to leave their native Yorkshire. Localism bedevilled the royalist war effort in the west as well. The 5,000 Welsh levies would not march beyond the River Severn, while the Cornish infantry preferred reducing Plymouth to marching east. Added to the king's tribulations was the undeniable strategic importance of Gloucester, still unconquered. At the centre of the Cotswold wool trade, it was in a commanding position on the River Severn, blocking communication between royalist Shrewsbury and Worcester on the northern reaches, and Bristol at the river's estuary. Gloucester also barred the way from the king's main armies to the iron foundries in the Forest of Dean and the region of South Wales where the Marquess of Worcester and his son were still recruiting.

[73] BL. Add. MS 18778 (Yonge's diary), fo. 19.
[74] Ibid., fo. 19v.
[75] Ibid., fo. 21v.

Gloucester seemed a fruit ripe for the plucking. With a population of less than 5,000, and a defending force of barely 1,500, its fortifications included little more than an insignificant moat and an old wall. The governor, Edward Massie, was rumoured not to be strongly wedded to the roundhead cause. His friend William Legge assured the king that if he appeared in force before the city Massie would surrender to him. After the fall of Bristol Gloucester did indeed appear doomed, and Massie did conspire to surrender it.[76] Both the corporation and Massie's own officers, however, were virtually unanimous in opposing capitulation. Their insistence on holding out stiffened Massie's backbone. For all his political ambivalence he mounted an effective defence with minimal resources. Already he had gone to the trouble to develop a gunpowder manufacturing capacity in the city. He supervised the destruction of suburban houses, as well as numerous barns, stables and orchards that were beyond the city's defences in order to create an obstacle-free killing zone. These houses constituted one-third of the city's stock.[77]

Prince Rupert was in favour of storming the city at once. Charles, appalled by the carnage at Bristol, would not countenance the idea. He was also anxious about the further bleeding of his main army, which was down to about 6,000 foot and 4,000 horse. His advice rejected, Rupert declined to command the besieging force, contenting himself with the command of the cavalry under the generalship of Lord Ruthin. The exact size of the besieging force is uncertain. In addition to the Oxford army there appear to have been about 5,000 Welsh on the west side of the city. A further 2,000 troops were raised in Gloucestershire, but as late as 10 August most of them still lacked arms. From the west Hopton on 4 September sent another 2,500 troops well supplied with ammunition and powder, but by then it was too late.[78] In fact, the combined royalist forces were less formidable than they appeared. Clarendon called them 'a miserable army' because of their recent losses. At the beginning of September for example, Rupert's own horse regiment was reported to consist of 300 men, of whom a mere 93 were adequately armed.[79]

Although Ruthin was later accused of sluggishness and lack of imagination, the records show that he conducted a vigorous siege, aggressively

---

[76] David Sidney Evans, 'The civil war career of Major-General Edward Massey (1642–1647)' (PhD thesis, University of London), 71–7.

[77] Stephen Porter, *Destruction in the English Civil Wars*, 77; Malcolm Atkin and Wayne Laughlin, *Gloucester and the Civil War: A City Under Siege*, 66.

[78] BL. Add. MS 18980 (Rupert Papers), fos. 106, 113.

[79] Clarendon, *Hist.*, Bk 7, 176; BL. Add. MS 18980, fo. 113 (Hopton to Rupert).

probing the city's defences, and subjecting it to a withering artillery assault. He at first terrorized the inhabitants, but also strengthened their will to resist. Breaches in the wall were quickly repaired. Fires were put out. Morale was sustained by staging several fasts during the 25-day siege, while Massie kept up the spirit of his troops by mounting frequent raids against the besiegers. Those who were inclined to capitulate were reminded how the royalists had violated their articles of surrender with the citizens and garrison of Bristol.

The besieged city was also sustained by the assurance that the Earl of Essex was on his way with a formidable relieving force. In London parliamentary leaders papered over their differences and persuaded the inhabitants of the metropolis that their fate was bound up with Gloucester's. It was preferable to pin down the king's forces there than have him march on the capital. A compulsory loan was exacted, to pay for the three new auxiliary regiments to replace the four handed over to Essex's army. Pym wrought the political miracle of getting the lord-general to forget his peace propositions, seize the chance to repair his military reputation, and also incidentally take Sir William Waller down a peg.

At Hounslow, a few miles west of London, Essex reviewed his resurrected army on 14 August. From there he marched into Buckinghamshire, picking up further reinforcements that swelled his numbers to 15,000. As he approached Gloucester he was shadowed by Wilmot with a small force of cavalry, and by Rupert with the main body of 4,000 royalist horse. The prince's attempt to cut off the London trained bands near Chipping Norton was unsuccessful. The pikemen stood their ground, while the firing of the musketeers broke the force of his attack. On 5 September Essex drew together the various columns of his army into Swedish formation, 800 to 1,000 men abreast and six lines deep on Prestbury Hill, about ten miles from Gloucester. From here he descended into the Vale of Gloucester, Rupert's cavalry harassing his front line but doing little harm. He arrived in the nick of time, Massie being down to his last three or four barrels of gunpowder. The king did not want to run the gamble of bringing Essex to battle there and then, with the attendant risk of a pincer movement from the combined troops of Essex and Massie. So he lifted the siege, and the triumphant lord-general entered the city on 8 September. Charles's hope was to fight Essex further afield in open country. But his troops had been fresh, while Essex's were fatigued and hungry after a long march, and probably inferior in numbers. Clarendon was scathing about the royalist refusal to fight at Gloucester.[80]

---

[80] Clarendon, *Hist.*, Bk 7, 238.

Essex's relief of the city had strategic significance. The retention of Gloucester as a base for parliamentary operations in the west prevented the royalists from integrating their strongholds in the west, Wales and the south Midlands into a militarily coherent force. Essex's success lifted many spirits; it was a symbolic turning point that broke the run of royalist victories.

The battle of Newbury

Two days after his arrival Essex quit the city, intending to return to London by a circuitous route. Charles moved to block his withdrawal, and the two armies followed roughly parallel paths, racing towards Newbury, through blustery weather, lashed by rain. If the king could secure this vital town first he would be able to prevent Essex's further progress towards the metropolis, and engage him on advantageous terms. Despite the melting away of 2,000 men on the way from Gloucester,[81] that is exactly what happened: on 19 September, with a flurry of hoofbeats and pistol shots, Rupert's horse swept into the town and drove off Essex's advance party. Fooled into thinking that the royalist foot were close behind, Essex halted his army, permitting the main body of the royalist army to enter Newbury. His men, who were already weary, starving, desperately thirsty, and yet 'pickled' by the rain, had to camp that night under a chill autumn sky.[82] The king's men were amply supplied with the food that had been stored in the town for their opponents, and many of them now slept in dry beds. Charles's army had successfully planted itself directly across Essex's path to the capital. Round one had been won decisively by the king; Essex, cut off from his base, would have to fight or starve.

Charles had been joined by more cavalry, some from Oxford, some from the west under Prince Maurice, fresh from his triumph at Exeter. In cavalry and artillery he had the advantage over Essex, while his infantry was almost as good. At the Council of War that night Rupert, again belying his reputation for impulsive rashness, argued against fighting on the following day. With Essex immobilized, they could afford to wait until more ammunition arrived from Oxford. The king inclined to agree with him, but both were overruled by events. With more audacity than intelligence some younger royalist officers provoked a number of actions.

---

[81] Clarendon, *Hist.*, Bk 7, 210.

[82] One captain was said to have offered 20 shillings for a drink of water: BL. Add. MS 18778 (Yonge's diary), fo. 53v.

What started as skirmishes quickly flared out of control until both armies
were wholly engaged. Despite the presence of many generals the royalists
fought the battle with little trace of tactics and no order of battle. Short
of powder, their field artillery was unable to inflict much harm on the
enemy.

The thread of the narrative of 20 September is difficult to disentangle,
chiefly because the main accounts flatly contradict each other.[83] To the
south of Newbury the ground rises gently in a series of small fields and
hedges for about a mile until it reaches a plateau. In places on the plateau
such as Wash Common and Endbourne Heath the ground was relatively
open. On the northern edge of the plateau a small ridge or spur known as
Round Hill juts out. Most of the royalist army was stationed between the
foot of the plateau and the River Kennet. Writing more than four years
after the event, Sir John Byron accused his fellow commanders of 'a most
gross and absurd' error, 'in not viewing the ground . . . and in not possess-
ing ourselves of those hills above the town by which the enemy was necessarily to march the next day to Reading, the regaining whereof afterwards
cost so much blood'.[84] This accusation is at least partly corroborated by
Lord Digby's account, published a few days or weeks after the battle, in
which he stated that during the night of the 19–20 September Essex had
managed to get his battery on 'a round hill', from which they were able to
command the whole plain before the town where the royal army stood,
'insomuch that unless we possessed ourselves of that hill, there was no
holding of that field'. Essex and his advisers had demonstrated shrewdness
and skill in choosing their ground.[85] Yet, according to the messenger who
reported to parliament just two days after the battle, the royalists had
not neglected to occupy the plateau overlooking the town. When Essex's
men attempted to scale it, 'we found they had placed their ordnance
and two troops of horse on either side and lined the hedges with dragoons'.[86] Whatever the truth of the matter, the royalist high command was
overconfident. Essex took advantage of their laxness, and sent a strong

---

[83] Of the modern accounts of the battle, perhaps the clearest is found in Frank Kitson's
Prince Rupert: Portrait of a Soldier, 147–53. Some of what follows draws on Kitson.
[84] Bodl. MS Clarendon 23, fo. 58v.
[85] *A Trve and Impartiall Relation of the Battaile betwixt his Maiesties Army and That
of the Rebells neare Newbery in Berkshire* (Oxford, 1643), E69/10, sig. A3.
[86] BL. Add. MS 18778 (Yonge's diary), fo. 54. This is perhaps corroborated by the
anonymous royalist officer who wrote that Rupert had ordered him to take his detachment to 'the hill on our left, from where we sent out scouting parties all night.' (Add. MS
18980, fo. 120). However, he may be referring to Trundle Hill rather than Round Hill.

detachment of two infantry brigades and a regiment of horse under Major-General Skippon with two light field-pieces, to deploy opposite them in the fields below the plateau. Skippon's task was to capture Round Hill. Essex commanded the other two brigades of infantry which, with Sir Philip Stapleton's horse, would advance onto the plateau itself. Someone then alerted him to the fact that the royalists, while guarding the plateau, had not physically occupied Round Hill. Under cover of darkness Skippon pushed forward one of his brigades with two light guns onto that position. Essex took his two brigades and established himself on the plateau at Wash Common. As daylight broke Skippon's guns opened fire on the royalists in the plain below. The king responded by assigning Rupert to secure Wash Common, and from there to dislodge the enemy from its commanding position. He seems to have succeeded in pushing Essex's two brigades back from the open ground on Wash Common into the small, hedged fields on the edge of the plateau, but the terrain prevented him from mounting the great whirlwind charges that before had always broken the enemy's resistance. Despite several assaults across hedge-blocked fields he was unable to achieve the breakthrough that would have dispersed their pikemen. Again and again Stapleton's horse were able to retreat behind manned squares of pikes when the pressure became too much for them.

On Round Hill the parliamentary main force had taken up well-protected positions behind hedges and houses; it was an arduous and bloody business for Sir John and Sir Nicholas Byron to dislodge them. After an initial mauling the foot called out 'horse, horse', prompting Sir John to advance with his two regiments. Finding that there was only a narrow gap in the hedge that barricaded the enemy, he ordered the gap widened. While he was supervising this operation his horse was shot in the throat, and he had to retire until he could find another mount. In the meantime Lord Falkland, 'more gallantly than advisedly' spurred his horse through the gap, where he was immediately killed by a musket ball in the abdomen. Falkland's death was greatly lamented, most of all by his dear friend Edward Hyde, the future Earl of Clarendon. In Viscount Falkland the royalists had lost one of their most intelligent and sensitive leaders. Only 34 years old when he died, he was a critical supporter of monarchy, but a warm defender of the Church of England. Appalled by the bloodshed of the war's first year, he looked for ways of bringing the conflict to a peaceful end. His foolhardy bravery at Newbury stemmed not from a desire to end his life as one contemporary suggested, but from a determination to prove that his advocacy of peace did not reflect physical cowardice.[87]

---

[87] Rushworth, *Hist. Coll.*, Vol. 5, 285.

It required three charges by Byron's cavalry before the roundhead foot were finally dislodged from the hill. The trained bands and auxiliary regiments from London performed heroically, not budging when royalist cannon fire cut through their ranks and 'men's bowels and brains flew in our faces'.[88] On open ground they presented a palisade of pikes, behind which the musketeers poured withering fire on the cavaliers, and gave their own scattered horse time to regroup. The pikemen stood fast against the charges of Byron's horse, each time obliging their attackers to wheel off. The roundhead horse were no match for their royalist counterparts, but their infantry saved the day.[89] By contrast, the royalist foot, after their initial battering, took fright, and behaved in Byron's words, like 'poltroons' and 'jades'.[90] Rupert attempted to conquer their timidity by calling on his officers to charge at the head of their troops, and led by his own example.[91] The king too joined the thick of the fighting. Wearing a soldier's grey coat he brought regiments onto the field, and personally fired two cannon.[92]

Essex made several attempts to regain the hill but was repulsed each time. The king then massed his entire army at the top of Endbourne Heath from which he controlled all the high ground above Newbury and blocked Essex's route to London. Rupert favoured staying where they were and renewing the fight the next day, when they would stand a good chance of finishing off the roundhead army as a fighting force once and for all. But already they had paid dearly for winning possession of the field: 1,000 men killed, including the earls of Carnarvon and Sunderland, and Viscount Falkland, as well as several other highly valued officers.[93] Fresh supplies of powder and ammunition had still not arrived from Oxford.[94] Another factor, not mentioned in the contemporary accounts, but which probably weighed on the minds of the king's advisers, was that Sir William Waller had finally left London with as many as 4,000 troops. Grudgingly he had taken up a position at Turnham Green, and from there perhaps moved to Windsor. Had he gone the extra 20 miles to Newbury, he could have given Essex a tremendous victory.[95] With all these factors weighing on his mind,

---

[88] Henry Foster, *A True and Exact Relation of the Marchings of the Two Regiments of the Trained Bands of the City of London* (1643), E69/15, sig. B3r.

[89] Clarendon, *Hist.*, Bk 7, 211.

[90] Bodl. MS Clarendon 23, fo. 59; Digby, *Trve and Impartiall Relation*, E69/10, sig. A3a.

[91] BL. Add. MS 62084B (Pythouse Papers), fo. 16.

[92] Foster, *A True and Exact Relation*, sig. B4.

[93] Folger Lib., MS V.a.216 (Life of John Lord Belasyse), unfol.

[94] BL. Add. MS 62084B (Pythouse Papers), fo. 16.

[95] Waller who had been provided with £4,000 refused, as late as 19 September, to march unless he was given a further £5,000: BL. Add. MS 18778 (Yonge's diary), fos. 50v, 53; Clarendon, *Hist.*, Bk 7, 213.

the king prepared for a withdrawal to Oxford. The road was open for Essex to reach Reading, and from there London.

The next day Essex evacuated Reading and completed the march to London. His men, with laurels in their hats, were greeted as conquering heroes by the cheering crowds that lined the streets. Essex himself was accorded the deference due to a prince, as the Lord Mayor and the Speaker, large deputations trailing behind them, paid him court at his great mansion in the Strand. He pretended magnanimously to make peace with Waller, though in the glow of victory he called in the independent commission that he had been forced to issue to his rival a month earlier. The House of Lords resolved that Waller should once more be answerable to the lord-general, who alone would have the power to grant commissions.[96]

Charles put a garrison into Donnington Castle overlooking Newbury to control the great western road from London to Bristol. He also re-occupied Reading, and then returned to his Oxford headquarters, where bonfires blazed out a regal triumph with the same conviction that Londoners had shown in hailing their noble earl. It was all a sham. Behind doors, as Clarendon tells us, there was

nothing but dejection of mind, discontent and secret mutiny; in the army, anger and jealousy amongst the officers, every one accusing another of want of courage and conduct in the actions of the field; and they who were not of the army, blaming them all for their several failings and gross oversights.[97]

Ever since her arrival from Holland the previous spring the queen, and her special friend Henry Jermyn, had exercised a baleful influence. She had virtually set up a rival court, pressuring the king into granting patronage appointments to her favourites and ignoring those who were more meritorious. Discovering in Prince Rupert a man who would not play the fawning courtier, she hated him, and looked for ways to destroy him.[98] Morale in Oxford sank precipitously, and the prince found pretexts for making himself more and more scarce.

Both sides celebrated Newbury; but in reality the strategic victory belonged to parliament. Gloucester had been saved; London was intact; Essex's refashioned army was still in the field; the king's forces had been

---

[96] *LJ*, Vol. 6, 242.

[97] Clarendon, *Hist.*, Bk 7, 238.

[98] For more light on Henrietta Maria's baleful influence see Michelle Anne White, *Henrietta Maria and the English Civil Wars*, esp. chs, 3, 5.

badly mauled. On the other side of the balance sheet parliament had lost Bristol, Exeter and other western towns; Waller's western army had been knocked out; Reading was abandoned. King and parliament were at an impasse, yet neither side was ready for peace. Instead, they chose to draw on forces from the other two kingdoms for the continuation of their quarrel. Much more English, Irish and Scottish blood remained to be shed before the outcome of the quarrel would become clear.

CHAPTER 7

The hinge year: 1643–44

In September 1643 Charles published a Declaration of thanks to the inhabitants of Cornwall, the most loyal of all his counties, for the courage, patience and support they had shown him. Yet for all the victories he had garnered over the past several months, he knew that he still faced 'so potent an enemy, backed with so strong, rich, and populous cities, and so plentifully furnished with men, arms, money, and provision of all kinds . . .'.[1] Conscious that parliament's alliance with the Scottish Covenanters would soon give it the strategic upper hand, the king too sought additional aid from outside the kingdom. Already he had received substantial sums of money and supplies from France and the United Provinces. For manpower he now turned to Ireland.

Ireland: the Cessation of September 1643

As early as the previous April, in the light of English parliamentary efforts to conclude a military alliance with the covenanting regime in Scotland, Charles had instructed his commander-in-chief in Ireland, James Butler, Earl of Ormond, to negotiate a cease-fire with the Catholic insurgents. A cease-fire would permit him to draw his Protestant army, which had now been tempered by over a year's fighting experience, across the Irish Sea to fight for him against his Puritan rebels.

How do we explain the new-found readiness of Protestant Ireland to supply the king with troops? In the spring of 1642 the tide had turned against the Catholic insurgents. The first contingent of Sir Robert Monro's Scottish army of 10,000 had arrived. The Westminster parliament had borrowed enough money from London merchants, with the promise of

[1] *CSPD 1641–43*, 484.

10 million acres of Irish land as security, to equip an invading force of 12,000. In addition the Dublin government had its own army of 22,000 men or more. Thus, before long there were armies of over 44,000 arrayed against the insurgents. The latter were able to muster 20,000 in 1643 – 1.3 per cent of the population of Ireland – and ultimately they would raise a total of 70,000 soldiers in the four provinces. But they were no match for the numbers or the ruthlessness of the Protestant settlers and their allies.[2]

By the end of March the Dublin forces had lifted the siege of Drogheda; the next month they beat the Irish under Viscount Mountgarret in open battle near Kilrush, south of the capital. This drove the insurgents out of the Pale. At the same time knowledge was spreading of Charles's proclamation of 1 January calling on the rebels to lay down their arms. The military fortunes of the insurgents deteriorated still further when Charles Coote in north Leinster and the Earl of Ormond, in the south, led raids ever deeper into their territory. By the summer Sir Phelim O'Neill, the leader of the Ulster rising was on the verge of disbanding the remnants of his army and the revolt seemed to be broken.

More than anyone it was the Earl of Ormond who was the instrument of its near defeat. 'The most illustrious cavalier' as Macaulay tagged him, Ormond was one of the largest and most influential landowners in Ireland. Of Catholic Old English stock, he had been raised a Protestant and become a protégé of Strafford in the 1630s. His wealth, his Protestantism and his immense social prestige made him Charles's natural choice for lieutenant-general. A minor drawback was his youth (he was only 33). His major defect – military incompetence – would not become fully manifest for several years. For the next decade he was to occupy the cockpit of Irish political and military affairs. Before long he disappointed the lords justices (the executive council of the Dublin parliament) by exhibiting more loyalty to the king than to them or the Westminster parliament, but at all times he kept his own interests firmly before his eyes. Recent work by William Kelly has brought out the devious complexity of the man. On the one hand he obeyed the king's command to disband Strafford's 9,000-strong Catholic army in deference to the wish of the Westminster parliament in March 1641, and informed Sir Henry Vane that he had done so.[3] But he also executed warrants from Charles, who did not really want the army disbanded, to commission nine colonels to recruit and transport regiments from it into

---

[2] Padráig Lenihan, 'The Catholic Confederacy 1642–9: an Irish state at war' (PhD thesis, University College, Galway), 5, 106.
[3] Bodl. MS Carte 1, fos. 426–7.

foreign service, ostensibly to rid Ireland of such disruptive, well-trained, and potentially subversive elements. Owing to a veto from Westminster the regiments were not allowed to leave the kingdom. Strafford's army thus remained for all practical purposes a coherent military force available for service at relatively short notice.[4] Significantly, it supplied two regiments to the insurgent army.[5] With his extensive connections among the Old English and other Irish Catholics, Ormond may well have been apprised of the planned rising ahead of time; significantly, he had ignored an urgent entreaty from the lords justices in October 1641 to come to Dublin, giving the capital a wide berth until almost two weeks after the insurgency had broken out.[6] There is reason to believe that if Ormond rather than the extremist Protestants William Parsons and Edmund Borlase had been at the head of the Irish government in 1641 the Old English leadership would not have become involved in the rebellion.[7] After some hesitation Charles decided to pursue an agreement with the Scottish Covenanters, and commanded Ormond to cooperate in suppressing the Ulster rebellion, which he was only too pleased to do.

In the spring of 1642 the Scots had already inflicted a series of defeats upon the insurgents, and by the end of June were in a position to link forces. The insurgent leaders were on the verge of fleeing the country when news arrived in July that Owen Roe O'Neill and Thomas Preston had landed with arms, money, officers and men in Donegal. O'Neill, 60 years old, boasted a record of distinguished service in the Spanish army. His family name (he was a nephew of the rebel Earl of Tyrone) and his lengthy exile endowed him with a charisma among the Gaelic population of Ulster. Preston, a few years younger than O'Neill, had also learned the art of war and assimilated Spanish religious views while fighting against continental protestants. In August the provincial assembly at Clones commissioned Owen Roe O'Neill general of the Ulster army, displacing Sir Phelim O'Neill, and he began to build up a disciplined fighting force. Preston was commissioned general of the Leinster army, while another returning emigré, Garret Barry, was made general for Munster. These professional officers

[4] Kelly, William Pius, 'The Early career of James Butler, twelfth earl and first Duke of Ormond (1610–1688)' (PhD thesis, University of Cambridge), 181.

[5] Lenihan, 'Catholic Confederacy', 97.

[6] Kelly, 'Ormond', 203. I am, however, sceptical of Kelly's suggestion that Ormond played key roles in both Antrim's plot, and the colonels' plot (ibid., 188ff). An unwavering Protestant, he always expressed disdain for Antrim's offers to help the king.

[7] Tadhg Ó hAnnracháin, *Catholic Reformation in Ireland: the Mission of Rinuccini 1645–49*, 80–1.

introduced the latest Swedish advances – a higher proportion of muskets to pikes, a thinner, more linear battle formation, smaller company-sized units, and the interspersing of musketeers among the cavalry. The reforms were not fully implemented until 1647, however, and none of them soon enough to enable the Confederates in Munster to stand up to Lord Inchiquin's regiments at Liscarroll in August 1642, when the Catholic levies were crushed by better-disciplined Protestant soldiers. What held back the Confederate armies throughout the decade was not primitive battle tactics, but a chronic shortage of cavalry.[8]

During 1642 the need for political as well as military organization of the Catholic war effort had become apparent. In April lawyers and Catholic clergy spearheaded the founding of the Confederate Assembly with its headquarters in Kilkenny, which coordinated the war until the Cromwellian invasion of 1649. The clergy, having previously denounced insurgent atrocities, now recognized the revolt as a just war waged against the puritans 'who have always, but especially in recent years, plotted the destruction of the Catholics, the destruction of the Irish, and the abolition of the king's prerogatives'.[9] In May they went further, declaring that Catholics who did not take part in the war were automatically excommunicated. They exhorted Old Irish and Old English Catholics to submerge their ethnic differences. In imitation of the Scots in 1638 and the English in 1641, they drew up an oath of association for the clergy to administer to all Catholics. Besides pledging to defend royal prerogatives, the privileges of parliament and the fundamental laws of the kingdom, the oath called for 'the free exercise of the Roman Catholic faith and religion'.[10] The Confederates went on to create a general council of clergy, nobility and lay people, and set up an elected national assembly to organize their financial and military affairs. The great majority of Catholic MPs who had sat in the Irish parliament before 1641 were elected to the Confederate Assembly. Three-quarters of Assembly members were of Old English origin, while only a fifth were Gaelic Irish and a handful were of New English origin. A high proportion were lawyers, merchants or the sons or brothers of peers. Their high socio-economic status partly explains their political moderation and their continual search for a compromise peace over the next seven years. The biography of Nicholas Plunkett, speaker of the Assembly, illustrates

[8] Padráig Lenihan, 'Celtic warfare in the 1640s', in John R. Young, ed., *Celtic Dimensions of the British Civil Wars*, 130–2.

[9] Quoted in *NHI*, Vol. 3, 197.

[10] Micheál Ó Siochrú, *Confederate Ireland 1642–1649: A Constitutional and Political Analysis*, 90, n.16.

this point. The most prominent confederate lawyer, he was connected to virtually every Old English family and to many of the New English as well. At heart a royalist, Plunkett would serve as an agent to negotiate a peace with Ormond. He was a suave and skilful politician, but his deep piety caused him to gravitate to the hard-line clerical party after the arrival of the papal nuncio Giovanni Battista Rinuccini in late 1645.[11] This points to the core problem that plagued the Confederation from beginning to end. Its members could never agree on a unified programme of action. The primary goal of some insurgents was to reclaim confiscated lands from the New English and Scots settlers. Fundamental to others was the restoration of the pre-Reformation privileges and immunities of the Catholic Church. Foremost in the minds of others was an end to civil war, and protection from militant English Puritanism through an alliance with the Stuart king.

For most of its history the Confederate Assembly did indeed profess loyalty to Charles I, but it also acted as if it was the sovereign authority in Ireland, passing laws, raising taxes, issuing coinage and dispatching envoys to other countries. It also set up a powerful, 24-member executive – the supreme council – with six members from each province. Some key executive members had close ties of blood or friendship with Ormond. They and other Confederate leaders who gravitated towards them and sought peace with the king were christened 'Ormondists'.[12]

At the same time that he maintained his connections with the Confederate Council, Ormond waged a power struggle within the Dublin administration, which was controlled by individuals extremely hostile to Catholic interests. The arch-anti-Catholic was the Lord Justice Sir William Parsons. Probably on Ormond's advice Charles dismissed Parsons in March 1643, and replaced him with the more compliant Sir Henry Tichborne. Later that summer Ormond expelled three other militant Protestants from the governing council and imprisoned them on a charge of supporting the English parliament against the king. Their detention removed the final obstacle on the royalist side to a truce with the Catholic Confederation. A further impetus came from the Catholic Earl of Antrim,

[11] Bríd McGrath, 'Parliament men and the confederate association', in Micheál Ó Siochrú (ed.), *Kingdoms in Crisis: Ireland in the 1640s*, 92, 95, 98–100; Ó Siochrú, *Confederate Ireland*, 114.

[12] Viscount Mountgarret the president was his great-uncle; Richard Bellings the secretary was his son-in-law; Viscount Muskerry was his brother-in-law and perhaps closest friend, while Gerald Fennell was his physician and friend: Kelly, 'Ormond', 192. For an excellent account of the workings of the Confederate Catholic government see Ó Siochrú, *Confederate Ireland*.

who, having married the Duke of Buckingham's widow, had excellent connections at Charles's court. His master plan was to forge an alliance between Irish royalists and Confederate Catholics to crush Monro's Scottish army in Ulster. He would then take his victorious army into the Western Isles to reclaim his ancestral lands from the usurper Archibald Campbell, Earl of Argyll. Antrim had the enthusiastic support of the queen, who finally got her way in April when Charles authorized Ormond to arrange a cease-fire with the Catholic party.[13]

Thanks to the peace faction's dominance of the Confederate Council, Ormond was able to conclude a cessation of hostilities by 15 September. The truce not only freed up troops for the royalist war effort in England; it enabled the Earl of Antrim to unleash his invasion of the Western Isles under his kinsman the Highland warlord Alasdair MacColla (or MacDonald), who brought 1,600 troops into Scotland. As we shall see, the alliance MacColla constructed with the Marquess of Montrose, enabled them to pull off a number of spectacular victories in 1644–45.[14]

Benefiting from better organization after the spring of 1642, the insurgents were able to blunt the Protestant offensives against them in Ulster and Leinster, which in any case had been debilitated by disease and a chronic lack of supplies from England. A further source of weakness was the refusal of Major-General Robert Monro to send his units south from Ulster into Leinster to help Ormond. This did not prevent Monro's army from administering a severe mauling to O'Neill's still green troops at Clones in the spring of 1643. Ulster stayed in Protestant hands for the next three years, despite the Confederate capture of the great fortress at Dungannon in October.

Meanwhile the negotiations for the Cessation – and the treaty itself – wreaked havoc with Irish politics. The lords justices, representing the Irish parliament in Dublin, were in no mood to give up their objective of crushing the Confederate Catholics, hoping that the Scottish Ulster army under Monro would rally behind them in doing so. For his own part Monro bitterly denounced the Cessation and rejected Ormond's demand to hand over the Earl of Antrim whom he had taken prisoner. Indeed, the Cessation appears to have galvanized Protestants in Ireland generally: the Scots under Monro, militant parliamentarians, most notably the lords

[13] Jane Ohlmeyer, *Civil War and Restoration in the Three Stuart Kingdoms: The Career of Randal MacDonnell, Marquis of Antrim, 1609–1683*, 119–20.

[14] For Antrim see Ohlmeyer, *Civil War and Restoration*, 133–44; John Lowe, 'The Earl of Antrim and Irish aid to Montrose in 1644', *Irish Sword*, 4 (1960), 197. For MacColla see David Stevenson, *Alasdair MacColla and the Highland Problem in the Seventeenth Century*.

justices, and New English settlers such as the Presbyterian landowner (and brother-in-law of John Pym) Colonel Sir John Clotworthy and his brother Captain James Clotworthy.[15] In London the Irish Adventurers chimed in with a denunciation, driven by the fear that any peace with the rebels of 1641 would mean the evaporation of their promised Irish acres. From the other side of the political fence the Confederates, failing to comprehend the intense pressures Ormond was under, excoriated him for his reluctance to negotiate toleration for Catholics. Thinking the king was a better friend than Ormond, the Confederates offered him £30,000 cash as well as soldiers, before the Cessation had even been signed.[16]

As it turned out, the Cessation accomplished little towards rescuing royalist fortunes in England over the following year. Already before it was signed two regiments of foot and two of horse had been removed from Ireland to bolster royal armies in England.[17] Initially the king stipulated that only English Protestants should be sent, and insisted that they all swear the Protestation of 1641, but before long the stipulation was forgotten, and Catholic troops were freely admitted. The soldiers who arrived materially helped the royalists in the north-west and the south-west, but in the larger view they were more of a liability than an asset. In the first place they were less well equipped than their English counterparts; their crossing was often obstructed by the parliamentary navy, which threw any Irish soldiers it captured into the sea; and once on English soil their loyalty to the king was shaky. Most seriously of all, they did great political damage to the royalist cause. From the start both English parliamentarians and Anglo-Scottish settlers interpreted Charles's Irish strategy as the enlisting of murderous Irish Catholics to wage war against British protestants. In Ulster government troops agreed with the Scots in characterizing the armistice as 'a masterpiece of the devil'.[18] And indeed, the loyalty of some of Charles's own troops was sorely tested by the spectacle of Irish soldiers debarking on the west coast of England. Conversely, some of those Protestant soldiers were shocked to discover how many Catholics there already were in the king's army, and decided to switch to parliament's side. In mid-July the Commons denounced all plans to subvert Protestant

---

[15] BL. Add. MS 18778 (Yonge's diary), fo. 84; HMC 36 *Manuscripts of the Marquis of Ormonde, . . . preserved at the Castle, Kilkenny*, new ser. Vol. 1, 67–70; NLI. MS 2308 (Ormonde Papers), fos. 389ff; *ODNB*, *sub* Clotworthy.

[16] Bodl. MS Carte 6, fo. 448.

[17] Carte, *Life*, Vol. 5, 445; Camden Society, *Diary of the marches . . . by Richard Symonds*, ed. C.E. Long, 254–5.

[18] Quoted by Wedgwood, *King's War*, 262.

Ireland, proclaiming 'that no earthly power is likely in humane reason to withstand this damnable plot but the power of the parliament of England'.[19]

In the end Irish intervention on behalf of the king was to be much less effective than Scottish intervention against him. From the autumn of 1643 to early 1644 7,740 mostly Protestant troops arrived on the west coast. Most of them were put under the command of Sir John Byron, but their career came to a quick end in January 1644 when they were captured or killed at the siege of Nantwich. Later a further 1,600 Catholic troops arrived in Scotland to assist MacColla. His leadership saw to it that their impact in Scotland was out of all proportion to their numbers. The grand total of Irish troops that came to the king's aid in his other two kingdoms in 1643–44 cannot have been higher than 11,000.[20]

When it came to Ireland Charles tried to square the circle. On the day he made Ormond lord lieutenant of Ireland (19 October 1643) he sent him a long set of instructions, so tortuously complex and contradictory that the most ingenious and willing servant in the world could not have implemented them. Regarding the Scottish Covenanters Charles's wishes were 'hugely' important. First, Ormond was to do everything in his power to hinder Scottish adherence to the Cessation. Why? If they signed they would then be able to withdraw Monro's army and use it in England. Yet as soon as the Scots breached the Cessation, the Confederate Irish were to be incited to fall upon them. Monro was also to be bribed not to leave Ireland, while the Scots settlers were to be threatened with extirpation if he did. With reference to the Confederate Irish, Ormond was directed to send the Munster army to Bristol to assist with 'a great design from the West'. He was to send the Leinster army to Lancashire to help reduce it and adjacent counties. The Confederation was also to be invited to lend

---

[19] *CJ*, Vol. 3, 166; *A Declaration of the Commons Assembled in Parliament Concerning the . . . Grand Rebellion in Ireland* (1643), E61/23, p. 22. See also Robert Matthew Armstrong, 'Protestant Ireland and the English Parliament, 1641–1647' (PhD thesis, Trinity College, Dublin), 102.

[20] Stoyle, *Soldiers and Stranger*, 209–10; James Scott Wheeler, *Cromwell in Ireland*, 21–2 and n.76; J.E. Auden, 'The Anglo-Irish troops in Shropshire', *Shropshire Archaeological and Natural Society Transactions*, 50 (1939–40), 49–64; BL, Add. MS 21506 (Civil war letters, 1633–55), fo. 44; Add. MS 18981 (Rupert papers), fo. 71. Joyce Lee Malcolm's estimates, based on parliamentary sources, are much too high: 'All the king's men: the impact of the crown's Irish soldiers on the English Civil War', *IHS*, 21 (1979), 263. Cf. Wheeler, 'Four armies in Ireland', 50; Wanklyn and Jones, *Military History*, 15.

ships to transport the troops. Emissaries from the Confederation, believing that the king was their friend, were expected to set out shortly for the royal court in Oxford. But because their appearance in Oxford would be a political embarrassment to the royalist cause, Ormond was to do his best to delay their departure.[21]

These instructions perfectly expressed the deviousness that would in the end prove Charles's undoing. They were so shameful that they had to be kept secret from almost everyone, even the privy council. Thus Secretary Nicholas reassured Lord Goring that 'all the forces that are arrived or sent for from Ireland are only the English soldiers, Protestants who are not able to live there . . .'.[22] At almost that very moment Charles was telling his closest adviser, George Lord Digby, to give Ormond the green light to negotiate with the Catholic grandee Theobald, Lord Taaffe for 2,000 Irish Catholic troops, and instructing the Earl of Antrim to raise a further 10,000 for England and 2,000 to assist the Earl of Montrose in Scotland.[23] With veiled exasperation Ormond observed that if Ireland were emptied of loyal troops it would be impossible to obstruct the departure of the Scots.[24]

England: the alliance with Scotland

Meanwhile, the constellation of difficulties confronting the Westminster parliament had brought many of its supporters to the brink of despair. The only bright spots that autumn were Essex's relief of Gloucester and his less-than-complete victory at Newbury, followed by Manchester, Cromwell and Fairfax's resounding triumph at Winceby in Lincolnshire. Essex's defeat of the royalists had been soured by the failure of Waller to come to his aid. Their attitude towards each other had changed from anger to hatred. Pressing home the political advantage he had gained from his recent battlefield successes, Essex indicted Waller for the loss of Reading and got the Lords to agree that he should surrender his commission and henceforth operate only under the earl's command. Royalist control of Newcastle had created a coal shortage, while their raids on coastal shipping exacerbated the trade depression, which in turn caused a shortage of excise revenue. The fleet could not put to sea because the cash was not

[21] Bodl. MS Carte 7, fo. 188-v.
[22] HMC 29, *Thirteenth Report, Portland MSS*, Vol. 1, 148.
[23] Carte, *Life*, Vol. 5, 529; *CSP*, Vol. 2, 165–6.
[24] Carte, *Life*, Vol. 6, 8.

there to pay it.[25] War weariness and disaffection to the cause were spreading throughout southern England. Waller's conscripted troops were refusing to obey his commands. In London army recruiters ran into such stubborn resistance that they had to carry on their work 'with barbarous violence'.[26]

The Solemn League and Covenant

Another calamity for parliament was the death of war leader John Pym from bowel cancer in December. A stern anti-Catholic, Pym had been one of Charles I's most formidable enemies since the summoning of parliament three years before. 'The promoter of the present rebellion and the director of the whole machine' was how the Venetian envoy described him.[27] Pym did not quit the stage of worldly affairs before he had helped bring to fruition parliament's single most important strategic measure of the whole war: the alliance with Scotland. While some such arrangement to halt the advance of popery had been openly mooted by members of the Junto since the autumn of 1642, the sense that an alliance was necessary had reached an even higher pitch of urgency in Edinburgh by the summer of 1643. There were three contributing factors to the Covenanters' sense of alarm. First, Monro's army in Ireland, which had received almost none of its promised English aid, found itself increasingly beleaguered by the Catholic forces. Secondly, there was the threat that Newcastle and his triumphant army might soon invade from the north of England. Finally, papers captured from the Earl of Antrim by the Scottish army in Ulster implicated prominent Scottish royalists including the Earl of Montrose in a plot against the covenanting regime. To English eyes it appeared that the Scots were unanimous in their desire for a covenanted relationship with them. In reality there had been a behind-the-scenes struggle lasting more than eighteen months in which the Marquess of Argyll and the radical nobles, backed by the lairds and burgesses, had outflanked conservatives and pragmatic royalists on the privy council. Radically dominated parliamentary committees had sprung up as the engine of the covenanting cause. It was these committees that were behind the summoning of the 1643 Convention of Estates and the promotion of the Solemn League and Covenant. The revelations of the Antrim Plot were decisive in discrediting the conservatives and pragmatists clustered around the Duke of Hamilton, and handing control of the Convention of Estates to Argyll and the radicals. With

[25] BL. Add. MS 18778 (Yonge's diary), fos. 60v-1.
[26] *CSPV 1643–47*, 94.
[27] *CSPV 1643–47*, 53.

Hamilton's subsequent withdrawal from the Convention the conservative–pragmatists were also leaderless. All obstacles in Scotland had now been removed to a covenanting alliance with the Westminster Parliament.[28]

In Westminster the Junto responded to Scots entreaties by sending a parliamentary delegation to Edinburgh led by Sir Henry Vane the younger. On the Scottish side it was radicals such as John Lord Balmerino, Sir John Smith and Archibald of Wariston who dominated the negotiations leading to the signing of the treaty. The talks lasted ten days, a remarkably short time, given that the English objective was simply military aid, while for the Scots a confederal union based on shared religious aims was essential. On 18 August the General Assembly and the Convention of Estates 'with much unanimity' agreed on 'a mutual league . . . for preservation of religion'. Scenes of great emotion accompanied the consummation of this historic pact. It was reported to the House of Commons that the Scottish lords 'fell weeping for half an hour' as they 'entered into Covenant to live and die with the parliament of England'.[29] After it was sent to London Argyll stayed in close touch with his radical counterparts in both houses until it had been adopted there as well. The political leaders in both kingdoms saw it in their interest to make common cause against Charles I; the Scots because he could no longer be trusted to respect covenanting hegemony in Scotland, the Junto because they were staring military defeat in the face. It is significant that the Scots wished to call the agreement a Covenant, with all the religious overtones of that word, while Sir Henry Vane underlined the primacy of military considerations by insisting on the word League. The price the Scots exacted for sending an army into England was the imposition of Presbyterianism throughout the Stuart kingdoms – Ireland as well as England. Here again Vane insisted on a modification: the English and Irish religious reformation should be framed 'according to the Word of God' – meaning the Bible – rather than the Scottish version of reformed Protestantism.[30]

From the Covenanters' vantage point, 'the Solemn League and Covenant was concerned with the transportation and imposition of the Scottish revolution on a British basis as the appropriate means of defending that revolution, in religious, military and constitutional terms'.[31] As

---

[28] Ohlmeyer, *Civil War and Restoration*, 121–4; Armstrong, 'Protestant Ireland', 107, 110; *LJ*, Vol. 6, 274–5.

[29] BL. Add. MS 18778 (Yonge's diary), fo. 20v.

[30] Rushworth, *Hist. Coll.*, Vol. 5, 478–9.

[31] John Young, *The Scottish Parliament 1639–1661: A Political and Constitutional Analysis*, 68.

Alan Macinnes has noted, the power to hold the Crown to account, by force if necessary, was also exported from Scotland to England.[32] In return for a closer, federative union Scotland was to send 20,000 troops to England for the war against the king. All their expenses were to be met by parliament. 'The coming of the Scots will add strength and reputation to the cause both at home and abroad', thought Walter Yonge. The immediate practical benefit from their coming would be the liberation of Newcastle and the coal supply for London. They could also be counted on to raise the siege at Hull, giving the Fairfaxes and the northern army badly needed relief.[33] On 25 September, shortly after the news came through that Charles had signed a Cessation of Arms with the Catholic Confederation in Ireland, MPs and members of the Assembly of Divines gathered at St Margaret's Church, Westminster to swear the covenant with Scotland. Charles's agreement with Irish papists would seal his doom; parliament's covenant with Scottish Presbyterians would effect its salvation.

The English were meant to bankroll the Scottish force, but the Scots knew better than to count on that – after all what had they ever been paid for Robert Monro's 10,000 men in Ulster? So dedicated were they to exporting their revolution that they were ready to foot most of the bill themselves, though they could ill afford to. Scottish revenues were never adequate, and in the end the Scots made themselves intensely disliked in the north of England by living off the land.[34]

Historians usually analyse the Solemn League and Covenant in terms of its politics and practicalities, rarely in terms of its emotional power and transcendent appeal. Yet it is the latter, embedded in the concluding sentences, which unleashed formidable political energy on both sides of the border.

we profess and declare, before God and the world, our unfeigned desire to be humbled for our own sins and for the sins of these kingdoms; especially that we have not as we ought valued the inestimable benefit of the Gospel; that we have not laboured for the purity and power thereof; and that we have not endeavoured to receive Christ in our hearts, nor to walk worthy of him in our lives, which are the causes of other sins and transgressions, so much abounding amongst us, and our true and unfeigned purpose, desire, and endeavour, for ourselves, and all others under our power and charge . . . [is] to amend our lives, and each one to

---

[32] Allan I. Macinnes, *The British Revolution, 1625–1660*, 150.

[33] BL. Add. MS 18778 (Yonge's diary), fo. 50.

[34] Stevenson, 'Financing', 102–5.

*go before another in the example of a real reformation, that the Lord may
turn away his wrath, and heavy indignation, and establish these churches
and kingdoms in truth and peace.*[35]

Has any revolutionary movement, apart from these Scottish and English
Calvinists, ever confessed a desire to 'be humbled for our sins' or 'receive
Christ into our hearts'?

England: the winter campaign: Alton, Arundel and Nantwich

The prospect of the imminent arrival of a large army from Scotland gave
a fillip to the Junto at Westminster. The resurgence of Essex's political
power proved ephemeral as Waller's war-party friends – Hesilrige chief
among them – saw to it that scarce resources went to building up his army,
not the earl's. Despite having to cope with a mutinous brigade of London
militia, whose loudest cry was 'Home! Home!', Waller rewarded his devo-
tees by administering a sharp defeat to Hopton's forces at Alton in Surrey
on 13 December. He followed this up by depriving Hopton of Arundel
Castle the next month, and then retired to winter quarters.

Meanwhile a much greater menace to the king was looming nearer the
royalist heartland of Wales and the west Midlands. The Cheshire Puritan
grandee, Sir William Brereton, had discovered a taste and no little aptitude
for military action. At the end of 1643 he was on the move, with a small
flying force, intent on challenging royalist dominance of north Wales.
Brereton was brought down to earth, however, by John Lord Byron,
whose forces had been swelled by the first contingents of Protestant troops
from Ireland. Byron destroyed Brereton's force with almost contemptu-
ous ease at Middlewich (26 December). Brereton then withdrew to
Manchester, where he awaited the arrival of Sir Thomas Fairfax who
had been despatched with a field army from Lincolnshire. Crossing the
Pennines with 2,300 horse and dragoons, he gathered another 2,500
infantry as he went. Together they moved on Nantwich, where the main
part of Brereton's little army was now under siege by Byron. The royalists
were camped in a broad circle around the town on both sides of the River
Weaver. Unaware of Fairfax's strength, Byron declined to abandon the
siege. Then he was hit by bad luck: a sudden thaw accompanied by heavy
rain on the night of 24–25 January. The melting snow turned the Weaver

---

[35] The Solemn League and Covenant, printed in Gardiner, *Const. Docs.*, 270–1.

into a torrent, and the solitary bridge spanning it was swept away. His army divided, Byron found himself obliged to fight in enclosed ground where his cavalry were nearly useless. Though they made a hard fight they were eventually overwhelmed, and 1,500 mostly Irish infantry were captured, of whom perhaps 700 went over to the parliamentary side. The episode demonstrated Fairfax's excellent generalship and Byron's limited military ability.[36]

The overthrow at Nantwich demoralized the royalist war effort in Cheshire and Shropshire; it put an end to Chester and North Wales as access points for Irish troops and it stopped the grand scheme of mobilizing the north-west under Rupert for an assault on the Scottish invaders. The royalists could no longer take any part of that region for granted. There were repercussions in the north-east as well. Shortly after Nantwich the Marquess of Newcastle wrote the king that he was beset by enemy forces in Yorkshire.[37] With the Scots on his doorstep and Fairfax on his way back from Cheshire, Newcastle had plenty of reason to panic.

At Westminster the transformation of the civil war into an archipelagic war of the three Stuart kingdoms was recasting the political mould. To the Northumberland–Holles grandees the intervention of the Scots spelt ruin for England. Yet the failure of the royal Court at Oxford to welcome the defections of the Earl of Holland and other peace peers in August, and the news of the Cessation of Arms with the Irish Catholic Confederation filled them with horror. Led by Northumberland, most of the remaining peace peers threw in their lot with Saye and the man who was beginning to fill the shoes of the ailing John Pym, Oliver St John. Essex, his political authority enhanced by his successes at Gloucester and Newbury, emerged with Holles, as the leader of the anti-Scottish faction. Here in embryo were the future Independent and Presbyterian parties. Whereas Pym had generally supported Essex's army in the past, St John favoured channelling parliament's resources to Waller, Manchester and the Scots.

The conflict of these two groupings is seen most starkly in the struggle over the creation of a new Anglo-Scottish executive body to direct the war and draw up terms for peace. No one could deny the need for unified strategic direction, but the Saye–St John group used the occasion to rein in

[36] The best account of Nantwich and surrounding events is by John Lowe, 'The campaign of the Irish royalist army in Cheshire, November 1643–January 1644', *Transactions of the Historic Society of Lancashire and Cheshire* (hereafter THSLC), 111 (1959), 47–76. See also Hutton, *Royalist War Effort*, 124–6.
[37] BL. Add. MS 18981 (Rupert Papers), fo. 42.

Essex's military and political ambitions. Called the Committee of Both Kingdoms, the new body included four members from Scotland, seven from the House of Lords and fourteen from the Commons. Essex's enemies saw to it that the committee was weighted with their own members: Northumberland, Saye, St John, Cromwell, Waller and Hesilrige among others, while Denzell Holles, was pointedly excluded. In spite of the fact that Essex himself was named to the Committee, it was no secret that it was essentially an anti-Essex body, dedicated to reducing his powers and if possible forcing him to resign his generalship.[38] The Scots, unimpressed with his patchy military record, backed the Saye–St John group, which further strengthened their hand at Westminster.

1644: the spring campaign

The West: Cheriton

Both sides geared up for the spring campaigning season amid mounting evidence of disaffection – to parliament in Surrey and Sussex;[39] to the king in Shrewsbury, Worcester, North Wales and the adjacent region.[40] Disaffection was not the only hindrance. When the Protestant Murrough O'Brien, Lord Inchiquin came to Oxford in February with an offer to raise another 6,000 troops in return for being made president of Munster, he was so shabbily treated that he left in disgust and soon afterwards transferred his allegiance to parliament.[41] His motive was less personal pique at being denied high office than the regretful conclusion that parliament was more serious about subduing the Irish rebels than the king would ever be. He had been shocked to note how much warmer a reception the delegates of the Catholic Confederation had received in Oxford from the king than he.[42] On parliament's side the war effort continued to be hampered by the persistence of Essex and Waller's mutually destructive quarrel.

After the battle of Newbury the royalist council of war had changed its English strategy from one of centralization to one of dispersal.[43] The

[38] *CSPV 1643–47*, 76, 78; Scott, *Politics and War*, 69–71.

[39] BL. Add. MS 18779 (Yonge's diary), fo. 51v.

[40] BL. Add. MS 18981 (Rupert Papers), fos. 28, 68; Bodl. MS Firth C6, fo. 122.

[41] BL. Add. MS 18981 (Rupert Papers), fo. 57v.

[42] Armstrong, 'Protestant Ireland', 144, 149.

[43] The following analysis is based on M.D.G. Wanklyn, 'Royalist strategy in the south of England, 1642–1644', *Southern History*, 3 (1981), 69–71, and Wanklyn and Jones, *Military History*.

most ambitious project involved the western army. Lord Hopton was to combine the forces of the Marquess of Hertford with reinforcements from the Oxford army and from Ireland to clear Dorset, Wiltshire and Hampshire of the enemy, and to advance towards London. To this end Hopton was made field marshal of the south-east, while Prince Maurice was instructed to assist him by raising forces in the counties farther west, and also to reduce Plymouth and Dartmouth, the last enemy garrisons in Devon. But Hopton lacked Waller's boldness and imagination; perhaps because of his wounds the previous summer, he seems never to have recovered his confidence. In December and January he had suffered humiliation at the hands of Waller at both Alton and Arundel. These reverses plus other blunders cost him a total of almost 2,000 men. They also cost him the confidence of the royalist high command. Maurice was appointed lieutenant-general of the south-east in February, which made him Hopton's immediate superior. Royalist strategic planning was thrown off balance by the transfer of 2,000 cavalry from Essex's to Waller's army in mid-March, and the news that Waller was planning to renew his offensive against Hopton. The Earl of Forth was sent with reinforcements from Oxford to take charge of operations against Waller. The two sides clashed outside the village of Cheriton. The royalists had taken up a strong defensive position, but were betrayed by the impetuosity of a young infantry officer, greedy for glory, who charged with his regiment down the slope, only to have it cut to pieces by a party of parliamentary horse under Sir Arthur Hesilrige. In the end Hopton was forced back by sheer weight of numbers, though with comparatively light losses. Waller had shown that the parliamentary cavalry was able to take on and beat the king's horse, but he derived no strategic advantage from his victory, and soon had to cope with the departure of his London trained-band regiments. Outnumbered again, he retreated to Farnham, where he stayed until Essex took the field in mid-May.

For their part the royalists had to cope with the counter-productive behaviour of Prince Maurice. Charles had decided to keep him and his army in Dorset and Devon, mainly to protect the queen, but also to besiege Lyme, which had been a base for parliamentary raiding in both counties. Henrietta Maria was nearing the end of her pregnancy, and was about to leave Oxford for Exeter where it would be easy for her to catch a boat for France should parliamentary forces press too close. Not until April did Maurice commence the siege. In May, however, the king's army was being driven back towards Oxford by Essex and Waller. Charles ordered Maurice to march to Bristol with his 600 troops, there to rendezvous with the main field army, but the prince disobeyed his uncle and stayed at Lyme.

In the ensuing campaign the two royalist armies were only saved from destruction by the blunders of their enemies.

The Midlands: Newark

Charles's failure to discipline his nephew had far-reaching consequences. From that point on the Council of War found its orders to provincial commanders often disobeyed, since the latter realized that they could flout orders with impunity. They rationalized their disobedience by claiming to be better informed about local conditions than the Council of War. This breakdown in the chain of command led, as we shall see, to the catastrophe at Naseby. Royalist headquarters were also pervaded with a mood of impending doom in the aftermath of Nantwich. 'We are sensible of the beginning and proceedings of this unnatural rebellion overspreading the face of the whole kingdom at one time . . .' wrote Robert Byron and the Lincolnshire commissioners.[44] It was the intervention of the Scottish army that tipped the balance. The necessity for Newcastle to mobilize his forces against the Scottish advance, together with the royalist defeat at Winceby the previous autumn and the subsequent fall of Lincoln and Gainsborough, had left the key fortress of Newark under Sir Richard Byron dangerously exposed. Sir John Meldrum had put together a besieging force of 7,000 against Byron's less than 2,000. To meet this emergency Prince Rupert had to be diverted from his assignment of recruiting in the north-west and sent to relieve Newark.

Drawing upon a force of 1,120 musketeers freshly arrived from Ireland and picking up detachments from every royalist garrison he passed, Rupert finally had a scratch army totalling 6,420. He arrived with his advance guard at the outskirts of Newark on 21 March. He had acted so fast that Meldrum scoffed at the report of his approach until it was too late. When the roundhead commander asked to treat, Rupert agreed, and allowed him to march away with his army, but without his siege artillery or hand weapons. 'By speed, surprise and a rapid seizure of every advantage, Rupert had achieved a brilliant victory.'[45] At Oxford bells rang out, bonfires blazed and congratulations rained down upon Rupert from all sides. The Marquess of Newcastle, styling himself 'your Highness's most passionate creature', fell over himself with praise, while the king credited him with 'no less than the saving of all the north'.[46] More prosaically

[44] BL. Add. MS 18981 (Rupert Papers), fo. 48v.
[45] Wedgwood, *King's War*, 300.
[46] Warburton, *Memoirs*, Vol. 2, 397.

Henry Jermyn reassured him that his success had consolidated his political position, while his friend Arthur Trevor gushed that he was 'absolutely the favourite of the court' and could count on being awarded the presidency of Wales.[47]

In the larger scheme of things Rupert's feat was less than glittering. True, he had gained valuable arms, and the royalists were always shorter of arms than men. True, Gainsborough, Lincoln, Sleaford and Crowland were quickly added to the royalist side of the ledger. But with a real army at his disposal Rupert's next step would have been to advance southward into the Eastern Association and dismantle the forces of Manchester, or at least stymie their attempt to link up with the Scots and the Fairfaxes. But since the arrival of the Scots the royalists in England found themselves completely outmatched. Most of Rupert's soldiers for example had to be returned to the garrisons from which they had been drawn, and he himself had to go back to Wales to resume his efforts to recruit a permanent army.

The North: Selby

At that moment the Marquess of Newcastle was having a fair amount of success keeping the Scots at bay. The city of Newcastle had still not capitulated, while the marquess with his main force retreated slowly southward, inflicting significant casualties as he went. Then came severely dismaying news from South Yorkshire.

By the end of March Sir Thomas Fairfax had raised 2,000 horse and 2,000 foot from Lancashire and was bringing them back to Yorkshire to add to his father's army. Lord Fauconberg wrote from York to Rupert beseeching him to come as quickly as possible to prevent their conjuncture, and thereby save Yorkshire for the king.[48] Panicky letters were also despatched to the Lincolnshire royalists exhorting them to bring their forces to prop up Newcastle's beleaguered army. But the men of Lincoln, from their localist perspective, saw more pressing reasons for staying put than contributing to the larger royalist strategy of concentrating forces in the north for a knockout blow against Scots and parliament.

With the aim of preventing the rendezvous of Sir Thomas and his father Ferdinando Lord Fairfax stationed in Hull, John Lord Belasyse the governor of York drew an army of 5,000 foot and 1,500 horse out of the city to

---

[47] BL. Add. MS 18980 (Rupert Papers), fo. 31 (misdated 1643); Add. MS 18981 (Rupert Papers), fos. 107, 113.

[48] Bodl. Lib., MS Firth C7, fo. 8.

take up a position in Selby, a small town on the River Ouse astride the route between Hull and the West Riding. He did this at the end of March, just after learning of the sudden weakening in the overall parliamentarian position effected by Rupert's action at Newark. From his base at Selby he attempted to capture the clothing town of Bradford, but was driven off by a smaller force under an able young commander, Colonel John Lambert. On 11 April the combined forces of Fairfax from the west, Lambert from Bradford, and Lord Fairfax from Hull (4,200 in all) moved against Selby. Again the northern parliamentarians boldly confronted a much larger force – this time half as large again – than their own. After two hours of intense fighting Sir Thomas forced his way past a barricade, and once inside the town overawed Belasyse's cavalry who fled, leaving their commander to be wounded and placed under arrest. The officers and infantry put up fierce resistance, however, resulting in heavy losses – 2,200 prisoners and 1,000 dead and wounded. A week later the Marquess of Newcastle wrote to the king that the disaster could have been averted had Lord Loughborough and Colonel George Porter reined in their localist inclinations, obeyed orders, and marched to Belasyse's aid. Instead they stayed put, enabling the Fairfaxes and Lambert to win a shining victory.

Selby was the crucial battle for the north of England.[49] The Yorkshire royalist field army was broken beyond repair, which compelled Newcastle to abandon his stand against the Scots in Durham and hasten back to York to prevent the city being overrun by the victorious Fairfaxes. As the diarist Henry Slingsby noted, the victory came in the nick of time for the parliamentary cause, because the Scots, after three months in unfriendly terrain, and starved of support, were nearly at the end of their tether. Since arriving in England their numbers had shrunk by 5–6,000.[50] They would have been forced to retreat to their own country had not the Fairfaxes' victory cleared the way for their southward march.[51] The Scots now united their forces with those of Lord Fairfax's northern army, and sat down before York on 22 April. Two weeks later they were joined by the Earl of Manchester and the Eastern Association army.

---

[49] P.R. Newman, 'The defeat of John Belasyse: civil war in Yorkshire, January–April 1644', *Yorkshire Archaeological Journal*, 52 (1980), 123–33; Jones, 'The war in the north', 232–9.

[50] Yonge reported that they were down to 14,000, but at Marston Moor they apparently numbered between 14,500 and 15,500: BL. Add. MS 18779 (Yonge's diary), fo. 101v.

[51] Slingsby, *Diary*, 106.

The summer campaign: Marston Moor

Behind the walls of the beleaguered city the Marquess of Newcastle prepared for a long siege, while pinning his hopes on Prince Rupert. Soldiers and civilians alike were issued a pint of beans, an ounce of butter and a penny loaf each day. As the besieged awaited the prince they bolstered their spirits by singing psalms in York Minster. Their music director was the distinguished composer William Lawes. A contemporary recalled the performances of his psalm settings as 'the very best harmonical music' that he had ever heard – a useful reminder that it was not only puritans who affirmed themselves by singing religious songs in time of war.[52]

The allies were expecting several thousand more reinforcements under Sir John Meldrum and the Earl of Denbigh, but Rupert's advance was so rapid that he easily outdistanced them. On 30 June the besiegers moved their forces to the west side of the city to block Rupert's approach along the Knaresborough Road. But Rupert unexpectedly streaked northwards, crossed the river Ouse at Boroughbridge on 1 July, and bore down on the unguarded northern gate of the city. The two-month siege was thus lifted by a manoeuvre that was 'by any standards a remarkable piece of generalship'.[53]

Divided in their counsel, the allies did not know whether to give battle at once, as the Fairfaxes advocated, or wait for the arrival of reinforcements as Leven urged. In the event they decided to retreat westward, and regroup their forces at a safe distance south of the Ouse near Long Marston. Having just got the news of Waller's defeat at Cropredy Bridge, the allied commanders feared that Rupert might head southwards to join with his uncle for an attack on Essex's army. They accordingly decided to retreat in the same direction.

Rupert in the meantime drew up his troops on Marston Moor in an open challenge to battle. He instructed Newcastle to have his own troops ready and in position by 4 o'clock the next morning. But when the time came Newcastle's troops were nowhere to be seen, and Rupert had lost the opportunity to attack before his foes could take up battle formation. Why had Newcastle dragged his feet? He may have been annoyed at being ordered around by a man half his age. He was also hoping that Montrose and Colonel Clavering would shortly arrive from the north with reinforcements to make up the numerical deficiency on the royalist side. According

---

[52] David Pinto, 'William Lawes at the Siege of York', *Musical Times*, 127: 1723 (1986), 581.
[53] Young and Holmes, *English Civil War*, 192.

to one account he had his foot drawn up by 2 a.m. ready to march out of the city, but was overruled by his second-in-command, General King (Lord Eythin), who said that they should not march until they had had their pay, 'whereupon they all quit their colours and disperse[d].'[54] Not only was it pay day for the York infantry, half of them were reportedly absent plundering the enemy's abandoned trenches, and therefore unavailable for mustering. But we must bear in mind that these mutinous, plundering troops were the very men – Newcastle's famous Whitecoats – who in the evening of that same day would stand in disciplined ranks until they were wiped out.[55] There was no reason why General King could not have brought these first-class soldiers back to order. Cholmley's account of this episode supports the view that General King was instrumental in wrecking Rupert's battle plans.

When they learned that Rupert wanted to fight, the allies abandoned their march to Tadcaster and retraced their steps. Simeon Ash records that 'hope of a battle moved our soldiers to return merrily . . .',[56] a corrective to the notion that fear is the only emotion with which soldiers approach the violence of battle. During the course of the day they took up positions on the ridge overlooking Marston Field, to the south of the Marston–Tockwith Road. Several thunder showers puncuated the afternoon. Once the allied soldiers were fully assembled they kept up their spirits in the humid heat by singing psalms.

Immediately in front of the allied foot was a large cornfield, but the ground as a whole was very little enclosed. On the right, facing Goring, the allied commanders placed Lord Fairfax's 3,000 horse in two lines, with his son Sir Thomas in command. A third line, 1,000 strong, consisted of three Scottish regiments under the Earl of Eglinton. On both wings the Scots were relegated to the rear because their smaller, lighter horses were considered unsuitable for the initial shock of a cavalry charge. In addition there were 600 musketeers interspersed in 12 platoons among the horse, as well as 500 dragoons. In the centre were most of the 19,000 foot arranged in 14 brigades, each of the three armies having positions in front and rear, but with Scots exclusively occupying the second line. The left wing under

[54] Bodl. MS Clarendon 23, fo. 153 (Sir Hugh Cholmley's account).

[55] On an earlier occasion when their uniforms were being fabricated Newcastle had suggested having the cloth dyed, but his soldiers, impatient to be on the move, 'requested my Lord, that he would be pleased to let them have it un-dyed . . . promising they themselves would dye it in the enemy's blood': Margaret Cavendish, Duchess of Newcastle, *The Life of William Cavendish Duke of Newcastle*, 84.

[56] *Continuation of True Intelligence* (1644), Beinecke Lib., Z17 65y.5, 4.

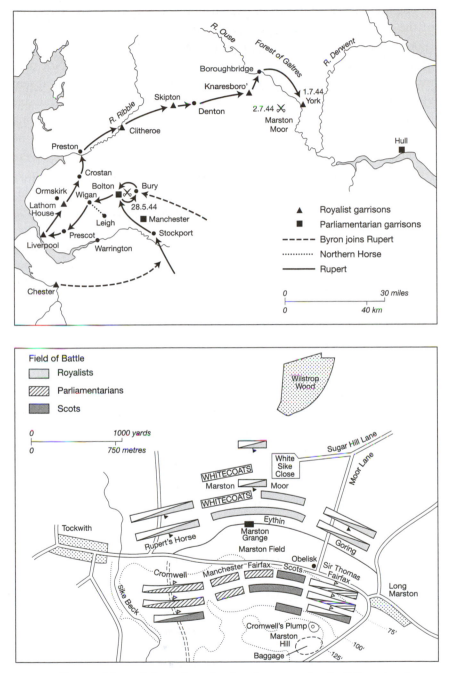

MAP 7 *Marston Moor: a) the region, showing the routes taken by i) Rupert and ii) Manchester, Fairfax and Cornwall; b) the battlefield, 2 July 1644*

Adapted from Young, Peter and Holmes, Richard, *The English Civil War: A Military History of Three Civil Wars, 1642–51* (Wordsworth Editions Ltd, 1999)

Cromwell consisted of eight regiments of horse and two of dragoons, arrayed in three lines. Cromwell personally commanded the first line consisting of his own Ironsides and two other of Manchester's regiments, as well as the Scots dragoons under Colonel Hugh Fraser on the extreme left. The second line also comprised Eastern Association regiments, while Major-General David Leslie led the third line of Scots. As on the right wing, the 4,000 horse and 500 dragoons were interspersed with 12 platoons of musketeers.

From their vantage point in a clump of trees – now known as Cromwell's Plump – the allied general staff had a good view of the enemy's position. It was clear to Leven that they substantially outnumbered their enemy – even after the arrival of Newcastle's Whitecoats – by a ratio of more than three to two.

Leven could see that Rupert had followed the conventional plan of stationing the infantry in the centre with the cavalry on the wings. The infantry stood behind a hedge that ran parallel to the road, while a ditch extending across much of their line gave added protection. Both Rupert and Leven, who had served under King Gustav II Adolph, followed the Swedish model of placing platoons of musketeers between the squadrons of horse. It was evidently Rupert's plan that should Cromwell charge first he would be obstructed by the ditch, and would face galling musket fire before he could make contact with the royalist horse.

Rupert had organized his army into four main bodies: right and left wings, centre and reserve. The right wing was under the immediate command of John Lord Byron, with the assistance of Sir John Urry, major-general of Rupert's horse. It numbered 2,400 horse and 500 musketeers drawn up in two main lines. Owing to his advantageous position behind the ditch, but also perhaps because of his inferior numbers (Cromwell had over 5,000 troops at his disposal on the allied left wing), Byron had been ordered by Rupert to stand and receive the charge of the enemy. Rupert's own regiment stood in the second line or reserve.

TABLE 7.1 *Army strength at Marston Moor*

Royalist forces		Parliamentary forces	
Rupert	9,200	Manchester	8,000
Newcastle	8,800	Fairfax	5,000
		Leven	14,500–15,500
Totals	18,000		27,500–28,500

The centre combined Rupert's and Newcastle's infantry, supported by Blakiston's cavalry brigade of 600 and 16 pieces of artillery. Given that 1,000 musketeers were drawn off to support the left and right wings of cavalry, the royalist centre contained under 10,000 foot. Because they were seriously outnumbered by the allied infantry, it was perhaps thought that the presence of a brigade of cavalry would encourage them. The centre included Rupert's Lancashire recruits, as well as two Irish regiments – Major-General Henry Tillier's and Colonel Broughton's 'Greencoats'. Newcastle's Whitecoats, owing to their late arrival from York, were deployed in the second and third lines. Expecting to attack rather than be attacked, they took up positions in front of a hedge lining Sugar Hill Lane.[57]

The left wing consisted of 2,100 northern horse under their general, Lord Goring, and their lieutenant-general, Sir Charles Lucas. Like Byron, Goring had 500 musketeers deployed in platoons to support his front line. Finally, Rupert had a reserve of some 700 horse under his direct command.

At about 9 a.m. Newcastle appeared on the battlefield with a troop of gentlemen. Rupert did not hide his disappointment: 'I wish you had come sooner with your forces, but I hope we shall yet have a glorious day.' The marquess informed him that General King was at that moment mustering the foot, and would bring them – '4,000 good foot as were in the world' – very shortly. Not until 4 p.m. did King show up, and then only with 3,000. Instead of apologizing for his tardiness he delivered a rebuke. 'Sir your forwardness lost us the day in Germany, where your self was taken prisoner.'[58] Rupert bit his tongue and ignored the older man's insolence. Nevertheless, the late arrival of the York infantry meant that the royalist centre was in disarray, and no distinctive order of battle could be achieved before the fighting began. 'Nothing', Peter Newman comments, 'could have inclined cautious old Leven to fight at once so much as this most . . . obvious failure by the royalist high command.'[59] Having lost the opportunity for a surprise attack, Rupert announced that they would postpone battle until the following morning. Newcastle asked him if the enemy might fall on them sooner, and the prince answered no. So the marquess retired to his coach and called for a pipe of tobacco. Rupert gave the troops permission to break ranks and sat down to his supper.

[57] Here I follow the analysis of Peter Newman in *Marston Moor, 2 July 1644: The Sources and the Site*, 35–6.
[58] Bodl. MS Clarendon 23, fo. 153v. King was referring to the battle of Lemgo in 1638.
[59] Newman, *Marston Moor*, 40–1.

It was now between 6 and 7 in the evening, and Leven through his per-spective glass could see the smoke curling up from the cooking fires in the royalist army. That, as well as his knowledge that he substantially out-numbered his foe, who were still not properly formed up, inspired him to take the offensive. A burst of cannon fire gave the signal for a simultaneous advance by the entire front line, over a mile-and-a-quarter (2 km) broad. As soon as they were halfway down the gentle slope the foot broke into a run, hoping to complete the remaining 1,000 yards before the royalist musketeers could get off more than one or two volleys. Added to the advantage of surprise was a clap of thunder and deluge of rain at the instant the advance began. Much of the infantry soldiers' match would have been extinguished in the downpour, but in any event the thin line of skirmishers behind the main hedge could not have hoped to hold out for long against formed hedgehogs of pikes.

Just to the left of centre Lawrence Crawford succeeded in outflanking his immediate opponents, while in the very centre of the allied front line one of Lord Fairfax's brigades broke through the hedge and pressed on against Rupert's main body. The Scots brigades on the right of centre must have come into contact with some of the Irish squadrons. But they made little headway, for to the right of them things were not going well. Sir Thomas Fairfax had charged gallantly, but the lane down which his troops rode was hemmed in by a hedge and a ditch, both lined with musketeers. These soldiers, and those stationed amongst Goring's squadrons 'did us much hurt with their shot'.[60] After a fierce contest in which Fairfax was slightly wounded and his horse shot, Goring was completely triumphant and the allied right wing was driven off the field. Lieutenant-General Sir Charles Lucas, who was still in position with the second line, now prepared to attack the right flank of the allied infantry, exposed by the rout of their cavalry. It was apparently at this point that the three allied generals – Lords Leven, Manchester and Fairfax – reckoned the battle lost and fled the field. But Lucas soon discovered that he was dealing with forces in good order, and the going was heavy. On the other wing the experience was as different as night from day. Cromwell was able to profit from Byron's blunder in pre-maturely rushing to meet his charge. By his impetuosity Byron both shielded the fire of his own musketeers and relieved Cromwell of the necessity to cross rough ground before engaging him. After a brief engagement in which Cromwell himself was wounded Byron's first line was driven from the field.

[60] Thomas Fairfax, 'A short Memoriall of the Northern actions' in BL. Harley MS 6390, fo. 37v.

Prince Rupert had been in the middle of supper when the allied armies advanced. He at once mounted, and surveying the scene, saw that he was needed on the right wing. Galloping forward through a crowd of fleeing troopers, some from his own regiment, he screamed 'Swounds! Do you run? Follow me.'[61] With that he charged into the thick of Cromwell's horse. For a few moments the battle hung in the balance as the cream of the two cavalries hacked at one another, neither willing to back away. At this point David Leslie and his three regiments – 'some few Scots in our rear' was how Cromwell carelessly labelled them[62] – joined the fray, falling on Rupert's flank. Rupert had no more reserves to bring up, and Cromwell, assisted by the impact of the Scots, was able to break through, 'scattering them before him like a little dust'.[63] Cromwell had retired briefly from the field to have his wound dressed.[64] It may therefore have been Leslie who was responsible for preventing the left wing from spreading out in headlong pursuit of the enemy, and reforming them for their next major task of the day.

The victorious second line of Goring's cavalry was now launching successive charges against the right flank of the allied foot as it stood locked in combat with Rupert's infantry. Sir William Blakiston's brigade of horse had also charged into the middle of the allied infantry and cut a swathe right up as far as the ridge summit, scattering the Scottish foot in all directions. But because it was an isolated action its spectacular success was more apparent than real. By now Cromwell was back on the field, joined by Sir Thomas Fairfax who had removed the white band from his hat, and passed through the enemy unrecognized, to get to his comrades on the other wing. The three leaders then took their regiments around behind their own units to attack Goring's horse in the rear. Coming up against the battle-seasoned Ironsides, Goring's troops broke and fled towards York. Here another weakness of the royalist army was exposed: it operated less like a unified force than as disjointed formations. Its units never managed to build on their individual successes.

With the right wing of the infantry relieved, one more task awaited Cromwell's and Leslie's weary troopers. Newcastle's Whitecoats, pinned against the hedge along Sugar Hill Lane between White Sike Close and

[61] Young, *Marston Moor*, 113.

[62] Abbott (ed.), *Cromwell*, Vol. 1, 287.

[63] Lion (Leonard) Watson, *A More Exact Relation of the late Battell Neer York* (1644), E2/14, 6.

[64] Austin Woolrych, *Battles of the English Civil War: Marston Moor, Naseby, Preston*, 74.

Moor Lane, could not flee, but neither would they surrender.[65] It had been well said of their white coats that they had 'brought their winding-sheets about them into the field'.[66] For a long while their pikemen stood firm against the battering rams of allied horse and foot. At length dragoons were called in to batter the bristling wall of pikes and pry open a gap for the cavalry to enter. But even when their square formation was finally broken the Whitecoats fought on, refusing quarter. Many wounded lay on their backs, still wielding their swords and pikes to gore the bellies of the horses that rode over them. Out of 3,000 Whitecoats all but 30 were slaughtered.

In the end the royalist death toll was 4,150, with the allies losing a mere 300 and taking an additional 1,500 prisoners, besides some 6,000 arms, all the royalist ordnance, powder and baggage, and about 100 battle standards. Rupert narrowly escaped capture, hiding in a beanfield until the coast was clear, and then staggering back to York under cover of darkness. The allies camped in the field where they sang their psalm of victory.

Marston Moor, the greatest battle ever to be fought on English soil, was soon recognized for its epochal implications. Simeon Ashe hailed it as a mighty chapter in the pan-European struggle between Roman Catholicism and reformed Christianity.

You cannot imagine the courage, spirit, and resolution that was taken up on both sides; for we looked, and no doubt they also, upon this sight, as the losing or gaining the garland: And Sir, consider the height of difference of spirits: in their army the cream of all the papists in England; and in ours, a collection out of all the corners of England and Scotland of such that had the greatest antipathy to popery and tyranny; these equally thirsting the extirpation of each other, and now the sword must determine that which a hundred years policy and dispute could not do . . . much like the encounters that were in the French war between the papist and the protestant.[67]

There were less epochal consequences as well. York surrendered two weeks later, and with it went the royalist presence in the north. A precious clause in the surrender articles guaranteed all churches and other buildings

[65] I accept Peter Newman's argument that the Whitecoats had not been driven into White Sike Close, but stood near where they had originally been stationed, south of Sugar Hill Lane: *Marston Moor*, 35–6, 42–3.

[66] Quoted in Woolrych, *Battles*, 77.

[67] *A True Relation of the Late Fight between the Parliament Forces and Prince Rupert, within Four Miles of Yorke* (1644), E54/7, sig. A2b.

from defacement. Sir Thomas Fairfax's respect for this clause saved York Minster's glass from the hands of iconoclasts. The loss of the north did not quench the optimism of Prince Rupert who determined to rally his men and rebuild his army. He took the few that were left across the Pennines to Chester. The lords Eythin and Newcastle, 'looking upon all as lost', chose exile in the United Provinces. 'I will not endure the laughter of the court', huffed Newcastle.[68]

On one level Newcastle was right: all *should* have been lost for the royalists. Lord Inchiquin in Ireland could see the writing on the wall. Already convinced that parliament was the better defender of Irish Protestantism, he let Marston Moor precipitate his defection from the king. Not only did he take with him all the leading Protestants in Munster; his switch of allegiance gave the valuable ports of southern Ireland into the hands of parliament, which immediately sent shiploads of arms to strengthen them. In England the combined armies of parliament and the Scots were expected to make short work of the remaining royalist forces in the south. That they were not able to do so said much about their strategic ineptness and disunity. In fact victory only exposed more glaringly the fissures in the parliamentary coalition. Writing to his brother-in-law, Cromwell exulted that his Ironsides had beaten the Prince's horse – 'God made them as stubble to our swords' – all but ignoring the contribution of the Scots who had made up more than half the allied coalition.[69] His emissary to London, the young cavalry captain Thomas Harrison, a man intoxicated with visions of the reign of Christ on earth, 'trumpet[ed] over all the city' the praises of Cromwell, to the intense annoyance of the Scots. At Westminster Cromwell's party, the Independents, enjoyed increasing support in the wake of his success. So did the policy that was nearest to his heart: liberty of conscience for religious separatists.[70]

The late summer and autumn campaign

Wales: Montgomery Castle

In the north-west meanwhile, Rupert's hopes of recruiting a new army in the north were disappointed. Wherever he went the prince found himself on barren ground. Leading his remnant across the Pennines, he got little

---

[68] Warburton, *Memoirs*, Vol. 2, 468.
[69] Abbott, *Cromwell*, Vol. 1, 287.
[70] Baillie, *Letters*, Vol. 2, 209, 211.

comfort from Cumberland and Westmorland, where the royalists were already demoralized by Marston Moor. His troops ran up against hostile parliamentary forces in Lancashire. They retreated, exhausted and hungry, into Cheshire. There they collided with Sir William Brereton who chased them into north Wales. It was now the turn of Sir Thomas Myddleton, the parliamentary sergeant-major-general for the region, to harass the dispirited royalists. At the beginning of August in the company of Thomas Mytton, the governor of Oswestry, he advanced upon Rupert's tiny army which had taken refuge in Montgomery Castle. Their numbers had been swelled to 2,000 foot and 1,500 horse by the arrival of John Byron from Chester. A pitched battle ensued; the outcome utter defeat for the royalists. Combined with Marston Moor it annihilated the royalists' military presence in Wales and in all England north of the Bristol Channel.

The remnants of Rupert's horse finally straggled into Oxford at the end of September.[71] They found that the royalist headquarters had been transformed by its energetic new deputy governor, Sir Henry Gage, from the ill-stocked, ill-guarded town that had almost fallen to Waller in June, into a well fortified, well provisioned fortress. Rupert's men may also have gained some comfort from the news that in the south-west their monarch had just executed his most brilliant manoeuvre of the war.

The south-west: Lostwithiel

Charles's achievement in late summer of 1644 was to consolidate his own forces, interpose them between the armies of Waller and Essex, and then isolate and liquidate Essex's army. His first step was to withdraw the substantial royalist garrisons from Reading and Abingdon, abandoning these outposts to parliament in May. Then at the end of June he duelled with Waller and beat him at Cropredy Bridge a few miles north of Banbury. The engagement was minor but the humiliation for Waller was major, for it broke the heart of his army, which promptly shrank from 8,000 to 4,000. Nursing his wounds, Waller withdrew sulkily to Farnham, while his army continued to waste away from hunger and disease.

Even though the king failed to drive his victory home, Cropredy helped him to prepare for greater things in the months ahead. Interestingly it was adoration for his wife and their unborn child that galvanized him into making a daring foray against the parliamentary forces in the west.

---

[71] BL. Add. MS 18981 (Rupert Papers), fo. 255. The sorry tale of the misfortunes of the northern royalist horse in August and September 1644 can be followed in Rupert's correspondence: ibid., fos. 233–70.

Parliamentary bumbling, the demoralization of its troops, and the ongoing antagonism between Essex and Waller, helped more than a little to make the king seem like an able general. The policy formulated by the Council of War was that the Oxford army, led by the king himself, would march into the south-west, link forces with Prince Maurice, Hopton and Grenville, and then, 16,000 strong, crush Essex before Waller could catch up with them.[72]

This policy was not difficult to consummate, given that neither parliamentary commander would cooperate with the other throughout 1644. Essex, instead of attempting a knockout blow against the king's remaining forces, thought it would be a grand idea to capture more territory in the south-west. The top prize would be Exeter, where he would take custody of Henrietta Maria, either to impeach her or use her as a bargaining counter in negotiations with the king. So he plunged westward, having already relieved Lyme which was under siege by Prince Maurice. Then, deaf to Waller's cries for help, he occupied Weymouth and Taunton, pushed on to Tavistock, and relieved Plymouth. It looked for all the world as if Essex was piling success upon success, but in truth his lines were now dangerously extended, and he ought to have known that he could not count on any help from his old rival Waller.

It did not take the royalists long to get Essex tangled up. Nearing Exeter, he found that his coveted prey, the queen, had eluded him, abandoning her newborn baby, and fleeing to France. The Committee of Both Kingdoms communicated Essex's request that Waller should 'take care of the king's army', before it could cause trouble to him, to which Waller retorted that he was in too weakened a condition to take care of anybody. In the Commons Edward Massie, governor of Gloucester, berated Waller for his inactivity. Nor was Sir Simonds D'Ewes, a partisan of Essex, impressed when Waller rushed back to explain himself to the House of Commons.[73]

Essex was also dragged down by the quality of his army. Not only the foot but the horse had been scraped from the bottom of the barrel. '[T]urbulent outlandish men . . . mere mercenaries' uninterested in religion or politics, and 'too oft insufferably insolent' was William Herbert's on-the-spot appraisal.[74] It did not help either that the people of Cornwall

---

[72] Such was the plan outlined by Digby on 12 July 1644: BL. Add. MS 30377 (letters from Digby and Charles II), fo. 1.

[73] BL. Harley MS 166 (D'Ewes diary, YCPH transcript), fos. 93, 106.

[74] Ibid., fo. 92.

were suspicious and hostile, nor that 'no gentlemen of the county come down to our assistance'.[75]

On 26 July Charles reached Exeter, disappointed that he could not embrace his beloved wife. The next day he was joined by Prince Maurice's army, 4,600 strong. On that same day Essex made the fateful decision to cross the River Tamar into Cornwall, as Richard Grenville's forces retreated before him. A week later he was at Lostwithiel. Charles was now at Liskeard and Grenville at Grampound, drawing the net tighter around him.

Why had the parliamentary commander-in-chief allowed himself to be trapped halfway across the narrowing peninsula of Cornwall? Partly because he thought that Waller would, at the end of the day, be shamed into coming to his rescue by attacking the king's rear. Or if not Waller, at least his lieutenant-general, John Middleton. Middleton did in fact get as far as Bridgwater in Somerset, but he was stopped there by Sir Francis Doddington. In a stunning display of loyalty to the king, the sheriff and other leading men of Somerset had supplied Doddington with 2,000 additional conscripts at the beginning of August.[76] Another factor influencing Essex's decision to push into Cornwall was the argument of his own lieutenant-general, John Lord Robartes, that the county was of supreme strategic importance. Sales of Cornish tin from the port of Falmouth gave the royalists precious revenue for the purchase of munitions. Robartes, a Cornishman, was also sure that his countrymen would rise for parliament as soon as Essex appeared at the head of a strong army. Cynics thought that Robartes had an ulterior motive: the protection of his own estates in the county.

In the event, Essex was bitterly disappointed. Not only did the Cornish fail to flock to his standard, they and their womenfolk withheld supplies and cut the throats of soldiers who straggled from the main force.[77] At the same time they were happy to provide the king with valuable intelligence about Essex's movements. To judge by the astonished delight of Sir Edward Walker, secretary of the council of war, Cornwall was exceptional among English counties in providing the royalists with so tangible a demonstration of popular support.[78]

Occupying an unaccustomed position of strength, the king chose this moment to tempt Essex with promises of 'eminent marks of my confidence

---

[75] Ibid., fo. 95v.

[76] BL. Harley MS 6802, fo. 254v.

[77] *Mercu. Civicus* (29 August–5 September 1644), E8/12, 634.

[78] Edward Walker, *Historical Discourses upon Several Occasions* (hereafter Walker, *Hist. Discourses*), 50.

and valour' if only he would join in the enforcement of a reasonable treaty, and help prevent the conquest of the kingdom by the Scots. The king's leading officers also wrote assuring Essex that they shared his aspirations: 'to defend his majesty's known rights, the laws of the kingdom, the liberty of the subject, the privilege of parliament, and the true Protestant religion'.[79] Essex replied that parliament had given him no authority to treat, and therefore it would be a breach of trust to engage in talks.

In reality there was a stronger yearning for peace in the king's camp than in Essex's. The royalist lieutenant-general of horse, Henry Lord Wilmot, an able soldier, but afflicted by a weakness for the bottle and a jealousy of Prince Rupert's ascendancy with the king, had talked openly of making peace by dethroning Charles and elevating the Prince of Wales in his place. He was supported by the general of the ordnance, Baron Harry Percy, brother to the Earl of Northumberland. Both men not only hated Rupert, but had also turned against Digby, who in the course of the summer had nimbly shifted to Rupert's side in order to please the king. When Charles wrote his peace letter to Essex, Wilmot contrived to add a secret personal message offering to organize support for him within the king's army, overthrow Digby and others who favoured war, and unite with Essex in taking the king to London.[80]

Someone leaked the message to Charles, who reacted decisively. On 8 August Wilmot was placed under arrest and Lord Goring, who had just arrived from the north, proclaimed general in his place. Percy resigned and Hopton was put in charge of the ordnance. The last stage of this shake-up was intended to be Rupert's appointment as commander-in-chief upon his return from the north.

Having rejected the royal olive branch, Essex prepared for battle. He was still pinning his hopes on the arrival of Lieutenant-General Middleton's reinforcements, and relief by sea from the Earl of Warwick. Both hopes were dashed. Unfavourable winds prevented Warwick from landing, while Middleton, his 3,800 reinforcements blocked by the Somerset militia at Bridgwater, had fallen back to Sherborne.

Charles's army by contrast, continued to grow. On 11 August Sir Richard Grenville arrived in his camp with 2,400 men. With 16,000 troops to Essex's 10,000 he chose 21 August to launch a concerted attack along a four-mile front, driving Essex's forces from several of their positions and

[79] *The Letters from His Maiesty, and from the Officers of His Majesties Army, to the Earl of Essex* (Oxford, 1644), E8/26, p. 4.
[80] Bodl. MS Firth C7, fo. 137.

drawing the net still tighter. In a transparent jab against Waller, Essex complained that if only 500 musketeers had arrived he could have gone on the offensive.[81] In reality he was now helpless, his army bottled up in a narrow tract of land five miles long and two miles wide. Desperately short of food and ammunition, and with no prospect of relief, he decided to fall back on the little port of Fowey, leaving his horse to try to break through royalist lines. At about 3 o'clock in the morning of 31 August Sir William Balfour sallied out of Lostwithiel at the head of 2,000 horse, past a detachment of sleeping musketeers, and onto the Liskeard road. That day they gave the slip to Cleveland's pursuing cavalry, and eventually reached the haven of Plymouth. This breathtaking feat was only possible because the royalists were strung out in a 15-mile perimeter around Lostwithiel in order to deny provisions to their foe.

Essex's foot, under Major-General Skippon, were now reeling backwards along the narrow lane leading to Fowey, as the king moved in to finish them off. Charles occupied Lostwithiel, and then pushed southwards, leading his troops in person and beating the enemy from hedge to hedge. By dusk Skippon's regiments, tired, hungry and demoralized at being deserted by the horse, began to disintegrate. Essex and Robartes – who more than anyone was the author of the disaster – had taken flight for Plymouth in a fishing boat. Charles, confident of victory, spent the stormy night under a hedge with his men. The next day Skippon asked to treat, and Charles, fearful of any delay that might allow reinforcements to arrive, granted him generous terms. His 6,000 soldiers were allowed to march off with their colours, but they had to abandon 5,000 arms, 42 cannon and all their gunpowder. One hundred soldiers signed on with the royalist army, while two-thirds of the rest disappeared during the nightmarish trek to Plymouth and Southampton. Along the way they were set upon by angry civilians who stripped them of their clothing and money, wounding and killing many.[82]

The western campaign culminating in Lostwithiel was the most thorough success achieved by the royalists during the whole civil war in England. Above all it was a personal triumph for the king. Charles, with his council of war, shaped the strategy that isolated, trapped and crushed the main parliamentary army in the south together with its hapless

---

[81] Rushworth, *Hist. Coll.*, Vol. 5, 702 (Essex to Sir Philip Stapilton, 3 September 1644).

[82] For a graphic eyewitness account of the retreat from Lostwithiel by Skippon's foot, see *A True Relation of the Sad Passages, between the Two Armies in the West* (1644), E10/27, 9–12.

captain-general.[83] Charles also coordinated armies and troop movements, eluded his pursuers and led his troops in combat. He has been criticized for allowing the parliamentary infantry to march away intact rather than liquidating them, but almost the same result was accomplished by their harrowing retreat through Cornwall. The only blot on his achievement was his inability to stop the parliamentary cavalry under Balfour from slipping through his lines.

The aftermath of Marston Moor and Lostwithiel

Charles knew better than to overestimate the magnitude of his Cornish victory, or pay heed to those who advised him now to advance on Kent and London. Sweet though it was, his win at Lostwithiel hardly balanced the great disaster of Marston Moor. Moreover, in its hour of triumph the temper of the king's army again turned ugly. Almost immediately 4,000 foot deserted, perhaps because it was harvest time. The cavalry were angered by lack of pay. By the end of September when Charles set out for Oxford, his and Prince Maurice's combined armies did not amount to more than 9,500 men.[84] His foes, in spite of their recent mauling, could boast far greater depth of strength. Essex's and Middleton's horse, united at Plymouth, totalled 6,000. Waller had another 4,000 horse and foot at Salisbury. Massie had 1,500 at Bath. Manchester, who had been ordered to come south, was hanging around Lincolnshire with 7,000 men of the Eastern Association. There were besides, several thousand soldiers in the major parliamentary garrisons between Plymouth and Reading who could be drawn out to form a wall against any royalist advance on London.

In the capital there were bitter recriminations and much political infighting in the wake of Essex's humiliation. The shame of Lostwithiel extinguished for the time being almost all his remaining political influence. In the House of Commons his enemies could scarcely conceal their glee. Waller's right-hand man, Sir Arthur Hesilrige – the hero of Cheriton – openly laughed and jeered when Essex's defeat was reported.[85] Whether it was Essex's simple incompetence as a general, or the failure of his subordinates, or his arrogance in disobeying parliament's prohibition against

---

[83] Ian Roy, 'The royalist council of war, 1642–6', *Bulletin of the Institute of Historical Research* (hereafter *BIHR*), 164.

[84] Walker, *Hist. Discourses*, 98.

[85] BL. Harley MS 166 (D'Ewes diary, YCPH transcript), fo. 112v.

entering Cornwall, or his poor judgement in following the bad, self-interested advice of Lord Robartes, his personal disgrace was inescapable. Waller did not fare much better. Many could see merit in Essex's attribution of his failure to Waller's sluggishness in coming to his rescue, conveniently ignoring the extreme weakness of the latter's army, bled by desertion, disease and lack of money. Others fixed the blame on Middleton for not crossing into Cornwall in time, conveniently overlooking the interception of Middleton's horse by the Somerset royalists under Doddington. With tempers frayed and resources stretched to the breaking point, the 'great clamour' which the Scots commissioner Robert Baillie so deplored was leading some to articulate a demand for the purging of parliament's military leadership, and the unification of its armies under centralized command.

CHAPTER 8

Hope revived: royalists counterattack, roundheads regroup, September 1644–May 1645

While the parliamentarians publicly lacerated and privately plotted against one another for their recent humiliations on the battlefield, the royalists soberly reckoned the far-reaching consequences of Marston Moor. When Newcastle finally capitulated before a Scottish assault in October, the whole of the north, a few small garrisons excepted, lay at parliament's feet. For the first time in three years the promise of coal for the hearths of shivering Londoners made the prospect of winter bearable. Their success at Newcastle restored the Scots' military reputation, while the power to control the supply of fuel to the capital gave them a valuable political counter as well.[1] Not only were the north, East Anglia and the south-east in parliament's hands, but the northern half of Wales, nursery of the king's infantry, had also fallen under their sway with the capture of Montgomery Castle by Sir Thomas Middleton, and John Lord Byron's disastrous attempt to take it back.

Reflecting the persistently low morale in the royalist camp, quarrelling and intrigue among commanders and courtiers once again rose to a crescendo. Several watched sullenly as Prince Rupert scaled ever higher in his uncle's esteem, apparently unharmed by the disaster of Marston Moor. Digby wrote to Rupert in mid-August that he would be elevated to

---

[1] *CSPV 1643–47*, 150; Baillie, *Letters*, Vol. 2, 238; Ancram, Sir Robert Kerr, *Correspondence of Sir Robert Kerr, First Earl of Ancram and His Son William, Third Earl of Lothian*, Vol. 1, 176.

commander-in-chief as soon as Lord Firth, who had just been given the sop of an earldom, could be brought to resign.[2] With the queen gone to France, Wilmot and Percy disgraced, Digby apparently backing him, and his best friend at Court, the Duke of Richmond, in the king's company again, Rupert appeared to be riding the crest of political power. Almost at once, however, the crest began to subside. Before the end of August his elder brother, Charles Louis, the elector Palatine, had arrived in London and was hob-nobbing with the parliamentary leaders. The rumour spread of a plan to supplant the English king with the unimpeachably Protestant prince elector. Under these circumstances the king shelved his plans to promote Rupert.

The Irish theatre

With few encouraging prospects in England, Charles looked again to his other two kingdoms for something that might kindle a flicker of hope. The one-year truce with the Irish Catholic Confederacy had been extended by three months, during which time Charles urged his lord lieutenant, Ormond, to negotiate a peace, no matter what the cost so long as it produced more troops to come and fight for him in England. The Catholic Irish, who had felt themselves stalemated by the signing of the 1643 truce, now saw their opportunity to profit from the king's weakness. Their demands were utterly reasonable and utterly unrealistic: complete freedom of religion, the appointment of Catholics to public office on an equal footing with Protestants, and the right to establish inns of court, universities and common schools. They also wanted an act of oblivion for all offences committed since the outbreak of civil war, while Poynings' Law, requiring all Irish legislation to be approved first by the king's privy council at Wesminster, and the 1642 act promising 10 million acres to Irish adventurers, should be repealed.[3] These demands were vehemently opposed by the Protestants who controlled the Dublin administration. Granting them, they maintained, would allow Irish Catholics, who constituted the overwhelming majority of the population, to 'assume all power into their own hands'.[4] For the better part of a year Charles refused to

---

[2] BL. Add. MS 18981 (Rupert Papers), fos. 218v–19 (printed with errors in Rupert, *Memoirs*, Vol. 3, 12).

[3] John T. Gilbert (ed.), *History of the Irish Confederation and the War in Ireland* (hereafter *Irish Confed.*), Vol. 3, 128–33, 324–7.

[4] And this, they added, 'after the murder of two hundred and fifty thousand Protestants': HMC 63, *Manuscripts of the Earl of Egmont*, Vol. 1, 219, 229.

commit himself to anything more than not persecuting Catholics if they returned to obedience.

The morass of Irish affairs was further deepened by the defection of Murrough O'Brien, Lord Inchiquin, governor of Munster, to the parliamentary side. This thunderbolt, together with parliament's announced policy of no compromise with the Irish rebels, strained the loyalty of other members of the Irish Protestant community to the king. Inchiquin's action decisively tilted the strategic balance in Ireland, and indeed throughout the three kingdoms. Not only did it give parliament important bridgeheads in Munster – at Cork, Duncannon and Youghal – it made for an effective military stalemate, since none of the protagonists in Ireland any longer had the preponderant strength needed to destroy their opponents.

The Confederates' bargaining position with the king was further undermined by the disastrous failure of their offensive against Monro's Scottish army in Ulster. Since Monro had refused to be a party to the Cessation, he was fair game for the Catholic Irish, who thought that they now had an opportunity to drive him and his army out of Ulster. They had grounds for their optimism. Thanks to a combination of death, desertion, disease and the return of three of his ten regiments to Scotland, Monro's numbers had been reduced to barely half his original 10,000.[5] The only obstacle to success was the refusal of Owen Roe O'Neill – the Confederation's general in Ulster – to cooperate with Thomas Preston, his counterpart in Leinster. Both men had fought in the Spanish army, where O'Neill had been senior to Preston. In the event the Confederate Supreme Council alienated both men by entrusting the command of the operation to a soldier of inferior talent, the Earl of Castlehaven. The three generals eventually managed to paper over their differences enough to move north in July with a combined strength of nearly 11,000 men. But by their dilatory conduct they allowed Monro to rally his forces, and augment them with regiments from the British settler or 'Laggan' army stationed in western Ulster, bringing his strength almost back to the original 10,000 men. The two armies then faced off at Charlemont for seven weeks, during which time neither side dared attack the other. Finally Castlehaven, his supplies running out, ordered his forces into winter quarters. He had just thrown away a rare chance of winning a major victory that might have counteracted the effect

---

[5] Hugh Hazlett, 'The recruitment and organisation of the Scottish army in Ulster, 1642–9', in H.A. Cronne, T.W. Moody and D.B. Quinn (eds), *Essays in British and Irish History in Honour of James Eadie Todd*, 126–7. See also Wheeler's admirable essay, 'Four armies in Ireland', 51–3, and his *Cromwell in Ireland*, 22–5.

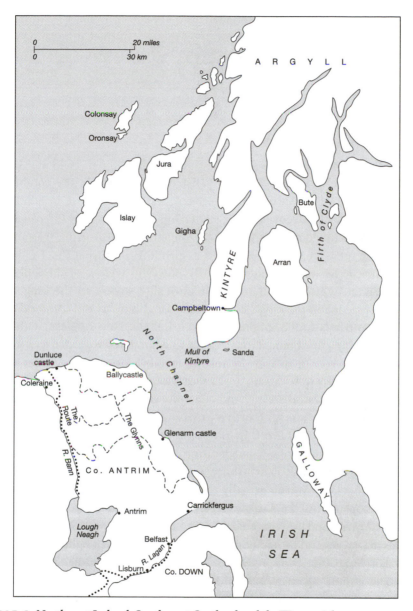

MAP 8 *North-east Ireland, South-west Scotland and the Western Isles*
(i.e. MacDonnell and Argyll territories)
Adapted from Young, Peter, *Edgehill, 1642 (Great Battles)* (Cassell Military, 1995)

of Inchiquin's defection and shifted the military balance in both Ireland
and Britain in the king's favour. For Monro defeat would have been
much more disastrous than for the Catholics, since the Covenanters in
Edinburgh were already overstretched by their commitments in all three

kingdoms and might have responded to a reverse in Ireland by ordering him home. A failure of strategic vision on the part of the Confederate generals, together with their reluctance to risk everything on a single throw of the dice, allowed Monro and his English Protestant supporters to preserve their position intact.

The Scottish theatre

While the 9,000 Irish troops sent by Ormond to England in 1643 and 1644 had made little difference to the royalist war effort there, the combined work of the Earl of Antrim and the Marquess of Montrose in Scotland severely shook up the covenanting leadership and blunted its offensives in the other two kingdoms. Randall MacDonnell, Earl of Antrim, was ambitious, vain, charming, unreliable and a spendthrift. During the 1630s he had married the wealthy and politically powerful widow of the Duke of Buckingham, which gave him almost unrivalled access to the king. Yet almost everyone in the king's council distrusted him, as did Ormond and most of Antrim's Catholic compatriots in Ireland. Nevertheless, with the queen's backing he obtained royal assent to what many regarded as a madcap scheme to recruit an army in Ireland, invade Scotland, join forces with the recent convert to royalism, the Earl of Montrose, beat up the Marquess of Argyll, his ancestral enemy, and generally create mayhem for the army of the Covenant. It was his fourth try in as many years to float such a plan, but this time he pulled it off. By the summer of 1644 he obtained the cooperation of the Catholic Confederation, whose chief motivation was to force Major-General Robert Monro to withdraw his army from Ireland. With this backing Antrim actually managed to recruit and transport over 2,000 troops across the narrow stretch of water separating his estates in County Antrim and the contested territory of the Western Isles of Scotland.[6] As his major-general he had nominated his kinsman the Highland warlord Alasdair MacColla, whose zeal for the cause was nourished by a longstanding enmity against Archibald Campbell, Marquess of Argyll, over territory in western Scotland. MacColla was a veteran soldier who had fought in both countries. A number of other officers could boast continental experience and were able to impart knowledge of modern warfare during the months when the troops, most of them musketeers, underwent their training. Judging by the stamina, courage and endurance they would display in Scotland, the training was effective.

[6] Ohlmeyer, *Civil War and Restoration*, 145, n.103.

Tippermuir

When they arrived in Scotland Montrose was nowhere to be found. He was lurking disconsolate at Carlisle after being cold-shouldered by Rupert when he asked the prince to detach 1,000 of his shattered cavalry so that he could carry the war into Scotland. Rupert's refusal was understandable. His priority in the summer of 1644 was to rebuild his army and defend the royalist heartland around Oxford and the west. Besides, Montrose was an ex-Covenanter, who so far had done little for the royalist cause. Arrogant and given to extravagant gestures, he and Antrim were seen as much of a piece. But when he heard of Alasdair MacColla's arrival he sped through the Lowlands and walked into the Irish camp at Atholl on 29 August. He had nothing to offer them but his leadership, knowledge of the terrain, and influence among his people. He also had a commission from the king giving him almost vice-regal powers in Scotland. Quickly he persuaded the clans of the region – the Robertsons and the Stewarts – that as the representative of the king of Scotland he deserved their backing. Two thousand more men rallied to his standard. Crossing into the Tay Valley, he next won over his own clan the Grahams, who had been sent out against the Irish. On 1 September 1644 Montrose came upon Argyll's forces arrayed against him on Tippermuir, a broad expanse of moor just west of Perth. Led by Lord Elcho, an inexperienced soldier, they were a hastily levied array of Lowland peasants and town dwellers perhaps 3,500 strong. The professional officers and regular soldiers of the Covenant were nearly all fighting in England and Ireland. Montrose's first test could not have been easier. When he sent his army forward the inexperienced government forces crumpled like paper and were then chased by the rebels and swiftly cut to pieces. On the Covenanters' left wing, after an initial volley of musketfire, which failed to halt the cavalry advance, Montrose's Highlanders hurled stones. They did this with such ferocity that they halted the cavalry. The Highlanders then used their swords to drive them from the field. There was then a general rout with the Highlanders and the Irish chasing the fleeing enemy all the way back to Perth, killing perhaps 500 and taking twice that number prisoner. 'Men might have walked upon the dead corpses to the town, being two long miles' wrote a royalist newswriter hyperbolically.[7] Their own losses were negligible.[8]

---

[7] Carte, *Orig. Letters*, Vol. 1, 73.

[8] This account of Tippermuir is based chiefly on the critical reassessment by Stuart Reid in *Campaigns of Montrose: A Military History of the Civil War in Scotland 1639–1646*,

The victory at Tippermuir led to the surrender of Perth, allowing the royalists to replenish their swords, ammunition and clothing. They attracted few recruits, however, which was to be a perennial problem for Montrose. The Irish were generally hated in Scotland because of their reputation for barbarous cruelty, and their Catholicism. Equally, MacColla's link with the Macdonald clan gave him little chance of drawing support from the Lowlands, where the Macdonalds were held in contempt. This clan and confessional dimension contributed an unprecedented level of savagery to the war in Scotland. Argyll was soon assembling another army at Stirling, whose mighty castle controlled central Scotland. Regiments were ordered home from England. With their shortage of cavalry still unremedied, the rebels rethought their plan to invade the Lowlands, and opted for Dundee instead. When the city rejected Montrose's summons to surrender on 6 September, he withdrew to the north-east, in the hope of rounding up more recruits.

Aberdeen

Despite their stunning victory at Tippermuir, Montrose and MacColla's royalist army was in parlous condition: with barely 1,500 or 1,600 foot and 60 to 80 horse at their command, they dared not leave the north. Argyll had moved his newly strengthened covenanting army out of Stirling and was soon on their tail. The committee at Aberdeen prepared to resist the royalists, and summoned the covenanting lairds of the shire to bring in their tenantry. About 2,700 men, including 300 horse, were mustered for the defence of the city. What they lacked was a competent leader. On 13 September Montrose sent a messenger with a drummer boy to treat for the surrender of the city. The two were rebuffed, and the drummer boy was pistolled by one of the troopers. Furious at this breach of the laws of war, Montrose vowed revenge and promised MacColla that his Irish troops, once victorious, could sack the city.

The battle, just outside the city, was soon launched. After a brief exchange of artillery and musketfire Montrose, leading from the centre, ordered his infantry to 'lay aside their muskets and pikes, and fall on with sword and durk [small dagger]'.[9] The ensuing fighting was prolonged, but

---

50–9. He convincingly reduces the disparity in numbers between the two sides, and downplays the importance of the so-called 'Highland charge'. Cf. Stevenson, *Alasdair MacColla*, 83–4, 126–9.

[9] Quoted by Reid, *Campaigns of Montrose*, 67.

contrary to legend, there was no wild Highland charge. In the end the government infantry were put to flight and over 500 slain. Royalist losses were minimal, and four days of bloodletting and pillage by MacColla's Irish followed in and around Aberdeen.[10] Since the city was the largest centre of royalism in the country, to sack it was a gross blunder on Montrose's part. As the story spread around Scotland it became still harder to recruit for the king, because of the universal detestation of MacColla's Irish Catholics. MacColla himself had not been present with his men at Aberdeen, having moved north-westwards to Kintore and Inverurie with the rest of the rebel army to await Argyll who was approaching fast.

After much marching and countermarching by the royalists Argyll caught up with them at Fyvie, about 25 miles (40 km) northwest of Aberdeen. With him were 4,000 infantry including two good foot regiments, and perhaps 900 cavalry. They outnumbered Montrose three to one, and he was still virtually bereft of cavalry. Seeing that his position was untenable, he fled southwards to Blair Atholl, much of his army melting away in the process. Argyll returned to Edinburgh, satisfied that he had nipped Montrose's rebellion in the bud.

In London the Scots commissioners were less sanguine about the news from the northern kingdom. They were acutely conscious of continuing English disappointment with their record since the beginning of the year. Their contribution to the decisive victory at Marston Moor had been overlooked or deliberately downplayed by Cromwell and others. It had taken them until October to overrun Newcastle with its crucial control of London's coal supply, and now they were having to withdraw regiments from the north of England because of serious trouble in their own back yard. That, combined with the recent defeat of the Earl of Essex, seemed to have put the Independents into the ascendant. Another humiliation was just around the corner for the troubled earl, one that would lead to an irresistible demand for a radical shake-up of parliament's military leadership.

---

[10] Buchan points out that the only contemporary list of the slain in Aberdeen, by the royalist chronicler John Spalding, contains no women, which raises the question of whether any women were actually killed. He also questions the assumption that the Irish engaged in an orgy of rape during their sack of the city: John Buchan, *The Marquis of Montrose*, 98. There is no mention of such an atrocity in Patrick Gordon of Ruthven, *A Short Abridgement of Britane's Distemper from the Yeare of God M.DC.XXXIX. to M.DC.XLIX*, 82–4.

The English theatre: Second Newbury

The king, pleased with his triumph in Cornwall, and buoyed up by the news of Montrose in Scotland and the political infighting in London, had begun to march confidently eastward, intent on relieving the besieged garrisons at Banbury, Basing and Donnington before retiring to winter quarters. Waller warned that London might be the king's next target.[11] He had tried to block the king's route, but as he explained to the Committee of Both Kingdoms, he could not do the job by himself; he must have Essex and Manchester and their combined forces to help him. Ordered to march westward, Manchester dragged his feet, protesting every mile of the way. Essex did little better. He had repaired his shattered army to the extent of reassembling a few hundred cavalry and less than 1,000 unarmed foot, but his animosity towards Waller was undiminished.

Humiliation was also meted out to Waller: at Andover Goring, with only 200 men, sent him and his forces packing under a drenching downpour. Manchester finally came to Waller's rescue at Basingstoke on 19 October, while Essex and his bedraggled forces arrived two days later. By now Cromwell, impatient with Manchester's lukewarmness for the struggle, was openly quarrelling with his superior officer. Essex was incapacitated by vomiting and diarrhoea. Waller had just called off the month-long siege of Donnington Castle at Newbury. The prospects were not good.

The king now filled the vacuum left by Waller by planting his army at Newbury. It had been arranged that Prince Rupert should come to his assistance from Bristol with 2,000 of the horse surviving from his own army and 2,000 foot from South Wales under Charles Gerrard. As yet there was no sign of Rupert, but Charles decided that he must relieve Banbury Castle, which was in desperate straits. He therefore posted the Earl of Northampton[12] with 800 horse to relieve the town. Northampton successfully raised the siege, but at a price: his absence reduced the king's

---

[11] Waller was wrong. Decipherment of Digby's letter to Rupert on 27 October shows that the king's primary objective was to regroup his forces around Oxford for the winter: BL. Add. MS 18981 (Rupert Papers), fo. 313. A key to the cipher used in this letter is in BL. Add. 30305, fo. 81v. I am indebted to Tim Wales for deciphering the letter, which is printed, but with crucial omissions, in Rupert, *Memoirs*, Vol. 3, 29–30. Rupert too was against pressing on to London, advising the king to march instead into the counties of the Eastern Association (Add. MS 18981, fo. 316).

[12] Not to be confused with his father, the second earl, who had been killed at Hopton Heath the previous year.

army at Newbury to just over 9,000 men.[13] Furthermore, Sir John Urry, the Scots officer who had previously defected to the king from parliament, now, because of some grievance, deserted the king for parliament, to whom he passed on strategically vital information. The knowledge that the king's army was smaller than they had thought gave parliament the confidence to go on the offensive before his reinforcements arrived. The parliamentary commanders were therefore ordered to converge on Newbury. Bolstered by 4,500 of the London trained bands, their numbers were in the neighbourhood of 22,000.[14] The parliamentary plan to cut off the king's path of retreat to Oxford made sense, but the combined armies were hampered by acute leadership problems. Since Essex was sidelined by illness supreme authority had been vested in a council, a notoriously bad way of conducting a battle.

The king, despite his inferior numbers, was in a fairly good position – too strong to attack head on. A scheme was therefore devised, probably by Waller, to attack his army simultaneously from front and rear. An outflanking column under Balfour, Skippon, Waller and Cromwell was sent in a wide circuit behind Donnington Castle, then down again, across the Lambourn, to Speen, where they were to fall on Prince Maurice's rear. It took the better part of a day for the 13,000 soldiers, nearly two-thirds of the army, to complete the march of 13 miles (20 km). The king's officers were fully aware of the flanking manoeuvre, and countered it by shifting Prince Maurice's troops west of Speen. They spent the morning of 27 October busily entrenching this position. The king was further strengthened by the fact that in spite of his shortage of cavalry, his troops between Shaw House and Speen were covered by the guns of Donnington Castle.

How were the two prongs of the parliamentary attack, over a mile apart, to be synchronized? It was agreed that as soon as Manchester heard Skippon's cannon go off at Speen, he was to unleash his troops against Shaw House. By mid-afternoon when Skippon's cannon announced their readiness to attack, the troops at Shaw were already worn out and

---

[13] The best contemporary account of the second battle of Newbury, from a royalist perspective, is found in Walker, *Hist. Discourses*, 110–16.

[14] Thomas Juxon, who was usually well informed, reported that the three parliamentary generals together mustered 10,000 horse and 12,000 foot: Camden Society, *The Journal of Thomas Juxon* (hereafter Juxon, *Journal*), *1644–1647*, eds Keith Lindley and David Scott, 59. The usual estimate, based on a later statement by Cromwell, and the parliamentary press, is around 19,000 in total: Gardiner, *GCW*, Vol. 2, 44; Wilfrid Emberton, *The English Civil War Day by Day*, 130. But the tendency of generals to minimize the size of their forces, particularly after a poor performance, should be borne in mind.

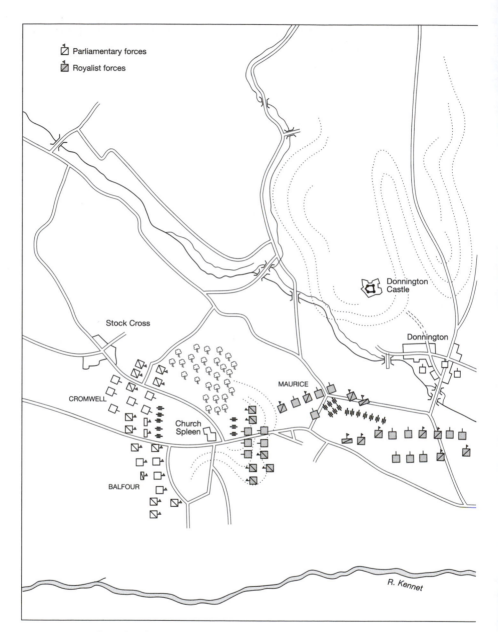

MAP 9   *Second Battle of Newbury, 27 October 1644*

Adapted from Ohlmeyer, Jane, *Civil War and Restoration in the Three Stuart Kingdoms: The Political Career of Randall MacDonnell, Marquis of Antrim* (Four Courts Press, 2001)

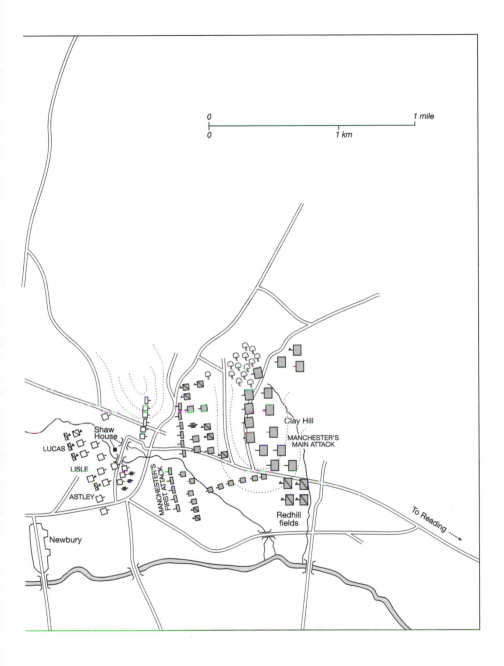

LUCAS

Shaw
House

LISLE

ASTLEY

Newbury

MANCHESTER'S
FIRST ATTACK

Clay Hill

MANCHESTER'S
MAIN ATTACK

Redhill
fields

To Reading →

0   1 mile

0   1 km

discouraged by continual skirmishing. Manchester did not respond to the pre-arranged signal. But Waller, already under fire from the guns of Donnington, exposed to heavy musket fire from the hedges, harassed by the king's cavalry, and with less than two hours of daylight remaining, could not wait. 'Their cannon made our ground very hot', he wrote, 'there was no way left but to fall on with horse and foot, and that without delay . . .'.[15] In spite of their fatigue they fell on resolutely. Essex's infantry, still smarting from their humiliation at Lostwithiel, joyfully retook the same cannon that they had surrendered there and sent the royalist foot reeling down Shaw road. Balfour also routed the king's western cavalry, which streamed past Charles himself, who vainly tried to rally them and was almost killed in the mêlée. Cromwell, puzzlingly, had been slow to intervene on his wing, and Goring had taken the initiative, charging Cromwell's squadrons and pushing them back. Meanwhile, Balfour's troopers had run into heavy musket fire from the hedges and ditches east of Speen, which had allowed the royalist cavalry under Sir Humphrey Bennet to rally and counterattack, throwing Balfour back to Speen. Fierce but inconclusive fighting continued in this sector until after nightfall.

On the other end of the battlefield, at Shaw House, Manchester finally launched his attack around 4 p.m. As was their custom, the troops of the Eastern Association advanced singing psalms,[16] but before long both his columns were thrown back, and the descending darkness spared the royalists from further assaults on either flank. Had the light not failed, the overwhelming numerical superiority of the parliamentarian army would almost certainly have won the day. Nevertheless, when the smoke cleared it was apparent that the king's soldiers had successfully defended their positions against an attacking force more than twice as large. Each side lost perhaps 500 men in a battle that was effectively a draw, but morally a defeat for parliament. In retrospect it is reasonably certain that had Charles not diverted troops to Banbury just before the battle, and had Prince Rupert arrived with forces from Bristol and Oxford by 27 October, they might have won a decisive victory against the dispirited and divided parliamentary armies.

In the cold light of dawn the king's officers could see that they must extricate themselves from Newbury as quickly as possible to avoid being

---

[15] Wadham College, Oxford, MS Coxe (Sir William Waller's Remarks – Experiences), 16, 20. I am grateful to Sandra Bailey and Oliver Pointer, librarians of Wadham, for permission to cite this MS.

[16] Walker, *Hist. Discourses*, 113.

crushed in a second attack. The king therefore entrusted his guns, baggage and wounded men to the care of Sir John Boys in Donnington Castle, and marched out through the 1,500-yard gap between Shaw House and Donnington. Yet another indictment of the parliamentary generals is their failure to cut the royalists' line of retreat, even though their entire army had to cross a narrow bridge between Speen and Donnington.

That same day (28 October) the parliamentary council of war met amid much recrimination. After a fruitless attempt by Waller, Hesilrige and Cromwell to pursue the retreating royalists with some detachments of horse, they turned their attention to Donnington Castle, where the tempting prize was the king's entire train of artillery. They summoned Sir John Boys to surrender. 'His sacred majesty had entrusted that place to his custody, and', he riposted, ''till His Majesty . . . should command him thence, he was resolved to live or die in the place.'[17] An attempted storm of the castle was repulsed with considerable loss.

Meanwhile, the king had reunited with Rupert and Northampton. On 5 November in Oxford he reviewed an assembled army of 15,000 men and announced the replacement of his aging, deaf and gouty General Brentford by Prince Rupert. Rupert found this an embarrassment, since it gave him superiority over the heir to the throne, Charles Prince of Wales. The king compromised by making his 14-year-old son commander-in-chief, and Rupert lieutenant-general of all his armies. Marching south with his augmented forces, the king arrived at Donnington on 9 November. He removed his guns from the castle and offered battle. The parliamentary council of war could not decide what to do, and was swayed by the gloomy words of the Earl of Manchester: 'If we fight [the king] 100 times and beat him 99 he will be king still, but if he beat us but once, or the last time, we shall be hanged, we shall lose our estates, and our posterities be undone.' 'My lord', objected Cromwell, 'if this be so, why did we take up arms at first? This is against fighting ever hereafter. If so, let us make peace, be it never so base.'[18] After beating off a half-hearted attack by the opposing cavalry Charles and Rupert completed their brilliant relief of Donnington. In a final gesture of scorn Prince Rupert sent a trumpeter to let his foes know that they were withdrawing, 'so that if it had been in their will, they might have fallen on our rear'.[19] But Manchester, Waller and Cromwell

---

[17] *Mercurius Aulicus* (2 November 1644), E18/11, 1241–2; Walker, *Hist. Discourses*, 115; Walter Money, *The First and Second Battles of Newbury and the Siege of Donnington Castle During the Civil War, A.D. 1643–6*, 145.

[18] *CSPD 1644–45*, 151, 159.

[19] Walker, *Hist. Discourses*, 118.

had no appetite for battle (Essex was in London), and allowed them to leave unchallenged.

Basing House too had been relieved, and so, his short-term objectives accomplished, the king went into winter quarters around Oxford.

The Self-Denying Ordinance

Now that this episode of battlefield infamy was behind them, the parliamentary commanders and their allies in both houses resumed their political struggle with even deadlier intent than before. Cromwell and Waller, confident of the support of London public opinion, unleashed an attack in the Commons on the Earl of Manchester, aiming at his removal as commander-in-chief of the Eastern Association. In the Lords Manchester rediscovered his fighting spirit and delivered a pointed indictment of Cromwell's military record, accused him of hating the Scots, of wishing to sabotage peace efforts, and of fomenting social and religious revolution: 'he hoped [he said], to live to see never a noble man in England . . . [and] expressed himself with contempt of the Assembly of Divines'.[20] The public debate dragged on for nearly two weeks while ruthless jockeying for position went on behind the scenes. One evening in early December the Earl of Essex summoned the Scots commissioners and a group of mostly peace-party MPs to a meeting at his house in the Strand. The meeting exposed the important shift of political alignments in the Long Parliament that had been taking place since October. The Scots, who had supported the war faction up to this juncture, had just switched to Essex's peace party. In the months to come the war faction would come to be labelled Independents, while the peace, or Essex, faction would be called Presbyterians. At no time, however, did the majority of MPs identify themselves with either political grouping.

Essex had called the private meeting because he shared Manchester's animus against Cromwell, and wanted to have him indicted as an incendiary. To his disappointment, the highly respected moderate Bulstrode Whitelocke counselled caution. Oliver Cromwell, he pointed out, was 'a gentleman of quick and subtle parts' with numerous friends in both houses. He was not a man to be trifled with. That was enough to put off the Scots commissioners, and the idea of an indictment was dropped.[21]

For Robert Baillie the campaign against the armies' aristocratic leadership constituted nothing less than 'a high and mighty plot of the Inde-

---

[20] Bodl. MS Tanner 61, fos. 205v–6.
[21] Whitelocke, *Memorials*, Vol. 1, 346.

pendent party to have gotten an army for themselves under Cromwell'.[22] This objective, of course, could not be admitted publicly. Instead, a broad coalition was constructed, comprising all of those who believed it necessary to win the war against the king by whatever means were most effective. On 9 December, before a crowded house, Zouch Tate, a Presbyterian MP, introduced the Committee of the Army's report on the lamentable losses of the previous few months. The chief problem was 'pride and covetousness', he said. Oliver Cromwell then moved the debate along by magnanimously admitting that like everyone else he had made mistakes, but urging the need to make a fresh start and win a decisive victory because 'the people can bear the war no longer, and will enforce you to a dishonourable peace'.[23]

The stage had been set for Tate, with the powerful backing of Sir Henry Vane, to introduce the celebrated resolution for a Self-Denying Ordinance. It called for all members of both houses to resign their military commands and civil offices. In appearance the resolution was even-handed, statesman-like and conciliatory: Manchester and Essex would have to go, but so would Cromwell, Waller, Hesilrige, Brereton, and other members of the war party. The resolution also shrewdly appealed to those MPs who were resentful that many of their colleagues were profiting from the war. With the opposition caught off guard, the ordinance quickly passed first reading in the Commons. It was when it came to spelling out its implications at the committee stage that deep divisions surfaced once more. Holles and Stapilton tried to pilot through an amendment exempting the Earl of Essex from the provisions of the ordinance. Vane and Evelyn mobilized against them, and they were overwhelmed, 100 votes to 93.[24] After this setback no attempt was made to exempt other peers such as Manchester and Warwick. A motion requiring all officers and government officials to swear the Solemn League and Covenant and adhere to the government's newly created Church was also turned aside.

In the Lords the Self-Denying Ordinance ran into much heavier weather. While a minority of war-party lords led by Viscount Saye and Sele supported it, the majority interpreted it as an insult to their honour. Unlike the MPs, who could resign their seats in the lower house if they wanted to continue their military commands, the peers had no such option. For the next three-and-a-half months the ordinance was stalled in the upper house.

---

[22] Baillie, *Letters*, Vol. 2, 246.
[23] BL. Add. MS 31116 (Whitacre's diary), fo. 178v; Rushworth, *Hist. Coll.*, Vol. 6, 3–4; Abbott, *Cromwell*, Vol. 1, 314.
[24] *CJ*, Vol. 3, 723.

The war party did not permit this obstruction to stop them from carrying through the re-organization of the war effort. The dissolution of the armies of Essex, Waller and Manchester, and the creation and equipping of a new army under new commanders and centralized control went on remorselessly throughout the winter.

The Uxbridge Treaty

It is against the backdrop of these military preparations that the stark futility of the peace negotiations at Uxbridge stands out. In November the Lords, under pressure from the Scots, had taken the initiative to broach a new peace with the king. The war-party leaders in the Commons, St John and Vane, had acquiesced because they knew they could count on the king to wreck it. Denzell Holles and the Scots in London thought that if they could persuade the king to abandon the Anglican church with its bishops, and accept Presbyterianism, they could all gang up on the Independents and destroy them politically. An indication of the chances of this strategy working was the scathing reception given to the parliamentary delegation that went to Oxford to meet the king in late November. The two things that Charles would never surrender were his Church and the militia. He was steeled in this determination by parliament's ruthlessness in sending Archbishop Laud to the scaffold for treason on 14 January 1645. The fate of his second chief councillor reminded him afresh of his guilt in the death of the first, Strafford. But he shared none of the guilt for Laud's blood. Therefore, the hand of divine justice 'must be heavier upon them and lighter upon us, looking now upon our cause, having passed through our faults'.[25]

At the same time that he was thinking these dark thoughts, he was telling Ormond to procure Irish troops for him on whatever terms he could, and exhorting the Duke of Lorraine to bring an army from France to rescue him. He also dispatched his commissioners, led by the Duke of Richmond, to meet with their parliamentary and Scottish counterparts at Uxbridge. So much did Charles despise his foes that he refused to call them a 'parliament' until he was outvoted by his own council. The parliamentary war party despised the royalists just as much, engaging one of their chaplains, Christopher Love, to preach a sermon insulting the king's commissioners as 'men of blood'.[26] For his part, Charles antagonized the

[25] Henry Parker (ed.), *The Kings Cabinet Opened* (1645), BL. Thomason, E292/27, 1.
[26] Clarendon, *Hist.*, Bk 8, 219.

Scots commissioners by refusing to discuss anything to do with their king-dom before consulting Montrose. The three main topics at Uxbridge were religion, the sword and Ireland.

Religion

Out of deference to the Scots, parliament demanded that the king should take the Covenant, assent to the abolition of bishops and Book of Common Prayer, and accept the establishment of Presbyterianism and the Directory of Worship. The king would hear of none of this, but under the influence of the Oxford clergy, agreed that the prayerbook might be modified, and that freedom should 'be left to all persons of what opinions soever in matters of ceremony'. He further agreed that bishops were to exercise 'no act of jurisdiction or ordination, without the consent and counsel of the presbyters, who shall be chosen by the clergy of each diocese'. Whether he meant it or not, Charles was publicly offering substantial toleration to Presbyterians and Independents.[27] The parliamentary commissioners displayed not the slightest interest in this offer, while the Scots commissioners and clergy, who were at Uxbridge in force, expressed passionate disappointment at the royalists' refusal to do away with bishops. Chancellor Loudon had promised that if the king gave way on the Church question the Scots would not trouble him about anything else.[28]

The sword

Parliament demanded that the militia and the navy should be permanently under its control. The most Charles would allow, and for which he was severely criticized by his wife,[29] was that the militia should be placed in the hands of a commission, whose members were to be named, half by parliament, half by the himself. After three years exclusive authority would revert to the him. Neither side would budge.

Ireland

Parliament demanded that the king's Cessation with the Irish be cancelled, and that the war in Ireland be waged by the English parliament alone,

---

[27] Rushworth, *Hist. Coll.*, Vol. 5, 872, 873.
[28] Clarendon, *Hist.*, Bk 8, 223.
[29] Henrietta Maria, *Letters of Queen Henrietta Maria*, ed. Mary Anne Everett Green, 288.

without obstruction from the king. The king's commissioners retorted that parliament had been guilty of a far graver dereliction of duty than he. They had levied troops and money for the war in Ireland and then used them to fight against the king at Edgehill and elsewhere, and to finance the Scottish invasion of England. Charles would be happy to end the Cessation if parliament would send over the men and money to prosecute the war vigorously against the Irish. Both sides were posturing and privately admitted as much. The discussions went nowhere.

The talks lasted until 22 February, when they ended with no agreement on any of the points at issue. Uxbridge was a barren treaty because of both sides' inflexibility and Charles's double dealing. On religion his commissioners' hands were tied by his vow to his wife never to 'quit episcopacy'. He had made a similar promise about 'that sword which God hath given into my hands'.[30] In any event, discussions about control of the sword had an air of utter unreality at a time when each side was arming itself to the teeth in readiness for the spring campaign. Still less was there any hope of concerting a policy to subjugate the Catholic Irish, given that Charles was at that moment secretly negotiating with the insurgents to send him troops for his war against parliament, and sweetening the deal with the promise to repeal the laws against Catholics once that war had been won.[31]

For most of the war party the treaty at Uxbridge was a side show to which they paid scant attention. The chief item on their agenda was creating a new army capable of smashing the king's forces once and for all. A sign of what was to come occurred on the day that the treaty was wound up. Colonels Laugharne and Mitton overran Shrewsbury for parliament, and in doing so broke the royalists' line of communication with Chester, and exposed the royalist heartland of north Wales, and the counties of Hereford and Worcester to frequent incursions by the enemy. The capture of Shrewsbury was a fillip to parliamentary morale, while it greatly depressed the king, as he confessed to Chancellor Hyde at the time.[32] Regardless of the brilliant successes of Montrose and MacColla in Scotland, Charles could foresee that he might well be captured in the near future. It would be doubly disastrous if he and the heir to the throne, Prince Charles, were captured together. To guard against this eventuality he dispatched his son to Bristol under the tutelage and protection of Hyde, Hopton and others.

[30] Parker (ed.), *Kings Cabinet*, 1.
[31] Ibid., 19.
[32] Clarendon, *Hist.*, Bk 8, 253.

The New Model Army

Common knowledge of the imminent failure of the Uxbridge treaty had the effect that the war party hoped for in London. Combined with the sobering news of a successful royalist attack on Weymouth, it forced the Lords to bow to the inevitable and approve the creation of a new army in the south with new commanders. War party strategy in the early months of 1645 was to pull the rug out from under the Lords' feet by starving the existing armies of funds, drawing off their officers, and transferring their units to the new force. The targeted strength of the New Model was 22,000 men, besides officers: 14,400 foot, 1,000 dragoons and 6,600 horse. The chief engine of finance for the new army was to be an assessment, or income tax, of £53,000 a month on the seventeen counties of East Anglia, the Midlands and the south-east that were under parliamentary control.[33]

The next step was to appoint the army's commanders. The Commons war party set about this sensitive task in complete disregard of the Lords' refusal to ratify the Self-Denying Ordinance. Over the opposition of the Holles–Stapilton faction Sir Thomas Fairfax, son of Ferdinando Lord Fairfax, was selected as commander-in-chief. Aged only 33, Fairfax could still boast lengthy military experience, having begun as a gentleman volunteer under Horace Lord Vere in the United Dutch Provinces in 1629. He was back in England in time for the outbreak of civil war, serving for more than two years in his father Lord Ferdinando's army. Already he had proven his brilliance at Winceby, Nantwich, Selby and Marston Moor. Never a great military strategist, he was nonetheless a courageous and inspirational battlefield commander who always drew undying loyalty from his troops. While he was well connected to the war party, his mild, taciturn manner, as well as his sterling military record, made him more palatable to moderates than more high-profile radicals such as Cromwell, Waller or Hesilrige. Next to be named was Philip Skippon, as major-general of the infantry. He had served in this capacity under Essex, as well as being sergeant-major-general of the London trained bands. Like Fairfax he could boast extensive continental military experience during the 1630s. He was widely admired for his courage, seasoned professionalism, and deep piety. His simple, inspirational addresses to his soldiers on the eve of battle were well known.

---

[33] This account of the founding of the New Model Army is based on Gentles, *NMA*, 10–25, and Ian Gentles, 'The choosing of officers for the New Model Army in 1645', *HR*, 67 (1994), 264–85.

A few days after his arrival from the north Fairfax submitted his list of nearly 200 officer nominations to the Commons. We do not know who advised him on the list, but it is difficult to believe that Cromwell and Sir Henry Vane did not play a key role. They may also have taken advice from Skippon and other trusted officers. All but eight of the nominees slipped through the Commons without division. Everyone knew that the real hurdle lay in the House of Lords. When the list was sent up to them with an urgent request for approval, they dug in their heels, and put the list to microscopic scrutiny lasting several days. In the end they demanded 57 changes, representing 30 per cent of the list. Over half the changes were among the former officers of Manchester's army, where political and religious polarization had been most intense. Almost all those whose demotion or expulsion was demanded and whose political orientation is known were radical or Independent. By contrast, virtually all those whom the peers wanted to introduce or promote to higher rank were moderates, Presbyterians, Scots, or kinsmen or protégés of Essex. The inescapable conclusion is that a great many of the proposed changes were politically motivated.

Faced with obstruction in the Lords, the war party devised a 'subtle ruse' to break the log jam. They prevailed on the London Common Council to make the £80,000 that they had already agreed to lend for the launching of the New Model conditional on there being no tampering with Fairfax's list. Financial pressure was reinforced by a high-powered delegation headed by Vane and St John which presented the peers with reasons for not altering Fairfax's list. After two days of fierce lobbying they were bluntly told that if they did not yield the Commons would go ahead without them. The moment had arrived for the war-party faction in the upper house led by Viscount Saye and Sele to swing into action. Invoking the proxy of Fairfax's own grandfather, the aged Lord Mulgrave, Saye was able to break the logjam and finally achieve passage of the list. All ten peers who opposed it, including Essex and Manchester, bitterly recorded their dissents.

The political significance of the triumph of Fairfax and his backers was not lost on informed observers. 'This very much weakens the Presbyterian and lord general's and Scots party', confided Thomas Juxon to his journal.[34] The enfeeblement of the Scots' political influence in England was tied closely to the troubles they were having at home with Montrose. 'It has much diminished our reputation already' moaned Robert

---

[34] Juxon, *Journal*, 75.

Baillie in London.[35] The decline in their reputation went hand-in-hand with their accelerating disenchantment with English politics. Juxon, who now sardonically called them 'our brethren the Scots', noted that they were refusing to be mustered, that their army was down to 5,000 – a quarter of what they had been a year before – and that they had switched their loyalty from the Independents, who they thought were growing too strong, to the Presbyterians, who shared their dislike for religious toleration.[36]

A few days later the Essex party was defeated on the question of whether Fairfax was obliged to preserve the king's safety on the battlefield. Ominously his commission was silent on this point. The omission of the obligation that had bound all previous commanders was an important turning point in the civil war. It signalled the abandonment of the fiction that parliament was fighting the king's evil counsellors rather than the king himself. In so far as it implied the possibility of converting England into a republic it was the first step in transforming the civil war into a revolution. Essex, Manchester and Warwick now resigned their commissions, and the next day (3 April) the Lords completed their capitulation by passing a slightly changed version of the Self-Denying Ordinance. Instead of barring MPs from military commands it simply obliged them to surrender whatever commands they held. It said nothing about reappointment. This opened a loophole through which the Committee of Both Kingdoms slipped the temporary extension of Cromwell's appointment at the end of April, and later, his commission to the vacant post of lieutenant-general of the cavalry. Why had this position been left vacant in the first place? Was it all part of a far-sighted Machiavellian scheme by Cromwell to best his political opponents while preserving a place for himself in the parliamentary army? Probably not. After Essex's exemption had been turned down it would have been unrealistic for Cromwell to count on having an exception made for himself. In December 1644 he doubtless reckoned that his own resignation was not too high a price to pay for the elimination of a whole bagful of aristocratic and other enemies. Yet once that objective had been accomplished, and with the advent of the spring fighting season, his desire for military action was rekindled, and he strained every sinew to stave off the day of his final dismissal. The Lords' opposition was implacable, however. Only Cromwell's brilliant role at Naseby on 14 June finally overturned their opposition and secured for him the generalship that by now he fiercely coveted.

[35] Baillie, *Letters*, Vol. 2, 234.
[36] Juxon, *Journal*, 75–6.

The exploits of Montrose

Inverlochy

The war party had been helped in their design to refashion parliament's war effort by the realization that with the Scots now preoccupied by their own civil war, the war in England against the king would have to be won largely without external help. While hammers and anvils were busy in London workshops forging new weapons of war, Montrose continued his daring exploits in the north of Scotland. At one level the war was a quarrel between the adherents of the Stuart king and the upholders of the Covenant. But for most of those fighting on the ground it was another bitter chapter in the ongoing warfare of the Scottish clans. At the beginning of the year Montrose had taken the battle into the heart of Campbell territory in the western Highlands. In the short term the strategy turned out to be an inspired one. The Campbells, under the leadership of the Marquess of Argyll, were prosperous and their power was increasing, though they were cordially detested by their neighbours. They had swallowed up the land of many lesser clans, and their sway now extended as far north and east as Lochaber and Perth. The Argyll fiefdom was well defended. South and west lay the sea, and the Campbells controlled Scotland's little navy. On the east, where it faced the lowlands, there were castles and sea-lochs to deter a would-be invader. To the north were high mountains and passes where it was all too easy to lose one's way. 'I had rather', said Argyll, 'lose a hundred thousand crowns than that any mortal man should know the way by which an army can enter into my country.'[37] But Montrose had with him a number of men who did know the way. Since October MacColla had raised another few hundred Irish recruits and perhaps as many as 1,000 men from the western clans – Camerons and Macdonalds – all of them eaten up by hatred for Argyll. Montrose had also gained a few cavalry from Angus under Sir Thomas Ogilvy. These men cared less for religion and monarchy than they did for vengeance against the clan Campbell. They were impatient to begin fighting, and Montrose realized that he would lose many of them if he put off his campaign until spring. Accordingly he divided his army into three divisions, led by MacColla, John Clanranald and himself. Leaving Blair Atholl in the east, he led his own division past the south banks of Loch Tay, through Glen Dochart and across the mountains to Glen Orchy. He then cut south to

[37] Quoted by Gardiner, *GCW*, Vol. 2, 152.

Loch Fyne and Inveraray, the leading town in Campbell territory. Wherever his army went it destroyed cattle, burnt houses to the ground, and butchered any fighting men who fell into its hands. Montrose now turned north, continuing to spoil as he traversed the long glen that leads to Loch Ness.

When Argyll at Edinburgh heard of the invasion of his territory he quickly rode to Invererary, confident that he could trap the invaders and wipe them out. But rampaging Macdonalds drove him to flee down Loch Fyne to his castle at Roseneath. It was time to call in the big battalions. William Baillie, who had fought on the continent under Gustav II Adolph, and established a distinguished record at Marston Moor and Newcastle, was summoned to bring back some of Leven's choice infantry from England and to replace Argyll as commander of the expedition against Montrose. He marched the infantry to Argyll at Roseneath, but the two men quarrelled over who was to have the senior command. Argyll, though an inferior soldier, got the Estates in Edinburgh to confirm him as supreme commander in the western Highlands, and Baillie was sent, with most of his infantry, to Perth to keep watch on the Highlands from the eastern side, leaving 1,100 of his men with Argyll. Argyll's real reason for resisting Baillie was that it would have been a humiliation to admit publicly that it had been necessary to call in an outside commander to save his own territory from its enemies. After Baillie's departure for Perth Argyll prevailed on his kinsman Sir Duncan Campbell of Auchinbreck, who was in Ireland with Monro, to rush back to his aid.

Montrose and MacColla were now heading northwards through Lorne and Lochaber. On the way their army was bled by desertion, as men headed for home with their plunder. By the time they had reached Kilchummin at the foot of Loch Ness they were down to less than 2,000 effectives. Beyond the top of Loch Ness was the garrison of Inverness, where the Earl of Seaforth commanded 5,000 Covenanters. Hearing that Argyll was not far behind at Inverlochy, with 3,500 men, Montrose and MacColla decided that they must quickly exploit the advantage of surprise to offset their numerical inferiority, and also to avoid being caught between Seaforth's and Argyll's forces. They opted to re-cross the mountains of Lochaber and march roughly parallel to the glen, concealed from view. The weather had suddenly turned very cold, and for part of the way they had to wade through snow up to their knees. By marching day and night, with only brief halts, they covered over 30 miles (50 km) in steep terrain in the space of 36 hours. By dusk on the second day they rounded the base of Ben Nevis and looked down on Inverlochy.

Argyll, having fallen from his horse and dislocated his shoulder, took refuge in his galley on the loch, leaving Auchinbreck to direct the battle. Montrose's men stayed on the alert all night long, then breakfasted on oatmeal moistened with snow. Before dawn the next day (2 February – Candlemas) MacColla's Irish soldiers, with their priests, fell to their knees, 'signing themselves and their weapons with the cross, entreating the celestial aid of the Queen of Heaven, fervently repeating the names of Saint Patrick . . . and Saint Brigid'.[38] The battle began at sunrise with a trumpet salute that told Argyll and his army that they faced, not a small contingent of Highland raiders, but the massed forces of Montrose and MacColla, who they had thought were still at Loch Ness. MacColla, on Montrose's right, led the attack, after stressing to his regimental commanders the absolute necessity of holding their fire until the very last moment, and to fire into the enemies' breasts.[39] The Irish soldiers obeyed their orders, allowed themselves to be fired on first, and then advanced to deliver a volley at much closer range with deadly effect. They followed it up with the manoeuvre known as the Highland charge. Throwing down their muskets they ran at Auchinbreck's men with drawn swords before they could get off a second volley. This reduced both wings of Lowlanders to immediate disorder. They fought fiercely for a while, but became confused and panicked when Argyll's standard was captured.[40] As many as 1,500 were killed, including Auchinbreck. On Montrose's side the handful of dead included the cavalry commander, Ogilvy. Argyll's flight while his clansmen were being butchered completed his military disgrace, since it was almost a repetition of his similar flight from Inveraray just a few months before.

For Montrose his sensational triumph brought a complete royalist victory within the bounds of possibility. Exultantly he wrote to Charles promising to bring him a large army to 'make the rebels in England, as well as in Scotland, feel the just rewards of rebellion'.[41] For most of the men who fought under Montrose, however, the victory had a different significance. It was one of the Highlanders' conquests – rare in Scottish history – over the Lowlanders. The Macdonalds savoured the sweetness of their revenge against the Campbells who had ruled the western Highlands with cruel arrogance for too long. They had little interest in going on to conquer more territory for the king. They and the Irish followers

---

[38] W. Forbes Leith (ed.), *Memoirs of Scottish Catholics during the XVIIth and XVIIIth Centuries*, Vol. 1, 321.

[39] Reid, *Montrose's Campaigns*, 85.

[40] Carte, *Orig. Letters*, Vol. 1, 76.

[41] Montrose, James Graham, Marquis of, *Memoirs*, ed. Mark Napier, Vol. 2, 487.

of MacColla also saw the defeat of the covenanting Campbells as a victory for Catholicism against heresy, turning a blind eye to the fact that Montrose too was a Protestant 'heretic'.

The victory brought Montrose more Highland recruits. As he marched northwards towards Inverness hundreds of men – Camerons, Grants, MacLeans, MacNeills and MacQuarries – flocked to his banner. George Lord Gordon was persuaded to desert the Covenanters, and brought with him a regular cavalry unit, but many of them were half-hearted, because of the confusing signals from his father the Marquess of Huntly, who wanted his third son Lewis to lead the Gordons. A number of fence-sitters like the Earl of Seaforth also joined him, with the primary motivation of protecting their estates. Their loyalty was doubtful. The Edinburgh parliament reacted to the setback at Inverlochy with horror, denouncing Montrose, MacColla and all 'the hellish crew' as traitors.[42] Another 1,500 men were recalled from the army in England, and 1,400 from Ireland. A new levy of 17,500 men was ordered within Scotland, but only a small fraction of that number ever materialized. The reality was that the Covenanters' resources were drastically overtaxed by wars in all three kingdoms, which in turn enfeebled their military efforts in every theatre. Sir John Hurry was appointed major-general of the forces in Scotland, over the objection of William Baillie.[43] The Scottish civil war had entered a new and more perilous stage for the covenanting regime.

Dundee

Montrose and MacColla spent the next few weeks roaming the Highlands, plundering and recruiting as they went, but still not daring to enter the Lowlands. By mid-March their infantry were 3,000 in number, and their cavalry 300, thanks mostly to the influx of regulars from Lord Gordon's regiment. They were shadowed by a slightly larger force of Covenanters under Sir John Hurry, who waited patiently as desertion once again began to exact its toll on an unstable army with no permanent base or source of funds, and no coherence beyond the charisma of its two leaders. In an effort to bolster morale Montrose led a raid on Dundee. The defences of the town were easily overrun, but as the soldiers dispersed through the streets in an orgy of plundering and drinking, scouts brought word that

[42] Alexander Peterkin (ed.), *Records of the Kirk of Scotland . . . from the Year 1638*, Vol. 1, 425.
[43] David Stevenson, *Revolution and Counter-Revolution in Scotland, 1644–1651*, 27–8.

Hurry's men, having completed a forced march from Perth, were nearly at the gates. Somehow Montrose stopped the plunder (the hardest thing for a commander to do), knocked his half-drunk men back together, and extricated them from the town. For several days he eluded both Hurry and Baillie, fading northward until he reached the fastness of Glen Esk. The discomfiture of Montrose at Dundee was celebrated by the Covenanters in London as a great victory. Not everyone was convinced. It was noted that he had raided this town on the edge of the Lowlands with impunity and then withdrawn relatively unscathed.

Auldearn

Montrose marched and countermarched to keep clear of the Covenanter commanders, Baillie and Hurry, while his own force continued to dwindle. By mid-April he had only 500 foot and 50 horse remaining. A few days later he discovered a welcome ally, James Gordon, Viscount Aboyne, second son of the Marquess of Huntly. As he moved north towards Skene he was joined by MacColla with fresh recruits from the Macdonald clan, and George Lord Gordon with a body of cavalry. The royalist force was back up to 2,000 foot or more and about 250 horse. For the first time Montrose had a significant body of cavalry. On the other hand, all the local gentry who hated the Gordons – Frasers, Forbeses, Rosses, Inneses, Crichtons – flocked to the covenanting standard of Baillie and Hurry. Their numbers in turn grew to 3,400 foot and 3–400 horse. The Earl of Seaforth, a man of essentially neutralist inclinations, ditched Montrose and bet on Baillie, who seemed favoured to win at this point. Baillie sent the turncoat Sir John Hurry in pursuit. Montrose, who habitually neglected adequate intelligence, was almost caught napping. When he was warned of an imminent attack there was barely enough time for MacColla to rouse two regiments – no more than 3–400 men – from their beds.[44] MacColla stationed his men on a low hill surrounded by marsh and bushes south-west of the village of Auldearn to try to hold off Hurry's men until Montrose could organize the rest of the army on the other side of the village to the east. He was quickly knocked off the hill by one of Hurry's regiments, and fell back into the village where, among the back yards he made a stand once more. He had almost given up the day for lost when help arrived. From a hillock to the south Aboyne led a squadron of cavalry, and charged into the

[44] SHS, James Fraser, *Chronicles of the Frasers*, ed. William Mackay, Vol. 47, 287, 294–5.

enemy's right flank. Lord Gordon hurled the other squadron of horse into their left flank. Disdaining to fire their pistols and carbines, they charged through the enemy horse with their drawn swords. The shock of cold steel crumpled the left wing of Hurry's cavalry.

Montrose had been observing the battle from Castle Hill immediately to the north of the village. The bulk of his infantry was drawn up, out of sight behind one of the hillocks on the other side. He now rode behind the lines to bring his men the news that the battle was almost won. This was a shrewd piece of deception, for it made them eager to join MacColla in winning glory. The counterattack of Montrose's infantry happened so fast that Hurry was caught off balance. Relieved at their delivery from imminent death, MacColla's men fought with renewed ferocity. The result was an extremely vicious encounter, in which Hurry's troops did not scatter upon contact with the enemy, but stood their ground and were cut down in their ranks and files.

Fully 2,000 Covenanter foot died that day. 'Ever and anon the cry and groans of men and women for their lost friends were universally heard', wrote the historian of the Frasers.[45] Montrose lost 200 common soldiers and 22 of his gentlemen. Royalists gloated over 'another great and happy victory'.[46] Several chroniclers and poets sang the praises of Alasdair MacColla as the warrior of Auldearn, but there were many others who performed feats of skill and bravery on the battlefield. As Stevenson observes, it was they, not the generals, who won the battle against a greatly superior enemy whose victory at the opening of the day seemed certain.[47] More than any other battle Auldearn

served to bring together the different groups and interests represented in Montrose's army. Irish and Highland foot with some Gordon support had fought off the initial enemy attack and thus saved the rest of the army. They in turn had been saved by the charges of the Gordon cavalry, and then by the arrival of the rest of the foot under Montrose. Alasdair had saved Montrose, then Montrose had saved Alasdair. All had shared in a most extraordinary victory.[48]

By a kind of billiard-ball effect, what had begun as three discrete rebellions and civil wars in each of Charles Stuart's kingdoms were, between 1643 and 1645, turned into full-blown wars between the kingdoms, with

---

[45] Ibid., 296–7.
[46] *Merc. Aul.* (25 May–8 June 1645), E288/48, 1611.
[47] Stevenson, *Alasdair MacColla*, 190.
[48] Ibid., 192.

each one playing a key role in the conflicts in the other two. In 1642 the Junto at Westminster had appealed to the Covenanters in Scotland to come to their aid, in the first instance by sending the largest army ever yet mobilized on British soil into England to rescue the ailing war effort against the king. This had prompted Charles to imitate their example by seeking external aid from Ireland (as well as France, the Netherlands and Denmark) for his campaign against the rebellious parliament in England. The public perception that the king was hand-in-glove with Irish papists provoked shock and horror in the other two kingdoms as well as dismaying significant numbers of his own supporters. The Cessation of September 1643, followed by Ormond's subsequent peace treaties with the Catholic Confederation, produced a disappointing harvest of recruits to the royalist armies, and did far more damage to Charles in terms of loss of public confidence than any good it did him on the battlefield. By contrast, the Scottish intervention in England did virtually no propaganda harm to the Junto at Westminster, and enabled them to turn their war effort around. The covenanting army was the crucial factor at Marston Moor, the greatest battle ever fought on British soil. The defeat suffered by the royalists lost them the northern half of the country, and marked the beginning of the end of their struggle against the forces of the English parliament. Fatally weakened by the liquidation of Newcastle's northern army, they were softened up at Marston Moor for the knock-out blow that parliament was to deliver less than a year later at Naseby.

It was not just the English royalists who were weakened by Marston Moor. The Covenanters too had been debilitated by their military involvement in the other two kingdoms. With most of their effectives fighting in Ireland and England, the regime was ill-prepared for a military challenge on its home ground. When the unlikely trio of the Earl of Montrose, the Earl of Antrim and Alasdair MacColla assembled a motley army of Gaelic Irish and Scots Highlanders, glued together by hatred of Protestants, resentment of the clan Campbell, and hunger for that clan's territory, they experienced unexpected success. The brilliant generalship of Montrose, backed up by the tenaciousness of MacColla's Highlanders, produced a series of stunning battlefield victories that shook the covenanting regime to its core, and obliged it to withdraw most of its forces from the other two kingdoms.

In the next two chapters we shall see how, by straining every sinew, the war party in the English parliament was able, in spite of the absence of their former Scottish allies and later their outright opposition, to subdue the armies of Charles I.

CHAPTER 9

The king vanquished, 1645–46

England: the spring campaign

Montrose's spectacular run of victories was almost the only good news to reach royalist headquarters in Oxford during the spring of 1645. While divisions at Court and in the Council of War deepened, and personal backbiting became nastier, parliamentarians subdued their animosities in the interests of fighting the war more effectively. Fed by the City's loan of £80,000, the recruitment, arming and provisioning of the army got off to a quick start. The parliamentary juggernaut gathered strength as 'every house in London' became 'stuffed up' with arms.[1]

The armies of Essex, Manchester and Waller were cannibalized to furnish manpower for the New Model. The diplomatic gifts of Philip Skippon, plus the promise of new clothes and weapons for the common soldiers, helped to make the potentially explosive business of extinguishing Essex's regiments run smoothly. Once the example had been set the regiments of the other two armies also allowed themselves to be absorbed without protest. However, the infantry recruited from the old armies only totalled 7,200 – just half the number needed. The rest had to be conscripted, or 'pressed' in the language of the day. The metropolitan region was told to raise 2,500 men, while most of the remainder were pressed in East Anglia and Kent. During the entire period of active fighting the New Model was continually bled by the desertion of its foot soldiers, which meant that new men were continually being pressed. This was a financial drain as well, since it cost between £2 and £2 10s. to recruit and clothe a foot soldier and deliver him to the army. There were good reasons why the

---

[1] Carte, *Life*, Vol. 6, 270 (Archbishop of York to the Marquess of Ormond, 25 March 1645).

foot, though not the horse, deserted in such large numbers. At 8d. a day for a private, the pay was not generous, and it was not always delivered on time. The life of a soldier on active duty was hard – carrying a 60lb pack and often sleeping under the open sky. Drawn from the lowest ranks of society, few of the common soldiers knew or cared about the reasons for fighting against the king. Colonel John Venn noted that 'most countries [counties] press the scum of all their inhabitants, the king's soldiers, men taken out of prison, tinkers, pedlars and vagrants that have no dwelling, and such of whom no account can be given. It is no marvel if such run away.'[2] When all the runaways are taken into account, the New Model had nearly reached its target in early June, standing at 20,000 men or more.

No matter how scintillating the triumphs of Montrose and MacColla, they could not offset the deepening gloom that enveloped royalist head-quarters at Oxford. The loss of Shrewsbury to parliament depressed the king for days since it cut communications with Wales, where so many soldiers had been recruited, and Chester, the vital port at which soldiers from Ireland were expected to debark. Added to this the Welsh economy was in ruins, and there was quarrelling between rival commanders, as well as a multitude of regional feuds. Wales, 'the nursery of the king's infantry', was in a state of near rebellion.[3]

The northern horse who had been led south by Rupert after Marston Moor were chafing at their long absence from home, and petitioned the king to be allowed to return on the pretext that they were needed to help their besieged comrades at Pontefract and Carlisle. Meanwhile one royalist commander after another – Lord Loughborough in Leicestershire, Sir Richard Byron at Newark, Lord Byron at Chester, Goring from Taunton – was complaining about the shortage of money and supplies.

A bad decision was taken to set up the 14-year-old Prince of Wales with a council and court of his own at Bristol. The arrangement seems to have been implemented partly to weaken Prince Rupert by establishing a rival power centre beyond his control. It split the royalist army at a time when parliament was welding its armies together. It also removed from the pres-ence of the king some of his key councillors – Hyde, Culpeper, Capel and Hopton.[4] Digby did not disguise his happiness at the removal of these men,

---

[2] *LJ*, Vol. 7, 268.
[3] Warburton, *Memoirs*, Vol. 3, 63.
[4] Richmond and Southampton had also been nominated to the prince's council but refused to go to Bristol.

who until then had acted as a brake on his policy initiatives, such as the alliance with the Gaelic Irish.

When the young prince arrived in the west he found a sorry state of affairs. Sir Richard Grenville, who had failed to reduce Plymouth, was blaming Sir John Berkeley, the governor of Exeter, for not coming to his aid. Neither of them would obey Goring, who was battering ineffectually at Taunton. The presence of the Prince of Wales gave all three of them an excuse for ignoring Prince Rupert's orders. Meanwhile, Cromwell was rampaging through the west with a brigade of 1,500 horse, to which were added steadily large numbers of horse, dragoons and foot, until by early May he was reportedly in command of 7,000 men.[5] After bloodying the Earl of Northampton's regiment he took Bletchingdon House without firing a shot. More significantly, he drove off several hundred draught horses, essential if the Oxford army was to leave its base. Equally serious, the news of Cromwell's success was inspiring 'swarms' of Londoners to flock to the parliamentary standard. His activities caused great anxiety among the royalist high command. Then the Committee of Both Kingdoms tightened the noose by instructing Cromwell to blockade Oxford while Fairfax took the bulk of the New Model Army to relieve Taunton.

Rupert, Goring and the Royalist Council of War met in Oxford at the beginning of May to concert a strategy for the coming campaign. Rupert argued for a march north, first relieving Chester, and then swinging east to attack the Scots army, now much smaller than before, which was besieging Pontefract. He was counting on Sir Thomas Fairfax not being able to move his New Model troops quickly enough to rescue the Scots. Once the covenanting Scots in England were disposed of it would be possible to join forces with Montrose, defeat the Covenanters in Scotland, and then march south to confront parliament's New Model Army. In his *History* Clarendon grudgingly recognized the cogency of Rupert's reasoning. Interesting confirmation is also found in the correspondence of the Scots commissioners in London, who were greatly troubled when the king's northern strategy became known to them.[6] The 7,000-strong royalist army rendezvoused at Stow-on-the-Wold on 8 May. The next day it was joined by Sir Jacob Astley with 3,300 foot, and by Colonel Bard with 300 foot. Charles Gerrard was expected to arrived shortly with his 2,000

[5] At the end of April Edward Nicholas had told Rupert that Cromwell was at the head of 2,500 horse and dragoons in the Oxford region: BL. Add. MS 18982 (Rupert Papers), fo. 48.

[6] Clarendon, *Hist.*, Bk 9, 29; *Correspondence of the Scots Commissioners in London*, ed. H.W. Meikle, *1644–1646*, 74, 77–8.

infantry and 700 cavalry recruits from South Wales, which would have made an army of impressive strength. Had this happened, and had the augmented army been kept together as one unit, Clarendon ruefully reflected, 'it is very likely that the summer might have been crowned with better success'.[7] Rupert's plan was discussed further. Sir Marmaduke Langdale threw his support behind the prince because his northern horse were itching to return home. The remainder of the Council favoured an advance into the west to meet Fairfax head on. Rupert feared that the quarrels of the western commanders had so debilitated the army that they and their forces would be of little use against Fairfax. He appeased Goring by bowing to the latter's demand to return to the west with his 3,000 troops to check Fairfax, and gave him a more extensive commission, perhaps in the hope of putting an end to the ceaseless bickering. The king too acquiesced in the splitting of his army. Goring was delighted, not least because he relished the prospect of exercising undisputed authority over Grenville, Berkeley and Hopton. By making this concession Rupert gained his point with the king: the Oxford army marched north. On its way it picked up additional troops from various garrisons, bringing its total up to 12,000, even without the reinforcements of Goring and Gerrard.

As soon as the Committee of Both Kingdoms heard that Charles was moving north with his main army they sent Colonel Vermuyden with 2,400 horse and dragoons to reinforce the Scots, and instructed Fairfax to leave a small brigade at Taunton, while wheeling his main force towards Oxford and linking up with Cromwell. The news of these troop movements caused the king to suspend his march to the north. He was not especially worried about Oxford, which by now was so well fortified that it would take Fairfax a long time before he could bring it to capitulate. The council reasoned that the best way to take the pressure off Oxford was by attacking a parliamentary stronghold in the vicinity. Goring was therefore instructed to bring his troops from the south-west for this purpose.[8] This order displeased Goring, and only confirmed him in his dislike for Rupert, even though the order did not emanate from him. With support from the Prince of Wales's council he defied the order, arguing that the king should return to Oxford, where Goring would meet him at the head of the western army and together they would put an end to Fairfax and his new army. It was a brazen attempt to defeat the northern strategy and shift the main

---

[7] Clarendon, *Hist.*, Bk 9, 29.
[8] BL. Add. MS 18982 (Rupert Papers), fos. 46, 48 (deciphered letters: Digby and Nicholas respectively to Rupert, 29 April 1645).

theatre of the war back to the south-west.[9] Already, before May was over, royalist strategy for the summer of 1645 was in ruins.

The town the royalists selected to teach Fairfax and parliament a lesson was Leicester. They besieged it with the Oxford army and summoned it to surrender. When the summons was rejected Rupert subjected the south wall to a four-hour artillery barrage that opened up a large breach. The town was then overrun and brutally sacked, without distinction between enemies and sympathizers.

The sack of Leicester caused extreme panic and recrimination in London. In fact it did greater objective harm to the king's cause than to parliament's. The king's army was reduced by nearly 200 dead, and by an even greater number of casualties. Many soldiers took the opportunity to run off with their plunder. The royalist infantry were further reduced by the necessity of leaving behind a garrison of several hundred men in Leicester. These combined factors brought the infantry component of the royalist army down from 5,000 to 3,500 – hardly enough to win a battle for the kingdom. Morale too was a problem in the wake of Leicester. The northern horse grew ever more restive at being kept in the south when they had thought that they were going to be marching to Yorkshire.

There was now an intense debate in the royalist council of war. The courtiers led by Digby argued for relieving Oxford, to rescue the Duke of York and the ladies who were sending them urgent entreaties. Rupert and his friends put this down to the jealousy the courtiers were feeling at the growing influence of the military faction on the council. He pointed out that Oxford was strongly fortified, that the governor, William Legge, had not requested relief, and that there was no sign of a conjunction of Cromwell and Fairfax's forces. The courtiers won the argument: in spite of Rupert, the military faction and the northern horse the army turned and marched for Oxford. On 7 June it reached Daventry. Then the news came that Fairfax had withdrawn his forces from the city. In the council of war Rupert prevailed once more, and the army prepared to bend its steps northward.

While preparations were made for this latest U-turn in royal policy the king and many of the officers amused themselves with hunting in the neighbourhood of Daventry. Charles was in a good mood. 'I may . . . affirm', he wrote to his wife, 'that . . . my affairs were never in so hopeful a way.'[10] Suddenly, on 12 June the news arrived that Fairfax was only five

---

[9] *CSPD 1644–45*, 506–7, 520–1.
[10] Parker (ed.), *Kings Cabinet*, 14.

miles off. While royalist scouts had been unaware of the looming presence of the New Model, parliament's chief scout, Leonard Watson, knew exactly the whereabouts and strength of the king's forces. Thanks to a double agent he was also able to keep Fairfax accurately informed of the disarray in the royalist council of war.[11] Once again parliamentary intelligence proved itself superior to royalist intelligence. Among the many captured letters in Watson's possession was one from Goring announcing that he would not be bringing his army to Charles's aid in the Midlands. It was this letter more than any other factor that resolved Fairfax and his council of war to engage the king's army without delay. The royalist council of war was hastily reconvened. Rupert repeated his advice to continue their march northward. They were heavily outnumbered: Goring and his cavalry had not come, nor was there any sign of Gerrard and his Welsh recruits. They should march towards the troops that were on their way from Newark and Melton. Digby and Ashburnham opposed him, arguing for an immediate attack. The king had just read Montrose's triumphant despatch announcing his victory at Auldearn, which swelled him with optimism once more. The ignorant arguments of the civilian councillors prevailed; the king decided for battle.

Naseby

Fairfax's withdrawal from Oxford, far from being a sign of defeatism, marked his liberation from the irksome rule of the armchair strategists in London. The Committee for Both Kingdoms, by its restless shifting of pieces over the chessboard of southern England had unwittingly created a vacuum at the centre. The main parliamentary forces were distributed between Taunton, where Colonel Weldon commanded a brigade of 5,000; Oxford, where Fairfax had 10,000; the north, where Colonel Vermuyden had been despatched with 2,500 to bolster the Scots; and the Isle of Ely, where Cromwell had just raised another 3,000 horse and foot. The whole confused strategy began to unravel when the Scots, anxious about the threat of Montrose, declined Vermuyden's help, and faded northwards towards Westmorland. This new weakness in the north had two significant ramifications. It dealt another blow to Scots political influence in London. It left Brereton vulnerable, causing him to abandon the siege of Chester. With Chester safe for the moment the king circled back southwards, in effect filling the vacuum at the centre. On 9 June the Committee of Both

---

[11] Bodl. MS Tanner 59, fo. 750.

Kingdoms acknowledged the futility of directing field operations and gave Fairfax the free hand he sought.

At this moment the London Common Council broached a question that no one had had the nerve to articulate in public: should not Oliver Cromwell – the hero of Marston Moor, the man who had done so much fighting and recruiting over the past several months – be given a military command? Acting on this cue Fairfax's council of war wrote urging that Cromwell be appointed to the vacant lieutenant-generalship of the cavalry. The Commons readily assented, but the Lords stalled. For Fairfax, Commons approval was sufficient and he made the appointment. On 13 June Cromwell rode into the New Model camp with 600 of the horse and dragoons that he had recruited in the Eastern Association. The strength of the New Model was now between 15,000 and 17,000 men.[12]

In the early morning of 14 June the two armies took up positions facing each other on two low hills just north of Naseby. Both sides adopted a simple order of battle, with cavalry on the wings and infantry in the middle. The one touch of tactical subtlety was the stationing of John Okey's crack dragoon regiment behind the hedges on the parliamentary left, at right angles to the line of battle.[13] From their concealed position they would be able to pour galling musketfire across the flank of Rupert's advancing horse. Fairfax drew his troops a hundred paces behind the brow of the hill in order to conceal their exact position from the king. The manoeuvre may have prompted Charles to think that Fairfax was fleeing and encouraged him to launch his attack, through low wet ground in the middle, and then uphill towards the enemy.

At 10 a.m. there was a brief exchange of cannon fire, and an hour later Rupert led the royalist right wing against Ireton on the parliamentary left. Ireton, though endowed with a formidable intellect, was an inexperienced and ineffectual cavalry commander. His regiments were quickly scattered, while he was wounded and taken prisoner. Okey's dragoons had only been able to save one of Ireton's regiments from the general rout. Soon the middle was in trouble as well. Major-General Philip Skippon was shot in the side, a wound from which it would take him almost a year to recover. The king's infantry under Astley rolled back Skippon's front line until they fell behind the reserves. The reserve regiments – Rainborowe's, Pride's and Hammond's – were made of sterner stuff, however, and held their ground, halting the royalist advance before all was lost.

[12] Glenn Foard, *Naseby: The Decisive Campaign*, 207.
[13] Peter Young, *Naseby, 1645*, 245.

Meanwhile on the parliamentary right wing Cromwell, from the highest position on the battlefield, led half his cavalry on a charge into Marmaduke Langdale's demoralized northern horse. He pushed them back, leaving the flank of the royalist foot vulnerable to attack. As Langdale's retreating horse streamed past him, Charles decided that he would personally try to save the day. Taking command of the reserves, he prepared to charge into Cromwell's flank. But the Earl of Carnforth quickly put a stop to this display of royal heroism. He rode up to the king, put his hand on his bridle, and with the words, 'Will you go upon your death?'[14] turned the king's horse to the side and out of harm's way.

Cromwell now effected a manoeuvre of which few cavalry commanders were capable at this time: he got his men to halt, re-form, wheel about and ride back to the battlefield. He then divided his horse into two squadrons, and with Fairfax's assistance charged into the king's infantry from opposite flanks. This relieved Skippon's foot, enabling them to recover the ground they had previously lost. Fairfax then reformed the whole parliamentary line for a second charge. At the sight of the monolithic approach of the New Model with its terrible superiority of numbers, the remainder of the king's army now turned tail and fled.

There can be no doubt about the crucial role played by Cromwell on Naseby field. First, his mere presence was an inspiration to the soldiers; secondly, he drew up the order of battle; thirdly, he erased the humiliation suffered by his son-in-law Ireton when he led a stunningly successful charge on the right and then reformed his men to rescue the beleaguered foot in the middle. Contemporary observers agreed, however, in awarding the laurels of the day to Fairfax. This may have been a tactful courtesy shown towards the commander-in-chief, but it also reflected his actual contribution. Thirteen years Cromwell's junior, but with the benefit of several years of continental and northern experience, he directed troop movements and responded to the unpredictable fluidity, the overwhelming rush of events, that were compressed into the two hours when the outcome of the English Revolution was decided. It was Fairfax who re-formed the whole line in the middle of the battle, and who synchronized the advance of horse and foot that finally won the day.

Measured in human lives, the victory was relatively cheap. The New Model lost 150 men, compared to 1,000 for the king. Virtually all the king's infantry were taken prisoner. He also lost 2,000 horses, his entire

---

[14] Clarendon, *Hist.*, Bk 9, 40.

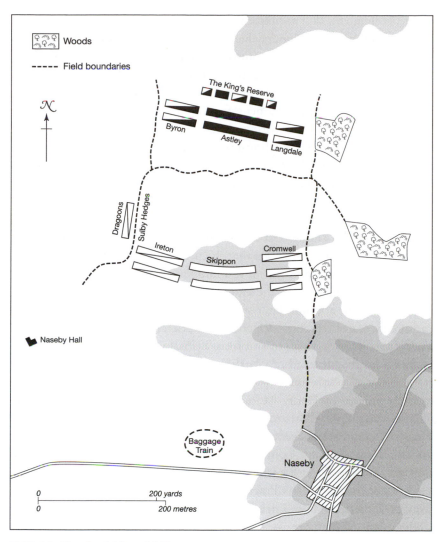

MAP 10 *Naseby, 14 June 1645*

artillery and baggage train, and his precious file of secret correspondence.
Most of the royalist cavalry got away intact.

In terms of numbers of combatants and casualties, Naseby was a far
less bloody battle than Marston Moor. Cromwell interpreted the stunning
victory as 'none other but the hand of God' and added the following
appeal to parliament: 'He that ventures his life for the liberty of his country, I wish he trust God for the liberty of his conscience, and you for the

liberty he fights for.'[15] The political consequences were incalculable. Scots, Presbyterians and Essex's party had not concealed their expectation, even their hope, that Fairfax and Cromwell would be trounced by the royalists. Afterwards, as Thomas Juxon noted, many in London 'were not very well pleased with this victory'.[16] The Scots suffered a further reduction of political clout, while Essex and Manchester were relegated to the shadows. The Independents enjoyed a correspondingly mighty access of political prestige. For his part Charles stubbornly declined to face up to reality, and continued to pursue the will-of-the-wisp of salvation by a combination of Irish Catholic and Scottish Highland military power, under the leadership of the newly emergent knight in shining armour, James Graham, now Marquess of Montrose. The man most responsible for keeping the king divorced from reality, Lord Digby, first did his utmost to pin the blame for Naseby on Rupert, disregarding the fact that the prince had advised against engaging with Fairfax and in favour of resuming the march to the north.

Most damaging of all to the king's cause was the delayed fuse that was ignited less than a month later with the publication of excerpts from his captured secret correspondence under the title *The Kings Cabinet Opened*. The letters, many of them to and from his wife, filled readers with a thrill of horror as they learned of Charles's duplicity, double-dealing and constant desire to please his wife. Accompanied by scathing editorial commentary penned by Henry Parker, they brought into the full light of day Charles's manifold efforts to secure outside help for his cause – from the kings of Denmark and France, the Prince of Orange, the Duke of Lorraine, and the Irish Catholic Confederation. The letters also exposed unmistakably his deep distrust of his own people and their parliament. They further documented his willingness to take away all penal laws against Roman Catholics in both England and Ireland if that would result in more soldiers fighting for his cause. No longer would Protestants in England give any credence to his reassurances that he was the stout defender of their faith. The gentry of Wales, for example were much cooler when he next tried to recruit among them.[17] More than anything else the publication of these letters confirmed the win-the-war party in their determination to go on with the struggle until they had obtained the king's unconditional surrender.

---

[15] Abbott, *Cromwell*, Vol. 1, 360.
[16] Juxon, *Journal*, 80.
[17] John Evelyn, *Diary of John Evelyn*, ed. William Bray, Vol. 4, 153, 167; Dodd, *Studies in Stuart Wales*, 95–7.

In military terms the next ten months were merely a mopping up operation after Naseby. Rupert recognized that the game was up and counselled the king to sue for peace rather than prolong the agony. Charles, still clinging to the mirage of a Celtic rescue, rejected Rupert's advice, and listened instead to the siren song of Lord Digby, who after a few moments of discouragement, continued to promise everyone who would listen that help was on the way and the royalist cause was just about to turn the corner to victory.

Scotland: Montrose vanquished

Sufficient to foster this delusion were another two dazzling victories by Montrose during the summer. Nothing had in fact happened to alter the basic fragility of Montrose's position in Scotland. For all his victories, he still lacked the depth of support to exploit them. Once more his army melted away as his soldiers insisted on going home with their booty. In effect he had been able to wage nothing more than a large-scale guerilla war, in which he had to retire to the mountains after every victory to replenish his depleted forces. While this drove the Edinburgh government to distraction it did little to advance Montrose's grand strategy of bringing an army out of Scotland to turn the tide of war in England. Despite her best efforts from Paris the queen was unable to raise the cavalry Montrose needed to invade the Lowlands. The Irish confederates too refused to send him more men. As far as they were concerned Alasdair MacColla's venture had failed because Monro's Scottish army had still not vacated Ireland.[18] Indeed, the Covenanters, despite their humiliation at Montrose's hands, declined to pull their armies out of England and Ireland in order to wage total war against him. Shrewdly they kept their wider strategy always in mind: to preserve, through their military presence, their influence on political events in the other two kingdoms.

Baillie, discouraged by his poor performance against Montrose, and resentful of the lack of confidence shown in him by the nobles and the Committee of Estates, tried to resign, but was prevented by the lack of anyone to take his place. Once more he marched north to confront the royalists, and the two armies met at Alford on 2 July. The pattern of Montrose's previous victories was repeated. After a short period of fierce fighting the Covenanters were routed with heavy losses in the pursuit,

---

[18] *CSP*, Vol. 2, 186; Carte, *Life*, Vol. 3, 380–1, 384; HMC 1, *Second Report*, part I (Marquis of Montrose MSS), 170.

while Montrose's sustained only a handful of casualties. These, however, included George Lord Gordon, a kindred spirit, and his most influential ally among the Gordons. For the Covenanters the humiliation at Alford was a heavy blow to morale, coming as it did in the wake of the New Model's sweeping victory at Naseby.

Once again Baillie, more disheartened than ever, tried to resign, and once again parliament turned him down. Parliament had shifted its venue to Perth to escape the plague, which had spread from Edinburgh to Stirling. While the Covenanters waited for Robert Monro to return from Ireland and replace Baillie at the head of the forces in Scotland, Viscount Aboyne (Huntly's second son) supplied Montrose with several hundred fresh cavalry, bringing the latter's overall numbers up to 5,000 – his all-time high. Montrose was determined not to repeat the previous pattern of victories, but this time to break into England and try to avert the final collapse of the royalist cause. He led his forces towards Glasgow, reaching Kilsyth, 11 miles north-east of the city, on 14 August. Then he sat down and waited for the Covenanters to catch up with him. The covenanting leadership, still nominally under Baillie, but overseen by a committee of the estates, was fatally riven by resentments and jealousies. Seeing their division, Montrose attacked. Again the Covenanters collapsed after only token resistance, and the fleeing soldiers were mown down by the hundreds. Most of the nobles scattered and the army itself disintegrated. Montrose looked to be the master of Scotland.

It was an illusion. After five consecutive, unanswered victories powerful men should have been flocking to his standard. Many did indeed promise loyalty, but they were playing a waiting game. Others were genuine in their professions of support: the Marquess of Douglas and the earls of Traquair, Wigtown, Annandale, Hartfell, Perth, Home and Roxburgh; but they were not able to supply what he needed most, recruits for his army. The Covenanters on the other hand, in spite of the shattering of their pride, still believed that they would be rescued by the return of their armies from England and Ireland. For the moment they were content to wait.

Waiting was a prudent course to take, for Montrose's army was now crumbling almost as quickly as it had grown. The Irish and the Highlanders wanted to leave, stash their plunder, and then go back to fighting against the Campbells. They were disappointed at not being allowed to pillage the temptingly rich city of Glasgow. MacColla and his departing Irishmen and Highlanders promised Montrose that they would return later, but the immediate result was that Montrose lost over 2,000 men, nearly half his army. Next there was trouble with the Gordons.

Aboyne insisted on going home to help his father against the Covenanters. This bled away several hundred cavalry. None of these groups – Irish, Highlanders, Gordons – appreciated that giving primacy to their localist concerns sealed Charles's doom in England, and ensured the eventual restoration of the Covenanters in Scotland.

Dénouement: England, July 1645–June 1646

All that summer in England Rupert did what he could to salvage the king's cause. Before the end of June he was in Barnstaple conferring with the Prince of Wales on the defence of the west. Charles retired to Wales, where he was warmly welcomed at Raglan Castle by the Marquess of Worcester. His son, the Earl of Glamorgan, was still negotiating with the Catholic Irish to send troops to revive the king's fortunes. Rupert soon determined that the situation in the west was worse than he had suspected. Goring, when he was not drinking himself into a stupor and neglecting the siege of Taunton, was alienating the local population by his failure to curb the outrages of his troops. Sir Richard Grenville and Sir John Berkeley continued to nullify each other's efforts with their endless quarrel.

Langport

Fairfax in the meantime retook Leicester and then wheeled around and set out for the west. He covered the 136 miles from Leicester to the Somerset border in fifteen days. Colonel Edward Massie, the governor of Gloucester, approached from the opposite direction with 2,200 horse and dragoons, and the two commanders set their sights on Taunton. Warned of their approach Goring had abandoned the siege of Taunton and fallen back to Langport. There Fairfax and Massie, with more than twice Goring's numbers, surrounded him. Goring held out in what seemed to be a strong position, at the top of a hedge-lined hill, that could only be scaled through a narrow lane along which no more than two men could ride abreast on horseback. In an audacious manoeuvre Fairfax sent 200 horse splashing across the stream at the bottom of the hill, and up the lane from hedge to hedge. When they reached the top they confronted Goring's whole brigade, who outnumbered them six or eight to one. They charged straight into it, and with the help of reinforcements soon overwhelmed the dispirited royalists. There were a few deaths, many prisoners and a great haul of horses, arms, cannon and ammunition. The king's cavalry were finished. 'To see this', exclaimed Cromwell, 'is it not to see the face of

God!'[19] In the space of less than a month the king's cause had been rendered utterly hopeless. At Naseby the king had lost most of his infantry. At Langport he lost his largest remaining contingent of cavalry. The war was effectively won.

Because Charles refused to recognize this brute fact, the war with its accompaniment of sieges, pitched battles, cold, hunger, sickness and anxiety carried on for another 11 months. Twelve days later Bridgwater was stormed and overrun, producing another fabulous haul of matériel, silver plate, jewels, tapestries and prisoners. The victory was the occasion for political dissension on the parliamentary side. The storming of the town was intended to be a joint venture by Fairfax's forces and Massie's brigade. Perhaps for reasons of political disaffection (Massie was a Presbyterian), his forces twice failed to join the attack, which caused annoyance to Fairfax's men and adverse comment in London. The Presbyterians at Westminster were discomfited by his poor showing.[20]

Bristol

Next Bath and Sherborne were overrun in late July and early August. Fairfax then turned his attention to Bristol, the second city of the kingdom, the king's chief port and his principal magazine. After the decision had been taken to invest the city the chaplains William Dell and Hugh Peters led the army in a day of fasting and prayer for divine blessing on the endeavour. There was no time to be lost. Montrose had just chalked up yet another victory against the Covenanters (Kilsyth, 15 August); Charles and Goring were approaching from the north and south respectively with the remains of the field army. Finally, the army's critics in London were again becoming vocal.[21]

With its massively fortified three-mile perimeter and ample supply of ordnance, ammunition and food Bristol looked to be an intimidating fortress. Yet the city was in a parlous condition. The morale of Rupert's garrison, bled by plague and desertion, was poor: the numbers of defenders had shrunk to only 3,500. There would be no external aid. Goring's progress from Devon had been blocked by Massie's brigade. The people of South Wales had been so put off by the misbehaviour of Charles Gerrard's

[19] Abbott, *Cromwell*, I, p. 365.
[20] See Gentles, *NMA*, 70, and passim for more detail on the New Model's western campaign in 1645–46.
[21] *CSPD 1645–47*, 96, 104–5.

men that they dispersed, unwilling to serve the king. In the north Carlisle, Pontefract and Scarborough had just fallen to parliament. While the king did succeed in occupying Hereford after its evacuation by the Scots, his 3,000 weary cavalry were now penned in by a formidable brigade under colonels Poynts and Rossiter. But after receiving a message from some of the Scots lords hinting at an alliance against the Independents, Charles began to dream of a grand alliance between Montrose and the Covenanters, augmented by the 10,000 troops he was certain would arrive any day from Ireland, and the remains of his army in England. He started preparing to go to Scotland to cement the alliance. When Rupert heard of the king's plans he wrote in horror to the Duke of Richmond who was with the king, saying that instead of pursuing wild fancies, Charles should begin serious negotiation with parliament. Charles wrote back with offended pride, conceding that objectively 'there is no probability but of my ruin', yet affirming his certainty 'as a Christian that God will not suffer rebels and traitors to prosper nor this cause to be overthrown'.[22]

Digby egged the king on in this conviction.[23] Inspired by the exciting news of Montrose's fifth victory, this time south of the Highlands (at Kilsyth), Charles had scraped together 2,000 horse and marched north hoping to link up with his Scottish paladin. He actually entered Yorkshire and got as far as Doncaster, but then word reached him of Convenanters approaching in force, and he thought better of the plan to rendezvous with Montrose. Instead, taking advantage of Fairfax's example in the west he made a foray into the heart of the Eastern Association. Then, hearing that the royalist city of Hereford was being hard pressed by the main body of the Scots army under Lord Leven he turned westwards to relieve it. Miserable from lack of food and pay, and conscious of the hatred of the local population, the Scots had just heard about Montrose's victory. When, to top it off, they got the news that a royalist army under the king himself was nearly upon them they judged that it was time to withdraw. Charles entered Hereford amidst the rejoicing of the populace.

At Bristol there was much less for royalists to rejoice about. Granted, Fairfax's New Model troops were down to less than 5,000, but they were joined by another 5,000 volunteers, some of them former clubmen,

---

[22] Rushworth, *Hist. Coll.*, Vol. 6, 132.

[23] As he put it to the Marquess of Ormond, while there had been many recent disasters, Hopton now had 6,000 men in Cornwall; he would soon be joining with Goring's 'army' and the 3,000 horse and foot besieging Plymouth, and was in no doubt 'but we shall give Fairfax as little joy of the west as Essex had the last year: Carte, *Life*, Vol. 6, 309.

out of Somerset and Gloucestershire. Their morale was high. Fairfax had great respect for Rupert as a soldier who had fought and suffered for the Protestant cause in Europe. The last thing he wanted was a bloodbath. He therefore sent a courteous invitation to the prince to surrender. There was no intention he assured Rupert of overthrowing monarchy. 'Sir, the crown of England is and will be where it ought to be', but 'the king, in supreme acts is not to be advised by men of whom the law takes no notice, but by his parliament, the great counsel of the kingdom'. If the prince would only spare the city by surrendering 'it would be an occasion glorious in itself and joyful to us, for the restoring of you to the endeared affection of the parliament and people of England'.[24] In spite of the grim outlook Rupert declined Fairfax's invitation. A six-day artillery bombardment followed, which failed to dent the high thick walls. The city was finally overrun in the most difficult way possible: by scaling the walls with ladders while the royalists poured round- and case-shot upon them. Only after the fall of Priors Hill Fort within the walls did Rupert finally surrender. He got no thanks from his royal master for his service on that day. Charles had now lost his main centre for the manufacture and import of ordnance. The verdict of the royalist secretary of war was that it represented 'the loss of all our magazines and warlike provisions, and so by consequence . . . of South Wales, the West, and all other places in the kingdom'.[25] Even Charles could see that the jig was up, and in his despair he fell prey to paranoid fantasies. At Westminster parliament had just voted Rupert's brother Frederick the Elector Palatine an income of £8,000 a year. Rupert's enemies at court fed the king rumours that Rupert and his friend William Legge, the governor of Oxford were engaged in a sinister plot to seize the royal headquarters, overthrow Charles and, with the cooperation of parliament, place Frederick on the throne.[26] Charles swallowed the lies, and believed that he had to act fast to avert a coup. Pitilessly he wrote to Rupert, the nephew he had loved and trusted for the past three years, hinting at betrayal, dismissing him, and ordering Sir Edward Nicholas to arrest him in Oxford.

The fall of Bristol also had far-reaching political repercussions in London. It instantly rehabilitated the reputation of Nathaniel Fiennes, who had been disgraced two years earlier for surrendering the city to Rupert. Recognizing that Fiennes had faced even greater difficulties than

---

[24] Sprigge, *Anglia Rediviva*, 98.
[25] Walker, *Hist. Discourses*, 137.
[26] *CSPD 1645–47*, 134.

Rupert, the Commons voted to restore him at once to his seat in parliament. The longer-term consequence was a widening of the breach between Independents and Presbyterians. For the New Model Bristol was a euphoric high point. In this mood Cromwell wrote to the Commons speaker appealing for liberty of conscience. 'Presbyterians, Independents, all have here the same spirit of faith and prayer . . . And for brethren, in things of the mind, we look for no compulsion, but that of light and reason.'[27] When parliament printed Cromwell's letter this passage was omitted. Cromwell's friends in the house retaliated by printing the suppressed portion and scattering it up and down the streets of the capital.[28]

Philiphaugh

Two days after the fall of Bristol, the royalists received a second hammer-blow, this time at the hands of the covenanting Scots under General David Leslie. Leslie had been at Nottingham when the news reached him of the disaster at Kilsyth in mid-August. At once his common soldiers insisted that they should all return to Scotland. By the time he crossed the border his numbers were about 6,000. Lord Leven had wanted to join him with troops from the west of England, but the parliamentarians begged him to stay, pleading that his departure would endanger all that the Scots had fought for over the past two years. The news that David Leslie was approaching the Borders in early September with a large part of the Scottish army in England prompted the earls of Home and Roxborough to desert Montrose. Nor was Charles any help. He could offer only thanks (to Montrose) and regrets that this was 'all my song to you'.[29]

On 12 September Montrose camped near Selkirk, unaware that Leslie was in hot pursuit. His tiny army consisted of 1,000 mostly untrained horse and 500 or so Irish infantry. Four factors made defeat inevitable: Leslie's army was four times as large and battle seasoned; Montrose's horse were untrained levies; Leslie took the royalists completely by surprise; many officers including Montrose were absent when the attack began.

By the time he reached the battlefield at Philiphaugh the horse had already fled. He did manage to rally a few of them and tried to help the Irish, who fought with the fierceness of men who knew that death was the

---

[27] Sprigge, *Anglia Rediviva*, 118.

[28] *The Conclusion of Lieut: General Cromwells Letter to the House of Commons concerning the Taking of Bristol* (1645), BL. 669.f.10/38.

[29] Gordon, *Britane's Distemper*, 146, quoted in Stevenson, *Revolution and Counter-Revolution*, 37.

only alternative to victory. Leslie paid them the tribute that he had 'never fought with better horsemen, and against more resolute foot'.[30] It was soon clear that the situation was hopeless, so Montrose fled with the horse. Of the Irish foot 250 were killed, while those who surrendered upon promise of quarter were shot, as were their wives (many of them pregnant),[31] children, cooks and horse boys. Some had escaped to the moors, but were rounded up and brought to Leslie's camp at Linlithgow. They were flung over the bridge of Avon, and either drowned in the river, as English settlers had been drowned at Portadown, or were stabbed with the pikes of the soldiers who lined the banks. Buchan comments, 'the records of the Irish rebellion hold no more horrid cruelties'.[32]

Time had run out for Montrose, just as it had for the king. There was no hope that he could reassemble his Irish and Highland infantry and his Gordon horse. After all, they had deserted him in his times of greatest victory; why should they rally to him after so devastating a defeat? In the larger political context it is arguable that Montrose actually did a disservice to the king by alienating moderate opinion in Scotland – those who were horrified by the conduct of his Irish Catholic and Highland allies. He also weakened the influence of the Scots in England by forcing them to divert money and men to subduing royalist rebels in their own back yard. The effect of this was to delay the formation of a strong party combining moderate Covenanters and royalists until 1648, by which time it was too late.[33]

The number of Scots killed in their own civil war of 1644–45 was about 10,000 – 1 per cent of the kingdom's population.[34] Beyond that were the extensive losses from disease and casualties suffered by the Scottish armies in England and Ireland. Finally, there was the grave suffering in the Lowlands, especially Edinburgh and Leith, from the bubonic plague. The Scots further punished themselves by the widespread material destruction that they inflicted upon one another, the systematic destruction of houses,

---

[30] *Three Great Victories* (1645), Wing T1093, sig. A4r.

[31] 'Big with child, yet none of them were spared, but all were cut in pieces . . . For they ripped up the bellies of the women with their swords, till the fruit of their womb . . . fall down upon the ground, weltering in the gory blood of their mangled mothers': Gordon, *Britane's Distemper*, 160.

[32] Buchan, *The Marquis of Montrose*, 195; W. Thompson, *Montrosse Totally Routed at Tividale in Scotland* (1645), E301/19; Gordon, *Britane's Distemper*, 158–63; G. Wishart, *Memoirs of Montrose*, 145–7; Henry Guthry, *Memoirs*, 201–4.

[33] Stevenson, *Revolution and Counter-Revolution*, 41.

[34] Ibid.

goods, animals and crops that only exacerbated suffering, starvation and death. Internecine violence did not abate in Argyllshire until two years after Philiphaugh, as the Catholic Confederation continued to send reinforcements and the Campbells wreaked revenge on them.

England: the royalist collapse

A week after the fall of Bristol, Digby had still not heard of the catastrophe at Philiphaugh, and had recovered his irrepressible optimism. He wrote to Jermyn and the queen that troops would soon be on their way – 20,000 from Scotland and 10,000 from Ireland. The Covenanters in England would come to their senses and make peace with the king. Charmed by Digby's silver tongue, Charles decided to quit Wales and march north in the hope of meeting Montrose. On the way he heard that Chester, his last seaport, and crucial for the landing of Irish troops, was likely to fall at any moment. He therefore changed course and made for Chester, arriving there with 1,000 troops on 23 September. The following day Langdale took about 3,000 cavalry out of the city with orders to attack the besiegers from behind. Before he could accomplish this objective he was met with a strong party of horse under General Poynts. They attacked Langdale's men in the flank, and soon put them to flight. Charles was profoundly shocked by the defeat of his cavalry, and even Digby was depressed. By now the news about Philiphaugh had trickled through. Although Chester had not yet fallen it no longer seemed a tenable headquarters. The king made for heavily fortified and garrisoned Newark. He commissioned Digby as lieutenant-general of all forces north of the Trent, and sent him to join Montrose, who was rumoured to be raising a new army. Not surprisingly Digby's mission turned into a fiasco in which his own secret correspondence was captured, and with their remaining few hundred troopers he and Langdale sailed to Ireland to accelerate the arrival of Irish troops. He was no more successful with this project than he had been as lieutenant-general of the north.[35]

Meanwhile Fairfax continued mopping up the west. Brigades were sent out under Thomas Rainborowe, Cromwell and Colonel Pickering to overrun Berkeley Castle, Devizes and Lacock House respectively. In November Cromwell added Winchester and Basing House to the list, putting a large number of the House's Catholic residents to the sword. If

---

[35] Ian Roy, 'George Digby, royalist intrigue and the collapse of the cause', in Gentles, Morrill and Worden (eds), *Soldiers, Writers and Statesmen*, 79–88.

Fairfax had been directing the storm perhaps the residents might have been spared. The storm of Basing prefigured the bloody conquests of Drogheda and Wexford four years later. Those garrisons were also put to the sword, not so much because of their refusal to surrender, but because they were thought to be Catholic. Tiverton in Devon was also regarded as a popish enclave. It too was refusing Fairfax's summons to surrender. Just as he was about to order a storm a round of cannon shot hit the chain of the drawbridge snapping it in two. The soldiers could scarcely believe their eyes as the drawbridge came crashing down. Without waiting for orders they raced across the drawbridge and took possession of the town. Following Fairfax's express instructions, they granted quarter to the terrified defenders.

It was now January 1646, and Fairfax pressed deeper into the west, his forces decimated by cold, sickness, hunger and desertion. On the 12 January Dartmouth was successfully stormed without artillery, and again quarter was granted in return for the surrender of the castle. As they turned north towards Torrington they heard that a large force of horse and foot was marching to meet them. Goring had already left for France, either to raise troops or to be cured of the pox,[36] and the army was now being led by Ralph Lord Hopton. On 17 February the two forces, of nearly equal strength (about 5–6,000 each) collided and fought a pitched battle by moonlight. Just after the New Model overran the town 80 barrels of gunpowder blew up in the church where Hopton had kept his magazine. Fairfax narrowly escaped death from one of the great webs of window lead that fell thickly near where he stood. With Fairfax's victory at Torrington the last remaining body of infantry in the field had been scattered. The fall of Chester around the same time (3 February) meant that there remained only two major fortresses in royalist hands – Newark and the king's headquarters at Oxford – and only one royalist force of any size in the field – the prince of Wales's 5,000 horse and 1,000 foot in Cornwall.

Fairfax was still apprehensive about Cornwall as a reserve of royalist manpower, while captured letters gave him cause to worry about the danger – illusory as it turned out – of a French landing on the south coast. Shrewd measures were taken to undermine enemy morale. Fairfax released all his Cornish prisoners and sent them home with two shillings in their pockets. The parliamentary chaplain Hugh Peters rode through his native county telling people that further resistance was futile, and publicising captured letters according to which 10,000 Catholic Irish troops would soon be on their way to succour Hopton. This advance work was abundantly

[36] This was the rumour in London: Juxon, *Journal*, 98.

rewarded when the New Model Army entered the county. Garrisons fell, the gentry switched sides, and the Prince of Wales retired to the Scilly Isles. Hopton agreed on 12 March to disband forces after Fairfax offered him terms that were a model of civilized humanitarianism.

Still Charles did not give up hope. Clinging doggedly to the belief that help might arrive any day from France, he ordered Lord Astley to bring his 3,000 men from Worcestershire and reinforce Oxford. Astley got as far as Stow-on-the-Wold when he was intercepted by Brereton's cavalry from the north, and some infantry from Gloucester. On 21 March he was overwhelmed and forced to surrender. The silver-haired, 67-year-old general sat on a drum and spoke to his captors. 'You have now done your work, and may go to play, unless you will fall out amongst yourselves.'[37] All that now remained to the king were a few secondary garrisons in Wales and the west Midlands.[38] Fairfax's chief remaining task was to invest Oxford. Before he could do this parliament ordered a day of Thanksgiving on 2 April to celebrate the wondrous year of victories since the New Model had first taken the field. Hugh Peters, the 'strenuous Puritan' was the invited preacher. In his three-hour sermon he exalted the New Model soldiers, 'the very off-scourings of the world',[39] who had delivered the nation from bondage and brought the blessings of peace. The challenge was now for the politicians to erect a just social order which would provide decent care for the sick and the poor, and a better justice system – with the laws in English, the courts decentralized, and imprisonment for debt abolished.[40] It was a vision that was unfortunately shared by few other parliamentarians.

Now that the army's military role was winding down Cromwell made his way back to London and resumed his seat in the Commons. As he passed through Westminster Hall his colleagues stared at him in awe.[41] It was common knowledge that the parliamentary Presbyterians and their clerical supporters in the City were far from jubilant over the achievements of the New Model Army. Nor were the Scots. Increasingly unhappy with both the Independents and the New Model, they had already put out feelers to the king. Charles, not wishing to surrender himself into the hands of the New Model, slipped out of Oxford in disguise. The city was finally handed over under generous terms that spared its intellectual and aesthetic treasures but earned Fairfax hard words in London. The defenders under

[37] Rushworth, *Hist. Coll.*, Vol. 6, 41.
[38] Hutton, *Royalist War Effort*, 196.
[39] Hugh Peters, *God's Doing and Man's Duty* (1646), E330/11, foreword, 9, 44–5.
[40] Peters, *God's Doing and Man's Duty*, 9.
[41] *Merc. Civicus*, 23–30 April 1646, E335/3, 2219–20.

their governor Sir Thomas Glemham were allowed to exit with maximum honour: 'colours flying, trumpets sounding, drums beating, matches lighted at both ends, bullet in their mouths, and every soldier [with] twelve charges of powder'.[42] By now it was known that the king had turned himself over to the Scots army near Newark. In London suspicion of the Scots darkened. The political wars were about to begin in earnest.

Ireland: September 1644–September 1646

Once the guns had been stilled and the remaining royalist garrisons handed over in England, parliament was reminded afresh of its unfinished business in Ireland. After the autumn of 1644 Ireland had remained almost quiet. In Ulster Monro's covenanting armies were content to retreat to their lairs and await better times. After the standoff at Charlemont neither Monro, nor Owen Roe O'Neill and his Gaelic Irish, nor the British Protestant Laggan army of Ulster had any further appetite for offensive action. In the south Thomas Preston kept an eye on the Protestant royalist forces under Ormond at Dublin, while in Munster Theobald Viscount Taaffe worried about Lord Inchiquin and the Munster Protestants' transfer of allegiance to the English parliament.

Charles worried that Ormond would not complete the arrangements for Confederate aid to his war effort in England, despite the king's repeated instructions to conclude a treaty with the Irish 'whatever it costs'. Ormond, however, was more interested in trying to exploit division within the Confederate Assembly and Council, and in playing one faction off against the other. With the arrival of spring, however, the Confederate armies once again began to flex their muscles. Thomas Preston marched into Munster, and in cooperation with Castlehaven conducted a pincer movement against Inchiquin's Protestant army. Preston took the garrison of Duncannon, which controlled the key port of Waterford on the east coast, while Castlehaven with 5,000 troops kept up pressure from the west. Losing patience with Ormond, Charles now sent his trusted emissary, the Catholic Earl of Glamorgan, to treat secretly with the Irish.

Glamorgan arrived in Ireland in late August of 1645. Great expectations attached to his mission. Charles was counting on him to reverse the verdict of Naseby with 'such succours . . . from that Kingdom [Ireland] which I have reason to expect'.[43] After conferring in Dublin with Ormond,

---

[42] Sprigge, *Anglia Rediviva*, 262.
[43] Henry Ellis, *Original Letters, Illustrative of English History*, Vol. 3, 311.

who was at least partly in the dark about his secret mandate, he travelled to Confederate headquarters at Kilkenny. His coming at once transformed the Irish political scene. Within a fortnight he had secured an agreement for 10,000 Irish troops to be sent to England to fight for the king. How did he achieve this breakthrough when Ormond had so signally failed? Apart from the trust he generated by being a Catholic, he had persuaded them that the king would satisfy all their demands, but that the agreement had to be kept secret, only to be published after the troops had been despatched and Charles had won the war. Ever since the Confederation had been formed the objectives of the clergy had been clear: Catholicism was not merely to be tolerated but reconstituted as the establishment religion of Ireland, with the complete transfer of rights, property and church buildings from the Protestant to the Catholic Church. Not only were these demands anathema to Ormond, he had stubbornly insisted that Church property seized from the Protestant clergy must be returned to them. It is sometimes overlooked that Ormond's hands were tied by the Protestants in the Dublin parliament who saw the vanquishing of the Catholic insurgency as their constant, overriding objective. This also explains why he only reluctantly agreed to allowing Catholics the quiet exercise of their religion, and set his face against any independence for the Irish parliament. In spite of these disappointments, the Catholic clergy were willing to accept Glamorgan's private guarantees that the king would satisfy their demands, including the one for the retention of Church property, after the war had been won.[44] Yet more than a few hard-line members of the Clericalist party were suspicious and insisted that only an open treaty with Ormond would be genuinely valid.

Glamorgan's treaty was blown apart by two events in October 1645. First, when the Archbishop of Tuam was killed near Sligo, a copy of Glamorgan's treaty was found on his body and forwarded to Ormond, though it did not reach him till Christmas Eve, and did not become known in Westminster until mid-January. Second was the arrival in Ireland of Giovanni Battista Rinuccini, the papal nuncio.

Rinuccini had a massive impact in Ireland. One of the finest products of the Catholic counter-reformation, he was highly educated and possessed of a brilliant intellect. He was also a charming, kindly, urbane and sophisticated man who had the added advantage of being privately wealthy.

---

[44] Seven of the thirteen Irish bishops who debated the Glamorgan treaty found it acceptable: Tadgh Ó hAnnracháin, 'Lost in Rinuccini's shadow: the Irish clergy, 1645–9', in Ó Siochrú (ed.), *Kingdoms in Crisis*, 179.

Twenty years earlier, at the age of 33, he had been made Archbishop of Fermo, and was now a seasoned administrator, assertive, shrewd and masterful in sizing up a situation. Coming from outside he had no trouble discerning that the king and Ormond were only trying to use the Irish Catholics for their own ends. He had a high concept of his papal mission, which was nothing less than 'to restore and reestablish the public exercise of the Catholic religion in the island of Ireland', and enormous confidence in the rightness of his vision.[45] He also carried in his pocket substantial papal subsidies, intended to assist the Confederate cause. Within two months he had persuaded the clergy that the Glamorgan treaty must be rejected. The cogency of his argument was vindicated by Ormond's arrest of Glamorgan in Dublin, and the king's repudiation of the secret treaty once its provisions were made public. Rinuccini's leadership of the Irish Church was uncontested until 1648. It did not require his intervention to scotch the Glamorgan treaty of 1645; nor did he have to twist many arms to get the clergy to insist on their supremacy in spiritual affairs vis-à-vis the Confederate General Assembly. This supremacy was held to include the right to interpret the Confederate oath of association and to excommunicate those who were held to have violated it. A key to Rinuccini's effectiveness was that he eschewed unilateral action, and was careful at all times to build an ecclesiastical consensus behind his policies.[46] Only one criticism can be made of his strategy. Unlike Pope Innocent X, Rinuccini tended to lose sight of the fact that even though Charles I and his lord lieutenant, Ormond, were Protestant heretics, their defeat in England would only release a more formidable enemy to fight against the Irish. Having conquered royalism, the Puritan English parliament would then be free to come and conquer Catholic Ireland. By refusing to do business with Protestants Rinuccini ran the risk of losing everything for the Catholics in Ireland.[47]

Meanwhile, in January 1646 the revelation of Glamorgan's promise to re-establish the Catholic church in Ireland had devastating political repercussions in London. Outraged by this new evidence of the king's duplicity the House of Commons received his urgent appeals for a personal treaty in stony silence. In private some of the Independent leaders were discussing his replacement on the throne by his younger son the Duke

---

[45] Quoted by Patrick J. Corish, 'Ormond, Rinuccini, and the confederates, 1645–9', *NHI*, Vol. 3, 317.

[46] Ó hAnnracháin, 'Lost in Rinuccini's shadow', 185–6.

[47] This point is perceptively made by Wedgwood in *The King's War*, 537.

of Gloucester, with the Earl of Northumberland as regent.[48] Reports were reaching London at the same time of yet another peace treaty negotiated between the queen's representative Sir Kenelm Digby and the pope, and signed in Rome on 20 November 1645. In return for a papal subsidy of 100,000 crowns of Roman money and the sending of 12,000 Irish troops to England to fight for the king, the Catholic church would be re-established with full property rights in Ireland. Knowledge of these concessions enabled Rinuccini to raise the stakes even higher when the Confederate Assembly met on 5 February 1646. He obtained Glamorgan's agreement to withdraw his own treaty in favour of the one concluded in Rome. The assembly agreed to extend the truce with the royalists until 1 May, and to send 3,000 troops to Chester for the king without delay. It was too late of course: on 3 February Chester had fallen, the last port through which troops for the king might have entered.

The news of Chester was not confirmed in Dublin until mid-March, but it impelled Ormond and the Confederate Council to reach a compromise, and a treaty was signed on 28 March. Subterfuge and deceit reigned for the next four months during which both sides agreed that the treaty should remain secret. Events during those months caused it to unravel. The fall of Chester made it seem pointless to try to ship troops to England. The seizure of Bunratty Castle in Munster by Protestant forces loyal to Inchiquin provided additional justification for keeping the troops in Ireland. Ormond's refusal to publish the religious articles of the treaty was a severe embarrassment to the peace faction led by the Marquess of Clanricarde, Viscount Mountgarret (president of the supreme council), and Viscount Muskerry. Seeing the weakness of their position Rinuccini went on the offensive, and laid down that rather than continuing to treat with Ormond and a defeated king, who was known to be negotiating with the covenanting Scots, they should now undertake the complete conquest of Ireland with their own forces. As Ó Shiocrú points out, this was not an extremist position, but the fruit of a pragmatic assessment of the geopolitical situation at that moment in the three Stuart kingdoms.[49] The Confederation already controlled most of the country. It ought to have been possible, with a little papal money, to make a coordinated effort to oust the Protestant parliamentarians under Inchiquin around Cork, the Protestant royalists under Ormond around Dublin, and the much

[48] CJ, Vol. 4, 409; SHS, The Diplomatic Correspondence of Jean de Montereul and the Brothers de Bellieure . . . 1645–48, Vol. 1, 114–15.
[49] Ó Shiocrú, Confederate Ireland, 107.

MAP 11 *Ireland, showing Confederate and Protestant territory*

Adapted from Gentles, Ian, *The New Model Army: In England, Scotland and Ireland, 1645–1653* (Blackwell Publishers, 1991)

enfeebled Scots Covenanters under Robert Monro, together with the small Laggan army of British Protestants in north-eastern and north-western Ulster respectively. But coordinated action was difficult in an organization whose members were so deeply divided on political and ecclesiological issues, and in which there was so much ingrained suspicion between the Ulster exiles under the leadership of O'Neill and the Leinster and Ulster Old English under Preston and Castlehaven. Another obstacle was the generals' egos. Both Preston and O'Neill were resentful that Castlehaven, a soldier inferior to both of them, had been made commander-in-chief of the Confederate army, but they could not get along with each other either. In any event, the attempt to cooperate in the summer of 1644 had been such a dismal failure that no one was keen to repeat the experiment.

Benburb

What Rinuccini then decided to do was put his eggs into two baskets: Preston's and O'Neill's. He gave twice as much to Preston as to O'Neill, but it was the latter investment that yielded the better dividend. Preston took Roscommon in Connacht, but did not attack Sligo as he was meant to. O'Neill by contrast, used the nuncio's money to put seven infantry regiments into the field for an extended campaign into eastern Ulster. The objective was to defeat Monro's Scots and capture a much-needed seaport, whether Belfast or Carrickfergus. On 5 June O'Neill stopped Monro's southward march at Benburb, a few miles north-west of Armagh. Monro's army, though enfeebled both in numbers and from lack of food, still wanted a trial of arms. The 3,500 Scots were fortunate in being bolstered by 2,000 soldiers from the British settler army in western Ulster. O'Neill, with the professionalism of a gifted and experienced infantry commander, drew up his troops where rough ground and furze bushes would hamper the attackers. They also had the benefit of confident exhortations from their priests who let them know that they were fighting for a cause greater than themselves – the survival of the Celtic race and their Catholic faith. The battle did not start until the late afternoon, and O'Neill's men held off the Scottish onslaught for over two hours. Then, with Monro's men suffering from exhaustion and thirst, and disorganized from their repeated assaults, O'Neill launched a counter-stroke with a fresh infantry regiment. The Scots were taken by surprise; the horse fled, and the infantry quickly followed their example. O'Neill's men took off in hot pursuit, and cut down their enemies without mercy. The body count was almost 3,000: over 1,800 Scots and 1,000 of the settler army lay dead. The Irish also captured significant quantities of ammunition and weaponry, which further improved their logistical position. The Scottish army, while not wiped out, was permanently crippled. It no longer had the capacity to launch an offensive campaign. The only Protestant force in Ulster strong enough to do that was the Laggan army of Sir Robert and Sir William Stewart. When the news reached Limerick, the nuncio led the whole population in singing a *Te Deum* of gratitude for the victory.

To press home the victory O'Neill ought to have continued marching north and stormed the Protestant garrison at Belfast. He had two free months in which to do it. Professional experience in the Netherlands, however, had taught him to be sparing of the lives of his men. In August he received an urgent message from Rinucinni to bring his troops south to Kilkenny to strengthen the nuncio's arm in his political struggle with the members of the Confederate Supreme Council. Obediently O'Neill led his army out of Ulster without reaping the full political or even military fruits of his one major victory in the Irish civil war.[50]

The reason for Rinuccini's urgent call for help was that the argument over the peace treaty with Ormond, which had been simmering for months, had now reached a crisis. In February the nuncio had got the supreme council to agree to postpone the treaty with Ormond until May. When he learned that the representatives of the Council had signed the treaty on 28 March, without the religious concessions deemed essential by the clergy, he was furious. The total collapse of the royalist cause in England made the treaty seem irrelevant. It was now pointless to send Confederate troops to help a king who did not possess an inch of territory on which to receive them. Secondly, what was the point in recognizing the authority of that king's lord lieutenant, when he had so little to offer? The king's defeat in England, combined with O'Neill's victory at Benburb, and Preston's capture of Bunratty, as well as the capture of Roscommon, added cogency to the nuncio's call for a complete conquest of the kingdom and the establishment of an independent Catholic state. The clergy were completely behind him, as was the leading general, Owen Roe O'Neill and to a lesser extent, Thomas Preston.

Yet by the beginning of August both Ormond and the Confederate Supreme Council had published the treaty. Not one of its 30 articles addressed the religious issue. The Confederate negotiators had been able to extract nothing more from Ormond than private assurances of toleration

---

[50] Wheeler, *Cromwell in Ireland*, 28.

for Catholics. Regarding the franchise, Catholics would apparently be permitted to vote provided they had been freeholders prior to the revolt of 1641. They would effectively be denied control of parliament. On the other hand there were a number of genuine concessions that had particular appeal for the Catholic Old English: an act of oblivion (except for particularly 'barbarous' crimes) for the revolt and subsequent civil war, security of tenure for Catholic landowners through a confirmation of the Graces of 1628, a reversal of Strafford's land confiscations, permission for Catholics to erect schools, a university and inns of court. But leading Confederate commanders, Preston and O'Neill were pointedly left out of the military structure of the new Ireland. Nor was there any guarantee of the right of Catholics to practise their religion publicly. For the moderate majority on the Supreme Council this had not been a stumbling block. To be allowed quietly to practise their creed without persecution was all they wanted. For Rinuccini and the clergy this willingness to accept informal assurances about religion after four years of war was intolerable. The cathedrals and parish churches, and the lands that went with them, had to be returned. Catholicism had to become the public, dominant religion of the nation. For Rinuccini it was a question of *splendore*, or public spectacle, which for him was a vital instrument of evangelism. *Splendore* meant processions through the streets, music, magnificent celebrations of the mass, the public washing of poor men's feet on the day before Good Friday by members of the hierarchy (himself included).[51]

Rinuccini now brought out his heavy artillery. On 12 August the ecclesiastical congregation of Ireland, meeting at Waterford, unanimously declared that the Ormond peace treaty, because of its lack of religious concessions, violated the oath of association. On 1 September he published a decree of excommunication against all who supported the treaty. Moderate members of the peace faction such as Patrick Darcy the lord chancellor and Nicholas Plunkett, chairman of the general assembly immediately fell into line, and crossed into the nuncio's camp. Preston's and O'Neill's rejection of the treaty completed the disintegration of the peace faction's authority. On 15 September the clergy ordered the leading proponents of the Ormond peace – men such as Muskerry, Fennell and Bellings – imprisoned. On 26 September they dismissed the existing Confederate government and established a new 17-member general council, subject to the later approval of the assembly.

[51] Ó hAnnracháin, *Catholic Reformation in Ireland*, 247–9.

Having carried all before him politically Rinuccini now turned his attention once more to military affairs and began to organize the conquest of Dublin.

Between 1644 and 1646 events in the three kingdoms had become increasingly tightly knit. In England both the parliamentary Junto at Westminster and the king had invited outside forces to invade the country on their behalf. For the Junto the measure had been a brilliant success, as the Scottish army made the critical contribution to the greatest battle of the English Civil War (Marston Moor, 2 July 1644). After that epochal event, however, their performance became lacklustre. For their part the Irish sent the king barely 9,000 troops, less than half the number they had promised, and their presence on English soil did little or no good for the royalist cause. The reorganization of England's war against the king under the banner of Sir Thomas Fairfax's New Model Army, backed by the newly emergent Independent party in the two houses, ensured the military collapse of Charles's cause in England. The royalist collapse had a knock-on effect in the other two kingdoms. The covenanting armies in Ireland and England, seeing their services no longer required, returned (in large part) to Scotland, where they made short work of Montrose, MacColla and the royalists. In Ireland the effect was quite different. The papal nuncio Rinuccini, perceiving more clear-sightedly than most that a militarily impotent king of England had virtually no negotiating power in Ireland, prevailed upon the Catholic Irish to make the conquest of their own country and the expulsion of foreign, Protestant elements their sole objective. The next 18 months would witness the frustration of Rinuccini's vision for Ireland, the re-alignment of the Covenanters' political loyalties towards the king, and the persistence of Scottish efforts to dominate the politics of England.

CHAPTER 10

The wars carried on by other means: the political struggles of 1646–48

The king had surrendered, fled his Oxford headquarters, and instructed the commanders of his remaining garrisons to throw in the sponge. The next 18 months would witness intense struggles in Westminster, Edinburgh, Kilkenny and Dublin that would effect political upheavals in all three kingdoms and culminate in the outbreak of renewed warfare among a profoundly altered constellation of forces. Never far from the centre of all these struggles was the figure of the king, who resorted to one subterfuge after another, as he strove to play off different factions in each kingdom, at the same time angling for aid from France and the papacy in his effort to wriggle free of his captors.

At Westminster the myriad items of unfinished business jostling for attention, as well as Charles's reluctance to recognize that his defeat on the battlefield required substantive concessions at the bargaining table, soon eclipsed any triumphalism over the ending of the war. Expressions of gratitude towards the New Model Army for its blaze of victories were few and far between. As early as January 1646 there had been sharp disagreement between the Essex-dominated Lords and the Vane-and-St John-dominated Commons over the ordinance to prolong the existence of the Committee for the Army and the treasurers at war, two institutions indispensable to the survival of the New Model. Not long afterwards the Presbyterian minister Thomas Edwardes gave vent to the fears of many when he published the first two installments of a three-volume work entitled *Gangraena*, a scurrilous catalogue of the heretical beliefs and practices of religious separatists. From the outset Edwardes took the New Model Army to be the chief agent in the spread of the separatist infection. His writings served to widen the distrust between the army and parliamentary Presbyterians.[1] In May, on the eve of Oxford's surrender the London Common Council, egged on by Essex's party and the Sion House conclave among the London Presbyterian clergy, addressed a Remonstrance to parliament calling for measures to check the growth of sectarianism and schism.[2] While warmly praising the Scots army's contribution to the defeat of the king they were silent about the New Model. Another sign of their growing wariness towards the army was the demand that the City should resume control of its own militia. In July the House of Lords ordered that the covenant be imposed throughout the army, and the ban on lay preaching enforced. The pro-army majority in the Commons blocked the initiative. Essex's party did not give up easily, and the conflict simmered throughout the summer. The Essex interest in both houses was encouraged to stay on the offensive by growing popular vexation over high taxes combined with the poor harvest of 1646, and a growing conviction that it was high time something was done about Ireland. No one denied the urgency of parliament's shedding some of its financial burdens; the argument now centred on which units should be disbanded first, and who should be sent to Ireland. At this juncture the Presbyterian peace forces were dealt a major setback. The Earl of Essex, after catching a chill while hunting in Windsor Forest, died on 14 September 1646. Parliament's first commander-in-chief, he had continued to wield enormous political influence even after being relieved of his military command in the spring of 1645. There was no one of Essex's stature to replace him, which made his death an 'irrecoverable loss' for the political Presbyterians.[3] His funeral, modelled on that of Prince Henry in 1612, was almost regal in its ostentatious pomp and extravagance. Leading Independents were conspicuously absent from the obsequies.[4]

Charles I and the Scots

Regardless of the fortunes of their English parliamentary Presbyterian friends, the Scots were determined to squeeze the maximum political advantage from their physical possession of the king. In fact talks had been

[1] Anne Hughes, *Gangraena and the Struggle for the English Revolution*, 106–7.
[2] For the role of Essex's parliamentary interest in the London Remonstrance of May 1646 see Juxon, *Journal*, 122.
[3] Juxon, *Journal*, 134–5, for the political implications of Essex's death.
[4] Ian Gentles. 'Political funerals during the English revolution', in Stephen Porter (ed.), *London and the Civil War*, 210–17. For a fuller treatment of Essex's funeral see John Adamson, *The Noble Revolt* (forthcoming).

going on between the king and senior officers of the covenanting army since as early as July 1645. The players included the Earl of Callander, an unscrupulous and ambitious politician, as well as Lord Lothian (a radical), and lords Sinclair and Montgomery. The inevitable rumours of a secret treaty between the Scots army and the king, though false, helped to poison relations between Covenanters and the English Independents. Matters were further complicated by French involvement. The new French agent in London, Montereul, pursued exploratory talks with Henrietta Maria, at the same time (July 1645) as he treated with the extreme Covenanter Lord Balmerino, one of the Scots commissioners in London. The agreement that the two men brokered was submitted to the queen, who in turn urged it on her husband. Charles would not hear of it. The great stumbling block, as always for Charles, was religion. He told his wife that to yield to the Scots on the Covenant or Presbyterian church government would be to 'go against my conscience and ruin my crown'.[5] Owing to parliament's mounting hostility to their army the Scots commissioners were more or less driven to continue trying for an understanding with the king. Not only was there growing parliamentary pressure for the Scots army to leave the country during 1646; there were also attempts to remove Robert Monro's army from Ulster.

The Scots' estrangement from the English parliament was compounded by the latter's resolute Erastianism – the policy of subordinating the Church to secular political authority. Equally disappointing to the Scots was parliament's ebbing interest in a confederal union between the two countries, which had been one of the cherished reasons for the Scots' initial participation in the English civil war. When the Scottish polemicist David Buchanan berated parliament for reneging on its commitment to closer union, the Commons ordered his pamphlet burnt by the common hangman. These stinging rebuffs drove the Scots closer to the king.

When Charles arrived at Montereul's lodging near Newark on 5 May 1646 he was already under the impression that he had an agreement with the Scots commissioners, brokered by the French resident. Lothian said that he knew of no such agreement, and Charles, having no written proof of his claims, found that he had been tricked by the French, whose main interest was in preserving a balance of forces in England and Scotland. He was now virtually a prisoner of the Covenanters. They for their part soon discovered that, far from restoring their political influence in London,

[5] Camden Society, *Charles I in 1646: Letters of King Charles the First to Queen Henrietta Maria*, ed. John Bruce, 23.

possession of the king only increased English fear and distrust towards them. This prompted them to take the precaution of removing Charles from Newark to their northern stronghold of Newcastle. There they worked on him to take the Covenant and accept a Presbyterian settlement. Leven's army had no interest in fighting for an uncovenanted king, and without Scottish military support the English Presbyterians would not join an alliance against the Independents and the New Model. Finding after repeated tries that the king was unbudgeable on religion, the Scots reluctantly concluded that he was more of a liability than an asset. They let parliament know that they were now ready to support the Newcastle Propositions, even though these did not meet Scottish expectations on religion. They were also willing to hand over the king and withdraw their army from England as soon as they were reimbursed for its expenses. Such was the policy of Argyll and the radical majority in the Scottish parliament. For the moment Argyll's political dominance was secure, but Hamilton, after his release in April (the king had imprisoned him for several months on suspicion of plotting with the enemy), at once began challenging it. Fearing that the army, once back in Scotland, would merely serve Argyll's interests, Hamilton tried to play the religious card, arguing before the Scottish parliament that the army should remain in England as a way of enforcing England's adherence to the Covenant. It should not leave the southern kingdom until religion was fully reformed there to Scotland's satisfaction. His hope was that the army might be used to protect the king against the Independents. All the while he was putting together a party of nobles and lairds who were prepared to fight for the king without forcing his conscience.[6] By 15 December his patient politicking appeared to pay off when Scotland's 'grand committee,'[7] the Committee for Common Burdens, declared itself in support of monarchical government and Charles's right to travel freely to London. However, the following day Argyll struck back with freshly mobilized support from among the gentry and burgesses in parliament, and a carefully orchestrated intervention from the Kirk. The bottom line for the Kirk was that the king must subscribe to the Covenant before there could be any alliance with him, or before he could be readmitted to Scotland. After this intervention the majority on the committee swung behind Argyll, and voted that the king must also accept the Newcastle Propositions if he wanted Scotland to do anything to help him. For the time being this put an end to Charles's negotiations with the Scots.

[6] Scott, *Politics and* War, 125; Woolrych, *Britain in Revolution*, 343.
[7] Quoted in Young, *Scottish Parliament*, 165.

His position on religion had become if anything more rigid than it had been half a year before.[8]

Ireland: the Ormond Peace and Rinuccini

While active warfare had stopped in England and Scotland, in Ireland it was going on in the traditional way. In the late summer of 1646, following O'Neill's shining victory at Benburb, Rinuccini began organizing the conquest of Dublin. The command of this risky undertaking ought to have been entrusted to O'Neill, but could not be because Preston's officers and men refused to recognize O'Neill's authority. So the two generals set off to besiege the capital, each leading his army on a separate route, and neither communicating with the other. Preston behaved duplicitously, corresponding secretly with Ormond during the very weeks when he was approaching Dublin. The Marquess of Clanricarde also sowed uncertainty among Confederate ranks by promoting his own scheme for a Confederate–royalist alliance, including the appointment of a Catholic lieutenant-general – himself. Plagued by division and mutual suspicion, the campaign against Dublin failed utterly. The arrival of a parliamentary fleet in Dublin Bay in November destroyed any chance of a successful conclusion to the siege, or of a treaty with Ormond. The lord lieutenant now turned his energies to making an accommodation with the victorious English parliament.

England: The Newcastle Propositions

In England in the autumn of 1646 members of both Houses bent their energies to negotiating a settlement with the king, overlooking for the moment the fact that the Scots controlled his person. The Newcastle Propositions, as they came to be known, leaned heavily towards the views and prejudices of the Independents, who were resolved never again to allow Charles to wield the power of the sword. There was a nod in the direction of Scottish sensibilities in the demand that the king swear the covenant, abolish the bishops, and accept whatever other religious reforms the two nations should agree upon. Catholicism was to be eradicated from

---

[8] As he confided to the French resident in London, Bellièvre, he was more convinced with every passing day 'that he committed a great sin when he abolished, seven years ago, the Scottish bishops and established Presbyterianism in their place', and that he was now being justly punished for this sin: SHS, Vol. 1, 364.

both kingdoms through a system of fines and penalties, and the compulsory education of Catholic children by Protestant teachers. When it came to the army and navy, the king was to surrender his authority to parliament, not for seven years, as in the Uxbridge propositions, but in perpetuity. The Scots' English allies at Westminster got this changed to 20 years, which was not a great concession on the part of the Independents, since 20 years was reckoned to be the remainder of Charles's life. Thirdly, all titles the king had created since January 1642 were to be voided, and the list of royalists exempted from pardon or targeted for the confiscation of their estates was made even longer than before. Finally, the king was to annul his Cessation of arms with the Irish, and the war in that kingdom was to be resumed under Westminster's direction. The Scots were to be excluded from any role in the war in Ireland, despite the presence of Monro's army in Ulster. At heart the Newcastle Propositions were a partisan Independent device to cut the confederal knot between Scotland and England.[9]

Charles, still clutching the hope that the French, the Irish and the Highlanders would come to his rescue, refused to abandon the Church, his crown and his friends. In rejecting Presbyterianism he was repudiating the advice of the majority of his own councillors, the French agent and his wife. He cherished the bishops, not just because they were divinely sanctified channels of grace, but also because they were a strong bulwark of monarchy. He never forgot his father's dictum: 'no bishop, no king'. Or, as he wrote to his sceptical councillors, 'people are governed by pulpits more than the sword in times of peace'; and again, 'religion is the only firm foundation of all power; that cast loose or depraved, no government can be stable. For where was there ever obedience where religion did not teach it?'[10]

Charles strung out the negotiations as long as he could, hoping for something to turn up. The Scots, tiring of the negotiating process, acutely conscious of their unpopularity in the north of England, and having their own agenda to pursue, decided to hand back the king and pull their troops out of England, on condition that parliament recoup the expenses they had run up over the preceding two-and-a-half years. After a good deal of haggling they lowered their demand from £1.3 million to £400,000, the first half to be paid before they left England. At the end of the day Argyll's

---

[9] David Scott, 'The "northern gentlemen", the parliamentary Independents, and Anglo-Scottish relations in the Long Parliament', *HJ*, 42 (1999), 365–70.

[10] *CSP*, Vol. 2, 243, 248 (Charles I to Jermyn, Culpeper and Ashburnham, 22 July, 19 August 1646).

radical party and the Kirk had prevailed: preserving the English alliance was of greater importance than upholding the rights of a king they could not trust. There is also evidence that Argyll had given up the dream of a confederal union. According to Clement Walker he abandoned the Westminster Presbyterians and threw in his lot with 'the Independent Junto', the aim being to win complete political independence for Scotland.

How was £200,000 to be raised from a bare and exhausted English treasury? The Independents decided to kill two birds with one stone. Without waiting for Charles's final answer to the Newcastle Propositions they hurried through an ordinance for the abolition of bishops, bludgeoning the Essex peers into submission along the way. They then rammed through a second ordinance to borrow money on the security of these bishops' lands and the excise. Those countless people who had already lent money to parliament on the public faith would, if they advanced the same sum again, receive a new bill for twice the original sum plus interest, and have first crack at the bishops' lands when they came onto the market. This fiscal innovation, known as doubling, would be used repeatedly in the sale of confiscated lands throughout the interregnum. People scrambled to double their previously worthless public faith bills, and it took a scant eight days to raise the funds to pay the Scots their first installment.[11] It then took until 11 February 1647 for Major-General Skippon to supervise the transport of the money to Newcastle, on which day the Scots handed over the king and exited the country.

Ireland

Ormond surrenders Dublin

With the failure of Rinuccini's scheme for the military conquest of Ireland, the Confederacy was in danger of collapse. To avoid this eventuality the nuncio reluctantly agreed to the release of the imprisoned councillors, and to the calling of a new general assembly. The assembly met in January 1647 and on 2 February formally and overwhelmingly rejected the Ormond Peace of the previous summer. It also accepted a new oath of association containing four amendments: that in any future agreement with Ormond:

---

[11] Ian Gentles, 'The sales of bishops' lands in the English Revolution, 1646–1660', *EHR*, 95 (1980), 574–5, 591.

1 There should be free and public exercise of the Catholic religion as in the time of Henry VII.

2 The Catholic clergy should have their jurisdiction, privileges and immunities as they had then enjoyed them.

3 All penal laws since 1538 should be repealed.

4 The Catholic clergy should have their churches on the same basis as the Protestants had held them on 1 October 1641, though with protection for Catholic owners of monastic and other church lands.

On 17 March a new supreme council was chosen, most of whose members were acceptable to Rinuccini. A shaky *modus vivendi* had been worked out between the clerical and peace parties. It was to be sorely tested in the summer ahead.

In Dublin Ormond was caught in a vice, squeezed on one side by the Confederates to re-open the treaty and grant favourable terms, and on the other by the Westminster parliament which was demanding that he hand over Dublin immediately and resign the lord lieutenancy. There was no question which side had the greater clout, and on 6 February Ormond secretly agreed to transfer Dublin to the forces of parliament. The reality of English power became palpable on 7 June 1647 when an army of 2,000 landed under the command of Colonel Michael Jones. Ormond topped that up by handing over the 3,000 foot of the Dublin garrison. A further 6,500 troops were promised from England. Twelve days later Ormond signed a treaty with the parliamentary commissioners; on 28 July he vacated Dublin Castle and sailed for England.

In Michael Jones parliament had at last discovered a defender of the Protestant interest in Ireland who was also an energetic soldier of first-class talent. The scion of a prominent Irish Protestant family, Jones had crossed over to England in 1644 to serve as an officer in the parliamentary army. He soon demonstrated his ability as he fought with distinction against the royalist forces in Wales and Cheshire, rising to the rank of colonel. In February 1646 he was appointed governor of Chester. Within less than two months of his arrival in Dublin Jones had consolidated his forces with the garrisons in Drogheda and southern Ulster, producing a total army of over 5,000 foot and 1,500 horse. His next objective was to expand parliament's power into the whole province of Leinster. The main obstacle was Thomas Preston's reasonably

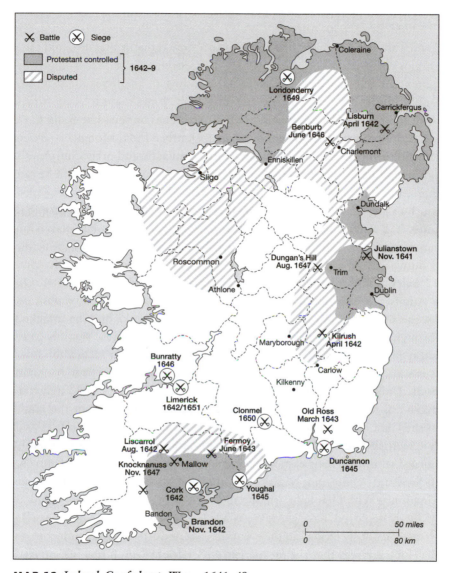

MAP 12 *Ireland: Confederate Wars, 1641–49*

Adapted from Young, John (ed.), *Ireland: Confederate & Protestant Territory: Celtic Dimensions of the British Civil Wars* (John Donald, 1997)

well-trained, well-paid and well-equipped Confederate army of Leinster. The two armies had their first encounter near Naas in late July. Preston's artillery fired two cannon shots, at which Jones's men fled in disorder back to the safety of Dublin.

Dungan's Hill[12]

Exhilarated by his minor triumph, Preston now thought that he could take Dublin while Jones was preoccupied with relieving Trim. Accordingly, he marched 5,000 troops south of Trim intending to cut Jones off from his Dublin supply base. But he was too impatient. Jones's south Ulster forces were soon due to depart; had he waited until that happened he could have faced the parliamentary general on much better terms. Moreover, Owen Roe O'Neill had informed Preston of the British forces' arrival in Jones's camp, and had offered help, counselling Preston not to move until he got there. Instead Preston broke camp at Portlester on 7 August and headed south-east towards Maynooth and Dublin, tempted by the intelligence that Jones had left behind only a skeleton garrison in Dublin. His plan soon came unstuck. Encumbered by the artillery train that was indispensable if he was to breach the walls of Dublin, he could march no more than 12 miles a day. Jones was soon on his tail and marching much faster. On 8 August Preston found himself obliged to take up a defensive position on the high ground of Dungan's Hill. His army could only be attacked through a narrow lane lined with impenetrable hedges, but his very impregnability circumscribed his own mobility. A further tactical blunder was stationing his 500-strong regiment of Redshanks away from his main body. Unlike the rest of Preston's army, which was mostly Old English in make-up, the Redshanks, under Glengarry, were drawn from the lands of the Clan MacDonald – County Antrim in Ulster, the Western Isles and the Scottish Highlands. They had a formidable reputation, most recently burnished during their exploits in the service of MacColla and Montrose in Scotland. Quite simply they were the best shock infantry in the three kingdoms. With their light armour and their celebrated spirit they could, if properly deployed, have given Preston the force and mobility he otherwise so conspicuously lacked. In the event they were wasted. A final unfortunate development was that the inexperienced Viscount Dillon had just arrived in camp with 300 horse. In deference to Dillon's aristocratic rank Preston gave him overall command of the three horse regiments, displacing the experienced and competent Mac Thomas.

Before Preston could bring these regiments through the bottleneck of the hedge-flanked road Jones hurled his own cavalry against him. Trapped by the enemy in front and their own comrades pressing against them from the rear, Preston's cavalry were mercilessly cut down. Only the prompt

---

[12] The best account of the battle is Pádraig Lenihan, 'The Leinster army and the battle of Dungan's Hill, 1647', *Irish Sword*, 18 (1991), 139–53.

action of their own foot soldiers behind the hedges, who opened a gap, enabled them to pour through to the relative safety of a cornfield. In their haste to save their skins they did not stop to regroup, but almost trampled the infantry and threw the whole army into a panic.[13]

On the other side of the battlefield Glengarry's Redshanks resisted the charge of a mixed force of English foot and horse, 'causing the bold enemy to stagger'.[14] Three times they did this, at which point Jones, seeing that there was no one to relieve them, pitted his whole army against the Redshanks. Refusing to retreat, all but 100 of the 800 were cut down where they stood. The rest of the infantry, now completely demoralized by the flight of the cavalry, and the fate of the Redshanks, retreated to a small bog, where they surrendered. Some of them were taken to Colonel Jones, who granted them quarter. The remaining 3,000, who surrendered to Colonel Henry Tichborne and Colonel John Moore, were put to the sword. In the restrained words of Pádraig Lenihan, the massacre 'was an act of unusual severity, even by the rough and ready standards of the time'.[15] By comparison, when Ormond and the Confederates had fought each other they customarily granted quarter to soldiers who surrendered. This is largely explicable by the absence of profound ideological divisions between the two sides. The army of Michael Jones, on the other hand, represented the radical, Independent wing of armed, triumphant, English Puritanism. Dungan's Hill was the graveyard of the Old English army of Leinster. Their massacre gave a foretaste of things to come.

When several hundred prisoners are taken into account, no more than 1,000 of Preston's soldiers escaped the carnage. The English lost about 60 men. Yet Jones was not able to press home his victory. Short of money, he had no option but to release his British auxiliaries. The Supreme Council of the Confederate Association recalled O'Neill and placed the Leinster horse at his disposal. His adoption of a scorched earth policy preoccupied the English so much that they were unable to take the offensive. Nevertheless, Dungan Hill (9 August) was a decisive turning point in the Irish civil war.

Knocknanuss

The other Old English army was that of Theobald, Lord Taaffe in Munster. Taaffe had long been accused by clericalists of having divided

[13] Carte, *Life*, Vol. 3, 319.
[14] Gilbert, *Contemp. Hist.*, Vol. 1, 155.
[15] Lenihan, 'Dungan's Hill, 1647', 151.

loyalties or worse. In support of their suspicion we have evidence that he was involved in a scheme by George Lord Digby to recruit Confederate soldiers from the Leinster and Munster armies for the French service.[16] However, so great was the mounting danger from Inchiquin that the Supreme Council threatened to dismiss Taaffe if he did not fight him. Inchiquin had already taken Dunvargan in May, putting Waterford under threat. Then on 14 September he stormed and sacked Cashel. His brutality at Cashel earned him the tag 'Murrough the Burner'. To avoid further humiliation to the Catholic cause Taaffe was shamed into giving battle on 13 November at Knocknanuss, near Mallow, County Cork. His numbers were greater than Inchiquin's, but there was no unity among them, with disparate infantry contingents from Munster, Taaffe's native Connacht, and Redshanks from western Scotland under Alasdair MacColla. It did not help matters that he deployed his 6,000 infantry in separate formations with a hill between them so that they lost sight of one another. MacColla, recently back from Scotland, got things off to a good start by charging with his Redshanks on the right, breaking the opposing wing and overrunning Inchiquin's artillery lines and baggage train. Instead of supporting MacColla's success, Taaffe's Munster contingent fired a single volley at their attackers, then broke and ran. Repeated cavalry charges by Inchiquin against the flank of the remaining infantry, together with the steady fire of two field guns, finally routed the remainder of the army. MacColla was felled where he stood, fighting with his men. Again no quarter was given, and almost as many prisoners were slaughtered as at Dungan's Hill. Inchiquin went on to capture all the major Munster towns except Waterford, Limerick and Clonmel. As Ó Siochrú points out, the disaster was the combined product of Taaffe's sheer incompetence and Inchiquin's considerable military talent.[17] Only the outbreak of the second civil war in England postponed the complete overrunning of Catholic Ireland by the parliamentary forces. There was to be little further English aid for over a year, while the scorched earth practices of O'Neill's army denied the parliamentarians supplies from their hinterland.

Nothing, however, could alter the fact that two of the three Confederate armies, both chiefly Old English in composition, had been shattered. Following Dungan's Hill O'Neill's army had to be called in to protect Leinster. The news of Knocknanuss threw the recently convened

[16] *Two Letters of the Lord Digby to the Lord Taaffe* (1647), BL. Thomason, E419/8, 6–8.
[17] Ó Siochrú, *Confederate Ireland*, 158.

assembly at Kilkenny into disarray, and voices were heard blaming the Confederates' humiliations on the uncompromising policies of Rinuccini. Yet such was the hostility towards the Old English within the Association that according to Ormond the 'violent and incorrigible party of . . . the nuncio, clergy, and Owen O'Neill' showed signs of being pleased with the result.[18] In effect the twin disasters of Dungan's Hill and Knocknanuss shifted the balance of power within the association decisively in the direction of O'Neill and the clerical party. The moderate, Old-English-dominated Supreme Council was thoroughly disheartened by the defeats, and moved, the following year, to come once again to an understanding with Ormond in mutual defence against revolutionary Puritanism. The assembly dissolved itself on Christmas Eve 1647, leaving a divided council and clergy to work out detailed instructions for aid-seeking embassies to France, Rome and Spain.

England

The New Model Army and the Levellers

The departure of the Scots from England the previous February, though it had been engineered by the Independents, had the effect of removing the last remaining reason for keeping the New Model Army in existence. For over half a year many people had been asking with mounting impatience why there was still a standing army in England when there was no longer a war for it to fight. The army's backers in parliament had managed to protect the New Model by insisting that the provincial armies should be disbanded first, and that the Scots must leave English soil before Fairfax's army was dismantled. Their first target was Colonel Edward Massie's Western Brigade, some 2,500 strong. No love had been lost between the New Model and Massie since the summer of 1645 when he felt that he had been unfairly used during the western campaign. The Essex–Holles faction had tried to take the brigade under its wing, expand it into a full-scale army, and thereby create a counterweight to the New Model. In spite of much behind-the-scenes lobbying the scheme came to nothing. The Commons Independents at length carried a motion, in the teeth of the Presbyterian majority in the Lords, to disband the brigade completely. The final insult was administered when New Model regiments under

---

[18] Carte, *Life*, Vol. 6, 547.

Fairfax and Ireton supervised the disbandment without bloodshed on the day before the Earl of Essex's interment (22 October 1646).[19]

In London on the other hand, the City's governors kept up their attack on the New Model for spreading sectarianism and anarchy. In the December 1646 municipal elections the army's supporters went down to defeat, making for a Common Council dominated by Presbyterians. Encouraged by this evidence of a sea change in London public opinion, the Presbyterian majority in the Lords rejected the Independent-sponsored ordinances for the continuance of the Committee for the Army, and the six-month extension of the assessment for the army's pay. The publication of Joshua Sprigge's panegyric to the exploits of the New Model Army, *Anglia Rediviva*, early in 1647, did nothing to stem the tide of popular hostility towards the army. Commercially the book was a flop, because most Londoners did not care to hear its message.[20]

The unfinished business of Ireland was now rising closer to the top of the parliamentary agenda. Powerful interests were calling for the kingdom's immediate subjugation and colonization. Chief among them were the Adventurers, who had advanced money in 1642 and 1643 for the suppression of the rebellion. There were also the Scots who had stationed and maintained an army of up to 10,000 in the province of Ulster for over four years. Their views, and those of other enemies of international popery were eloquently represented in Sir John Temple's influential publication of 1646, *The Irish Rebellion*.[21] Yet at the same time there were elements of the public who were rather less enthusiastic about the policy of Irish conquest. Popular opinion, for all its horror at the alleged atrocities of 1641–42, was dismayed at the prospect of another major war and its concomitant, high taxes. Relations between parliament and the Adventurers had already cooled in the summer of 1645 when parliament rejected out of hand the proposal for a massive extension of land confiscations. A third factor was that Ormond had shrewdly kept open the lines of communication with the Essex–Holles interest in parliament through the Marquess of

---

[19] Juxon, *Journal*, 138. The disbanding of the brigade, and the politics surrounding it, are clearly set out in Evans, 'Civil war career of Major-General Edward Massey', (PhD thesis, University of London), 194–5, 210–11.

[20] The tireless London book collector George Thomason did not bother to acquire a copy. Sales were so poor that the army had to bail out the printer, John Partridge, to the tune of £150 'for the losses he sustained by *Anglia Rediviva*': Chequers MS 782, fo. 42v.

[21] Temple was a spokesman for the Lisle Independent interest, but his optic on Irish popery was shared by Presbyterians and Scots if not by the followers of Ormond.

Clanricarde, Essex's half-brother who was also a Catholic Old-English peer and a loyal Ormondist.

Militating against the policy of moderation towards Ireland was the current ascendancy of the Independent party, borne aloft by the stunning successes of its military arm, the New Model Army. The strategy actually adopted at Westminster during the winter of 1646–47 was the one advocated by John Temple and ultimately realized in the Cromwellian conquest of 1649–50. Enactment of the strategy was entrusted in the first instance to Philip Sidney, Viscount Lisle, son of the Earl of Leicester and nephew of the Earl of Northumberland. He was a man closely identified with the anti-Scottish party at Westminster and with the political Independents – Northumberland, Saye, Wharton, St John, Vane, Sir John Evelyn of Wiltshire and the leading officers of the New Model. Nominated by the Commons as lord lieutenant in January 1646, he did not actually reach Ireland until February 1647. He was expected to have overall command of the expeditionary force drawn from the ranks of the New Model. The Scots would be excluded from any further role in the reconquest of Ireland, as the Newcastle Propositions firmly underlined in July 1646. The policy of restricting prosecution of the Irish war exclusively to the English parliament would be reaffirmed in the army's Heads of Proposals when they were laid before the king a year later.[22]

In early 1647, however, the Presbyterian peace faction had temporarily recovered its ascendancy in both houses of parliament, thanks to general war-weariness and dismay at the growth of religious sectarianism. Its leaders believed that they held the key to the two intractable problems of the day: Ireland and the New Model Army. On 18 February, after a gruelling, all-day debate, they carried a motion in the Commons stipulating that apart from garrison forces only 5,400 horse and 1,000 dragoons would be kept up in England. The infantry of the New Model Army would have the choice of going to Ireland or being disbanded. Resurrecting the principles of the Self-Denying Ordinance they also laid down that no member of the Commons should henceforth hold a military commission. Nor would there be exemptions any longer for army officers who were loath to swear the Solemn League and Covenant. Cromwell, Ireton, Harrison and Fleetwood were immediately affected by these motions. As the New Model

---

[22] See Patrick Little's valuable essay, 'The English parliament and the Irish constitution, 1641–9', in Ó Siochrú (ed.), *Kingdoms in Crisis*. However, I am not persuaded by his argument for 'the essential conservatism of parliament's attitude towards Ireland' (120).

Army faced imminent extinction, radical Independents in the metropolis, soon to be known as Levellers, tried to rally support for it. In their so-called Petition of Many Thousands they exhorted parliament not to 'lay by that strength which . . . hath hitherto made you powerful to all good works'. In a separate tract they described the New Model as 'a refuge pillar for the oppressed and distressed commons of England'.[23]

Within the army itself the rank and file were seized with paranoia towards the two houses. Their growing conviction was that only the army and a remnant of the civilian population were still adhering to God's ways, by which they meant taking a hard line against the king, suppressing popery and promoting ease for tender consciences. In an attempt to assuage their resentments the officers formulated a petition in February focusing on practical issues:

1 Full payment of pay arrears, in addition to regular pay until disbandment.

2 No conscription of enlisted soldiers for service outside the kingdom.

3 An act of parliament (sealed by the king) guaranteeing indemnity against prosecution for all acts of war.

Pay, conscription and indemnity: these would constitute the connecting thread of most army statements until the outbreak of the second civil war in 1648. Had the Presbyterian peace faction addressed these demands in a timely fashion and handled the soldiers with tact they might have achieved their goal of dissolving the New Model Army. As it was, tact was not their concern, nor were they willing to offer the army a fair deal. Convinced that they had the nation at their back they were confident that they could ride roughshod over the army's grievances with impunity. Their first impulse upon hearing of the officers' petition was to order it suppressed. When they learnt that their order was apparently being flouted they exploded with rage. On 29 March 1647 Denzell Holles scribbled a motion accusing the promoters of the petition of 'tending to put the army into a distemper and mutiny', and threatening to proceed against them 'as enemies to the state and disturbers of the public peace'. The motion passed in a thin house.[24]

[23] Don M. Wolfe (ed.), *Leveller Manifestoes of the Puritan Revolution*, 138; *A Warning for All the Counties of England* ([24 March] 1647), E381/13, 9.

[24] *CJ*, Vol. 6, 127; *Old Parliamentary History* – or, *The Parliamentary or Constitutional History of England* (hereafter *OPH*), Vol. 15, 344–5.

The Declaration of Dislike, as it came to be known, was the crossing of the Rubicon for Holles and the Presbyterian peace party. Their systematic hostility transmuted the army's already sharp political consciousness into revolutionary militancy. The Declaration of Dislike was added to the existing list of grievances. The label 'enemies of the state' was an attack on their honour. Denial of the right of petition was an intolerable restriction. At the same time they began talking to civilian sympathizers in the nascent London Leveller movement. A radical outgrowth of the Independent party, the Levellers were a movement of mainly urban radicals who advocated political and social reform. They attracted the label 'Leveller' because of the misperception that they favoured levelling social distinctions and abolishing private property. Their leading spokesman was John Lilburne, a soapboiler and gentleman's son from Durham. Some soldiers got hold of his pamphlets, and were heard quoting them as 'statute law'.[25]

Simultaneous with the confrontation between parliament and the New Model Army was the crisis affecting Viscount Lisle's lord lieutenancy in Ireland. From the province of Ulster came reports that Monro's Scottish army had declared for the king. In Munster Inchiquin was lobbying his friends in the Holles–Stapilton peace faction to blacken Lisle's reputation by portraying him as a religious radical. The aim was to scotch the renewal of his appointment, which expired on 15 April 1647. The campaign was surprisingly effective, owing in no small part to the dominance of Holles over the lower house. By the last week of March Lisle's allies had lost control of the Derby House Committee for Irish affairs. Its sittings abruptly ceased on 26 March, while the battle for control of the Irish campaign was fought out on the floor of the two houses. The rout of what Thomas Juxon called 'Northumberland's party' began at that time. Lisle was dismissed as lord lieutenant. The career soldier Colonel Michael Jones was nominated to replace Ormond as governor of Dublin. On 7 April the Derby House Committee was radically restructured to give a clear majority to the pro-Scottish, Presbyterian peace party led by the Earl of Warwick, Holles and Stapilton. The campaign against the Confederates would continue, but without the hostility to the Old English and to the Protestant Irish which had been the hallmark of Lisle's regime. It was a triumph for Inchiquin's Irish lobby at Westminster, but its sweetness would not be savoured for long.[26]

[25] HMC 29, *Thirteenth Report, Portland MSS*, Vol. 3, 156.
[26] This paragraph is based on John Adamson's pioneering essay, 'Strafford's ghost: The British context of Viscount Lisle's lieutenancy of Ireland', in Ohlmeyer, ed., *Ireland from Independence to Occupation*, 152–5.

The Presbyterian triumph was evanescent chiefly because of Holles's mishandling of the New Model Army. Rather than address the army's grievances he opted to build up a counter-force to overawe and if necessary destroy it. The first element in this counter-force was to be the trained bands of London. The power to nominate the City militia committee was handed back to the corporation, which immediately excluded radical Independents from its revamped committee. The second element in Holles's counter-force was to be the northern army, now under the command of Major-General Sedenham Poynts. He was instructed to draw it up in readiness to crush the New Model. The third element comprised those soldiers from the New Model who were willing to go to Ireland. The foot were quartered in strategic locations not far from the capital, while the horse, whose numbers had reached 400 by the beginning of June, were incorporated into the London trained bands. At the same time a committee of safety was set up to organize additional troops from the counties, and to mobilize the large number of reformados (disbanded, unpaid officers) swirling about the capital. Finally, as we shall see shortly, there were the Scots. It was hoped that they could be prevailed upon once again to march an army into England, this time to back the Presbyterians.

Holles's projected coalition had all the solidity of a house of playing cards, and it mirrored the fundamental lack of realism underlying his approach. When it came to political manoeuvre Saye and Sele, Vane and Cromwell easily outclassed Holles, Stapilton and Warwick. More important, the rank and file of the New Model did not stand idly by while their destruction was being plotted in parliament. Their next move came when the eight cavalry regiments stationed in East Anglia met together and elected two representatives – soon to be known as agitators – from each regiment. They denounced the design 'to ruin and break this army in pieces', demanded the redress of the army's grievances, and told Fairfax that their chief reason for taking up arms in the first place had been so that 'the meanest subject should fully enjoy his right, liberty and proprieties in all things'.[27] The officers had already published their own petition in which they too asserted that they had fought for 'the removal of every yoke from the people's necks'.[28]

The action of these cavalry regiments was quickly emulated throughout the army. By June the higher officers decided to canalize the energies of the

[27] *The Apologie of the Common Souldiers* (3 May 1647), E385/18, 2–4; *A Second Apologie of All the Private Souldiers* (1647), E385/18, 7–8.
[28] *The Petition and Vindication of the Officers . . . to the House of Commons* (27 Apr. 1647), E385/19, 1.

revolutionary rank and file into a General Council of the Army, consisting of four agitators – two officers and two privates – from every regiment, plus the general officers. The General Council met for the first time in July 1647 and was not dissolved until January 1648.[29] At the same time a printing press was purchased for the army and a team of writers enlisted to draft pamphlets that would argue the army's case before the public. Envoys were sent to forge links with other forces and 'well-affected friends' throughout the kingdom. There were many arguments over policy, but overall the higher officers worked in concert with the agitators during the late spring and summer of 1647.[30] Their energies were directed towards neutralizing the attempts of the Holles–Warwick pro-Scottish faction to divide and weaken the army. About 7 per cent of the officers and 4 per cent of the rank and file left the army or were driven out and replaced because of their Presbyterian sympathies. The men who were promoted to their places – men such as Harrison, Pride, Tomlinson, Goffe and John Cobbett – were of lower social status and politically more militant.

The most decisive of the army's moves to prevent its own extinction was the seizure of the king. Since being handed over by the Scots earlier in the year he had been held under army guard at Holdenby, Northamptonshire. At the end of May Cornet George Joyce of Fairfax's horse regiment came to Cromwell's house in Drury Lane and laid before him a plan to march to Holdenby and replace the guards under the Presbyterian Richard Graves with troops whose loyalty the Independents could count upon. Armed with Cromwell's blessing Joyce accomplished his mission without a hitch. To avoid arrest by Holles's party Cromwell fled London and took refuge with the army. Joyce, fearing that he and his men might be overpowered by a superior force, then took it upon himself to remove the king to a safer location. Charles acquiesced, and suggested that they make for Newmarket, because its air 'did very well agree with him', and doubtless too because it happened to be the site of army headquarters and of the army's forthcoming rendezvous.[31] When Joyce arrived with his royal prisoner Fairfax did not punish him as the parliamentary Presbyterians demanded, but he did take care to keep the king out of sight during the army rendezvous. Much later Fairfax would claim that he had

---

[29] The definitive account of the General Council and its role in the revolution is Austin Woolrych, *Soldiers and Statesmen: the General Council of the Army and its Debates, 1647–1648*.

[30] For a detailed analysis of the army's political activities in 1647 see Gentles, *NMA*, chs 6 and 7.

[31] Rushworth, *Hist. Coll.*, Vol. 6, 516.

been the helpless tool of political activists between 1647 and 1649, but his failure to resign as commander-in-chief, along with his many actions which forwarded the army's political agenda belie that claim.

Holles's anti-New Model coalition now rapidly began to unravel. Moderate forces in the City and parliament demanded conciliatory measures. The trained bands refused to obey their new Presbyterian officers. A party of New Model agitators journeyed to York, where they persuaded the northern army to arrest Major-General Poynts and throw in their lot with their southern comrades. Though strongly tempted to send the slimmed-down covenanting army south once again to assist the English Presbyterians against their Independent foes, the Committee of Estates held back. Scottish perception of their interests was becoming increasingly divergent from that of its erstwhile allies in England. As soon as they had turned over the king, and withdrawn their army north of the Tweed in February, the Scots could not agree on what to use it for. As leader of the conservatives and crypto-royalists Hamilton wanted it to become the core of a new force that would rush to the aid of Charles I. For public consumption he gave out that the army was needed to complete the reformation in England. Argyll, spokesman of the radicals, and close ally of the Kirk, worried about the pervasive signs of increasing royalism in Scotland, and therefore promoted the purging and refashioning of the army to make it more politically reliable. For public consumption he gave out that he wanted the army reduced in order to make it less of a burden to the people. Argyll won. The Scottish parliament voted that the army should be 'new modelled' into a leaner force of 1,200 horse, two companies of dragoons (200 in all), and 6,000 foot. The reliable Covenanter, Lieutenant-General David Leslie, was made commander-in-chief. Anyone suspected of royalist sympathies was frozen out. Argyll had forged himself a reliable military instrument. Just in the nick of time too, for in March 1647 the parliament dissolved itself. After fresh elections it would not meet again until February 1648.

A sign of political climate change in Scotland came with the selection of the new 76-member Committee of Estates that was to govern between parliaments. There was a small but decisive shift in the balance of power away from Argyll's radicals towards Hamilton's coalition of conservatives and pragmatic royalists. The most telling indication of this shift was the election of the notorious Earl of Traquair, a man whose name had long been anathema to the Covenanters. The scene was now set for a bitter power struggle between Argyll and Hamilton.[32] Before embarking on that struggle,

[32] Young, *Scottish Parliament*, 184–5.

however, Argyll lost no time in deploying his new-modelled army to clean out the last pockets of royalist rebellion in Scotland. In March he sent Leslie north against the Marquis of Huntly. The royalist castles in the north-east promptly surrendered, and all Irish soldiers found within them were put to the sword. Then, with the bubonic plague licking at their heels, Leslie and the army moved west to purge Campbell territory of its remaining rebels. At Kintyre on 24 May they scattered the rebel army. MacColla fled with his Irish troops to Islay leaving their Highland comrades to fend for themselves. About 300 Highlanders barricaded themselves in Dunaverty Castle. When they surrendered Leslie yielded to his soldiers' pressure for vengeance, and allowed the Highlanders to be massacred. He then cleared the remaining rebels out of Islay and Mull, plundering and massacring the Irish as he went. MacColla had already fled to Ireland, where he was killed not long afterwards at Knocknanuss. By October 1647 there were no enemies of the Covenant in arms in Scotland. Decimated by the plague, ravaged by the destruction of crops, livestock and buildings, bankrupted by its military interventions in the other two kingdoms, and weakened by incessant bloodletting, Scotland was in a state of utter physical and moral exhaustion. Small wonder that the Committee of Estates shrank at the thought of using its much diminished army to stir up once again the maelstrom of civil war in England.

The Estates were in any case stalemated in the summer of 1647. On the one hand the commissioners in London protested strenuously against the abduction of the king and made a commitment to rescue him. Under Lauderdale's inspiration the Earl of Dunfermline was despatched to France to urge Henrietta Maria to send the Prince of Wales to Scotland to lead an army into England on the king's behalf. There was only one drawback to the scheme: neither Hamilton nor Argyll would sign on. Argyll had no enthusiasm for helping the king, while Hamilton's fear was that the army, under Argyll's and Leslie's thumb, would merely try to impose the extreme covenanting programme on Charles if ever he fell into their hands. Hamilton's aim was to have Leslie's army disbanded or purged before giving any thought to launching an expedition against the king's English enemies. Besides, during the summer of 1647 the king was more interested in exploring what the New Model Army could do for him than in being rescued by the Scots.

The New Model Army's rendezvous at Newmarket on 4–5 June turned out to be an intoxicating experience of fraternal unity. Relieved that the higher officers had joined with them, the soldiers greeted Sir Thomas Fairfax with rapturous joy as he visited and addressed each regiment in turn. On the second day they all entered into a covenant to stick together until all their grievances had been redressed. The safety of the soldiers and the freeborn people of England would have to be guaranteed by a water-tight provision of indemnity, as well as the expulsion from power of those who had abused the army and endangered the kingdom. Judgment on these issues would be exercised by the General Council of the Army. The Solemn Engagement as this covenant was titled became the army's talis-man for the next two climactic years.

Between June and November there was close cooperation and unity of purpose between officers and rank and file. The general staff supplied the funds that supported the agitators in activities as diverse as the purchase of a printing press, the publication of pamphlets, travel, and the arrest of Major-General Poynts. On 14 June Fairfax issued the *Declaration or Representation of the Army* which justified the army's political mobiliza-tion on the grounds that 'we were not a mere mercenary army hired to serve any arbitrary power of a state, but called forth and conjured by the several declarations of parliament to the defence of our own and the people's just rights and liberties'.[33] The most likely author of these ringing words was Oliver Cromwell's son-in-law, Commissary-General Henry Ireton. The landless son of a Nottinghamshire gentleman, Ireton was a dedicated Puritan who had served in Essex's and Manchester's armies before being commissioned in the New Model. In 1643 he had met Oliver Cromwell, later marrying his daughter Bridget. Between 1647 and 1649 he would emerge as the army's chief theoretician, writer and political draftsman.

Agitators and general staff continued their collaboration in drawing up the articles of impeachment against 11 leading Presbyterian MPs who had campaigned to disband the army. The impeachment was a comprehensive indictment of the Presbyterian leadership for plotting a counter-revolution against the army and its Independent backers in both houses.[34] Before the MPs could be brought to trial they withdrew from the house and went into hiding.

Massie, Holles and other hard-line Presbyterians continued to pursue their counter-revolutionary schemes from their hiding places. They pinned their hopes on the City trained bands and the reformados from Massie's brigade who were still camped out near the houses of parliament. To counter this hostile activity Fairfax deployed his troops in an arc around London. When the General Council met for the first time at Reading on

[33] *The Army Book of Declarations* (1647), E409/25, 39.
[34] BL. Egerton MS 1048, fos. 51–80.

16 July the agitators pressed for a march on London to enforce the army's demands on parliament. They were particularly indignant about the continued imprisonment of John Lilburne, Richard Overton and other radical friends of the army.

The higher officers counselled caution, and tried to enlist the agitators' support for their draft settlement with the king, known as the Heads of the Proposals. Constituting the most interesting terms the king was ever offered, the document had been put together by Ireton in consultation with Lords Wharton and Saye in an effort to divert the king from a settlement with the Scots or English Presbyterians. It was dramatically more generous than the Newcastle Propositions of a year earlier. Parliament was to control the armed forces for 10 years instead of 20; it would nominate chief officers of state for 10 years instead of perpetuity; bishops, rather than being abolished, would merely lose their coercive power; the Book of Common Prayer would be permitted so long as its use remained voluntary; no more than five royalists would be excluded from pardon. But the army went far beyond the Newcastle Propositions in its ideas for parliamentary reform. Henceforth parliaments would be biennial, and the current one would be dissolved within a year. Seats would be redistributed strictly according to taxation. The burdens of the common people would be lightened by the abolition of the hated excise, the forest laws, trade monopolies and imprisonment for debt. Tax rates would be equalized. The people were also to enjoy the right of petition and the right not to incriminate themselves in criminal trials. These social reforms almost certainly reflected the influence of the Levellers on army thinking.

One reason for bending over backwards to be generous to the king was the army's awareness of the growing popular longing to have him back on the throne. If they could effect a rapprochement with Charles and escort him triumphantly to the capital the projected Presbyterian counter-revolution would collapse. When a high-level army delegation conferred with him on 28 July, however, they were met with 'sharp and bitter language'. Why did Charles turn so abruptly negative? Why did he recklessly cast aside his best-ever chance of a settlement? In part it was because he mistakenly thought that the army needed him more than he needed it. 'You cannot be without me: you will fall to ruin if I do not sustain you', he warned the officers.[35] Charles also, as always, had other cards up his sleeve. Through his wife he was already in talks with the Scots, and now that the war on the continent was at last drawing to a close, he was

---

[35] Edmund Ludlow, *Memoirs*, Vol. 1, 160.

confident that the long-awaited troops from France would soon be on their way. Nor had he given up on the Confederate Irish.

As the king strung the army along in unprofitable negotiations the counter-revolutionaries in London seized the initiative. What triggered their action was the Commons' appeasement of the army: on 22 July it had voted to return the London militia committee to the Independents who had controlled it before 4 May. When parliament assembled on Monday 26 July both houses were besieged by an angry crowd demanding the return of the militia to the Presbyterian committee. The Lords rebuffed a delegation of aldermen, who then went home, leaving the crowd to its own devices. A small group of extremists drawn from the Presbyterian clergy, militia officers and common councilmen then turned the demonstration into an attempted seizure of power. First the crowd invaded the lords' chamber, and forced the peers to recall the motion returning the London militia into Independent hands. Next they broke into the Commons and forced them to do the same. The lower house was subjected to the further humiliation of being kept in their places until they resolved that the king should immediately be brought to London. Although Holles later denied having anything to do with the rape of parliament he certainly made good use of it. Before the end of the month Holles and his cronies were in the saddle once again, directing the resistance to the New Model.[36]

The crowd's assault on parliament instantly vindicated the agitators' call for a march on London. The speakers of both houses, as well as 57 MPs and 8 peers trekked to Fairfax's headquarters and took refuge with the army. Despite the bravado displayed by Massie and Poynts any thoughts of offering military resistance to the invading army soon collapsed like a punctured balloon. The occupation of London on 4 August was a bloodless operation, made easier by the radical Southwark militia who controlled London Bridge. Two days later Fairfax escorted the speakers and members of both houses back to Westminster. The soldiers decked their hats with laurel and church bells pealed in triumph as the procession wound its way through the streets to the palace of Westminster.

The restored parliament did not immediately do the army's bidding. While the Lords were now firmly pro-army, it was not till the end of the month that the Commons obeyed the demand to repeal all votes passed between the mob attack of 26 July and the army occupation of London on 6 August. The royalist lord mayor, John Gayre, and three of his

[36] BL. Add. MS 37344 (Whitelocke's annals), fo. 101.

aldermanic supporters were thrown in the Tower, while the army imposed its own nominee for lord mayor, John Warner. The Presbyterian lieutenant of the Tower was replaced by the radical Independent Colonel Robert Tichborne. Most important of all, the purged Independents returned to their seats on the London militia committee. The most visually spectacular demonstration of the army's control of the capital was the demolition of the lines of communication, the 11-mile ring of forts and earthworks that had been erected at immense cost in human labour in 1643. On one matter the City remained recalcitrant, however: paying its arrears on the monthly assessment for the army. It owed more on this account than any of the counties.

With its objectives mostly accomplished, the army withdrew from London and established headquarters at Putney, five miles up the River Thames from Westminster. The recruitment of new soldiers to fill the many vacancies in its regiments resulted in a significant number of urban radicals enlisting for the sole purpose of influencing the army's political agenda. By the end of September many of the rank and file were unhappy at the continuing problem with pay and at the slow pace of political reform. New agitators or agents emerged in five cavalry regiments, although they did not replace the ones who had been elected the previous spring. Several more regiments would soon throw up new, more radical agitators. In mid-October the new agents lobbed a grenade into the deliberations of the General Council of the Army in the form of a pamphlet entitled *The Case of the Armie Truly Stated.*[37] Proclaiming that 'the great mansion house of this commonwealth . . . [is] on fire' the agitators also blamed the grandees for failing to look after the army's material needs, and for rendering it odious to the people. Nothing had been done to bring about the abolition of monopolies, tithes or the excise tax. Such measures of social justice necessarily awaited a political revolution grounded in the principle that 'all power is originally and essentially in the whole body of the people of this nation'. The revolution they envisaged would entail the dissolution of the present corrupt parliament, biennial elections, votes for 'all the freeborn' men of England, religious liberty and freedom from conscription. General Fairfax, recognizing that the protestors were actuated

---

[37] Recently John Morrill and Phil Baker have made a strong case for trooper Edward Sexby of Fairfax's own horse regiment as primary author of the pamphlet, chiefly on the grounds of its suffusion with biblical language: 'The case of the armie truly restated', in Michael Mendle (ed.), *The Putney Debates of 1647: The Army, the Levellers and the English State,* 115ff.

by goodwill, agreed that their manifesto should be taken up by the General Council.[38]

The Case of the Armie was duly referred to a committee of field officers and agitators, who were instructed to vindicate the army 'from the aspersions cast upon them by the said paper'. On 27 October, the day before the General Council was to hear the committee's report, Robert Everard delivered to headquarters a new document entitled *An Agreement of the People*. It had been approved that same day at a meeting of the agents of the five regiments, in addition to other soldiers, plus John Wildman and 'divers country-gentlemen'. Whether its primary author was William Walwyn or John Wildman,[39] its brevity, clarity and sophistication made it a far more memorable document than *The Case of the Armie*. It contained two concepts that were novel in English political thought. The first was the idea of a written constitution that would gain higher authority than any mere act of parliament through the signatures of all the freeborn men of England. The second was the concept of powers that were reserved to the people, meaning that they could not be exercised by any government. Because of the people's reserved powers no government could impose military conscription, legislate on religious matters, violate the principle of equality before the law, or question or punish anyone for what they had said or done during the civil war.

As soon as the agreement came up for debate Edward Sexby, who had been one of the army's core activists since the previous spring, took the rhetorical offensive. Parliament was rotten, he charged, and Cromwell and Ireton guilty of servility towards it and the king. 'Your credits and reputation hath been much blasted', he shouted.[40] The two generals defended themselves, and after this preliminary skirmishing the Council proceeded to a consideration of *An Agreement of the People*. Again there was a contest for rhetorical control of the debate. The agents accused the grandees of bending the knee to king and parliament. But Cromwell and Ireton turned the tables by labelling the agents in effect anarchists and communists. Universal manhood suffrage, which was what the *Agreement* seemed to imply, according to Ireton, would give power to the vast majority of the population who owned no property, and thereby lead to the abolition of

---

[38] Wolfe, *Leveller Manifestoes*, 222.

[39] William Walwyn, *The Writings of William Walwyn*, eds. Barbara Taft and J.R. McMichael, 31; and Woolrych, *Soldiers and Statesmen*, 215, think it was Walwyn, as do I; while John Morrill and Phil Baker, in Mendle (ed.) *Putney Debates*, 121, opt for Wildman.

[40] Camden Society, *The Clarke Papers* (hereafter *CP*), ed. C.H. Firth, Vol. 1, 227–8.

property. Thomas Rainborowe, the truculent infantry colonel who had recently quarrelled with Cromwell over his desire to be appointed vice admiral of the navy, took up cudgels for the rank and file. So what if the *Agreement* was 'a huge alteration' as Cromwell said? 'If writings be true there hath been many scufflings between the honest men of England and those that have tyrannized over them.' So what if it put property in jeopardy? There was a higher principle at stake. In words that still ring in our ears after more than three-and-a-half centuries he proclaimed,

Really I think that the poorest he that is in England hath a life to live as the greatest he; and therefore truly, sir, I think it's clear, that every man that is to live under a government ought first by his own consent to put himself under that government; and I do think that the poorest man in England is not at all bound in a strict sense to that government that he hath not had a voice to put himself under.[41]

For all the rhetorical posturing there was a genuine attempt on both sides to reach a consensus and preserve the unity of the army. There were lengthy prayer meetings. Committees met. People apologized for their heated words. The General Council finally agreed, with only three dissenting votes, that the franchise should be granted to all soldiers, as well as all other men who were not servants or beggars. The other provisions of the *Agreement* were embraced, including the revolutionary concept of reserved powers, but not the notion of an unalterable constitution signed by the people. In effect a reformed parliament would remain the ultimate arbiter of constitutional forms. The dilemma of how to guarantee the soldiers a watertight act of indemnity for everything they had done in the war remained unresolved. Weary of debate and alarmed by the increasingly hostile denunciations of the king being voiced within the army, Cromwell opined that forms of government were but 'dross and dung in comparison with Christ'.[42] The reality was that the grandees had lost the argument in the General Council, not only over forms of government, but, more critically, over whether to continue treating with the king. On 8 November Cromwell carried a motion that the agitators should return to their regiments. What enabled him to do this was the support of Fairfax who enjoyed universal respect within the army, the widespread worries about army unity, and the promise that there would be a rendezvous of the army to hear and approve the recommendations of the General Council.

[41] Ibid., 301.
[42] See ibid. after p. 367. He was loosely quoting St Paul's letter to the Philippians 3:8.

Agitators and Levellers had assumed that there would be a single rendezvous. In the event the general staff opted for three. The regiments were widely dispersed, and it would be awkward to summon them all to one meeting point. Radicals felt betrayed by the decision to divide the army into three, but they decided to concentrate on influencing the one being held closest to London, in Corkbush Field near Ware, Hertfordshire. Energetically the London Levellers staged meetings in and around London to mobilize weavers and other tradesmen to attend the rendezvous en masse to push for the *Agreement of the People*. Within the army radicals strove to persuade regiments that had been assigned to other rendezvous to turn up at Corkbush Field on 15 November.

On the morning of that day the general officers rode to the rendezvous with a high sense of apprehension. Would the soldiers accept the Remonstrance they had prepared for them, or would they shout it down in favour of the *Agreement of the People*? Considering the frenetic political activity of the previous weeks, as well as the mounting evidence of royalist feeling among the infantry, they had reason to be worried. Before they arrived in Ware an assortment of unauthorized people, both military and civilian, were already there to meet them. John Lilburne and Richard Overton had made the journey, as had Major Thomas Scott, the recruiter MP for Aldborough, and Thomas Rainborowe, who was no longer a member of the army. Leveller agents were busily collecting signatures to the *Agreement* among the seven regiments who were authorized to be there. Fairfax was confronted with a delegation headed by Rainborowe demanding that he embrace the *Agreement* in the army's name. A bit later Harrison's regiment appeared on the field uninvited and without their officers. They wore copies of the *Agreement* pinned to their hats with the slogan 'England's Freedoms, Soldiers' Rights' written on the outside. But their defiance collapsed when Fairfax rebuked them and Cromwell swooped down and began ripping the papers from their hats. Then Colonel Robert Lilburne's regiment suddenly appeared on the field, also without its officers, and the men also wearing the *Agreement* in their hats. When the major from another regiment tried to restore discipline he was met with a hail of stones and retired with a broken head. At this Cromwell put himself at the head of a flying wedge of officers who rode into the ranks with swords drawn, breathing fury against the mutineers. Their display of courage and ruthlessness was enough to cow the soldiers, and the offending papers disappeared. The other two rendezvous, on 17 and 18 November, passed without incident. Significantly there were eight more regiments, including some of the ones with the most notorious records for political turbulence in the army, that were not invited to any rendezvous. Five civilian Levellers were imprisoned at the order of the House of Commons, while in the army the ringleaders of the Ware mutiny were rounded up, court martialled and condemned to die. Fairfax pardoned all but Private Richard Arnold, who was shot at the head of his regiment by two of his co-conspirators.

The grandees now sat down and composed a Representation to Parliament on behalf of the army. In measured words they made plain their anger at parliament's failure to support the army financially, ensure indemnity for the soldiers, and look after wounded soldiers or the widows and orphans of the slain. Shaken by the political agitation of the previous nine months, parliament finally took effective steps to meet the army's demands. But they also got the grandees to agree to a major disbandment of 20,000 troops, mostly from among the garrison and provincial forces, in return for meeting their other demands. Remarkably, this great disbandment was carried out in January and February 1648, just a few weeks before the outbreak of the second civil war. It involved the emptying of fortresses from Northumberland to Cornwall, the dissolution of all but five regiments in the northern army, and the reduction of 4,000 men from the original New Model regiments. A similar number who had flocked into the army after the occupation of London were also sent home. There is evidence that the high command used the occasion of the great disbandment to weed out soldiers suspected of political radicalism or disaffection.

The reduction of the parliamentary army's numbers by almost 50 per cent in early 1648 was an impressive administrative achievement, all the more so since it kept the original New Model regiments intact. It was proof that parliament and army had heard the groans of the people against heavy taxation and free quarter, and were serious about lightening the burden of both. By the spring of 1648 the military high command had trimmed the parliamentary army into a leaner, less costly and more politically homogeneous body of men.

All the efforts towards order and settlement were overshadowed by the flight of Charles I on the evening of 11 November from his confinement at Hampton Court. Fear of assassination by army radicals was only one element in his decision to flee. More important was his desire for freedom so that he could concert military resistance against his foes in parliament. He had evidently hoped to enter London in triumph, or meet up with the Scots at Berwick, or board a ship for the continent. Instead, thanks to the incompetence of his advisers, he blundered into the hands of Colonel Robert Hammond, governor of the Isle of Wight, who, instead of allowing him to roam freely, kept him in close custody at Carisbrooke Castle for the next year.

The Engagement of Charles I with the Scots

Close custody did not mean that he could not receive visitors. Well before he arrived on the Isle of Wight Charles had begun serious talks with three of the Scots commissioners who were most sympathetic to his plight – Lauderdale, Lanark and Loudoun. They were emphatic that he could be master of Scotland, but only if he would give way on religion. Charles, who could not stop wrestling with his conscience, advised them to have secret talks with Ormond, since he was ready to mount a royalist campaign in Ireland if the Scots invaded England. Charles had already primed Ormond on what he wanted done in Ireland, and shortly afterwards Ormond and two of the commissioners met at a secret location outside London to coordinate strategy for the following year.[43] By 15 December the draft of an Engagement between the king and the Scots commissioners had been agreed upon.[44] His final rapprochement with the Scots was clinched by parliament's passage of the Four Bills. This legislation had been drafted by lords Saye and Wharton on behalf of the Independent Junto as a means of showing up Charles as a man of bad faith, and tightening the vice on him. The first bill gave parliament permanent control over the militia; the second revoked Charles's declarations against parliament; the third cancelled the honours he had recently granted, and the fourth gave parliament the right to adjourn itself to any place it pleased. The Scots by contrast were flexible about every issue except religion, and professed dismay that the Four Bills said little about that subject. Charles manipulated the commissioners into making concessions by giving the impression that he was about to accept the Four Bills. In return for the king's agreement to maintain the covenant and establish Presbyterianism in England for three years, neither he nor his English subjects would be obligated personally to take the covenant. The radicals led by Loudoun in effect joined the Hamiltonians in abandoning the religious demands of the Newcastle Propositions. In civil matters Charles promised to ratify the acts of the 1644–47 Scots parliament and to settle the debts due from the English parliament to Scotland. He would also 'endeavour a complete

---

[43] HMC 36, *Ormonde MSS*, Vol. 2, 353–5.
[44] *CSP*, Vol. 2, 380–1; Burnet, *Hamilton*, 323–4, 331.

union of the kingdoms' or at least establish free trade between them. In return the Scots commissioners were quite happy to agree to the disbandment of all armies, and the restitution of the king's authority over the militia, as well as his power to veto parliamentary bills, and they would bring him to London for a personal treaty with parliament. If the English parliament did not yield peacefully Scotland would send an army to compel its acquiescence and restore the king to his government. There was only one catch: the Committee of Estates and the Kirk had yet to approve the extra concessions that the commissioners had promised. Nonetheless, on the day after Christmas the Engagement was signed, and with great solemnity wrapped in lead and buried in the garden of Carisbrooke Castle until it could be safely carried out of the island. The next day Charles dismissed the emissaries from Westminster and their Four Bills.

The Independent Junto's reaction was swift and harsh. On 3 January 1648 it piloted through the Vote of No Further Addresses to the king, with the proviso that any person who negotiated with him without permission would be guilty of high treason. Deeply suspicious of the activities of the Scots commissioners, the Junto also proceeded to terminate the existence of the Committee of Both Kingdoms. The Scots commissioners then departed for Edinburgh, having made arrangements for a rising in England, to be coordinated with a Scottish invasion.

During these months Ormond too had been in direct communication with the king. At the end of August 1647 Charles had confirmed him in the office of lord lieutenant. Later, at Hampton Court he had instructed Ormond to concert strategy with the Scots commissioners, which Ormond did. The Independent Junto, increasingly wary of Ormond, forbade him any further access to the king, but in January 1648 Charles wrote authorizing him to try again to reach a peace with the Confederate Irish. Ormond then sent Colonel John Barry to Ireland to see if he could win over Inchiquin to the royalist cause. Once in Ireland, Colonel Barry made progress with Inchiquin. The President of Munster was unhappy with the Independent, army-backed control of parliament, and was looking for a way of switching sides again. Before he could do this he had to overcome the resistance of a number of his officers who were principled Protestants, opposed to any accommodation with the Confederate Catholics. On 3 April 1648 Inchiquin assembled his army and told them that he had decided to stand up against the king's enemies. The small minority of officers who resisted him he imprisoned. On the other side of the fence the rapprochement between royalists and Confederates was spoiled by the papal nuncio, Rinuccini, who proclaimed the excommunication of any who took part in it. Open war between the clericalist and peace or Ormondist parties soon followed.

Conclusion

The eighteen months following the termination of the first English civil war witnessed a political revolution at Westminster as the Independent party, sustained by the might of the New Model Army, overcame their conservative Presbyterian opponents in both houses. This transformation of the political landscape in England spurred political reactions in Scotland under the Hamiltonians, and in Ireland under the Ormondists. Yet the strenuous attempts of the disparate groups that feared and hated the Independent Junto to forge a coalition around the king were dogged by misfortune at every turn. The great stumbling block was religion. Much as they were bound together by a shared commitment to monarchy and a loathing for the anarchic implications of religious liberty, the adherents of the Kirk were repelled by the prospect of shedding blood on behalf of an uncovenanted king. Much as they desired to collaborate in restoring the king to his rightful throne, the Protestant followers of Ormond and Inchiquin, and the moderate Catholics in the Confederate national assembly, found the prospect of fighting side by side, even against detested English puritans, almost more than they could stomach. For their part, the clericalists in the assembly denied that there could be any value in rallying behind a captive heretic king who could not even bring himself publicly to endorse the rights of Catholics against an intolerant persecuting Puritanism.

In truth Charles I was no nearer to squaring the religious circle at the beginning of 1648 than he had been four years earlier. Despite attracting much public sympathy for his plight he had made almost no headway in shaking the Independent Junto's grip on the levers of power in his greatest kingdom. All he could boast was the fluctuating support of a shaky majority of the Scottish and Irish political nations. Yet thanks to his negotiating skills the War of the Engagement, also known as the second English civil war, was about to commence.

CHAPTER 11

The War of the Engagement – 1648

Scotland

The Engagement hammered out between Charles and the Scots commissioners ran into trouble almost as soon as it had been buried on the Isle of Wight. The Committee of Estates accepted it, but took the precaution of delaying its implementation until parliament met on 2 March. Before that date vociferous voices were raised against the treaty. The Kirk pronounced the king's religious concessions inadequate, and threw its weight behind a peace movement spearheaded by women in Edinburgh and Leith 'who carry a great sway, especially at home, do cry for peace, and say their husbands shall not fight'.[1]

When parliament assembled royalist nobles who had previously taken little part in public affairs showed up, adding their voices to a clear majority for the Engagement. Argyll's faction reacted bitterly to its unaccustomed minority status and attempted to stir up opposition within the Kirk and the army. An army petition against the Engagement had to be abandoned, however, when too many of the leading officers declined to sign it.

The Kirk nonetheless put forward a cogent critique of the Engagement. Why was war to be waged on behalf of the king against the English parliament when Charles himself was not being required to accept the Covenant? If the war was to be a religious one, as the Engagers pretended, how could they act in alliance with a king who had turned down their most basic demand? The Engagers had no answers for these questions.[2] When, on 20 April, parliament approved a declaration of war against England the Kirk riposted that it could see no just grounds for war. That did not stop

---

[1] Quoted in Stevenson, *Revolution and Counter-Revolution*, 99.
[2] Ibid., 104.

the hundreds of English cavaliers who had already flocked to Edinburgh from setting to work. The committee for dangers sent a contingent of these cavaliers under Sir Marmaduke Langdale to occupy Berwick and another under Sir Philip Musgrave to occupy Carlisle at the end of April.

On top of the strenuous opposition of the Kirk, the Engagers had to contend with the intervention of the English Independents. The Junto sent a delegation to explain English government policies and campaign to keep the two nations united. It redoubled intelligence activity; intercepting many royalist and Engager letters, as well as blocking many of the king's replies.[3]

Not until the beginning of May – over four months after the Engagement had been signed – did the Scottish parliament authorize the levying of a new army. Its strength was set at 27,750 foot and 2,760 horse and it was to be assembled by the end of the month. David Leslie's army was to be absorbed into it, and Monro's army in Ireland was invited to send troops. Hamilton displaced Leven as commander-in-chief, while Callander had to be content with being second in command. David Leslie declined to serve, and the Kirk was not slow to denounce the levies. Argyll also did what he could to thwart recruitment, and was rumoured to have been in touch with Cromwell and other Independent leaders requesting their help in suppressing the Engagers. Opposition was strongest in the Kirk's strongholds in Fife and the west, especially Galloway, Ayrshire and Glasgow. In the streets of Edinburgh the Duke of Hamilton was set upon by women hurling stones and insults.[4] This open and vehement opposition to the recruitment of the new army had a predictable effect: it 'made the soldiers very heartless' at 'the curses the ministers thundered against [them]'. The Engager majority in parliament struck back, 'conjuring' the Kirk 'not to . . . fall into the episcopal disease of meddling in civil affairs'.[5] The projected invasion of England was inevitably slowed down by all the opposition, and the anti-Engagers were able to count some significant gains from their activity. In June Chancellor Loudon returned to their fold. The anti-Engager campaign was successful too in exploiting popular ambivalence towards a non-covenanting king and harnessing it to the general war-weariness that pervaded the country. The Engagers also made things more difficult for themselves by turning down the services of those who had taken part in previous royalist risings. They did this in the hope of

---

[3] Burnet, *Hamilton*, 339.
[4] *Montereul Correspondence*, Vol. 2, 503.
[5] Burnet, *Hamilton*, 348–9.

persuading the Kirk that they did not countenance malignants. Monro's army in Ireland also responded with half-hearted enthusiasm to the call to arms. The final brake on the Engager mobilization effort was that its army was poorly led. Hamilton, the pragmatic royalist, was intelligent enough, but he distrusted his own judgement, and allowed himself to be dominated by others. Thus the Earl of Callander, a more single-minded royalist, and a professional soldier with long military experience in the Low Countries, took it upon himself to criticize all of Hamilton's suggestions and to press his own ideas as indispensable to the army's success.[6]

In spite of these less-than-ideal circumstances the Earl of Lauderdale made a compelling case for entering England sooner rather than later: several royalist risings there had already been crushed, and unless they acted quickly the remaining royalist forces would also be defeated. The army was ordered to rendezvous on 4 July. The turnout was disappointing; those who did come were mostly untrained; ammunition was short and artillery nonexistent; the contingents from Ireland had not yet landed. The 9,000 troops that the Duke of Hamilton led across the border on 8 July showed little promise of being able to stand up to the battle-hardened men of the New Model Army.

Ireland

The twin defeats of Dungan's Hill and Knocknanuss left the Catholic Confederation paralysed with despair. O'Neill's army had to be called in to protect Leinster. Many voices in the Kilkenny Assembly were heard blaming the Confederates' disarray on the uncompromising policies of Rinuccini. The assembly dissolved itself on Christmas Eve 1647, leaving a divided council and clergy to work out detailed instructions for aid-seeking embassies to France, Rome and Spain. Searching frantically for a solution, the council could think of nothing better than to offer the government of Ireland to Queen Henrietta Maria and the Prince of Wales, as proxies for their captive king.

In January 1648 Charles authorized Ormond to try again to reach a peace with the Confederate Irish. The king's grand strategy was that his old and new friends in the two smaller kingdoms should come together to reverse his recent defeat in England. The Duke of Hamilton and the Marquess of Ormond were to construct an alliance to challenge and over-throw the Independent Junto at Westminster.

---

[6] Ibid., 354–5.

In the winter of 1647–48 the best news for the royalists coming out of Ireland was that Murrough O'Brien Baron Inchiquin, President of Munster, was again wavering in his allegiance. Ormond accordingly sent Colonel John Barry to Munster to see if he could nudge this formidable commander into declaring himself for the royalist cause.[7] Barry found himself pushing at an open door. The president of Munster was unhappy with the Independent, army-backed control of parliament, but a number of his officers were principled Protestants likely to oppose an accommodation with the confederate Catholics. Inchiquin too, unlike the *politique* Ormond, whose opposition to Catholic claims was based on political considerations, was hostile to Catholicism on principle. On 3 April 1648 Inchiquin assembled his army and told them of his decision to oppose the king's enemies in England. Several dozen of his officers were indignant at this second transfer of allegiance, and tried to stir up a mutiny. Able commander that he was, Inchiquin nipped the mutiny in the bud. Then, with Ormond's approval, he negotiated a cessation of arms with the Catholic Confederation, which was proclaimed on 20 May. It was hoped that this rapprochement would pave the way for a united royalist Ireland that would snatch the king from his captivity in England.

This hope was to be cruelly disappointed. The Cessation of May 1648 inflamed such dissension among the Catholic Confederation that it nullified any moves to mobilize troops to fight for the king in England. Rinuccini and the clerical party ('nuncioists') were aghast that the moderates and peace-party adherents preferred to settle with the heretic who had recently desecrated Cashel Cathedral than work together with Owen Roe O'Neill and his Catholic troops. They pointed out that the Cessation violated the Confederation's Oath of Association, and threatened excommunication against any who embraced it. This ignited civil war within the Confederation. Owen O'Neill and his army found themselves pursued by forces led by Lord Taaffe, Sir Phelim O'Neill and Alexander MacDonnell acting for the moderates in the assembly.

Most interpreters of these events have found the clerical party guilty of rigid intolerance and high-handedness. From their own perspective, however, the followers of the nuncio had ample reason for distrusting the royalists. Not only had Ormond dealt savagely with the insurgents in 1642, he continued to play a destructive role through the rest of the 1640s. Far from promoting peace he had encouraged Confederate divisions by

---

[7] Bodl. MS Carte 22, fos. 5, 51–2 show that Ormond and Inchiquin were in frequent contact in early 1648.

refusing to make concessions on religious issues. Granted that he was under fierce pressure from Protestant royalists such as the lords justices and members of the Dublin parliament, yet at the end of the day his unyielding policy towards the Confederation was the fundamental reason why the king obtained virtually no military assistance from Ireland after 1644. Ormond had compounded his failing by surrendering Dublin to the Westminster parliament in July 1647. This action was disastrous for royalist interests in Ireland and delayed for almost two more years a peace settlement there.[8]

The whole bitter conflict revealed the mutual incomprehension that now existed between the royalists and moderates ('Ormondists') on the one hand, and the Catholic hardliners ('nuncioists') on the other. The division was only partly ethnic. Virtually all of the nuncioists were Gaelic Irish. The Ormondists were a true coalition, including most of the Old English and some Gaelic Irish yoked in an uneasy alliance with Protestant royalists. Many Catholics supported the truce with Inchiquin on account of war-weariness and the spread of disease, which was cruelly straining Ireland's ability to field so many armies.

Few historians have noticed that the conflict triggered by the Cessation in Munster was exactly what Inchiquin had intended. As he revealed in a letter to Ormond, the primary reason for agreeing with the Confederates in Munster was to 'divide betwixt them'. Exposing his incomprehension of the Gaelic Irish, he went on to express astonishment at how they 'do greedily embrace the infusions of their disaffected clergy . . . who vehemently contend against the re-establishing of his Majesty's authority in this kingdom'.[9]

When it came to 'dividing betwixt them' Inchiquin succeeded beyond his wildest hopes. At the end of May Rinuccini excommunicated the Catholic supporters of the Inchiquin truce. Two weeks later Owen Roe O'Neill and the Army of Ulster declared war on the Supreme Council. This morass of murderous factionalism was made more serpentine by the arrival of the Marquess of Antrim in late July. His goals were overridingly personal: to protect his fiefdoms in Ulster and the Western Isles, and to prevent the return of his rival Ormond from France. Accordingly he threw in his lot with Owen Roe O'Neill, proposing that they should collaborate to overrun Kilkenny and install a new Supreme Council subservient to Rinuccini and the nuncioists. But with characteristic ineptitude Antrim

---

[8] Ó Siochrú, *Confederate Ireland*, 248–9.
[9] Bodl. MS Carte 22, fo. 165.

was unable to prevent the interception of a number of his most self-incriminating letters. O'Neill's invasion of Kilkenny was a failure, and by early August, after wreaking considerable destruction, he was driven out by the combined forces of Preston and Inchiquin.[10]

England

The first overtly royalist uprising broke out in England in May 1648, but the second civil war may be said really to have begun on the day that Charles I fled from Hampton Court, 11 November 1647. As far as the New Model Army officers were concerned Charles had broken his parole. For Cromwell and Ireton it was the last straw. They jettisoned any further attempts to come to an understanding with him and directed their efforts to re-unifying the army and honing it once more into an effective fighting machine. The army grandees were in an ugly mood. Sir John Berkeley, Charles's emissary, got a frigid reception when he paid a visit to army headquarters at Windsor Castle. Privately he was informed that the officers were talking of bringing the king to trial. Intelligence activities were stepped up, resulting in a copious harvest of letters between royalists and their newfound Scottish allies.

Apprehension of renewed warfare also prompted the army grandees to ask that Rainborowe should take up his vice admiralty in the Downs. It was crucial to have a trusted man in charge of the navy on the south coast to block any royalist attempt to rescue the king by sea. When a majority of the peers refused to give their assent to the motion the Independent majority in the Commons simply overrode them and instructed Rainborowe to take command of the ships guarding the Solent. At the same time the Independent Junto worked to bolster Argyll's anti-Engagement faction in Scotland by sending it money and offers of English support. More daringly, and in great secrecy, they also renewed overtures to the king, violating their own Vote of No Addresses. Aiming to detach him from the Engagement, they tried to reach an agreement with him, probably on the basis of the Heads of Proposals. No agreement materialized, but by playing this triple game they retained the army's confidence, weakened the Hamiltonian Engagers and mollified English Presbyterians.[11]

No political manoeuvres, however, could overcome pervasive popular weariness with the burden of taxes needed to keep the army on a war

[10] Ohlmeyer, *Civil War and Restoration*, 210–11.
[11] Scott, *Politics and War*, 163–4.

footing. People hated the tyranny of county committees, and the violation by Westminster of the traditional rights of the county. Many chafed too at the cultural repressiveness of the Puritan regime, exemplified by the ordinance of 1644 abolishing the public celebration of Christmas. That ordinance was like a bomb with a delayed fuse, which exploded on Christmas Day 1647 in Canterbury when the mayor of the city tried to compel markets and shops to stay open on that day. There was spontaneous rioting, quickly exploited by cavaliers who declared their desire to ally with the Scots and restore the king to his throne. The Kentish parliamentary colonel Anthony Weldon needed 3,000 of the county's trained bands to quell the riot. Ipswich was the scene of another pro-Christmas uprising, and there were also pro-Christmas stirrings in London. As John Morrill has justly observed, the more the puritans tried to abolish Christmas the more certain their eventual downfall became.[12]

Even the great disbandment of February 1648, whereby parliament shed 20,000 troops – nearly half its military establishment – failed to assuage popular anger against an oppressive regime. Free quarter continued to be a monumental grievance, not lessened by the ordinance of 24 December 1647, which in theory eliminated it. Royalist printed propaganda proliferated, much of it satirical. Parliament reacted by attempting to impound royalist news-sheets and arrest their printers, sellers and authors. The propaganda was deemed damaging enough to justify the hiring of a parliamentary writer to attack the royalists through the mouthpiece of a revived *Mercurius Britanicus*.[13] A Dorset petition of June 1648 summed up what was on many people's minds. Without referring to the army it complained about taxes, county committees and the loss of liberties. The king, said the men of Dorset, should be restored so parliament would 'no longer be called master without a head'.[14] Even London was not immune from royalist agitation. Both men and horses were recruited there for projected risings in the provinces. By the end of the winter the political temperature in the metropolis was at fever point. On the anniversary of the king's coronation (27 March) bonfires were lit, coaches stopped, and their occupants obliged to drink the king's health, while an effigy of Colonel Hammond, the king's gaoler, was dragged through the streets, drawn, quartered and burnt.[15] On the Sunday after

[12] Morrill (ed.), *Reactions, 1642–1649*, 114.

[13] Lois Potter, *Secret Rites and Secret Writing: Royalist Literature 1641–1660*, 17.

[14] Printed in Morrill, *Revolt of the Provinces*, 207.

[15] Bodl. MS Clarendon 31, fo. 42.

Easter (9 April) 3–4,000 apprentices surged down Fleet Street chanting 'Now for King Charles'. A detachment of New Model horse rode out to meet the apprentices, and herded them back inside the City gates. The next day Fairfax sent more troops into the City to quell the uprising. By the time they had done their work several apprentices and watermen lay dead in the streets.

It proved easier to keep order in the capital than to extinguish smouldering anger in the countryside. In some respects the risings against parliament looked like a reassertion of the old festive culture. Defiant celebrations of Christmas, the drinking of healths, Sunday games, bonfires, maypoles and horse races were enlisted as organizing tools against a centralizing Independent Junto and its hated army. The rights of the locality were a common thread binding many of the petitions and demonstrations. But the second English civil war was more than just a localist revolt against centralist tyranny. David Underdown has shown how engagement with traditional festive culture was frequently a vehicle for the expression of serious royalist commitment. Underlying the celebratory manifestations of 1648 were serious messages about restoring the king to his former power and dignity, and re-establishing the Church of England as a precondition of recovering the imagined harmony and stability of the past. This traditionalist, hierarchical vision of England was contested by 'honest radicals' with a national consciousness, and increasingly republican leanings. They held sway in Warwickshire, Somerset, Suffolk, Lancashire and elsewhere throughout 1648.[16] Their revolutionary stance was intellectually buttressed by writers such as John Milton, Henry Parker, Marchmont Nedham, Richard Overton and William Walwyn; parliamentary spokesmen such as Viscount Saye and Sele, Henry Marten, Thomas Chaloner and Thomas Scot; and preachers such as John Goodwin, William Dell, John Saltmarsh and Hugh Peters.[17]

---

[16] Underdown, *Revel, Riot and Rebellion*, 230–2, 260–1; Brian Lyndon, 'Essex and the king's cause in 1648', *HJ*, 29 (1986), 19; Hughes, *Warwickshire*, 220–1, 254.

[17] Much fine work has been published recently on English revolutionary republicanism. See for example, David Norbrook, *Writing the English Republic: Poetry, Rhetoric and Politics 1627–1660*; Jonathan Scott, 'What were Commonwealth Principles?', *HJ*, 47 (2004); Nigel Smith, *Literature and Revolution in England, 1640–1660*; Blair Worden, 'English republicanism', in J.H. Burns and Mark Goldie (eds), *The Cambridge History of Political Thought 1450–1700*; Blair Worden, *Roundhead Reputations: The English Civil War and the Passions of Posterity*; David Wootton (ed.), *Republicanism, Liberty and Commercial Society 1649–1776*.

Most worrying for parliament was the number of key counties where royalists gained the upper hand in 1648. Essex for example, had been a pillar of strength to the parliamentary cause in the first civil war. But on 22 March the Chelmsford grand jury adopted a peace petition calling for a personal treaty with the king; 2,000 men carried the petition to Westminster where they were coldly rebuffed. In May the Grand Jury met again and adopted an Engagement and Declaration, refusing to collect any more taxes or admit any more soldiers to the shire, and pledging its adherents to defend King Charles and 'the known laws of this kingdom'.[18]

Dissatisfaction also seethed in the formerly parliamentarian city of Norwich. The boiling point came on 23 April when soldiers arrived to fetch the mayor to Westminster to explain why he had permitted royalist festivities on the anniversary of Charles's coronation, and why he had sanctioned the election of 'malignant' – meaning royalist – aldermen. The crowd that gathered to protest soon raged out of control. Militants seized the city magazine and started to bring out gunpowder to use against the soldiers. Whether by accident or not, the magazine was set on fire, igniting a mighty explosion that killed over 100 people. Order was only restored with difficulty by nightfall.

Suffolk was the third county in the parliamentary heartland to flare into revolt. A crowd had gathered round a traditional maypole in Bury St Edmunds when a troop of Thomas Fairfax's cavalry regiment rode up. Shouting 'for God and King Charles', the crowd laid into the troopers and chased them out of town. They then shut the town gates, barricaded the streets and seized the magazine. Fortunately for the troopers there was still a solid stratum of parliamentary support in Suffolk, and many of the county militia rallied to their side. At length the rising was brought under control, although later the same month the leading parliamentary MP for the county, Sir Thomas Barnardiston, informed the Lords that cavaliers were still active in Suffolk, while others had migrated to nearby Newmarket, where they congregated 'under pretence of horseracing'.[19]

As a consequence of the great disbandment Fairfax's resources of manpower were stretched to the limit. Two regiments of foot had to be assigned to Newcastle under Sir Arthur Hesilrige to guard that city against the expected Scottish incursion. Half a regiment of foot held Oxford, while a full regiment garrisoned Gloucester. North Wales was patrolled by a

---

[18] Rushworth, *Hist. Coll.*, Vol. 7, 1101; *LJ*, Vol. 9, 244; Lyndon, 'Essex and the King's cause', 21, 24.
[19] *LJ*, Vol. 10, 302.

regiment of horse, while a mobile force of one foot and three horse regiments under Ferdinando Lord Fairfax's brilliant protégé, the young Yorkshire Colonel John Lambert, covered the north, watching for the Scots and keeping local royalists in awe. Lambert's northern brigade was further strengthened when New Model Colonel Thomas Sheffield's horse regiment, sent to Cheshire to guard against a thrust by Langdale, swung across to join it. These deployments left Fairfax with just over 7,000 troops to hold the capital and the south-east.[20]

In the early spring of 1648 much the gravest threat for parliament lay on the west side of the country. There were royalist 'insolencies' in the city and county of Worcester. There were also royalist mobilizations, said to number in the thousands, in Devon and Cornwall, which kept Sir Hardress Waller, the Anglo-Irish MP and New Model infantry colonel, anxious and busy during these months.[21] At his disposal were only one regiment of horse, one of foot, and 200 dragoons to keep the whole of the south-west under control. Plymouth mutinied against him as its new governor. Exeter too was hostile, obliging parliament to withdraw its soldiers from the city for the time being. Colonel Alexander Popham was sent next door to his native country of Somerset to keep the royalist infection from spreading there. Surveying the south-west, and stunned by the depth of neutralist and cavalier spirit he encountered wherever he turned, Waller marvelled that the region was not 'all in one flame'.[22]

In the shadow of this gathering military peril the New Model officers resorted to the morale-boosting remedy in which they had greatest confidence: a prayer meeting. On 27 April they kept a solemn fast at Windsor. Following an interruption on 28 April the prayer meeting resumed on the 29th. For two days the officers pondered the 'sad dispensation' they witnessed on every side. Many spoke and prayed, but it was Cromwell who focused their efforts when he urged all present 'to a thorough consideration of our actions as an army, as well as our ways particularly, as private Christians, to see if any iniquity could be found in them . . . that if possible we might . . . remove the cause of such sad rebukes as were upon us'. The breakthrough came on the third day when Lieutenant Colonel Goffe, one of the most pious officers in the army, rose to speak. Taking Proverbs 1:23 ('Turn you at my reproof . . .') for his text he announced that all the mishaps that had befallen them were their

---

[20] Young and Holmes, *English Civil War*, 276–7.
[21] Folger MS X.d.483(23) (Bennett Papers); Bodl. MS Carte 67, fo. 160.
[22] *CJ*, Vol. 5 569; David Underdown, *Pride's Purge: Politics in the Puritan Revolution*, 92.

punishment for not following the ways of the Lord. Only by listening to God's voice could they achieve peace of mind and freedom from fear. There now occurred an extraordinary scene: Goffe, who was respected by radicals and conservatives alike evidently spoke with such eloquence and intensity that everyone in the room broke down. 'None was able to speak a word to each other for bitter weeping, partly in the sense and shame of our iniquities of unbelief, base fear of men, and carnal consultations (as the fruit thereof) with our own wisdoms, and not with the word of the Lord.' The unrestrained collective tear shedding brought emotional catharsis. Hard on the heels of catharsis came unity. Without dissent the officers agreed that they must go out and fight their enemies 'with an humble confidence in the name of the Lord only, that we should destroy them'. They further agreed that it was their duty 'to call Charles Stuart, that man of blood, to an account for that blood he had shed, and mischief he had done . . . against the Lord's cause and people in these poor nations'.[23]

As soon as the meeting broke up the officers dispersed to fight royalist insurgency in Wales, Cornwall, the north, Kent, Surrey and Essex. Four months would elapse before they met again under the same roof.

Potentially the most alarming setback to the parliamentary cause was the defection of eight of its warships to the king in late May.[24] The mutiny had been triggered by a combination of material grievances and anger at the Independents' 'overrunning, disarming, and plundering [of] the country, as if it were a conquered nation'.[25] Now the king's party had a naval force at its disposal. The queen, the Prince of Wales and other members of the royalist party wanted to use it to escort the prince to assist Hamilton and his army. But Hyde and other anti-Scots members of the king's council, who backed the established Church and loathed the Presbyterian Covenant, insisted that the prince and the fleet should be sent either to Ireland with Ormond or to the insurgents in Wales. The queen and the pro-Scots faction prevailed, but the seamen themselves were so anti-Scots that the naval force was of no service. After mounting a short-lived blockade of the Thames estuary it returned to Holland, deeply unhappy, and contributed nothing further to the royalist war effort.[26]

[23] William Allen, *A Faithful Memorial of that Remarkable Meeting of Many Officers of the Army in England at Windsor Castle, in the Year 1648* ([27 April] 1659), BL. E979/3, 2–5.

[24] Kenyon and Ohlmeyer (eds), *Civil Wars*, 182–3.

[25] J.R. Powell and E.K. Timings (eds), *Documents Relating to the Civil War 1642–1648*, 354.

[26] Scott, *Politics and War*, 176–7.

Wales

In Wales it was the attempt to disband the parliamentary troops of Major-General Rowland Laugharne and Colonel John Poyer that put the spark to the tinder. Both men had already shown signs of disaffection to the Independent Junto, and sympathy towards the Presbyterians if not the royalists. Their soldiers were dissatisfied with the terms offered them, and Poyer had also made many enemies during his governorship of Pembroke Castle. He now offered his allegiance to royalist agents who gave him a ready welcome. On 24 March Fairfax ordered a brigade headed by New Model cavalry colonel Thomas Horton to bring Poyer to heel. But with Laugharne's support Poyer chased off the first detachment from the brigade, and then swept through the county crying up the Book of Common Prayer, deploring the king's imprisonment, and demanding that he be brought to London for a personal treaty with parliament. This unvarnished royalism evoked a passionate response from the Welsh. During April Poyer continued to gather strength in south Wales. Worried about Horton's ability to subdue the revolt, Fairfax sent Cromwell with another two horse and three foot regiments to bolster him. Forewarned of Cromwell's approach, the Welsh royalists opted to engage Horton before he could be reinforced. They fell upon him, 7,000 strong, at St Fagans just outside Cardiff. Horton was outnumbered three to one, but the royalists could only call upon 500 cavalry, which they stationed in the rear to keep the infantry from turning tail. Although they fought tenaciously, they were no match for Horton's cavalry and dragoons. His sweeping victory surprised everybody, and he followed it up by taking Tenby Castle. The political fall-out from this battlefield verdict was almost instantaneous. Royalist morale plummeted, while in London Presbyterian opinion gave up on the king and resigned itself to the invincibility of the New Model Army.

Cromwell joined Horton on 11 May, and set about besieging Chepstow and Pembroke Castles. The former he stormed successfully on 25 May, but Pembroke's thick walls kept him mired in a two-month siege during which he had to call in heavier and heavier artillery. Pembroke was not overrun until 11 July.

While Cromwell and Horton were preoccupied in Wales, the royalists redoubled their efforts to assault the capital. On 16 May a large contingent of armed men from Surrey, at least 3,000 strong, and well armed, arrived at Westminster to petition for a personal treaty with the king. A group of them invaded Westminster Hall, and began fighting with the guards, killing one of them. Reinforcements were rushed in from Barkstead's and

Rich's regiments; in the ensuing mêlée five or six petitioners were killed and a great many wounded.

At the same time as the clash with the Surrey petitioners Kent rebelled. In order to meet that threat Fairfax had no choice but to remove both his field regiments from London, in addition to Colonel Robert Tichborne's Tower regiment of foot. He was able to denude London of its occupying forces safe in the knowledge that the City militia was controlled by his politically reliable infantry major-general, Philip Skippon. With Skippon at the helm the militia could be counted upon to do the army's will.

Maidstone

It was the Kentish rising that obliged Fairfax to shelve his plan of marching north against Hamilton's Engagers. After Horton's victory in Wales the royalists in Kent had intended to await the Scottish invasion before unleashing their rebellion. However, they were unable to keep their rank and file under control. In a rage over the opening of the trial of the Christmas rioters on 10 May, the insurgents rose up and swept through the county, taking one town after another. Assistance from revolted naval ships in the Downs, and the defection of many moderates from the parliamentary cause assisted the insurgents to seize country magazines and coastal castles. They occupied Rochester, Deal, Walmer and Sandwich and laid siege to Dover. The Commons tried to defuse the anger of the revolted ships by ordering the Earl of Warwick to replace the hapless Rainborowe, who had been sent packing by the crew of his own ship. Behind the scenes, meanwhile, Lord Saye and Sele, acting for the Derby House Committee for Irish Affairs, which had emerged as the chief executive body in the state after the abolition of the Committee of Both Kingdoms, concerted with Fairfax the military plan to crush the insurgency. The nightmare scenario for Saye and the New Model officers was that Kent might become the springboard of a royalist assault on London. On 29 May about 10,000 rebels assembled on Burham Heath, between Rochester and Maidstone, and elected as their leader George Goring's father, the Earl of Norwich, who had just arrived from France with the Earl of Holland. They decided to advance on Blackheath, almost next door to London, the following day. Their numbers included men from Surrey and Essex, as well as 'butchers, dyers, clothworkers, and some of the looser sort' from London.[27]

---

[27] *News from Kent* (1648), E445/27, 3.

Fairfax and the Derby House Committee resolved to meet the challenge head on. Marching with barely 4,000 troops, the captain-general met Norwich's mongrel force of 'cavaliers, citizens, seamen and watermen' on 30 May.[28] Lacking the appetite for a bloody fight with veterans of the New Model, 1,000 rebels suddenly decided that they were only petitioners after all, and surrendered. The others retreated to their homes or fell back to Rochester. Fairfax for his part decided to target the main royalist concentration at Maidstone. After despatching a horse regiment to relieve the besieged fortress of Dover, he approached Maidstone by a roundabout route. Hidden by thick woods, he was able to keep the insurgents ignorant of his movements, until suddenly his presence was discovered four miles to the west of the town. On 1 June he was before the gates. His advance guard of dragoons, hearing shouts of 'For God, King Charles and Kent' from within the town, impetuously unleashed their assault at once, undeterred by a heavy rain shower. To their surprise they ran up against resolute resistance from the troops that had been raised a scant ten days before. Pitched fighting began a mile outside the town, and it took two hours before the defenders were driven from hedge to hedge back inside. Once Fairfax's men surmounted the barricades they had to fight street to street, for the royalists exacted a heavy price for every foot of ground they ceded. One reason the defenders fought so grimly was that most of them were not local men, but 'seamen, apprentices, . . . commanders and cavaliers that have formerly been in arms against the parliament'.[29] In the narrow streets they used their cannon with deadly effect, cutting down 30 men, including a captain lieutenant in Hewson's foot regiment. Fairfax himself led his men through the greatest danger on horseback, all the while suffering excruciating pain from gout. By 1 a.m. the defenders were overpowered and the town was still.

Maidstone was a critical victory for parliament. Credit is due to Fairfax for his careful planning and personal valour, and also to the performance of his veteran troops. In addition it helped that his force outnumbered the enemy by almost two to one. On paper there were 11,000 armed royalists in Kent, but they had been dispersed throughout the county. When word got round about the defeat at Maidstone most of the rest opted to desert. Those who stuck with Norwich trudged over Rochester Bridge and made for Blackheath. By then their numbers were down to 3,000. Any hope of

[28] Ibid., 5.
[29] *A Letter . . . of the Fight between His Excellency's the Lord Fairfax Forces at Maidstone and the Kentish Forces* (1648), E445/37, 5–6.

linking up with cavaliers in the City was stymied by Skippon who fortified London Bridge, closed the gates and stopped all ferryboats across the Thames. Norwich therefore changed plans and headed for Essex. By morning 1,500 of his troops had reached the opposite shore, some by swimming, others on horseback.

The little band of royalist insurgents now began their trek to Chelmsford and Colchester, hoping to pick up support along the way. Fairfax dispatched Colonel Edward Whalley with a small force of cavalry into Essex to shadow Norwich, while he remained to supervise the pacification of Kent. Once Dover Castle was relieved and the other coastal castles retaken the royalist remnant scattered to other counties. Essex now became the main scene of action, while half a dozen other eastern counties were aflame with revolt. Petitions unfriendly to parliament emanated from Sussex and Dorset at the same time that the revolted ships of the navy were an ever-present threat. Royalist strategy in June was to exploit the insurgency in Essex to gain control of London. That this was not a pipe dream is indicated by the highly unstable political situation in the metropolis over the next two months. The newly appointed sheriffs and lieutenant of the Tower were all high Presbyterians. The Presbyterian aldermen and militia officers imprisoned after the July 1647 counter-revolution had been set free. These gestures of appeasement by the Independent Junto were intended to avert a Presbyterian–royalist alignment. But they did not stop the expelled MPs Denzell Holles, William Waller and Edward Massie from creeping back, the latter two to recruit actively for the royalist cause. Munition trains on their way to Fairfax's forces were attacked and overturned by royalist apprentices on 19 June. Thereafter military supply wagons had to give the City a wide berth on their trips to Essex. London was no longer a safe lodging place for royalist prisoners of war, as it had been until 1646. A petition to bring Charles to London received wide support, and on 7 August the Common Council went so far as to call the Scots Engagers 'our brethren' and to commend the programme recently published by the Prince of Wales. The chief reason why there was no counter-revolutionary uprising in London in the summer of 1648 was Major-General Skippon's ability to control the capital with the trained bands and a freshly recruited regiment of cavalry. Skippon not only kept a lid on anti-parliamentary ferment; he also strangled the flow of men and matériel to the Essex royalists.

Skippon was called upon as well to assist in countering the looming royalist threat in Surrey. The Earl of Holland and the Duke of Buckingham had set up headquarters in Kingston where they strove to rally support from the southern counties. Their hope was that the Prince of Wales would sail up the Thames and galvanize their campaign, but he never showed up. In the event the royalist dream for the southern counties was shattered when Colonel Michael Livesey led a force from Kent augmented by the Hertfordshire militia and detachments of cavalry from Rich's, Ireton's and Skippon's regiments. At the beginning of July he clashed with the royalists at Kingston and scattered them, killing Buckingham's son and capturing the Earl of Holland.

The siege of Colchester

The royalists' penultimate hope was Colchester. The presence of Norwich's 5,000 hard-bitten men, a mere two days' march from London, gave Fairfax and the Derby House Committee many sleepless nights between June and August. The supreme importance of this theatre is signalled by the fact that the Committee of the Army was sent to take up quarters there for the duration of the siege.[30] While disenchantment with the parliamentary regime may have been less general in Essex than in Kent, it was the Essex royalists, who staged a more effective struggle than did their counterparts in Kent and Surrey.

We have seen how in the spring of 1648 the Essex grand jury petitioned for disbandment of parliament's armies and pledged to defend King Charles. When in early June Lord Norwich crossed into their county, 1,000 members of the trained bands, led by colonel and former deputy lieutenant of the county Henry Farr, transferred their loyalty from parliament to the king, and arrested the members of the county committee at Chelmsford, holding them hostage until the end of the summer. A few days later Norwich met Sir Charles Lucas, who held a commission from the Prince of Wales to command royalist forces in Essex. They were joined by Lord Capel, former commissioner of array for Hertfordshire, Sir George Lisle, a gentleman of fortune, and several gentry from various counties. Together they made their way to Lucas's native town, Colchester. Unlike Norwich Lucas was an officer of real military talent, who speedily put the town into a state of defence.

Colonel Whalley had to content himself with guarding the road to London, linking up with Sir Thomas Honeywood's 1,200 horse and foot from the county trained bands who had remained loyal to parliament, and awaiting the arrival of Fairfax with reinforcements. Although still racked

---

[30] NA. SP28/55, fo. 337.

with gout, Fairfax advanced with lightning speed, crossing the Thames at Tilbury on 11 June, and arriving at Colchester by the 12th. The royalist garrison paid the price for lax intelligence when they awoke the next day to find their enemy within musket shot of the suburbs. But they answered Fairfax's summons to surrender with a characteristic piece of cavalier bravado. Referring to Fairfax's ailment, Norwich told the parliamentary trumpeter that his master need not worry, for he 'would cure him of all diseases'.[31] Lucas then hastily drew up the men in battle order across the London road, preparing to meet the enemy head on. Fairfax hurled Barkstead's brigade at this target, confident that the outcome would be as quick and telling as it had been at Maidstone. To his disappointment Barkstead's men were repulsed three times. At length Lucas's men retreated inside the walls of the town, then turned on their pursuers and drove them back through the town's gates with heavy losses. After the fierce, eight-hour battle the royalists had been reduced by between 150 and 500 men captured, wounded or killed, while Fairfax had lost about 500 dead or wounded.

Fairfax now had to face up to the disagreeable truth that Colchester would not be an easy nut to crack. Another unsuccessful assault would put London in jeopardy, or permit the royalists to escape to the north and join Sir Marmaduke Langdale and the Scots. Fairfax therefore had no recourse but to resign himself to a long siege, the kind of warfare he liked least. His soldiers spent most of the next 11 weeks investing the town with a line of trenches and stockades punctuated with angled and star-shaped bastions. The defenders for their part busied themselves repairing the town's decaying walls, and where there were no walls, casting up ramparts and counterscarps. If the royalists' main hardship was an ever-dwindling food supply, the besiegers were sorely tested by having to camp out of doors during an exceptionally miserable cold wet summer.

Fairfax could not have encircled Colchester without a major infusion of manpower from county forces. His New Model troops, augmented by the Tower of London regiment of Colonel Needham, added up to just over 4,000. In addition he acquired 2,640 troops from the Essex militia and 3,600 from Suffolk, for a total of about 10,000.[32] Midway through the siege his army was augmented by a further 1,500 men recruited by Major-General Skippon in London.[33] In sum, at least half Fairfax's army before

---

[31] Rushworth, *Hist. Coll.*, Vol. 7.

[32] B.P. Lyndon, 'The parliament's army in Essex, 1648', *JSAHR*, 59 (1981), 145.

[33] *Merc. Melancholicus* (17–24 July 1648), E453/43, 127.

Colchester comprised county forces. These numbers testify to a solid base of support for parliament among the inhabitants of Essex and Suffolk. By contrast, despite the addition of some 1,000 foot from the Essex trained bands, Norwich and Lucas's royalist garrison had shrunk to 4,000 inadequately armed men at the beginning of the siege, and the shrinkage continued as the summer wore on.

The siege of Colchester is remembered as the bitterest episode of the civil wars in England. Its sheer length was a major factor in the development of the boundless contempt that each side expressed for the other. Fairfax's men were infuriated by the royalists' alleged use of 'poison bullets' – musket balls that had been chewed and rolled in sand or boiled in copperas.[34] Civilians were treated without mercy. Fairfax refused to let women and children leave the town, because he wanted as many mouths as possible to consume the town's dwindling provisions. When a group of women did slip out his troops stripped them naked and drove them back in. Both sides razed to the ground suburban houses and set them on fire so as to keep them from falling into enemy hands.[35] Early in the siege Fairfax choked off the town's profitable trade with London, and cut the water supply, melting down the lead pipes for bullets.

By 19 August, long since having slaughtered their horses, the royalists were now dining off dogs and rats. When the besiegers flew a kite over the town on 24 August spreading the news of Cromwell's recent triumph against the Scots at Preston, the last reason for holding out expired. Driven on by the threat of mutiny from the ranks, the officers had no recourse but to accept Fairfax's requirement that they 'surrender at mercy'.[36] This phrase, as everyone understood, meant that mercy could be denied to any or all who threw down their arms. The besieging soldiers had the satisfaction of seeing Lucas and Lisle shot to death. The noble prisoners – lords Norwich, Capel and Hastings – were turned over to be judged by parliament.

Fairfax has often been criticized for the severity he showed in withholding mercy from Lucas and Lisle, yet he enjoyed the solid support of his council of war and of parliament. He was also justified under the laws of war at the time.[37] An officer who continued to hold an untenable position, thereby causing unnecessary bloodshed, forfeited his right to quarter. Equally, an officer taken prisoner and then released could be executed if he

[34] Lyndon, 'The parliament's army in Essex', 233.
[35] Porter, *Destruction in the English Civil Wars*, 68.
[36] HMC 38, ser. 35, *Fourteenth Report*, app. 9 (Round MSS), 290.
[37] Barbara Donagan, 'Atrocity, war crime and treason in the English Civil War', *AHR*, 99 (1994), 1144, 1155–9.

took up arms a second time against the enemy who had released him. This applied to Sir Charles Lucas, who had been taken prisoner at Marston Moor in 1644. A further piece of damning evidence against Lucas was that in the first civil war he had ordered at least 20 parliamentary defenders at Stinchcombe, Gloucestershire, put to death in cold blood.

The political legacy of Colchester was an unwavering conviction on the part of most higher officers who had attended the siege that the king, as the ultimate author of the suffering and bloodshed which they and their comrades had undergone, must be brought to account for his crimes. Their abiding bitterness stemmed in part from the fact that their victory at Colchester had been a near thing. The town had become a rallying point for royalist diehards, Londoners in particular. The Prince of Wales had nearly succeeded in sailing up the Thames with 11 warships to attack London.[38] The strategy of pinning down almost half of parliament's mobile forces had worked for nearly three months. Thanks to the perseverance of Norwich and Lucas's men the northern royalists and Scots invaders were handed the chance to overrun the north of England. By their divided counsel and military incompetence they threw that chance away.

Preston

How had this happened? That the great conflict in the north had been so long delayed was due to the manifold difficulties experienced on both sides. Colonel John Lambert, with only 3,000 fighting men at his disposal, had no choice but to play for time until Cromwell could be spared from Wales to bolster him. The last of the Welsh rebels, who were holed up in Pembroke Castle, took an annoyingly long time to surrender. Even after Horton's stunning victory at St Fagans there had been plenty of work left for Cromwell and his 6,500 men in Wales. Chepstow and Tenby castles had to be taken before the main centre of royalist resistance – the medieval fortress of Pembroke Castle – could receive his full attention. Pembroke's massive stone walls enabled its 2,000 defenders to defy four times as many besiegers, who were deficient in the only thing that mattered: artillery. Cromwell was prevented from taking effective action against Pembroke's walls until heavy pieces from the army's depot at Wallingford arrived in early July. On the day they did he unleashed his assault, and Pembroke surrendered a week later (11 July).[39]

[38] Gardiner, GCW, Vol. 4, 174.
[39] Powell, The Navy in the English Civil War, 151; Powell and Timings (eds), Documents, 342.

The royalist collapse in Wales came not a moment too soon. The Duke of Hamilton had already been in England for three days at the head of 9,000 men. More than two months earlier Sir Marmaduke Langdale with only 100 troops had seized the fortress at Berwick, while his companion Sir Philip Musgrave needed only 16 men to overrun Carlisle. At the beginning of June Langdale scored another notable triumph when 20 men in disguise wormed their way into the great fortress at Pontefract and wrested it from the parliamentary garrison.

Although Langdale had annoyed his Scottish allies by rushing in before they were ready, the stirring welcome he encountered in every county except Lancashire seemed to vindicate his boldness. In the gloomy reckoning of Lambert's secretary the cavaliers outnumbered roundheads twenty to one in the north-east. Sir Arthur Hesilrige at Newcastle complained bitterly about Westminster's seeming unconcern about the plight of the north.

In the end, though, Langdale's stunning exploits were neutralized by the careful, unspectacular work of John Lambert. Patiently he added to his numbers, at the same time playing cat and mouse with Langdale to keep him off balance and prevent him from uniting with Hamilton's army.[40] In the process he laid a firm foundation for Cromwell's sensational successes in August.

The Scottish invasion was doomed from the start. It was already several weeks too late to help the risings in England and Wales. Its tardiness was of course caused by the relentless opposition of the Kirk, and its insistence that going to war on behalf of Charles I made a mockery of the Solemn League and Covenant. The Engagement's cause was also hampered by its leadership: the second-rate Duke of Hamilton and the third-rate Earl of Callander. Hamilton's timidity suited the arrogant, opinionated Callander perfectly. By his overbearing behaviour he fuelled dissension among the lower officers, undermined the army's respect for Hamilton, and ultimately destroyed its effectiveness as a fighting force.[41] Many regiments had been filled up with untrained recruits, while the army as a whole was short of ammunition, artillery and money. It was therefore reduced to plundering the countryside through which it marched to feed itself. This parasitism foreclosed any hope of engendering popular support for the royalist cause among the population of the north-west, who in any case had been made allergic to the Scots by the three-year occupation of the north from 1644 to 1647. Five years earlier the north had been a bastion of royalism, but

---

[40] SNA, GD 406/1/2348 (Hamilton Papers).
[41] Burnet, *Hamilton*, 355.

Charles threw this advantage away by enlisting Scots to fight his English subjects.

Finally, the invaders were plagued throughout their adventure by 'constant, rainy, stormy and tempestuous weather'.[42] Drenching rains in the north of England made the summer of 1648 the wettest in living memory. Rivers and streams that were easy to ford in normal years became raging torrents; roads turned into quagmires; match and powder were soaked; and life for the rank and file, shivering in their sodden clothes, became a living hell. The weather discouraged the English parliamentarians too, but they at least were fighting on home ground.

Once across the border Hamilton's first error was not to engage Lambert, whom he vastly outnumbered. This failure meant that he was unable to join forces with Langdale. He also blundered by choosing to march down the western route through Lancashire rather than the eastern route through Yorkshire. He did this in the hope of taking Manchester, which was ably defended and had resisted all attempts on it during the first civil war. He next thought he would link up with a projected rising in Cheshire under Lord Byron, but this was in fact aborted. Lancashire, with its several Puritan towns, was the northern county least sympathetic to the royalists. Its inhabitants had also been put off by the brutality of Rupert's forays. Another negative factor was the county's many enclosures, hedges and ditches, which made the terrain difficult for cavalry. The cavalry were the pride of the Engager army, and would have found greater scope for their talents in the more open country of Yorkshire. Because of the scarcity of forage Hamilton had little choice but to allow his horse to enlarge their quarters and advance ahead of the foot. When the crunch came his main army was strung out along a thin line more than 20 miles long. Thus dispersed, they were in no position to administer a concentrated blow to the enemy when it was needed.

Hamilton also threw away the badly needed reinforcement that Major-General George Monro might have given him. At the beginning of August Monro met Hamilton at Kendal to receive orders for the 2,000 or so men he had brought from Ireland. The only condition he stipulated was that he should report to Hamilton alone and not to either of the lieutenant-generals. Instead of giving a straight answer to Monro's demand, Hamilton weakly evaded the issue by ordering him to keep his men at the border, ostensibly to guard an artillery train, which was expected momentarily.

---

[42] Sir James Turner, *Memoirs of his Own Life and Times*, 78.

Cromwell was now on the move to join Lambert. He had set out immediately after the fall of Pembroke Castle. When his first 30 troops of horse (numbering nearly 2,400) arrived at Lambert's quarters they brought the latter's numbers up to 9,000, and Hamilton had almost lost the chance to exploit his numerical superiority. Uncertain what to do, he remained at Kendal, which allowed Lambert and Cromwell to complete the union of their forces. The size of their combined army was in the neighbourhood of 14,000 effectives.[43]

By 16 August Cromwell was marching, 'where the knotted muscles of the high Pennines relax into the pastoral slopes and fertile closes of the lower Ribble'.[44] In consultation with his council of war he made the daring choice to stay on the north side of the Ribble, thereby cutting off Hamilton's line of retreat back to Scotland and ensuring that there would be a decisive engagement.

Until almost the last moment neither Langdale nor the Scots had any inkling of the peril they were in. Most of Hamilton's cavalry had advanced south to Wigan, leaving only a small rearguard to protect the dispersed infantry. Langdale and his compact force of 3,600 were stationed six miles to the east of Hamilton's army. Monro's army was located somewhere to the north, but nobody seemed to have any idea where.

By the night of 16 August Langdale had been alerted to Cromwell's proximity; hurriedly on the following morning he began pulling back towards Preston. When he realized that a battle could not be avoided he took up a defensive position across the road outside the town. The site was inhospitable to cavalry, as the road was waterlogged and lined on either side with enclosed fields and ditches. Cromwell, enjoying a superiority of two or three to one, stationed a pair of his crack horse regiments on the lane running through the middle of Langdale's position. They were sandwiched between two layers of infantry, with cavalry on both wings and at the rear.

Langdale now spurred his horse for Preston, where he met the two Scottish commanders with most of the Scottish foot drawn up. Callander belittled his fears, and Hamilton surmised that he was only threatened with a probing attack that he ought to be able to deal with. The Scots com-

---

[43] The generally accepted figure for Cromwell's strength prior to Preston – 9,000 – is based on Cromwell's letter to the Speaker of 20 August. However, Lambert alone had already achieved this number, while we know that Cromwell contributed a further 5,000, mainly infantry. This is precisely the number given in a letter from Lambert's quarters at the end of July: Rushworth, *Hist. Coll.* Vol. 7, 1211. Thus the Scots–royalist superiority in numbers at Preston was not as great as historians have assumed.

[44] Woolrych, *Battles*, 166.

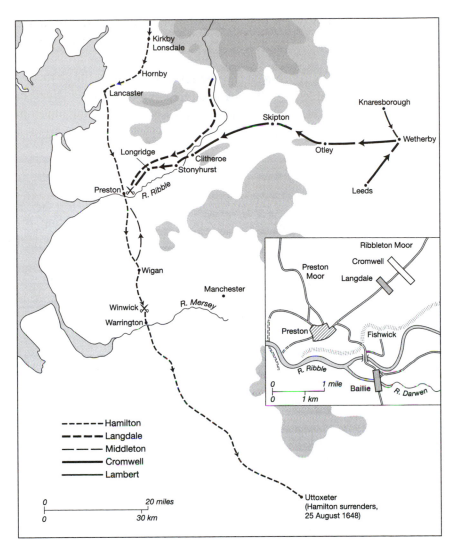

MAP 13 *The Battle of Preston, 17 August 1648*

Adapted from Gentles, Ian, *The New Model Army: In England, Scotland and Ireland, 1645–1653* (Blackwell Publishers, 1991)

manders had not recalled their horse from Wigan, and, astoundingly, were resolved to continue marching south with the foot. From his vantage point further north Sir George Monro had been warned by Philip Musgrave that Cromwell was bearing down on the royalist–Scots forces. Monro also transmitted this intelligence several times to Hamilton, but the duke's biographer assures us that none of the messages ever reached him.[45]

---

[45] Burnet, *Hamilton*, 368.

Monro – thinking that Cromwell intended to knock him off first – retreated northward, making it even less likely that he could bring aid to either Langdale or Hamilton.

The failure of Monro's intelligence to get through to the duke proved fatal. It made it possible for Callander and Hamilton to dismiss Langdale's worries. Thus, at the very moment when Cromwell was launching his full-scale attack on the English royalists the Scottish foot were tramping across the bridge over the Ribble.

In a preliminary skirmish between Cromwell's and Langdale's armies, the parliamentarian captain and diarist, John Hodgson, detected that one of the newly raised royalist infantry companies had already lost heart. They were shooting at the skies, and as soon as they made contact with the enemy they threw down their arms and retreated to the main body of their army. Nevertheless, the main battle went on for almost six hours, and most of Langdale's foot acquitted themselves honourably. The enemy, as he later boasted, 'never saw any foot fight better than mine did'.[46] During the battle Langdale sent urgent requests for help, but the Scots did not respond. Eventually, as the reports piled up, Hamilton was persuaded that Langdale was truly facing the whole of Cromwell's army. He therefore decided to halt the foot and give battle on Preston Moor. He summoned General Middleton to bring the cavalry up as soon as possible. The plan might have worked, except that at this moment Callander rode up from the bridge and angrily asked Hamilton why he had halted the foot. To draw up on Preston Moor was folly; the cavalry could not arrive in time; denied mounted support the Scottish foot would be ridden down by Cromwell's horse. Far better to finish sending all the foot across the river. They would then have the Ribble between them and the enemy, and could be joined by the horse. The reunited army would then have every chance of success. As he did so often, Hamilton allowed himself to be swayed by his overbearing second-in-command. Callander's arguments were plausible, even if fatally defective in two respects. They entailed totally abandoning Langdale's army to its fate, and presupposed well-executed manoeuvres on the part of an ill-disciplined army.

Callander got his way, and Langdale saw most of his infantry destroyed or taken prisoner, while his cavalry scattered northward, hoping to unite themselves with Monro's brigade. The great bulk of Hamilton's infantry, sitting immobile on the south side of the Ribble, were still unscathed, but

---

[46] Chetham Society, *Tracts Relating to Military Proceedings in Lancashire during the Great Civil War*, 268.

they were profoundly dispirited by the news from Preston and the realization that their leaders' vacillation had prevented them from doing anything to prevent the catastrophe.

Cromwell now proceeded to attack the 600 musketeers defending the bridge over the Ribble. They were easily swept back to the south side, and Cromwell prepared to press his advantage. At the end of a day's fighting he had captured about 4,000 of the enemy and killed over 1,000. Most of Hamilton's army was still intact, however, and Cromwell's task was to make sure that it did not slip past him and escape northward.

At a hurried royalist council of war Callander worsened an already perilous state of affairs by advocating a night withdrawal southwards to rendezvous with Middleton's cavalry. Even though Baillie and Turner, two of the more level-headed members of the council, pointed out the pitfalls of such a move, Hamilton fell in with Callander. A night withdrawal is an extremely difficult operation for even the best-trained army under ideal circumstances. Here it meant uprooting a shivering, hungry and exhausted body of infantry and sending them down mud-clogged lanes in the middle of a wet black night. The ammunition wagons had to be left behind, but the order to blow them up was not passed on, so that they fell into enemy hands. They also failed to make contact with Middleton's cavalry, who had ridden in the opposite direction by a different route.

Cromwell was now in hot pursuit with 5,500 troops; he caught up with Hamilton at Winwick. There ensued a desperate struggle in which 1,000 Scots were slaughtered and several times that number taken prisoner. Callander now persuaded Hamilton to abandon the infantry so that the cavalry could either return to Scotland or make themselves useful to the English royalists. Another 4,000 captives, together with the bridge at Warrington, fell into Cromwell's lap.

Parliament's army was now burdened with almost 10,000 prisoners, and was almost as worn out as the remnant it was pursuing. With 1,000 fresh horse, Cromwell wrote, we could make quick work of them, 'but truly we are so harassed and haggled out in this business, that we are not able to do more than walk an easy pace after them'.[47] Confident of his ability to fight on two fronts, Cromwell divided his cavalry, dispatching Lambert southward to round up the last of Hamilton's force, while he turned north with eight regiments to deal with Monro. Lambert's task was accomplished for him by the county militias. On 22 August at Uttoxeter Hamilton gave himself up to the governor of Stratford.

[47] Abbott, *Cromwell*, Vol. 1, 637.

The root causes of the débâcle of Preston reach deeper than the inability of English royalists and Scots Engagers to coordinate their military efforts. The inhabitants of northern England disappointed the royalists by their failure to rally to the king's standard in meaningful numbers. Not to be overlooked was the strategic skill of Cromwell and Lambert, and the bravery of their men – New Model veterans and county regiments alike. The parliamentary commanders had forces that were in good spirit and well supported logistically. Underpinning this logistical strength was the unspectacular work of parliamentary committees and state servants during the previous three years. The Committee of the Army under the chairmanship of Northumberland's 'man of business' Sir Robert Scawen, assisted by the Treasurers at War (men such as the London merchants John Blackwell and Sir John Wollaston) and backed up by key members of the Derby House Committee such as Northumberland, Saye and Sele, Wharton, Vane and St John had seen to it that money and supplies had been channelled to the army in timely fashion. Fairfax, Cromwell and Lambert then deployed these resources to best advantage by concentrating overwhelming force at a single point, while exploiting the geographical dispersion of their foes. As much as anything, however, the royalist project of 1648 was undermined by the fierce antagonism of the Kirk, the Marquess of Argyll and other key Scottish leaders to the Engagement. By the vehemence of their opposition they hobbled the recruitment of the Engager army, and in so doing imposed a fatal delay on the invasion.

The collapse of the Engager army was the signal for civil war to break out in Scotland. When news of Hamilton's defeat arrived several thousand men from western Scotland advanced on Edinburgh in what became known as the Whiggamore raid. Their leaders included Loudon, Leven and David Leslie. The Committee of Estates immediately ordered George Monro to gather his men from Ireland and any remnants of Hamilton's army that he could find, and rendezvous at Berwick. Forces raised under Lanark in Scotland were told to meet at Jedburgh. The Committee of Estates then quit Edinburgh to join Lanark and Monro on the Borders to avoid capture by the westerners. Their position became hopeless, however, when Cromwell marched his forces into Scotland. The Engagers faded northward and seized Stirling, while the westerners tried to persuade Cromwell not to enter the country. He brushed aside their objections, observing that they still needed his assistance to prevent the Engagers from recruiting a new army. Before the end of September Argyll had prevailed on the westerners to give way and disband so as to rid the kingdom of Cromwell's army. The Engagement had crumbled to dust, in great measure because of disenchantment with the king and the realization that he had no intention of abolishing episcopacy and imposing the Covenant on England. Indeed, Charles had never wavered from his conviction that the Covenant was incompatible with his kingly authority and therefore displeasing to God. By the time of Preston most Engagers had lost their trust in Hamilton and his brother Lanark, as well as the king.

Nevertheless, for all his shortcomings and failures, Hamilton had achieved 'a limited but dramatic counter-revolution'.[48] The extreme Covenanters had been ousted from government by votes in parliament and the Committee of Estates. The Engagers' destruction in Scotland only came after their military defeat in England. It would be the Covenanters themselves over the next two years who would fritter away the popular support they had managed to build up, and bring back the royalist party stronger than before.[49]

In Ireland the factions in the Catholic Confederation were crippling themselves with internecine civil war during the summer and autumn of 1648. In public printed statements the combined peace party and moderate majority vented such fury against the papal nuncio for his alleged wrecking of Irish unity that they helped eventually to drive him out of Ireland.[50] Yet the divisions which Ormond and Inchiquin had deliberately fostered inflicted at least as much damage upon themselves as the Confederates. The civil war in Munster hindered the effort to organize support for the king. Antrim's efforts to sabotage Ormond's mission were another setback. On top of these factors were the difficulties Ormond experienced in accumulating money, ships and supplies, which forced him to postpone his departure from France for many months. By the time he arrived in Ireland at the end of September the second civil war in England had been over for several weeks. Ormond nevertheless pressed on, his first priority being to help Inchiquin quell a mutiny among his Protestant officers who were violently opposed to letting the Catholic Church gain legal status, much less acquire any buildings or landed property. By mid-November the mutinous officers had been dismissed and order restored in Inchiquin's army. The royalist court in exile, demoralized and quarrelsome, now pinned all its hopes on Ormond's negotiations with the Association of Confederate

[48] Gerald Aylmer (ed.), *The Interregnum*, 5.
[49] Stevenson, *Revolution and Counter-Revolution*, 116–22.
[50] The vindictiveness of these public statements has to be read to be believed: e.g., Bodl. MS Carte 22, fos. 108 & 158.

Catholics. The big stumbling block continued to be religion; in addition, Ormond had to cope with the systematic efforts of Colonel Michael Jones, governor of Dublin, to divide the anti-royalist nuncioists in the association from the Ormondists. Towards the end of November, for example, Jones supplied Antrim with ammunition and allowed him to pass through his lines to join Owen Roe O'Neill in Ulster.

At the end of November Ormond offered the association essentially what he had put on the table in 1646: freedom for Catholics to practise their religion, but no public recognition of their rights. He told them that penalties would not be imposed on them but that changing the law to recognise their rights would have to wait until a future parliament. For several agonizing weeks he refused to budge from this position even though the power he wielded was minimal. The impasse was not broken until almost the eve of the king's trial, when Ormond agreed to Roman Catholic property rights, appointment to government office and army commands, and continued possession of all garrisons, towns, forts and castles in their present possession. Other sticking points, such as the Confederate demand for the repeal of Poynings' law would be decided by the next parliament, in which Catholics would be eligible to sit.[51] These concessions did the trick. At the end of December the association told Ormond that in view of the desperateness of the king's condition the General Assembly was prepared to hasten approval of the treaty. Yet simultaneously Inchiquin was warning Ormond about continuing opposition to the treaty among his remaining officers.[52]

In spite of all the obstacles a treaty was signed on 17 January 1649, dissolving the Confederate government and replacing it with 12 'commissioners of trust' to manage affairs in Confederate areas, under Ormond as lord lieutenant. The Ulster Scots also agreed to put themselves at Ormond's disposal. The Catholic clergy were still divided, conscious of the profound disapproval of the nuncio, and O'Neill made it clear that he would sign no treaty to which the nuncio was not a party. Neither Rinuccini nor Ormond wanted to have anything to do with each other, and so Rinuccini, seeing that his usefulness was at an end, set sail from Galway on 23 February, never to return to Ireland. His mission had been a failure, but it is difficult to see how it could have been otherwise. He left the Irish as he had found

---

[51] Bodl. MS Carte 23, fos. 84–9. The intensity of the negotiations, as well as their agonizingly slow progress can be followed in MS Carte, 23, fos. 62, 66, 70, 80, 84–9, 90, 96, 100, and Gilbert, *Irish Confed.*, Vol. 7, 186.

[52] Bodl. MS Carte 23, fos. 123, 121.

them: deeply divided, and buffeted by external forces over which they had little control.

With its rickety coalition of Protestant royalists, Ulster Scots Covenanters and divided Catholics, Ireland now braced itself for the coming hurricane.

CHAPTER 12

Regicide and republic

The sodden English summer of 1648 gave way to an even wetter autumn. Disastrous harvests deepened the unease of the chief actors in the unfolding political crisis. Distraught by the economic havoc wreaked in the recent war, the Common Council of London petitioned parliament to make a treaty with the king and come to an understanding with the army. For the moment the city fathers avoided the unpleasant reality that achieving one objective ruled out the other.

The Newport Treaty

On 18 September negotiations with the king opened at the town hall of Newport on the Isle of Wight. It was the fourth round of peace talks in less than six years, and it was in technical violation of the Vote of No Addresses of the previous January, but a great deal of water had passed under the bridge since then. Rather than inducing any mood of triumphalism, victory in the War of Engagement had brought home to the parliamentary regime how deeply unpopular it was, and how ubiquitous its enemies were in all three kingdoms. The parliamentary Presbyterians had regained the upper hand, chiefly owing to their advocacy of negotiations for a definitive end to the war. They hoped to restore Charles with his wings clipped to the bone, and a Reformed Church settlement acceptable on both sides of the Scottish border. Surely the king would recognize the totality of his defeat; surely he would make the concessions required of a twice-vanquished enemy. It was in this spirit that the 15 parliamentary commissioners rode to Newport. They were a mixed bag, including prominent Independents such as the Earl of Northumberland, Viscount Saye and Sele and Sir Henry Vane, as well as the Commons Presbyterian leader, Denzell Holles. Among those advising the king were the Duke of Richmond and the Earls of Hertford, Lindsey and Southampton. From his vantage point in France Secretary Nicholas was pessimistic that the talks could have any good outcome.

Early in the negotiations Charles agreed to surrender the militia to parliament for 20 years, a period generally expected to encompass his remaining lifetime. He thereby gave up the power of the sword, which, as his wife had often reminded him, was the essence of sovereignty. Yet it was religion that proved to be the insuperable stumbling block, as it had been for the previous three-and-a-half years. This would not have been the case had Charles been a conventionally sensible man. In August parliament had passed an ordinance establishing a thoroughgoing, intolerant Presbyterian system of Church government in England. All the king had to do was say yes to this fait accompli. Alive to the danger of interference by an enraged New Model Army, two of the Presbyterian commissioners, Denzell Holles and Sir Harbottle Grimstone fell to their knees, their eyes brimming with tears, and implored the king to yield on the religious question.[1]

Even the king's advisers exhorted him to face up to reality and give parliament its way on religion. In doing so they were asking Charles to violate his most deeply held convictions. During six years of civil war he had been unwavering in his defence of the Reformed Church of England, with its Book of Common Prayer and its government by bishops, as a true Church. Charles was never more candid about his innermost thoughts than when he communicated with his son and heir. Writing to the Prince of Wales in the summer of 1646 he spelled out why defence of the Church was his single most important principle.

[T]he chiefest particular duty of a king is to maintain the true religion (without which he can never expect to have God's blessing), so I assure you that this duty can never be right performed without the church be rightly governed ... For take it as an infallible maxim from me that as the church can never flourish without the protection of the Crown so the dependency of the church upon the Crown is the chiefest support of regal authority ... Wherefore my first direction to you is to be constant in the maintenance of episcopacy.[2]

---

[1] Sir Richard Bulstrode, *Memoirs and Reflections upon the Reign and Government of King Charles the Ist and K. Charles the IId*, 172–3.
[2] Bodl. MS Clarendon 91, fo. 30-v.

When in October 1648 Charles's trusted advisers told him that he had no alternative but to acquiesce in the abolition of bishops – it had been two years after all since parliament had abolished them and put their lands on the auction block – he found himself in such 'a great perplexity' that he broke down and wept.[3] Rather than accept such a violation of his conscience, Charles determined on an escape from the Isle of Wight. He was also hoping for Ormond to conclude his alliance with the Confederate Catholics in Ireland. That is why he spun out the negotiations, giving way on Ireland, surrendering episcopacy for three years, but refusing to swear the Solemn League and Covenant, and demanding the restitution of his revenues and an act of oblivion for both sides. On 27 October the Commons rejected the whole of Charles's proposal, though both houses voted to prolong negotiations until the beginning of December.

The Army and the Levellers

The parliament and the army, united in war just a few months before, were now completely at odds over how the king should be handled. While the war had shaken many parliamentarians with the revelation of how unpopular they were, it had only deepened the army officers' anger against a king who had defied the clear message of providence and through his obduracy needlessly put their lives in jeopardy once again. Important voices among the officers – future fifth monarchist Colonel Thomas Harrison, and future Quaker Captain George Bishop – had condemned the king as a 'man of blood' as long ago as the Putney Debates a year earlier. The agitator Edward Sexby had chimed in with the comment that nothing they did would please the king except cutting their own throats. Cromwell had allowed that it might well be God's will to destroy the king, but that did not necessarily mean that the army should be the instrument of that will. Besides, at the moment 'the sons of Zeruiah were too hard for him'.[4] This reference to the Old Testament was an oblique way of saying yes, Charles is a murderer, but he still has too many powerful friends for the army to be able to call him to account.[5] Cromwell's objection was pragmatic rather

---

[3] Francis Peck, *Desiderata Curiosa*, Vol. 2, 392. For an illuminating discussion of Charles's position on religion throughout the four treaties of the 1640s see Smith, *Constitutional Royalism*, 139–40, 143–56.

[4] *CP*, Vol. 1, 417. Cromwell was citing 2 Samuel 3:39.

[5] For a penetrating discussion of Cromwell's attitude to regicide see John Morrill and Phillip Baker, 'Oliver Cromwell, the regicide and the sons of Zeruiah', in Jason Peacey, ed., *The Regicides and the Execution of Charles I*, 14–35.

than principled. In January 1648, when the king's Engagement with the Scots became public knowledge, Cromwell declared to his fellow MPs that 'they should not any longer expect safety and government from a man whose heart God had hardened'.[6] At their Windsor prayer meeting the army officers had branded Charles Stuart a man of blood who had defiled the land, which could not be cleansed 'but by the blood of him that shed it'.[7] The army committed itself to putting the king on trial at the first opportunity.

After the war furnished clinching evidence that Charles was the man against whom God had witnessed, the officers could not comprehend why he should be treated as anything less than a moral leper. The suspicion overtook them that Holles, Warwick and others in parliament who were driving on the peace treaty with the king intended also the destruction of the army. Looking about for friends, they found them among the London Levellers who in their 'Large Petition' of 11 September denounced the forthcoming Newport Treaty and called for justice upon 'the capital authors . . . of the . . . late wars'.[8] Fairfax moved his headquarters from Colchester to St Albans, significantly closer to London, as professional army watchers were quick to note.[9] Army militants now combined with political radicals to orchestrate an influx of petitions and letters from regiments and garrisons up and down the country calling for justice against the authors of the recent war. Many also supported the Levellers' brand of radical social reform.

Tension within the army was heightened at the end of October by the killing of Colonel Thomas Rainborowe. After the fall of Colchester he had been sent northward with his regiment to assist in the siege of Pontefract. At Doncaster royalist agents had kidnapped him and run him through with their swords when he tried to tear himself loose in the street. A fortnight later his body was brought to London where the funeral became a show of Leveller strength. Nearly 3,000 supporters reportedly joined the procession as it wound its way through the streets of the City.

In this emotionally charged atmosphere Fairfax summoned the Council of Officers to the abbey church of St Albans, among other things to review

[6] D.E. Underdown (ed.), 'The parliamentary diary of John Boys, 1647–8', *BIHR*, xxxix (1966), 156–7; Abbott, *Cromwell*, Vol. 1, 575. Yet, as David Scott reminds me, there is evidence that only a few months later the wily Cromwell was involved in the Independents' secret negotiations with Charles.

[7] Again they were citing the Old Testament: Numbers 35: 33.

[8] Wolfe, *Leveller Manifestoes*, 289.

[9] Worcester College MS 114 (Clarke Papers), fo. 77v.

several regimental petitions. Judging the time to be ripe, Commissary-General Henry Ireton introduced a draft paper soon to be known as the Remonstrance of the Army. Ireton's drastic solutions did not win immediate assent; indeed, a number of colonels declared that they 'desire[d] nothing more than to see . . . the hearts of the king and people . . . knit together in a threefold cord of love'.[10] What enabled Ireton to overcome the moderates in the council of officers was a combination of outside radical pressure, and the imminent threat of a parliamentary pact with the king that would have left the army high and dry.

Since the beginning of November the Levellers had been meeting with a group of 'gentlemen Independents' at the Nag's Head Tavern. In response to their pressure Ireton agreed to endorse the Leveller Agreement of the People that he had so vehemently opposed a year before. To thrash out the details of this new projected constitution for England a committee of 16 was appointed, with equal representation from Levellers, army, London Independents and the 'honest party' in the House of Commons. Ireton was as good as his word. When the Remonstrance of the Army was laid before the Commons on 20 November it both commended the Leveller petition of 11 September and called for a written constitution based on an Agreement of the People. The clerk needed four hours to read out the 25,000-word document, after which the Presbyterian majority curtly declined to debate it, evidently expecting that it would soon be rendered irrelevant by a treaty with the king. Stung by the Commons' casual attitude to their blueprint for settlement, the officers who had been hovering all day at the door of the House pursued the MPs down the stairs threatening that if the Remonstrance was not debated promptly they 'might take what followed'.[11]

Since the Remonstrance was the master plan for the army's actions in the critical months ahead, and since it contains the chief theoretical justification for the coup d'état known as Pride's Purge, it merits more attention than it has received from most historians of the revolution. It opens with an appeal to the principle that the public safety is the highest law (*salus populi suprema lex*). This is the army's justification for speaking out on political matters. At the heart of the Remonstrance is a sweeping indictment of the king as a covenant breaker, and of parliament for having any truck with him. The king's great crime has been the flouting of his obligation, enshrined in his coronation oath, to protect the people's rights

[10] *The Representations and Consultations of the Generall Councell of the Armie at St. Albans* ([14 November] 1649), E472/3, p. 3.
[11] Gentles, *NMA*, 274.

and liberties. By annihilating these rights through the exercise of his own absolute will and power he has freed the people from their duty to obey him. More pointedly, the king, after having been once defeated in his attempts to overthrow the public interest, resumed the struggle, causing renewed bloodshed and desolation. Most damningly of all, his refusal to call off Ormond even during the Newport Treaty has demonstrated once again that he can never be trusted. Therefore, 'we may justly say he is guilty of the highest treason against law among men . . . and . . . guilty of all the innocent blood spilt thereby'. Only if judgement is executed against him will the wrath of God be appeased. Trying to unite the king and parliament is like trying to join 'light with darkness . . . good with evil'.[12] In a startling admission of the king's popularity the Remonstrance underlines the danger of permitting him to return to London: 'The King comes in with the reputation among the people of having long graciously sought peace.'

One apparent obstacle to bringing the king to judgement remained: the Solemn League and Covenant, which obligated those who had sworn it to preserve the king's person and authority. Ireton's answer was that in case of conflict the duty to preserve the king must yield to the higher duty to defend religion and the public interest. While it clearly foresaw the king's condemnation, the Remonstrance did not explicitly prescribe the abolition of monarchy. Yet it ended with a call for the dissolution of the present parliament, electoral redistribution according to population, and annual or biennial elections. There was to be a new constitution, the Agreement of the People, which implicitly abolished monarchical government, and only those who subscribed to it would be eligible to participate in the country's political life.

At the Isle of Wight army intelligence was fully apprised of the king's plans to escape. The officers accordingly transferred him from Carisbrooke to the much securer castle at Hurst a few miles along the coast on a lonely promontory jutting into the Solent. At this juncture it was Ireton and his backers who were in control of the army's political strategy. Yet Fairfax, despite his later denials, did not resist the momentum of events. For example, he signed the letter explaining the army's disobedience in marching on the capital as a natural consequence of parliament's high-handed refusal to consider its demands.[13]

[12] *A Remonstrance of His Excellency Thomas Lord Fairfax . . . and of the Generall Councell of Officers Held at St Albans the 16 of Nov., 1648*, E473/11. The quotations above are taken from the version printed in *OPH*, Vol. 18, 183–4, 187. See also Scott, *Politics and War*, 187.

[13] Worcester College MS 114 (Clarke Papers), fo. 115 (29 November 1648).

Pride's Purge

Initially the officers had intended to dissolve parliament, but their friends in Westminster persuaded them to opt instead for a purge. Lord Grey of Groby visited army headquarters at St Albans on 23 November, in all likelihood to discuss the list of MPs to be purged. Two days later the army shifted its headquarters to Windsor Castle, which would shortly become the king's prison, and which also had a large arsenal to recommend it. Once at Windsor the officers convened a prayer meeting. As observers by now appreciated, Fairfax's officers were never more potentially dangerous than when they wrestled with the Lord in prayer. After being spiritually fortified they returned, on 28 November, to the debate on political strategy. There was no disagreement that they should occupy the capital. With admirable but doomed courage the Commons majority ordered the army to withdraw 40 miles from London. Instead the army mustered, 7,000 strong, in Hyde Park on Friday 1 December, and advanced to Westminster the same afternoon. While the City trembled at the thought of rapine and plunder the Commons majority continued defiant.

On Monday 4 December the Council of Officers had still not decided exactly how to deal with the Commons, continuing to cherish the hope that the MPs would purge themselves of 'corrupt and apostasised members'.[14] The army's friends, aware of their minority status, preferred a solution imposed from without. The House spent the whole of that day in acrimonious debate, first condemning the army's removing the king to Hurst Castle, and then turning to the king's answer to the Newport Propositions. They knew that the position they took regarding his answer would have far-reaching consequences. Most MPs stayed for the stormy, all-night sitting. Not until 8 a.m. on 5 December, crushed with fatigue, did they vote that the king's answer was 'a ground for the House to proceed upon, for the settlement of the peace of the kingdom'.[15]

The army reacted swiftly to this slap in the face. Fairfax refused to see a delegation of six MPs who came to explain the Commons vote to the Council of Officers. In consultation with their friends in the House the officers marked out between 80 and 90 MPs for arrest. Many of those on the list were prudent enough to stay away the next day, but on that morning (6 December) Colonel Thomas Pride cordoned off the House with the men of his own and Nathaniel Rich's regiments, and then, with the assistance of the MP Lord Grey of Groby, arrested 41 MPs. The officers called

[14] Rushworth, *Hist. Coll.*, Vol. 7, 1345, 1348; Bodl. MS Tanner 57, fo. 450.
[15] *CJ*, Vol. 6, 93.

upon the remainder to proceed to 'the execution of justice, to set a short period to your own power, [and] to provide for a speedy succession of equal Representatives according to our late Remonstrance'.[16]

The arrival of Cromwell

Later that day Oliver Cromwell rode in from the north and took up residence in one of the king's bedrooms in Whitehall. About the purge he declared that 'he had not been acquainted with this design; yet since it was done, he was glad of it, and would endeavour to maintain it'.[17] This and other enigmatic statements have given rise to conflicting interpretations of Cromwell's role in the events leading up to the trial and execution of the king. When did he make up his mind that the king must die? Why did he stay in the north during the critical months from September to November when the army was debating and resolving questions of the highest importance at St Albans and Windsor? The first thing to be noted is that Cromwell's responsibilities in the north were anything but trivial. He had had to ensure that there was a political as well as a military solution to the war with Scotland, and that the northern kingdom remained quiet. He had to supervise the siege of Pontefract, one of the strongest castles in England, and he was also in charge of the garrisons at Berwick, Carlisle and Newcastle. On 28 November Fairfax wrote instructing him to come to headquarters with all convenient speed on account of 'the very great business now in agitation'.[18] He left almost immediately, but he was slowed by the four regiments that accompanied him on his march as far as Bedfordshire.

---

[16] Gentles, *NMA*, 281–3. The best account of the events of 6 December 1648 remains Underdown's *Pride's Purge: Politics in the Puritan Revolution*, ch. 6.

[17] Edmund Ludlow, *Memoirs*, ed. Colin Firth, Vol. 1, 211–12. David Scott has discovered a pay warrant with Cromwell's signature, dated 2 December, which would seem to indicate that he was in London before the purge: NA. SP28/251, unfol. However, we know that Cromwell was in Nottinghamshire on 1 December, and it would have been almost impossible for him to travel, with his bodyguard of 60 troopers, from Mansfield to London in a day. Ludlow had little love for Cromwell, and there is no reason to suppose that he would have cooperated in a conspiracy to conceal the fact of Cromwell's presence in London in the days leading up to Pride's Purge. The most likely explanation for the pay warrant is that Cromwell added his signature – which appears at the bottom of the warrant – some days after the others had signed. I am grateful to David Scott, Jason Peacey and John Morrill for discussion on this point.

[18] *CP*, Vol. 2, 63.

Between the time of the Newport Treaty and the king's trial Cromwell kept open his lines of communication with both radicals and moderates. When Lilburne came north in September he met with Cromwell and the two men stayed in touch throughout the autumn. Cromwell gave implicit support to the Leveller petition of 11 September; he advised on the negotiations over the Agreement of the People; and his regiment was known to be especially receptive to Leveller agitation. At the end of November he and the officers at the siege of Pontefract met with the parliamentary gentry of the four northern counties and agreed upon a petition to parliament calling for justice upon delinquents. Earlier that month he had written to Colonel Robert Hammond, the king's gaoler, assuring him that he had not turned into a Presbyterian but was merely trying to come to an accommodation with those of the Scots who were non-cavalierish. Bowing to Hammond's own opinion, he allowed that a peaceful settlement with the king was desirable, but 'peace is only good when we receive it out of our Father's hand . . . War is good when led to by our Father'.[19] Peace with this king was not, for all he could tell, in God's hand. Strong but not conclusive evidence confirming this interpretation is supplied by Lilburne writing six months later about his effort to get Cromwell to agree that the sole end of the civil wars had been to establish the people's rights and freedoms under a just government. Lilburne was bluntly told at the Nag's Head Tavern by Independents who had spoken to Cromwell's 'creature' that the army's desire was 'to cut off the king's head . . . and force and thoroughly purge, if not dissolve the Parliament'.[20] Two weeks later Cromwell wrote to Fairfax commending his regiment's petition and his officers' 'very great zeal to have impartial justice done upon offenders'.[21] He also commended the Army's Remonstrance of 20 November, expressing doubt that any good could be expected from 'this man against whom the Lord hath witnessed'.[22]

John Morrill and Philip Baker, who have recently reviewed all the evidence about Pride's Purge and the king's trial agree that Cromwell wanted the king put on trial and deposed if he would not abdicate. He had no wish to see monarchy abolished, and though he wanted the king dead, he feared

---

[19] Abbott, *Cromwell*, Vol. I, 677.

[20] Lilburne, *Legall Fundamentall Liberties*, reprinted in Wolfe, *Leveller Manifestoes*, 411–12. The 'creature' was a Mr Hunt.

[21] Abbott, *Cromwell*, Vol. 1, 690.

[22] Ibid., 698–9.

that cutting off his head might shipwreck everything the army wanted to achieve, because of all the forces arrayed against regicide.[23]

Who were the forces that opposed executing or even trying the king for capital crimes? Recent work has underlined how protean they were, and how nervous the officers must have been as they prepared themselves to lay violent hands on their anointed monarch. Royalists reminded anyone who would listen that king killing was frowned on in Scripture. Furthermore, so flagrant a defiance of the popular desire for a peaceful settlement would mean that a standing army would have to be kept perpetually on foot, which would entail heavy taxation and 'lasting war with Scotland and Ireland'.[24] Even after it was purged, the supposedly revolutionary remnant of the House of Commons had refused to repeal the motions that had provoked Pride's Purge until Fairfax answered their demand for the release of the imprisoned members. Fairfax did not favour them with an answer. There was also the House of Lords, unanimously opposed to the Purge and trial on account of their apprehension that an England without a king would soon be an England without an upper house. London's Presbyterian clergy unleashed a blizzard of paper in December and January, reinforced by thunderous pulpit denunciations of the army and all its works. The officers can only have squirmed as City ministers hammered home the point that under the Solemn League and Covenant parliament and army were sworn to protect the person of the king. Reneging on this covenant with God, they warned, would have the direst consequences.[25] Among these were the spread of sectarianism and religious anarchy. The Levellers too were vociferously opposed to trying the king, in contradiction to the position they had taken in their September petition. They warned that the overthrow of monarchy under the auspices of the army could portend nothing other than a political dictatorship by the army.[26] Within the army council were a number of officers who were troubled that killing the king violated the Solemn League and Covenant and defied the wishes of the vast majority of the nation. They also urged that having a weak, discredited king under their direct control would leave them in a stronger position than if they killed that king. They would then have to cope with a young

---

[23] Morrill and Baker, 'Oliver Cromwell, the regicide and the Sons of Zeruiah', 29. See also Scott, *Politics and War*, 186.

[24] BL. Add. MS 36913 (Aston Papers), fos. 166v, 168–9.

[25] Elliot Vernon, 'The quarrel of the covenant: the London Presbyterians and the regicide', in Peacey (ed.), *Regicides*, 209–14.

[26] Andrew Sharp, 'The Levellers and the end of Charles I', in Peacey (ed.), *Regicides*, 192–4.

claimant to the throne over whom they had no power. The Prince of Wales, at large on the continent, 'potent in foreign alliances and strong in the affections of the people' would be a far more dangerous customer.[27]

The navy

External threats loomed, if anything, larger than domestic opposition to the trial and condemnation of the king. The naval revolt of the previous May had given the royalists the core of a new fleet of their own. By August that fleet numbered 11 warships and several armed merchantmen, and had been given safe haven in Dutch ports by Charles I's son-in-law, the Stadtholder Prince William II of Orange-Nassau. The shaky allegiance of the remaining parliamentary ships had been rendered even shakier by the Prince of Wales's assumption of the command of the fleet, and his nomination of Prince Rupert as his commander-in-chief. Conscious of the unreliability of his crews, parliament's admiral, the Earl of Warwick, had sailed back to the Downs in late November without engaging the royalists at Helvoetsluys on the Dutch coast, though he did detach four ships from their fleet. Rupert leapt at the opportunity afforded by Warwick's departure to send several small frigates to sea, and then set sail himself with ten ships in late January, to establish a royalist base at Kinsale on the Irish south coast.[28] The unmastered royalist fleet posed an ever-present danger to the parliamentary regime in the winter and spring of 1648–49. A sobering reminder of the reality of that danger was the quiet opposition of Warwick to bringing Charles to the block. His position seems to have been that leading royalists, not the king, should be required to expiate the sins of the second civil war.[29] In token of their respect for Warwick's importance the MPs hastened to back his request for improved funding and expansion of the navy.

Ormond

More worrying than the activities of the royalists at sea was their resurgence in Ireland, and the diplomatic developments that accompanied it.

---

[27] Bodl. MS Eng.c.6075, 155/1, 'A deliberation on the execution of justice vppon HR', fo. 7v; Bodl. MS Clarendon 34, fo. 13-v.

[28] Bernard Capp, 'Naval operations', in Kenyon and Ohlmeyer (eds), *The Civil Wars*, 184, 186–7.

[29] John Adamson, 'The frighted junto: perceptions of Ireland, and the last attempts at settlement with Charles I', in Peacey (ed.), *Regicides*, 43.

On 18 December Isaac Dorislaus brought news to parliament of a treaty that the States General of the Dutch Republic had concluded with the Confederate Catholics of Kilkenny for 'mutual trade and commerce'.[30] A commercial pact between rebel-held Ireland and the world's greatest maritime power had clear strategic implications. A treaty between Kilkenny and the Irish royalists under Ormond was said to be imminent. The nightmare scenario of an Irish, royalist and Dutch naval alliance must have imprinted itself in more than a few parliamentary imaginations in London. The Marquess of Ormond was already working to create a joint royalist–Confederate fleet. This constellation of foes threatened to encircle southern England from the Irish Sea to the northern approaches to the Channel. Any attack on Confederate shipping carried the danger of triggering a war with the Dutch.

Ireland was the kingdom that parliament had not yet bent to its will. How great a danger did it pose to the regime at Westminster? Although Ormond had been commissioned by the king to organize Ireland for the royalist cause as long ago as October 1647, it had taken him another year just to set foot in Ireland once again. He immediately signed a fresh truce with the Confederates and set about constructing a military alliance to wage war against the 'Independent Party' in England.[31] Not until the following summer would it become clear that Ormond, his ramshackle coalition rent by the bitterest religious divisions, was a paper tiger. For the time being Marchamont Nedham and other royalist newsbook writers were able to frighten Londoners with the 'news' that Colonel Jones was on the verge of surrendering Dublin, and that Chester would be the next target of a resurgent royalism. Hard on the heels of a seaborne assault on Chester would come a rendezvous between Irish and Lancashire royalists. With hindsight we know that this was all a chimera, but in late December 1648 it seemed to assume a menacing reality with the arrival of reports of 'a bloudy Fight at Sea between the English and the Irish', in which a Confederate fleet had captured 14 merchant ships.[32] From his base at Helvoetsluys on the Dutch coast Prince Rupert was playing havoc with English shipping.[33] Early in January Rupert slipped out of port with nine ships and made for Ireland. Morale was so low in the parliamentary navy

---

[30] CSPD, 1648–49, 340.

[31] A Declaration of the Lord Lieutenant General of Ireland ([27 November] 1648), E473/25, 4.

[32] Articles Exhibited against the King ([29 December] 1648), E536/21, 5; Mod. Intelligencer (14–21 December 1648), E477/14, sig. Mmmmmmmm2v.

[33] Bodl. MS Tanner 57, fo. 449, printed in Powell, The Navy, 186.

that no attempt was made to intercept him. A few days earlier Ormond and Inchiquin warned Fairfax's officers and parliament that if so much as 'one hair of his Majesty's head fall to the ground by their means' they would take 'speedy revenge upon them and their posterity'.[34] The revolutionaries had ample grounds for fear at the potential consequences of cutting off the king's head.

Fear was mixed with anger as they contemplated the evidence of what they construed to be the king's incorrigible perfidy. His refusal to call off Ormond seemed to make nonsense of the majority view in the Commons that the king's concessions at Newport were the basis for a 'safe and well-grounded peace'. As a petition from Hewson's regiment to Fairfax put it, the king was 'the grand Enemy and great abettor of Ormond in Ireland, his son [Prince Charles] in Holland, and any other party that hath but a sword to draw for his destructive designs'.[35] Ormond was again fingered as a principal antagonist in the army's final indictment of the king just before Christmas: 'the king hath granted commissions to the Prince, as also to ORMOND and his associate Irish Rebels, which are not recalled to this day'.[36]

At the same time the officers strove to mend fences with the ten or twelve peers who had loyally backed the New Model Army since the spring of 1645 and the Self-Denying Ordinance – most notably the earls of Northumberland, Salisbury, Denbigh and Pembroke, and Viscount Saye and Sele. They 'gave attendance', and paid respectful attention to the opinions and requests of the Earl of Warwick. Client MPs such as Rudyerd and Fiennes (son of Viscount Saye) were among those released from prison, while Michael Oldisworth, Pembroke's patronage secretary, was spared the unpleasantness of prison in the first place, even though he had actively promoted the Newport Treaty. Pembroke was appointed constable of Windsor Castle, making him, in name at least, the king's gaoler.

The officers also received a delegation of four peers – Denbigh, Pembroke, Salisbury and Northumberland – at army headquarters to discuss the future settlement of the kingdom.[37] This was the meeting that led

---

[34] *Merc. Melancholicus* (25 December 1648–1 January 1649), E536/27, 7.

[35] *Two Petitions Presented to His Excellency the Lord Fairfax* (24, 25 November 1648), E473/23, 7.

[36] *Heads of the Charge against the King, Drawn up by the Generall Councell of the Armie* ([24 December] 1648), E477/25, 5.

[37] Bodl. MS Clarendon 34, fo. 12. I concur with John Adamson that 'North' was not Lord North, but the Earl of Northumberland: 'The frighted junto', 45 and n.37.

to the Denbigh mission to the king later in the month. Charles was apparently offered his life if he would agree to the status of nominal monarch, an English Doge of Venice stripped of all but ceremonial powers. More urgently he had to promise to cancel Ormond's threatened invasion from Ireland. Denbigh arrived at Windsor on Christmas Day, but his mission was rebuffed. Charles, confident that 'his Irish subjects will come in their time and rescue him', saw little need to bargain with a militant war-party peer.[38]

Cromwell, meanwhile, had been working assiduously to dampen opposition to the army's assault on parliament, and its plans for bringing the king to justice. He knew the critical importance of broadening support for the army's course of action. In the week or two after the purge many MPs boycotted the House, causing attendance to dip perilously close to the quorum of 40. Consequently, once the purged House had repealed the vote in favour of a personal treaty with the king, denounced the king's answer to the Newport propositions, and taken steps to pay the army's arrears, the army returned the compliment by releasing nearly half the imprisoned MPs, and readmitting a number of others who had been secluded. Cromwell himself put in a lot of time meeting with moderate MPs Bulstrode Whitelocke and Sir Thomas Widdrington and inviting them to draw up proposals for the settlement of the kingdom. Flattered by his attention, the two lawyers set to their task with a keen sense of their own importance. They did not realize that Cromwell was keeping them harmlessly busy while the army got on with its deadly agenda. Nothing ever came of Whitelocke's and Widdrington's proposals.

Cromwell also dedicated much time to several meetings with the Duke of Hamilton, imprisoned in Windsor Castle. His hope was to pry out of him information as to the identity of 'his correspondents in England' when he had been preparing the Scottish invasion.[39] It was common knowledge that these correspondents included the king himself. Hamilton's refusal to betray his sovereign meant that Cromwell's time was wasted.

There were many in the army who hoped that a way could be found to avoid executing the king. Hugh Peters, one of the mouthpieces of the high command put it about that the army would not prove so unreasonable as men imagined. Indeed, at the end of December officers opposed to putting the king to death introduced a prophetess, Elizabeth Poole, to the army

---

[38] *His Majesties Last Proposals to the Officers of the Armie* ([28 December] 1648), E536/13, 1.

[39] Burnet, *Hamilton*, 379.

council. She told of a vision that led her to infer that the army could try and even depose the king, but not shed his blood. She was heard with respect. Perhaps it was such crumbs of news that led Marchamont Nedham to inform Secretary Nicholas that no more than six members of the Council were driving on 'this horrid treason', but he was deceiving himself.[40] Meanwhile, the City's Presbyterian ministers had stepped up their campaign by adding protest meetings accompanied by prayer and fasting. Cromwell, Ireton and Peters, who knew the potency of these latter weapons, went about the city confronting the ministers in person, trying to gag them with threats of military force. Several more regiments were marched into London. When the Common Council tried to appease the army with 100 barrels of 'good strong beer' and two cartloads of bread, butter and cheese, the officers were unimpressed. Tired of seeing their men sleep on bare boards they wheeled artillery into position at Blackfriars, while they raided the parliamentary treasuries in Goldsmiths', Weavers' and Haberdashers' Halls. In St Paul's soldiers warmed themselves at great fires on the cathedral floor, fuelled by carved timber, scaffolding and other materials which they found to hand. When the City implored Fairfax to remove the troops he sardonically replied that their continued presence would facilitate the collection of London's large assessment arrears.

The army was now feeling more confident about moving against the king. The municipal elections of 21 December had barred from voting all those who had supported the king or even signed the petition calling for him to be brought to London. The result of these exclusions was a Common Council dominated by radical militia officers who backed the army to the hilt. Two or three days later the army published another indictment of the king as the 'capital and grand offender and author of our troubles . . . [who] is guilty of all the trouble, loss, hazard and expense of the blood and mischiefs that have happened by the late wars in this kingdom'.[41] The Rump parliament fell in line with the army, voting to

---

[40] Bodl. MS Clarendon 34, fo. 13-v. In this report to Secretary, Nicholas Nedham claimed that the letter opposing the regicide had been sent from Cromwell to Pride, and that in it he threatened to organize the assassination of the six pro-regicide ringleaders. The notion is palpably absurd. Nedham is a much better guide to parliamentary politics than he is to army politics in 1648–49. According to Jason Peacey, Nedham was also convinced that the grandees planned to have a 'duke of Venice' rather than a royal martyr. Threats of death were only meant to 'bend him to their cue': Jason Peacey, ' "The counterfeit silly curr": money, politics, and the forging of royalist newspapers during the English Civil War', *Huntingdon Library Quarterly* (hereafter *HLQ*) 67 (2004), 43.

[41] *Heads of the Charge against the King*, E477/25, 5–6.

consider 'how to proceed in a way of justice against the king and other capital offenders'.[42]

By the end of the year, convinced by the news from the United Provinces and Ireland that the king was continuing to plot their destruction, the army council and their revolutionary colleagues in the Rump agreed that the king would be brought to trial. Was this only a ploy to frighten him into submission? Did they hope that the prospect of execution would induce him to call off Rupert and Ormond? Debate continued in both the army and the House over whether he should be executed or merely deposed; whether he should be replaced by his third son, Prince Henry, or whether there should be a king at all. For public consumption Cromwell continued to cultivate ambiguity, but with menacing undertones. When he spoke in the Commons debate on whether to try the king for his life he declared,

[I]f any man whatsoever had carried on this design of deposing the king and disinheriting his posterity, or if any man had yet such a design, he should be the greatest traitor and rebel in the world. But since the providence of God hath cast this upon us, I cannot but submit to providence, though I am not yet provided to give you my advice.[43]

On 27 December there appeared the first public signifier that the debate over the king's fate had been finally settled within the army's inner councils. By an order of the Council of War Charles was no longer served on the knee in Windsor Castle; all ceremonies of state were eliminated and the number of his attendants was reduced.

The Agreement of the People

While preparations for the solemn drama of the overthrow of monarchy approached their climax, another drama, less compelling, but of almost equal political import was unfolding only a few steps away from the houses of parliament. The army with its political and religious advisers was drafting a new constitution for England. By mid-December the Committee of Sixteen had completed its revision of the Agreement of the People and submitted it to the Council of Officers. John Lilburne later put it about that the army was bound to adopt the committee's draft, but he is contradicted by the title page of the published version, which made it

---

[42] *CJ*, Vol. 6, 102–3.
[43] Bodl. MS Clarendon 34, fo. 72.

crystal clear that it was for the *consideration* of the officers. Moreover he raised no objection at the time when the officers began to debate it. At least 160 officers and civilians, including 30 clerics, are known to have attended the debates on the agreement, which consumed the better part of a month between mid-December and mid-January. All the participants seemed to share the conviction that they were taking part in deliberations of the greatest historical importance. They believed that providence had handed them an unrepeatable opportunity to shape the political and spiritual destiny of their country.

The draft agreement assumed that monarchy and House of Lords had ceased to exist. The present parliament would dissolve before the end of April 1649. Future parliaments would be elected according to a new electoral map that reflected the present distribution of population. Electors would be male householders assessed for poor relief who were not royalists, servants or wage-earners, and who had signed the agreement. An executive, called the Council of State, appointed by parliament and responsible to it, would govern in the intervals between biennially elected parliaments. At the heart of the agreement was the list of powers reserved by the people to themselves. Parliament would have no right to compel people's religious practice, conscript them for military service, question them for their actions during the civil war, violate the principle of equality before the law, or punish where there was not an existing law. No member of parliament would be able to handle public money. The agreement also guaranteed freedom of commerce, jury trials and a maximum interest rate of 6 per cent per annum, and it abolished the excise tax, imprisonment for debt, tithes and capital punishment – except for murder.[44] At Putney in 1647 the higher officers had entered strenuous objections against franchise and electoral reform. But modifications had been made, and Ireton had moved to the left during the intervening year. The drafters of the new version of the agreement had also taken the measure of political realities. All who had supported the king in any way would be denied the vote for seven years. Anyone who opposed the agreement would be permanently excluded. Ireton's chief reason for supporting this second version of the agreement was that he saw in it the necessary bulwark against the election of a royalist parliament and the recall of the king. While most historians have overlooked the restrictive nature of the franchise under the second

---

[44] Rushworth, *Hist. Coll.*, Vol. 7, 1358–61. For a discussion of the Second Agreement and its political context see Ian Gentles, 'The Agreements of the People in their political contexts, 1647–1649', in Mendle (ed.), *Putney Debates*, 148–74.

agreement, its many critics at the time did not. Even the editor of the friendly newsbook, *The Moderate*, conceded that the agreement would initially disenfranchise a large segment of the people.[45]

The issue that inspired the most impassioned debate at Whitehall was not the franchise, but religious liberty. There were many ringing statements against the magistrate having any power over men's consciences, but it was left to Ireton, who never suffered himself to be browbeaten by the majority, to speak up for the state's responsibility in religious affairs. No libertarian, Ireton was animated at all times by the vision of a godly commonwealth. It had been a function of the magistrate to restrain sin since ancient times, he pointed out, and nothing had happened recently to abrogate that function.

Ireton's frequent and lengthy interventions showed that the agreement mattered to him. If the staging of the debate had been merely a sop to the radicals, a 'children's rattle' in Lilburne's bitterly cynical phrase, to distract them while the grandees got on with the real business of the day, disposing of the king, it is hard to see why the commissary-general expended so much time, and made himself so disliked, in his efforts to make the agreement say what he wanted it to say. In the end he won his point: under article nine there would be religious freedom for all (except Anglicans and papists), but Christianity would be the public religion of the nation, with a ministry maintained out of state funds. This article foreshadowed the Cromwellian Church of the 1650s with its loose national structure and large measure of toleration for sectarians.

There were other minor modifications, but the lower officers rallied to defeat Ireton's attempts to delete the prohibition against *ex post facto* legislation, and to give parliament power over moral questions. The amended version, henceforth known as the Officers' Agreement, was laid before the Commons on the opening day of the king's trial, 20 January. The army's high-level delegation was led by Lieutenant-General of the Ordnance, Thomas Hammond. After giving him a respectful hearing the Commons ordered the agreement printed, and promised to deal with it soon. They did not keep the promise, and the officers never reminded them of it. Some historians have concluded that the whole episode was a charade, and that the higher officers never intended the agreement to be implemented. We have already seen why this interpretation is simplistic. On the other hand

---

[45] *The Moderate* (14–21 November 1648), E473/1, 154. See also *A Warning, or a Word of Advice to the City of London* ([30 November] 1648), E474/6, 3, for an admission that 'the major party . . . are not to have any vote'.

it is true that the agreement had few passionate supporters. Even the Levellers were less worked up about the structure of government than about decentralizing political power and liberalizing the laws. The gathered churches, who might have been expected to endorse it, were more interested in establishing the reign of Christ than fashioning a new political constitution. As for the members of the Rump parliament, apart from an understandable reluctance to sign their own marching orders, many of them were so startled by the bitter opposition to trying the king that they concluded that now was not the time for radical democratization of the machinery of government. Nor was there any groundswell of support from the army's rank and file. The most dedicated support for the agreement had come from the lower officers, who by their persistence had won several victories in the Council of Officers against Ireton and the grandees. These victories may have caused the latter to become lukewarm in their support for a document they had earlier taken quite seriously. Whatever the case, the agreement was pushed to the political sidelines and soon forgotten by everyone except John Lilburne.

The king's trial

On 28 December the charge against the king was read out on the floor of the House of Commons. It was a comprehensive indictment, broadly similar to the one promulgated by the army four days earlier. The ordinance for erecting a High Court of Justice to try the king was ready by the beginning of January and sent to the upper house. The peers threw it out, as they did the Commons resolution that 'by the fundamental laws of this kingdom, it is treason in the king of England to levy war against the parliament and kingdom of England'.[46] In the hope of bringing the machinery of revolution grinding to a halt the Lords then adjourned themselves for a week. The Commons retaliated with a declaration that the people 'are, under God, the original of all just power', and that the Commons, as their representatives, possessed supreme power, and that whatever they decided had the force of law, whether or not the Lords assented. They had just turned England's parliament into a unicameral body.

The High Court of Justice comprised 135 commissioners, of whom 29 were serving army officers. Efforts to make the court broadly representative of the social and legal elite were a failure. None of the half-dozen nominated peers or the lord chief justices attended any of its sittings.

---

[46] *CJ*, Vol. 6. 110.

Perhaps most embarrassingly, the army's commander-in-chief, Thomas Lord Fairfax, came to the first meeting on 8 January but refused to sit down, and attended no further meetings. Several other army officers failed to turn up, pleading pressure of work. Colonel Algernon Sidney, governor of Dover Castle, threw cold water on the proceedings with the biting observation that not only could the king be tried by no court; no one could be tried by this court. He then retired to his father's house at Penshurst to sit out the trial.

The chronic absence of nearly half the commissioners demonstrates that many shared Sidney's doubts. A small knot of revolutionaries who had banished their own doubts hounded the rest and kept them to the agenda. Some were soldiers – Cromwell, Ireton and Harrison. Some were MPs – Henry Marten, Thomas Scot, John Lisle, Thomas Chaloner and John Blakiston. The noisiest was the redoubtable Hugh Peters, who, alternating between bouts of manic frenzy and melancholic sickness, dashed to and fro between Westminster and the City, stirring up his colleagues and confuting their foes. The recently elected Common Council of London, under the radical leadership of Colonel Robert Tichborne, played its part in suppressing public disaffection. There was also steady military pressure from the forces outside London on the Rump and the Council of Officers not to falter in their resolve. But the grandees also had to rein in those who threatened to upset the process by their clamour for complete revolution now. Cromwell, conscious of the debt he owed the radical peers for past support, resisted attempts to abolish the House of Lords while the trial was in mid-career.

As the final details of the trial were thrashed out the revolutionary caucus met day and night, sometimes in rooms near Westminster Hall, sometimes in taverns like the Star in Coleman Street, and occasionally in Ireton's lodgings in Windsor. The last pre-trial meeting took place in the Painted Chamber in the palace of Westminster on the morning of 20 January. Suddenly came the announcement that the king had just landed at the stairs on the river leading up to Sir Robert Cotton's House. Cromwell went to the window to watch, and was stunned to realize that they had still not decided how they would answer Charles if he challenged their authority to try him. His fellow commissioners fell silent, except for Henry Marten. Never at a loss for words, the republican MP said they would inform the king that they acted 'in the name of the commons in parliament assembled, and all the good people of England'.[47] After reading over

---

[47] *A Complete Collection of State Trials and Proceedings for High Treason*, ed. Francis Hargrave, Vol. 2, 392.

and approving the charge as it had been drawn up by the solicitor John Cook the commissioners adjourned to Westminster Hall, England's greatest public building since its construction in the twelfth century.

It was 2 p.m. when the 68 commissioners processed into the hall. While 12 halberdiers went to fetch the king, the clerk read the roll-call of commissioners. First on his list was the army's commander-in-chief. 'He has more wit than to be here', shouted Lady Fairfax from behind her mask in one of the galleries. After the roll-call the king appeared, tightly escorted by the halberdiers. The president of the court, the Cheshire attorney John Bradshaw, signalled to John Cook to read the charge. Its reading took about ten minutes, the essence being that Charles as king of England had been 'trusted with a limited power to govern', yet he had engineered 'a wicked design to erect and uphold in himself an unlimited and tyrannical power to rule according to his will, and to overthrow the rights and liberties of the people'. In prosecuting this design he had 'traitorously and maliciously levied war against the present parliament and the people'. Most damning of all, in spite of being twice defeated in war, he was plotting to plunge the kingdom into bloodshed a third time. He had not ceased issuing commissions to the Prince of Wales and other royalists, 'and to the Earl of Ormond, and to the Irish rebels . . . associated with him, from whom further invasions upon this land are threatened'. He was therefore to be impeached as a 'tyrant, traitor and murderer, and a public and implacable enemy to the Commonwealth of England'.[48]

Charles answered the charge with a question: by what *lawful* authority had he been summoned before them? Bradshaw merely reiterated the gist of the charge and ordered him to answer 'in the name of the people of England, of which you are *elected* king'. Charles pounced on this piece of novel constitutional theory. 'England was never an elective kingdom, but a hereditary kingdom for near these thousand years.' Moreover, 'I do stand more for the liberty of my people than any here that come to be my pretended judges.' Rattled by this unexpected eloquence, Bradshaw halted the proceedings and ordered the prisoner removed. This dramatic confrontation was repeated twice more on 22 and 23 January, after which the commissioners went into secret session in the Painted Chamber to deal with their own crisis of self-confidence. It was decided to call witnesses against the king, and fresh attempts were made to get Sir Thomas Fairfax to attend the next session.

[48] Rushworth, *Hist. Coll.*, Vol. 7, 1396–8.

During these days Fairfax's public career hit rock bottom. A first-class general, he was out of his depth when it came to political manoeuvre. Radical in sympathy, he had not shrunk from chairing the revolutionary General Council of the Army in 1647, and had willingly led the invasions of London in August 1647 and December 1648. While Cromwell assumed a steadily higher political profile, Fairfax had still retained control of army appointments. He instinctively distrusted the Levellers, and had been one of the handful of officers to resist the adoption of Ireton's November 1648 Remonstrance. Yet he remained at his post during and after Pride's Purge. He drew the line, however, at trying his anointed sovereign. Why had he even allowed his name to stand as a commissioner for the trial? Perhaps it was a blunder, perhaps he hoped that he could be a force for moderation, but when the truth hit home to him that his colleagues were implacably determined to put the king to death, he boycotted the court and bent all his efforts to derailing its proceedings.

It is possible that had Charles been willing to recognize the authority of the court, enter a plea, and order Ormond to cease his mobilization, the commissioners would have been willing to work out a deal that would have spared the king's life.[49] But Charles remained obdurate to the end. On Wednesday 24 January, after a closed session, the commissioners empowered a seven-man committee to draw up the sentence of death. At the next public sitting, on Saturday 27 January Lady Fairfax created a second commotion from the gallery and was hustled out. Charles, finally realizing that his stalling and bluffing had only exasperated his tormentors and further imperilled his situation, asked for permission to address the Lords and Commons jointly in the Painted Chamber. Perhaps at last his intention was to offer abdication in return for his life. However, the commissioners knew that granting such an appeal they would undo the work of Pride's Purge and undermine everything the Rump had done since 6 December. Bradshaw had no choice: he rejected the king's request.

The sentence was then read and the 67 commissioners present stood up to affirm their assent. The king was shattered, not so much by the sentence of death, for which he had prepared himself, as by the words 'tyrant, traitor and murderer'. He asked to be heard once more, but Bradshaw rebuffed him and ordered his removal. His exit was punctuated by

---

[49] Sean Kelsey, 'The trial of Charles I', *EHR*, 118 (2003), 601, 614–15; Sean Kelsey 'The death of Charles I', *HJ*, 45 (2002), 729, 734; Adamson, 'The frighted junto', 59–61.

Lieutenant Colonel Axtell's men crying 'Execution! Justice! Execution!' Others wept openly.[50]

On Sunday both sides girded themselves for the climax of the hastening tragedy. The soldiers, radical clergy, and many of their Presbyterian opponents fasted. At St James's the soldiers were treated to a homiletic extravaganza by Hugh Peters on the grisly text, 'thou art cast out of thy grave like an abominable branch, and as the raiment of those that are slain, thrust through with a sword'.[51] The officers were absorbed with a last-minute appeal from the Dutch ambassadors to save the king's life. The meeting, which took place at Fairfax's house, was nugatory. Cromwell arrived in the company of two troops of horse. Did he mean to intimidate Fairfax as royalist sources suggested, or was he merely taking special care for his own safety?[52] Fairfax did not intimidate easily. Early the following day he summoned a council of war, at which he laboured to persuade his fellow officers to postpone the execution. They were unmoved. The Scots commissioners in London weighed in with strongly worded appeals to both Fairfax and Cromwell to call off the execution.[53] Their letters had no effect except to increase Fairfax's moral agony.

The judges then signed the death warrant, but the signatories fell so far short of the number that had stood up to condemn the king that on the same day (Monday 29 January), Cromwell stood at the Commons door with the warrant in his hand, trying to catch those who were evading their duty. Some MPs slipped by him, but he pursued them into the house saying, 'those that are gone in shall set their hands, I will have their

---

[50] *The Bloody Court, or the Fatall Tribunall* (1649), 6–10, cited by Jason Peacey, 'Reporting a revolution', in Peacey (ed.), *Regicides*, 171.

[51] Isaiah 14: 19–20.

[52] Cromwell's arrival at Fairfax's house accompanied by two troops of horse has hitherto gone unnoticed by historians. The royalist newswriter on 31 January seems to suggest that the incident occurred on Sunday 21 January ('Sunday was se'nnight'), when 'Cromwell put a guard upon Fairfax, accusing him of an intention to deliver the king': Carte, *Orig. Letters*, Vol. 1, 212; in which case it could not have been connected with the meeting with the Dutch ambassadors. Aaron Guerdon, writing some four or five months later, stated explicitly that Cromwell was at Fairfax's house on Sunday 28 January, but said that he arrived at night, with the purpose of counteracting the preaching of the Presbyterian ministers: *A Most Learned, Conscientious and Devout Exercise* ([25 June] 1649), 8. I owe this reference to the kindness of John Morrill.

[53] *Acts of the Parliaments of Scotland during the Commonwealth*, Vol. 6, pt 2, 697. I am indebted to John Morrill, both for this reference and for conversations about the regicide.

hands now'.[54] By the end of the day the total had reached 59, of which 18 were army officers in current service. Most of the leading officers signed, including Cromwell, Ireton, Pride and Harrison. Notable among the non-signatories, apart from Fairfax, were Major-General Philip Skippon and Colonel Fleetwood.[55] Prominent among the MPs who signed were Henry Marten, Sir John Danvers, Sir John Bourchier, John Blakiston, William Purefoy, Thomas Scot, Gregory Norton and Thomas Chaloner.

Charles was escorted from St James's to Whitehall on the bitterly cold morning of Tuesday 30 January. He was kept waiting until 2 p.m. in the banqueting house that Inigo Jones had designed for him while the Commons rushed through a bill making it illegal for anyone to proclaim a new king. Meanwhile Fairfax and the Dutch ambassadors vainly continued their efforts to postpone the execution. Once the Commons bill had been enacted Charles was escorted onto a raised scaffold draped in black outside the Banqueting House. A great crowd had gathered to witness the first public execution of an English king, but Charles was separated from this sea of faces by densely packed ranks of mounted troopers. Speaking briefly he proclaimed his innocence, asked God to forgive those who had brought about his death, and affirmed that he was dying 'a Christian according to the profession of the Church of England'.[56] When the axe descended, severing in a single stroke his head from his body, a tremendous, involuntary groan rose from the crowd. It was their expression of horror at the unprecedented act of national parricide. They were not allowed to linger with their grief. At once troops of horse swept down Whitehall from opposite directions scattering everyone in sight. Within minutes the streets were empty.

While the nation was still paralysed with shock at the king's death the new rulers acted quickly to consolidate their power. On 1 February the remnant of the House of Commons decided that no one who had voted on 5 December that the king's offers were a ground for settlement should be allowed to sit until he had recorded his dissent from that motion. Five days later, overriding Cromwell's earlier objection, they voted to abolish the House of Lords. The next day the office of king was also eliminated. At the same time the chief executive body of the previous two years, the Derby House Committee, was replaced by a larger Council of State. Several peers were welcomed onto the Council – Pembroke, Salisbury, Mulgrave and

---

[54] *State Trials*, Vol. 2, 392.
[55] Colonel John Lambert, another non-signatory, was at Pontefract at the time.
[56] *King Charls His Speech upon the Scaffold*, 11.

Grey of Warke, but parliament made a point of rejecting two of the most prominent regicides – Henry Ireton and Thomas Harrison. This last measure was intended to communicate the Rump's intention to take a more conservative tack in the future. One-third of the new executive body had military associations; some were hardliners such as Cromwell and Hesilrige; others such as Fairfax and Skippon were, in the context of 1649, moderates. Ironically it had been Ireton who drafted the text of the Engagement that had to be sworn by every member of the Council of State from which he was excluded. Those who took the Engagement declared their approval of the High Court of Justice, of the trial and execution of the king, and of the abolition of monarchy and House of Lords. A number of nominees balked at giving retroactive approval to illegal acts. To win over Fairfax the Rump gave him permission to write his own version of the Engagement. In it he made no mention of what had been done, merely undertaking to defend the present government 'without king and House of Peers'.[57]

By mid-February the ship of state appeared to be on a steady course. The regime was ready to direct its attention to the outside world. At the top of the agenda was Ireland and the sprawling royalist coalition under the prestigious leadership of the country's greatest magnate, James Butler, Marquess of Ormond. It is to this kingdom that we now turn.

---

[57] Blair Worden, *The Rump Parliament, 1648–1653*, 180–1.

CHAPTER 13

Ormond, Cromwell, the Levellers and Ireland

Ormond and the Association of Confederate Catholics

The treaty with the Association of Confederate Catholics (17 January 1649) was Ormond's most creative act of statesmanship.[1] Yet it was won at the price of exacerbated tensions among the Protestant members of his royalist coalition. To mollify them Ormond found it necessary to pledge that he would not slacken his defence of the Protestant religion and the royal prerogative. He found it hard to explain how he could do this and satisfy the Catholics at the same time.

For their part the Confederates had to quell the ongoing tensions inside their own ranks between clericalists (nuncioists) and moderates (Ormondists). Ever since the spring of 1648 they had been divided over how to respond to the royalist charm offensive being waged by Ormond, Rupert and others to win support for a mighty effort to restore the king. In May the royalist navy was augmented by the ships that revolted from the parliamentary fleet. By August it had swelled to 20 ships. But it was effectively neutralized by the Earl of Warwick, who kept it hemmed in at Helvoetsluys on the Dutch coast. Not until 21 January 1649 was Prince Rupert able to slip out of port and take most of the fleet to establish a new base at Kinsale on the Irish south coast. In combination with the ships brought by Prince Maurice the royalist fleet now numbered 28 sail, with more ships being built at Wexford. A west-country sea captain complained in February that 'those Irish men of war lie constantly so in the throat of the Channel between Scilly and the Land's End that no ship can pass'

---

[1] For a more pessimistic interpretation see Ó Siochrú, *Confederate Ireland*, 185–204. I am nevertheless indebted to Ó Siochrú's analysis for much of what follows.

except in the night or at dusk.[2] The activities of these men of war were a major irritant to English shipping, but Rupert did not have enough strength for a blockade of Dublin, which is what Ormond needed if he was to bring the garrison there to its knees.

Two other factors were even more effective in checkmating Ormond's efforts to achieve the military upper hand: first, the superb competence of the parliamentary commander in Dublin, Colonel Michael Jones, and secondly, the continuance of the Catholic civil war which pitted Owen Roe O'Neill and the Marquess of Antrim against the armies of the Confederation. When the leaders of the Catholic Association signed a Cessation with Inchiquin in May 1648, O'Neill had fallen into line behind the papal nuncio Rinuccini who had once again pronounced a decree of excommunication against all who had made peace with the brutal Protestant heretic. In June O'Neill and his Ulster army of 4–5,000 soldiers had declared war on the association. A month later the Marquess of Antrim had turned up in Ireland and added 2,000 Scots and Irish Catholics to O'Neill's army. Antrim had an intensely personal animus against Ormond, being convinced that he could have done a much more effective job of uniting Catholic Ireland behind the king had he, rather than Ormond, been named lord lieutenant. At the end of the summer of 1648 the Confederate General Assembly pronounced an anathema against the papal nuncio, and asked him to leave the country. Rinuccini did not at once quit Ireland, but he did leave Kilkenny, to establish new quarters at Galway on the west coast. On 30 September, the day of Ormond's arrival in Ireland, the Confederate Assembly also denounced O'Neill as a traitor and called upon all who were loyal to the king to pursue and destroy him. They pointed out that he had engaged in treacherous dealings with the bitter enemies of the Catholic population, such as Colonel Michael Jones,[3] 'and in an hostile and rebellious manner marched with his . . . army, killing, burning, pillaging, plundering and destroying his majesty's faithful subjects'.[4] This was essentially true. At the end of October the assembly had also prepared a protestation to the pope accusing the nuncio of destroying the unity of the association. The pope's failure to grant any more money to the association strengthened the hand of the Ormondists and completed the isolation of the nuncioists in the Assembly.

In the autumn of 1648 the royalist coalition had to allocate precious resources to the task of expelling O'Neill's garrisons from western Leinster

---

[2] HMC 29, *Thirteenth Report, Portland MSS*, Vol. 1, 510.
[3] See p. 350.
[4] Bodl. MS Carte 22, fo. 261.

and northern Munster. It took the combined Munster and Connacht armies of Inchiquin and Clanricard respectively to accomplish the task. The strategic consequence of having to fight O'Neill was that the push for Dublin was delayed for many months. Michael Jones profited from the Catholic civil war to strengthen his position in the Pale. With 5,000 soldiers he cleared out all Catholic garrisons within a 50-mile radius of Dublin. Sir Charles Coote, the parliamentarian commander in south-western Ulster, did the same there, marching deep into Confederate territory, killing people and driving off cattle. Clanricarde and O'Neill were too busy fighting each other for control of western Leinster to offer him any resistance.

News from England in December of the king's imminent trial finally overcame most of the animosities between royalists and Confederates. The Confederate Assembly's president Sir Richard Blake informed Ormond that they were ready to sign the treaty. Embodied in its 35 clauses were a number of significant gains for the Confederates. Not only did Catholics win freedom of religion, security of tenure and exemption from recusancy fines, their clergy were allowed to retain possession of the church buildings and property they presently occupied. Final resolution of the question of church property was put off until the next Irish parliament. Catholics were then expected to make up the majority of MPs, since they would have the right to vote and stand for election. The way was also cleared for the repeal of Poynings' law. An act of oblivion was promised that went beyond the one sketched in the 1646 treaty. It now extended to all acts committed before, on or since 23 October 1641, the day on which the Ulster rising had begun. This clause had the effect of exonerating leaders such as Sir Phelim O'Neill, and several Old English leaders who had taken part in plots during that year. Remarkably too, there were concessions to the Ulster Irish, which meant that the whole policy of plantation settlement could be challenged in parliament. The guarantee that the royalists would not wriggle out of these concessions after their own purposes had been served was the existence of an army, predominantly Catholic in make-up. In contrast to 1646 the function of this army was not to invade England, but to *withstand* an invasion from England. The Association of Confederate Catholics came to an end, and supreme power within royalist and Catholic Ireland now passed to Ormond and 12 Catholic 'commissioners of trust'.[5] Both Blake and Ormond hailed the treaty with extravagant rhetoric, the former trumpeting that it would 'restore this nation in its former lustre', the latter rhapsodizing that 'there are no bounds to your hopes' now that they had all been joined together in a new 'bond of unity'.[6]

[5] Scott, *Politics and War*, 190.
[6] Gilbert, *Irish Confed.*, Vol. 7, 181–3.

Had the 1649 treaty not been nullified by the implacable hostility of the Westminster parliament it might have paved the way for an Ireland at peace with itself and with the rest of the world. Apart from the changes already noted, the treaty provided for places of 'command, honour, profit, and trust in his majesty's armies in this kingdom' to be conferred impartially on Catholics and non-catholics. Roman Catholics, like Protestants, would enjoy the right to arm themselves. They would have permission to 'erect and keep free schools for education of youths of this kingdom'. Trade monopolies would be abolished. Tax assessments would be carried out by joint committees of Catholics and Protestants in every county. Judges would be nominated by a 14-member executive committee chaired by the lord lieutenant but dominated by Catholics.[7]

To sum up, what the treaty gave Ireland was national autonomy under English kingship. If implemented it would have ushered in an era of religious toleration and social justice far more extensive than that practised in England during the 1650s. It might even have enabled Ireland to avoid the bouts of murderous bloodshed that have punctuated its history from that day to this. Again, however, any such dream was check-mated by the determination of the English republic to bring Catholic Ireland to heel. Within months the country, bereft of its king, had to face invasion and renewed civil war.

The immediate challenge facing Ormond and his Commissioners of Trust was to recruit soldiers and raise the excise, customs and assessments for the coming summer's war effort. The military chain of command was simplified. Gone were the independent provincial forces; in their place a unified command with Ormond as lord-general, and Inchiquin and Castlehaven as lieutenant-generals of horse. The size of the unified army was 15,600, consisting of 2,600 horse and 13,000 foot.[8] George Monro's

---

[7] The complete text of the treaty is printed in Gilbert, *Irish Confed.*, Vol. 7, 184–211.

[8] The coalition army was composed of the following:

	Horse	Foot
Inchiquin	700	3,000
Taaffe	800	4,000
Preston	700	2,000
Clanricard	400	4,000
Totals	**2,600**	**13,000**

Source: Bodl. MS Tanner 57, fo. 513, printed in *Tanner Letters*, ed. Charles McNeill, 302.

Scots would later add 4,000 to that number, and the royalist Sir Robert Stewart's Laggan army of Donegal and north-west Ulster another 1,000 or so. As a veteran of the Swedish service in the 1630s, Stewart brought invaluable military experience to the royalist coalition. But the most effective units in this disparate force were Inchiquin's 3,700 horse and foot, the only ones to have proven themselves consistently in the heat of battle. In fact this royalist–catholic force was less formidable than its numbers might suggest. The endemic mistrust of Catholics towards Inchiquin, and vice versa, meant that real unity was seldom realized on the ground.

Another source of fractiousness was Antrim. So consuming was his personal animus against Ormond that not even the political earthquake which saw the king on trial for his life was enough to persuade him to abandon the clerical faction and return to his royalist allegiance. On the contrary, as soon as the republican regime was established in London the clerical faction, presumably with Antrim's blessing, sent Patrick Crelly, the abbot of Newry, to negotiate with it on their behalf. Crelly's mission was facilitated by the Spanish ambassador in London, Alonso de Cárdenas, who had several leading Independents – including the regicides Henry Marten, Tom Chaloner and Thomas Scot – on his payroll.[9] In fact the republican regime welcomed these negotiations as a means of buying time until it was in a position to undertake the complete reconquest of Ireland.

The counterpart to these high-level negotiations with the Independents in London were the links in Ireland between the Catholic leaders O'Neill and Antrim on the one hand and the parliamentary Protestant colonels George Monck, Sir Charles Coote and Michael Jones on the other. Both sides benefited from this improbable alliance, which meant that they did not have to worry about hostility from each other, and could focus their energies on fighting Ormond. For Ormond the alliance had the effect of diverting royalist energies away from what ought to have been their principal objective – taking Dublin.

Viewed from Westminster the grand coalition forged by Ormond was anything but defensive. Grouping together under one tent Catholics and Protestants, new Scots and British, it seemed the latest example of royalism's obstinate refusal to accept the verdict of two civil wars. Inchiquin, Robert Monro the Marquess of Clanricarde and the moderate and peace party majority among the Catholic Confederates may have regarded its primary purpose as the defence of Ireland, but Ormond, the Prince of

---

[9] This astonishing discovery is buried in a footnote in Jane Ohlmeyer's immensely learned *Civil War and Restoration*, 220, n. 104.

Wales, Prince Rupert, Henrietta Maria and a host of royalist exiles in the low countries and France had greater ambitions. These were nothing less than the overthrow of the republican regime in England and the capture of the throne for the murdered king's son.[10]

The Westminster parliament took measures to meet the royalist menace. It voted to send out 40 warships and 30 armed merchantmen manned by 6,000 sailors. Unlike the royalists it had the economic muscle to realize its targets. Parliament next addressed its personnel problem. Dissatisfied with Warwick's cautiousness, on 23 and 24 February it dismissed him and appointed three army colonels, Edward Popham, Robert Blake and Richard Deane as joint admirals and generals at sea. This shake-up at the top was accompanied by sweeping administrative and staffing changes. The new officer corps was moulded from the small radical group among the old captains, and from radicals among the merchant shipmasters energetically recruited by Sir Henry Vane and his admiralty colleagues.[11]

On 22 May ten parliamentary warships arrived off the Irish south coast and at once bottled up Rupert's fleet in Kinsale harbour. The blockade was maintained until October, paralysing the royalist navy and ending Ormond's dream of cutting the supply lines between Dublin and England.

Ormond also faced disturbing challenges from within the country. In early February Confederate Catholic commissioners sent him panicky reports that O'Neill's army was 'multiplying daily', increasing 'like a snow ball', thanks to the assistance of 'malignant clergy . . . acting and fomenting sedition wherever they go'.[12] Before the end of the month O'Neill was on the offensive again, overruning Westmeath and Longford, and threatening to invade Connacht. At this point there were half-hearted efforts at a rapprochement between Ormond and O'Neill. O'Neill held out for the restoration of the land of six Ulster counties to the Catholic Irish as his price for joining the royalist coalition. Whatever the justice of this demand, had Ormond yielded it would have blown apart the entire land settlement of Ireland and caused a rebellion among his Protestant supporters. There could be no meeting of minds.

In March therefore, Inchiquin was sent with an army of 4,000 infantry towards Athlone to block O'Neill's advance into Connacht. This troop movement was coordinated with Clanricarde's sending of 1,000 men to county Galway to prevent O'Neill from crossing to the west in that district.

[10] Carte, *Life*, Vol. 6, 596.
[11] Capp, 'Naval operations', 187.
[12] Gilbert, *Contemp. Hist*, Vol. 1, 769.

Castlehaven took another army of 5–6,000 from Tuam into Queen's County to overrun several of O'Neill's garrisons there. These manoeuvres, in conjunction with the accession of the Ulster Scots and the Laggan force in western Ulster forced O'Neill back into his own Ulster heartland where he offered to make common cause with his hitherto bitter Protestant enemies Coote and Monck. They too were beleaguered, Coote having been reduced to a few garrisons around Derry in north-western Ulster, and Monck to a few around Dundalk in the south-east of the province. Together with Jones's forces in the Pale they were the last hold-outs against a united royalist Ireland. At Dundalk Monck negotiated a three-month truce with O'Neill. In July, as Inchiquin advanced against him, Monck appealed to O'Neill for military support. O'Neill said that he would come to Monck's aid but that he was short of gunpowder. Monck promised the needed powder provided O'Neill sent a detachment to collect it. As the powder was being escorted by 1,400 troops back to O'Neill's camp, Inchiquin attacked the convoy, many of whom were drunk at the time, killed several hundred, drove off the rest, and captured the precious powder. The disaster was made irretrievable for Monck by the desertion of most of his garrison to Inchiquin. On 24 July 1649 he surrendered Dundalk and returned to England where he was unfairly criticized in parliament for having negotiated with the Catholic Irish. As a result of Inchiquin's operations all of Ulster's major ports except for Derry were now in royalist hands.

With the fall of Dundalk, Derry should not have been far behind. But only a commander as hard-bitten as Inchiquin could have overawed the redoubtable Sir Charles Coote. As it was, the task fell to the Laggan army and George Monro with his mixed force of Scots Highlanders, Ulster British and a few Irish who were loyal to Sir Phelim O'Neill. They lacked siege artillery; nor were they able to stop Coote from being supplied by sea until, early in July, Monro brought some light field guns that were capable of interdicting the ships sailing into Derry. At the very moment when Coote's situation had become desperate O'Neill's army arrived on the scene, in retreat from Inchiquin at Dundalk. The two armies combined were able to drive off Monro's Scots and Sir Robert Stewart's Laggan army. The 20-week siege of Derry was over. Parliament's superior seapower had made a crucial contribution by getting supplies to Derry at critical moments. A more telling factor, however, had been the internecine conflict between the Catholic armies. The royalist forces in Ulster were now dispersed, vulnerable to the invading army that was finally on its way. The actions of O'Neill and Antrim were the root cause of all these distractions. Thanks to those two men Michael Jones continued to be the ruler of Dublin.

Yet time was running out for Jones, as he never tired of reminding parliament. He and Ormond had been striving to gain the advantage over each other since the latter's return to Ireland at the end of September 1648. With slender resources Jones had been waging war on several levels: diplomatic subversion to keep Catholics and royalists divided among themselves; frequent forays into enemy territory to destroy property and crops, and render the enemy nervous and demoralized; constant haranguing of his parliamentary masters in Westminster so that they could have no excuse for imagining that his needs were less than desperate; and a propaganda war against his chief antagonist, Ormond, in order to establish publicly the justice of the cause for which he had risked everything.[13]

Throughout the spring of 1649 Jones continued to bolster O'Neill's army and exacerbate the conflict between O'Neill and Ormond. In a letter to Cromwell dated 6 June he diplomatically thanked the general for seeing to the arrival of supplies just in time to save the parliamentary war effort in Ireland.[14] Ormond, however, despite all his difficulties, was managing to tighten the noose around Dublin. By the beginning of July the only strongholds still holding out against the royalists were Derry, Dundalk, Trim and Drogheda. Inchiquin, demonstrating once again his superior military talent, made quick work of Dundalk, Trim and Drogheda. By mid-July he was able to rejoin the main royalist army before Dublin, bringing its strength to nearly 11,000 soldiers. With Rupert's little fleet still bottled up in Kinsale harbour, however, Westminster was able to keep Jones supplied by sea.

Ormond knew also that Cromwell was on his way with a crack force to relieve Jones and do battle with the royalist besiegers – it was essential to capture Dublin before Cromwell arrived. In addition, he knew that there was serious discord in Dublin, and that Jones's troops were now deserting in large numbers.[15] Still, ineffectual as ever, he hesitated to unleash an all-out assault against the city. As we shall see, Ormond's timidity and lack of resolution was to make the Cromwellian conquest possible.

---

[13] The public debate between Ormond and Jones can be followed in *A Trve Copy of Two Letters . . . from the Earle of Ormond to the Honourable Colonell Michael Jones* (Dublin, 1649), E529/28.

[14] Bodl. MS Carte 118, fos. 44v–5.

[15] It was 'credibly reported' that 500 of Colonel Monck's 700 horse had crossed over to the enemy, mainly for money: *Modest Narrative* (21–8 July 1649), E566/7, 131.

Preparations in England

But why was it taking Cromwell so long to get to Ireland? No one doubted that the expedition was high on the Commonwealth's agenda for several reasons. Ormond and his royalist coalition had to be defeated. The slaughter of thousands of English settlers in 1641 had to be avenged. England's sovereignty over the kingdom had to be re-asserted. Less than a month after the king's execution parliament had appointed a high-level committee of Cromwell, Vane, Marten, Colonel John Jones and Thomas Scot to organize the expedition. The committee called for an expeditionary force of 12,000. Everyone assumed that Cromwell would lead the army, but he temporized for as long as possible. Aware that Ireland was a graveyard for English military reputations, and approaching his fiftieth birthday, he also knew that during his absence he would have little influence on political events in England. He therefore laid down stringent conditions before he would consider accepting the commission. Not only must the army be well financed, as commander-in-chief he must have plenary power, civil as well as military. He must also have his own substantial purse to spend as he saw fit. Above all he must have an iron-clad guarantee that the Irish project would continue to have top priority in Westminster. It took a marathon prayer meeting with his fellow officers before Cromwell consented at the end of March to accept the high command. In April lots were drawn to select the four New Model regiments that would form the core of the expeditionary army. Many additional men had to be pressed in order to bring it up to its intended strength.

The Leveller mutiny

The grandees were embarrassed to discover that many of the men in the four selected regiments had no desire to go to Ireland, despite generous financial inducements. Some of them simply wanted to avoid the high odds of meeting a violent death. Others were influenced by the Leveller argument that they should not let their officers rush them out of the kingdom until English rights and liberties had been enshrined in an Agreement of the People. Only then would it be appropriate for them to go over as the missionaries of an authentic social revolution.[16] A few had genuine sympathy with the plight of the Irish. The eloquent Major John Cobbett asked his fellow soldiers:

---

[16] *The English Souldiers Standard* ([5 April] 1649), E550/1, 9.

What have we to do with Ireland, to fight and murther a people and nation . . . which have done us no harm, only deeper to put our hands in blood . . . ? We have waded too far in that crimson stream (already) of innocent and Christian blood.[17]

The whole New Model had been seething with unrest for several months, partly on account of the continuing shortage of pay, and partly on account of the subversive activity of the London Levellers. John Lilburne had returned in Feburary from Durham where he had been laying claim to the timberland voted to him by parliament. He was indignant that the king had been put to death before there were any structures in place to check a new tyranny of the grandees. Over the next few months he and Richard Overton published repeated, recklessly vitriolic diatribes against the Commonwealth's political and military leaders. They called for the restitution of the General Council of the Army, and for the soldiers to exercise their supposed right to overthrow their officers and elect new ones. Lilburne and Overton's reward for promoting this radical vision of military democracy, and for fomenting mutiny within the ranks, was to be thrown in the Tower of London along with their fellow Leveller leaders Walwyn and Prince, on a charge of treason. Undaunted, they intensified their propaganda campaign among the soldiers, while petitions were organized and demonstrations by women and apprentices staged outside the House of Commons. By April 1649 the metropolis was in a state of high tension. In an effort to insulate as much of the army as possible from Leveller influence the grandees moved some units to the outskirts. When the order to do this came down to Colonel Edward Whalley's horse regiment, one troop mutinied by seizing their colours and barricading themselves in the Bull Inn. A large sympathetic crowd gathered, and the situation looked as though it would spin out of control, but the mutiny collapsed with the arrival of Fairfax on the scene 'furiously breathing forth nothing but death to them all'. The following day the ringleader of the mutiny, Robert Lockyer, was sentenced to die. Lockyer's heroic behaviour at his execution won him the admiration of many. A crowd reportedly numbering 4,000, among whom were several hundred soldiers, followed

---

[17] *The Souldiers Demand* (Bristol [18 May] 1649), E555/29, 12–13. For the reasons for ascribing this anonymous pamphlet to Major Cobbett, see Gentles, *NMA*, 533, n.74. For the Levellers and Ireland see Norah Carlin, 'The Levellers and the conquest of Ireland in 1649', *HJ*, 30 (1987), 269–88.

his funeral procession. Green ribbons, the symbol of Leveller allegiance, were worn prominently on many shoulders.[18]

Radical agitation in the army now intensified.[19] Corporal William Thompson rallied 300 men around Banbury, but Colonel John Reynolds snuffed out their uprising before they could join the larger group who were converging on the Oxfordshire village of Burford. The main mutiny was concentrated in the horse regiments designated for Ireland – Scrope's, Ireton's and Horton's – but it had spilled over into several others. Fairfax and Cromwell knew that prompt action was essential if the mutiny was not to spread throughout the cavalry. On 9 May they mustered 4,000 troops in Hyde Park, then marched south to Bagshot, Surrey, meaning to intercept the mutineers who were on their way from Bristol via Salisbury to Oxfordshire. Late in the night of 14–15 May the generals pounced on the 900 sleeping mutineers in Burford and put down their uprising with the loss of only one life on each side. Three of the ringleaders were later shot to death after a court martial, while the others were cashiered. While the number of men routed at Burford was less than 1,000 there were several times that many disaffected soldiers distributed throughout the Midlands and western England.

Monied men, magistrates and the political nation in general heaved a collective sigh of relief when they heard the news from Burford. The decisive crushing of the Levellers meant that the limits of the revolution had been drawn. The Agreement of the People would not become England's constitution; parliament would not be dissolved, nor would tithes be abolished, or free trade introduced. For this achievement the grandees were rewarded with honorary degrees in Oxford and a sumptuous banquet in London. With civil peace imposed at home the rulers of the English republic now directed their attention to Ireland. The military expedition could at last go ahead unhindered and the Irish Adventurers could look forward to cashing in on their investment.

The Cromwellian invasion

There was no time to be lost, as Colonel Michael Jones continually stressed. Yet there were unavoidable delays. The charisma of Cromwell's leadership had not stopped large-scale desertion from the regiments selected for Ireland. In order to make up the quota of 12,000, men had to

---

[18] Gentles, 'Political funerals', 218–20.
[19] For a detailed account of the Burford mutiny see Gentles, *NMA*, 329–49.

be pressed almost to the moment of embarkation. Financing and equipping the expedition was if anything a greater headache. Arms were twisted in the City, producing a loan of £150,000. Cromwell hectored parliament into charging £400,000 on the future receipts of the excise. The dean and chapter lands attached to England's cathedrals were put on the auction block for the sole purpose of financing the reconquest of Ireland. Their sale would realize over £1.1 million. Three months later, in July, the Crown lands were also put up for sale, chiefly to reduce the arrears of the parliamentary army, but in effect also to increase the state's financial viability as it prepared for the challenge of Ireland. By raising over £1.4 million the sales of Crown lands did much to defuse discontent in the army.

Cromwell left London for the west coast amidst great pomp on 9 July. Once he arrived in Bristol he spent the next month mustering his regiments, and awaiting the £100,000 that was his minimum requirement for crossing the Irish Sea. When at length the Council of State appreciated that Cromwell would not be budged from this demand it scrambled to raise the cash, even though it meant robbing the navy to do so. The navy was nevertheless crucial to Cromwell's success. Colonel Blake was already keeping Prince Rupert blockaded in Kinsale harbour. Two more squadrons patrolled Dublin and the seas to the north. In addition, some 130 ships were enlisted to transport the 12,000 men, as well as their arms, ammunition and vast quantities of biscuit, beer, salt, wheat, rye, oats, peas, barley, cheese, raisins and rice. The 56 pieces of artillery included nine of the largest cannon available. To make the muskets and cannon operational there were 600 barrels of powder as well as 900 carriage and draft horses. Ormond's army could boast only a fraction of this matériel.

The resources that were poured into the conquest of Ireland illustrate both the expansionist energy released by the English revolution, and the superior financial muscle of the republic. At the start of the expedition it had been fondly imagined that Ireland could be conquered on a monthly budget of £20,000, and that this sum would only be required for a few months. Less than a year later it was found to have cost twice that much, and final conquest still lay far in the future.[20] Looking ahead, the full cost of subjugating Ireland between 1649 and 1656 came to £6.8 million.[21] Once a territorial foothold had been secured, taxes began to be levied in Ireland in order to make the country pay for its own conquest. Still, the impossibility of raising the gigantic sums necessary led the Commonwealth

[20] NA, SP25/118, unfol., abstract at beginning of volume.
[21] Wheeler, 'English army finance and logistics 1642–1660', 205, 211–12.

in 1652 to resort to paying its military and civilian creditors in Irish land, and attempting – but soon abandoning – the transplantation of the native population to the poorest of the four provinces, Connacht.

There was another dimension to Cromwell's preparation of the Irish project: diplomacy. Not only did he stay in close touch with Michael Jones, he was also kept informed about Monck's truce with Owen Roe O'Neill, and passed on the details to the Council of State. Cromwell also welcomed Roger Boyle, Lord Broghill, Inchiquin's great rival in Munster, into the English Protestant camp, commissioning him master of the ordnance in Ireland. Broghill played a key role in winning over a number of Munster towns to Cromwell's side.[22] He also prevailed upon a number of disgruntled officers in Inchiquin's army to postpone their resignations until Cromwell was ready to exploit them for maximum political advantage. On 13 August all was ready and the wind was right. Cromwell set sail from Milford Haven for Dublin. It was his good fortune that Michael Jones had prepared the ground well for the arrival of his superior officer.

Rathmines

Colonel, later Lieutenant-General Michael Jones was a former royalist who had crossed over to parliament's side after Ormond had negotiated the Cessation with the Confederates in 1643. After fighting for parliament in England he had been sent to receive the garrison of Dublin from Ormond when the latter handed it over in 1647. In the spring and early summer of 1649 he watched with mounting apprehension as Ormond's royalist coalition army, from its base at Rathmines, drew closer to Dublin. Ormond, however, displaying the poor judgement that repeatedly confirmed his inferiority as a military commander, decided to send his best officer, Murrough O'Brien, Lord Inchiquin, to take the fortresses of Drogheda, Trim and Dundalk. By doing this he divided his forces and became distracted from his main objective. Inchiquin was successful, and was back before Dublin by mid-July. But during his absence Jones sent out frequent sallies against his besiegers. These sallies had the effect of throwing Ormond's troops off balance and demoralizing them. Still lacking the nerve to launch a frontal assault on Dublin, even though he had 15,000 troops and knew that Cromwell's arrival was only weeks away, Ormond again sent Inchiquin away, this time to clear the remaining

[22] Patrick Little, *Lord Broghill and the Cromwellian Union with Ireland and Scotland*, 53, 60–1.

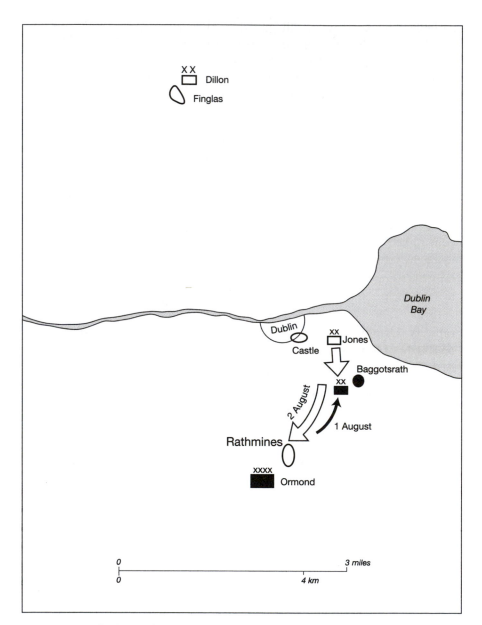

MAP 14 *Rathmines, 2 August 1649*
Adapted from Wheeler, James Scott, *Cromwell in Ireland* (Palgrave Macmillan, 2000)

parliamentary garrisons from the Pale. After this was accomplished he acceded to Inchiquin's request to withdraw 1,100 horse from Rathmines to their home province of Munster, because of his fear that Cromwell might land there rather than at Dublin. The absence of this most ruthless and effective commander further sapped Ormond's will to meet Jones head on. According to Castlehaven, Inchiquin's absence was the chief factor in the ensuing disaster.[23]

Emboldened by the evident timidity and mediocrity of his chief antagonist, Jones prepared to attack the royalists' forward position at Baggotsrath Castle, less than a mile from the city. He had just received two additional regiments from Chester, which enabled him to commit 5,200 troops to this sortie. It was the morning of 2 August, and Ormond had just gone to bed after staying up all night writing letters. When he was woken up by the sound of gunfire at Baggotsrath, he leapt on his horse and tried to rally the troops that were already fleeing from the attack. It was impossible to stop them. Nor could he persuade Lord Dillon to come to the rescue with his 2,500 infantry on the north side of Dublin. With astonishing rapidity Ormond's whole remaining army disintegrated before the onslaught of Jones's forces. Rathmines was a stupendous reversal of royalist fortunes, with incalculable psychological and strategic consequences. Jones's men killed up to 4,000 royalist soldiers, including many of Inchiquin's Munster infantry, and took 2,500 prisoners, as well as capturing Ormond's artillery train, papers, ciphers, supplies, money and baggage. Rathmines was the last major battle fought by the Old English forces of the Confederation, even though the Earl of Clanricarde's army of 3,000 remained intact in Connacht. The British royalists in Ulster under Lord Montgomery, and the Scots under George Monro were also in control of Ulster. But no one was willing or able to do Ormond any good. Only Owen Roe O'Neill's 5,000-strong army could have reinforced him, but O'Neill excused himself with the plea that his hands were tied until the end of August, when his truce with Sir Charles Coote expired.

Ormond now relocated his headquarters to Tecrogan, half way between Dublin and Drogheda. From there he reinforced Drogheda, and pursued his efforts to win O'Neill to his side. Negotiations were painfully slow, and when O'Neill finally began to march southwards he was too late to affect the outcome at Drogheda. The town lay athwart the road from Dublin to Ulster, and was strategically important. Before the end

---

[23] Castlehaven, James Touchet, Earl of, *Memoirs of the Irish Wars* (1684) (hereafter Castlehaven, *Memoirs*), 144.

of August Ormond had replaced its Irish commander with the English Catholic officer and veteran of the Thirty Years' War, Sir Arthur Aston. Aston was a man of impeccable royalist credentials who had successfully defended Reading and Oxford, and was known for his unshakable hatred of parliamentarians. The four regiments that Ormond gave him were about equally divided between Catholics and Protestants. The garrison, however, continued to be short of money, match and shot. When Ormond held a council of war at the town on 23 August the officers voted ten to three to defend the town against attack. Of these ten, only one – Aston – would actually be present for its defence. Ominously, the three votes against holding out were all cast by colonels of the garrison. They would shortly make the supreme sacrifice.

Drogheda

Continuing to divide his eggs among several baskets, Ormond stationed 3,000 troops at Tecrogan, too far from Drogheda to be of any material use to Aston. He later justified this indecisive strategy by explaining that his troops were in such low spirits that he did not dare bring them closer to the scene of action. Perhaps he was right. Cromwell, meanwhile, was preparing to advance from Dublin. One of his first acts on arriving in Ireland was to issue strict orders to his soldiers against taking free quarter or plunder. He also promised the peasantry that if they brought food or supplies to his army they would be paid in ready money. He backed up his promise by hanging several soldiers for looting within weeks of his arrival. This policy, even though it was only honoured for a few months, served the valuable purpose of winning much of the populace in Leinster and Munster to the parliamentary side.

For all Cromwell's massive superiority in money, men and matériel, the outcome at Drogheda was not a foregone conclusion. Protected by a steep ravine on the south-east side, the town also boasted a 20-foot high medieval wall ranging between four and six feet thick. When Aston contemptuously rebuffed the summons to surrender Cromwell unleashed his heavy artillery, opening up two breaches in the south and east walls. He then sent his infantry into the breaches, but they met unexpectedly heavy resistance and were hurled back, tumbling down the steep ravine below the walls. At this point Cromwell took personal charge, rallied his men, and led them on foot in a second charge. As the last daylight ebbed away they overran the enemy's entrenchments and took control of the city. Some of Aston's men, hearing the shouted offer of quarter from the invaders, surrendered and were taken prisoner. But others continued to resist, and

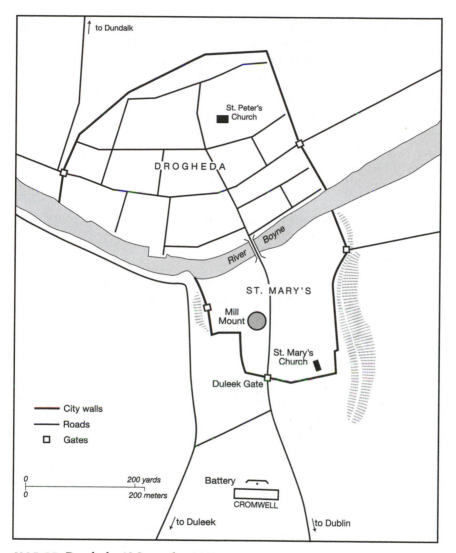

MAP 15 *Drogheda, 10 September 1649*

Adapted from Gentles, Ian, *The New Model Army: In England, Scotland and Ireland, 1645–1653* (Blackwell Publishers, 1991)

Cromwell, 'in the heat of action', as he later confessed, 'forbade them to spare any that were in arms in the town'.[24] His own close brush with death as he led the second storm may have triggered this command. Some soldiers and their officers, dismayed by his instruction, let their prisoners escape, but their isolated acts of humanity scarcely redeemed a night of terror. In a strict sense Cromwell was justified by the rules of war at the

[24] Abbott, *Cromwell*, Vol. 2, 126.

time, which sanctioned the killing of all the defenders of a garrison that had refused a summons to surrender. However, the killing continued the following day when resistance was all but at an end. The officers, most of whom had been taken prisoner, were killed in cold blood, including Edmund Verney, the scion of an ancient English Catholic family, and Sir Arthur Aston, who was said to have been clubbed to death with his own wooden leg.

The final death toll was probably around 3,000, including 2,800 of the 3,100-strong garrison, and every priest and friar, as well as perhaps 100 civilians. A few soldiers escaped death and were shipped to Barbados. Parliamentary losses were about 150. The horror of Drogheda remains imprinted in the minds of Irish people to this day. It was the moral low point of Cromwell's life. The unease he felt over the massacre can be read in the ambivalent message he transmitted to Parliament:

I am persuaded that this is a righteous judgement of God upon these barbarous wretches, who have imbrued their hands in so much innocent blood, and that it will tend to prevent the effusion of blood for the future, which are satisfactory grounds to such actions, which otherwise cannot but work remorse and regret.[25]

Apart from its questionable theology, Cromwell's statement is shot through with error. How could a town that at no time had been in the hands of the Confederate Catholics be held responsible for the massacre of British Protestants in 1641? Half Drogheda's defenders were themselves Protestant, and many were English. Nor did the slaughter at Drogheda, as some historians have assumed, do much, if anything, to prevent further bloodshed.

Drogheda was the second hammer blow to Ormond's royalist coalition. Yet rather than complain about the savagery of his foes Ormond mournfully construed the misfortune as God's punishment for royalist sins.[26] It was a while before he also appreciated the fatal consequence of Drogheda for his leadership. It destroyed the confidence of the Catholic Confederates in his abilities as a general, as well as their confidence in British Protestants as a whole. Equally, it exacerbated the distrust of Catholic towns such as Wexford, Waterford and Limerick to the extent that they would no longer admit Ormond's soldiers or obey his orders.[27]

---

[25] Ibid., 127.
[26] Carte, *Orig. Letters*, Vol. 2, 412.
[27] Clarendon, Edward Earl of, *The History of the Rebellion and Civil Wars in Ireland*, 95.

The loss of Drogheda also transformed the strategic landscape in Ireland. It cleared the road to Ulster, enabling Colonel Robert Venables to lead a column of 5,000 men to join Sir Charles Coote in the conquest of the northern province. Trim and Dundalk fell in rapid succession, leaving Cromwell to concentrate on the east-coast ports in Leinster and Munster. For his part Ormond clung to the hope that a Fabian strategy of avoiding pitched battles, combined with the effects of wet weather, disease and hunger, would weaken the invaders to the point where they could be picked off in small actions. But even with all these factors working in his favour, Ormond was ill-equipped to exploit them. Many Catholic officers, taking the measure of English military superiority, had begun leaving the country for Spain. Their exodus continued until the conquest was complete in 1652. The Catholic towns, seeing the writing on the wall, stopped sending assessment money to the treasury at Kilkenny. The Marquess of Clanricard wrote from Connacht, declining to send troops or money to Ormond because he needed all his resources to fend off Coote's forces from Sligo. Clanricarde's own troubles were compounded by an outbreak of plague in Galway. Ormond's negotiations with Owen Roe O'Neill to bring his 4,000 troops south proceeded with agonizing slowness. In the event it hardly mattered, for O'Neill was by now a dying man.

Cromwell, after resting his army for a few days, left Dublin and headed south, collecting garrisons as he went. These conquests drank up men, since every new garrison required between a few dozen and a few hundred soldiers to defend it. The shrinkage of his field army was accelerated by the ravages of dysentery. Before the end of September 4,000 men had fallen ill, and many died. By its nature dysentery attacks violently and without warning. On 3 November, for example, many of the soldiers, under attack by Inchiquin's army at Glascarrig, were forced to fight with their breeches down because of the 'flux'.[28] Cromwell not only lost several thousand soldiers to disease that autumn; two of his most valued officers were felled by it – Lieutenant-General Michael Jones and Colonel Thomas Horton.

Wexford

In spite of all these losses Cromwell's army still outnumbered Ormond's by about two to one, which meant that he could go where he pleased. He chose as his next objective, the port town of Wexford – the main harbour

---

[28] Ludlow, *Memoirs*, Vol. 1, 239.

for the Irish privateers who had taken a heavy toll of English merchant shipping during the 1640s. The town also stood out in English minds for its fervent Catholicism. But, terrified by the fate of Drogheda, the town was now riven with faction, a minority openly advocating capitulation. The hard-line Confederates carried the day against them, and sent a message to Ormond that they wanted reinforcements, but only Catholic ones. He complied, sending two regiments of Castlehaven's Ulster foot, about 1,500 men in all.

By the end of September Cromwell was outside the town, with a secure line of communications along the coastal road to Dublin and complete command of the sea. His army, now about 8,000 strong, would be down to 6,000 by mid-October. Unlike Ormond, however, he was backed up by the resources of an incomparably richer state. Even though recruitment constantly fell short of targets, in October 1649 and February 1650 several thousand fresh soldiers were sent to Ireland.[29] At the same time, Ireland, where as late as 1650 the price of provisions actually remained lower than in England,[30] became the recipient of massive quantities of wheat, rye, oats, biscuit, beer, cheese and salmon to feed the invading army.

Under the best of circumstances Wexford would have been a hard nut to crack. Its garrison had swelled to 4,800 defenders; two fingers of land and a fort protected its harbour from the north and south; on the west it was ringed with heavy stone walls lined with earth; at its south end stood a strong castle on high ground. Once again Michael Jones demonstrated his immense utility to Cromwell: with a small detachment he overran the fort, opening the harbour to English warships and supply vessels which brought in the siege train and supplies for the army. The governor of Wexford, David Sinnott, returned a delaying answer to Cromwell's summons to surrender. He believed that time was on his side, knowing that Cromwell's army was every day being weakened by disease. So he made high demands for liberty of worship and the maintenance of clerical privileges. Cromwell impatiently rejected these demands.

A few days later Cromwell used this artillery to blast a hole in the castle walls. This display of firepower alarmed the defenders and prompted the townsfolk to flee. Sinnott sued for terms, asking to withdraw his garrison intact to Ross with arms, ammunition and horses, and for privateers to be

---

[29] Wheeler states that by October 4,000 men had been recruited, and by the following February nearly 9,000 had been sent to Ireland: Wheeler, *Cromwell in Ireland*, 94. He cites NA, SP25/118/139-48 & *CSPD 1649–50*, 591 – but the latter are merely warrants to raise men. Cf. Gentles, *NMA*, 364.

[30] Gilbert, *Contemp. Hist.*, Vol. 3, 167; *CSPD 1650*, 60.

permitted to sail to wherever they saw fit. These were impossible demands: Cromwell could not permit a garrison of this size to march off and reinforce the main royalist army, or the merchant privateers who had already wreaked such havoc to get off scot free.

In the midst of these talks, however, the governor of the castle, which was outside the town walls, yielded it up without consulting his superiors. The parliamentary soldiers lost no time in occupying the castle, and training their guns on the town. The defenders of Wexford then capitulated. Not waiting for orders, Cromwell's men hoisted themselves over the walls with pikes and scaling ladders, and took possession of the town within half an hour. Some of the defenders made a stand in the marketplace but were overcome and slain on the spot. Another 300 who tried to escape across the harbour drowned when parliamentary troops opened fire on them and their boats sank. Any priests or friars unfortunate enough to cross the attackers' path were butchered. Many townspeople also lost their lives.

Cromwell estimated the death toll at around 2,000 on the royalist side and less than 20 on his own. Even though Sinnott had made impossible demands, the slaughter nevertheless occurred – without Cromwell's orders – while negotiations were still in progress. This violated the laws of war at the time. The massacre also had grave practical consequences. Instead of gaining a vital economic centre whose industries and population could have been used to sustain future operations, the English took possession of a desolate and ruined place. Cromwell's failure to stop the slaughter hurt the discipline of his army at a time when discipline was essential to the English campaign. Finally, the gravest consequence was that the example of Wexford, far from terrorizing other garrisons into surrendering, stiffened their resolve, prolonged the war and increased bloodshed.[31]

After Wexford Cromwell's effective force was down to 5,600 men, some of whom had to be left behind to garrison the town. With reinforcements, money and supplies arriving very slowly from England, and with his soldiers now on half pay, army discipline deteriorated rapidly. His situation would have been desperate but for the near-collapse of his foes. Ormond, having lost about 4,000 soldiers at Rathmines, 2,800 at Drogheda, and 2,000 killed or dispersed at Wexford, had seen his field army dwindle to fewer than 3,000 men. Not only had he lost large quantities of cannon and supplies, but also three warships, and one of the key ports in Ireland. The only remaining royalist naval force was Prince

---

[31] Wheeler, *Cromwell in Ireland*, 98; Gentles, *NMA*, 365–7.

Rupert's fleet at Kinsale, about 60 miles south of Wexford. But shortly after the fall of Wexford, Rupert stole out of Kinsale with seven of his ten vessels and escaped to Portugal. The royalists posed no further naval threat to either Ireland or Britain. Hard on the heels of Wexford came the betrayal of five Munster towns, including Cork, Youghal and Kinsale. Their capitulation was the fruit of Cromwell's arrangement with Lord Broghill the previous spring. By mid-November Inchiquin had lost virtually all his Protestant troops and Ormond was disgraced in Catholic eyes. Cromwell on the other hand had gained excellent winter quarters, just when his forces had been drastically weakened by sickness and losses in the field.

Waterford

After Wexford Cromwell's next major target was Waterford, another 35 miles down the coast. Waterford at that time was Ireland's second city. Its fervently Catholic citizenry had made of it a thriving commercial centre second only to Dublin in population and wealth. Situated on the River Suir, its ample harbour was guarded by two forts: Duncannon on the east and the smaller and decayed Passage on the west. On 17 October Cromwell was before New Ross, which guarded the approaches to Waterford, and summoned the governor, Major Lucas Taaffe. When Taaffe asked for liberty of conscience for the populace Cromwell set him straight on the English understanding of this concept:

concerning liberty of conscience, I meddle not with any man's conscience.
But if by liberty of conscience you mean a liberty to exercise the mass,
I judge it best to use plain dealing, and to let you know, [that] where the
parliament of England have power, that will not be allowed of.[32]

He then underlined the futility of further talk by firing his cannon, at which Taaffe immediately yielded. As his troops marched out of the town 500 from one of Inchiquin's Protestant regiments crossed over to Cromwell's side.

On 15 October Cromwell had despatched Major-General Henry Ireton with a force of several thousand men to capture Duncannon Fort. Ormond had anticipated Ireton's arrival by sending his lieutenant-general of horse, the Earl of Castlehaven, with reinforcements there. He also replaced the existing governor of the fort with Colonel Edward Wogan, a Protestant

---

[32] Abbott, *Cromwell*, Vol. 2, 146.

native of Kildare, who had fought for parliament, and then changed sides in 1647. This operation was to be the most successful that Ormond supervised during the whole 1649–50 campaign.

Its most remarkable aspect was the repulse that Wogan administered to Lieutenant-General Michael Jones. A brilliant tactician, who was also blessed with extraordinary personal magnetism, Wogan had the qualities of a born soldier. When he saw Jones's 2,000 men beginning to invest his garrison he devised a ruse. He got Castlehaven to ferry 80 cavalry to him from Passage. When he deployed these troops in his next sortie, Jones, who until then had believed that Wogan possessed only infantry, jumped to the conclusion that Ormond had suddenly arrived with the field army, and hastily withdrew. This setback was most unwelcome to Cromwell. 'Crazy in my health', as he reported to parliament, and with his army demanding to return to winter quarters, he paused before launching his planned assault against Waterford.[33] Meanwhile, Ormond had finally come to an agreement with Owen Rowe O'Neill, which bore fruit in 1,300 troops to augment the defence of the town. Cromwell, his army down to barely 3,000 troops fit for action, and nearly ten men per company falling sick every night, decided to abandon the attempt on Waterford. On 2 December he left under pelting rain, 'it being as terrible a day as ever I marched in, all my life'.[34]

Waterford has the distinction of being the only Irish city that successfully resisted a siege by Oliver Cromwell. This unique setback is explained in part by the determination of Ormond and his officers (Wogan in particular) to hold the town, but also by the shrewdness of the mayor and inhabitants in admitting only Ulster Catholics to man their defences. Thanks to Wogan's successful defence of Duncannon fort Cromwell was deprived of his artillery. The resistance at Waterford also demonstrates that the 'effusion of blood' at Drogheda and Wexford, rather than cowing the Irish into submission, had sharpened the resolve of royalists and Confederates alike to resist the invader with every ounce of their strength.

At the end of 1649, however, Waterford was the only bright spot on an exceedingly sombre canvas for the Catholic–royalist coalition. Cromwell and Jones had overrun most of the towns and garrisons in Leinster and Munster; colonels Robert Venables and Sir Charles Coote had efficiently reduced Ulster to obedience – this despite the formidable reputation of O'Neill's army, and the not inconsiderable obstacle of George Monro with

[33] Ibid., 160.
[34] Ibid., 176.

his Scots army and his British allies in Sir Robert Stewart's Laggan army. Before September was out Venables had taken Dundalk, Carlingford and Newry. In October he pushed farther north, and captured Lisnagarvey, Antrim and Belfast with little resistance.

The other side of the pincer movement against Ulster was led by Sir Charles Coote, who launched a campaign from his base in Derry against the royalists in Coleraine. Once he had overrun the town he lived up to his reputation for brutality by massacring most of the garrison regardless of their religion. The Laggan army now disintegrated, and Monro's force shrank to 3,000. At the beginning of December Venables and Coote combined their forces and advanced on the royalists near Lisnagarvey, 20 miles south of Carrickfergus. The battle quickly turned into a rout in which over 1,500 royalists were killed. Coote next took Carrickfergus on 13 December, turning the Scottish garrison and their families out into the winter cold. Except for Enniskillen, which did not surrender until the following March, Ulster was now under English rule. O'Neill and his army, which had previously roamed through western Ulster, had begun marching south in October to assist Ormond in Munster. In effect, from August 1649 to early 1650 the largest Gaelic Irish army played almost no role in defending Ireland from its English Puritan invaders.

For all his remarkable success in denying victory to Cromwell at Waterford, the aura of defeat still weighed heavily on Ormond's shoulders. Defeat compounded by mistrust. More than anything, according to Clarendon, it was the defection of the Protestant forces in the towns of Munster that 'introduced a spirit of jealousy and animosity in the army, which no dexterity . . . could extinguish or allay'.[35] Increasingly the Irish were heard to say they could trust no one who did not go to mass.[36] In a bid to arrest the corrosion of trust within the coalition the bishops met at Clonmacnoise, where they issued a call for Irish unity against the terrible enemy, Cromwell. This drew from the lieutenant-general a ferocious counterblast.

Your covenant is with death and hell . . . You are a part of Antichrist . . . You have shed great store of [blood] already, and ere it be long, you must all of you have blood to drink; even the dregs of the cup of the fury and the wrath of God, which will be poured out unto you![37]

Evidently relying on Sir John Temple's tendentious and inflammatory *Irish Rebellion* (1646) he lectured the bishops that their country had prospered

---

[35] Clarendon, *History of the Rebellion in Ireland*, 99.
[36] Bodl. MS Clarendon 38, fos. 155, 282.
[37] Abbott, *Cromwell*, Vol. 2, 197, 199.

under English rule. This was a gross distortion of history, as Cromwell ought to have known. He had been in the House of Commons in the spring of 1641 where he had heard Pym's elaborate indictment of Strafford for his misgovernment of Ireland. He would therefore have had an inkling of the grievances of the native population against their English overlords.[38]

Kilkenny and Clonmel

The winter of 1649–50 was mild in Ireland. The arrival of large quantities of oats from England meant that Cromwell did not have to wait for the growth of spring grass to move his cavalry and artillery horses. The pause in December and January also rested his men and restored the army's strength by the addition of several thousand soldiers who deserted from Inchiquin's Munster army, and 5,000 fresh recruits from England. The English soldiers also benefited from excellent – by the standards of the day – medical care. Hospitals in Dublin and Munster allowed many soldiers to recuperate and rejoin their regiments in time for the winter campaign in February.[39]

News of the mounting threat from Scotland – it had recognized Charles II as king of all three nations and was preparing to wage war on his behalf – made speed imperative. Using well the time remaining to him, Cromwell, helped by Lord Broghill and Henry Ireton, devoted February to overrunning many inland towns and garrisons in Munster. At the same time Colonel John Hewson, the new governor of Dublin, led a force of 3,000 men south-west from the capital to join Cromwell in a pincer movement against Kilkenny. The handsome headquarters of the Catholic Confederate Association, Kilkenny, was also the chief inland town of Ireland. Ormond was well to the west, trying to rally support in Limerick. Castlehaven, with his roving army of 4,000 men at Ballyragget, 12 miles to the north, stood by helplessly. His Ulster regiment refused to reinforce the garrison, citing the plague raging within as their reason.[40] Castlehaven's appeal to Lord Dillon to join him with forces from Leinster was equally unavailing. To all appearances, the governor, Sir Walter Butler, faced a hopeless situation. Yet he refused to surrender, vowing to 'maintain this city for his majesty'.[41] That this was not mere rhetorical bluster is proved by the skilful determination with which he conducted his defence. By noon

[38] Corish, 'The rising of 1641', 344.
[39] Wheeler, *Cromwell in Ireland*, 119.
[40] Castlehaven, *Memoirs*, 156.
[41] Denis Murphy, *Cromwell in Ireland: A History of Cromwell's Irish Campaign*, 297.

on 25 March Cromwell's artillery had opened a breach in the southern wall. Butler's counter-measures revealed that the Irish were now becoming adept at neutralizing the English heavy guns. Around the area of the breach they had thrown up two counterworks of earth, strongly pallisaded. When Cromwell flung his men into the breach under the leadership of Axtell and Hewson, the Irish, who were more than ready, poured withering fire on them from the safety of their palisades and beat them off. Not acknowledging the ingeniousness of the defence, Cromwell blamed his men for not performing 'with usual courage'. A second assault was also abortive, and each time the defences were repaired. A third order to attack was disobeyed, but by now Butler could see that the end was in sight, so he re-opened negotiations. Cromwell, in a hurry to move on to Clonmel, granted generous terms. This exemplified his new policy of leniency aimed at persuading the Catholic populations and garrisons that they could trust him not to massacre them and their priests if they would yield to terms.

The siege of Clonmel which began a month later demonstrated afresh the maturing Irish ability to withstand the shock of parliament's heavy guns. So skilful was the defence directed by Hugh O'Neill (cousin to Owen Roe), that he inflicted on Cromwell the severest check of his military career. Ormond had installed O'Neill there in December, with 1,300 Ulster Catholic troops, but his inability to supply the garrison made its surrender inevitable. Clonmel was a populous, well-fortified town, about 25 miles upstream from Waterford on the River Suir. After a three-week siege Cromwell again resorted to the argument of heavy artillery: he blasted a hole in the northern wall. Not idle, O'Neill had enlisted every available person within the town to erect a twin set of walls out of rubbish, stones, timber and mortar, running back 80 yards from either side of the breach. At the end of the lane thus fashioned he dug a deep ditch, and then planted his own guns behind it. As luck would have it there was a row of houses behind one of the makeshift walls. These he filled with soldiers whom he instructed to fire from the upper storeys on the invaders when they came through the breach.

Ignorant of these preparations, Cromwell ordered the attack to begin on the morning of 16 May. For four hours he poured men through the deadly breach, but time and again they were mowed down by O'Neill's pikemen and musketeers. At the end of the day 1,500 parliamentary soldiers lay dead, and the town's resistance had still not been broken. Later that night, however, O'Neill and his Ulster regiment slipped out of the town. They were out of ammunition, and knew there was no hope of relief from either Ormond or Castlehaven. Cromwell, unaware that the defenders

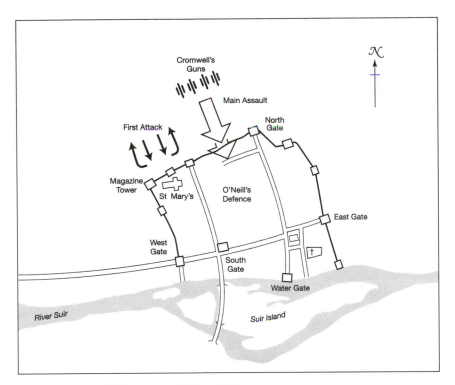

MAP 16 *Siege of Clonmel, April–May 1650*
Adapted from Wheeler, James Scott, *Cromwell in Ireland* (Palgrave Macmillan, 2000)

had flown, let the town surrender on easy terms. Only after he had ratified the agreement did he discover the deception, but he stuck to his word.

A week later Cromwell left Ireland after a stay of barely nine months. He had come intending a quick conquest through the application of overwhelming force. His policy had been to shed blood in order to save it later on. Despite his initial devastating victories, despite his diplomatic triumphs in winning over the towns of Munster, despite matchless support from Sir Charles Coote in Ulster, Lieutenant-General Michael Jones in Leinster and Lord Broghill in Munster, his campaign of conquest became ever more costly. His well-paid and well-supplied army shrank alarmingly, both from the dysentery and other diseases that tore through its ranks, and from the necessity to leave behind defenders for every garrison he conquered. Replacements from England never arrived fast enough. Had it not been for substantial defections by Protestant royalists he would have had almost no men left to put in the field by the end of 1649. The following spring virtually none of the soldiers he had brought with him were still in service.[42] By the time he left Ireland Cromwell had liquidated half of Ormond's army and bent many towns to his will, but he had never fought a battle in the field. That honour was reserved to Michael Jones and Sir Charles Coote.

In theory the war should have been winding down, given the severe mauling suffered by the forces of the royalist–Catholic coalition. Ulster and Leinster were firmly under parliamentary control, while in Munster the Irish held only Waterford, Duncannon, Limerick and the fastnesses of Kerry. The only province they could still call their own was the poorest, Connacht. Yet the war went on for more than two additional years. This was partly due to the absence of Cromwell's able generalship – his son-in-law Ireton who succeeded him was much less gifted. It is also explained by the necessity for the conqueror to tie up more and more of his troops in the 350–400 garrisons that peppered the Irish landscape. For their part, the Irish were becoming more adept at resisting sieges. Defeated in the field, and controlling very little territory, they turned increasingly to guerrilla warfare. This was a type of combat that the English found very difficult to deal with.

Scarrifhollis

To make matters worse for both sides bubonic plague was now raging across the breadth of the country. It had begun on the west coast, but was now claiming several hundred lives a week in Dublin. Of graver consequence for the Catholic–royalist coalition was the chronic mistrust of the clerical party towards royalists, and the general mistrust of Catholics towards all Protestants. The point is illustrated by the manner in which Owen Roe O'Neill's successor was selected. O'Neill had died of tetanus[43] in November 1649, and the provincial Confederate Assembly of Ulster had insisted that it, not commander-in-chief Ormond, would nominate his successor. After a lengthy wrangle it commissioned Heber MacMahon, Bishop of Clogher. Devoid of military experience, MacMahon was chosen for his imagined ability to unite the various Catholic factions in the province. His major-general, Henry Roe O'Neill (son of Owen Roe), advised him to avoid pitched battles, save lives and wear out the English by delay.

---

[42] *A Letter from Sir Lewis Dyve to the Lord Marquis of Newcastle, giving to his Lordship an Account of the Whole Conduct of the King's Affairs in Ireland . . . to 1650* (The Hague, 1650), E606/7, 50.

[43] Jerrold Casway, *Owen Roe O'Neill and the Struggle for Catholic Ireland*, 252.

MacMahon thought he knew better. In June 1650 he led the Ulster army, consisting of 4,000 foot and 600 horse, towards Londonderry, aiming to divide and confront the forces of Sir Charles Coote and Colonel Robert Venables. Encouraged by some initial successes, he advanced deep into enemy territory, but neglected to establish either an adequate supply base or train of siege artillery. He caught up with Coote near Lifford on 2 June. Coote, with only 800 foot and 600 horse, seemed vulnerable. A smart skirmish took place in which the Irish bested 200 of Coote's cavalry. Surprisingly, MacMahon did not exploit his advantage by attacking Coote's main force which was completely outnumbered. Instead, he continued to march west, ending up at Scarriffhollis, about five miles south-west of Letterkenny. Coote withdrew to Derry where he used the gift of time to bring in the foot regiments of Venables and Fenwick as reinforcements. MacMahon on the other hand unwisely divided his forces by sending detachments out to forage and capture a remote castle.[44] Coote now advanced against him. He found the Irish troops drawn up on a mountain-side, impossible to get at. MacMahon's officers were for sticking to the Fabian tactics of the late Owen Roe, and waiting for the English to exhaust their supplies. The bishop accused them of cowardice, and moved his army lower down the mountainside in order to engage the enemy. The battle opened (on 21 June 1649) with a fierce infantry engagement that ended with the Irish hemmed in and unable to manoeuvre. Before they fled 2,000 had fallen on the battlefield. Hundreds more were killed during the rout by Coote's cavalry. The final toll was 3,000 Irish and only 100 English. Owen Roe O'Neill's precious Ulster army was wiped out, and most of its officers, including Henry O'Neill, were slain on Coote's orders, even though they had been promised quarter on the battlefield. MacMahon himself was captured a few days later, and on Coote's orders hanged, drawn and quartered. His severed head was set on the gate at Londonderry. Without officers or weapons it was now impossible to rebuild the Ulster army. It was the greatest military disaster suffered by the Irish since their defeat at the hands of Mountjoy at the end of the Nine Years' War in 1601.[45]

Thanks to the impetuosity and inexperience of its clerical leader, the main Catholic army in Ireland had been lost. Not surprisingly, most of

---

[44] Richard Bagwell, *Ireland under the Stuarts and During the Interregnum*, Vol. 2, 229.

[45] Wheeler, *Cromwell in Ireland*, 172; *A Declaration of the Irish Armie in Ulster* ([12 July] 1650), E 607/14, 17–24. Coote sent the heads of the five leading commanders as trophies to Londonderry: *Severall Proceedings in Parliament* (4–11 July 1650), E 777/22, 579, sig. Gggg2v; *Perf. Passages of Every Daies Intelligence from the Parliaments Army* (5–12 July 1650), E 777/24, 12–13; Gilbert, *Contemp. Hist.*, Vol. 2, 87–8.

the remaining garrisons in Leinster and Munster tumbled into parliament's lap that summer: Tecroghan, Killmallock, Athy, Carlow, Waterford, Duncannon. Those Irish still bent on resistance withdrew to Connacht and to Kerry in western Munster. The defeats of the summer of 1650 deepened Irish disillusionment with the royalist cause in general and with Ormond in particular. The news from England that Charles II had not only sworn the Covenant in return for Scots Presbyterian support, but had denounced the 1649 treaty between Ormond and the Catholic Confederates, had a devastating impact. The Irish bishops disowned Ormond, ordered him to leave the country, and threatened to excommunicate anyone who persisted in adhering to him. The final straw was Cromwell's sensational victory at Dunbar (3 September 1650), which completed the discrediting of the royalist cause in Ireland. In December Ormond and his friend Castlehaven sailed for France. The Earl of Clanricarde had already taken over most of the responsibilities of military command.

The events of the summer of 1650 explain why the Irish bishops counselled their flock to make peace with the conqueror rather than continue loyal to a deeply compromised and hopelessly enfeebled royalist cause. In reality a majority of the Irish people would have been happy to see an end to the killing and the physical destruction of their country. There was only one stumbling block: the English republic's refusal to let them retain their property or practise their religion. Cromwell's declaration of January 1650 had made it brutally clear that the price of 'exercising the mass' would be a struggle to the death. The instructions issued to the parliamentary commissioners for Ireland in December of the same year prove that that policy was still in force. They were to propagate the gospel and suppress 'idolatry, popery and superstition'.[46] The following year the republican government turned a deaf ear to Henry Ireton's appeal to relax this policy, and so Ireland descended deeper into the maelstrom of violence.[47]

Limerick

When Cromwell quit Ireland at the end of May 1650 he left his son-in-law Henry Ireton in charge with the title lord deputy. A month later Edmund Ludlow joined Ireton as lieutenant-general of horse. For the rest of the

[46] *The Acts and Ordinances of the Interregnum*, eds C.H. Firth and R.S. Tait (hereafter *A & O*), Vol. 2, 494; BL Egerton MS 1048, fos. 192–3.
[47] For evidence of the Council of State and parliament's inaction on Ireton and the parliamentary commissioners' recommendation, see Bodl. MS Tanner 56, fo. 253 and *CSPD 1651*, 147, 175.

summer they swept up the Munster garrisons that were still holding out. It was a maddening business: for every unit decapitated another seemed to spring up hydra-like in its place. Inchiquin raised 3,000 recruits in Kerry during July, while the Marquess of Clanricarde was able to put 4,500 men in the field in Connacht in October. The formidable Hugh O'Neill was in charge of the garrison at Limerick, while Lord Dillon governed Athlone. Large and well defended, Limerick boasted a position of great natural strength. Sitting athwart the River Shannon where it divides, Limerick's sturdy walls were shaped like an hourglass. These geographical advantages were vitiated by the bitter factionalism that seethed within its walls.

Ireton was aware of the divisions inside the city, and confident that he could exploit them and accomplish the surrender of both Limerick and Athlone before winter. Yet he failed on both fronts and had to withdraw to winter quarters. Had he tried a vigorous attack on Limerick at any time during the preceding months he could almost certainly have toppled it. O'Neill had no ammunition.[48]

In the spring of 1651 a flotilla of parliamentary ships sailed up the Shannon bringing both provisions and heavy guns. Although he was now supplied in a fashion that the Irish could only dream of, Ireton was still incapable of bringing the town to its knees. During the spring and summer of 1651 parliament sent an additional 9,000 troops to Ireland, but disease, cold and hard marching, as well as enemy attacks 'much wasted' them. By the end of October, 2,000 men had died before Limerick alone.[49] Throughout the siege Ireton had to contend with dedicated efforts to relieve the town by forces under Lord Muskerry and Colonel David Roche. In addition, the concentration of parliamentary forces at Limerick and in Connacht gave roving enemy bands the chance to make trouble in Leinster. In August there were reports of 2,400 Catholic troops within six miles of Dublin. Finally, Ireton and Waller were hampered by their inflexible refusal to allow anyone in the town who had been involved in the 1641 rebellion to escape capital punishment. Had they been willing to bend on this point Limerick would have capitulated many months earlier than it did.[50]

It is difficult to avoid the suspicion that had Cromwell, or Michael Jones, or Sir Charles Coote been in charge of the siege instead of Ireton it

---

[48] John G. Simms, *War and Politics in Ireland, 1649–1730*, 23.

[49] R. Dunlop (ed.), *Ireland under the Commonwealth*, Vol. 1, 74.

[50] Folger Lib. MS X.d.483(100), Sir Hardress Waller to Colonel Robert Bennett, 11 September 1651.

would have been over much more quickly. Enjoying ample matériel and superior numbers, any of these commanders would have found a way of exploiting the fact that the population of Limerick was dying from starvation and the plague, and that most of them wanted to sue for peace. Ireton, even though he disposed of 8,000 troops before Limerick, in comparison with Hugh O'Neill's 2000 within the town, was indecisive. After one abortive attempt at a storm he fell back on starvation as his weapon of choice. Although he had also boasted a substantial train of artillery since the spring of 1651, it was not until the end of October that he finally located a length of the town wall that was not reinforced by an earthen backing. Once he trained his guns on it the masonry collapsed, the defenders gave up, and the siege was over. Shortly afterwards Ireton himself succumbed to a fever and died a few days later.

Guerrilla warfare, 1651–52

By the time of Ireton's death the war had already entered a new phase. The fall of Limerick, combined with the news of Charles II's crushing defeat at Worcester demoralized the Irish. The capture of Clare Castle by Ludlow on 5 November and of Galway by Coote the following May meant that virtually all the 350–400 forts and garrisons in the country were in English hands.[51] Yet, control of the garrisons paradoxically weakened parliament's grip on the country. Pinned down by their responsibilities, the soldiers found it increasingly unsafe to venture outside the walls of their fortresses. The Irish forces, whose numbers never seemed to diminish, adopted a classic pattern of guerrilla warfare against the occupying power. Though defeated in the field and deprived of their urban strongholds, they roamed at large, spreading terror when and where they chose.

Dispossessed native outlaws known as tories were reported to be driving away cattle on the outskirts of Dublin as early as June 1650, the same month that O'Neill's Ulster army was destroyed. Three months later the provinces of Munster, Leinster and Ulster were 'much infested with tories'. Characteristically, they conducted lightning raids that were over before the parliamentary infantry could engage them. They then retreated to bogs, woods or mountains where cavalry could not venture. Whatever arms and munitions they needed they captured from the enemy. The violence and disorder they were able to foment seemed unending. The root cause, as parliament's commissioners acknowledged, was the republic's refusal to give the Irish guarantees for the security of their estates. As a consequence,

[51] For evidence about the number of garrisons see Gentles, *NMA*, 544, n.163.

by 1652 the country was in a state of economic near-collapse. Cattle were almost wiped out, while four-fifths of the fertile land lay waste and uninhabited.

Yet the fighting went on, and the parliamentary commissioners appealed to London for still more recruits. In 1652 the English army in Ireland had grown to over 33,000 – nearly three times the number Cromwell had brought over in 1649. Many of them were now being recruited among the Gaelic Irish as Micheál Ó Siochrú has discovered.[52] It was reported at the end of 1651 that besides a generally hostile populace there were still 30,000 men in arms against parliament. In Ulster and Connacht 5,000 Irish fought under Clanricarde against Coote and Venables, while in Munster Lieutenant-General Edmund Ludlow confronted a similar number under Lord Muskerry. In Leinster Colonel Grace led 3,000 men against the parliamentary colonels Richard Ingoldsby and Daniel Abbott. All the time there were countless minor skirmishes, involving up to 2,000 Irish fighters. Yet this was the very period when 34,000 Irish soldiers were leaving the country to enlist in continental armies.[53]

In this guerrilla phase of the war the parliamentary commanders imitated the tactics of their enemies, denying them food and striving to turn the rural population against them. By April 1652 every vestige of the tolerance and compassion espoused by Whalley, Ireton and Ludlow just a year earlier had vanished.[54] A joint meeting of army officers and parliamentary commissioners at Kilkenny blamed their own lenity for encouraging the obstinate resistance of the Irish. Indicting the whole nation for 'blood-guiltiness', they professed to be 'deeply . . . affected with the barbarous wickedness of . . . these cruel murthers and massacres'.[55]

But the war did reach a formal conclusion. Notwithstanding their retributive attitude towards the Catholic Irish, the parliamentary commissioners signed articles of peace for all four provinces in May and June 1652. A general pardon was issued except to those implicated in the 1641 massacre, and to 'priests, jesuits, or others in popish orders'. Yet at the end of the year we still hear of 11,000 armed men keeping up the resistance against parliament.[56]

---

[52] Micheál Ó Siochrú 'English military intelligence and the Wars of the Three Kingdoms', *Historical Studies*, 25 (forthcoming, 2006). I am grateful to Micheál Ó Siochrú for letting me have this information in advance of publication.
[53] *NHI*, Vol. 3, 362.
[54] Bodl. MS Tanner 56, fo. 253.
[55] Bodl. MS Tanner 53, fo. 20.
[56] Bodl. MS Clarendon 44, fo. 137.

The land settlement

If the Irish were a blood-guilty people then in English eyes it was justifiable to clear them out and replace them with a new population. This was not a new idea: it was anchored upon the plantation scheme of 1642, which in turn was a continuation of the process that had been begun in the 1580s.[57] The republic's project was to invite all the Irish Adventurers – those who had lent money for the conquest of Ireland in return for the promise of up to 2.5 million acres of land – to come and settle on their property. The soldiers, who were owed £1.75 million, were to be given land in lieu of their arrears. Sixteen counties were to be reserved for these purposes, in addition to a pale extending from the River Boyne just north of Dublin, south to the River Barrow – roughly half the province of Leinster. Even peasants who laid down their arms and accepted parliament's protection were not to be allowed to cultivate land in those areas. This impractical policy was soon relaxed, and peasants were allowed to take up tenancies in the pale. The Irish Catholic gentry, however, were completely dispossessed of their lands.

In spite of the misgivings of the Adventurers, most of whom had little appetite for settling in a desolate, war-torn land, parliament passed the Act for the Settlement of Ireland on 12 August 1652. The body of the act was given over to specifying categories of people who were denied pardon as to life and estate. At least 80,000 people were liable to the death penalty under its provisions.[58] While little attempt was made to hound the people denied pardon, all Catholic landowners, with rare exceptions, were transplanted to Connacht. More than half the landmass of Ireland – 11 out of 20 million acres – was transferred to Adventurers and soldiers.[59]

From 1651 onward Ireland was afflicted with a hunger greater even than that of the 1840s.[60] Starvation, compounded by the first epidemic of bubonic plague in half a century, decimated the population. The new settlers were dismayed to discover that they were occupying a graveyard: the collapse in population had reduced land values almost to zero.[61] That is why in the end so few English took up residence in Ireland. About 500 of the 1533 Adventurers and 7,500 of the 35,000 soldiers eligible to do

[57] Canny, *Making Ireland British*, 553.
[58] S.R. Gardiner, 'The transplantation to Connaught', *EHR*, 14 (1899), 703.
[59] Karl S. Bottigheimer, *English Money and Irish Land: The Adventurers in the Cromwellian Settlement of Ireland*, 117, 139–40; *NHI*, Vol. 3, 359–61, 369.
[60] Lenihan, 'The Catholic Confederacy, 1642–9', 532–40.
[61] Gentles, *NMA*, 383–4.

so bought land and settled in Ireland.[62] The reluctance of Cromwellian soldiers to concretize the English republican vision of a Protestant yeomanry tilling the soil of Ireland effectively sabotaged parliament's hopes of ending the strategic threat posed by a disaffected native population. As William Petty, the English administrator and statistician would acknowledge 20 years later, the experiment of making Ireland British proved to be a costly failure.[63]

[62] Bottigheimer, *English Money and Irish Land*, 63, 140.
[63] Canny, *Making Ireland British*, 578.

CHAPTER 14

War between Scotland and England, 1650–51

After Cromwell and Lambert had humiliated the Scots at Preston and Uttoxeter in the summer of 1648, they pressed their victory home by invading Scotland and moulding the regime to their will. While he was in Edinburgh Cromwell insisted that all 'malignants' – meaning Engagers – be excluded from military or civil office. In obedience to this diktat Engagers were purged from the Committee of Estates and replaced by radicals acceptable to Cromwell. Writing to Colonel Robert Hammond, Cromwell noted how in Scotland 'a lesser party of a parliament hath made it lawful to declare the greater part a faction, and made the parliament null, and call a new one, and to do this by force . . . Think of the example and consequence.'[1] Not for the first time England was about to model itself on Scottish political practice. When the Scots parliament resumed its sitting in January 1649 it was subjected to 'a very long speech' by the Marquess of Argyll on 'the breaking of the malignants' teeth'. He left it to Wariston to 'break their jaws', by which he meant destroy their arguments utterly.[2] Inspired by the two leaders of the radical Covenanting or Kirk party, parliament proceeded to repeal all acts of the previous session (March–June 1648), and all acts of the Committee of Estates (June–September 1648). At a stroke the period of the Engagers' dominance of Scottish politics vanished like a bad dream. As if this cleansing of the body politic were not drastic enough, an Act of Classes was passed just three days before the execution of Charles I (27 January 1649). All holders of government office, whether civil or military, who had supported the Engagement of December 1647, were removed.

---

[1] Abbott, *Cromwell*, Vol. 1, 678.
[2] Sir James Balfour, *Historical Works*, Vol. 3, 377.

Events in England, however, soon made many Covenanters rethink their repudiation of Engagement royalism. There was general alarm throughout the northern kingdom when it became known that the New Model Army had purged the House of Commons and engineered the trial of Charles I. The Scots commissioners in London were instructed to protest against the violence shown to parliament, but to say or do nothing that could give grounds for a new war between the kingdoms. Although they embraced the Calvinist doctrine that Charles, like any other ruler, could be called to account by lesser magistrates, they affirmed that 'the business of greatest consequence was the king's preservation'.[3] Argyll and Wariston attempted to continue discreetly supporting Cromwell and the New Model, but their cover was rudely blown away by the actual beheading of Charles on 30 January, which flagrantly defied the sentiment of the vast majority of the Scottish people.

The king's death profoundly affected Scottish attitudes towards the Westminster Junto. When parliament reconvened on 5 February it immediately proclaimed his son king not just of Scotland, but of England, France and Ireland as well. Covenanting confederalism and the Scottish yearning for religious uniformity on the Presbyterian model throughout the three kingdoms was still very much alive. Many of Argyll's supporters assumed that Charles II would be treated as a figurehead monarch, but there was as yet no tolerance of former Engagers: they continued to be purged without let-up. At the same time they wrote to their new king asking him to ignore the calumnies and shun the company of the 'ungodly', meaning royalists, who were blaming Presbyterianism, for his father's death.[4] A diplomatic mission set sail in March to meet him in Holland in order to persuade him to accept Presbyterianism and become a covenanted king. Meanwhile, the radicals consolidated their grip on the levers of power. A Committee of Dispatches, whose members were all radical Covenanters, was named in May to look after foreign affairs. Except for Argyll, the nobility had been all but eliminated from the covenanting regime, their places taken up by men of much lower social and economic status.

In the elaborate minuet that they performed over the next year both Covenanters and king repeatedly tried to double-cross each other. While the Covenanters kept on purging royalists, the king attempted to use the threat of an invasion by the Marquess of Montrose to intimidate the Covenanters into relaxing their harsh condition – the unqualified embrace of Presbyterianism – for admitting him to the kingdom.

[3] Ibid., 386.
[4] SNA, GD 406/1 (Hamilton MSS), 2128.

To the Covenanters' alarm Montrose was already at that moment in The Hague whispering in Charles's ear. Montrose had assured Charles, 'that I shall never have end, friend, nor enemy, but as your pleasure, and the advancement of your service shall require'.[5] It would have taken a heart of stone for Charles to turn his back on a man who made such an impassioned declaration, but in the end Montrose would be shabbily rewarded for his unstinting loyalty.

The Committee of Estates did everything in its power to destroy Montrose's influence with the king, furiously denouncing him as an oath-breaker who had invaded his country (in 1644), burnt it, wasted it and spilt his countrymen's blood. For all these sins, he had never shown 'the smallest sign of repentance'.[6] In response to this and other acrimonious communications Charles advised the Covenanters that moderation was more likely to convince him of the genuineness of their desire to restore him.[7] For as long as Montrose and the Scottish royalists posed a real threat to the covenanting regime Charles had the upper hand in negotiations with them. Encouraged by risings at Inverness, Stirling and Atholl, Charles renewed Montrose's commissions as lieutenant governor and captain-general of Scotland, and for good measure heaped on him the honour of Admiral of Scotland. More seriously, he authorized Montrose to negotiate with foreign powers for an invasion of Scotland, promising to do nothing without the latter's advice.[8] The pro-monarchist cast of public opinion, together with the recognition that kings and nobles had more in common, in terms of upholding traditional social relations, than he had previously thought, finally wrought a change in Argyll's thinking. By the summer of 1649, if not earlier, he had come to appreciate the need for serious negoti-ations with the king. Charles too, having learned of the complete rout of Ormond's forces by Cromwell, and realizing that France, Spain and the papacy could not be counted on for anything beyond words, now appre-ciated that Scotland was his last hope of regaining the throne.

Shared weakness in the face of the military threat from England at length brought the two sides together. The stumbling blocks to an agree-ment were so huge that it took months of agonizing negotiation, together with the Cromwellian triumph in Ireland, finally to surmount them. They were chiefly religious. The Kirk, before they would let Charles sail to Scotland, insisted that he agree to the imposition of Presbyterianism and

---

[5] *CSP*, Vol. 2, 470 (18/28 January 1649).
[6] *CSP*, Vol. 2, 474.
[7] SNA, GD406/1/1867 (Hamilton MSS).
[8] Montrose, *Memoirs* (Napier), Vol. 2, 706; Carte, *Orig. Letters*, Vol. 1, 357.

the Solemn League and Covenant in all his kingdoms. Parliament further stipulated that he must agree to swear at his coronation to observe and preserve religion as then established in Scotland and to rule according to the word of God and the constitution of the kingdom, and accept both the National Covenant of 1638 and the Solemn League and Covenant of 1643, together with the duty to advance them in all his kingdoms. He was not to bring evil councillors (such as Montrose) to Scotland, and he was to agree to anything else required for the good of the kingdom.

For all its outward intransigence towards the young king, the covenanting regime needed Charles almost as much as he needed it. Lacking foreign friends, beset by the threat of invasion from both royalists and republicans, the Covenanters were acutely conscious of how little they, and how much the king, were liked by their own people. By early 1650 Argyll and most of the nobles were pushing hard for an agreement with Charles II. Yet they were unable to overcome the majority of their fellow Covenanters who continued to enfeeble the regime by ever more drastic purges and arguments over taxation.

In the meantime Charles thought that he could terrify the Kirk party into relaxing their demands by authorizing a military invasion of northern Scotland. 'Proceed vigorously and effectually in your undertaking' he wrote to Montrose in January 1650.[9] In fact Montrose had spent the better part of a year canvassing the continent for money, men and arms. He had met with modest success in Brandenburg, Denmark and Sweden. In mid-March he landed in the Orkneys with 1,200 armed infantry and a handful of horse at his back. Bolstered by reports of Montrose's progress, Charles refused to renounce his treaty with the Irish, or promise to sign the covenants, or stop receiving communion on his knees according to the Anglican rite, or give up his habitual partying and dancing till daybreak.[10] Whatever we make of the young king's social habits, his military strategy was poorly thought out. The royalists did not command enough arms, supplies or money for one campaign, never mind two. Had he been a competent leader Charles would have turned his back on Ireland, suspended talks with the Covenanters until he knew the outcome of Montrose's expedition, and given priority to Montrose by committing everything he had to the invasion of Scotland.[11]

[9] Carte, *Orig. Letters*, Vol. 1, 358; Napier, *Montrose*, Vol. 2, 752.

[10] Stevenson, *Revolution and Counter-Revolution*, 161, n.1.

[11] James Maclean, 'Montrose's preparations for the invasion of Scotland, and royalist missions to Sweden, 1649–1651', in Ragnihild Hatton and M.S. Anderson (eds), *Studies in Diplomatic History*, 16.

His insouciant arrogance was soon stopped in its tracks by the misfortune of war. Help that Montrose had expected from Highland royalists with whom he had kept in regular contact over several months – the Mackays, Seaforth's Mackenzies, the Macleods, the Marquess of Huntly, the Earl Marischal and John Middleton – did not materialize.[12] The key to the Scottish royalists' holding back was their understandable inclination to wait and see what sort of treaty Charles negotiated with the Covenanters before committing themselves.[13] Nor were there any hard-bitten Irish infantry to back up Montrose as there had been in 1644–45. This time all the advantages were with the Covenanters. Now that they were no longer maintaining armies in England and Ireland, they could send their best cavalry against him, which they did at Carbisdale on 27 April. The Covenanters were so confident of victory they only committed about 250 horse and a little over 400 foot. Before setting out Lieutenant Colonel Strachan steeled his men by leading them in psalm singing, scripture reading and prayer, and assuring them that victory was theirs.[14] Events would soon bear him out. When scouts reported that Montrose was approaching he hid all but one of his troops of horse. The royalist scouts then informed Montrose that there were only a few covenanting horse in the vicinity. As Montrose prepared to attack, Strachan then brought out all his horse and fell on the royalists. Enjoying the advantage of surprise, the 650 Covenanters completely routed a force nearly twice as large, killing 4–500, while a further 200 drowned in the River Shin and over 400 were captured. The Covenanters lost only one trooper. A week later Montrose himself was seized and taken to Edinburgh. Loyal to the end, he declined to reveal that he had acted under a commission from the king. He had to suffer the disgrace of hanging, beheading and quartering. His head was displayed over Edinburgh tollbooth, and the other parts of his body in Stirling, Glasgow, Perth and Aberdeen.

On 15 May Charles, unaware of Montrose's defeat, wrote to him to lay down his arms because he had come to an agreement with his Scots subjects: the treaty that he had been negotiating since March with the Scottish parliamentary commissioners at Breda in Holland was on the point of being signed.[15] He also promised Montrose to do all in his power to protect him. A week later, under pressure from the Scots commissioners he

[12] Carte, *Orig. Letters*, Vol. 1, 348.
[13] Carte, *Orig. Letters*, Vol. 1, 363–4.
[14] Edward Furgol, *A Regimental History of the covenanting Armies, 1639–1615*, 328.
[15] For the treaty negotiations see *CSP*, Vol. 2, appendix, li–lxv. The treaty was concluded in June 1650.

disowned responsibility for Montrose's invasion. As the historian of these events has observed, once having authorized the invasion 'it was insulting of Charles' to countermand his previous orders at such a late date. He must have known that there was not the remotest chance of his fresh, contradictory orders reaching Montrose in time to help him.[16]

In fact Charles did not crumple all at once. He continued to hold out for the liberty of the Irish to practise their popish religion, and against adopting Presbyterian worship. As in other arenas of conflict during the previous 15 years, religion was the great barrier to agreement. Eventually, however, Charles recognized that his only way of getting to Scotland was to take the covenants, denounce popery, cast off his 'malignant' councillors, and accept as replacements those whom the Kirk would certify as being 'of a blameless and Christian conversation'.[17] So he swallowed the bitter pill, and put his name to the Treaty of Breda in June 1650. No one was under any illusion as to the hypocrisy this entailed on both sides. One of the parliamentary commissioners confided to his diary, 'we knew from clear and demonstrable reasons that he hated [the covenants] in his heart . . . He sinfully complied with what we most sinfully pressed upon him'.[18] Another jaundiced observer of the proceedings wrote that it was pleasant

to see how they endeavour to cheat and cozen each other. The king strokes them till he can get into the saddle, and then he will make them feel his spurs for all their old jade's tricks they have played his father . . . and they know it, and therefore will not agree that he shall back them [i.e. mount them] with his heels armed.[19]

Just as the Covenanters feared, Charles arrived in Scotland to a rapturous welcome. Amidst the dancing and bonfires, they shuddered to think that what the merrymakers really wanted was for the king to overthrow the Kirk party, not ally himself with it. Not only did they insist on removing Hamilton and Lauderdale from his entourage, they also forbade Charles to go near the army. Still, at the beginning of August he accepted the invitation of some officers to visit the forces at Leith, where he was received with joy. Shaken by this outpouring of affection, Wariston and other members of the Committee of Estates ordered him to leave since he

---

[16] Maclean, 'Montrose's preparations for the invasion of Scotland', 27.

[17] *CSP*, Vol. 2, appendix, lxii–lxiv.

[18] *Diary of Alexander Jaffray*, ed. John Barclay, 55.

[19] SHS, *Letters and Papers Illustrating the Relations between Charles II and Scotland in 1650*, ed. S.R. Gardiner, 80.

was competing with God for popularity, and undermining their notions of godliness.

The Scots' unquenchable 'predilection for ideological schism'[20] can only have given comfort to the leaders of the parliamentary army in England. Ever since the Scots proclaimed Charles II king of all three kingdoms, the Rump parliament knew that an armed confrontation was unavoidable. News of the imminent treaty at Breda prompted an urgent message to Cromwell to return from Ireland to meet this dire threat to English security. On 20 June the Council of State grasped the nettle and resolved on a pre-emptive invasion of Scotland. It assumed that Fairfax and Cromwell would lead the expedition together, but Fairfax, who had been drifting towards Presbyterianism since before the regicide, had scruples about attacking the Long Parliament's old ally, and declined the invitation. Consequently, Cromwell now became commander-in-chief of the entire parliamentary army.

He moved quickly to prepare logistically, politically and spiritually for the expedition. After fasting with his officers and attending a five-sermon marathon, he mobilized 16,300 men as well as the money and matériel to underpin them. He then embarked on a letter-writing campaign to undermine the Scottish people's allegiance to the Covenant, and the key Covenanters' allegiance to the king. To the Scots he promised that they had nothing to fear from his army. To the Covenanters, 'our brethren', he expressed 'tenderness', imploring them to soften their religious rigidity, and scolding them for having dealings with a faithless king. The next few months would demonstrate his effectiveness at planting doubts in sincere minds.

The Scots for their part girded themselves for war. First, their general David Leslie stripped the border region between the river Tweed and Edinburgh of its food and evacuated its population. He also entrenched his army behind a nearly impregnable fortified line running from Edinburgh to Leith. Secondly, he built up his army to over 20,000 men by the beginning of September. This he accomplished in spite of the Kirk's insistence on purging malignants and ungodly men. Using the example of the Old Testament commander Gideon, the clergy argued that a small godly army would prove superior to a larger army of dubious moral and religious purity.[21] Several days in August were devoted to expelling 80 officers and 4,000 men who failed to pass the religious and political tests. The

---

[20] Macinnes, *The British Revolution*, 191.

[21] Judges 7 and 8 for the story of how Gideon conquered the Midianites after purging his army as the Lord commanded.

Covenanters have been harshly criticized for insisting on ideological purity in the army, but there are numerous historical examples of small elite forces bound together by intensive training, and religious or ideological unity, that have performed better than larger, less tightly disciplined entities. Indeed, small forces of Covenanters had recently won sensational victories against the royalists at Balvenie in May 1649 where they were outnumbered ten to one,[22] and at Carbisdale in April 1650, where the odds against them were almost two to one. It was less the purging of their army than the bad conscience of key Covenanters – Wariston, Strachan and Ker – who had been holding secret talks with Cromwell's officers in July, that would contribute to Leslie's humiliation at Dunbar.[23]

Cromwell crossed the River Tweed on 22 July, and a week later was before Leith, barely eight miles north-west of Edinburgh. But torrential rain, shortage of food, and the Scots' refusal to be drawn outside their walls compelled him to fall back to Musselburgh, where his troops found themselves harried in the middle of the night by crack units of Scots cavalry. After this bruising encounter Cromwell decided to suspend military activity for a while and resume the battle for his adversaries' hearts and minds. He wrote to the General Assembly of the Kirk, taxing them with intolerance and berating them for their alliance with Charles, 'a covenant made with death and hell'. 'Is it therefore infallibly agreeable to the Word of God, all that you say? I beseech you, in the bowels of Christ, think it possible you may be mistaken.' With caustic brevity the Covenanters asked him, 'would you have us to be sceptics in our religion?'[24]

Following another four weeks of playing cat and mouse with Leslie west of Edinburgh Cromwell was forced to withdraw to Dunbar. His troops were in a sorry state: 'provisions . . . being once more near exhausted and gone, the nights cold, the ground wet, the bloody-flux and other diseases prevailing in the army, and the Scots hitherto refusing to fight'.[25] Sickness and desertion had reduced his army to barely 11,000 in the space of six weeks. More dauntingly, Cromwell had never faced as accomplished a commander as Leslie, and at the beginning of September it looked as if he had been out-generalled. With the Scots snapping at their heels his troops found themselves pushed against the sea, encamped in the midst of swamps and bogs. Facing a foe twice their size, it seemed only a matter of

---

[22] Stevenson, *Revolution and Counter-Revolution*, 147–8.
[23] Ibid., 175.
[24] Abbott, *Cromwell*, Vol. 2, 303, 305.
[25] *Perfect Passages* (9–13 September 1650), E780/6, 71.

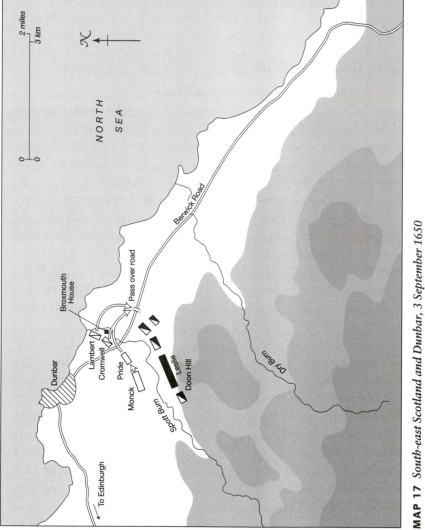

MAP 17 *South-east Scotland and Dunbar, 3 September 1650*

Adapted from Gentles, Ian, *The New Model Army: In England, Scotland and Ireland, 1645–1653* (Blackwell Publishers, 1991)

time before they were encircled and devoured. His council of war now gave all its attention to the desperate question of how to get back to England alive. To keep their morale from breaking the officers unleashed a torrent of prayer and God-seeking. In the midst of this crisis they were also borne up by the prayers of the faithful in England, most notably from a number of all-night prayer meetings of London officers led by Colonel Thomas Harrison.[26]

The Battle of Dunbar[27]

On 1 September the Scots army occupied the high ground known as Doon Hill overlooking Dunbar. In response to clerical pressure for a decisive engagement, Leslie sent a detachment to cut off the pass at Cockburnspath, six miles south-east of Dunbar. The only mode of escape for the English was now evacuation by sea. In reality Cromwell's position was less precarious and Leslie's more vulnerable than at first appeared. The English were protected from surprise attack by a little stream that tumbled through a narrow glen about 40 feet deep. They were also out of range of the Scots artillery. The only way Leslie could attack was to bring his army down the hill to the plain south-east of the town on the other side of the stream. Moreover, the high ground on which the army was stationed was cruelly exposed to wind, cold and wet. Confident that he had Cromwell on the run, Leslie came down the hill on the morning of 2 September. In the process he transferred two-thirds of the left wing of his cavalry to the right, causing the whole right wing to edge down towards the sea. His army was now strung along a front one mile long. His intention was to fall on the flank or rear of Cromwell's cavalry as they tried to retreat towards England.

Far from retreating, Cromwell unexpectedly took the offensive. This was thanks mainly to the reconnoitering work of Lambert and other commanders. With their experienced eyes they could tell that the Scots left wing was crowded against the steep slope of the glen. Given the quality of their soldiers they believed that a concerted assault on Leslie's right wing had a good chance of succeeding before the left could rally to its assistance. For this audacious plan to work they had to get the bulk of the army past the front of the enemy's line. This they did during the night of 2–3 September. They were assisted by wet windy weather, which muffled the

---

[26] Folger Lib., X.d.483(63) (Bennett Papers).
[27] For a more extended analysis of the battle of Dunbar, see Gentles, *NMA*, 392–8.

sound of their troop movements. The Scots, oblivious to what was taking place only a few yards away, relaxed their watch. The musketeers extinguished their match and lay down beneath the newly reaped corn to snatch a few hours of sleep, while many of the officers sheltered in farmhouses and tents behind the lines.

It was 4 a.m. and Cromwell's manoeuvre was nearly complete by the time the Scots had caught wind of what the English were up to and were sounding the trumpets to rouse their men. The attack was led by the men of Lambert's brigade, who were met with a resolute charge down the hill by Scots cavalry armed with lances. The English recoiled a little under the shock, but quickly rallied. Just before 6 a.m. the full sun appeared over the sea, and Cromwell shouted in the words of the psalmist, 'Now let God arise and his enemies shall be scattered!' The horse and foot were quickly engaged all over the field. Soon the Scots found themselves hemmed in and panic gripped their ranks. Captain Hodgson heard Cromwell exult, 'I profess they run!' After a second combined charge by New Model cavalry and foot regiments the Scots' right wing collapsed. This main action was over by 7 a.m. As Hodgson observed, they 'routed one another after we had done their work on their right wing'.[28] Seeing the cream of the infantry overcome, the rest of the foot flung down their weapons and scattered terrified in all directions. The English cavalry then rode among these panic-stricken men, making them, in Cromwell's words 'as stubble to their swords'.[29] The New Model horse next encircled the left wing of the Scots horse, which until now had not struck a blow in the battle. It was short work for the Ironsides to cut through these demoralized men.

The English could scarcely believe that an enemy more than twice their size would just crumble before their eyes. Cromwell 'did laugh so excessively as if he had been drunk; his eyes sparkled with spirits'.[30] His exuberance was understandable, for he had once again demonstrated his superior generalship in massing overwhelming force at a single point. His daring stroke against a much larger army was facilitated by the fine calibre of the English troops. English seapower, which up to that moment had brought him a fairly steady stream of supplies, preserved his army from starvation and kept it battle ready.[31] English control of the seas was in turn made

---

[28] Slingsby, Sir Henry, *Original Memoirs Written during the Great Civil War; Being the Life of Sir Henry Slingsby and Memoirs of Capt. Hodgson*, 147–8.

[29] Abbott, *Cromwell*, Vol. 2, 324.

[30] John Aubrey, *Miscellanies upon Various Subjects*, 160.

[31] Bernard Capp, *Cromwell's Navy: The Fleet and the English Revolution 1648–1660*, 67.

possible by English economic might. While the wars of the last decade had caused serious strain for England they had left Scotland prostrate. The simple fact is that the English Exchequer found a total of £1.2 million to pay for Scotland's conquest in 1650–51.[32] The Scottish treasury resorted to many of the same expedients as the English – monthly assessments, an excise tax, forced and voluntary loans – but cannot have raised more than a tenth of the English total. Furthermore, by 1650–51, the people of Scotland were in a state of economic suffocation, thanks to a public debt running into the millions of pounds Scots, that had been incurred for all the wars fought by the Covenanters.[33]

Dunbar was Cromwell's most one-sided victory. The Scots army suffered 3,000 slain and almost 10,000 taken prisoner. If we can believe English reports Cromwell did not lose more than 20 men. The strategic and political consequences of this lopsided result were far-reaching. Having lost almost half his soldiers, Leslie could no longer hold the fortified line between Edinburgh and Leith, both of which fell to Cromwell. The Committee of Estates, the Kirk Assembly and the military high command all withdrew to Stirling. Renewed infighting erupted between the Kirk party and the Committee of Estates, whom the Covenanters blamed for trying to compromise with the royalists. Moderates and royalists in turn blamed the Covenanters for causing Leslie's defeat by their purging of the army and continual interference in military affairs. Radical Covenanters calling themselves Remonstrants and led by colonels Archibald Strachan and Gilbert Ker, now attempted to construct their own power base in the shape of a new army of godly men recruited from around Glasgow in the west. But they could not prevent the rapprochement between Charles and the moderate majority known as Resolutioners. The union between them was symbolically consummated with Charles's coronation on New Year's Day 1651. It was no churchman, but the Marquess of Argyll, who placed the crown on the young king's head at Scone. A great royalist–nationalist revival now seized the country, and within half a year the Kirk party was swept from power.[34]

It was reported that royalists rejoiced at the news of Dunbar. Charles II was so pleased that he fell on his knees and gave thanks.[35] The royalists'

[32] NA, Treasurers at War Accounts, 28 March 1645–25 December 1651, E351/302, fo. 5v.

[33] Stevenson, 'Financing', 118–23. There were 12 Scots pounds to each pound sterling.

[34] David Stevenson (ed.), *Government under the Covenanters*, 58.

[35] Clarendon, *Hist.*, Bk 8, 23; *Merc. Politicus* (12–19 September 1650), E613/1, 259.

accession to power did not occur overnight, nor did it prevent Scotland's continuing humiliation at the hands of the English republic. The formation of a royalist–Covenanter coalition was obstructed at first by Charles's panicky reaction to a rumour that a band of Remonstrants led by Colonel Strachan was plotting to abduct him and hand him over to Cromwell. He resolved to protect himself by rallying a force of royalists and Engagers to secure Perth and take command of Leslie's army. When the Committee of Estates got wind of this they immediately demanded a purge of his household. Charles then embarked on an escapade known as 'the Start'.[36] With ill-judged impetuosity he jumped on his horse and fled Perth for the north, where he hoped to join forces with the Marquess of Huntly. The Committee of Estates reacted decisively, despatching 600 troops after him. They overtook him before he could get beyond the South Esk and courteously persuaded him to come back to Perth. As Gardiner observes, Charles by his conduct 'had demonstrated that he was an unfit leader in any enterprise which demanded secrecy and decision'.[37]

There were enough nobles intent on national reconciliation, however, that Charles's madcap adventure was soon overlooked. Nobles who had been associated with the Engagement were gradually admitted to parliament, though Callander and Lauderdale were still barred from civil office. The next step was the establishment of a new Committee of Estates at the end of year. Again, despite the admission of a number of Engager and Pragmatic Royalist nobles, 'the radical regime still maintained its ascendancy'.[38] But by March 1651 the partisans of patriotic accommodation felt strong enough to face down the radical nobles. Increasingly, national interests promoted by the gentry and burgesses trumped the interests of theocracy and religion. The fundamental political shift was signified by the appointment on 28 March of new colonels for the southern shires: all were former Engagers or royalists. By 2 June the political revolution was complete when the Acts of Classes of 1646 and 1649 were both repealed, opening the way to complete rehabilitation of royalists and Engagers, and their readmission to political life. In effect the Committee of Estates transformed itself into a conservative, royalist body. All 16 of its noble members were exclusively royalist; the power of the Church was correspondingly diminished.[39] Between the Engagement of December 1647 and the royalist

---

[36] Clarendon, *Hist.*, Bk 8, 48.
[37] S.R. Gardiner, *History of the Commonwealth and Protectorate 1649–1656*, Vol. 1, 338.
[38] Young, *Scottish Parliament*, 272.
[39] Ibid., 269–70, 272, 278–9, 285, 287, 289.

recapture of power in the spring of 1651 Scottish politics, hammered on the anvil of civil war and melted in the blast furnace of invasion and conquest, had come full circle. Never again would a triumphalist Presbyterian clergy be allowed a role in Scotland's high politics.

After Dunbar, Cromwell wasted little time savouring his triumph, but immediately resumed his theological offensive against the Covenanters. He chalked up some notable conversions to the cause of religious toleration and republicanism, among them radical Covenanters Alexander Jaffray of the Committee of Estates, and colonels Strachan and Ker of the Glasgow-based Western Association. The Western Association was an organization of dissidents, critical of Leslie's conduct at Dunbar and alienated by the rapprochement of the Committee of Estates with the royalists. One fruit of the Cromwellian conversions of these disaffected radicals was their promulgation of the Western Remonstrance, which denounced the new policy of fighting for Charles II. Some of Strachan and Ker's officers went further, and openly embraced English Independency. Before the end of the year, however, Cromwell had grown impatient at the slowness of theological progress, and resolved to employ military means to bring the Western Association to heel. On 30 November a brigade led by Colonel Lambert marched to Hamilton where they clashed with the Western army under Ker and destroyed it. This second military disaster revived the doubts among extreme Covenanters that in resisting Cromwell they were resisting the will of God. One man who thought along these lines was Sir Walter Dundas, governor of Edinburgh Castle. Cromwellian argument backed up with Cromwellian siege guns brought him to surrender the castle on Christmas Eve 1650.

The covenanting–royalist regime was granted a few months' breathing space in early 1651 owing to the ill-health of its chief antagonist. 'I grow an old man', Cromwell had confided to his wife after Dunbar, 'and feel infirmities of age marvellously stealing upon me.'[40] In February 1651 he succumbed to dysentery. It took him two months to get over that, only to fall ill of kidney stones and several fits of ague. Not until June did his physicians certify that his health was restored.

The Scots used the respite furnished by Cromwell's illness to attempt to put their political and logistical houses in order. As an expedient to accommodate professed royalists whom they were still not ready to admit to the Committee of Estates, parliament created a Committee for the Army

[40] Abbott, *Cromwell*, Vol. 2, 329.

which it staffed with royalists. While the Committee of Estates convened in Stirling, the Army Committee sat in Perth, each treading on the other's toes in the joint effort to raise men, money and supplies. As Stevenson points out, the creation of the Army Committee in March 1651 marked an important stage in the transformation of the Kirk-party regime into a full-fledged royalist regime. The next stage followed hard on the heels of the first: at the beginning of April parliament asked Charles to take command of the army. A further stage was the repeal of the Acts of Classes, and the condemnation of the Western Remonstrance at the beginning of June. During these months the Army Committee made herculean efforts to raise food, horses, muskets, pistols, gunpowder and lead for a counter-offensive against the English occupiers. Again and again they had to admit failure, for the simple reason that the country had already been squeezed dry. Try as they would they could never find money and food to keep the army in being for more than ten days at a time. In desperation the members of the committee lent from their own pockets to buy provisions to feed the soldiers and keep them from deserting.[41] No matter what expedient they employed there was never enough food to maintain the army anywhere near its targeted strength of 36,000 men. The chronic shortage of food and money meant that the army's numbers were in a constant state of hemorrhage. The Army Committee's stirring proclamation that 'religion, the king's person and authority and the preservation of Scotland and all Scots are being fought for', cut little ice with many of the new soldiers.[42] Matters were not helped by the foot-dragging of the Marquess of Argyll, who had little love for the increasingly royalist regime. His failure to bring out his men had a knock-on effect with neighbouring Highlanders who also became reluctant to take the field, fearing that the Campbells would raid their territory when they were gone.[43]

Cromwell by contrast had received fresh recruits from England, bringing his army up to 21,000. There was no trouble keeping it supplied. Confident in his logistical support Cromwell took the field again in July, sending 4,000 men across the Firth of Forth under colonels Lambert and Robert Overton. Benefiting from Cromwell's feints towards the west and Stirling, Lambert attacked the main Scottish army at Inverkeithing as

---

[41] See Stevenson (ed.), *Government under the Covenanters*, 112–35, 162–3 for the sometimes frantic efforts of the Committee for Managing the Affairs of the Army to find food in early 1651.

[42] Ibid., 141.

[43] Ibid., 140.

it was attempting to get back to Stirling and defend the capital from Cromwell's incursion. Once again Cromwell's gifted understudy won a stunning victory, slaughtering 2,000 Scots and taking a further 1,400 prisoner, while losing hardly a man of his own.

Profiting from Lambert's success Cromwell now crossed the Forth into Fife, Scotland's richest county. By 1 August he was before Perth, where he obtained a bloodless victory the next day. Within the space of two weeks, Cromwell and Lambert had transformed the military situation. They had fooled the Scots as to their intentions, mauled their main army, and by establishing themselves in Perth, cut them off from all hope of reinforcements and supplies from the north. Strategically, Inverkeithing was a more decisive battle than Dunbar. The risk that the remainder of the army at Stirling would invade England was one that Cromwell and Lambert had taken with open eyes. Cromwell's paramount objective was to force the Scots into the field: the last thing he wanted was a war of sieges and attrition. By quitting Stirling the Scots played into his hands.

The Battle of Worcester

With hindsight we may question why the Scots and their king imagined they could gain anything from invading England. Unaware that their annihilation was imminent, the Scots could cite several reasons why they might plausibly hope for success. The republic's ablest troops and officers were well behind them, unable to stop their advance on London. Ahead of them would be mostly militia units and untried recruits. They also hoped to exploit the disillusionment of many people in England with republican rule. Had not the combined monthly pay of the republic's armies in England, Ireland and Scotland reached the astronomical figure of £157,000 in the month of August alone?[44] Surely the English people could be counted upon to rise up and rebel against such oppression. There were other reasons as well for leaving Scotland. Charles had become weary of bullying Presbyterians. Invasion offered an escape from surroundings that he found personally intolerable. Those who accompanied him had few illusions about their prospects. The second Duke of Hamilton confessed to his niece that the army 'must either starve, disband or go with a handful of men into England'. Their hope was 'willingly [to] lay down their lives as Christ did his'. To a friend he candidly admitted 'we have one stout argument,

[44] *CJ*, Vol. 6, 617.

despair'.[45] Since, like so many other royalist letters, this one was intercepted, the English knew exactly the state of morale in the Scottish army.

Hamilton's intuition was correct: the invasion was doomed before it began. Once the royalist army left Stirling, perhaps 20,000 strong,[46] the soldiers deserted by the thousands. When it crossed the border it was down to 12–13,000, an ethnically diverse body of 'Jockies, Walloons or redshanks [Celtic inhabitants of the Scottish Highlands or Ireland]', but very few English.[47] The further they marched from Scotland the more their numbers shrank, from dysentery as well as desertion. Hardly anyone reported to Charles's standard after he crossed into England at the beginning of August. North-west England's greatest royalist magnate, the Earl of Derby, for example, could muster no more than 1,500 troops. It did not help that Charles's officers were 'miserably divided'. The untrustworthy Duke of Buckingham thought he should be general of the horse in place of David Leslie. David Leslie for his part was 'sad and melancholic' throughout the whole march. When the crunch came at Worcester he held his troops back from the fray.[48]

Yet the republican regime was reputed to be deeply unpopular as the English people staggered under the weight of accumulated debt and ever higher taxes. Why did they not welcome their king in 1651? Apart from a general loathing of the Scots as 'a beggarly nation', there were four principal reasons. First, there had already been a premature and isolated rising in Norfolk in December 1650 which had been easily suppressed. Secondly, the royalist conspiracy in England had been cracked in March 1651 with the arrest of two ringleaders who spilled the beans to their captors. The plan had been for a coordinated uprising of Lancashire royalists under the Earl of Derby assisted by a Scottish incursion, together with a popular rising of servants and apprentices in London under the direction of certain noblemen and Presbyterian ministers. Their object was to restore the MPs secluded at Pride's Purge and then prevail upon the new king to accept the Newport Treaty. The rooting out of this conspiracy points to the continuing excellence of the republic's intelligence operation. Thirdly, expected help from the continent never materialized. Add to that the fourth factor, that the invading force was weak in numbers, ill-armed, poorly supplied

---

[45] SNA, GD 406/1/5956; Henry Cary (ed.), *Memorials of the Great Civil War in England from 1646 to 1652*, Vol. 2, 305.

[46] *OPH*, Vol. 20, 19.

[47] *Merc. Politicus* (21–8 August 1651), E640/23, 1026.

[48] Clarendon, *Hist.*, Bk 8, 62, 74.

and badly led, and it is abundantly obvious why most English people in 1651 decided to give this latest invitation to counter-revolution a miss.[49]

Once in England Charles had to cope with Lambert and Harrison, each leading brigades of 3–4,000 horse and dragoons harassing his rear and shepherding him westward, away from London. The despised county militias also played a significant role in annoying the royalist invaders. The rallying of so many men to the republic's defence proves that however unpopular parliament may have been, the Scots royalist invaders were more unpopular still.

On his way south Charles won a minor victory when he drove off Harrison's and Lambert's combined forces and captured Warrington Bridge. This was more than outweighed by the annihilation of the Earl of Derby's whole contingent at Wigan by the Cheshire infantry and Robert Lilburne's cavalry regiment. It was now nearly the end of August; after 23 days on the road Charles's men were worn out and dispirited. The king would have liked to press on to London, but at Worcester his men sat down and refused to budge. If the citizens gave him a cordial welcome, they had little to offer him in the way of tangible support. Worcester's fortifications were in disrepair, and before he could begin to repair them Cromwell had taken up a position just outside the city with an army whose numbers would soon swell to three times those of the king. About a quarter of the parliamentary force was made up of county militias.

Cromwell had such an abundance of manpower that he did not need to spend time on a siege. He divided his army in two in order to conduct a pincer movement against his enemy. On the west bank of the River Severn, he placed 11,000 troops under Colonel Charles Fleetwood. The main body of his army he kept at Perry Wood near Spetchley, south-east of the city. Early on the morning of 3 September he launched a combined assault against Scottish positions west and south of the city. This assault succeeded in its objective of forcing the king to bring his remaining troops out of the city to join the battle. Charles led a charge in person against Fleetwood's left wing where they were trying to cross Powick Bridge. At first he was successful, but when he rode to his main body, who were struggling with Fleetwood's right wing and Cromwell's reinforcements, he found them in disorder. Subjected to withering fire from parliamentary musketeers, he had to retreat into the city.

It was now late afternoon, and the second phase of the battle, the struggle on the city's eastern side, commenced. After regrouping within the

---

[49] David Underdown, *Royalist Conspiracy in England, 1649–1660*, 42–7.

city walls, Charles went on the offensive, sending most of his army thundering out of St Martin's and Sidbury gates for an attack on the parliamentary position at Red Hill. He was initially rewarded for his boldness with success, but soon Cromwell was back, leading his troops into the fray. It took three hours of close fighting before the royalists were driven back behind the city walls.

After sundown began the third phase of the battle, the fight for Worcester itself. Cromwell now hurled all his troops against the city, keeping none in reserve. There was bitter, bloody fighting from street to street, but it was soon over. Before long the royalist foot threw down their arms and scattered. The horse under the king's own command continued to dispute the streets. Later royalist witnesses were unanimous in saluting the king's suicidal courage as he rode among his men, 'calling every officer by his name' and giving them 'all the encouragement . . . a magnanimous General could afford'.[50] Hamilton and Middleton were wounded, while many other officers were either dismounted or slain. The king himself seemed to prefer death in this hopeless struggle to capture and an ignominious trial. Eventually he was persuaded to flee with an improvised lifeguard of 600 mounted men, which he later reduced to 60. After a six-week trek, much of it spent hiding in Catholic households, he reached the south coast, where he boarded a ship for France.

With the flight of the king the battle came to an end by 8 p.m. The next day Worcester and its environs were a scene of desolation. Its streets were choked with the corpses of men and horses; the stench of death was everywhere. Between 2,000 and 3,000 royalists, but fewer than 200 parliamentarians had lost their lives. For several days the remnants of the Scots cavalry were hounded from town to town and cut to pieces as they attempted to regain their native country.

This overwhelming popular antagonism to the Scots invaders is another sign of how little support Charles had garnered for his project of reclaiming his kingdom. The contrast with 1639 is instructive. In that year many had welcomed the Scottish army that had humiliated Charles I when it invaded and occupied the northern counties. The anger shown in 1651 to the alien soldiers, together with the massive outpouring of militia support at the battle of Worcester, tells of the widespread if temporary favour enjoyed by the Commonwealth. In the aftermath of Worcester parliament attempted to consolidate its popularity by reducing the size of the military establishment, thereby cutting its outlay by over £420,000 a year.[51]

[50] *CSP*, Vol. 2, 562; Bodl. MS Clarendon 42, fo. 152v.
[51] *CJ*, Vol. 7, 25.

A week after the battle Cromwell arrived in London to a hero's welcome. As he rode through the streets, accompanied by all the country's magistrates, he was greeted by shouting crowds; cannon and musketry saluted his arrival at Whitehall. The next day 4,000 of the prisoners taken at Worcester were paraded through the capital, after which their punishments were meted out. The Earl of Derby and four others were executed. The toll of executions would have been one higher had not Hamilton already died of gangrene in the leg. Other leaders such as Lauderdale and Leslie were kept in confinement until the Restoration, though Massie and Middleton effected their escape. Some of the common soldiers were sentenced to servitude in Ireland and Bermuda, while the rest, if they had not already died in England, were eventually sent home.

Before Worcester had even been fought Colonel George Monk and his 5–6,000 troops had extinguished the last embers of resistance in Scotland. On 14 August Stirling Castle fell to him thanks to his adroit use of mortars and heavy cannon. He also sent Colonel Matthew Alured to take Alyth, where the remnant of the Committee of Estates were holed up. The last major stronghold was Dundee. This time, because bad weather frustrated the artillery barrage at the end of August, Monk opted for a storm – his troops butchering between 400 and 800 townspeople in the process. The surviving population was plundered for a fortnight.

Conclusion

The reasons for Scotland's downfall were similar to Ireland's. The country was politically and religiously divided, economically exhausted, and so deficient in population after over a decade of war in all three kingdoms, that it had little chance of withstanding the withering blast of the English republic's military machine. In the face of imminent invasion, and conscious of the renewed threat of Highland royalist insurgency under the leadership of Montrose, Argyll had abandoned the purity of his former anti-Engager stance, and spoken up for a rapprochement with Charles II. But he had failed to carry with him an important segment of the radical Kirk party. Based in the region around Glasgow, these radicals metamorphosed into the Western Association and issued a call for loyalty known as the Western Remonstrance, which gave them the tag Remonstrants. The moderate Covenanters under Argyll, who became increasingly identified with Charles II and the former Engagers were called Resolutioners. Infighting between Remonstrants and Resolutioners severely compromised the Scottish effort to turn back the Cromwellian invaders.

The Presbyterian clergy had insisted on a drastic purging of the army in the summer of 1650, and then their political heirs, the Western Remonstrants, had indulged in carping criticism of General Leslie for his humiliation at Dunbar. Some Remonstrants went so far as to embrace English Independency. It is hardly surprising that their army was easily liquidated by Lambert at Hamilton. Even when the Committee of Estates had achieved a semblance of unity against the invader–occupier it ran up against an insurmountable problem of shortages: there was never enough food, money, matériel or men to stand up to the well-furnished troops of Cromwell's army. Nor were matters helped by Argyll's diminishing enthusiasm for an increasingly royalist regime. In the end an inexperienced king led the remnant of a ravaged Scottish army to its destruction deep in the English heartland at Worcester. Scotland's reward was 11 years of harsh, if administratively efficient military tyranny.

After Worcester, Scottish political independence was at an end. So many high-ranking prisoners had been taken there and at Alyth that as Marchamont Nedham scoffed, 'the nobility of Scotland that are at liberty may all sit about a joint-stool'.[52] By the end of the year eight commissioners had been named to administer Scotland under the following terms:

1 religious toleration;

2 political union with England;

3 reparations to be paid out of the estates of the Crown and leading Scottish royalist landowners; and

4 amnesty for most tenants and vassals.

The onus for the war was formally placed, not on the Scottish nation as a whole, but on its social and political leaders. In contrast to its policy of repression and punishment in Ireland, the English republic extended the hand of friendship to the mass of the people of Scotland. This policy was an attempt to safeguard the revolution in England by exporting some elements of it to Scotland. Like the Covenanters before them, the Rump parliament had grasped the point that the greater security lay in union and uniformity between the two countries.[53]

---

[52] *Merc. Politicus* (11–18 September 1651), E641/20, 1076.
[53] F.D. Dow, *Cromwellian Scotland, 1651–1660*, 32.

CHAPTER 15

Audit of war: the human and material cost

Introduction

In his book *Plagues and Peoples* the Chicago historian William McNeill postulates that throughout its history humanity has been beset by two sorts of parasites. First there are micro-parasites: the various bacteria and viruses that dwell in the human body, feed off it, and sometimes kill it. Then there are macro-parasites: robbers, pirates, princes, aristocracies and, in the modern era, the nation-state in its multifarious manifestations.[1] The macro-parasitism of the state is at its most intense during times of war, civil war and revolution. To examine the extent of this macro-parasitism in Britain and Ireland during the upheavals of the mid-seventeenth century is, at least indirectly, to raise the question: 'Was the English Revolution worth it?' I shall attempt to answer the question under four headings: deaths and wounds, property damage, taxation and property confiscations, and free quarter and plunder.

Deaths and wounds

At the beginning it must be acknowledged that the whole question of the mortality caused by the English Revolution is bedevilled by uncertainty and confusion. Charles Carlton tells us that there were 84,830 battle deaths in England and Wales, though he disarmingly concedes that his figures for all three kingdoms ought to be taken with 'a pinch of caution and pound of scepticism'.[2] My own opinion – reinforced by conversations

---

[1] William H. McNeill, *Plagues and Peoples*, 5–6.
[2] Carlton, *Going to the Wars*, 204, 214.

with other students of the civil wars – is that Carlton's figures are on the high side, and should be shaved to 75,000, if not less, for England and Wales. French historical demographers have estimated that in seventeenth-century Europe only 10–25 per cent of military deaths occurred in battle.[3] The rest were caused by disease – dysentery ('the bloody flux'), typhus ('spotted' or 'camp' fever), typhoid and bubonic plague – and accidents. Another military historian suggests, more cautiously, that deaths from disease outnumbered deaths from wounds and accidents by 'a bit less' than six to four; i.e. less than 1.5 to 1.[4] Based on a reading of the British and Irish evidence, I would support this lower ratio. Certainly the 'wastage' figures that we have for English civil war armies seem to bear out that there was a good deal of non-battlefield attrition. A seventeenth-century army in England or on the continent was fortunate if it shrank at a rate of less than 2 per cent per month from disease and desertion. Essex's army, which numbered about 14,000 effectives at Edgehill, was down to 5,500 by July 1643, a mere nine months later, with a further 3,000 infantry incapacitated by illness. This represents a monthly wastage rate of 4 per cent.[5] When the army of Scottish Covenanters entered England in January 1644 it numbered 21,500 men. Four months later it was down to 14,000, a wastage rate of 7.5 per cent per month.[6] The New Model Army shrank from a peak strength of 24,800 at the end of May 1645 to 13,800 by the end of July the same year. This represented a wastage of 14 per cent per month. Only a few hundred men had died in battle; the rest had been wounded, run away, or succumbed to disease.[7] In the Eastern Association Army the wastage was 2 per cent per month between June and October 1644; in Warwickshire the cavalry wasted away at a rate of 3 per cent per month, while the infantry declined by 7 per cent.[8]

For England at least, desertion appears to have been a greater source of attrition than disease. Yet there is ample evidence of the devastating toll exacted by disease in the 1640s and 1650s. In 1643, for example, typhus fever was spread by the king's and the Earl of Essex's armies along the Thames Valley with devastating effect. Burials skyrocketed in Berkshire in

---

[3] André Courvisier, 'Guerre et mentalités au xviie siècle', XVIIE Siècle, 38 (1985), 222. For Jacques Dupâquier see Parker, *Military Revolution*, 53.
[4] Frank Tallett, *War and Society in Early-Modern Europe, 1495–1715*, 106.
[5] *LJ*, Vol. 6, 160.
[6] BL. Add. MS 18779 (Yonge's diary), fo. 101v.
[7] Gentles, *NMA*, 39.
[8] Holmes, *The Eastern Association*, 168–9; Hughes, *Warwickshire*, 200.

1643 and 1644, 72 per cent above the previous 20-year average.[9] Again, in 1649 Lancashire suffered a severe subsistence crisis. The county was visited with 'sword, pestilence and famine, all at once afflicting that country above other parts of the nation, by means whereof . . . many people have perished and died'.[10] In wartime Oxford sickness and death held sway, thanks to the military presence, bad housing and polluted water. Other towns such as Bristol and Colyton were also gravely affected. Typhus was rampant in Oxford by the summer of 1643, and plague took hold the following year. Burials increased six-fold over their pre-war annual average.[11] There was also 'a serious population crisis' in the early 1640s in 5 of the 14 parishes studied by the Cambridge Population Group.[12] In Scotland troops returning from the siege of Newcastle brought the plague with them, creating a national epidemic that carried off between 2 and 3 per cent of the population (20–30,000 people).[13] In Ireland too war mortality was exacerbated by bubonic plague. It arrived at Galway from Spain in July 1649, the first outbreak in half a century. From Galway it spread across the whole country except for Ulster, reaching Dublin in 1651. Its spread was undoubtedly accelerated by the fact that it hit precisely when large-scale movements of soldiers and refugees across the island were beginning.

Regarding Ireland, the wars were 'nothing less than a demographic catastrophe'.[14] The warfare in Ireland lasted longer that it did in the other two kingdoms, and was much bloodier. Commonly the death rate during a battle or a siege might reach one-third or one-half of those involved. Prisoners of war were routinely put to the sword. Cromwell was not the first commander to slaughter whole garrisons, including civilians. When Sir Charles Coote stormed Sligo in 1646 he refused quarter and killed both soldiers and civilians. The Confederate commanders responded in kind.

---

[9] Mary J. Dobson, *A Chronology of Epidemic Disease and Mortality in Southeast England, 1601–1800*, 49; Joan A. Dils, 'Epidemics, mortality and the civil war in Berkshire, 1642–6', in Richardson (ed.), *The English Civil Wars: Local Aspects*, 145, 148, 154. The 72 per cent figure is derived from the data on p. 154.

[10] Dobson, *Chronology of Epidemic Disease*, 51.

[11] Ian Roy and Dietrich Reinhart, 'Oxford and the civil wars', in Nicholas Tyacke (ed.), *The History of the University of Oxford*, Volume iv: *Seventeenth-Century Oxford*, 710; Ian Roy and Stephen Porter, 'The population of Worcester in 1646', *Local Population Studies*, 28 (1982), 38.

[12] Hughes, *Warwickshire*, 258.

[13] Michael Flinn (ed.), *Scottish Population History*, 133, 136–7, 147.

[14] Pádraig Lenihan, 'War and population, 1649–52', *Irish Economic and Social History*, 24 (1997), 9–11, 18, 19–21.

Strikingly, when General Charles Fleetwood became lord deputy in the 1650s he ordered that if a Protestant was murdered by a Catholic, the people responsible were to be handed over within 24 hours, or four hostages would be seized and shipped to Barbados as slaves, while every other person in the district would be transported to Connacht or Clare.[15] According to the most recent estimate Ireland's population shrank by 15–20 per cent or about 300,000 between 1641 and 1652, with the bulk of the deaths concentrated in the years from 1649 to 1652.[16] Not only were lives lost to killing in war, starvation and disease; once the wars were over many Irish, numbering in the thousands, were transported to the West Indies and Virginia. A further 27,000 were sent to join the Spanish and other continental armies.[17] If we accept Lenihan's figure for Ireland, shave Carlton's for England and Scotland (increasing them by a ratio of 1.4 to account for non-battle deaths), and multiply the battlefield deaths by 1.2 to account for casualties, we can estimate the human cost of the revolution and wars in the three kingdoms between 1640 and 1652 (see Table 15.1).[18]

TABLE 15.1 *Deaths and casualties due to the English revolution and wars in the three kingdoms, 1640–52*

	In battle	Disease and accident	Total deaths	Deaths as a % of population	Casualties
England	75,000	105,000	180,000	3	90,000
Ireland			300,000	15–20	
Scotland	25,000	35,000	60,000	6	30,000
Total			540,000	7	

[15] John Morrill, 'The Britishness of the English revolution 1640–1660', in R. Asch (ed.), *Three Nations – a Common History? England, Scotland, Ireland and British History c. 1600–1920*, 114.

[16] Lenihan, 'War and population, 1649–52', 19, 21. William Petty in 1672 put the figure at 618,000 or 40 per cent of the population in 1640.

[17] Patrick J., Corish, 'The Cromwellian regime, 1650–60', in *NHI*, Vol. 3, 62–3; Eamonn Ó Ciardha, 'Woodkerne, tories and rapparees in Ulster and north Connaught in the seventeenth century' (MA thesis, University College Dublin), 47.

[18] The ratio of 1.4 reflects Tallet's suggestion that deaths from disease outweighed those from wounds and accidents by 'a little less than' 1.5 to 1. The use of 1.2 to express the ratio between casualties and deaths is derived from Carlton's finding of 1.27 for the battle of Edgehill.

Assuming that the pre-war population of the three kingdoms was 7.5 million, we have an overall mortality of 7 per cent due to the wars. Even the English and Scottish mortality of 3 and 6 per cent respectively represents a much higher death rate than Britain suffered during the world wars of the last century, which was well under 2 per cent. Yet it falls well short of the 15–20 per cent mortality that ravaged Germany in the Thirty Years' War.[19] On top of all the deaths were those who were wounded but survived. In modern wars the number of wounded normally far exceeds the number of dead. In the seventeenth century, when medicine was much more primitive, the ratio between wounded and dead was much closer. Carlton determined that there were 1.27 wounded for every man who died at Edgehill.[20] If, again using conservative assumptions, we apply a ratio of 1.2 we arrive at figures of just over 90,000 wounded for England and Wales, and 30,000 for Scotland. Since Irish mortality has not been disaggregated, it is difficult to calculate the number of wounded, but a plausible estimate would be in the region of 80,000 to 100,000. In each of the three kingdoms, then, there were tens of thousands of men who for years after the wars bore in their bodies tangible reminders of what they had undergone, whether it was a limp, a lingering ache, deafness, disfigurement, or a missing arm, leg, hand or eye. Aside from the long-term suffering there was the loss of productive work, and the cost of caring for these maimed soldiers and their families.[21] Some of them were lucky to receive state pensions, but the majority had to fall back on relatives, friends and neighbours for support.[22]

By whatever standard we use it was a high price to pay for overthrowing an arbitrary king, crushing the menace of popery, and conducting an 18-year experiment in republican government.

---

[19] In the First World War British military deaths were 722,785 or 1.6 per cent of a population of 44,714,000: Brian Bond, *The Unquiet Western Front*, 24; B.R. Mitchell, *British Historical Statistics*, 13. In the Second World War British military deaths numbered 357,116 or 0.7 per cent of a population of 47,762,000: Central Statistical Office, *Annual Abstract of Statistics, 84 (1935–1946)*, 7; W. Franklin Mellor (ed.), *Casualties and Medical Statistics*, 835; Geoffrey Parker, *The Thirty Years' War*, 211.

[20] Carlton, *Going to the Wars*, 221.

[21] For the short-term costs of caring for the wounded see NA. SP28/136, part 11, fos. 3v–8v, and part 16, fo. 11 (Edgehill); and SP28/173, unfol. (Naseby); and Philip Tenant, 'Parish and people: south Warwickshire in the civil war', in Richardson (ed.), *English Civil Wars*, 172.

[22] Geoffrey L. Hudson, 'Disabled veterans and the state in early modern England', in David A. Gerber (ed.), *Disabled Veterans in History*, 134–5.

Yet it must be confessed that there is an evidential wrinkle, having to do with the estimates for England. The wrinkle comes in the shape of E.A. Wrigley and R.S. Schofield's magisterial *Population History of England.* Embarrassingly, this study shows no population decline in England from 1640 until the second half of the 1650s. On the contrary, population appears to grow at an annual rate averaging between a fifth and a third of 1 per cent for the whole 20-year interregnum.[23] This picture of slight growth rather than decline appears to be corroborated by Mary Dobson's study of the three south-eastern counties: Essex, Kent and Sussex, which reveals average or even low mortality from epidemic diseases between 1641 and 1652.[24] We also know that towns such as Worcester and Gloucester did not experience excessive mortality during the 1640s; indeed, their populations swelled, thanks to people crowding in from the suburbs and countryside.[25]

These contradictory pieces of evidence can perhaps be accounted for. Carlton's estimate of the number of deaths caused by the civil wars in England and Wales, even if it is too high, represents only 6 per cent of the 1.3 million deaths that Wrigley and Schofield estimate occurred in England during the 1640s. Furthermore, Wrigley and Schofield do show that 1643 and 1644 were years of relatively high mortality.[26] The south-eastern counties studied by Dobson were for the most part insulated from the battles of the civil war. Except for the siege of Colchester in 1648 these counties did not undergo the experience of troops marching back and forth, spreading disease and destruction, the way the west, the south-west, the Midlands and the north did. Regarding Wrigley and Schofield's national survey, it needs to be recalled that their study is based on 404, or fewer than 5 per cent, of England's more than 9,200 parishes; moreover, all London parishes were excluded. Yet we know that London contributed tens of thousands of recruits to the parliamentary army. Wales contributed many thousands to the royalist army, and it too is not included in Wrigley and Schofield's study. Roger Finlay tells us that christenings in London fell by over a third in the 1640s, while London's population over the 20-year interregnum fell by 35,000.[27] Another consideration is that the deaths of many soldiers who fell and were buried on the battlefield were not recorded

[23] Wrigley and Schofield, *Population History of England*, 208–9.
[24] Dobson, *Chronology of Epidemic Disease*, 9.
[25] Roy and Porter, 'Population of Worcester in 1646', 37–8.
[26] Wrigley and Schofield, *Population History of England*, Table 2.3, 497–8. I am grateful to Professor Wrigley for discussion of this point.
[27] Roger Finlay, *Population and Metropolis*, 53; Beier and Finlay (eds), *London 1500–1700*, 42.

in any parish register.[28] Finally, there is the chilling, matter-of-fact statement by Richard Gough that three Shropshire villages sent 20 men to fight for the king in the civil war, 13 of whom did not return.[29] One can only reflect on the consequence of this demographic attrition on the three village economies, not to mention the emotional impact on the men's families, friends and lovers.

Property damage

Before the advent of high explosives the extent of property damage in war was limited. Stephen Porter, in his authoritative study of property destruction during the civil wars in England, estimates that at least 150 towns and 50 villages suffered war damage. A total of 10,000 houses were destroyed in cities and towns and a further 1,000 in villages.[30] Compare this with the more than 3.5 million houses damaged or destroyed in Britain during the few months of the German bombing Blitz in 1940.[31] A population less than ten times greater than it had been three centuries earlier lost nearly 350 times as many houses. The civil-war figure also pales beside the 13,000 houses lost just in London during the Great Fire of 1666.[32] Yet in a society much poorer than our own the economic cost was significant. Losses averaged from £30 to £250 per house, depending on the area of the country, and whether they were suburban or town-centre properties. If we assign an arbitrary value of £100 to each house, the loss of residential properties alone cost England £1,100,000. A further 150–200 country houses were destroyed, as well as a handful of castles – Corfe, Bridgnorth, Pontefract, Banbury, Kenilworth, Pembroke, Sudeley and Montgomery. Relatively little damage was wreaked against ecclesiastical structures. Cheapside Cross was pulled down in London in 1643, as was the market cross in Abingdon in 1644. Besides the systematic iconoclasm carried out by the Earl of Manchester's agent William Dowsing in East Anglia, about 30 parish churches throughout England suffered destruction at the

---

[28] For example, there were probably over 500 burials at Abingdon, none of which was noticed in the parish records: Peter Harrington, *English Civil War Archaeology*, 109.

[29] Gough, *History of Myddle*, 71. The same villages sent a handful of recruits to the parliamentary army. Only one of these was wounded; none was killed (p. 73). Of course it is not necessarily the case that all of those who did not return were killed; some may have emigrated or settled elsewhere after the wars.

[30] Porter, *Destruction in the English Civil Wars*, 65–6, 89, 130.

[31] A.J.P. Taylor, *English History, 1914–1945*, 502.

[32] Stephen Porter, *The Great Fire of London*, 71.

hands of soldiers. There was also extensive damage done to 13 cathedrals: Canterbury, Rochester, Winchester, Peterborough, Lincoln, Worcester, Chichester, Lichfield, Exeter, Salisbury and Gloucester, Westminster Abbey and St Paul's. St Paul's suffered more than any other. Parliamentary soldiers brought down part of its south transept with its roof; the portico was let out for shops, and its carving broken up with axes and hammers. In December 1648 soldiers were lodged in the nave; they tore the carved wainscotting from the walls and lit bonfires on the floor to keep warm. Later in the interregnum the nave was used to stable cavalry horses.[33]

The damage to country houses, castles, churches and cathedrals cannot have been worth less than £400,000,[34] bringing our conservative estimate for property destruction in England and Wales to £1.5 million. Property destruction in Ireland has not been systematically studied, but it was clearly more terrible than in England and Wales. Allowing for the lower populations of Ireland and Scotland, and their correspondingly lower property values, we would probably be safe to estimate property destruction in the other two kingdoms in the neighbourhood of £500,000 and £200,000 respectively. This yields an estimated grand total of £2.2 million for property destruction in the three kingdoms.[35] This does not include crops or livestock. Nor does it include the destruction and decay of the country's infrastructure. On almost every estate the maintenance of farm buildings and other forms of fixed capital was neglected, not least on account of the absence of tenants and their labourers who were off serving with the armies.[36] Bridges were often destroyed to obstruct the progress of enemy armies. Bridges and highways often fell into disrepair 'by reason of the distractedness of the times'. The administrative infrastructure that underpinned poor relief, social control, justice and economic regulation, also broke down, most notably in Ireland, but also throughout Scotland and England. Everyone suffered, most of all those at the bottom of society: maimed soldiers, the helpless ('impotent') poor, orphans, the aged.[37] The

---

[33] Gentles, *NMA*, 109–10.

[34] I have assumed that country houses would have been worth on average at least £1,000–1,500 in replacement cost; castles £4–10,000 each; parish churches £1,000; and cathedrals between £2,000 and £10,000.

[35] I emphasize that these are my own estimates. Stephen Porter is far too cautious a scholar to attempt to put a price tag on the phenomenon that he has so authoritatively described.

[36] Christopher Clay, 'Landlords and estate management in England', in Thirsk (ed.), *Agrarian History*, Vol. 5, 2, *1640–1750: Agrarian Change*, 123.

[37] John Morrill, *Cheshire 1630–1660*, 92.

breakdown of law and order was manifested in the destruction of parks, theft of timber, poaching of game, uprooting of enclosing hedges and breaking open of prisons and houses of correction. Often this type of destruction anticipated as well as accompanied the formal outbreak of armed conflict. John Castle wrote about 'the ball of wildfire that is kindled here', referring to the collapse of law and order in London in the summer of 1640.[38]

Another consequence of war was the 'decay of trade'. Trade could come to a halt in anticipation of war, as when clothiers from many counties complained in 1641 of the deadness of the cloth trade, which they attributed to 'the tediousness of putting justice in execution'.[39] Or trade could be halted as a deliberate policy, as when Edward Massie, governor of Gloucester, stopped all trade up the Severn in order to put the squeeze on royalist headquarters at Oxford, as well as Bristol and other centres.[40] Or it could be caused by military raiding parties.[41] Or it might just be the unforeseen consequence of war, as the London Militia Committee observed in late 1643: 'our rich men are gone . . . trade is decayed, and shops shut up'.[42] Less cloth reaching London meant less cloth to export. What was exported was more vulnerable to the depredations of privateers. After 1647 the Dutch took advantage of political disarray in the three kingdoms to make inroads in English trade in the Baltic, the Mediterranean and the Far East.[43] Whatever the reasons for the decay of trade, the consequences were relentless: severe economic depression and unemployment, especially in the industries that depended on exporting their products.

In England destruction was concentrated in provincial towns and cities. The countryside suffered relatively little, as did London, which never came under assault. At least one in ten of those living in provincial cities and towns saw their houses destroyed. The centres of most extensive destruction were Exeter, Newcastle-upon-Tyne, York, Leicester, Hereford, Gloucester, Worcester and Carlisle. Bristol underwent the unfortunate experience of twice being taken by assault – in 1643 and 1645. The larger towns of south Wales were also afflicted. Pembroke was a particular target because of its role as a key parliamentarian garrison in the first Civil War

---

[38] Huntington Lib., Ellesmere Collection (Bridgwater MSS), EL 7835.

[39] HMC 3, *Fourth Report* (House of Lords MSS), 62; *LJ*, Vol. 4, 237.

[40] Ian Roy, 'England turned Germany? The aftermath of the civil war in its European context', *TRHS*, 5th ser. 28, 137.

[41] See for example, Bodl. MS Tanner 62, fo. 147.

[42] *CJ*, Vol. 3, 315.

[43] Jonathan Israel, *Dutch Primacy in World Trade*, 200–7.

and the lengthy siege of the castle in 1648. Leicester was subjected not only to bombardment and assault but a brutal sack by Prince Rupert. Barely two weeks later it was bombarded a second time by the troops of the New Model, fresh from their triumph at Naseby. The royalist fortress at Newark, strategically situated athwart the intersection of the Great North Road and the River Trent, sustained an assault and two major sieges, which saw one-sixth of the town destroyed.

A large amount of this destruction was the consequence of siege warfare. Land had to be cleared for earthworks, sconces and bastion traces around fortified towns. Fences, hedges, orchards and garden walls were demolished. Buildings also had to be removed immediately inside town walls in order to clear an unobstructed passage so that troops could move swiftly from one sector to another to reinforce threatened points during an assault. Outside town walls suburban housing and adjacent villages were a prime target for demolition in order to provide defenders with a clear field of fire around their fortifications. In addition, clearance of buildings around a defensive perimeter deprived besieging marksmen of cover and so reduced their effectiveness. It also made it difficult and hazardous to set up artillery batteries. Similar difficulties arose if the besiegers wished to tunnel under a town's defences. Finally, the clearance of buildings deprived the besiegers of accommodation, obliging them to fall back on tents or huts. In cold or wet weather, such temporary shelter induced illness and low morale among the besieging troops. For all these considerations contemporary writers recommended that every structure, as well as trees and hedges within half a mile of a town's defences, should be removed. We know that at Oxford, Bristol, Wallingford, Worcester and Exeter the ground was cleared for 600 yards to three miles beyond these towns' defences.[44]

Another source of property destruction was raids by soldiers on towns to encourage them to pay their taxes, or punish them for failing to do so, or worse, for paying taxes to the enemy.[45] Setting buildings on fire was the preferred punishment. The destruction of hay and grain in the surrounding territory was another. Crop destruction was practised on a gigantic scale by all parties to the conflict in Ireland. In July 1651 the parliamentary commissioners in Ireland reported to the Council of State in London that cattle had almost disappeared and that four-fifths of the most fertile land lay waste and uninhabited.[46] So devastating was the destruction that, in

[44] Porter, *Destruction*, 18–24.

[45] Stephen Porter, 'The fire-raid in the English Civil War', *War & Society*, 2 (1984), 31–4.

[46] Dunlop (ed.), *Ireland under the Commonwealth*, Vol. 1, 7–8.

combination with other factors such as crop failure, it caused prices to rocket in the early 1650s and hunger was pervasive. The price of wheat in Ireland, for example, was five times higher in 1652 than in 1640.[47] Indeed, there had been such a glut of cattle, wool and barley in some parts of the country in 1640 that it had been very difficult to find buyers for them.[48] In Scotland in 1649 butter, cheese, meat, wheat, barley, oats and peas could only be had at 'very exorbitant rates' that had 'never been seen in this kingdom before'.[49] In fact, wherever soldiers took up residence food prices shot up, reflecting the strain their presence put on the local economy.[50]

Not only did trade often slow to a crawl and prices explode; credit also dried up as monied men grew fearful of lending. There was a flight of gold in all three kingdoms caused by merchants and financiers seeking safe havens for their capital. Thus in Dublin in 1644 the Marquess of Ormond was reduced to exchanging ammunition for wheat, 'so scarce a commodity is money in this place'.[51] All the towns within a six-mile radius of the capital had been burnt, while Dublin itself was ravaged by the continuous quartering of thousands of troops from 1642 onward. Many property owners abandoned their houses and fled the city.[52]

The war deprived thousands of people of shelter. In Exeter for example, it converted 'whole streets into ashes'. Between a third and a half of the city's inhabitants were left homeless, and for all these poor, distressed people, 'the civil war had proved an unmitigated disaster'.[53] Property values tumbled, partly because of destruction, but also because of the decay of trade, the conscription of many men into the armies, the abandonment of dwellings in combat zones, and the lack of hands to till the soil.

So great was the fear instilled by marauding soldiers that farmers were afraid both to plant crops and bring produce to market. In County Meath

---

[47] Lenihan, 'War and population, 1649–52', 8. A note of caution: wheat was not a staple food in mid-seventeenth-century Ireland. Milk and oatmeal were, but we have no indices for them.

[48] HMC 63, *Egmont MSS*, Vol. 1, 121, 139.

[49] Sir James Balfour, *Historical Works*, Vol. 3, 408–9.

[50] See for example, John Aston's experience at Berwick in 1639: Aston, *Diary*, 21.

[51] NLI. MS 2311 (Ormonde Papers), 156.

[52] Raymond Gillespie, 'War and the Irish town: the early modern experience', in Pádraig Lenihan (ed.), *Conquest and Resistance: War in Seventeenth Century Ireland*, 300–4.

[53] Mark Stoyle, ' "Whole streets converted to ashes": property destruction in Exeter during the English civil war', in Richardson (ed.), *The English Civil Wars*, 136–7, 138, 140.

at the beginning of 1647 five landowners wrote to Lord Lieutenant Ormond about their losses: 'our tillage neglected, no man daring to plough, and no markets frequented to enable us to make use of any thing we have'.[54] A similar phenomenon was reported from Durham and Northumberland after the second Bishops' War and the Scottish occupation of these counties.[55] Widespread unemployment was noted. In Warwickshire, in the aftermath of Edgehill there was an alarming increase in the number of beggars and pedlars.[56] Yet against the literature of lament must be set the finding of agrarian historians that during the years of most intense fighting in England (1642–45), agricultural prices were actually lower than average. Field crop and livestock prices only rose sharply from 1646 to 1649, which, not surprisingly, were also poor harvest years.[57] It must also be borne in mind that the clothing, leather and metal industries prospered by supplying the needs of the various armies.

Taxation and land confiscations, or, the macroparasitism of the state

As we saw in Chapter 4, the English people were taxed many times more heavily during the 1640s than ever before.

The figures shown in Table 15.2, all derived from records in the National Archives, demonstrate that the Long Parliament and interregnum governments extracted nearly £30 million from the English people, or an average in excess of £1.7 million a year. This does not include that portion

TABLE 15.2 *Total known government revenue, England, 1643–59*[58]

	£
Taxation	22,467,127
Land confiscations	7,152,501
Total	29,619,628

[54] NLI. MS 2314 (Ormonde Papers), 394.

[55] HMC 3, *Fourth Report* (House of Lords MSS), 57.

[56] Tenant, 'Parish and people, 182.

[57] Thirsk (ed.), *Agrarian History of England and Wales*, Vol. II, 828, 840.

[58] Wheeler, 'English army finance', 174; Habakkuk, 'Public finance and the sale of confiscated property', 87.

of the weekly and monthly assessment revenue which was spent locally, and consequently went unnoticed in the central records. It may have amounted to a further £5 million. Moreover, the governments always spent more than they took in – during the decade from 1649 to 1659, more than £2.5 million a year. With no further capital assets to sell, they fell deeper and deeper into debt. By 1659 the government owed its military forces at least £2.2 million, in addition to untold amounts for unredeemed public faith bills. On the eve of the restoration of the monarchy the English state had become an undischarged bankrupt.[59]

This, however, is not the end of the tale. Colossal though the totals are, they only represent those sources of state revenue that can be documented. There are other sources that have left only the occasional footprint in the archives, but whose magnitude is perhaps comparable to the ones we have just analysed. The chief unaudited sources comprise free quarter and plunder.

Free quarter and plunder

We will never know the precise cash value of what the English people forked out in the form of food and lodging for the soldiers who were billeted upon them. But there are a few suggestive clues. It is clear that soldiers almost never paid for their quarters. Petitioners from Bedfordshire, a county that saw comparatively little fighting, claimed in 1645 that free quarter and plunder by soldiers had cost £50,000 up to that point. Soldiers in Cheshire extorted £120,000 in free quarter by the end of the first civil war in 1646, almost half what the county raised in taxes. Cheshire villages claimed to have lost plundered goods worth an additional £90,000. In Warwickshire the costs of free quarter and plunder 'rarely amounted to less than half as much again as taxation, and often to much more'. Fragmentary evidence from Buckinghamshire suggests that in the years up to 1646 that county may have coughed up more than three times in free quarter what it did in assessments.[60] Given that the Long Parliament and the interregnum regimes were chronically unable to pay their armies in every year between 1642 and 1659, it is perhaps not rash to suggest that the evidence from these four counties of a massive resort to free quarter and plunder is typical. The papers of the Indemnity Committee corroborate

---

[59] Wheeler, 'English army finance', 187–9.
[60] H.G. Tibbutt, *Bedfordshire and the First Civil War, with a Note on John Bunyan's Military Service*, 15; Carlton, *Going to the Wars*, 281; Morrill, *Revolt in the Provinces*, 120; Morrill, *Cheshire*, 107; Hughes, *Warwickshire*, 256.

this impression.[61] Not only did soldiers exact free quarter, they helped themselves to whatever they deemed militarily necessary. The number one item on their list was horses, followed by hay and provender. The loss of teams of horses could all too easily bring a farm's operations to a halt, especially at harvest time.[62] Soldiers also confiscated carts and wagons for transport, as well as metal, wool and woollen cloth. Often short of food, they would also round up available supplies of corn, cheese, poultry, sheep and cattle to sate their appetites. There were frequent reports of soldiers poaching deer and other game, adding to the distress of many landowners. One of the consequences of plunder was that tenants could not, or would not, pay their rents. Land in effect was drained of its value.[63] Both plunder and free quarter also imposed an emotional cost on their victims. The feeling of violation and powerlessness that they left in their wake caused immeasurable psychological harm.[64]

A very conservative estimate is that free quarter was worth at least half the roughly £12 million that was raised from the assessments. Plunder, being less systematic, was worth perhaps half the value of free quarter. It is thus a safe assumption that the population of England and Wales were obliged to yield a further £9 million on top of everything that they paid in taxation to the parliamentary governments.

This brings to just under £39 million the monetary cost over 17 years to the people of England and Wales of overthrowing monarchy and establishing parliamentary, republican government. We need to bear in mind that this price tag does not take account of further tangible but incalculable costs such as the inflationary effect of scarcity aggravated by war. At the outbreak of armed conflict the flight of precious metals from London depreciated the English currency, and hampered the exchange of goods by the shortage of bullion. From 1643 onwards there were frequent laments about the 'decay' or 'deadness' of trade.[65] Commercial stagnation inevitably entailed the loss of jobs. There were doubtless many men who joined the armies of either side because it was the only work they could find.

What of the royalists? They too contributed to the cost of the revolution by extracting money and resources from the country to support their war effort. At the beginning of the conflict many of the nobility and gentry

[61] Gentles, *NMA*, 129–30 and *passim* (ch. 5).
[62] See BL. Add. MS 31116 (Whitacre's diary), 145 (24 August 1643).
[63] See for example, Ian Beckwith, *Gainsborough during the Great Civil War*, 23; Clay, 'Landlords and estate management', in Thirsk (ed.), *Agrarian History*, Vol. 5, 2, 125–8.
[64] Carlton, *Going to the Wars*, 266–74, 281–2.
[65] D.H. Pennington, 'The cost of the English Civil War', *History Today*, 8 (1958), 133.

gave and lent large sums to the royal treasury. The marquesses of Worcester and Newcastle each asserted that their support of the king cost them over £900,000. The sources of voluntary support were soon exhausted, and from then on royalist finance became a story of catch-as-catch-can. The queen's jewels were pawned in Holland. The Court of Wards continued to function in Oxford, and made a modest contribution to the king's revenue. Soon the royalist council in Oxford found itself imitating parliamentary expedients to bring in revenue. Weekly and monthly loans were exacted in the areas under royalist control. Quite often people living in contested territory found themselves paying taxes to both sides.[66] The lands of the king's enemies were sequestrated, and their rents funnelled into his treasury. An excise tax was levied in imitation of parliament's. From the beginning the royalist treasury imposed it on both foreign and domestic commodities, and on a much wider range of articles, including essential food items, notably salt, meat, bread, butter and cheese.

We know that the king's army for the Edgehill campaign in 1642 cost £5,000 a week, meaning that the royalists got by on half what it cost parliament to put Essex's army into the field. We also know that the royalist treasurer at war, John Ashburnham, spent £180,000 up to October 1643.[67] For the first two years of the first civil war the royalists were able to find enough money to match parliament in the size of its armies, and also to equip them with clothes, weapons, ammunition and supplies. However, by the spring of 1645 royalist finances were exhausted, and what little money was still being raised was raised locally. In default of a regular supply of cash from headquarters, Rupert, Hopton, Goring and other commanders resorted to free quarter, and when that failed, to outright plunder. It may be an optical illusion produced by parliament's domination of the print media, but the impression remains that the plundering of royalist troops was more extensive and ruthless than that carried out by their parliamentarian counterparts. On the other hand it would be hard to believe that the rapacity of the royalists could have exceeded in nastiness and thoroughness that inflicted by the occupying Scottish army in the north between 1644 and 1646. Scottish atrocities, and the suffering they left in their train, were for the most part overlooked in the London press, though not by the Yorkshire county committee, which reported them frequently to parliament.[68]

---

[66] Martyn Bennett, *The Civil Wars in Britain and Ireland, 1638–1651*, 178.
[67] Roy, 'Royalist army', 225, 242.
[68] Bodl. MS Tanner 60, fos. 361, 368, 400, 556.

As we have noted, the absence of surviving financial records makes it impossible to arrive at an exact estimate of the monetary cost of the royalist war effort in England.[69] For the first four years of fighting, up to the end of the first civil war, royalist expenditure, including free quarter, plunder and straightforward borrowing may have equalled half of parliament's £2.5 million a year. For the next two years, until the end of the second civil war, it may have been in the neighbourhood of one-quarter of parliamentary expenditure. This gives a total of £6.25 million for royalist expenditure in the first two civil wars. That leaves the third civil war of 1651 still to account for. Although Charles II did manage to bring an army of perhaps 15,000 into England, it was financed and recruited mainly in Scotland. The royalists fought the third civil war on a shoestring. Even with the heroic contribution of the Earl of Derby it is doubtful if royalist expenditure exceeded £250,000. This yields a grand total of £6.5 million as the amount that the royalist war effort cost England between 1642 and 1651 in taxation, borrowing, free quarter and plunder. The two sides thus may have spent something like £45 million during the revolutionary period 1642–60. Add to this our conservative estimate of £1.5 million for the value of property destroyed during the civil wars, and we reach a grand total of £46.6 million. Again, it needs to be stressed that this estimate takes no account of the incalculable damage done to the English economy by the frequent stoppage of trade and the loss of employment that the fighting inevitably entailed. Even if we rounded up our total to £50 million we would still probably be underestimating the monetary cost of the wars in England and Wales. All classes were hit hard by this extra financial burden, none more so than the landed class. They were 'stripped of their reserves of readily realizable assets, burdened with debts, with the value of their estates impaired, and not infrequently having suffered other losses, which might range from the destruction of their houses to lost educational or marriage opportunities for their children'.[70]

The total of £46.6 million for the 17 years between late 1642 and late 1659 yields an average of £2.74 million per year. This was more than triple the average state revenue of £800,000 per year between 1626 and 1640, and more than double the annual £1.2 million that Charles II was voted

---

[69] The two principal scholars who have addressed the question of royalist civil war finances are Roy 'The royalist army', especially pp. 225–6, 236 and 242; and Engberg, 'Royalist finances during the English Civil War, 1642–1646', 87–96. Neither scholar hazards an estimate for the total cost of the royalist war effort.

[70] Clay, 'Landlords and estate management', 2, 153–4.

but failed to receive during the first 20 years after his Restoration.[71] If we are looking for the beginnings of the fiscal–military state, surely they are located in the 1640s rather than the 1690s.[72]

If our estimates are unavoidably imprecise for England and Wales, they are even more so for the other two kingdoms. It is nonetheless worth trying to reach some notion of their order of magnitude.

Scotland

Scotland was at war in at least one, and sometimes all three kingdoms at once, for 13 years, from 1639 to 1651. This tiny nation of a million people held Charles I and his English army to a standoff in 1639; sent them packing in 1640; despatched an army of 10,000 to Ireland in 1643, another of 21,500 to England in 1644, and another of 10,000 in 1648; mobilized 20,000 to fight the Cromwellian invasion of 1650, and another 15,000 under Charles II to invade England for the third time in 1651. From 1644 to 1645 there was also a bitter civil war between Covenanters under the leadership of the Marquess of Argyll, and royalists led at different times by the Earl of Antrim, Alasdair MacColla and the Marquess of Montrose. Their military adventures in the other two kingdoms were far beyond their financial ability, but they were persuaded to undertake them by the promise that English sympathizers – the radical nobles in 1640, and the Long Parliament in 1643 and 1644 – would pay their costs. In the event they received only a fraction of what they were promised by the English, with the consequence that they ended up living off the land both in Ulster and the north of England, and bankrupting their own treasury.

The people of Scotland were taxed as never before to pay for the wars in the three kingdoms, as we have seen in Chapter 4. Like the English they began with voluntary contributions and borrowing, followed by a 10 per cent tax on all forms of wealth, and then forced loans, and finally an excise tax. Like the English the Scots had also to put up with free quarter, forced levies and plunder. Two major burghs were sacked – Aberdeen by Montrose in 1644 and Dundee by Monck in 1651. For many merchants,

---

[71] C.D. Chandaman, *The English Public Revenue, 1660–1688*, 272.

[72] Average state revenue was one-third higher (£3.64 million per year) during the Nine Years' War (1689–97), and twice as high (£5.36 million per year) during the War of the Spanish Succession (1702–13): Michael J. Braddick, *The Nerves of State: Taxation and Financing of the English State, 1558–1714*, 10, 33. State expenditure in the last two wars reached £5.46m. and £7.06 respectively: John Brewer, *Sinews of Power: War, Money and the English State*, 30.

especially those of Edinburgh who were moneylenders as well, the wars brought financial ruin. The leading Edinburgh merchant and financier of the Covenant, Sir William Dick of Braid, ended his life in a debtors' prison in England in the 1650s.[73] Being on the losing side, the Scots found themselves devastated and impoverished, both by their own civil war, and by the costs incurred from their interventions in English and Irish affairs.

The main areas of devastation within Scotland were the central and south-western Highlands. The process dated from the summer of 1640, when the Earl of Argyll, authorized by the Covenanters, began to harry the disaffected in the central Highlands. He laid waste the estates of suspected royalists in Atholl, the Braes of Angus and Lochaber. Civil strife and devastation reached a pitch of unparalleled intensity with the arrival in the summer of 1644 of the Earl of Antrim's expedition from Ulster, commanded by his kinsman Alasdair MacColla. The Irishmen ravaged the lands of their clan enemies, the Campbells, during the terrible winter of 1645–46.

So great was the devastation of the south-western Highlands that the covenanting regime had to ship large quantities of malt and meal to rescue the displaced and destitute population from starvation in early 1646. Reparations of £15,000 (£180,000 Scots) were paid to the chief of the Campbells and £30,000 (£360,000 Scots) to other landowners. A relief fund for widows and orphans in Breadalbane was set up. Townships in the central Highlands were also laid waste by the marching and countermarching of the armies of Montrose and his covenanting pursuers between 1644 and 1646. In April 1646, according to the Fraser chronicler, 'betwixt the bridge end of Inverness and Gusachan, 26 miles, there was not left in my country a sheep to bleet, or a cock to crow day, nor a house unruffled'.[74] This despoliation is reflected in the movement of grain prices. Scottish grain prices, low in the mid-1640s, doubled after 1646, and reached record heights in 1649–50.[75]

Scotland's population in the mid-seventeenth century was about a fifth that of England, and its people on average were much poorer than the English. On the other hand, Scotland suffered a much higher per capita death toll than England in the three kingdoms wars, owing to its greater commitment to the struggles. Bearing in mind all these factors, and using

[73] Michael Lynch, *Scotland: A New History*, 280.
[74] SHS, *Chronicles of the Frasers*, 315.
[75] Rosalind Mitchison, 'The movements of Scottish corn prices in the seventeenth and eighteenth centuries', *EcHR*, 2nd ser. 18 (1965), 283.

England's £46.6 million as a benchmark, we arrive at a figure for Scotland of: £46.6m. × $^1/_5$ (for population) × $^1/_3$ (for lower per capita wealth) × $1^1/_4$ (to account for Scotland's heavier tax rate) plus £1.5m (the amount Scotland had to borrow for her extra-territorial actions). The total comes to £5.4 million.[76]

Ireland

In Ireland the wars may be said to have lasted eighteen years, beginning with the Ulster rising in late October 1641, and dragging on until the downfall of the Protectorate in 1659. Patrick Corish was surely right to call them 'the war[s] that finished Ireland'.[77] Reporting in 1650, Henry Ireton said that in stretches of 30 miles he had seen no life but only ruin and desolation. By the end of the war farming had almost ceased, and even cattle – hitherto Ireland's most valuable export – had to be imported. This occurred not as an accident of war, but as a direct consequence of the parliamentary army's policy of denying the enemy the means of subsistence. This scorched earth policy meant that by 1652 four-fifths of fertile land lay waste and uninhabited. Justice Cooke did not exaggerate when he declared in the same year that the country was 'a white paper . . . ready to have anything writ on it that the state shall think fit'.[78] True, fighting formally ceased with the 'Settlement' Act of 1652, but the destruction of life and property continued, with the Catholic Irish fighting a guerilla war of resistance against English attempts to continue the plantation policies of Elizabeth, James and Strafford. In fact the Cromwellian objective was more ambitious: nothing less than the replacement of a Celtic Catholic population by a British one, the Catholics being confined to the poorest of the four provinces, Connacht. The policy ultimately failed, but not before it had exacted an immense toll in both treasure and human lives.

In the absence of financial records for the four major armies that fought in Ireland between 1641 and the Cromwellian invasion of 1649 we can only guess at the cost of those eight years of warfare. With Cromwell's expedition, however, we are on firmer ground. Of the total cost of the Cromwellian conquest (£6.8 million between 1649 and 1656), £1,941,000

---

[76] In 1657 General Monck pointed out that Scotland, with a fifth of England's population, was paying a quarter of England's assessment, a rate 25 per cent higher: Lesley M. Smith, 'Scotland under Cromwell: a study in early modern government' (D.Phil. thesis, University of Oxford), 89.

[77] *NHI*, Vol. 3, 357.

[78] HMC 63, *Egmont MSS*, Vol. 1, 514.

was paid in cash by the Irish themselves from their assessment, fines, customs and excise.[79] A further £3 million was paid by the Irish in the form of confiscated land – 2.5 million acres, representing about a quarter of the surface area of the country. In effect the Irish paid nearly three-quarters (73 per cent) of the cost of their own conquest.

Land confiscations were on a much larger scale than in England. The contemporary statistician and administrator William Petty tells us that by the 1650s 11 of Ireland's 20 million acres had been seized. Much of this confiscation preceded the wars of the 1640s, but we do know that 700,000 acres were assigned to the London merchants, financiers and gentlemen who had invested £360,000 in the conquest of Ireland. Another 400,000 acres were kept for the government, while 1.7 million acres were set aside to pay off military arrears – which by the mid-1650s amounted to over £1.5 million – and debts incurred for arming and supplying the navy which came to £200,000.[80]

In addition there is free quarter and plunder, which were probably levied at the same rate as in England. If, reckoning conservatively, the value of free quarter was equivalent to the amount raised by the Irish assessment, we should add £1,309,000 to the total, plus half that amount (£654,500) for plunder, bringing to £6,904,000 the amount that the Irish paid for their own conquest. There is also the question of how much the Confederate Catholics, and – after their collapse – the guerrilla fighters who continued the struggle throughout the 1650s, spent on resisting the conquest. Their overwhelming popular support must be weighed against the virtual disappearance of their taxing power by the middle of 1650. To credit them with the ability to raise and spend one-seventh of the sum

TABLE 15.3 *Irish land confiscations, 1642–60*

	Acreage	Assigned value (£)	Purpose
	696,087	360,000	reimbursement of the 1,500 Irish Adventurers
	404,000	[400,000 – est.]	government use
	1,727,500	1,750,000	army arrears, public faith debts
Totals	2,827,587	2,510,000	

[79] NA. SP63/281, fos. 1–9, cited by Wheeler, 'English army finance', 211.

[80] Bottigheimer, *English Money and Irish Land*, 135–6, 150.

TABLE 15.4 *The material cost of the three-kingdom wars in Ireland, 1641–59*

	£
The wars of the four armies, 1641–49	3,653,000
The Cromwellian conquest and its aftermath	7,884,000
Property destruction	500,000
Destruction of crops and livestock	1,000,000
Total	13,037,000

raised by the conqueror – £980,000 – would seem not to exaggerate the case.[81] This gives a grand total of £7,884,000 as the amount spent by both sides during the Cromwellian conquest. On top of this is the amount of destruction wreaked by both sides in order to weaken the war-making ability of their foe. The deliberate destruction of crops and livestock seems to have been far more extensive, systematic and ruthless in Ireland than it was in England. On the other hand, Ireland was poorer, and its population perhaps a third that of England. Therefore, we reckon, again conservatively, that the value of destroyed property (houses, castles, churches and fortifications) was £500,000, and the value of destroyed crops and livestock a further £1 million.[82] For the period before the Cromwellian invasion (1641–49), when four armies were actively engaged, the cost of civil war cannot have been less than one-sixth the English total of £2.74 million per year, or £3,653,000 over eight years.[83]

This figure, somewhat higher than one-quarter of the cost we derived for England, is likely an underestimate.

[81] The proportion one-seventh is quite arbitrary, based on the impression that after Cromwell arrived the royalist and Gaelic Irish, in their weakened condition, could not have raised more than 15 per cent of the resources that the invader was able to commandeer.

[82] I am grateful to Micheál Ó Siochrú for discussion of these estimates, and for emphasizing how much greater the destruction of crops and livestock appears to have been in Ireland than in England.

[83] The proportion of one-sixth was arrived at by reckoning that Ireland's population was one-third of England's, and assuming that its per-capita income was one-half.

TABLE 15.5 *Estimated material cost of the revolution and wars in the three kingdoms, 1638–59*

	£ millions
England	46.6
Scotland	5.4
Ireland	13.037
Total	65.037

Summary of material costs

By adding all our totals together, we arrive at a grand total for the material cost of the wars of the three kingdoms of £65.037 million (see Table 15.5).

Conclusion

It must be emphasized that the purpose of this exercise is not to create the impression that we have yet more than a rough idea of the human or material cost of the wars of the three kingdoms. Its objective is more modest: to stir up discussion of the order of magnitude of these costs. Perhaps the attempt made in this chapter will stimulate other scholars to probe more deeply, employ more sophisticated techniques and provide a more accurate estimate of the material and human cost to the people of Britain and Ireland of the English Revolution and the three-kingdom wars.

It is unarguable that the wars exacted a heavy toll of human life and material wealth in all three kingdoms. What of the long-term impact of these losses? Did any of the three kingdoms suffer enduring or permanent setback? Was the balance of wealth and power among the kingdoms altered? Did the costs of the war retard or advance Britain's emergence as a great power?

The disproportionate suffering of Ireland, culminating in her complete subjugation to England in the wake of the Glorious Revolution of 1688–91, certainly inhibited her economic freedom, and probably her growth as well. Curiously, though, Ireland's population appears to have bounced back with surprising speed. Fastest growth occurred between 1652 and 1659, with another surge in the 1680s. Population growth then stalled for more than half a century, and resumed after 1755.[84] By 1841

---

[84] *NHI*, Vol. 3, 454; R.A. Houston, *Population History of Britain and Ireland, 1500–1750*, 18.

Ireland's population was 8.2 million – four to five times what it had been in 1640, or five to six times what it had been in the wake of the devastation of the 1640s and early 1650s.[85] Scotland recovered more slowly, and her economy was prostrate for several decades after the end of the wars. Yet her population is thought to have reached 1.23 million by 1691.[86] What rescued Scotland economically, culturally and demographically was the union with England in 1707, which in turn facilitated Scotland's full participation in the industrial revolution. Given that England suffered proportionately less, not only in deaths and casualties, but also in wealth and property lost, it is no surprise that the wars reinforced her hegemony over the three kingdoms. But it is striking that England's population was much slower to recover than Ireland's; indeed it stagnated and declined slightly until the end of the seventeenth century, not reaching its 1657 level again until the 1730s.[87] Yet there can be little doubt that the mid-century wars helped to vault England (later Britain) into its position as a leading power in Europe during the course of the eighteenth century. At times of crisis Britain was able to mobilize a larger share of the national product than France, with the result that she decisively beat France in three major wars, at the beginning, the middle and the end of the eighteenth century. As Niall Ferguson observes, war has been the motor of financial change, and military expenditures have been the principal cause of fiscal innovation throughout history.[88] It was the wars of the 1640s that witnessed a number of these innovations. The excise tax, which was the first sales or value-added tax, generated a steadily increasing stream of revenue for the state treasury. More dramatic was the flood of cash produced by the weekly and monthly assessments. For the first time people were taxed according to a realistic appraisal of their real and personal wealth, and they became accustomed to much higher levels of tax than ever before. That they were willing to do so was in part due to the introduction of the principle of the executive's accountability to the legislature for spending. This was achieved by the creation of the Committee of Accounts in 1644. Although post-Restoration politicians were wary of its civil war antecedents, by the eighteenth century the Commons had rediscovered the language of accountability.[89] Another antecedent was the monthly assessment, which

[85] K. Theodore Hoppen, *Ireland since 1800: Conflict and Conformity*, 37.

[86] Houston, *Population History*, 17.

[87] Wrigley and Schofield, *Population History of England*, 532–3.

[88] Niall Ferguson, *The Cash Nexus: Money and Power in the Modern World, 1700–2000*, 14, 23.

[89] Henry Roseveare, *The Financial Revolution, 1660–1760*, 7; Paul Seaward, 'Parliament and the idea of accountability in post-Restoration England'.

was essentially similar to the land tax of the later seventeenth and eighteenth centuries. As we now know, Britain financed its great wars against France more through taxation than borrowing.[90] Again, despite the popular cry, 'No Standing Armies!', England after 1688 did return to the precedent set during the 1640s, and equipped herself once again with a large standing army. This was possible in part because half a century earlier a powerful parliament had both asserted its right, and shown itself competent, to tax the nation on a colossal scale, and wage aggressive wars with striking success. In short, the wars in the three kingdoms played a critical role in the financial modernization of England, and her promotion to major-power status in the early eighteenth century. All this, of course, would have been small comfort to the hundreds of thousands of people caught up in the wars, who paid so heavy a price for their involvement in them.

[90] Brewer, *Sinews of Power*, 88.

Epilogue

There are only two forces in the world – the sword and the spirit.
In the long run the sword will always be conquered by the spirit.

Napoleon

Recent work on the French, Russian and Chinese revolutions has emphasized how comprehensively the new orders that emerged from these upheavals betrayed the peasants and workers who had helped bring them into being. Similarly, the new republican order that took charge of the former Stuart kingdoms betrayed the apprentices, husbandmen, yeomen, artisans and tradesmen who had initially supported it. The intoxicating rush of energy and creativity unleashed by the revolutionary events of 1640–41[1] soon gave way to popular disenchantment at the staggering price exacted by the war against monarchy. That price was paid in ever more crushing taxes, higher prices, the 'decay of trade', the destruction of property, and a continually mounting death toll as civil wars gave way to wars of subjugation and conquest. From the time of the Saye–Pym Junto until the eve of the Restoration the new order rode roughshod over the rule of law, filling the gaols, then turning great houses and ships into prisons to be stuffed with the enemies of the regime, and seizing and putting up for sale millions of pounds worth of Crown, Church and royalist land.

Four-fifths of the republic's standing armies were stationed in Ireland and Scotland during the 1650s. Although both countries were allowed to send representatives to the Westminster parliament, this did not alter their status as colonies groaning under an oppressor's heel. General Charles

---

[1] This theme is fully explored in David Cressy, *England on Edge: Crisis and Revolution 1640–1642.*

Fleetwood might never have been brought to lament that 'God hath blasted [us] and spit in [our] faces'[2] if the Commonwealth had not fatefully chosen this policy of colonization. So expensive did it prove that in the end the regime was bankrupted. Bankruptcy brought about political collapse, which in turn hastened the restoration of monarchy. Ultimately the peoples of Britain and Ireland agreed with Thomas Hobbes: the risk of royal tyranny was a less fearful prospect than the present reality of a rebel regime accompanied by religious, political and financial disorder.

The tragedy of the English Revolution and the three-kingdom wars is that the conflict was begun with high-minded fervour on all sides. Tens of thousands of rank-and-file soldiers, as well as thousands of officers put their lives on the line because of their devotion to the king, or their vision of a godly commonwealth, or their yearning for freedom of conscience, political rights and economic liberty.[3] Many officers on both sides made huge financial sacrifices in order to preserve intact the troops or companies of men they had recruited and trained. More than a few of these officers and men looked forward with positive excitement to the prospect of battle, which is a useful reminder that the first concern of soldiers is not always the protection of their own skins. We know from Simeon Ashe and other observers that many were impatient for battle – on the march to Edgehill, at First Newbury and at Marston Moor, for example.

The other side of the coin is that even greater numbers of men, chiefly foot soldiers, had to be coerced into military service. Impressed soldiers, because their morale was lower, and because they were mostly low-paid infantry, often succumbed to disease, and were inclined to desert at the drop of a hat. Apart from the committed minorities on both sides, popular allegiance in these wars was in constant flux. In the north of England or the Midlands, for example, plunder and rapine could turn a previously friendly population into enemies of the Scots or the royalists respectively. By the same token heavier and heavier tax demands could stimulate a longing for the stability and predictability of monarchical rule, even in the parliamentary strongholds of London and East Anglia.

If Charles I had conquered his parliamentary opponents, as he came close to doing in 1643, their leaders would have been executed for treason.

[2] CP, Vol. 4, 220.
[3] For striking evidence of the dedication of some common soldiers to the Crown see Mark Stoyle, 'Memories of the maimed: the testimony of Charles I's former soldiers, 1660–1730', History, 88 (2003), 223–4. For the religious dedication of the Irish Confederate armies see Pádraig Lenihan, 'Catholicism and the Irish confederate armies: for God or King?', Recusant History, 22 (1994–95), 190, 196.

Because it was the king who went down to defeat, the treason of 1640 was forgotten, while the king's uxoriousness, deviousness and double-crossing treachery were exposed to public view. His futile attempt to square the religious circle – courting Catholic aid wherever he could find it, while trying to placate his Protestant followers in all three kingdoms – was in the end a major factor in his undoing.

A little-noticed aspect of the English revolution is the strong emotions that burst out at times of intense stress. People sang, shouted and prayed aloud as they besieged parliament, signed petitions and covenants, or prepared themselves for battle. Often they broke down and wept. In Edinburgh in April 1648 there was 'abundance of tears, sighs and sobs' from nobles and people alike when they queued up to sign the National Covenant.[4] At the Glasgow Kirk Assembly in November of the same year the Earl of Traquair wept as he spoke, and 'drew water from many [people's] eyes' who 'apprehended the certainty inevitable of these tragedies which now are in doing'.[5] In August 1643 the Lords of Scotland 'fell weeping for half an hour' when they committed themselves to the Solemn League and Covenant with the English parliament.[6] The following month Sir Simonds D'Ewes felt 'hot tears' roll down his cheeks as he listened to the letter read out in the House of Commons from the Kirk Assembly of Scotland commending the Solemn League and Covenant to the English parliament.[7] This shedding of tears on both sides of the border was a neat fulfillment of Samuel Rutherford's eschatological dream of two sisters, 'Britain's Israel [Scotland] and Judah [England] . . . coming together weeping and asking the way to Sion'.[8] Supporters of the king too could burst into tears of exaltation, as at Selby when he addressed them on the eve of the Second Bishops' War.[9]

It was not only religious or military exaltation that evoked powerful emotion. Taxpayers could be reduced to tears by the intolerable burden of taxation.[10] Men could grieve at having made a wrong choice. After the

---

[4] Wariston, *Diary*, 331.

[5] Baillie, *Letters*, Vol. 1, 141.

[6] BL. Add. MS 18778 (Yonge diary), fo. 20v (printed in C. Thompson [ed.], *Walter Yonge's Diary*, Vol. 2, 31).

[7] BL. Harley MS 165 (D'Ewes diary) fo. 177v.

[8] *Peaceable and Temperate Plea for Paul's Presbyterie in Scotland*, sigs. Av–A2, cited in John Coffey, *Politics, Religion and the British Revolutions: The Mind of Samuel Rutherford*, 245–6.

[9] Huntington Lib., Ellesmere Collection (Bridgewater MSS), EL 7856.

[10] For an example from Hertfordshire see Luke, *Letter Books*, 599.

defeat of Hamilton's Scottish army in the War of the Engagement (August 1648) Chancellor Loudoun wept tears of contrition for having betrayed the Covenant by becoming an Engager.[11] The 340 Leveller mutineers taken prisoner at Burford in May 1649 reportedly broke down when they learned that they had all been condemned to death.[12] People also mourned their human losses, above all the loss of their king. It did not rain on the day of his execution, 'yet it was a very wet day in and about the City of London by reason of the abundance of affliction that fell from many eyes for the death of the king'.[13] The general of the New Model Army, Sir Thomas Fairfax, so abhorred what the army had done that 'to his dying day [he] never mentioned it but with tears in his eyes'.[14]

The shedding of tears is a reliable guide to what people hold most dear. During the English revolution it usually had to do with religion or personal attachments. In this regard it is worth pondering three memorable occasions when Charles I is known to have wept: in May 1641 when he agonized over whether to sign Strafford's attainder;[15] in February 1642 when he parted from his wife at Dover;[16] and at the Newport Treaty in the autumn of 1648 when his advisers told him that he must give up the bishops in order to save his throne and his life.[17] Judging by these episodes the things that mattered most to Charles were his friends, his wife and the Church.

Cromwell too was renowned for weeping – when he spoke at the opening of Barebone's Parliament in 1653 for example. Calvin had given powerful religious sanction to the shedding of tears as a necessary sign of repentance.[18] This may explain why Cromwell's well known propensity for weeping attracted the charge of hypocrisy. As Richard Overton put it, 'You shall scarce speak to Cromwell about anything but he will lay his

---

[11] Balfour, *Historical Works*, Vol. 3, 395; *CSP*, Vol. 2, 463.

[12] In the event only three were executed: *A Declaration of the Proceedings of his Excellency the Lord General Fairfax in Reducing the Revolted Troops* (23 May 1649), E556/1, 10–11.

[13] *Kingdomes Weekly Intelligencer* (30 January–6 February 1649), E541/17, 1241. I owe this reference to Nicole Greenspan.

[14] BL. Harley MS 6390, fo. 4v.

[15] Woolrych, *Britain in Revolution*, 182.

[16] *CSPV 1640–1642*, 196; *CSPV 1642–1643*, 5.

[17] Peck, *Desiderata Curiosa*, Vol. 2, 392; Sir Philip Warwick, *Memoires of the reigne of King Charles I. with a Continuation to the Happy Restauration of King Charles II*, 326.

[18] Susan James, 'Reason, the passions and the good life', in Daniel Garber and Michael Ayers (eds), *Cambridge History of Seventeenth-Century Philosophy*, Vol. 2, 1377.

hand on his breast, elevate his eyes, and call God to record, he will weep, howl and repent even while he doth smite you under the first rib'.[19]

There is another aspect of the English revolution that is little commented on: missed opportunities. In 1639 Charles could have nipped the Scottish rebellion in the bud by attacking the Covenanter army. Another opportunity was missed two years later. By the end of 1641 it seemed that both Scotland and England were on the verge of a momentous transformation of absolute, divine-right kingship into constitutional, parliamentary monarchy. The king had consented to the statutory dismantling of the whole apparatus of prerogative government. He had agreed to govern with parliament and not against it. But both sides were plagued by the suspicion that their foes were not merely political adversaries, they were traitors. Because of this unquenchable mistrust, the chance of a peaceful transition to constitutional monarchy was passed up, and king and parliament went to war against each other.

In Ireland, after Owen Roe O'Neill's stunning victory in 1646 against Monro's Scottish Ulster army at Benburb, the Confederate forces were presented, for the first time since 1641, with a real chance to overrun Dublin. Rinuccini and O'Neill's failure to consolidate their power in the wake of Benburb, by purging the Ormondists from the Confederate government and placing Preston's Leinster army under O'Neill's command, meant that the opportunity to take the weakly defended Dublin garrison was lost. Confederate control of Dublin would have put them in a very strong position vis-à-vis their foes in England and Scotland.

In the early months of 1647 the Presbyterian peace party were in control of the parliament at Westminster. Scotland was exhausted; the Confederates were losing their grip in Ireland, and the Independent war-party Junto was demoralized. All that was needed in order to effect a permanent peace with the king was a respectful attitude towards the New Model Army, including a serious commitment to reducing its arrears of pay. Instead the short-sighted Presbyterian leaders opted for a policy of gratuitous aggression against the New Model. By provoking a military revolt they enabled the Independents to climb back into the saddle and resume their dominance of parliament.

In the summer of 1647, when the political situation was at its most fluid, Charles missed perhaps his best opportunity by turning his back on the army's Heads of the Proposals. His preferred tactic of continuing to

---

[19] *The Hunting of the Foxes*, printed in G.E. Aylmer (ed.), *The Levellers in the English Revolution*, 149.

strive to divide his foes, while building a military alliance with disaffected elements in Scotland, would seal his fate in little over a year.

Ireland's final lost opportunity may have occurred in January 1649 when the Marquess of Ormond signed a treaty with the representatives of Ireland's Catholic population. Had this treaty been implemented the Catholics would have recovered their property, enjoyed religious and political freedom, and perhaps lived at peace with their English neighbours, both at home and across the sea. Unfortunately the new revolutionary government at Westminster was not interested in embracing any such opportunity.

A more realistic lost opportunity was Scotland's chance for independence. It is almost certain that had the Scots wished to seize it in the aftermath of the regicide the remnant of the Westminster parliament would have left them alone. The rulers of Scotland chose instead to insist on confederal union with England.

Little over a decade later the English people, supported by their counterparts in Scotland and Ireland, emerged from their 18-year republican experiment as if from a bad dream. The memory of the three kingdoms' mid-century troubles would long haunt their rulers. Yet what is remarkable is the rapidity with which the people of England, Ireland and Scotland recovered from the economic, demographic and psychological impact of their experiment with new forms of government and religion. This recovery is striking testimony to the resilience of the human spirit in the face of seemingly overwhelming adversity.

Abbreviations

Abbott, *Cromwell*	W.C. Abbott (ed.), *The Writings and Speeches of Oliver Cromwell*, 4 vols (Cambridge, MA, 1937–47)
A & O	*The Acts and Ordinances of the Interregnum*, eds C.H. Firth and R.S. Rait, 3 vols (London, 1911)
Add.	Additional
AHR	American Historical Review
Baillie, *Letters*	Robert Baillie, *The Letters and Journals*, ed. David Laing, 3 vols (Bannatyne Club, Edinburgh, 1841)
BIHR	*Bulletin of the Institute of Historical Research*
Bodl.	Bodleian Library
BL	British Library
Burnet, *Hamilton*	Gilbert Burnet, *The Memoires of the Lives and Actions of James and William Dukes of Hamilton* (London, 1677)
Carte, *Life*	Thomas Carte, *Life of James Duke of Ormond*, 6 vols (Oxford, 1851)
Carte, *Orig. Letters*	Thomas Carte (ed.), *A Collection of Original Letters and Papers, Concerning the Affairs of England, From the Year 1641 to 1660*, 2 vols (Dublin, 1759)
CJ	*Journal of the House of Commons*
Clarendon, *Hist.*	Edward, Earl of Clarendon, *History of the Rebellion and Civil Wars in England*, ed. W. Dunn Macray, 6 vols (Oxford, 1888)
CP	*The Clarke Papers*, ed. C.H. Firth, 4 vols (Camden Society, new series, 49, 54, 60, 62, 1891–1901)

CSPD	*Calendar of the State Papers, Domestic Series*
CSPI	*Calendar of the State Papers, Ireland*
CSPV	*Calendar of the State Papers, Venetian Series*
CSP	*State Papers Collected by Edward, Earl of Clarendon*, eds R. Scrope and T. Monkhouse, 3 vols (Oxford, 1767–86)
EcHR	*Economic History Review*
EHR	*English Historical Review*
Gardiner, *Const. Docs.*	Samuel Rawson Gardiner, *Constitutional Documents of the Puritan Revolution 1625–1660*, 3rd edn (Oxford, 1906)
Gardiner, *Hist.*	S.R. Gardiner, *History of England, 1603–1642*, 10 vols (London, 1883–84)
Gardiner, *GCW*	S.R. Gardiner, *History of the Great Civil War*, 4 vols (London, 1893)
Gentles, *NMA*	Ian Gentles, *The New Model Army in England, Ireland and Scotland, 1645–1653* (Oxford, 1992)
Gilbert, *Contemp. Hist.*	John T. Gilbert (ed.), *A Contemporary History of Affairs in Ireland, from 1641 to 1652*, 3 vols (Irish Archaeological and Celtic Society, Dublin, 1879–80)
Gilbert, *Irish Confed.*	John T. Gilbert, *History of the Irish Confederation and the War in Ireland*, 7 vols (Dublin, 1890)
HJ	*Historical Journal*
HLQ	Huntingdon Library Quaterly
HLRO	House of Lords Record Office
HMC	Royal Commission on Historical Manuscripts
HR	*Historical Research*
IHS	*Irish Historical Studies*
JBS	*Journal of British Studies*
JMH	*Journal of Modern History*
JSAHR	*Journal of the Society for Army Historical Research*
Juxon, *Journal*	*The Journal of Thomas Juxon, 1644–1647*, eds Keith Lindley and David Scott (RHS, Camden 5th series, Vol. 13, 1999)

LJ	*Journal of the House of Lords*
Merc.	*Mercurius*
NA	National Archives (London). Formerly the Public Record Office
NAS	National Archives of Scotland
NHI, Vol. 3	T.W. Moody, F.X. Martin and F.J. Byrne (eds.) *The New History of Ireland. Volume III: Early Modern Ireland 1534–1691* (Oxford, 1976)
NLI	National Library of Ireland
NLW	National Library of Wales
ODNB	*Oxford Dictionary of National Biography*, eds. H.C.G. Matthew and Brian Harrison, 60 vols (Oxford, 2004)
P & P	*Past & Present*
Procs	*Proceedings*
RO	Record Office
Rupert, *Memoirs*	*Memoirs of Prince Rupert and the Cavaliers*, ed. Eliot Warburton, 3 vols (London, 1849)
Rushworth, *Hist. Coll.*	John Rushworth, *Historical Collections*, 8 vols (London, 1721–72)
SHR	*Scottish History Review*
SHS	Scottish History Society
SP	State Papers
THSLC	*Transactions of the Historic Society of Lancashire and Cheshire*
TRHS	*Royal Historical Society, Transactions*
Walker, *Hist. Discourses*	Edward Walker, *Historical Discourses upon Several Occasions* (London, 1705)
Whitelocke, *Memorials*	Bulstrode Whitelocke, *Memorials of English Affairs*, 4 vols (Oxford, 1853)
Wing	Wing, Donald, *Short Catalogue of Books . . . 1641–1700* (2nd edn, New York, 1998)
Worc.	Worcester College Library, Oxford
YCPH	Yale Center for Parliamentary History

Bibliography

A. Primary sources

1. Manuscripts

Beinecke Library, Yale University, Osborn shelves

fb 155 (Stanford MSS, John Browne's commonplace book)
fb 156 (John Browne Papers, 1642–49) [not 1640–45 as given in the catalogue]
fb 157 (Stanford MSS, misc. I, 16th and 17th centuries)
Osborn MSS
76.12.3 (Lord Howard of Escrick Papers 1640–41)

Bodleian Library, Oxford

MS Add. D.114 (A Collection of Original Papers relating to the Siege of Oxford, &c.)
MSS Ashmole 800, 830
MSS Carte (Ormond Papers) 1, 2, 6, 7, 19, 20, 22, 23, 67, 68, 80, 87, 118
MSS Clarendon 22, 23, 31, 34, 38, 42, 44, 91
MS Eng.c.6075, 155/1 ('A deliberation about the Execution of Justice vppon HR')
MS Fairfax 132
MSS Firth C6–C8
MSS Nalson 1–23 (State Papers, 1640–60, calendared in HMC *Portland* 1 and 2)
MSS Rawlinson D141 (Englands Memorable Accidents, 1637–44), D942 (book of civil war colours), Poet 71, 211 (royalist poetry)
MSS Tanner, 53–65 (Lenthall papers)

British Library

Add. MS 5460–1 (Sabran's despatches)

Add. MS 11045 (Newsletters addressed to Lord Scudamore, 1639–40)

Add. MS 11744 (Poems, etc. by Thomas Lord Fairfax)

Add. MS 12098 (Letters to the Treasurers at War)

Add. MS 14308 (Arms and banners of the trained bands of London, 1647)

Add. MS 15567 (Anonymous memoirs formerly attributed to the Second Earl of Manchester)

Add. MS 16730 (Plans of fortified towns and battlefields in England)

Add. MSS 18777–80 (Walter Yonge, Journals of Proceedings in the House of Commons, 19 September 1642–10 December 1645, transcribed by Christopher Thompson [2 vols, The Orchard Press, Wivenhoe, 1986])

Add. MSS 18980–2 (Prince Rupert Correspondence)

Add. MS 19398 (Royal and noble autographs, 1399–1646)

Add. MS 19399 (Royal and noble autographs, 1646–1768)

Add. MS 21506 (Letters and papers chiefly relating to the civil war, 1633–55)

Add. MS 22546 (Naval Papers, 1643–77)

Add. MS 22619 (Collections relating to Norwich, Vol. 1, 1633–1730)

Add. MS 25277 (Political and Miscellaneous Papers, 17th and 18th centuries)

Add. MS 27962 K(1) (Salvetti Correspondence, 1642–44)

Add. MS 30305 (Fairfax Family Correspondence, 1518–1700)

Add. MS 30377 (Letters from Digby and Charles II, 1644, 1649)

Add. MS 31116 (Whitacre's diary)

Add. MS 33596 (Original letters and autographs of eminent persons, 1587–1835)

Add. MS 34253 (Civil War Papers, 1640–47)

Add. MS 36913 (Sir Thomas Aston Papers 1532–1696)

Add. MS 37344 (Whitelocke's annals)

Add. MS 46931A (Egmont Papers, January–May 1647)

Add. MS 62084B (Pythouse Papers)

Add. MS 63743 (Letters to William, Earl of Craven, Vol. 1, 1649–71)

Add. MS 63788B (Civil war MSS)

Add. MS 70108 (Harley Papers)

Add. MS 71448 (Letters from Thomas, third Lord Fairfax to James Chaloner, 1651–59)

Add. MS 72437 (Trumbull Papers, Vol. 196 – parliamentary and confiscated royalist papers)

Add. MS 72438 (Trumbull Papers, intercepted royalist letters, etc.)

Add. MS 78255–7 (Sir Richard Fanshawe and Sir Robert Long papers, 1645–50)

Add. MS 78268 (Evelyn Papers: Sir Edward Nicholas correspondence, 1640–69)

Egerton MS 787 (Letter Book of Sir Samuel Luke, 1643–1645, Vol. 3)

Egerton MS 1048 (Parliamentary documents, 1624–59)

Egerton MS 1761 (Orders of State for Ireland, 1650–54)

Egerton MS 2545 (Nicholas Papers)

Egerton MS 2643, 2646–7 (Barrington Papers)

Harley MSS 164–6 (Sir Simonds D'Ewes's parliamentary diary, 1642–45, transcribed by YCPH)

Harley MS 6390 (Fairfax Actions in the Civil War)

Harley MSS 6802, 6852 (Papers of the Royalist Council of War, 1644, 1643–48)

Harley MS 7001 (Original Letters of State, warrants, etc., 1633–1724)

Harley MS 7038 (T. Baker, misc. collections)

Sloane MS 1519 (Original letters, 1574–1667)

Sloane 1983B (Miscellaneous papers)

Sloane MS 5247 ('Cornetes' of the Earl of Essex's army and of the Scottish and Irish forces in the time of the Commonwealth)

Stowe MS 840 (Colchester Collections, etc.)

Cambridge University Library

Baker MSS 27(Mm.1.38), 30(Mm.1.41), 36(Mm.1.47) (Earl of Manchester papers, 1643–44)

Chequers Court, Buckinghamshire

MS 782 (William Clarke's account book 1649–59) [also published by Harvester microfilm, *Clarke Manuscripts*, ed. G.E. Alymer (Brighton, 1977)]

Corporation of London Records Office

Common Council Journal Vol. 40

Common Hall Book No. 1 (1642–46)

Repertory 56 (1642–43)

Dr Williams's Library

MS Modern Folio 7 (Original watercolours of Civil War colours)

Folger Shakespeare Library, Washington DC

V.a.14–15 (Thomas Fairfax, sermon notes., c. 1662–67)
V.a.216 ('A briefe relation of the life and memoires of John Lord
    Belasyse')
X.c.29 (Letter of Sir Henry Vane to a foreign prince, 3 January 1639–40)
X.d.144 (letter from the Earl of Pembroke to Ferdinando Lord Fairfax,
    11 February 1644–45)
X.d.483 (Papers of Colonel Robert Bennett, 1605–83)

House of Lords Record Office

Hist. Coll. 65 (Draft Letters and Warrants of King Charles I 1644–45
    [Edward Walker Papers], 2 vols)
Main Papers (various dates)
Manuscript Journal of the House of Lords, no. 14
Parchment Collection, Box 8 (11 January 1642–11 March 1642: Petition
    of inhabitants of Westminster, 20 December 1642, for an
    accommodation between king and parliament)

Huntington Library, San Marino, California

Hastings Collection, Irish Papers, 1630–40: HA 14061, 15009, 15172
    (Bramhall letters); HA 1435–42 (Conway, Edw, 2nd Visct Conway)
HA 15306, 15308, 15309, 15396 (Col. George Monck, commander-in-
    chief of the Ulster forces)
Ellesmere Collection, Earl of Bridgewater MSS (Irish Papers)
    EL 7711–7877 (John Castle, newletters, 1639–40)

Leeds Castle, Maidstone, Kent

Civil War Letters, 1642–49

National Archives, London (NA) (formerly The Public Record Office (PRO))

AO1/361/15, 16 Audit Office, Goldsmiths Hall, Treasurers' Accounts,
    Revenue from Sequestrated Delinquents' Estates, 1643–55

AO1/1706/90–2 Audit Office, Declared Accounts, Navy, Sir Henry Vane, treasurer, 13 May 1645–12 May 1649

AO15/4 Audit Office, Enrolment Books, Committee of the Revenue, 1636–49

E351/603/87 Exchequer, Accounts of Sir John Dethick, Treasurer for the Sale of Crown Lands [1662]

E351/1275 Exchequer, Pipe Office, Declared Accounts, Army 1647 (Robert Scawen)

E407/8/169 Exchequer of Receipt, Miscellaneous rolls, books and papers (Petition to Parliament from the inhabitants of Westminster as to the civil war. c. 1642–43)

PRO31/3/73–89 Baschet transcripts, Paris, January 1642–December 1649

SP21/26 Derby House Committee for Irish Affairs, Order Book, November 1646–September 1648

SP24/1–76 (Indemnity Committee Papers)

SP25/118 (Council of State, charges for war in Ireland, 1 March 1649–16 February 1650)

SP28/1–120 (Army pay and supply warrants, 1624–51)

SP28/136 (Edgehill)

SP28/171–3 (Northants)

SP182–6 (Warwick's accounts)

SP28/251 (Army pay warrants)

SP63/281 (Irish State Papers)

WO47/1 (Ordnance Office, Journal of Proceedings, 1 April 1644–11 August 1645)

National Library of Ireland

MSS 2307–14 (Ormonde MSS vols 7–14: 15 July 1640–23 March 1647)

MS 2541 (Colonel William Cadogan papers, 1640–49)

New College Oxford

MS 9501 (Diary of Robert Woodeford, 1637–41)

Scottish National Archives, Edinburgh (formerly Scottish Record Office (SRO))

GD406/1 (Hamilton MSS 1563–1712)

Surrey Record Office, Guildford Muniment Room
MS 85/5/2 (Nicholas Papers, 1641–68)
MS 52/2/19 (Nicholas Family papers, 1641–98)
Loseley MSS

Wadham College, Oxford
MS Coxe 16 (Sir William Waller's Remarks – Experiences)

Worcester College, Oxford
MSS 41, 67, 114 (Clarke Papers)

2. Printed books

Abbott, W.C. (ed.), *The Writings and Speeches of Oliver Cromwell*,
    4 vols (Cambridge, MA, 1937–47)
The Acts and Ordinances of the Interregnum, 1642–1660, eds C.H. Firth,
    and R.S. Rait, 3 vols (London, 1911)
*The Acts of the Parliaments of Scotland and the Government during the
    Commonwealth*. Vol. 6. pt 2. A.D. M.DC.XLVIII.–A.D. M.DC.LX
    (Lords Commissioners of Her Majesty's Treasury, Edinburgh, 1872)
Ancram, Sir Robert Kerr, first Earl of and William, third Earl of Lothian,
    *Correspondence of Sir Robert Kerr, First Earl of Ancram and his son
    William, Third Earl of Lothian*, 2 vols (Edinburgh, 1875)
Aston, John, *Diary*, Surtees Society Publications, 118 (London, 1910)
Aubrey, John, *Miscellanies upon Various Subjects* (London, 1784)
Auden, J.E. (ed.), 'The Anglo-Irish troops in Shropshire', *Archaeological
    and Natural Society Transactions*, 50 (London, 1939–40), 49–64
Bagwell, Richard, *Ireland under the Stuarts and during the Interregnum*,
    2 vols (London, 1909)
Baillie, Robert, *The Letters and Journals*, ed. David Laing, 3 vols
    (Edinburgh, 1841)
Baker, Sir Richard, *A Chronicle of the Kings of England from the Time
    of the Romans Government unto the Death of King James* (London,
    1679)
Balfour, Sir James, *Historical Works*, 4 vols (Edinburgh, 1825)
Baxter, Richard, *Reliquiae Baxterianae*, ed. Matthew Sylvester (London,
    1696)
Beaven, Alfred B., *The Aldermen of the City of London*, 2 vols (London,
    1908, 1913)

Beinecke Library, British Tracts

Bellings, Richard, *History of the Irish Confederation and the War in Ireland, 1641–1643*, ed. John T. Gilbert, 2 vols (Dublin, 1882)

Boys, John, 'The parliamentary diary of John Boys', ed. D.E. Underdown, *BIHR*, xxxix (1966), pp. 141–64

Bulstrode, Sir Richard, *Memoirs and Reflections upon the Reign and Government of King Charles the Ist. and K. Charles the IId.* (London, 1721)

Burnet, Gilbert, *The Memoires of the Lives and Actions of James and William Dukes of Hamilton* (London, 1677)

Calendar of State Papers, Domestic Series, 1637–53

Calendar of State Papers, Ireland, 1633–60

Calendar of State Papers, Ireland: Adventurers for Land, 1642–59 (London, 1903)

Calendar of State Papers, Venetian Series, 1642–47

Camden Society, *Letters and Papers of the Verney Family Down to the End of the Year 1639*, ed. John Bruce, 56 (London, 1853)

Camden Society, *Charles I in 1646: Letters of King Charles the First to Queen Henrietta Maria*, ed. John Bruce, 63 (London, 1856)

Camden Society, C.E. Long, ed., *Diary of the Marches . . . by Richard Symonds*, 74 (London, 1859; repr. with introduction by Ian Roy, 1997)

Camden Society, *The Clarke Papers*, ed. C.H. Firth, 4 vols, new ser. 49, 54, 60, 62 (London, 1891–1901)

Camden Society, *The Hamilton Papers*, ed. Samuel Rawson Gardiner, new ser. 27 (London, 1880)

Camden Society, Camden Miscellany 9. *Hamilton Papers*. Addenda, ed. Samuel Rawson Gardiner, new ser. 53 (London, 1895)

Camden Society, Camden Miscellany 33. *Seventeenth-Century Political and Financial Papers*, 5th ser. 7: 'The letters of Sir Cheney Culpeper, 1641–1657', ed. M.J. Braddick and Mark Greengrass (London, 1996)

Camden Society, *The Journal of Thomas Juxon, 1644–1647*, eds Keith Lindley and David Scott, 5th ser. 13 (London, 1999)

Carte, Thomas, (ed.) *A Collection of Original Letters and Papers, Concerning the Affairs of England, From the Year 1641 to 1660*, 2 vols (Dublin, 1759)

Carte, Thomas, *The Life of James Duke of Ormond*, 6 vols (Oxford, 1851)

Cary, Henry (ed.), *Memorials of the Great Civil War in England from 1646 to 1652*, 2 vols (London, 1842)

Castlehaven, James Touchet, Earl of, *The Earl of Castlehaven's Memoirs of the Irish Wars (1684), with The Earl of Anglesey's Letter from a Person of Honour in the Countrey* (1681) (repr. New York, 1974)

Cavendish, Margaret, Duchess of Newcastle, *The Life of William Cavendish, Duke of Newcastle*, ed. C.H. Firth (London, 1886)

Central Statistical Office, *Annual Abstract of Statistics*, 84 *(1935–46)* (London, 1948)

Chetham Society, *Tracts Relating to Military Proceedings in Lancashire during the Great Civil War*, ed. George Ormerod, Chetham Society, Vol. 2 (London, 1844)

Clanricarde, Ulick Bourke, Marquess of, *The Memoirs and Letters of Ulick, Marquiss of Clanricarde and Earl of Saint Albans* (London, 1757)

Clarendon, Edward, Earl of, *The History of the Rebellion and Civil Wars in Ireland* (Dublin, 1719–20)

Clarendon, Edward, Earl of, *State Papers Collected by Edward, Earl of Clarendon*, eds Richard Scrope, T. Monkhouse, 3 vols (Oxford, 1767, 1773, 1786)

Clarendon, Edward, Earl of, *The History of the Rebellion and Civil Wars in England*, ed. W. Dunn Macray, 6 vols (Oxford, 1888)

Collins, Arthur, *The Peerage of England*, 5th edn, 8 vols, W. Strahan *et al.* (London, 1779)

A Complete Collection of State Trials and Proceedings for High Treason, 4th edn, ed. Francis Hargrave, 11 vols (London, 1776–81)

Correspondence of the Scots Commissioners in London 1644–1646, ed. Henry W. Meikle (Roxburghe Club, Edinburgh, 1917)

The Journal of Sir Simonds D'Ewes, ed. Willson Havelock Coates (New Haven, CT, 1942)

Dorney, John, *A Briefe and Exact Relation of the . . . Siege laid before the City of Glocester* (London, 1643)

Dunlop, Robert (ed.), *Ireland under the Commonwealth*, 2 vols (Manchester, 1913)

Edwardes, Thomas, *Gangraena*, 3 parts (London, 1646)

Ellis, Henry, *Original Letters, Illustrative of English History*, 1st series, 2nd edn, Vol. 3 (London, 1825)

Elton, Geoffrey, 'A high road to civil war?', in *Studies in Tudor and Stuart Politics and Government*, Vol. 2 (London 1974), 164–182

Evelyn, John, *Diary of John Evelyn*, ed. William Bray, 4 vols (new edn by Henry B. Wheatley, London, 1906)

Fairfax Correspondence, ed. Robert Bell, Vols 3 and 4 (London, 1849)

Firth, C.H. (ed.) 'The siege and capture of Bristol by the royalist forces in 1643', *JSAHR*, 4 (1925)

Forbes Leith, William (ed.), *Memoirs of Scottish Catholics during the XVIIth and XVIIIth Centuries*, 2 vols (London, 1909)

Gardiner, S.R., *History of England, 1603–1642*, 10 vols (London, 1883–84)

Gardiner, S.R., *History of the Great Civil War*, 4 vols (London, 1893)

Gardiner, S.R. (ed.), *The Constitutional Documents of the Puritan Revolution, 1625–1660*, 3rd edn (Oxford, 1906)

Gauden, John, *The Bloody Court; or, The Fatall Tribunall* (London, 1660)

Gilbert, John T. (ed.), *A Contemporary History of Affairs in Ireland from 1641 to 1652*, 3 vols (Irish Archaeological and Celtic Society, Dublin, 1879–80)

Gilbert, John T. (ed.), *History of the Irish Confederation and the War in Ireland*, 7 vols (Dublin, 1890)

Gordon, Patrick of Ruthven, *A Short Abridgement of Britane's Distemper, from the Yeare of God M.D.C.XXIX to M.D.C.XLIX* (Aberdeen, 1844)

Gordon, James, *History of Scots Affairs, from MDCXXXVII to MDCXLI*, 3 vols (Aberdeen, 1841)

Gough, Richard, *The History of Myddle*, ed. David Hey (Harmondsworth, 1981)

Grey, Zachary, *An Impartial Examination of the Fourth Volume of Mr. Daniel Neal's History of the Puritans* (London, 1739)

Guthry, Henry, *Memoirs* (2nd edn, Glasgow, 1748)

Hardwicke, Philip York, 2nd Earl of, *Miscellaneous State Papers from 1501 to 1726*, 2 vols (London, 1778)

Henrietta Maria, *Letters of Queen Henrietta Maria*, ed. Mary Anne Everett Green (London, 1857)

HMC 1 *Second Report*, Pt. 1: Duke of Montrose MSS (1874); Pt 2: Duke of Manchester MSS (London, 1881)

HMC 3, *Fourth Report* (London, 1874), House of Lords MSS

HMC 4, *Fifth Report* (London, 1876), House of Lords MSS

HMC 21 *Supplementary Report*, Hamilton MSS 2, 1563–1794 (London, 1932)

HMC 29 *Thirteenth Report*, Portland MSS, Vol. 1 (London, 1891)

HMC 31 *Thirteenth Report*

HMC 36 *Manuscripts of the Marquis of Ormonde, . . . preserved at the Castle, Kilkenny*, new ser., Vol. 2 (London, 1899); *Manuscripts of the Marquis of Ormonde*, new ser., Vol. 1 (London, 1902), 2 (London, 1903)

HMC 38 *Fourteenth Report*, Appendix 9 (Round MSS)

HMC 63 *Manuscripts of the Earl of Egmont*, Vol. 1 (London, 1905)

HMC 77 *Lord De L'Isle and Dudley*, Vol. 6 (Sidney Papers) (London, 1966)

HMC 78 *Manuscripts of Reginal Rawdon Hastings, esq.*, Vol. 2 (London, 1930)

Hobbes, Thomas, *Behemoth, or the Long Parliament*, ed. F. Tonnies (2nd edn, New York, 1969)

Hopton, Ralph, *Bellum Civile*, ed. C.F.H.C. Healey, Somerset Record Society, Vol. 18 (London, 1902)

House of Commons Journal, Vols 3–7, 1640–53

House of Lords Journal, Vols 5–10, 1640–49

Hutchinson, Lucy, *Memoirs of the Life of Colonel Hutchinson*, ed. J. Sutherland (London, 1973)

Diary of Alexander Jaffray, 3rd edn, ed. John Barclay (Aberdeen, 1856)

Kirkton, James, *The Secret and True History of the Church of Scotland from the Restoration to the Year 1678* (Edinburgh, 1817)

Lightfoot, John, Works: Vol. 13: *The Journal of the Proceedings of the Assembly of Divines from January 1, 1643, to December 31, 1644* (London, 1824)

Ludlow, Edmund, *Memoirs*, ed. C.H. Firth, 2 vols (Oxford, 1894)

Luke, Samuel, *The Letter Books of Sir Samuel Luke 1644–45*, ed. H.G. Tibbutt (London, 1963)

Marshall, Stephen, *Meroz Cursed* (London, 1642)

May, Thomas, *The History of the Parliament of England: which Began November the Third, M.DC.XL. with a Short and Necessary View of Some Precedent Years* (London, 1647)

Military Orders and Articles Established by His Maiesty for the better Ordering and Government of His Majesties Army (Oxford, 1643)

Mitchell, B.R., *British Historical Statistics* (Cambridge, 1988)

Montrose, James Graham, Marquis of, *Memoirs*, ed. Mark Napier, 2 vols (London, 1856)

Montrose, James Graham, Marquis of, *Memoirs*, ed. George Wishart (Edinburgh, 1756)

Nalson, John, *An Impartial Collection of the Great Affairs of State, from the Beginning of the Scotch Rebellion in the Year Mdcxxxix to the Murther of King Charles I*, 2 vols (London, 1682–83)

[Parker, Henry (ed.) *The Kings Cabinet Opened* (London, 1645)]

Parker, Henry, *Scotlands Holy VVar* (London, 1651)

The Parliamentary or Constitutional History of England (commonly known as *The Old Parliamentary History*), 24 vols (2nd edn, London, 1762–63)

Peck, Francis, *Desiderata Curiosa*, 2 vols (London, 1779)

Peterkin, Alexander (ed.), *Records of the Kirk of Scotland, . . . from the Year 1638*, Vol. 1 (Edinburgh, 1838)

Peters, Hugh, *Gods Doing and Mans Duty* (London, 1646)

Powell, J.R. and E.K. Timings (eds), *Documents Relating to the Civil War 1642–1648*, Navy Records Society, Vol. 105 (London, 1963)

The Pythouse Papers, ed. William Ansell Day (London, 1879)

Ricraft, Josiah, *A Survey of Englands Champions and Truths Faithfull Patriots* (London, 1647)

The Royalist Ordnance Papers, 1642–1646, ed. Ian Roy, Oxfordshire Record Society, 2 pts (London, 1963–64, 1971–73)

Rushworth, John, *Historical Collections*, 8 vols (London, 1692, 1721–22)

Rutherford, Samuel, *Quaint Sermons* (London, 1885)

SHS, *Letters and Papers Illustrating the Relations between Charles II and Scotland in 1650*, ed. S.R. Gardiner (London, 1894)

SHS, *Diary of Sir Archibald Johnston Lord Wariston 1639*, Vol. 26 (London, 1896)

SHS, *The Diplomatic Correspondence of Jean de Montereul and the Brothers de Bellievre . . . 1645–48*, ed. J.G. Fotheringham, Vols 29, 30 (London, 1898–99)

SHS, Fraser, James, *Chronicles of the Frasers*, ed. William Mackay, Vol. 47 (London, 1905)

SHS, *Government under the Covenanters*, ed. David Stevenson, 4th ser. Vol. 18 (London, 1982)

Slingsby, Sir Henry, *The Diary*, ed. Daniel Parsons (London, 1836)

Slingsby, Sir Henry, *Original Memoirs Written during the Great Civil War; Being the Life of Sir Henry Slingsby and Memoirs of Capt. Hodgson* (Edinburgh, 1806)

Spalding, John, *The History of the Troubles and Memorable Transactions in Scotland and England, from M.DC.XXIV to M.DC.XLV*, 2 vols (Edinburgh, 1828–29)

Spenser, Edmund, *A View of the Present State of Ireland, 1596*, ed. W.L. Renwick (London, 1934)

Sprigge, Joshua, *Anglia Rediviva, England's Recovery* (London, 1647)

Swadlin, Thomas, *The Soldiers Catechisme Composed for the King's Armie* (Oxford, 1645)

Symmons, Edward, *Scripture Vindicated* (Oxford, 1644)

The Tanner Letters, ed. Charles McNeill (Dublin, 1943)

Temple, Sir John, *The Irish Rebellion* (London, 1646)

Thomason Collection. The pamphlets and newsbooks in this collection are too numerous to be listed individually. In the footnotes Thomason items are recognizable by the pressmark beginning either with E (for newsbooks, pamphlets and books) or 669 (for broadsides).

Thompson, W., *Montrosse Totally Routed at Tividale in Scotland* (London, 1645)

Turner, Sir James, *Memoirs of his Own Life and Times* (Edinburgh, 1829)

Pallas Armata. Military Essayes of the Ancient Grecian, Roman, and Modern Art of War. Written in the Years 1670 and 1671 (London, 1683)

Venn, Thomas, *Military and Maritime Discipline in Three Books: Book I. Military Observations or Tacticks put into Practice for the Exercise of Horse and Foot* (London, 1672)

Verney, Frances Parthenope (ed.), *Memoirs of the Verney Family during the Civil War*, 2 vols (London, 1892)

Wagstaffe, Thomas, *A Vindication of K. Charles the Martyr* (3rd edn, London, 1711)

Walker, Edward, *Historical Discourses upon Several Occasions* (London, 1705)

Walwyn, William, *The Writings of William Walwyn*, eds Barbara Taft and Jack R. McMichael (Athens, GA, 1989)

Warburton, Eliot (ed.), *Memoirs of Prince Rupert and the Cavaliers*, 3 vols (London, 1849)

Warwick, Sir Philip, *Memoires of the Reigne of King Charles I. with a Continuation to the Happy Restauration of King Charles II* (London, 1701)

Washbourn, John, *Bibliotheca Gloucestrensis: a Collection of Scarce and Curious Tracts, Relating to the County and City of Gloucester; Illustrative of, and Published during the Civil War* (Gloucester, 1825)

Whitelocke, Bulstrode, *Memorials of the English affairs*, 4 vols (Oxford, 1853)

Whitelocke, Bulstrode, *Diary*, ed. Ruth Spalding (London, 1990)

Wing, Donald, *Short Title Catalogue of Books . . . 1641–1700*, 4 vols (2nd edn, New York, 1998)

Wolfe, Don M. (ed.) *Leveller Manifestoes of the Puritan Revolution* (New York, 1944)

Young, Peter (ed.), ' "The praying captain" – cavalier's memoirs', *JSAHR*, 35 (1957), 3–15, 53–70

B. Secondary sources

1. Books

Adamson, John, *The Noble Revolt* (forthcoming, 2006)

Asch, Ronald G. (ed.), *Three Nations – a Common History? England, Scotland, Ireland and British History c. 1600–1920* (Bochum, 1993)

Atkin, Malcolm and Wayne Laughlin, *Gloucester and the Cvil War: A City under Siege* (Stroud, 1992)

Aylmer, Gerald (ed.), *The Interregnum* (London, 1974)

Aylmer, Gerald (ed.), *The Levellers in the English Revolution* (London, 1975)

Barber, Sarah and Steven Ellis (eds), *Conquest and Union: Fashioning a British State, 1485–1725* (London, 1995)

Barnard, T.C., *Cromwellian Ireland: English Government and Reform in Ireland 1649–1660* (Oxford, 1975)

Barnard, T.C., Toby Fenlon and Jane Fenlon (eds), *The Dukes of Ormonde, 1610–1745* (Woodbridge, 2000)

Beckwith, Ian, *Gainsborough during the Great Civil War* (Gainsborough, 1969)

Beier, A.L. and Roger Finlay (eds), *London 1500–1700: The Making of the Metropolis* (Harlow, 1986)

Bennett, Martyn, *The Civil Wars in Britain and Ireland, 1638–1651* (Oxford, 1997)

Bennett, Martyn, *The Civil Wars Experienced* (London, 2000)

Bond, Brian, *The Unquiet Western Front* (Cambridge, 2002)

Bottigheimer, Karl S., *English Money and Irish Land: The 'Adventurers' in the Cromwellian Settlement of Ireland* (Oxford, 1971)

Braddick, M.J., *Parliamentary Taxation in Seventeenth-Century England* (Woodbridge, 1994)

Braddick, M.J., *The Nerves of State: Taxation and the Financing of the English State, 1558–1714* (Manchester, 1996)

Bradshaw, Brendan and John Morrill (eds), *The British Problem, c. 1534–1707: State Formation in the Atlantic Archipelago* (London, 1996)

Bradshaw, Brendan and Peter Roberts (eds), *British Consciousness and Identity: The Making of Britain, 1533–1707* (Cambridge, 1998)

Bradshaw, Brendan, Andrew Hadfield and Willy Maley (eds), *Representing Ireland: Literature and the Origins of Conflict, 1534–1660* (Cambridge, 1993)

Brenner, Robert, *Merchants and Revolution: Commercial Change, Political Conflict, and London's Overseas Traders, 1550–1653* (Cambridge, 1993)

Brewer, John, *Sinews of Power: War, Money and the English State, 1688–1783* (London, 1989)

Brotherstone, T. (ed.), *Covenant, Charter and Party* (Aberdeen, 1989)

Brown, Keith M., *Kingdom or Province? Scotland and the Regal Union, 1603–1715* (London, 1992)

Brunton, Douglas, and D.H. Pennington, *Members of the Long Parliament* (London, 1954)

Buchan, John, *The Marquis of Montrose* (Edinburgh, 1913)

Burgess, Glen, *Absolute Monarchy and the Stuart Constitution* (New Haven, CT, 1996)

Burne, Alfred H. and Peter Young, *The Great Civil War: A Military History of the First Civil War, 1642–1646* (London, 1959)

Canny, Nicholas, *Kingdom and Colony: Ireland in the Atlantic World 1560–1800* (London, 1988)

Canny, Nicholas, *Making Ireland British 1580–1650* (Oxford, 2001)

Capp, Bernard, *Cromwell's Navy: The Fleet and the English Revolution 1648–1660* (Oxford, 1989)

Carlton, Charles E., *Going to the Wars: The Experience of the British Civil Wars 1638–1651* (London, 1994)

Carlin, Norah, *The Causes of the English Civil War* (Oxford, 1999)

Casway, Jerrold I., *Owen Roe O'Neill and the Struggle for Catholic Ireland* (Philadelphia, 1984)

Chandaman, C.D., *The English Public Revenue, 1660–1688* (Oxford, 1975)

Clarke, Aidan, *The Old English in Ireland, 1625–42* (Ithaca, NY, 1966)

Coate, Mary, *Cornwall in the Great Civil War and Interregnum, 1642–60* (Truro, 1963)

Coates, Ben, *The Impact of the English Civil War on the Economy of London, 1642–50* (Aldershot, 2004)

Coffey, John, *Politics, Religion and the British Revolutions: The Mind of Samuel Rutherford* (Cambridge, 1997)

Collinson, Patrick, *The Birthpangs of Protestant England: Religious and Cultural Change in the Sixteenth and Seventeenth Centuries* (Basingstoke, 1988)

Cressy, David, *England on Edge: Crisis and Revolution 1640–1642* (Oxford, 2006)

Cronne, H.A., T.W. Moody and D.B. Quinn (eds), *Essays in British and Irish History in Honour of James Eadie* (London, 1949)

Cust, Richard, *Charles I: A Political Biography* (Harlow, 2005)

Cust, Richard and Ann Hughes (eds), *Conflict in Early Stuart England* (Harlow, 1989)

Davies, Julian, *The Caroline Captivity of the Church: Charles I and the Remoulding of Anglicanism, 1625–1641* (Oxford, 1992)

Dobson, Mary J., *A Chronology of Epidemic Disease and Mortality in Southeast England, 1601–1800* (London, 1987)

Dodd, A.H., *Studies in Stuart Wales* (Cardiff, 1952)

Donald, Peter, *An Uncounselled King: Charles I and the Scottish Troubles, 1637–1641* (Cambridge, 1990)

Dow, F.D., *Cromwellian Scotland 1651–1660* (Edinburgh, 1979)

Eales, Jacqueline, *Puritans and Roundheads: The Harleys of Brampton Bryan and the Outbreak of the English Civil War* (Cambridge, 1990)

Eales, Jacqueline, *Community and Disunity: Kent and the English Civil Wars, 1640–1649* (Faversham, 2001)

Edwards, Peter, *Dealing in Death: The Arms Trade and the British Civil Wars* (Stroud, 2000)

Elton, Geoffrey, *Studies in Tudor and Stuart Politics and Government*, 4 vols (Cambridge, 1974)

Emberton, Wilfrid, *The English Civil War Day by Day* (Stroud, 1997)

Everitt, Alan, *The Community of Kent and the Great Rebellion, 1640–60* (Leicester, 1973)

Ferguson, Niall, *Virtual History: Alternatives and Counterfactuals* (London, 1997)

Ferguson, Niall, *The Cash Nexus: Money and Power in the Modern World, 1700–2000* (New York, 2001)

Finlay, Roger, *Population and Metropolis* (London, 1981)

Firth, C.H., *Cromwell's Army* (4th edn, London, 1962)

Fissel, Mark, *The Bishops' Wars: Charles I's Campaigns against Scotland, 1638–1640* (Cambridge, 1994)

Fletcher, Anthony, *A County Community in Peace and War: Sussex 1600–1660* (London, 1975)

Fletcher, Anthony, *The Outbreak of the English Civil War* (New York, 1981)

Fletcher, Anthony and Peter Roberts (eds), *Religion, Culture and Society in Early Modern Britain: Essays in Honour of Patrick Collinson* (Cambridge, 1994)

Fletcher, Anthony and John Stevenson (eds), *Order and Disorder in Early Modern England* (Cambridge, 1985)

Flinn, Michael (ed.), *Scottish Population History* (London, 1977)

Foard, Glenn, *Naseby: The Decisive Campaign* (Whitstable, 1995)

Freist, Dagmar, *Governed by Opinion: Politics, Religion and the Dynamics of Communication in Stuart London 1637–1645* (London, 1997)

Furgol, Edward M., *A Regimental History of the Covenanting Armies 1639–1651* (Edinburgh, 1990)

Garber, Daniel and Michael Ayers (eds), *The Cambridge History of Seventeenth-Century Philosophy*, 2 vols (Cambridge, 1998)

Gardiner, S.R., *History of England from the Accession of James I to the Outbreak of the Civil War 1603–1642*, 10 vols (London, 1883–84)

Gardiner, S.R., *History of the Great Civil War 1642–1649*, 4 vols (London, 1893)

Gardiner, S.R., *History of the Commonwealth and Protectorate 1649–1656* (4 vols, London, 1903)

Gentles, Ian, *The New Model Army in England, Ireland and Scotland, 1645–1653* (Oxford, 1992)

Gentles, Ian, John Morrill and A. Blair Worden (eds), *Soldiers, Writers and Statesmen of the English Revolution* (Cambridge, 1998)

Gerber, David A. (ed.), *Disabled Veterans in History* (Ann Arbor, MI, 2000)

Griffin, Margaret, *Regulating Religion and Morality in the King's Armies 1639–1646* (Leiden, 2004)

Grosjean, Alexia, *An Unofficial Alliance: Scotland and Sweden 1569–1654* (Leiden, 2003)

Hall, James, *A History of the Town and Parish of Nantwich* (Nantwich, 1883)

Harrington, Peter, *English Civil War Archaeology* (London, 2004)

Hatton, Ragnhild and M.S. Anderson (eds), *Studies in Diplomatic History* (London, 1970)

Hibbard, Caroline, *Charles I and the Popish Plot* (Chapel Hill, NC, 1983)

Hibbert, Christopher, *Cavaliers and Roundheads: The English at War, 1642–1649* (London, 1993)

Hill, Christopher, *The English Revolution 1640* (London, 1940)

Hill, Christopher, *Intellectual Origins of the English Revolution* (Oxford, 1965)

Hill, Christopher, *The World Turned Upside Down* (London, 1972)

Hill, Christopher, *The English Bible and the Seventeenth-Century Revolution* (London, 1993)

Hill, James Michael, *Celtic Warfare, 1595–1763* (Aldershot, 1993)

Holmes, Clive, *The Eastern Association in the English Civil War* (London, 1974)

Holmes, Clive, *Seventeenth-Century Lincolnshire* (Lincoln, 1980)

Holmes, Geoffrey, *Augustan England: Professions, State and Society, 1680–1730* (London, 1982)

Hoppen, K. Theodore, *Ireland since 1800: Conflict and Conformity*, 2nd edn (Harlow, 1999)

Houston, R.A., *The Population History of Britain and Ireland, 1500–1750* (Cambridge, 1995)

Hughes, Ann, *The Causes of the English Civil War* (London, 1991, 1998)

Hughes, Ann, *Politics, Society and Civil War in Warwickshire, 1620–1660* (Cambridge, 1987)

Hughes, Ann, *Gangraena and the Struggle for the English Revolution* (Oxford, 2004)

Hutton, Ronald, *Royalist War Effort 1642–1646* (Harlow, 1982)

Israel, Jonathan, *Dutch Primacy in World Trade* (Oxford, 1989)

James, Mervyn, *Society, Politics and Culture: Studies in Early Modern England* (Cambridge, 1986)

Kearney, Hugh F., *Strafford in Ireland 1633–41: A Study in Absolutism* (Manchester, 1959)

Kent, Joan R. *The English Village Constable 1580–1642* (Oxford, 1986)

Kenyon, John, *The Civil Wars of England* (London, 1988)

Kenyon, John and Jane Ohlmeyer (eds), *The Civil Wars: A Military History of England, Scotland, and Ireland 1638–1660* (Oxford, 1998)

Kitson, Frank, *Prince Rupert: Portrait of a Soldier* (London, 1994)

Kyle, Chris R. and Jason Peacey (eds), *Parliament at Work: Parliamentary Committees, Political Power and Public Access in Early Modern England* (Woodbridge, 2002)

Lansberry, F. (ed.), *Politics and Government in Kent, 1640–1914* (Woodbridge, 2001)

Laslett, Peter, *The World We Have Lost* (London, 1965)

Lee, Maurice, Jr., *The Road to Revolution: Scotland under Charles I, 1625–1637* (Urbana, IL, 1985)

Lenihan, Pádraig (ed.), *Conquest and Resistance: War in Seventeenth-Century Ireland* (Leiden, 2001)

Little, Patrick, *Lord Broghill and the Cromwellian Union with Ireland and Scotland* (Woodbridge, 2004)

Lynch, Michael, *Scotland: A New History* (London, 1992)

Mac Cuarta, Brian (ed.), *Ulster 1641: Aspects of the Rising* (Belfast, 1993)

Macdougall, Norman (ed.), *Scotland and War A.D. 79–1918* (Edinburgh, 1991)

Macinnes, Allan I., *Charles I and the Making of the Covenanting Movement 1625–1641* (Edinburgh, 1991)

Macinnes, Allan I., *The British Revolution, 1625–1660* (London, 2005)

McNeill, William H., *Plagues and Peoples* (New York, 1976)

Maltby, Judith, *Prayerbook and People in Elizabethan and Early Stuart England* (Cambridge, 1998)

Manning, Brian, *The English People and the English Revolution* (2nd edn, London, 1991)

Manning, Roger B., *Swordsmen: The Martial Ethos in the Three Kingdoms* (Oxford, 2003)

Mason, Roger A. (ed.), *Scots and Britons: Scottish Political Thought and the Union of 1603* (Cambridge, 1994)

Mellor, W. Franklin (ed.), *Casualties and Medical Statistics* (London, 1972)

Mendle, Michael, *Henry Parker and the English Civil War* (Cambridge, 1995)

Mendle, Michael (ed.), *The Putney Debates of 1647: The Army, the Levellers and the English State* (Cambridge, 2001)

Merritt, J.F. (ed.), *The Political World of Thomas Wentworth, Earl of Strafford, 1621–1641* (Cambridge, 1996)

Money, Walter, *The First and Second Battles of Newbury and the Siege of Donnington Castle during the Civil War, A.D. 1643–6* (2nd edn, London, 1884)

Moody, T.W., F.X. Martin and F.J. Byrne (eds), *A New History of Ireland: Early Modern Ireland*, Vol. 3, *1534–1691* (Oxford, 1976)

Morrill, John, *Cheshire 1630–1660* (Oxford, 1974)

Morrill, John, *Revolt of the Provinces: Conservatives and Radicals in the English Civil War 1630–1650* (London, 1976)

Morrill, John, *Revolt in the Provinces: The People of England and the Tragedies of War, 1630–1648* (London, 1999)

Morrill, John, *The Nature of the English Revolution* (Harlow, 1993)

Morrill, John (ed.), *Reactions to the English Civil War 1642–1649* (London, 1982)

Morrill, John (ed.), *Oliver Cromwell and the English Revolution* (Harlow, 1990)

Morrill, John (ed.), *The Scottish National Covenant in its British Context, 1638–1651* (Edinburgh, 1990)

Morrill, John (ed.), *The Oxford Illustrated History of Tudor and Stuart Britain* (Oxford, 1996)

Murdoch, Steve, *Britain, Denmark-Norway and the House of Stuart, 1603–1660* (East Linton, 2000)

Murdoch, Steve (ed.), *Scotland and the Thirty Years' War, 1618–1648* (Leiden, 2001)

Murdoch, Steve and A. Mackillop, *Fighting for Identity: Scottish Military Experience c. 1550–1900* (Leiden, 2002)

Murphy, Denis, *Cromwell in Ireland; a History of Cromwell's Irish Campaign* (Dublin, 1890)

Newman, Peter, *Marston Moor, 2 July 1644: The Sources and the Site* (Borthwick Papers no. 53, York, 1978)

Newman, Peter, *The Old Service: Royalist Regimental Colonels and the Civil War, 1642–1646* (Manchester, 1983)

Norbrook, David, *Writing the English Republic: Poetry, Rhetoric and Politics 1627–1660* (Cambridge, 1999)

O'Brien, Ivar, *Murrough the Burner: Muachadh na dTóiteán: Life of Murrough, Sixth Baron and First Earl of Inchiquin, 1614–74* (County Clare, 1991)

Ó hAnnracháin, Tadhg, *Catholic Reformation in Ireland: the Mission of Rinuccini 1645–49* (Oxford, 2002)

Ó Siochrú, Micheál, *Confederate Ireland 1642–1649: A Constitutional and Political Analysis* (Dublin, 1999)

Ó Siochrú, Micheál (ed.), *Kingdoms in Crisis: Ireland in the 1640s* (Dublin, 2001)

Ohlmeyer, Jane H., *Civil War and Restoration in the Three Stuart Kingdoms: the Career of Randal MacDonnell, Marquis of Antrim, 1609–1683* (Cambridge, 1993)

Ohlmeyer, Jane H. (ed.), *Ireland from Independence to Occupation, 1641–1660* (Cambridge, 1995)

Ohlmeyer, Jane H. (ed.), *Political Thought in Seventeenth-Century Ireland: Kingdom or Colony* (Cambridge, 2000)

Orr, D. Alan, *Treason and the State: Law, Politics and Ideology in the English Civil War* (Cambridge, 2002)

Oxford Dictionary of National Biography, eds H.C.G. Matthew and
    Brian Harrison, 60 vols (Oxford, 2004)

Parker, Geoffrey, *The Thirty Years' War* (London, 1984)

Parker, Geoffrey, *The Military Revolution* (2nd edn, Cambridge, 1996)

Peacey, Jason (ed.), *The Regicides and the Execution of Charles I*
    (Basingstoke, 2001)

Peck, Linda Levy, *Court Patronage and Corruption in Early Stuart
    England* (Boston, 1990)

Perceval-Maxwell, Michael, *The Outbreak of the Irish Rebellion of 1641*
    (Montreal, 1994)

Porter, Stephen, *Destruction in the English Civil Wars* (Stroud, 1994)

Porter, Stephen, *The Great Fire of London* (Stroud, 1996)

Porter, Stephen (ed.), *London and the Civil War* (London, 1996)

Potter, Lois, *Secret Rites and Secret Writing: Royalist Literature
    1641–1660* (Cambridge, 1989)

Powell, J.R., *The Navy in the English Civil War* (London, 1962)

Prestwich, Menna (ed.), *International Calvinism 1541–1715* (Oxford,
    1985)

Reid, Stuart, *The Campaigns of Montrose: A Military History of the Civil
    War in Scotland 1639–1646* (Edinburgh, 1990)

Richardson, R.C. (ed.), *Town and Countryside in the English Revolution*
    (Manchester, 1992)

Richardson, R.C. (ed.), *The English Civil Wars: Local Aspects* (Stroud,
    1997)

Roberts, Stephen K., *Recovery and Restoration in an English County:
    Devon Local Administration 1646–1670* (Exeter, 1985)

Roseveare, Henry, *The Financial Revolution, 1660–1760* (London, 1991)

Russell, Conrad, *The Causes of the English Civil War* (Oxford, 1990)

Russell, Conrad, *The Fall of the British Monarchies* (Oxford, 1991)

Russell, Conrad (ed.), *The Origins of the English Civil War* (London,
    1973)

Scott, David, *Politics and War in Three Stuart Kingdoms, 1637–1649*
    (2004)

Scott, Jonathan, *Algernon Sidney and the English Republic, 1623–1677*
    (Cambridge, 1988)

Scott, Jonathan, *Commonwealth Principles: Republican Writing of the
    English Revolution* (Cambridge, 2004)

Sharpe, Kevin, *Criticism and Compliment: The Politics of Literature in
    the England of Charles I* (Cambridge, 1987)

Sharpe, Kevin, *The Personal Rule of Charles I* (New Haven, 1992)

Simms, John G., *War and Politics in Ireland, 1649–1730* (London, 1986)

Smith, David, *Constitutional Royalism and the Search for Settlement, c. 1640–1649* (Cambridge, 1994)

Smith, David, *A History of the Modern British Isles, 1603–1707* (Oxford, 1998)

Smith, Nigel, *Literature and Revolution in England, 1640–1660* (New Haven, 1994)

Smuts, R. Malcolm, *Court Culture and the Origins of a Royalist Tradition in Early Stuart England* (Philadelphia, 1987)

Smuts, R. Malcolm, *The Stuart Court and Europe* (Cambridge, 1996)

Sommerville, J.P., *Royalists and Patriots: Politics and Ideology in England 1603–1640* (2nd edn, London, 1999)

Stevenson, David, *The Scottish Revolution 1637–1644* (London, 1973)

Stevenson, David, *Revolution and Counter-Revolution in Scotland, 1644–1651* (London, 1977)

Stevenson, David, *Alasdair MacColla and the Highland Problem in the Seventeenth Century* (Edinburgh, 1980)

Stevenson, David, *The Covenanters: The National Covenant and Scotland* (Edinburgh, 1988)

Stevenson, David, *King or Covenant? Voices from the Civil War* (East Lothian, 1996)

Stone, Lawrence, *The Crisis of the Aristocracy, 1558–1641* (Oxford, 1965)

Stone, Lawrence, *The Causes of the English Revolution* (London, 1972)

Stoyle, Mark, *Loyalty and Locality: Popular Allegiance in Devon during the English Civil War* (Exeter, 1994)

Stoyle, Mark, *Soldiers and Strangers: An Ethnic History of the English Civil War* (New Haven, 2005)

Tallett, Frank, *War and Society in Early-Modern Europe, 1495–1715* (London, 1992)

Taylor, A.J.P., *English History, 1914–1945* (Oxford, 1965)

Terry, Charles Sanford, *The Life and Campaigns of Alexander Leslie First Earl of Leven* (London, 1899)

Thirsk, Joan (ed.), *The Agrarian History of England and Wales*, Vol. 4, *1500–1640* (Cambridge, 1967)

Thirsk, Joan (ed.), *The Agrarian History of England and Wales*, Vol. 5, *1640–1750: Agrarian Change* (Cambridge, 1985)

Thomas, W.S.K., *Stuart Wales: 1603–1714* (Llandysul, 1988)

Tibbutt, H.G., *Bedfordshire and the First Civil War, with a Note on John Bunyan's Military Service* (Elstow, 1956)

Trevor-Roper, H.R., *Religion, The Reformation and Social Change* (London, 1967)

Tuck, Richard, *Natural Rights Theories: Their Origin and Development* (Cambridge, 1979)

Tyacke, Nicholas (ed.), *The History of the University of Oxford*, Vol. 4: *Seventeenth-Century Oxford* (Oxford, 1997)

Underdown, David, *Royalist Conspiracy in England, 1649–1660* (New Haven, CT, 1960)

Underdown, David, *Pride's Purge: Politics in the Puritan Revolution* (Oxford, 1971)

Underdown, David, *Somerset in the Civil War and Interregnum* (Newton Abbot, 1973)

Underdown, David, *Revel, Riot, and Rebellion: Popular Politics and Culture in England, 1603–1660* (Oxford, 1985)

Underdown, David, *Fire from Heaven: the Life of an English Town in the Seventeenth Century* (London, 1992)

Underdown, David, *A Freeborn People: Politics and the Nation in Seventeenth-Century England* (Oxford, 1996)

Walter, John, *Understanding Popular Violence in the English Revolution: The Colchester Plunderers* (Cambridge, 1999)

Wanklyn, M.D.G. and Frank Jones, *A Military History of the English Civil War, 1642–1646: Strategy and Tactics* (Harlow, 2005)

Webster, Tom, *Stephen Marshall and Finchingfield* (Chelmsford, 1994)

Wedgwood, C.V., *The King's Peace, 1637–1641* (London, 1955)

Wedgwood, C.V., *The King's War, 1641–1647* (London, 1958)

Wedgwood, C.V., *Thomas Wentworth, First Earl of Strafford, 1593–1641* (London, 1961)

Wedgwood, C.V., *The Trial of Charles I* (2nd edn, London, 1968)

Wheeler, James Scott, *Cromwell in Ireland* (Dublin, 1999)

Wheeler, James Scott, *The Making of a World Power: War and the Military Revolution in Seventeenth Century England* (Stroud, 1999)

White, Michelle Anne, *Henrietta Maria and the English Civil Wars* (Aldershot, 2006)

Wood, Andy, *The Politics of Social Conflict: The Peak Country, 1520–1770* (Cambridge, 1999)

Woolrych, A.H., *Battles of the English Civil War: Marston Moor, Naseby, Preston* (London, 1961)

Woolrych, A.H., *Soldiers and Statesmen: the General Council of the Army and its Debates, 1647–1648* (Oxford, 1987)

Woolrych, Austin, *Britain in Revolution, 1625–1660* (Oxford, 2002)

Wootton, David (ed.), *Republicanism, Liberty and Commercial Society 1649–1776* (Stanford, 1994)

Worden, Blair, *The Rump Parliament 1648–1653* (London, 1974)

Worden, Blair, *Roundhead Reputations: The English Civil War and the Passions of Posterity* (London, 2001)

Worthington, David, *Scots in Habsburg Service, 1618–1648* (Leiden, 2004)

Wrigley, E.A., and R.S., Schofield, *The Population History of England, 1541–1871: A Reconstruction* (Cambridge, MA, 1981)

Young, Alan R., *Emblematic Flag Devices of the English Civil War 1642–1660* (Toronto, 1995)

Young, John R., *The Scottish Parliament 1639–1661: A Political and Constitutional Analysis* (Edinburgh, 1996)

Young, John R. (ed.), *Celtic Dimensions of the British Civil Wars* (Edinburgh, 1997)

Young, Peter, *Edgehill, 1642* (Moreton-in-the-Marsh, Gloucs., 1967)

Young, Peter, *Naseby, 1645* (London, 1985)

Young, Peter and Richard Holmes, *The English Civil War: A Military History of the Three Civil Wars 1642–1651* (London, 1974)

2. Articles and chapters in books

Adamson, John, 'England without Cromwell: what if Charles I had avoided the Civil War?', in Niall Ferguson (ed.), *Virtual History: Alternatives and Counterfactuals* (London, 1997)

Adamson, John, 'Strafford's ghost: The British context of Viscount Lisle's lieutenancy of Ireland', in Jane Ohlmeyer, *Ireland from Independence to Occupation, 1641–1660* (Cambridge, 1995)

Adamson, John, 'The frightened junto: perceptions of Ireland, and the last attempts at settlement with Charles I', in Jason Peacey (ed.), *The Regicides and the Execution of Charles I* (Basingstoke, 2001)

Ashton, Robert, 'From cavalier to roundhead tyranny, 1642–9', in John Morrill (ed.), *Reactions to the English Civil War 1642–1649* (London, 1982)

Auden, J.E., 'The Anglo-Irish troops in Shropshire, *Shropshire Archaeological and Natural Society Transactions*, 50 (1939–40), 49–64

Aylmer, G.E., 'Collective mentalities in mid-seventeenth-century England: II. royalist attitudes', *TRHS*, 5th ser. 37 (1987), 1–30.

Bennett, Martyn, 'Contribution and assessment: financial exactions in the English Civil War, 1642–1646', *War & Society*, 4 (1986), 1–11

Brown, Keith M., 'Aristocratic finances and the origins of the Scottish revolution', *EHR*, 104 (1989), 46–87

Burke, James, 'The New Model Army and the problems of siege warfare, 1648–1651', *IHS*, 27 (1990), 1–29

Canny, Nicholas, 'In defence of the constitution? The nature of Irish revolt in the seventeenth century', in *Culture et Pratiques Politiques en France et en Irlande XVIe–XVIIIe siècle*. Actes du Colloque de Marseille, 28 septembre–2 octobre 1988 (Centre de Recherches Historiques, Paris, 1990)

Canny, Nicholas, 'The attempted Anglicisation of Ireland in the seventeenth century: an exemplar of "British History"', in J.F. Merritt (ed.) *The Political World of Thomas Wentworth, Earl of Strafford, 1621–1641* (Cambridge, 1996)

Capp, Bernard, 'Naval operations', in John Kenyon and Jane Ohlmeyer (eds), *The Civil Wars: A Military History of England, Scotland, and Ireland 1638–1660* (Oxford, 1998)

Capp, Bernard, 'The war at sea', in John Kenyon and Jane Ohlmeyer (eds), *The Civil Wars: A Military History of England, Scotland, and Ireland 1638–1660* (Oxford, 1998)

Carlin, Norah, 'The Levellers and the conquest of Ireland in 1649', *HJ*, 30 (1987), 269–88

Clarke, Aidan, 'The Earl of Antrim and the First Bishops' War', *Irish Sword*, 6 (1963), 108–15

Clarke, Aidan, 'Ireland and the general crisis', *P & P*, 48 (1970), 79–99

Clarke, Aidan, 'The government of Wentworth, 1632–40', in *NHI*, Vol. 3

Clay, Christopher, 'Landlords and estate management in England', in Joan Thirsk (ed.), *The Agrarian History of England and Wales*, Vol. 5(2), *1640–1750: Agrarian Change* (Cambridge, 1985)

Clifton, Robert, 'Fear of popery', in Conrad Russell (ed.), *The Origins of the English Civil War* (London, 1973)

Clifton, Robin, 'The popular fear of Catholics during the English Revolution', *P & P*, 52 (1971), pp. 23–55

Cooper, J.P., 'Strafford and the Byrnes' country', *IHS*, 15 (1966–67), 1–20

Corish, Patrick, J., 'Ormond, Rinuccini, and the confederates, 1645–9', *NHI*, Vol. 3

Corish, Patrick, J., 'The Cromwellian regime, 1650–60', in *NHI*, Vol. 3

Corish, Patrick, J., 'The rising of 1641 and the Catholic confederacy, 1641–5', *NHI*, Vol. 3

Courvisier, André, 'Guerre et mentalités au xviie siècle', *XVIIe Siècle*, 38 (1985)

Cressy, David, 'The Protestation protested, 1641 and 1642', *HJ*, 45 (2002), 251–79

Cressy, David, 'Revolutionary England, 1640–1642', *P & P*, 181 (2003), 35–71

Cust, Richard, 'News and politics in early seventeenth century England', *P & P*, 112 (1986), 60–90

Dils, Joan A., 'Epidemics, mortality and the civil war in Berkshire, 1642–6', in R.C. Richardson (ed.), *The English Civil Wars: Local Aspects* (Stroud, 1997)

Donagan, Barbara, 'Codes and conduct in the English civil war', *P & P*, 118 (1988)

Donagan, Barbara, 'Atrocity, war crime and treason in the English Civil War', *AHR*, 99 (1994), 1137–66

Donagan, Barbara, 'Halcyon days and the literature of war: England's military education before 1642', *P & P*, 147 (1995), 65–95

Donald, Peter, 'New light on the Anglo-Scottish contacts of 1640', *HR*, 62 (1989), 221–9

Eales, Jacqueline, 'Kent and the English civil wars, 1640–1660', in F. Lansberry (ed.), *Politics and Government in Kent, 1640–1914* (Woodbridge, 2001)

Edwards, Peter, 'The supply of horses to the parliamentarian and royalist armies in the English Civil War', *HR*, 68 (1995), 49–66

Engberg, Jens, 'Royalist finances in the English Civil War', *Scandinavian Economic History Review*, 14 (1966), 73–96

Finlay, Roger and Beatrice Shearer, 'Population growth and suburban expansion', in A.L. Beier and Roger Finlay (eds), *The Making of the Metropolis: London 1500–1700* (Harlow, 1986)

Firth, C.H. (ed.), 'Sir Hugh Cholmley's narrative of the siege of Scarborough 1644–5', *EHR*, 32 (1917), pp. 568–87

Firth, C.H., 'The siege and capture of Bristol by the royalist forces in 1643', *JSAHR*, 4 (1925), 180–203

Fletcher, Anthony, 'The coming of war', in John Morrill (ed.), *Reactions to the English Civil War 1642–1649* (London, 1982)

Furgol, Edward M., 'Scotland turned Sweden: the Scottish Covenanters and the military revolution, 1638–1651', in John Morrill (ed.), *The Scottish National Covenant in its British Context, 1638–1651* (Edinburgh, 1990)

Furgol, Edward, 'The civil wars in Scotland', in John Kenyon and Jane
    Ohlmeyer (eds), *The Civil Wars: A Military History of England,
    Scotland, and Ireland 1638–1660* (Oxford, 1998)
Gardiner, S.R., 'The transplantation to Connaught', *EHR*, 14 (1899),
    700–34
Gentles, Ian, 'The sales of crown lands during the English Revolution,
    1649–1660', *EcHR*, 2nd ser. 26 (1973), 614–35
Gentles, Ian, 'The sales of bishops' lands in the English Revolution,
    1646–1660', *EHR*, 95 (1980), 573–96
Gentles, Ian, 'Why men fought in the British civil wars, 1639–1652',
    History Teacher, 26 (1993), 407–18
Gentles, Ian, 'The choosing of officers for the New Model Army in 1645',
    HR, 67 (1994), 264–85
Gentles, Ian, 'Political funerals during the English revolution', in Stephen
    Porter (ed.), *London and the Civil War* (London, 1996)
Gentles, I. 'The iconography of revolution: England, 1642–1649', in
    Ian Gentles, John Morrill and Blair Worden (eds), *Soldiers, Writers
    and Statesmen of the English Revolution* (Cambridge, 1998)
Gentles, Ian, 'The Agreements of the People in their political contexts,
    1647–1649', in Michael Mendle (ed.), *The Putney Debates of
    1647: The Army, the Levellers and the English State* (Cambridge,
    2001)
Gillespie, Raymond, 'The Irish economy at war, 1641–1652', in Jane
    Ohlmeyer (ed.), *Ireland From Independence to Occupation,
    1641–1660* (Cambridge, 1995)
Gillespie, Raymond, 'War and the Irish town: the early modern
    experience', in Pádraig Lenihan (ed.), *Conquest and Resistance:
    War in Seventeenth-Century Ireland* (Leiden, 2001)
Glow, Lotte, 'The Committee of Safety', *EHR*, 80 (1965), 289–313
Glow, Lotte, 'Pym and parliament: the methods of moderation', *JMH*, 36
    (1964), 373–97
Habakkuk, H.J., 'Public finance and the sale of confiscated property
    during the interregnum', *EcHR*, 2nd ser. 15 (1962–63), 70–88
Hacker, Barton C., 'Women and military institutions in early modern
    Europe: a reconnaissance', *Signs*, 6 (1981), 643–71
Hatcher, John, 'Understanding the population history of England,
    1450–1750', *P & P*, 180 (2003), 83–130
Hazlett, Hugh, 'The recruitment and organization of the Scottish army in
    Ulster, 1642–9', in H.A. Cronne, T.W. Moody and D.B. Quinn (eds),
    Essays in British and Irish History in Honour of James Eadie Todd
    (London, 1949)

Hopper, A.J., ' "The Readiness of the People": The Formation and Emergence of the Army of the Fairfaxes, 1642–3', *Borthwick Institute of Historical*, Research paper no. 92 (1997)

Howell, Roger, Jr., 'The structure of urban politics in the English Civil War', *Albion*, 11 (1979), 111–27

Hudson, Geoffrey L., 'Disabled veterans and the state in early modern England', in David A. Gerber (ed.), *Disabled Veterans in History* (Ann Arbor, MI, 2000)

Hughes, Ann, 'Coventry and the English Revolution', in R.C. Richardson, *Town and Countryside in the English Revolution* (Manchester, 1992)

Hutton, R., 'The failure of the Lancashire cavaliers', *THSLC*, 129 (1980), 47–62

James, Susan, 'Reason, the passions and the good life', in Daniel Garber and Michael Ayers (eds), *The Cambridge History of Seventeenth-Century Philosophy*, Vol. 2 (Cambridge, 1998)

Kelsey, Sean, 'The trial of Charles I', *EHR*, 118 (2003), pp. 583–616

Kelsey, Sean, 'The death of Charles I', *HJ*, 45 (2002), pp. 727–54

Kishlansky, Mark, 'Charles I: a case of mistaken identity', *P & P*, 189 (2005), 41–80

Lake, Peter, 'Antipopery: the structure of a prejudice', in Richard Cust and Ann Hughes (eds), *Conflict in Early Stuart England* (Harlow, 1989)

Langelüddecke, Henrik, ' "The chiefest strength and glory of this kingdom": arming and training the "Perfect Militia" in the 1630s', *EHR*, 118 (2003), 1264–303

Lenihan, Pádraig, 'Catholicism and the Irish confederate armies: for God or King?', *Recusant History*, 22 (1994–95), 182–98

Lenihan, Pádraig, 'The Leinster army and the battle of Dungan's Hill, 1647', *Irish Sword*, 18 (1991), 139–53

Lenihan, Pádraig, 'War and population, 1649–52', *Irish Economic and Social History*, 24 (1997), 1–21

Lenihan, Padráig, 'Celtic warfare in the 1640s', in John R. Young (ed.), *Celtic Dimensions of the British Civil Wars* (Edinburgh, 1997)

Lindley, Keith, 'The impact of the 1641 rebellion upon England and Wales, 1641–5', *IHS*, 18 (1972), 143–76

Lindley, Keith, 'Irish adventurers and godly militants in the 1640s', *IHS*, 29 (1994), 1–12

Little, Patrick, 'The English parliament and the Irish constitution, 1641–9', in Micheál Ó Siochrú (ed.), *Kingdoms in crisis: Ireland in the 1640s* (Dublin 2001)

Lowe, John, 'The campaign of the Irish royalist army in Cheshire, November 1643–January 1644', *THSLC*, 111 (1959), 47–76

Lowe, John, 'The Earl of Antrim and Irish aid to Montrose in 1644', *Irish Sword*, 4 (1960), 191–8

Lowe, John, 'Charles I and the confederation of Kilkenny, 1643–9', *IHS*, 14 (1964), 1–19

Lyndon, Brian, 'Essex and the king's cause in 1648', *HJ*, 29 (1986), 17–39

Lyndon, Brian, 'The parliament's army in Essex, 1648', *JSAHR*, 59 (1981), 140–59, 229–41

Maclean, James, 'Montrose's preparations for the invasion of Scotland, and royalist missions to Sweden, 1649–1651', in Ragnhild Hatton and M.S. Anderson (eds), *Studies in Diplomatic History* (London, 1970)

Malcolm, Joyce Lee, 'All the king's men: the impact of the crown's Irish soldiers on the English Civil War', *IHS*, 21 (1979), 239–64

Marston, J.G., 'Gentry honor and royalism in early Stuart England', *JBS*, 13 (1973), 21–43

Mason, Roger, 'Aristocracy, episcopacy and the revolution of 1638', in T. Brotherstone (ed.), *Covenant, Charter and Party* (Aberdeen, 1989)

McCafferty, John, ' "God bless your free Church of Ireland": Wentworth, Laud, Bramhall and the Irish Convocation of 1634', in J.F. Merritt (ed.), *The Political World of Thomas Wentworth, Earl of Strafford, 1621–1641* (Cambridge, 1996)

McGrath, Bríd, 'Parliament men and the confederate association', in Micheál Ó Siochrú (ed.), *Kingdoms in Crisis: Ireland in the 1640s* (Dublin, 2001)

Milton, Anthony, 'Thomas Wentworth and the political thought of the Personal Rule', in J.F. Merritt (ed.), *The Political World of Thomas Wentworth, Earl of Strafford, 1621–1641* (Cambridge, 1996)

Mitchison, Rosalind, 'The movements of Scottish corn prices in the seventeenth and eighteenth centuries', *EcHR*, 2nd ser. 18 (1965), 278–91

Morrill, John, 'The Britishness of the English revolution 1640–1660', in R. Asch (ed.), *Three Nations – a Common History? England, Scotland, Ireland and British History c. 1600–1920* (Bochum, 1993)

Morrill, John, 'Politics in an age of revolution, 1630–1690, in John Morrill (ed.), *The Oxford Illustrated History of Tudor and Stuart Britain* (Oxford, 1996)

Morrill, John and Phillip Baker, 'The case of the armie truly restated', in Michael Mendle (ed.), *The Putney Debates of 1647: The Army, the Levellers and the English State* (Cambridge, 2001)

Morrill, John and Phillip Baker, 'Oliver Cromwell, the regicide and the sons of Zeruiah', in Jason Peacey (ed.), *The Regicides and the Execution of Charles I* (Basingstoke, 2001), 14–35

Murphy, John A., 'The politics of the Munster Protestants, 1641–49', *Journal of the Cork Historical and Archaeological Society*, 76 (1971), 1–20

Newman, P.R., 'The defeat of John Belasyse: civil war in Yorkshire, January–April 1644', *Yorkshire Archaeological Journal*, 52 (1980), 123–33

Noonan, Kathleen M., ' "The cruell pressure of an enraged, barbarous people": Irish and English identity in seventeenth-century policy and propaganda', *HJ*, 41 (1998), 151–77

Nusbacher, Aryeh J.S., 'Civil supply in the civil war: supply of victuals to the New Model Army in the Naseby campaign, 1–14 June 1645', *EHR*, 115 (2000), 145–60

Ó Danachair, Caoimhín, 'Montrose's Irish regiments', *Irish Sword*, 4 (1959–60), 61–7

Ó hAnnracháin, Tadgh, 'Lost in Rinuccini's shadow: the Irish clergy, 1645–9', in Micheál Ó Siochrú (ed.), *Kingdoms in Crisis: Ireland in the 1640s* (Dublin, 2001)

Ó Siochriú, Micheál, 'The Duke of Lorraine and the international struggle for Ireland, 1649–1653', *HJ*, 48 (2005), 905–32

Ohlmeyer, Jane, ' "The Dunkirk of Ireland": Wexford privateers during the 1640s', *Journal of the Wexford Historical Society*, 12 (1988–9), 23–49

Ohlmeyer, Jane, 'Irish privateers during the civil war, 1642–1650', *Mariner's Mirror*, 76 (1990), 119–33

Ohlmeyer, Jane, 'The "Antrim Plot" of 1641 – a myth?', *HJ*, 35 (1992), 905–19

Ohlmeyer, Jane, 'The "Antrim Plot" of 1641 – a rejoinder', *HJ*, 37 (1994), 431–37

Ohlmeyer, Jane H., 'Strafford, the "Londonderry Business" and the "New British History" ', in J.F. Merritt (ed.) *The Political World of Thomas Wentworth, Earl of Strafford, 1621–1641* (Cambridge, 1996)

Ohlmeyer, Jane, 'The civil wars in Ireland', in John Kenyon and Jane Ohlmeyer (eds), *The Civil Wars: A Military History of England, Scotland, and Ireland 1638–1660* (Oxford, 1998)

Orr, D. Alan, 'Sovereignty, supremacy and the origins of the English Civil War', *History*, 87 (2002), 474–90

Peacey, Jason, 'Reporting a revolution', in Jason Peacey (ed.), *The Regicides and the Execution of Charles I* (Basingstoke, 2001)

Peacey, Jason, ' "The counterfeit silly curr": money, politics, and the forging of royalist newspapers during the English Civil War', *HLQ*, 67 (2004), 27–58

Peacock, Edward, 'Notes on the life of Thomas Rainborowe', *Archaeologia*, 46 (1881), 9–64

Pennington, D.H., 'The cost of the English Civil War', *History Today*, 8 (1958), 126–33

Perceval-Maxwell, Michael, 'The "Antrim Plot" of 1641 – a myth? A response', *HJ*, 37 (1994), 421–30

Phillips, Gervase, 'Irish Ceatharnaigh in English service, 1544–1550, and the development of "Gaelic Warfare" ', *JSAHR*, 78 (2000), 163–72

Pinto, David, 'William Lawes at the siege of York', *Musical Times*, 127: 1723 (1986), 579–83

Porter, Stephen, 'The fire-raid in the English Civil War', *War & Society*, 2 (1984), 27–40

Ranger, Terence, 'Strafford in Ireland: a revaluation', *P & P*, 19 (1961), 26–44

Reeve, John, 'Secret alliance and Protestant agitation in two kingdoms: the early Caroline background to the Irish rebellion of 1641', in Ian Gentles, John Morrill and A. Blair Worden (eds), *Soldiers, Writers and Statesmen of the English Revolution* (Cambridge, 1998)

Roy, Ian, 'George Digby, royalist intrigue and the collapse of the cause', in Ian Gentles, John Morrill and A. Blair Worden (eds), *Soldiers, Writers and Statesmen of the English Revolution* (Cambridge, 1998)

Roy, Ian, 'The royalist council of war, 1642–6', *BIHR*, 35 (1962), 150–68

Roy, Ian, 'England turned Germany? The aftermath of the civil war in its European context', *TRHS*, 5th ser. 28 (1978), 127–44

Roy, Ian and Dietrick Reinhart, 'Oxford and the civil wars', in Nicholas Tyacke (ed.), *The History of the University of Oxford*, Volume IV: *Seventeenth Century Oxford* (Oxford, 1997)

Roy, Ian and Stephen Porter, 'The population of Worcester in 1646', *Local Population Studies*, 28 (1982), 32–43

Russell, Conrad, 'The British background to the Irish rebellion of 1641', *HR*, 61 (1988), 166–82

Russell, Conrad, 'The Scottish party in the English parliament, 1640–2 OR the myth of the English Revolution', *HR*, 66 (1993), 35–52

Sacks, David Harris, 'Bristol's "wars of religion" ', in R.C. Richardson, *Town and Countryside in the English Revolution* (Manchester, 1992)

Scott, David, 'Politics and government in York, 1640–1662', in R.C. Richardson, *Town and Countryside in the English Revolution* (Manchester, 1992)

Scott, David, ' "Hannibal at our gates": loyalists and fifth columnists during the Bishops' Wars – the case of Yorkshire', *HR*, 70 (1997), 269–93

Scott, David, 'The "northern gentlemen", the parliamentary Independents, and Anglo-Scottish relations in the Long Parliament', *HJ*, 42 (1999), 347–375

Seaward, Paul, 'Parliament and the idea of accountability in post-Restoration England', unpublished paper delivered to the conference on Parliaments, Peoples and Power, Yale University, 7 April, 2005

Seel, Graham, 'Cromwell's trailblazer? Reinterpreting the Earl of Essex', *History Today*, 45, 4 (1995), 22–8

Shagan, Ethan Howard, 'Constructing discord: ideology, propaganda, and English responses to the Irish rebellion of 1641', *JBS*, 36 (1997), 4–34

Sharp, Andrew, 'The Levellers and the end of Charles I', in Jason Peacey (ed.), *The Regicides and the Execution of Charles I* (Basingstoke, 2001)

Sharp, Buchanan, 'Rural discontents and the English revolution', in R.C. Richardson, *Town and Countryside in the English Revolution* (Manchester, 1992)

Sheils, William, 'Provincial preaching on the eve of the civil war: some West Riding fast sermons', in Anthony Fletcher and Peter Roberts (eds), *Religion, Culture and Society in Early Modern Britain: Essays in Honour of Patrick Collinson* (Cambridge, 1994)

Simms, Hilary, 'Armagh', in Brian Mac Cuarta (ed.), *Ulster 1641: Aspects of the Rising* (Belfast, 1993)

Spufford, Margaret, 'The cost of apparel in seventeenth-century England, and the accuracy of Gregory King', *EcHR*, 53 (2000), 677–705

Steele, Margaret, 'The "politik Christian": the theological background to the National Covenant', in John Morrill (ed.), *The Scottish National Covenant in its British Context, 1638–1651* (Edinburgh, 1990)

Stevenson, David, 'The financing of the cause of the Covenants, 1638–1651', *SHR*, 51 (1972), 89–123

Stewart, David, 'Sickness and mortality rates of the English army in the sixteenth century', *Journal of the Royal Army Medical Corps*, 91 (1948), 23–35

Stoyle, Mark, ' "Sir Richard Grenville's creatures": the New Cornish tertia, 1644–46', *Cornish Studies*, 2nd ser. 4 (1996), 26–44

Stoyle, Mark, ' "Whole streets converted to ashes": property destruction in Exeter during the English civil war', in R.C. Richardson (ed.), *The English Civil Wars: Local Aspects* (Stroud, 1997)

Stoyle, Mark, 'Memories of the maimed: the testimony of Charles I's former soldiers, 1660–1730', *History*, 88 (2003), 204–26

Styles, Philip, 'The city of Worcester during the civil wars, 1640–60', in R.C. Richardson (ed.), *The English Civil Wars: Local Aspects* (Stroud, 1997)

Tenant, Philip, 'Parish and people: south Warwickshire in the civil war', in R.C. Richardson (ed.), *The English Civil Wars: Local Aspects* (Stroud, 1997)

Terry, C.S., 'The visits of Charles I to Newcastle in 1633, 1639 and 1646–7, with some notes of contemporary history', 83–145; 'The Scottish campaign in Northumberland and Durham', 146–79; 'The siege of Newcastle-upon-Tyne by the Scots in 1644', 180–258; all in *Archaeologia Aeliana*, 21 (1894)

Thirsk, Joan, 'The farming regions of England', in Joan Thirsk (ed.), *The Agrarian History of England and Wales*, Vol. 4, *1500–1640*

Underdown, David, 'The chalk and the cheese: contrasts among the English clubmen', *P & P*, 85 (1979), 25–48

Underdown, David, 'The problem of popular allegiance in the English Civil War', *TRHS*, 5th ser. 31 (1981), 69–94

Vernon, Elliot, 'The quarrel of the covenant: the London Presbyterians and the regicide', in Jason Peacey (ed.), *The Regicides and the Execution of Charles I* (Basingstoke, 2001)

Wanklyn, M.D.G. and Brigadier P. Young, 'A king in search of soldiers: Charles I in 1642. A rejoinder', *HJ*, 24 (1981), 147–54

Wanklyn, M.D.G., 'Royalist strategy in the south of England 1642–1644', *Southern History*, 3 (1981), 54–79

Wheeler, James Scott, 'The logistics of the Cromwellian conquest of Scotland 1650–1651', *War & Society*, 10 (1992), 1–18

Wheeler, James Scott, 'Four armies in Ireland', in Jane Ohlmeyer (ed.), *Ireland From Independence to Occupation, 1641–1660* (Cambridge, 1995)

Wood, Andy, 'Beyond post-revisionism? The civil war allegiances of the miners of the Derbyshire "Peak Country" ', *HJ*, 40 (1997), 23–40

Worden, Blair, 'English republicanism', in J.H. Burns and Mark Goldie (eds), *The Cambridge History of Political Thought 1450–1700* (Cambridge, 1991)

Wormald, Jenny, 'The creation of Britain: multiple kingdoms or core and colonies?', *TRHS*, 6th ser. 2 (1992), 175–94

Young, Peter, 'The royalist army at the battle of Roundway Down, 13th July, 1643', *JSAHR*, 31 (1953), 127–31

3. Theses (PhD except where otherwise noted)

Armstrong, Robert Matthew, 'Protestant Ireland and the English parliament, 1641–47' (Trinity College Dublin, 1995)

Braddick, Michael Jonathan, 'Parliamentary lay taxation c. 1590–1670: local problems of enforcement and collection, with special reference to Norfolk' (University of Cambridge, 1988)

Cliftlands, William, 'The "Well-Affected" and the "Country": politics and religion in English provincial society, c. 1640–c. 1654' (University of Essex, 1987)

Costa, D.A. 'The political career of Sir Arthur Hesilrige' (Oxford University, D.Phil. thesis, 1989)

Darman, Peter M., 'Prince Rupert of the Rhine: a study in generalship, 1642–1646' (University of York, M.Phil. thesis, 1987)

Evans, David Sidney, 'The civil war career of Major-General Edward Massey (1642–1647)' (University of London, 1993)

Henderson, Frances M.S., 'New material from the Clarke manuscripts: political and official correspondence and news sent and received by the army headquarters in Scotland, 1651–1660' (Oxford D.Phil. thesis, 1998 [2 vols])

Jones, Jennifer, 'The war in the north: the northern parliamentarian army in the English civil war 1642–1645' (York University [Toronto], 1991)

Kelly, William Pius, 'The early career of James Butler, twelfth earl and first Duke of Ormond (1610–1688), 1610–1643' (Cambridge University, 1997)

Lenihan, Pádraig, 'The Catholic Confederacy 1642–9: an Irish state at war' (University College, Galway, 1995)

Mahony, Michael Patrick, 'The Presbyterian party in the Long Parliament, 2 July 1644–3 June 1647' (Oxford University, D.Phil. thesis, 1973)

Maltby, Judith Diane, 'Approaches to the study of religious conformity in late Elizabethan and early Stuart England: with special reference to Cheshire and the diocese of Lincoln' (University of Cambridge, 1991)

Newman, Peter, 'The royalist armies in northern England, 1642–45' (University of York, 1978 [2 vols])

Nusbacher, Aryeh J.S., 'The triple thread: supply of victuals to the army under Sir Thomas Fairfax 1645–1646' (University of Oxford, D.Phil. thesis, 2001)

Ó Ciardhá, Eamonn, 'Woodkerne, tories and rapparees in Ulster and north Connaught in the seventeenth century' (University College Dublin, MA thesis, 1991)

Peacey, Jason Tom, 'Henry Parker and parliamentary propaganda in the English civil wars' (Cambridge University, 1994)

Roy, Ian 'The Royalist Army in the First Civil War' (University of Oxford, D.Phil., 1963)

Scally, John Joseph, 'The political career of James, third Marquis and first Duke of Hamilton (1606–1649) to 1643' (Cambridge University, 1993)

Smith, Lesley M., 'Scotland and Cromwell: a study in early modern government' (Oxford D.Phil., 1979)

Stent, R.W., 'Thomas Rainsborough and the army Levellers' (University of London, M.Phil., 1975)

Sumner, Anne, 'George Lord Digby' (Cambridge University, 1987)

Wheeler, James Scott, 'English army finance and logistics 1642–1660' (University of California, Berkeley, 1980)

Index